JOHN CONSTANTINE, HELLBLAZER: IN THE LINE OF FIRE

JOHN CONSTANTINE, HELLBLAZER: IN THE LINE OF FIRE

PAUL JENKINS WRITER

SEAN PHILLIPS AL DAVISON ARTISTS

MATT HOLLINGSWORTH JAMES SINCLAIR PAMELA RAMBO COLORISTS

CLEM ROBINS LETTERER

SEAN PHILLIPS COVER ART AND ORIGINAL SERIES COVERS

LOU STATHIS EDITOR – ORIGINAL SERIES
AXEL ALONSO ASSISTANT EDITOR – ORIGINAL SERIES
SCOTT NYBAKKEN EDITOR
ROBBIN BROSTERMAN DESIGN DIRECTOR – BOOKS
LOUIS PRANDI PUBLICATION DESIGN

SHELLY BOND EXECUTIVE EDITOR – VERTIGO
HANK KANALZ SENIOR VP – VERTIGO AND INTEGRATED PUBLISHING

DIANE NELSON PRESIDENT
DAN DIDIO AND JIM LEE CO-PUBLISHERS
GEOFF JOHNS CHIEF CREATIVE OFFICER
AMIT DESAI SENIOR VP – MARKETING AND FRANCHISE MANAGEMENT
AMY GENKINS SENIOR VP – BUSINESS AND LEGAL AFFAIRS
NAIRI GARDINER SENIOR VP – FINANCE
JEFF BOISON VP – PUBLISHING PLANNING
MARK CHIARELLO VP – ART DIRECTION AND DESIGN
JOHN CUNNINGHAM VP – MARKETING
TERRI CUNNINGHAM VP – EDITORIAL ADMINISTRATION
LARRY GANEM VP – TALENT RELATIONS AND SERVICES
ALISON GILL SENIOR VP – MANUFACTURING AND OPERATIONS
JAY KOGAN VP – BUSINESS AND LEGAL AFFAIRS, PUBLISHING

JACK MAHAN VP – BUSINESS AFFAIRS, TALENT
NICK NAPOLITANO VP – MANUFACTURING ADMINISTRATION
SUE POHJA VP – BOOK SALES
FRED RUIZ VP – MANUFACTURING OPERATIONS
COURTNEY SIMMONS SENIOR VP – PUBLICITY
BOB WAYNE SENIOR VP – SALES

JOHN CONSTANTINE, HELLBLAZER: IN THE LINE OF FIRE

DC COMICS, 1700 BROADWAY, NEW YORK, NY 10019
A WARNER BROS. ENTERTAINMENT COMPANY
PRINTED IN THE USA. FIRST PRINTING.
ISBN: 978-1-4012-5137-6

LIBRARY OF CONGRESS CATALOGING-IN-PUBLICATION DATA

JENKINS, PAUL, 1965- AUTHOR.
JOHN CONSTANTINE HELLBLAZER. VOL. 10, IN THE LINE OF FIRE / PAUL JENKINS ; [ILLUSTRATED BY] SEAN PHILLIPS.
    PAGES CM
ISBN 978-1-4012-5137-6 (PBK.)
1. GRAPHIC NOVELS. I. PHILLIPS, SEAN, ILLUSTRATOR. II. TITLE. III. TITLE: IN THE LINE OF FIRE.

PN6728.H383J47 2015
741.5'973—DC23

2014039173

SUSTAINABLE
FORESTRY
INITIATIVE

Certified Sourcing
www.sfiprogram.org
SFI-01042
APPLIES TO TEXT STOCK ONLY

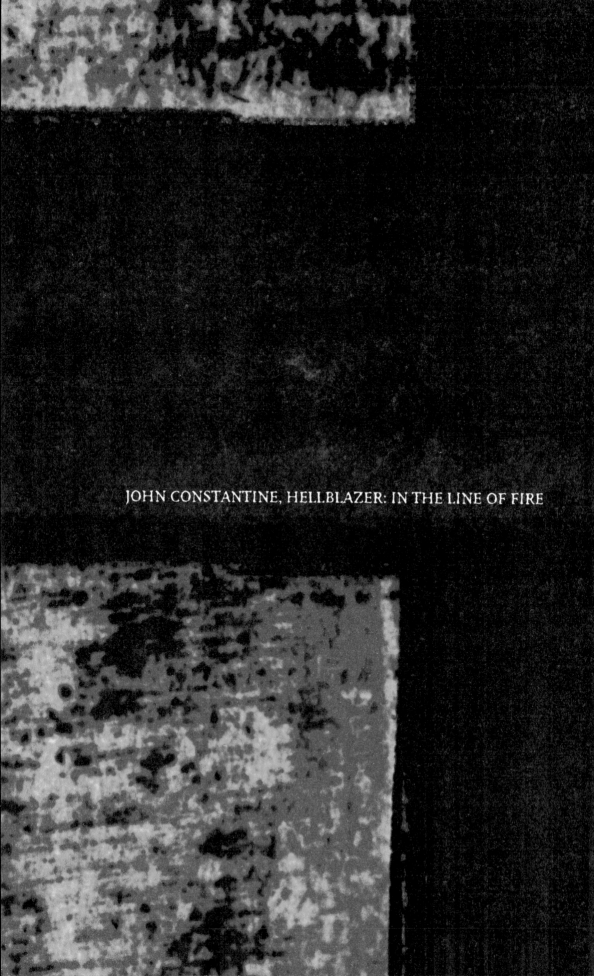

JOHN CONSTANTINE, HELLBLAZER: IN THE LINE OF FIRE

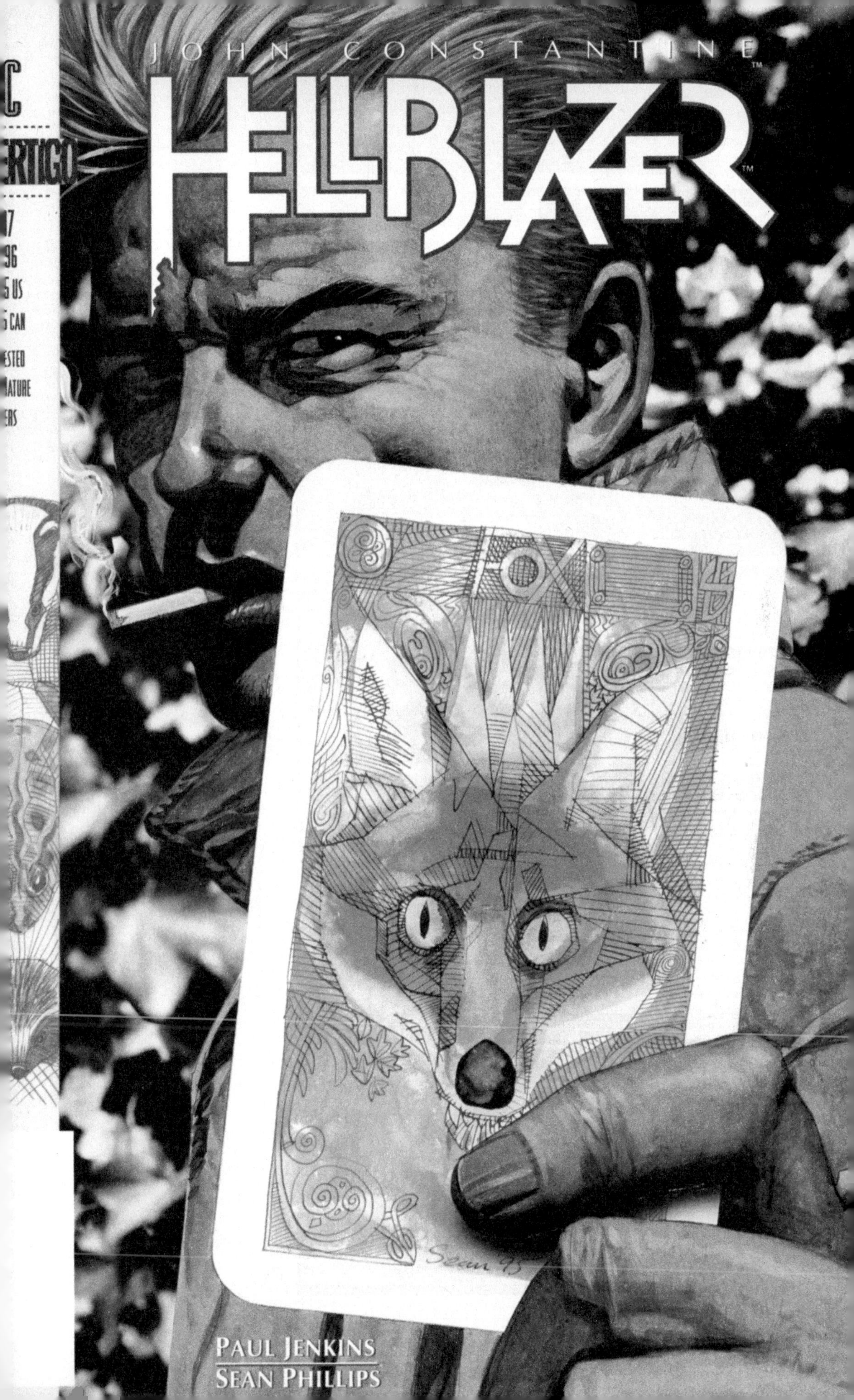
JOHN CONSTANTINE
HELLBLAZER
PAUL JENKINS
SEAN PHILLIPS

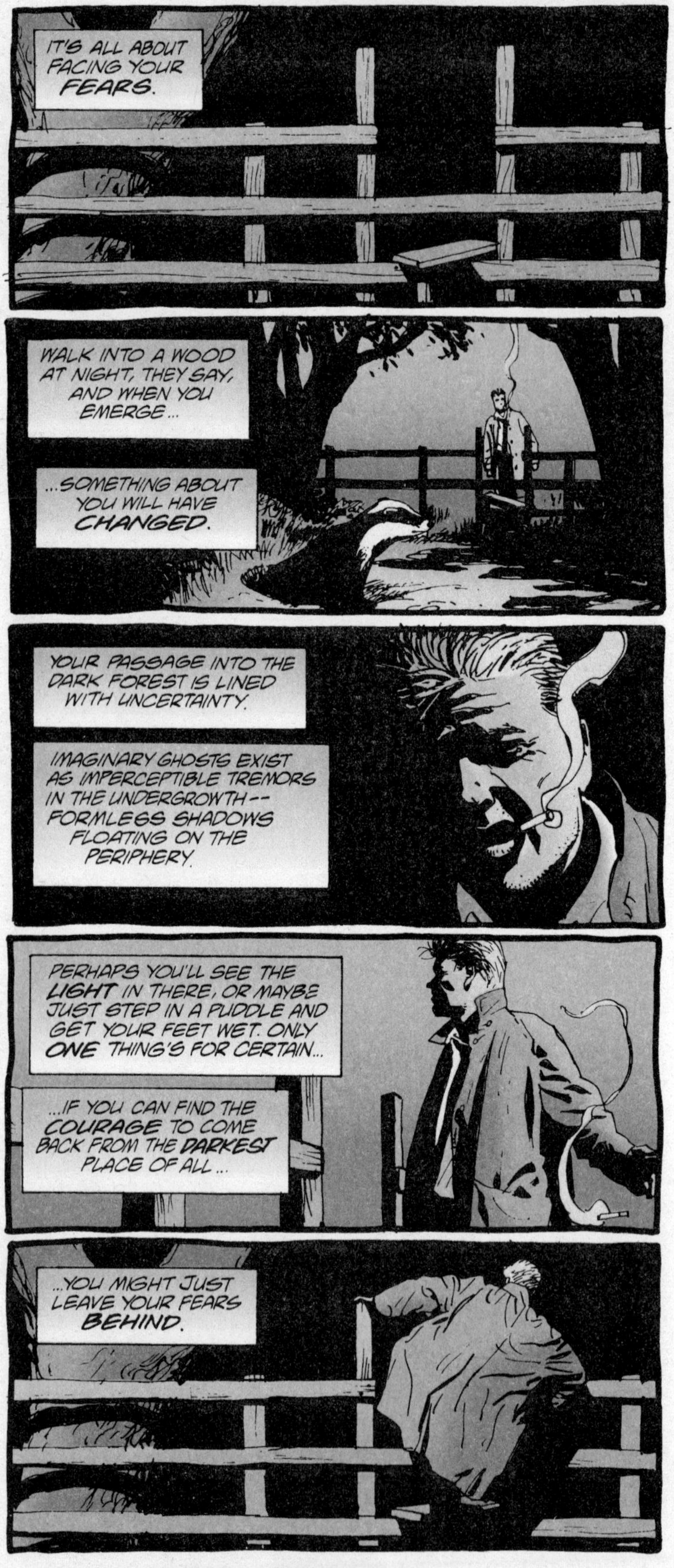
IT'S ALL ABOUT FACING YOUR FEARS.
WALK INTO A WOOD AT NIGHT, THEY SAY, AND WHEN YOU EMERGE...
...SOMETHING ABOUT YOU WILL HAVE CHANGED.
YOUR PASSAGE INTO THE DARK FOREST IS LINED WITH UNCERTAINTY.
IMAGINARY GHOSTS EXIST AS IMPERCEPTIBLE TREMORS IN THE UNDERGROWTH-- FORMLESS SHADOWS FLOATING ON THE PERIPHERY.
PERHAPS YOU'LL SEE THE LIGHT IN THERE, OR MAYBE JUST STEP IN A PUDDLE AND GET YOUR FEET WET. ONLY ONE THING'S FOR CERTAIN...
...IF YOU CAN FIND THE COURAGE TO COME BACK FROM THE DARKEST PLACE OF ALL...
...YOU MIGHT JUST LEAVE YOUR FEARS BEHIND.

the NATURE of the BEAST

Paul Jenkins Writer

Sean Phillips Artist

Matt Hollingsworth Colorist

Clem Robins Letterer

Axel Alonso Asst. Editor

Lou Stathis Editor

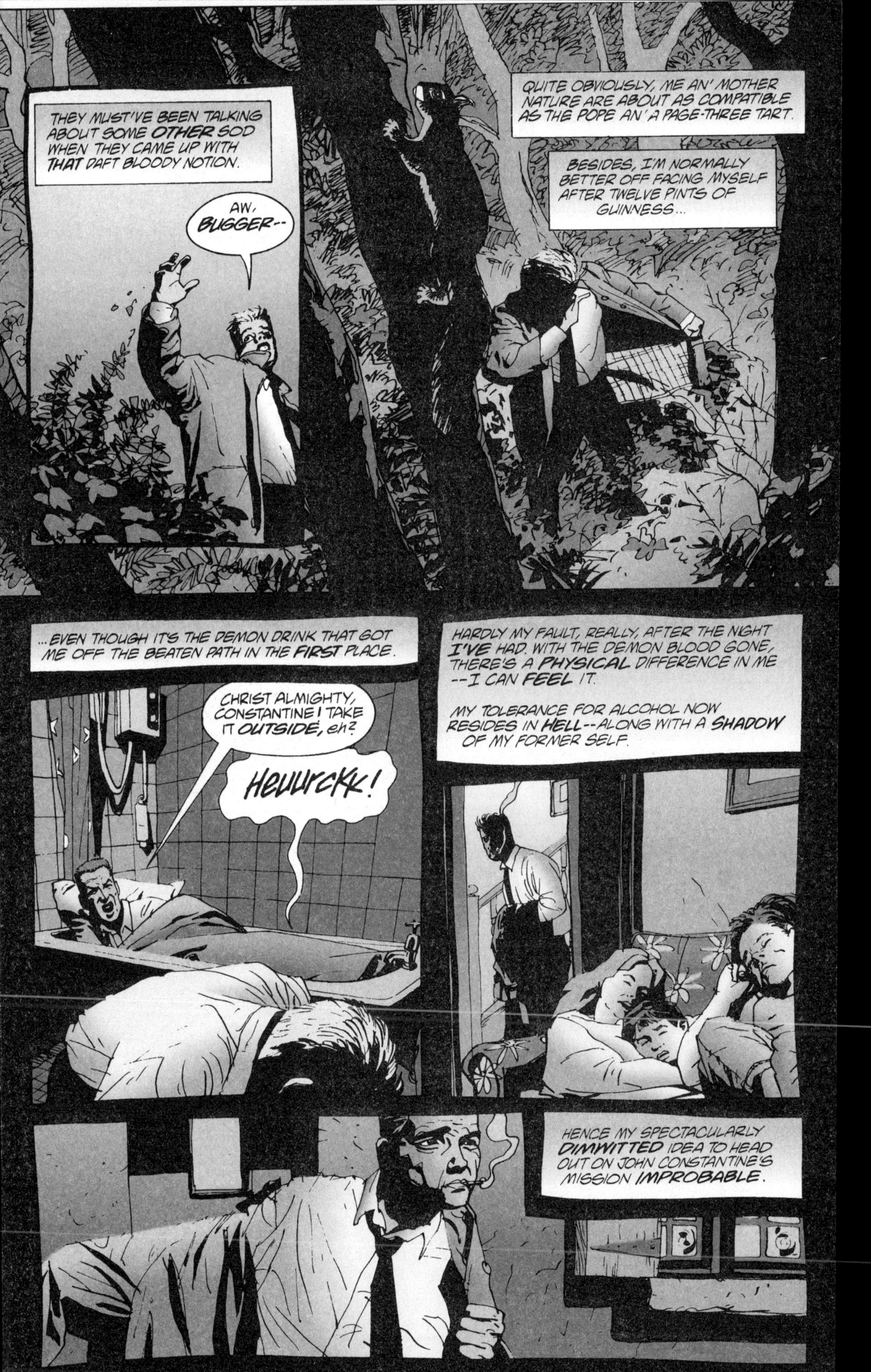
THEY MUST'VE BEEN TALKING ABOUT SOME OTHER SOD WHEN THEY CAME UP WITH THAT DAFT BLOODY NOTION.
AW, BUGGER--
QUITE OBVIOUSLY, ME AN' MOTHER NATURE ARE ABOUT AS COMPATIBLE AS THE POPE AN' A PAGE-THREE TART.
BESIDES, I'M NORMALLY BETTER OFF FACING MYSELF AFTER TWELVE PINTS OF GUINNESS...
...EVEN THOUGH IT'S THE DEMON DRINK THAT GOT ME OFF THE BEATEN PATH IN THE FIRST PLACE.
CHRIST ALMIGHTY, CONSTANTINE! TAKE IT OUTSIDE, eh?
HEUURCKK!
HARDLY MY FAULT, REALLY, AFTER THE NIGHT I'VE HAD. WITH THE DEMON BLOOD GONE, THERE'S A PHYSICAL DIFFERENCE IN ME --I CAN FEEL IT.
MY TOLERANCE FOR ALCOHOL NOW RESIDES IN HELL--ALONG WITH A SHADOW OF MY FORMER SELF.
HENCE MY SPECTACULARLY DIMWITTED IDEA TO HEAD OUT ON JOHN CONSTANTINE'S MISSION IMPROBABLE.

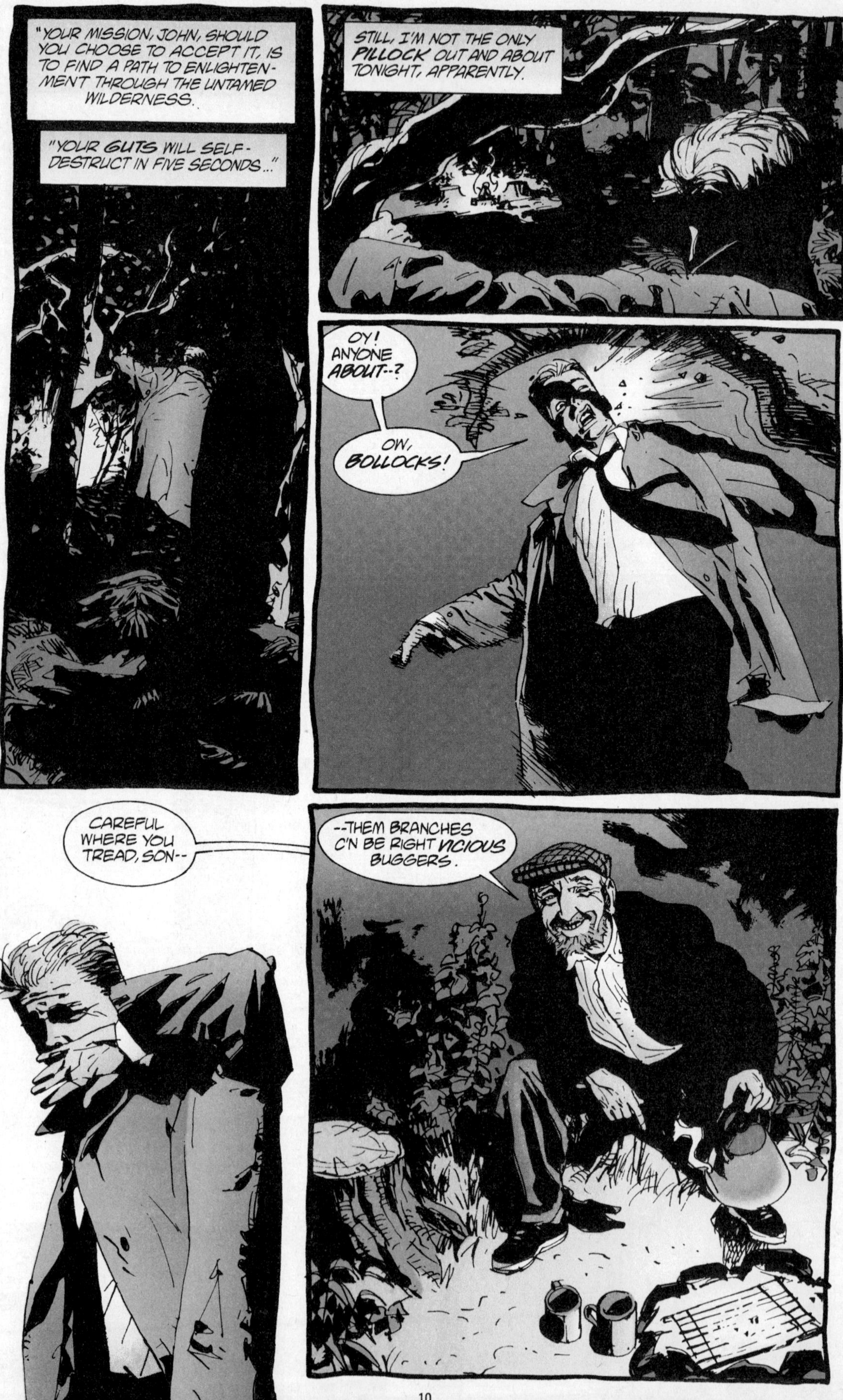
"YOUR MISSION, JOHN, SHOULD YOU CHOOSE TO ACCEPT IT, IS TO FIND A PATH TO ENLIGHTENMENT THROUGH THE UNTAMED WILDERNESS.
"YOUR GUTS WILL SELF-DESTRUCT IN FIVE SECONDS..."
STILL, I'M NOT THE ONLY PILLOCK OUT AND ABOUT TONIGHT, APPARENTLY.
OY! ANYONE ABOUT--?
OW, BOLLOCKS!
CAREFUL WHERE YOU TREAD, SON--
--THEM BRANCHES C'N BE RIGHT VICIOUS BUGGERS.

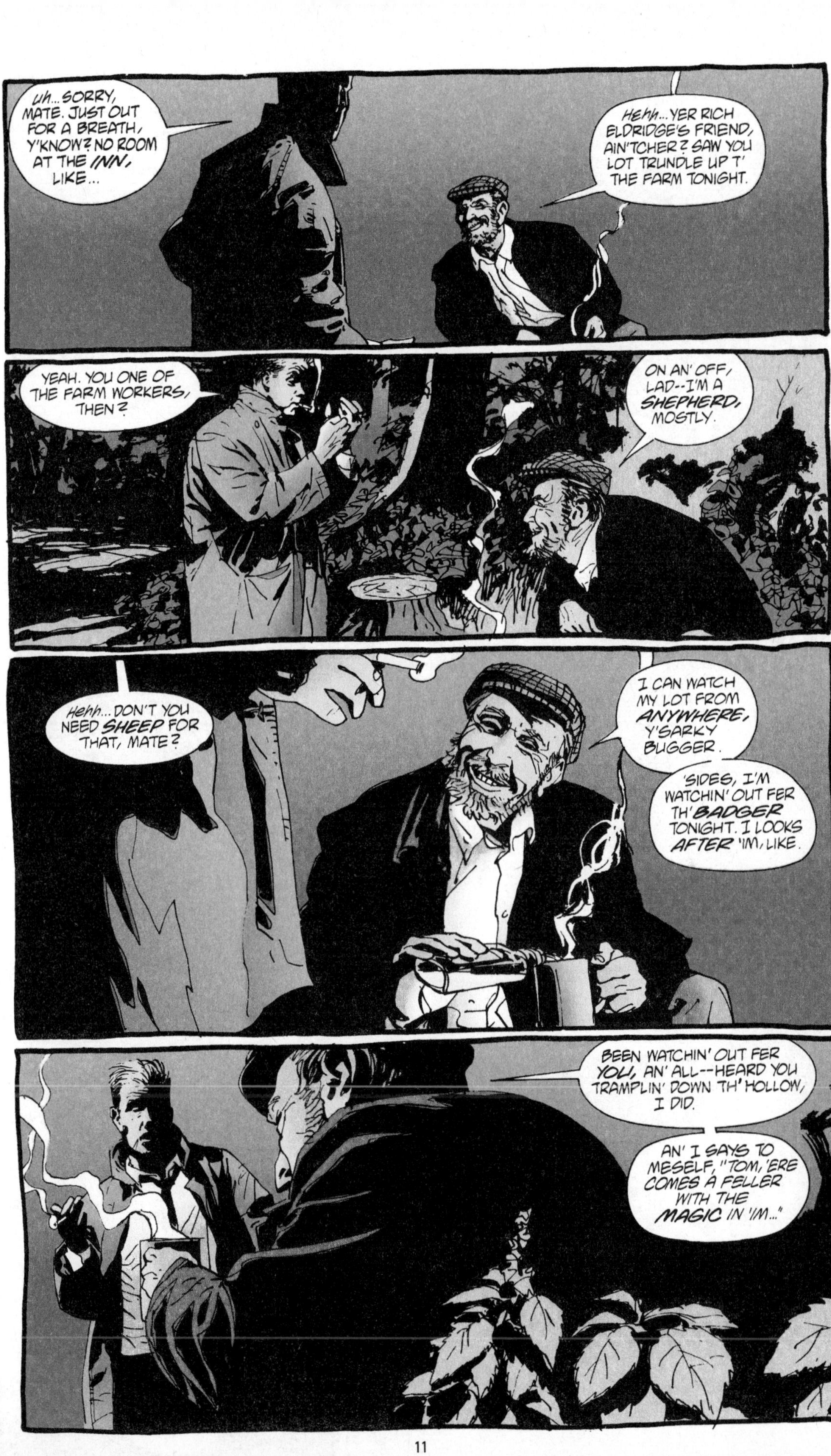
Uh... SORRY, MATE. JUST OUT FOR A BREATH, Y'KNOW? NO ROOM AT THE INN, LIKE...
Hehh... YER RICH ELDRIDGE'S FRIEND, AIN'TCHER? SAW YOU LOT TRUNDLE UP T' THE FARM TONIGHT.
YEAH. YOU ONE OF THE FARM WORKERS, THEN?
ON AN' OFF, LAD--I'M A SHEPHERD, MOSTLY.
Hehh... DON'T YOU NEED SHEEP FOR THAT, MATE?
I CAN WATCH MY LOT FROM ANYWHERE, Y'SARKY BUGGER.
'SIDES, I'M WATCHIN' OUT FER TH' BADGER TONIGHT. I LOOKS AFTER 'IM, LIKE.
BEEN WATCHIN' OUT FER YOU, AN' ALL--HEARD YOU TRAMPLIN' DOWN TH' HOLLOW, I DID.
AN' I SAYS TO MESELF, "TOM, 'ERE COMES A FELLER WITH THE MAGIC IN 'IM..."

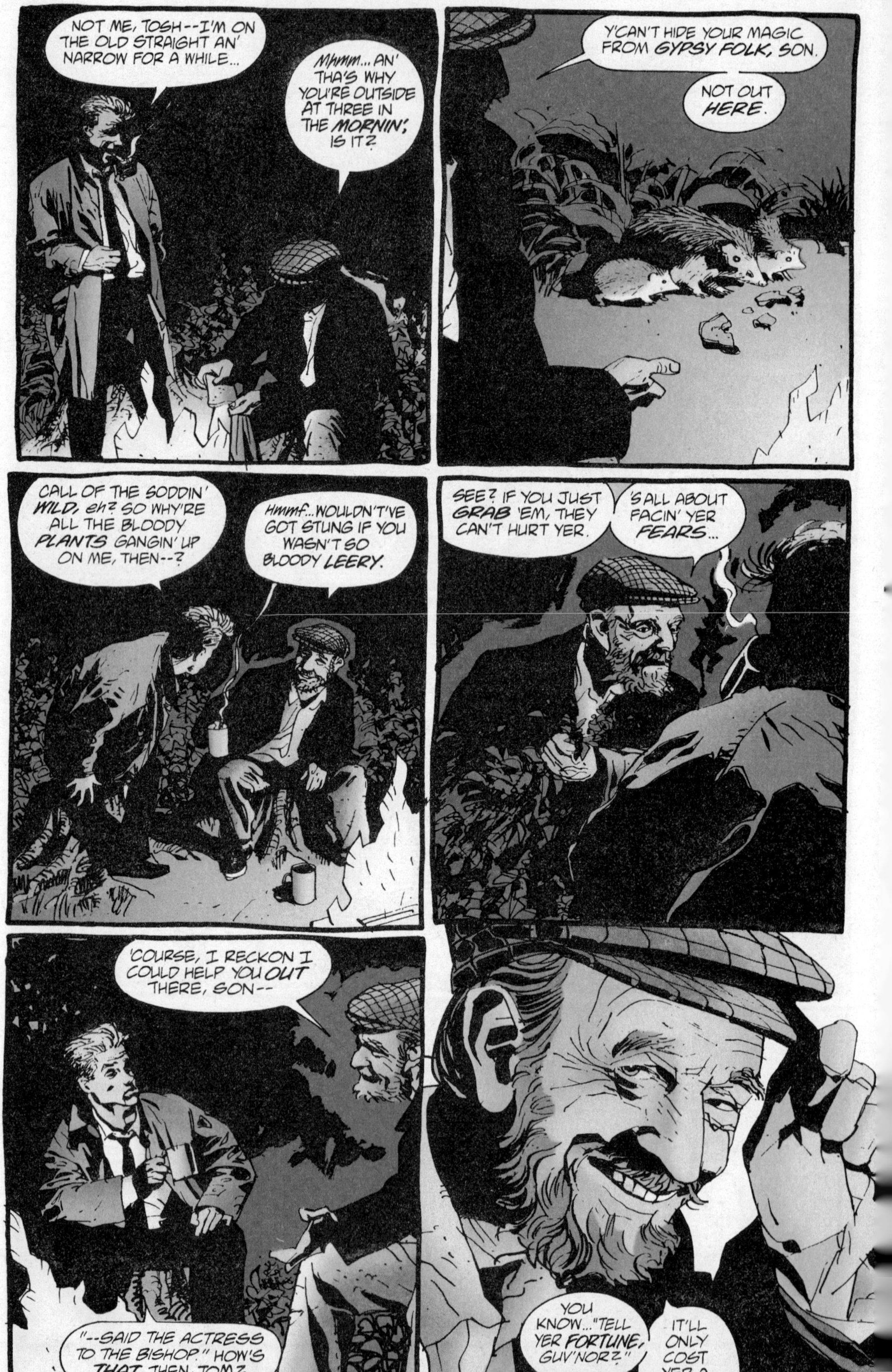
NOT ME, TOSH--I'M ON THE OLD STRAIGHT AN' NARROW FOR A WHILE...
MMMM... AN' THA'S WHY YOU'RE OUTSIDE AT THREE IN THE MORNIN', IS IT?
Y'CAN'T HIDE YOUR MAGIC FROM GYPSY FOLK, SON.
NOT OUT HERE.
CALL OF THE SODDIN' WILD, EH? SO WHY'RE ALL THE BLOODY PLANTS GANGIN' UP ON ME, THEN--?
HMMF... WOULDN'T'VE GOT STUNG IF YOU WASN'T SO BLOODY LEERY.
SEE? IF YOU JUST GRAB 'EM, THEY CAN'T HURT YER.
'S ALL ABOUT FACIN' YER FEARS...
'COURSE, I RECKON I COULD HELP YOU OUT THERE, SON--
"--SAID THE ACTRESS TO THE BISHOP." HOW'S THAT, THEN, TOM?
YOU KNOW... "TELL YER FORTUNE, GUV'NOR?"
IT'LL ONLY COST YER A TENNER.

heh...NOT LIKELY, MATE. I'VE HAD ENOUGH OF THAT LARK FOR ONE NIGHT.

LISTEN, THANKS FOR THE CUPPA AN' ALL THAT--

WHAT, YOU SCARED OF A DODDERY OLD BUGGER LIKE ME, OR OF SPENDIN' TEN BLOODY QUID?

TELL YOU WHAT--WE'LL PUT A LITTLE BET ON IT, eh? JUST TO PROVE TOM'S BEIN' HONEST, LIKE...

LET'S SAY AN OLD MATE OF YOURS SHOWS UP BEFORE WE'VE FINISHED --RECKON YOU'D TAKE THAT BET FOR A TENNER?

FUNNY, INNIT? YOU SPEND YOUR WHOLE LIFE LOOKING AT SOMETHING IN A CERTAIN WAY-- LIKE TAROT CARDS, FOR INSTANCE.

THERE'S MORE CHANCE OF SEEING THE FUTURE IN A PACKET OF CORNFLAKES, AS FAR AS I'M CONCERNED.

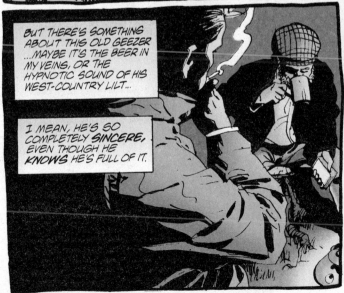

BUT THERE'S SOMETHING ABOUT THIS OLD GEEZER ...MAYBE IT'S THE BEER IN MY VEINS, OR THE HYPNOTIC SOUND OF HIS WEST-COUNTRY LILT...

I MEAN, HE'S SO COMPLETELY SINCERE, EVEN THOUGH HE KNOWS HE'S FULL OF IT.

AND SO, MUCH TO MY OWN SURPRISE...

ALL RIGHT, THEN -- I'M GAME FOR A LAUGH.

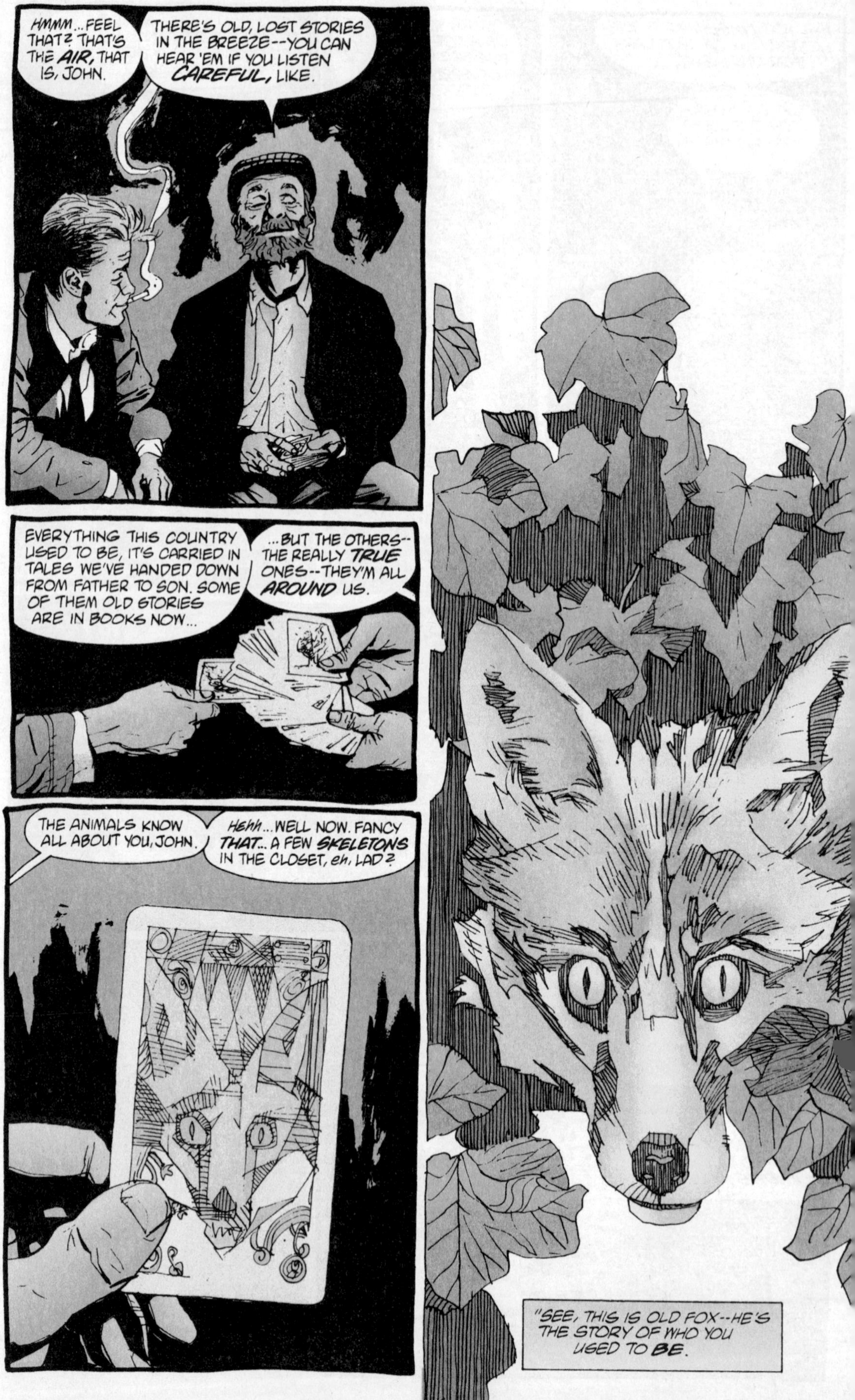
HMMM... FEEL THAT? THAT'S THE AIR, THAT IS, JOHN.
THERE'S OLD, LOST STORIES IN THE BREEZE--YOU CAN HEAR 'EM IF YOU LISTEN CAREFUL, LIKE.
EVERYTHING THIS COUNTRY USED TO BE, IT'S CARRIED IN TALES WE'VE HANDED DOWN FROM FATHER TO SON. SOME OF THEM OLD STORIES ARE IN BOOKS NOW...
...BUT THE OTHERS--THE REALLY TRUE ONES--THEY'M ALL AROUND US.
THE ANIMALS KNOW ALL ABOUT YOU, JOHN.
Hehh... WELL NOW. FANCY THAT... A FEW SKELETONS IN THE CLOSET, eh, LAD?
"SEE, THIS IS OLD FOX--HE'S THE STORY OF WHO YOU USED TO BE.

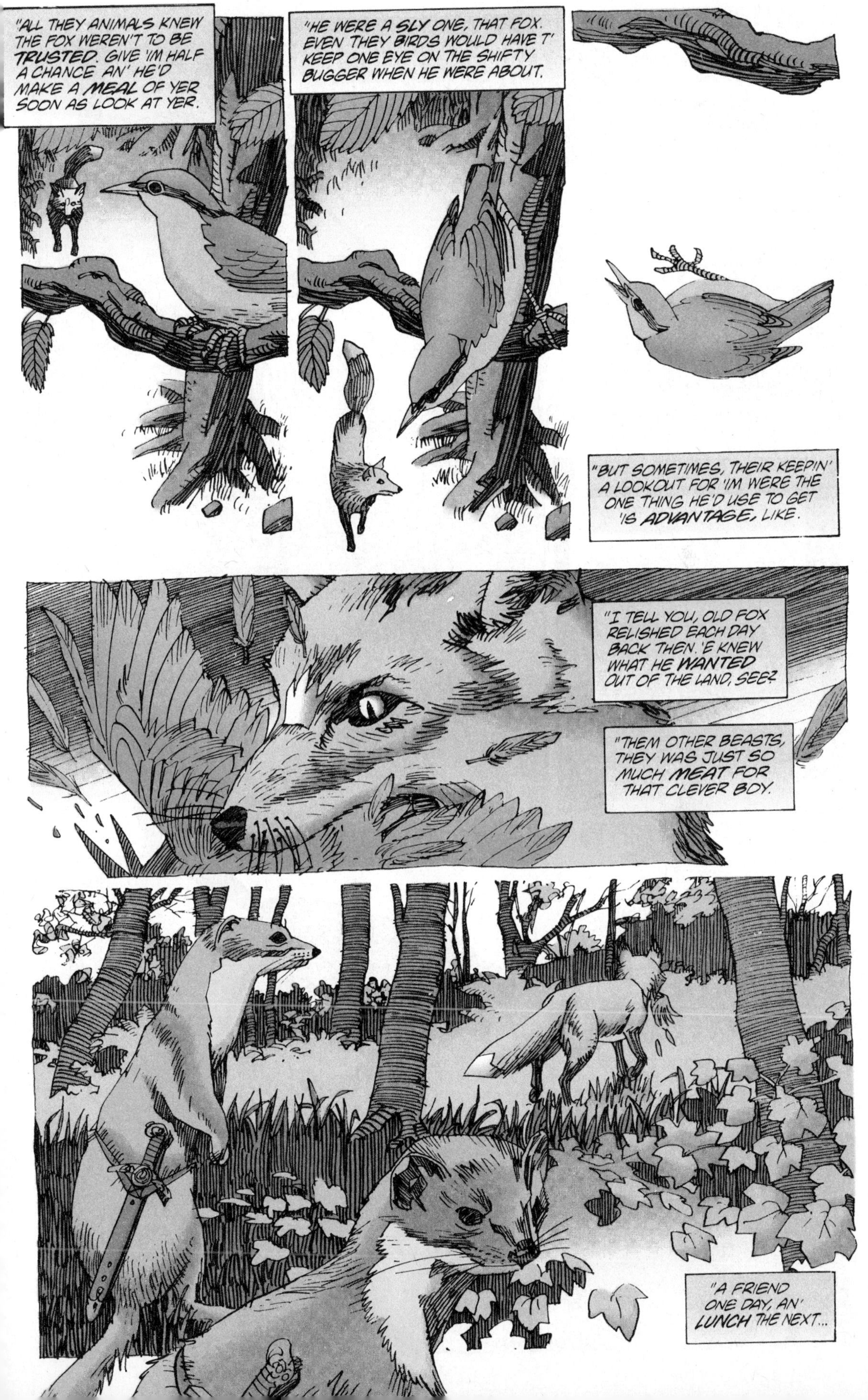
"ALL THEY ANIMALS KNEW THE FOX WEREN'T TO BE TRUSTED. GIVE 'IM HALF A CHANCE AN' HE'D MAKE A MEAL OF YER SOON AS LOOK AT YER.
"HE WERE A SLY ONE, THAT FOX. EVEN THEY BIRDS WOULD HAVE T' KEEP ONE EYE ON THE SHIFTY BUGGER WHEN HE WERE ABOUT.
"BUT SOMETIMES, THEIR KEEPIN' A LOOKOUT FOR 'IM WERE THE ONE THING HE'D USE TO GET 'IS ADVANTAGE, LIKE.
"I TELL YOU, OLD FOX RELISHED EACH DAY BACK THEN. 'E KNEW WHAT HE WANTED OUT OF THE LAND, SEE?
"THEM OTHER BEASTS, THEY WAS JUST SO MUCH MEAT FOR THAT CLEVER BOY.
"A FRIEND ONE DAY, AN' LUNCH THE NEXT...

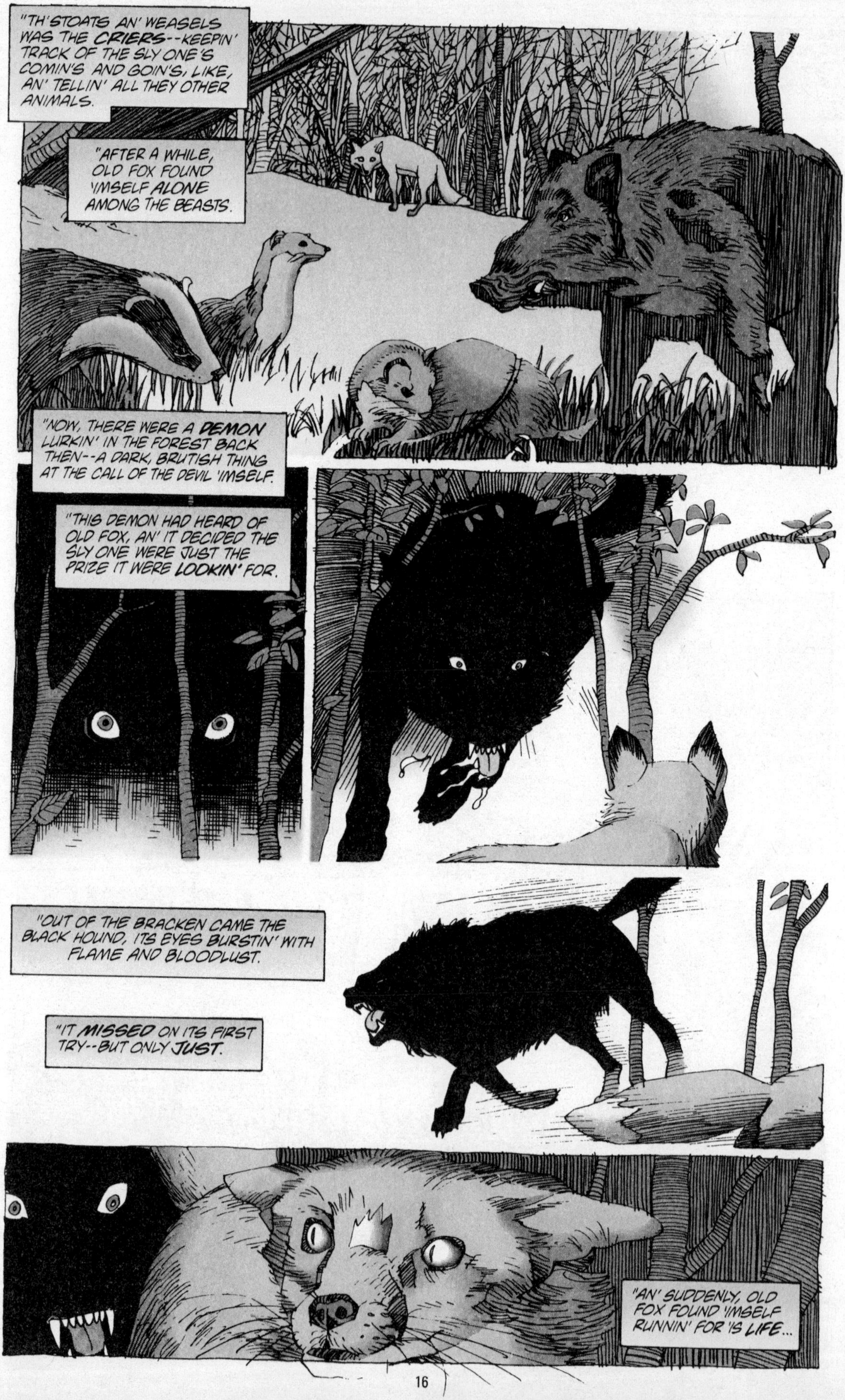
"TH' STOATS AN' WEASELS WAS THE CRIERS--KEEPIN' TRACK OF THE SLY ONE'S COMIN'S AND GOIN'S, LIKE, AN' TELLIN' ALL THEY OTHER ANIMALS.
"AFTER A WHILE, OLD FOX FOUND 'IMSELF ALONE AMONG THE BEASTS.
"NOW, THERE WERE A DEMON LURKIN' IN THE FOREST BACK THEN--A DARK, BRUTISH THING AT THE CALL OF THE DEVIL 'IMSELF.
"THIS DEMON HAD HEARD OF OLD FOX, AN' IT DECIDED THE SLY ONE WERE JUST THE PRIZE IT WERE LOOKIN' FOR.
"OUT OF THE BRACKEN CAME THE BLACK HOUND, ITS EYES BURSTIN' WITH FLAME AND BLOODLUST.
"IT MISSED ON ITS FIRST TRY--BUT ONLY JUST.
"AN' SUDDENLY, OLD FOX FOUND 'IMSELF RUNNIN' FOR 'IS LIFE...

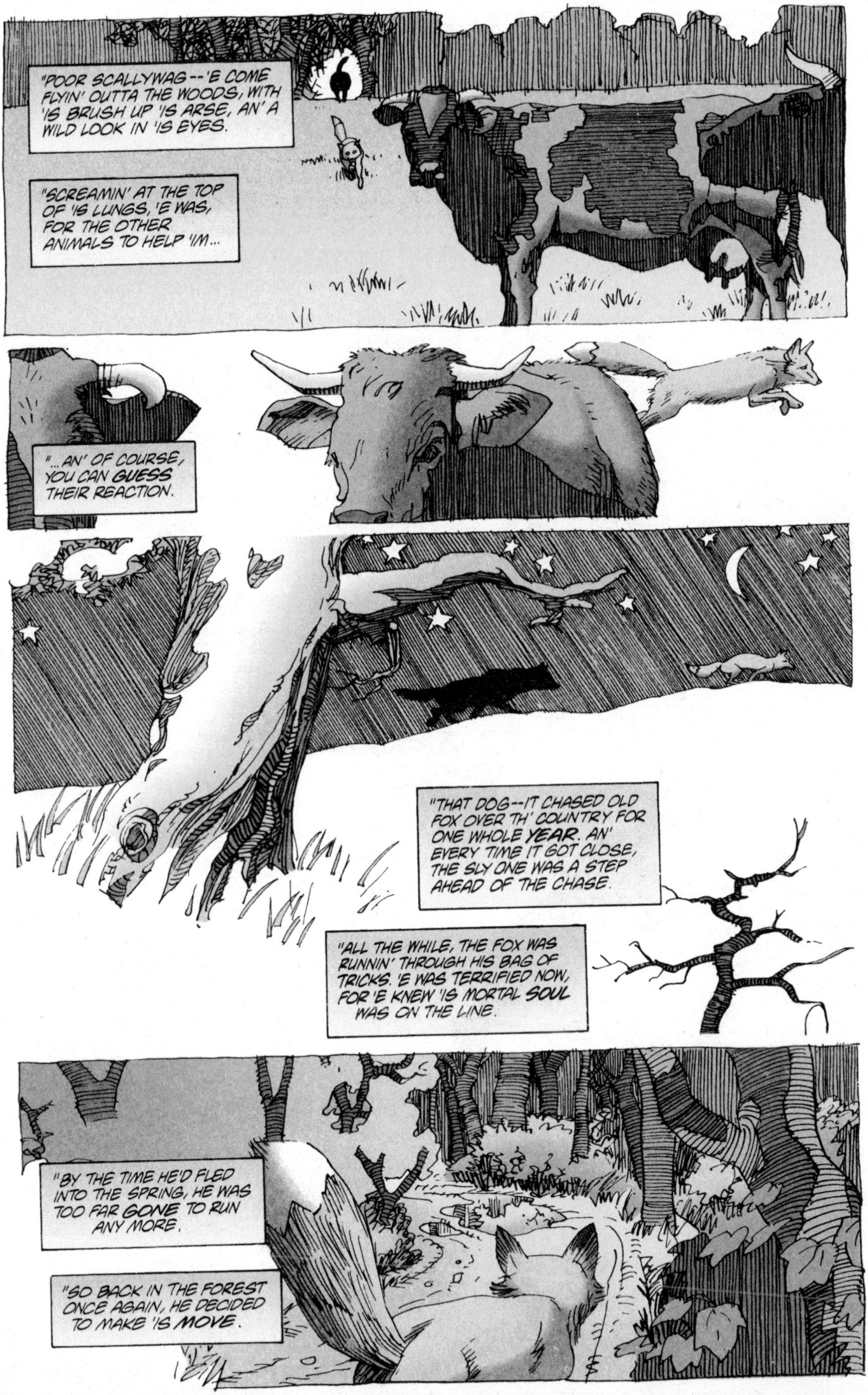
"POOR SCALLYWAG--'E COME FLYIN' OUTTA THE WOODS, WITH 'IS BRUSH UP 'IS ARSE, AN' A WILD LOOK IN 'IS EYES.
"SCREAMIN' AT THE TOP OF 'IS LUNGS, 'E WAS, FOR THE OTHER ANIMALS TO HELP 'IM...
"...AN' OF COURSE, YOU CAN GUESS THEIR REACTION.
"THAT DOG--IT CHASED OLD FOX OVER TH' COUNTRY FOR ONE WHOLE YEAR. AN' EVERY TIME IT GOT CLOSE, THE SLY ONE WAS A STEP AHEAD OF THE CHASE.
"ALL THE WHILE, THE FOX WAS RUNNIN' THROUGH HIS BAG OF TRICKS. 'E WAS TERRIFIED NOW, FOR 'E KNEW 'IS MORTAL SOUL WAS ON THE LINE.
"BY THE TIME HE'D FLED INTO THE SPRING, HE WAS TOO FAR GONE TO RUN ANY MORE.
"SO BACK IN THE FOREST ONCE AGAIN, HE DECIDED TO MAKE 'IS MOVE.

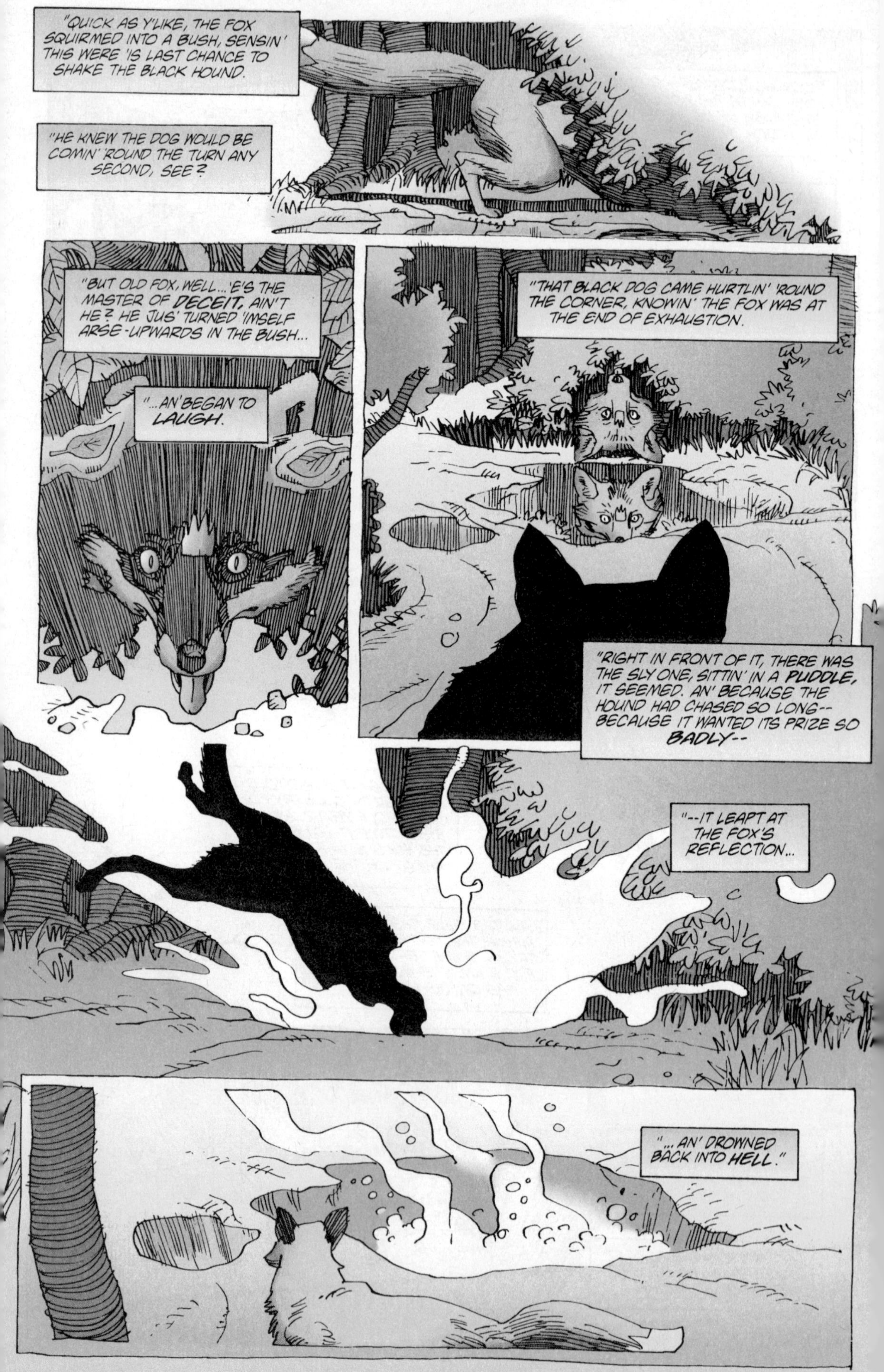
"QUICK AS Y'LIKE, THE FOX SQUIRMED INTO A BUSH, SENSIN' THIS WERE 'IS LAST CHANCE TO SHAKE THE BLACK HOUND.
"HE KNEW THE DOG WOULD BE COMIN' 'ROUND THE TURN ANY SECOND, SEE?
"BUT OLD FOX, WELL... 'E'S THE MASTER OF DECEIT, AIN'T HE? HE JUS' TURNED 'IMSELF ARSE-UPWARDS IN THE BUSH...
"...AN' BEGAN TO LAUGH.
"THAT BLACK DOG CAME HURTLIN' 'ROUND THE CORNER, KNOWIN' THE FOX WAS AT THE END OF EXHAUSTION.
"RIGHT IN FRONT OF IT, THERE WAS THE SLY ONE, SITTIN' IN A PUDDLE, IT SEEMED. AN' BECAUSE THE HOUND HAD CHASED SO LONG-- BECAUSE IT WANTED ITS PRIZE SO BADLY--
"--IT LEAPT AT THE FOX'S REFLECTION...
"... AN' DROWNED BACK INTO HELL."

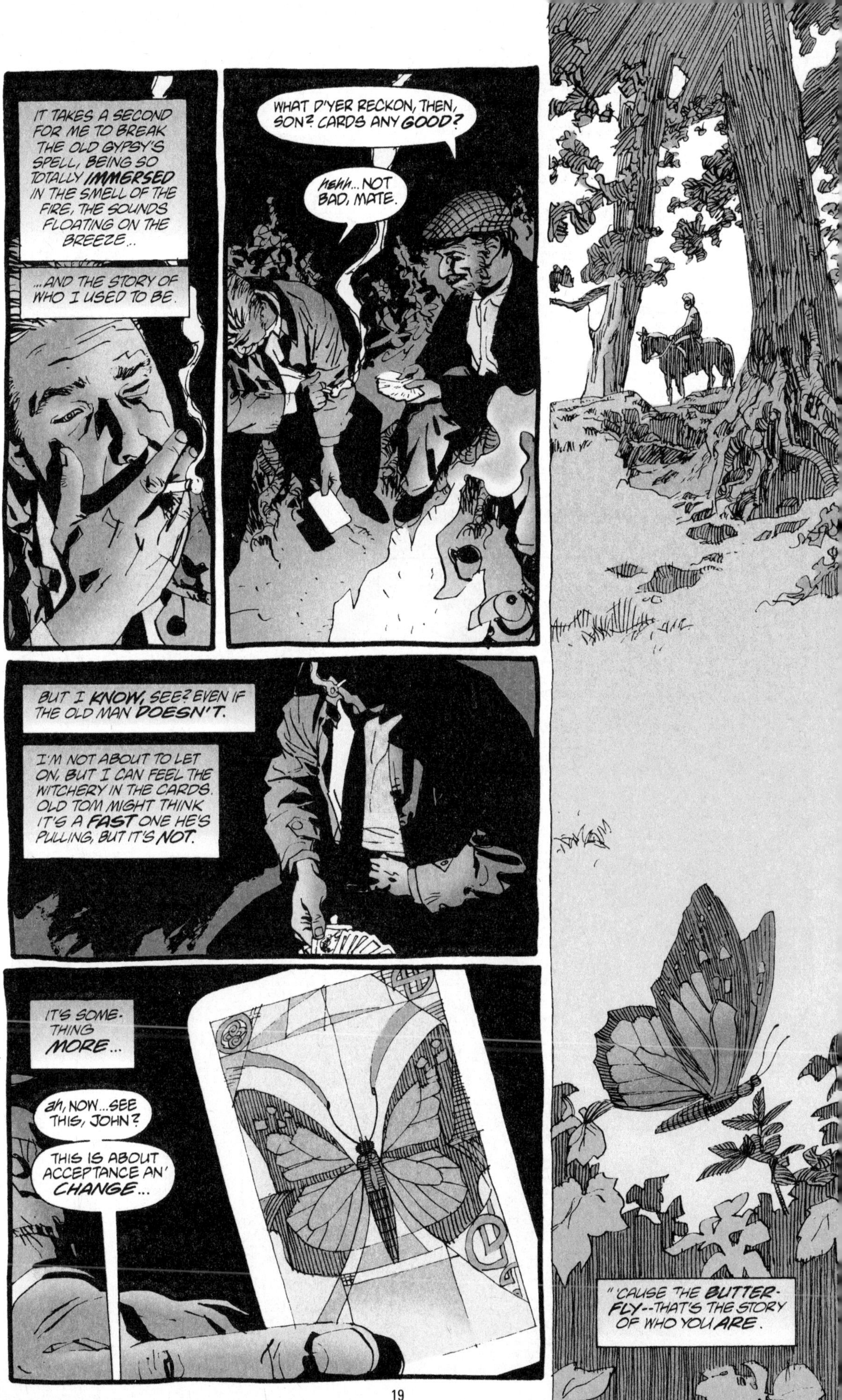

IT TAKES A SECOND FOR ME TO BREAK THE OLD GYPSY'S SPELL, BEING SO TOTALLY IMMERSED IN THE SMELL OF THE FIRE, THE SOUNDS FLOATING ON THE BREEZE...
...AND THE STORY OF WHO I USED TO BE.
WHAT D'YER RECKON, THEN, SON? CARDS ANY GOOD?
HEHH... NOT BAD, MATE.
BUT I KNOW, SEE? EVEN IF THE OLD MAN DOESN'T.
I'M NOT ABOUT TO LET ON, BUT I CAN FEEL THE WITCHERY IN THE CARDS. OLD TOM MIGHT THINK IT'S A FAST ONE HE'S PULLING, BUT IT'S NOT.
IT'S SOMETHING MORE...
AH, NOW... SEE THIS, JOHN?
THIS IS ABOUT ACCEPTANCE AN' CHANGE...
"CAUSE THE BUTTERFLY--THAT'S THE STORY OF WHO YOU ARE.

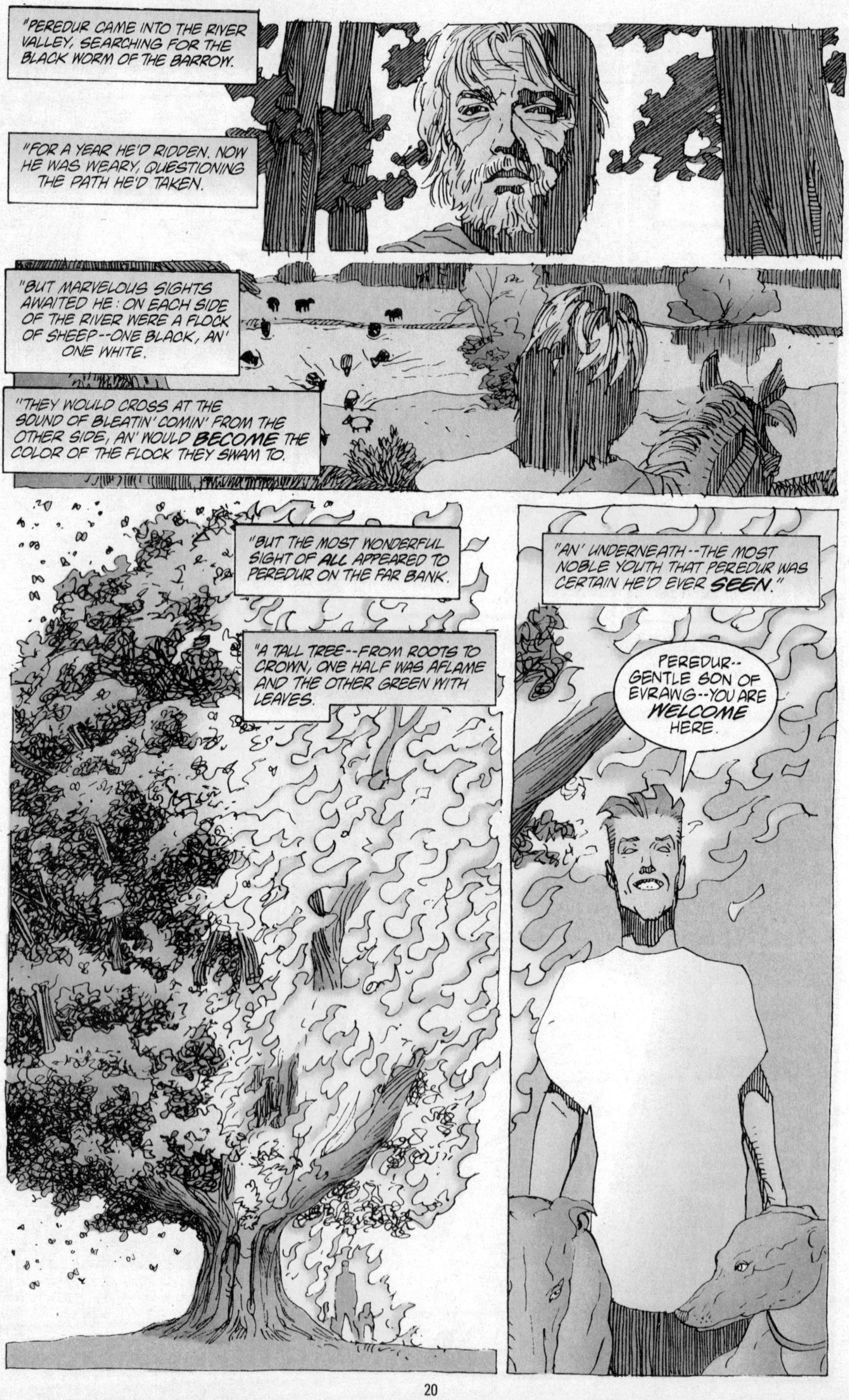
"PEREDUR CAME INTO THE RIVER VALLEY, SEARCHING FOR THE BLACK WORM OF THE BARROW.
"FOR A YEAR HE'D RIDDEN. NOW HE WAS WEARY, QUESTIONING THE PATH HE'D TAKEN.
"BUT MARVELOUS SIGHTS AWAITED HE: ON EACH SIDE OF THE RIVER WERE A FLOCK OF SHEEP--ONE BLACK, AN' ONE WHITE.
"THEY WOULD CROSS AT THE SOUND OF BLEATIN' COMIN' FROM THE OTHER SIDE, AN' WOULD BECOME THE COLOR OF THE FLOCK THEY SWAM TO.
"BUT THE MOST WONDERFUL SIGHT OF ALL APPEARED TO PEREDUR ON THE FAR BANK.
"A TALL TREE--FROM ROOTS TO CROWN, ONE HALF WAS AFLAME AND THE OTHER GREEN WITH LEAVES.
"AN' UNDERNEATH--THE MOST NOBLE YOUTH THAT PEREDUR WAS CERTAIN HE'D EVER SEEN."
PEREDUR--GENTLE SON OF EVRAWG--YOU ARE WELCOME HERE.

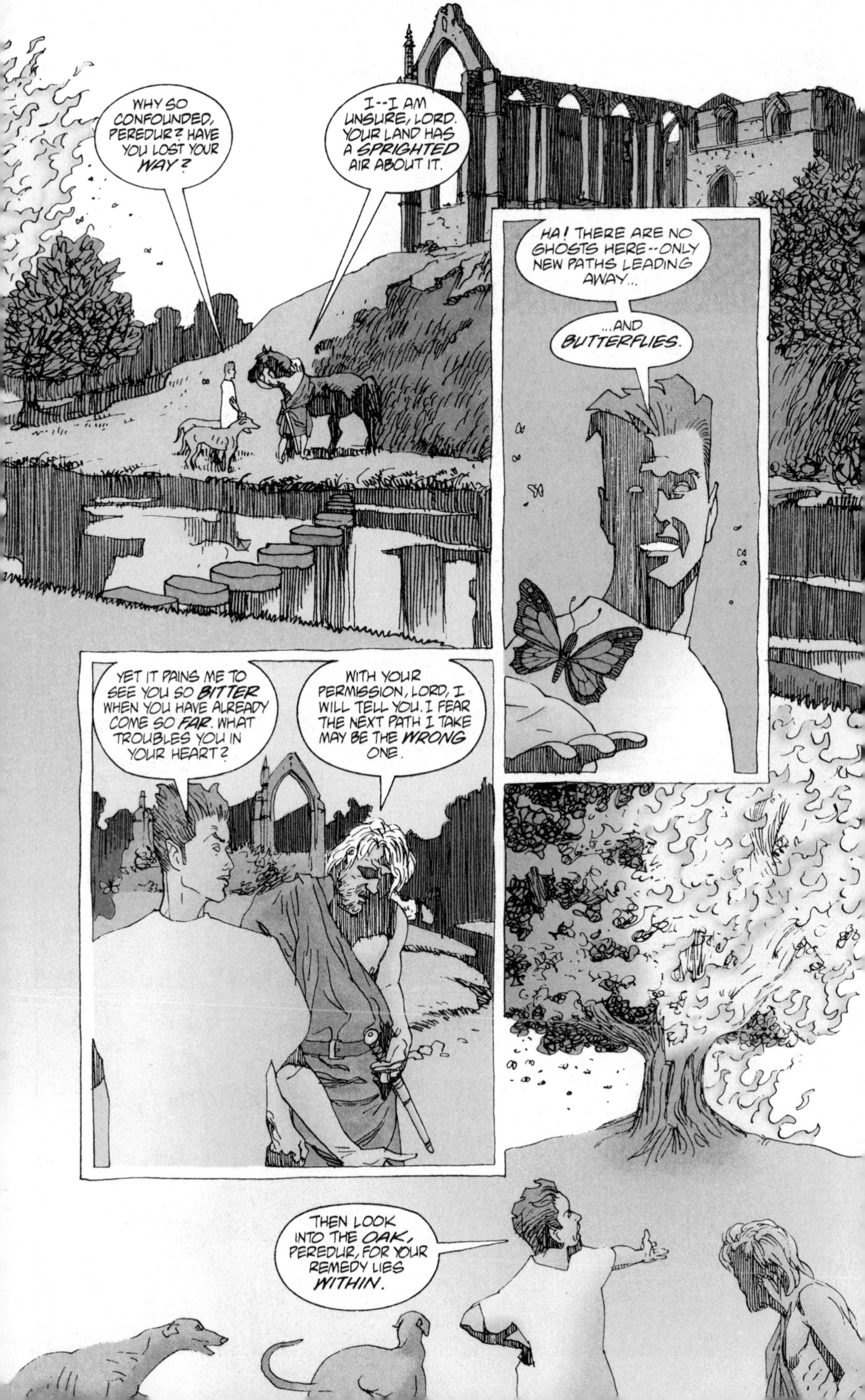
WHY SO CONFOUNDED, PEREDUR? HAVE YOU LOST YOUR WAY?
I--I AM UNSURE, LORD. YOUR LAND HAS A SPRIGHTED AIR ABOUT IT.
HA! THERE ARE NO GHOSTS HERE--ONLY NEW PATHS LEADING AWAY...
...AND BUTTERFLIES.
YET IT PAINS ME TO SEE YOU SO BITTER WHEN YOU HAVE ALREADY COME SO FAR. WHAT TROUBLES YOU IN YOUR HEART?
WITH YOUR PERMISSION, LORD, I WILL TELL YOU. I FEAR THE NEXT PATH I TAKE MAY BE THE WRONG ONE.
THEN LOOK INTO THE OAK, PEREDUR, FOR YOUR REMEDY LIES WITHIN.

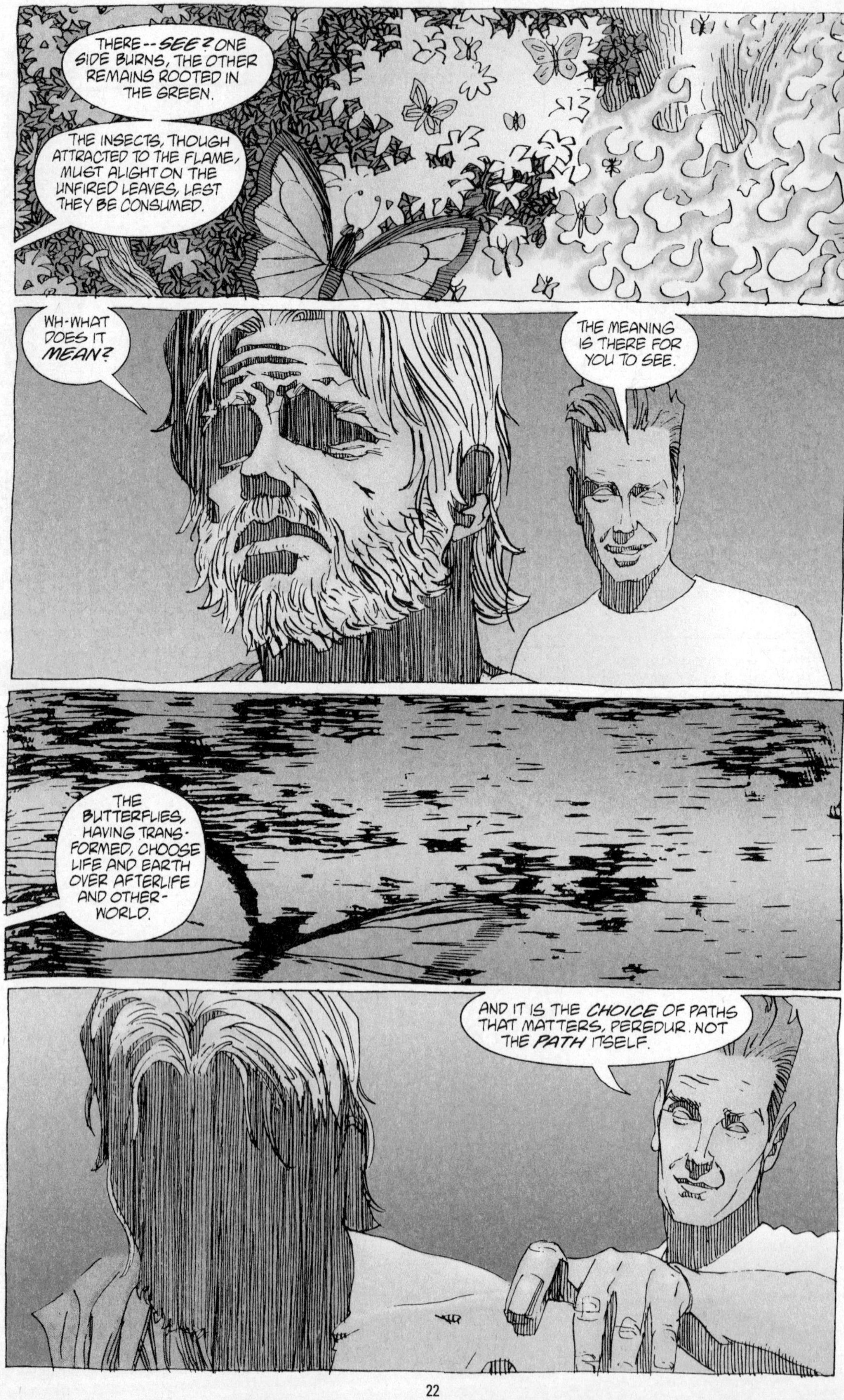
THERE -- SEE? ONE SIDE BURNS, THE OTHER REMAINS ROOTED IN THE GREEN.
THE INSECTS, THOUGH ATTRACTED TO THE FLAME, MUST ALIGHT ON THE UNFIRED LEAVES, LEST THEY BE CONSUMED.
WH-WHAT DOES IT MEAN?
THE MEANING IS THERE FOR YOU TO SEE.
THE BUTTERFLIES, HAVING TRANS-FORMED, CHOOSE LIFE AND EARTH OVER AFTERLIFE AND OTHER-WORLD.
AND IT IS THE CHOICE OF PATHS THAT MATTERS, PEREDUR. NOT THE PATH ITSELF.

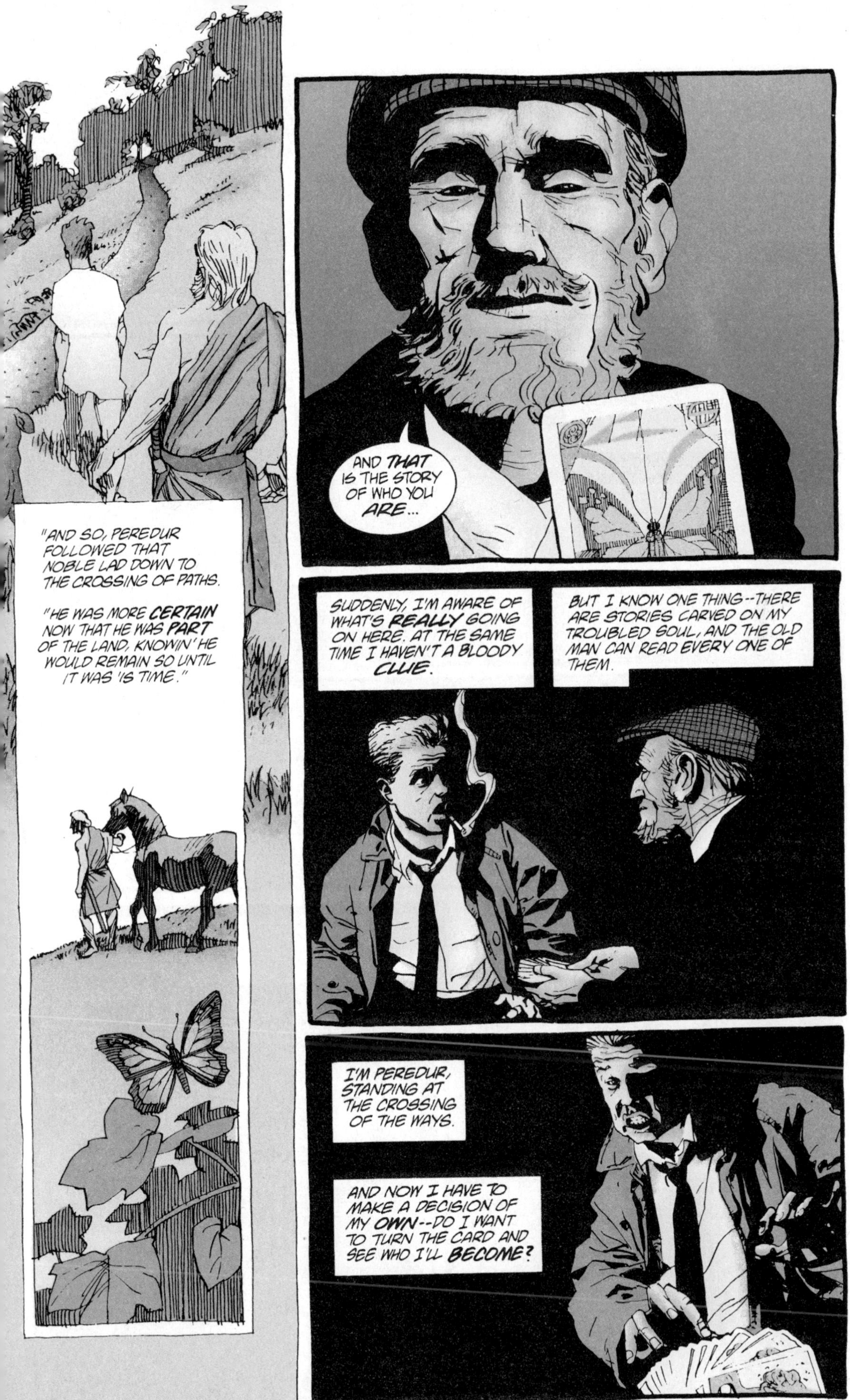
"AND SO, PEREDUR FOLLOWED THAT NOBLE LAD DOWN TO THE CROSSING OF PATHS.
"HE WAS MORE CERTAIN NOW THAT HE WAS PART OF THE LAND, KNOWIN' HE WOULD REMAIN SO UNTIL IT WAS 'IS TIME."
AND THAT IS THE STORY OF WHO YOU ARE...
SUDDENLY, I'M AWARE OF WHAT'S REALLY GOING ON HERE. AT THE SAME TIME I HAVEN'T A BLOODY CLUE.
BUT I KNOW ONE THING--THERE ARE STORIES CARVED ON MY TROUBLED SOUL, AND THE OLD MAN CAN READ EVERY ONE OF THEM.
I'M PEREDUR, STANDING AT THE CROSSING OF THE WAYS.
AND NOW I HAVE TO MAKE A DECISION OF MY OWN--DO I WANT TO TURN THE CARD AND SEE WHO I'LL BECOME?

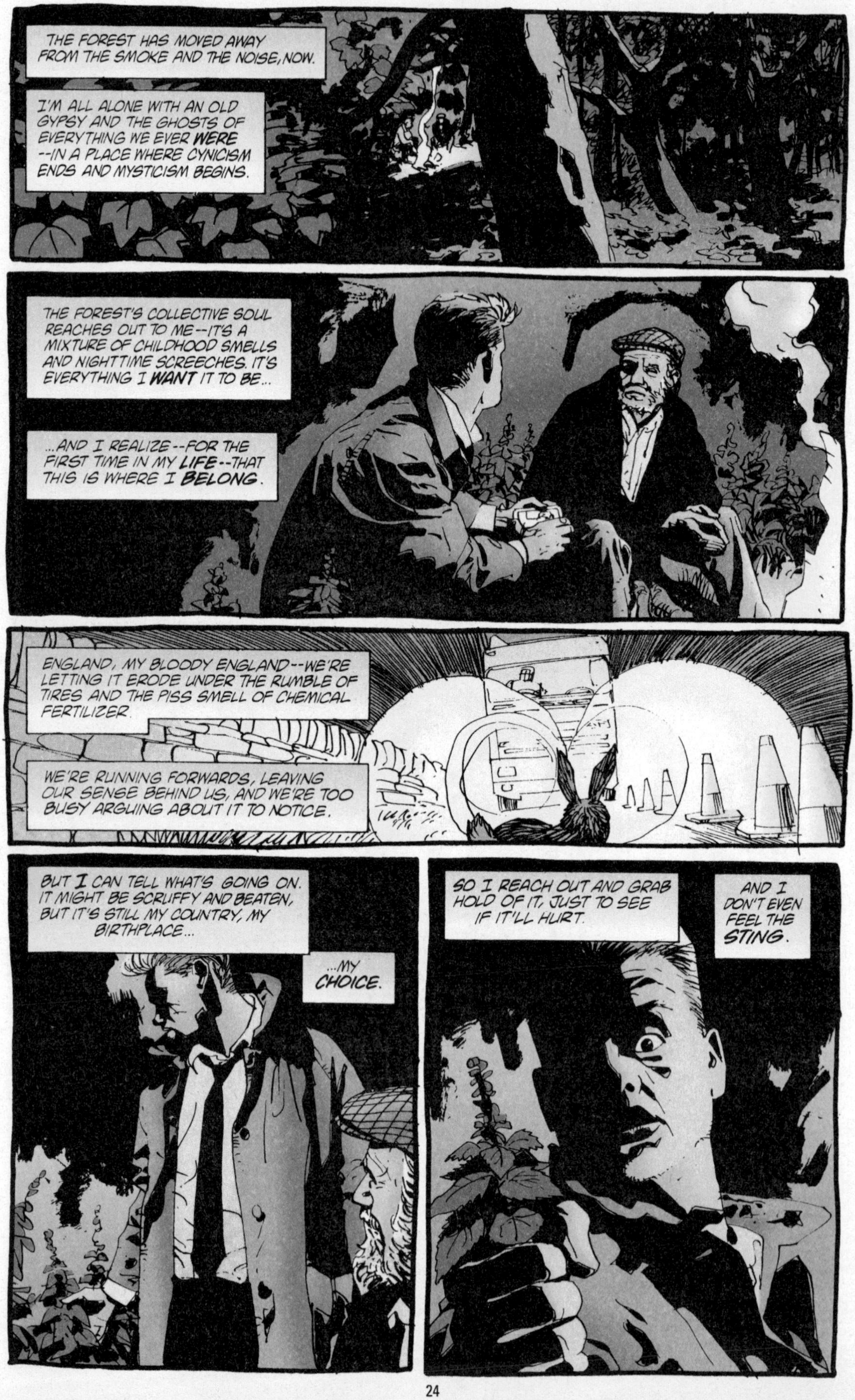
THE FOREST HAS MOVED AWAY FROM THE SMOKE AND THE NOISE, NOW.
I'M ALL ALONE WITH AN OLD GYPSY AND THE GHOSTS OF EVERYTHING WE EVER WERE --IN A PLACE WHERE CYNICISM ENDS AND MYSTICISM BEGINS.
THE FOREST'S COLLECTIVE SOUL REACHES OUT TO ME--IT'S A MIXTURE OF CHILDHOOD SMELLS AND NIGHTTIME SCREECHES. IT'S EVERYTHING I WANT IT TO BE...
...AND I REALIZE--FOR THE FIRST TIME IN MY LIFE--THAT THIS IS WHERE I BELONG.
ENGLAND, MY BLOODY ENGLAND--WE'RE LETTING IT ERODE UNDER THE RUMBLE OF TIRES AND THE PISS SMELL OF CHEMICAL FERTILIZER.
WE'RE RUNNING FORWARDS, LEAVING OUR SENSE BEHIND US, AND WE'RE TOO BUSY ARGUING ABOUT IT TO NOTICE.
BUT I CAN TELL WHAT'S GOING ON. IT MIGHT BE SCRUFFY AND BEATEN, BUT IT'S STILL MY COUNTRY, MY BIRTHPLACE...
...MY CHOICE.
SO I REACH OUT AND GRAB HOLD OF IT, JUST TO SEE IF IT'LL HURT.
AND I DON'T EVEN FEEL THE STING.

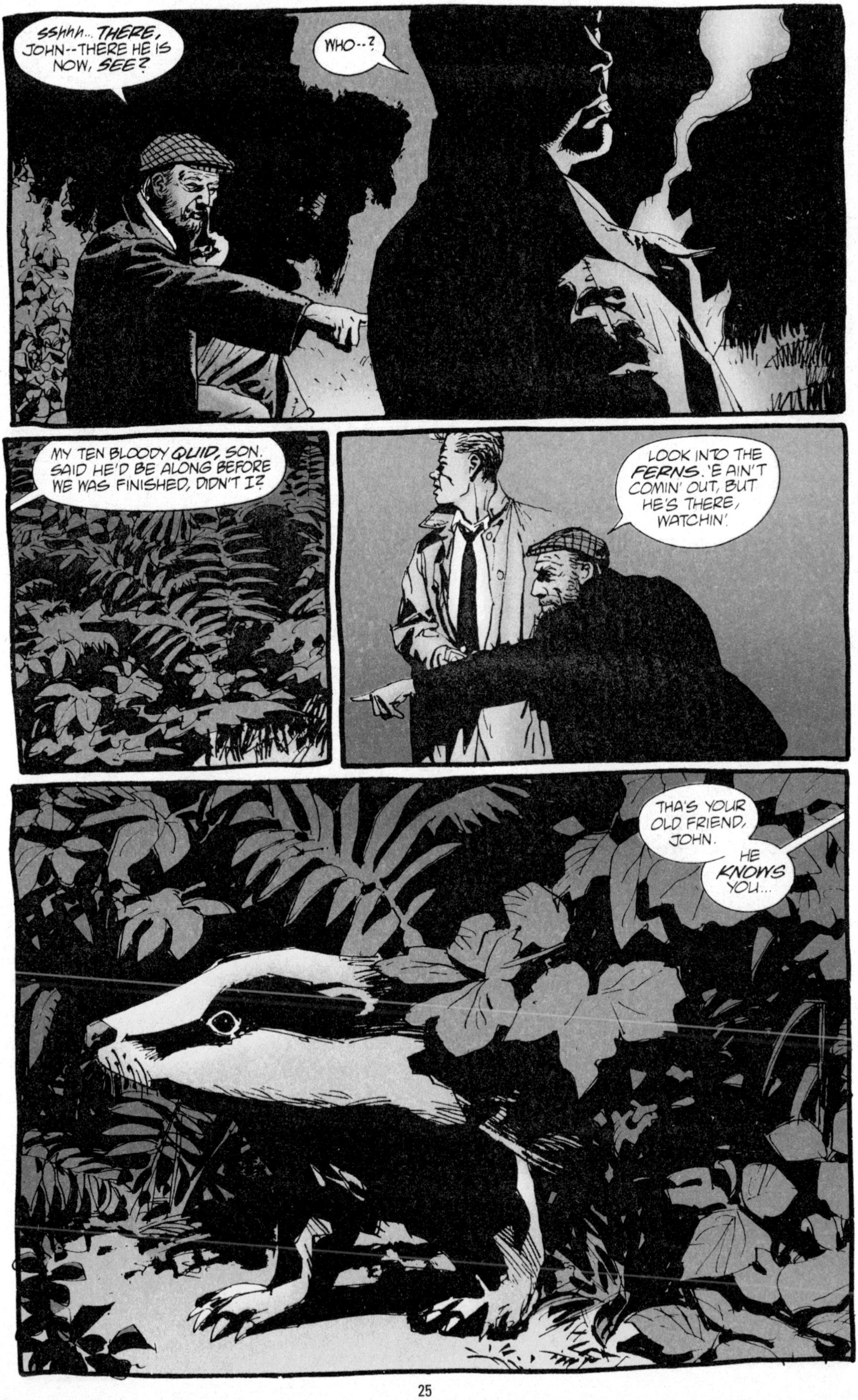
SSHHH... THERE, JOHN--THERE HE IS NOW, SEE?
WHO--?
MY TEN BLOODY QUID, SON. SAID HE'D BE ALONG BEFORE WE WAS FINISHED, DIDN'T I?
LOOK INTO THE FERNS. 'E AIN'T COMIN' OUT, BUT HE'S THERE, WATCHIN'.
THA'S YOUR OLD FRIEND, JOHN.
HE KNOWS YOU...

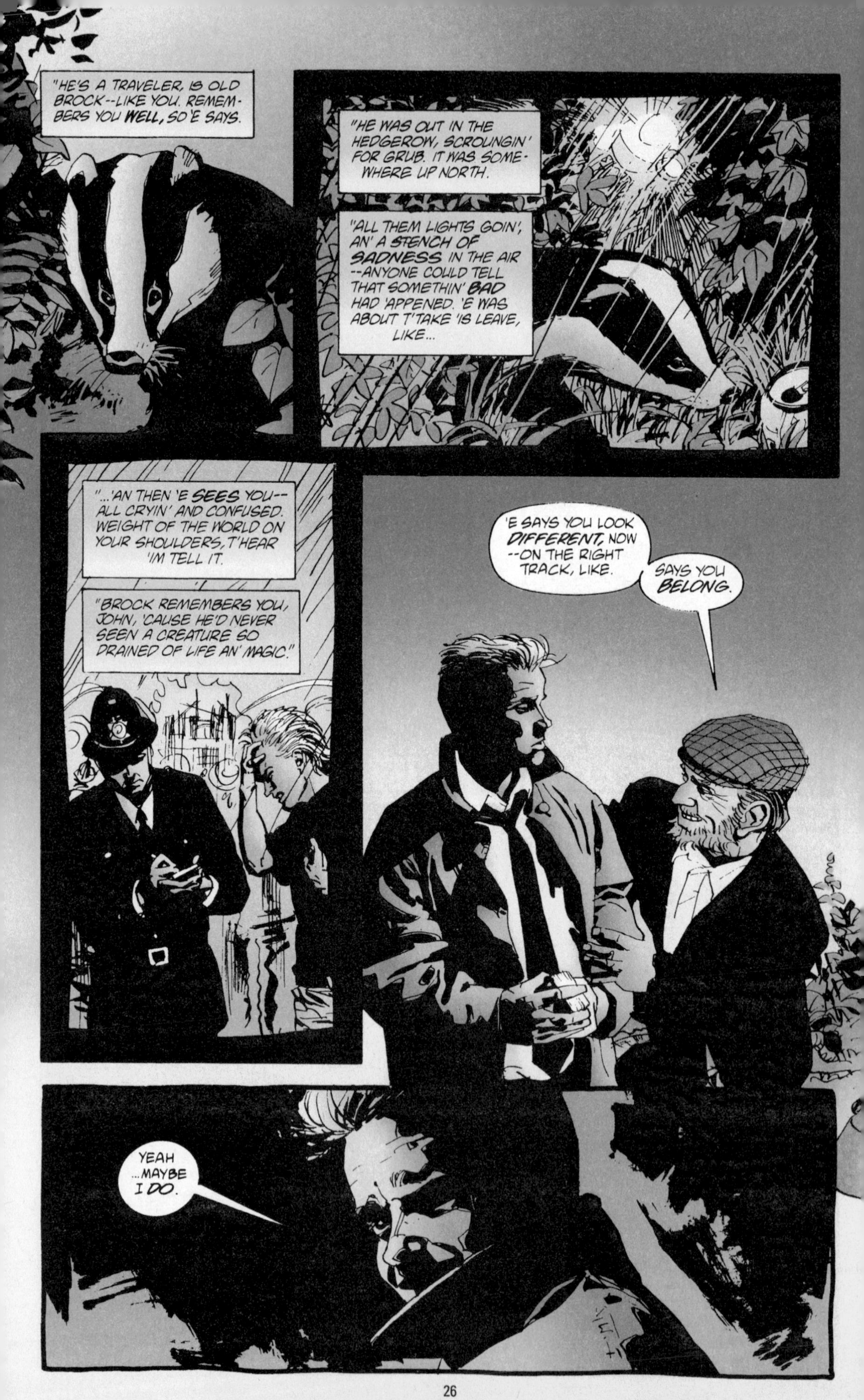
"HE'S A TRAVELER, IS OLD BROCK--LIKE YOU. REMEMBERS YOU WELL, SO 'E SAYS.
"HE WAS OUT IN THE HEDGEROW, SCROUNGIN' FOR GRUB. IT WAS SOMEWHERE UP NORTH.
"ALL THEM LIGHTS GOIN', AN' A STENCH OF SADNESS IN THE AIR --ANYONE COULD TELL THAT SOMETHIN' BAD HAD 'APPENED. 'E WAS ABOUT T' TAKE 'IS LEAVE, LIKE...
"...'AN THEN 'E SEES YOU-- ALL CRYIN' AND CONFUSED. WEIGHT OF THE WORLD ON YOUR SHOULDERS, T'HEAR 'IM TELL IT.
"BROCK REMEMBERS YOU, JOHN, 'CAUSE HE'D NEVER SEEN A CREATURE SO DRAINED OF LIFE AN' MAGIC."
'E SAYS YOU LOOK DIFFERENT, NOW --ON THE RIGHT TRACK, LIKE.
SAYS YOU BELONG.
YEAH ...MAYBE I DO.

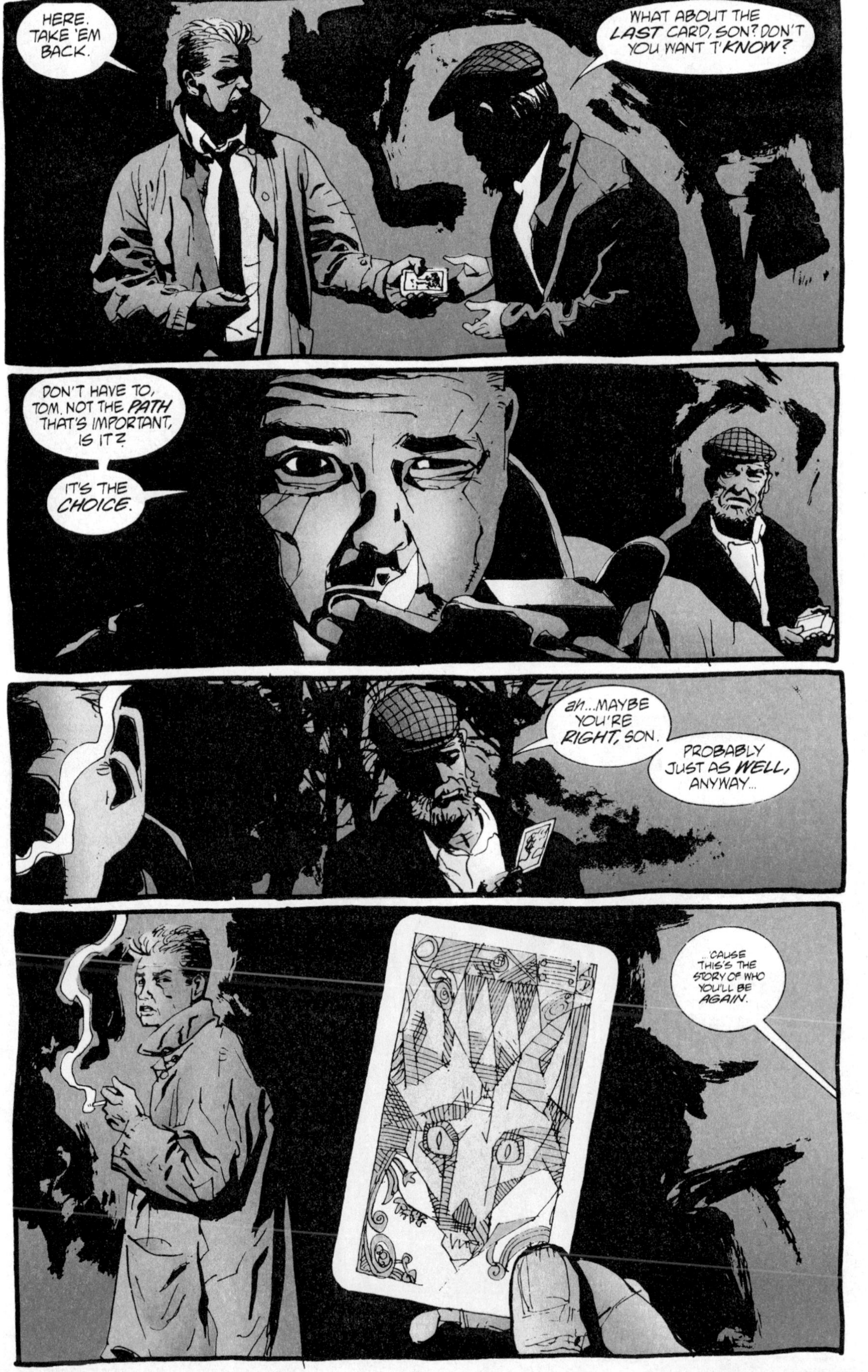

HERE. TAKE 'EM BACK.
WHAT ABOUT THE LAST CARD, SON? DON'T YOU WANT T'KNOW?
DON'T HAVE TO, TOM. NOT THE PATH THAT'S IMPORTANT, IS IT?
IT'S THE CHOICE.
ah...MAYBE YOU'RE RIGHT, SON.
PROBABLY JUST AS WELL, ANYWAY...
...'CAUSE THIS'S THE STORY OF WHO YOU'LL BE AGAIN.

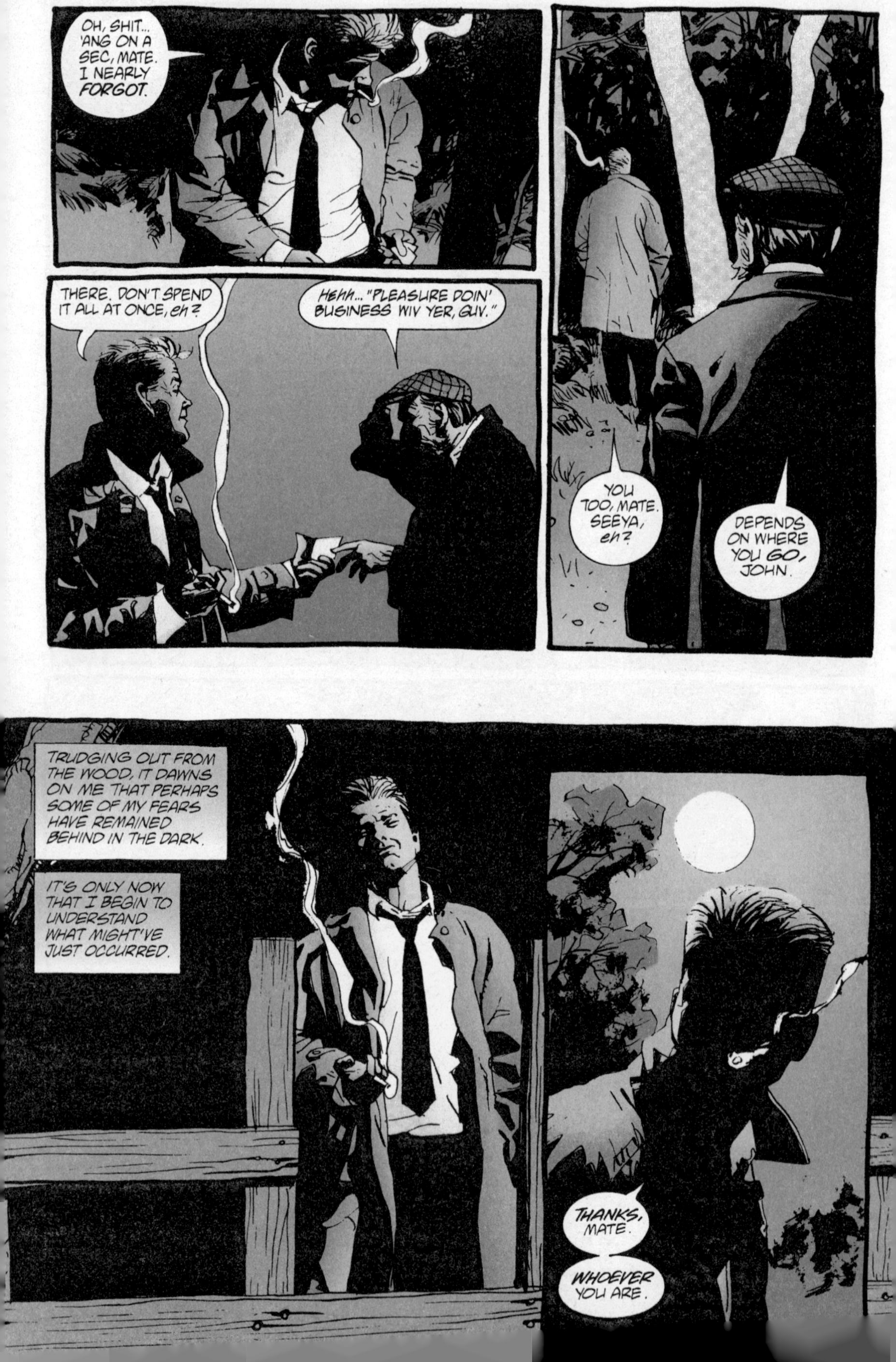
OH, SHIT... 'ANG ON A SEC, MATE. I NEARLY FORGOT.
THERE. DON'T SPEND IT ALL AT ONCE, eh?
Hehh... "PLEASURE DOIN' BUSINESS WIV YER, GUV."
YOU TOO, MATE. SEEYA, eh?
DEPENDS ON WHERE YOU GO, JOHN.
TRUDGING OUT FROM THE WOOD, IT DAWNS ON ME THAT PERHAPS SOME OF MY FEARS HAVE REMAINED BEHIND IN THE DARK.
IT'S ONLY NOW THAT I BEGIN TO UNDERSTAND WHAT MIGHT'VE JUST OCCURRED.
THANKS, MATE.
WHOEVER YOU ARE.

HE CALLED ME *JOHN,* SEE?

AND I NEVER ONCE TOLD HIM MY *NAME.*

MAKE GOOD USE OF YOUR CHOICE, JOHN CONSTANTINE.

PERHAPS YOU WILL FOLLOW THE *CHILDREN,* AFTER ALL...

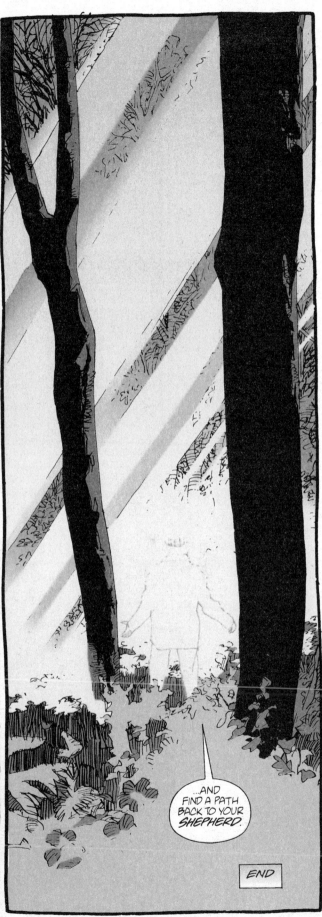

...AND FIND A PATH BACK TO YOUR *SHEPHERD.*

END

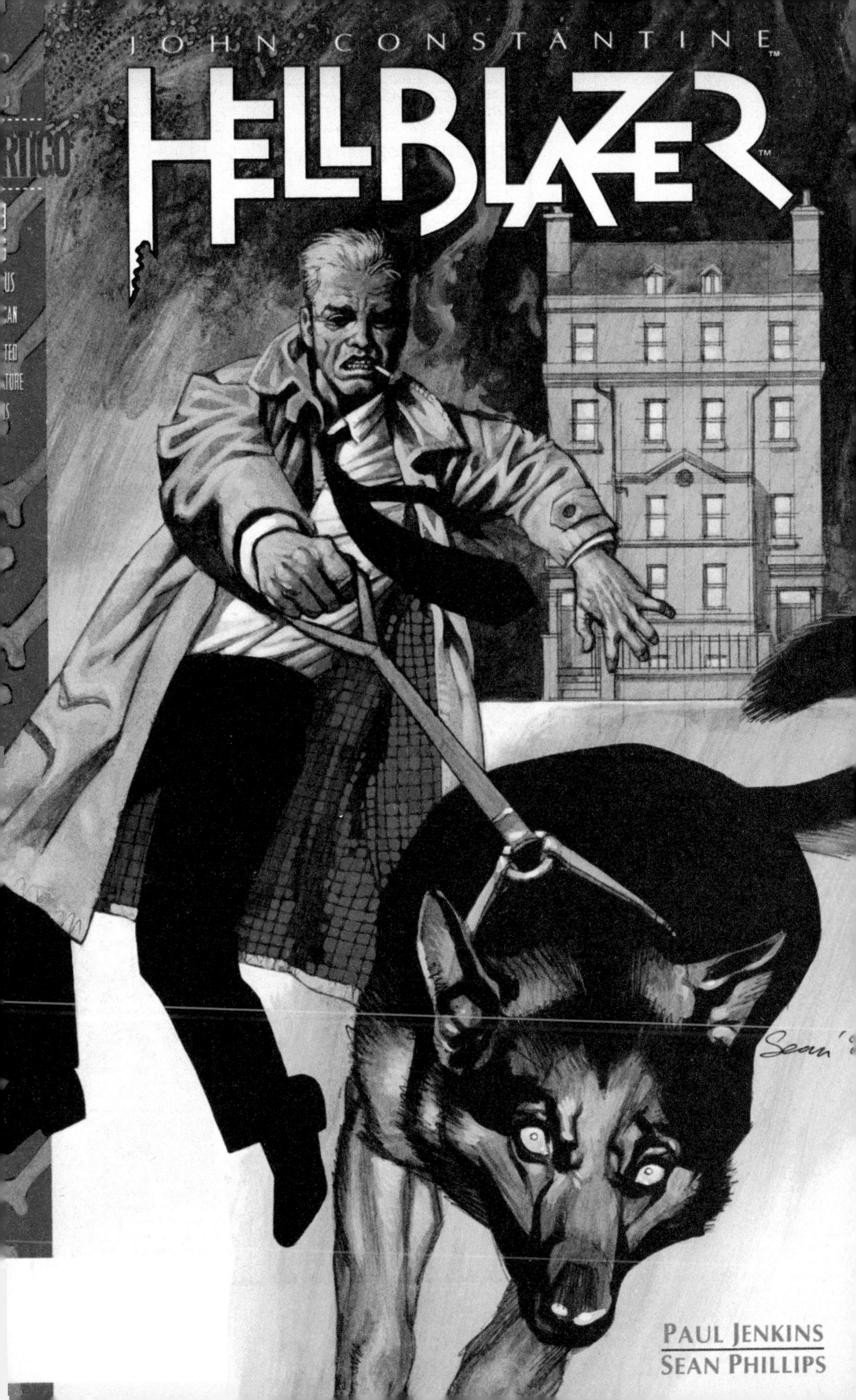
JOHN CONSTANTINE
HELLBLAZER
PAUL JENKINS
SEAN PHILLIPS

walking the dog

Paul Jenkins Writer

Sean Phillips Artist

Matt Hollingsworth Colorist

Clem Robins Letterer

Axel Alonso Asst Editor

Lou Stathis Editor

DAY ONE OF A WEIRD BLOODY WEEK, AND THE GODS'VE BEEN *DRINKING* AGAIN...

COME ON, CONSTANTINE-- SHAKE A *LEG*, WILL YER?

UHH...BLIMEY, STRAFF. WHASSUP, MATE?

M-ME MUM...SHE'S DONE IT *AGAIN*--

I SHOULD'VE *EXPECTED* THIS, SHOULDN'T I? I MEAN, EVER SINCE I GOT BACK FROM BORLEY, I'VE FAR EXCEEDED MY *COMFORT* QUOTA.

JUST 'CAUSE *I'VE* CHANGED, IT DOESN'T NECESSARILY FOLLOW THAT ANYONE *ELSE* HAS.

JOHN--BACK 'ERE! 'LO, SANGIV.

MAKE WAY FOR THE ANGEL OF *MERCY*, SANGIV, MATE!

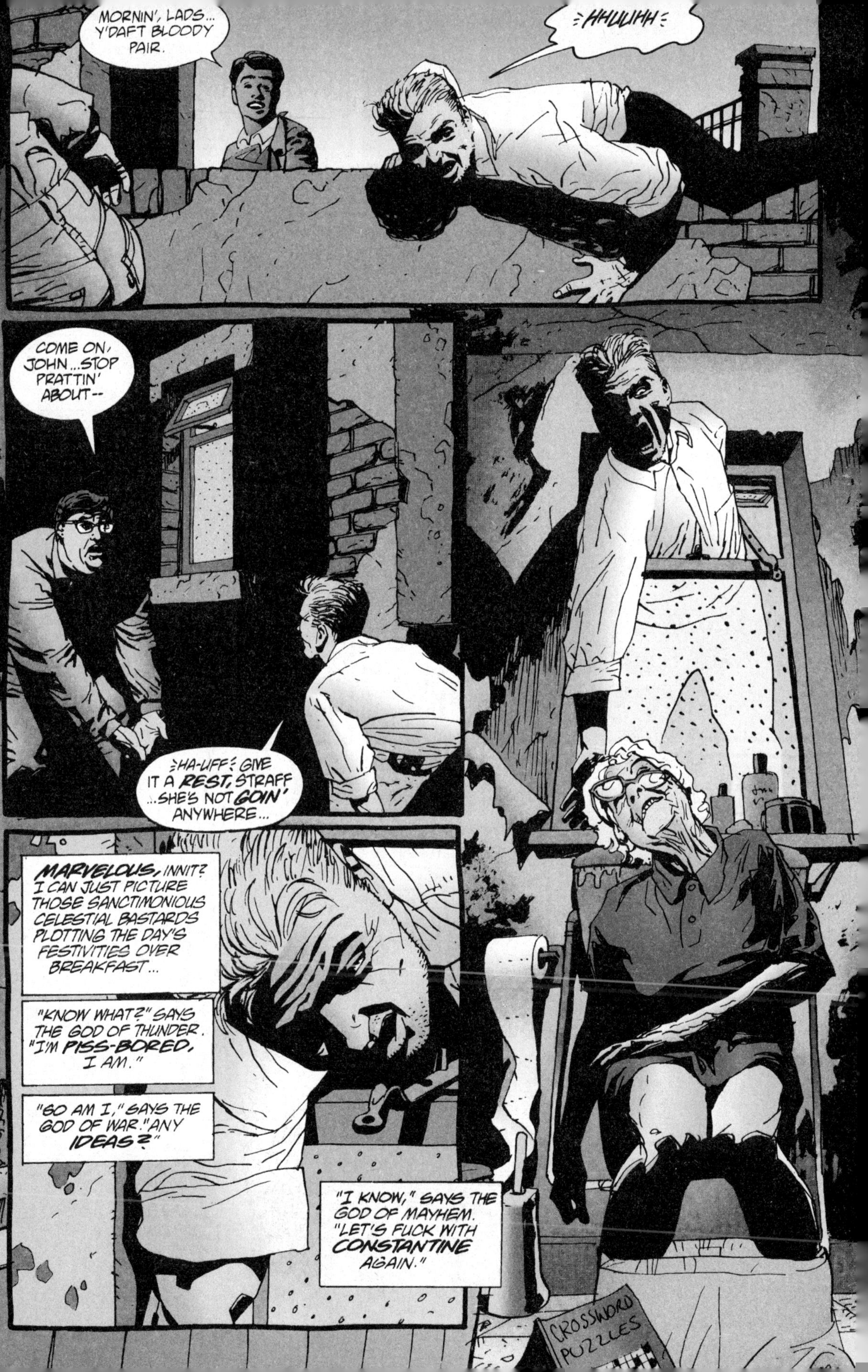
MORNIN', LADS... Y'DAFT BLOODY PAIR.
HHUUHH
COME ON, JOHN... STOP PRATTIN' ABOUT--
HA-UFF GIVE IT A REST, STRAFF ...SHE'S NOT GOIN' ANYWHERE...
MARVELOUS, INNIT? I CAN JUST PICTURE THOSE SANCTIMONIOUS CELESTIAL BASTARDS PLOTTING THE DAY'S FESTIVITIES OVER BREAKFAST...
"KNOW WHAT?" SAYS THE GOD OF THUNDER. "I'M PISS-BORED, I AM."
"SO AM I," SAYS THE GOD OF WAR. "ANY IDEAS?"
"I KNOW," SAYS THE GOD OF MAYHEM. "LET'S FUCK WITH CONSTANTINE AGAIN."
CROSSWORD PUZZLES

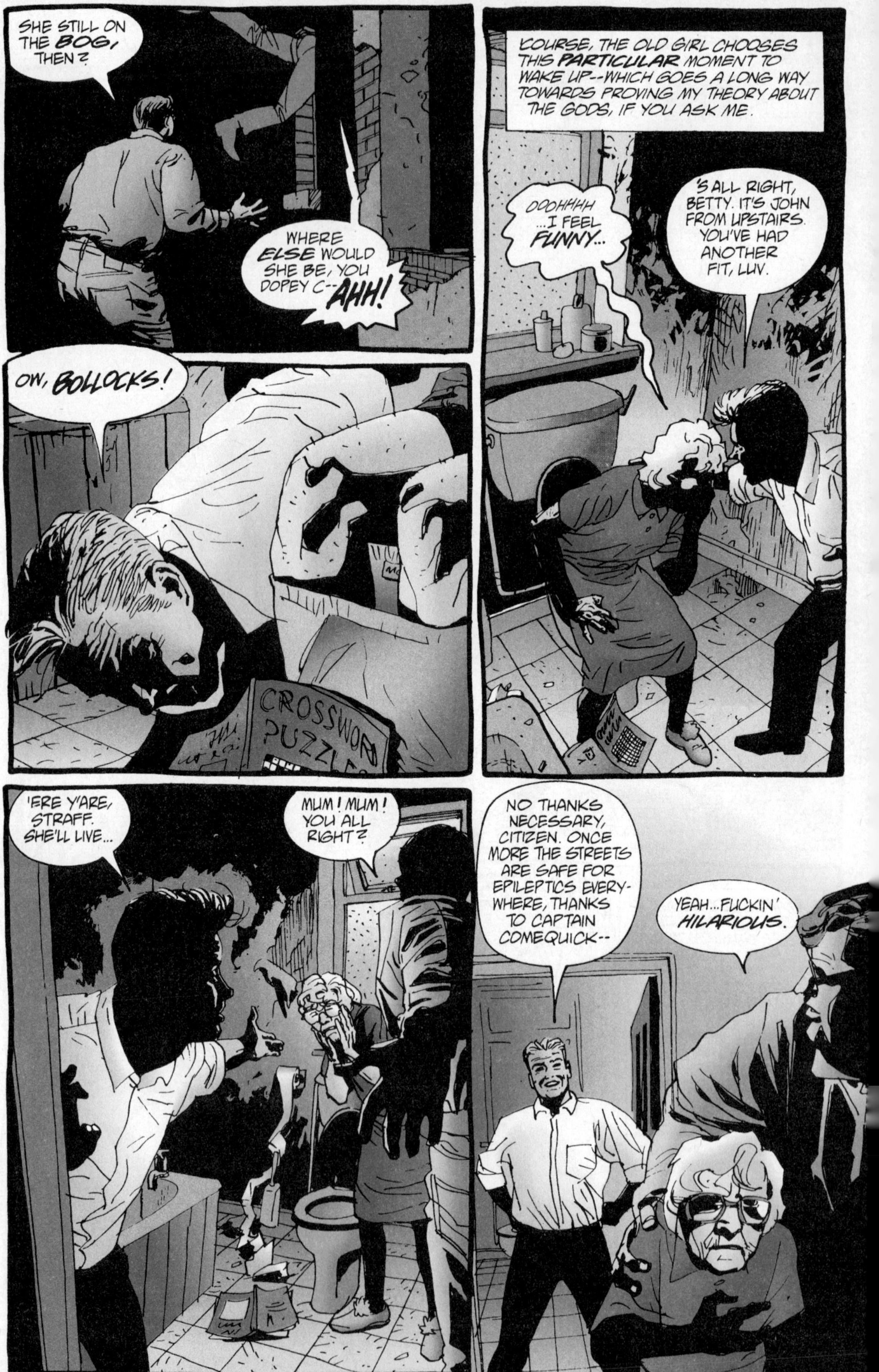
SHE STILL ON THE BOG, THEN?
WHERE ELSE WOULD SHE BE, YOU DOPEY C--AHH!
'COURSE, THE OLD GIRL CHOOSES THIS PARTICULAR MOMENT TO WAKE UP--WHICH GOES A LONG WAY TOWARDS PROVING MY THEORY ABOUT THE GODS, IF YOU ASK ME.
OOOHHHH ...I FEEL FUNNY...
'S ALL RIGHT, BETTY. IT'S JOHN FROM UPSTAIRS. YOU'VE HAD ANOTHER FIT, LUV.
OW, BOLLOCKS!
CROSSWORD PUZZLE
'ERE Y'ARE, STRAFF. SHE'LL LIVE...
MUM! MUM! YOU ALL RIGHT?
NO THANKS NECESSARY, CITIZEN. ONCE MORE THE STREETS ARE SAFE FOR EPILEPTICS EVERY-WHERE, THANKS TO CAPTAIN COMEQUICK--
YEAH...FUCKIN' HILARIOUS.

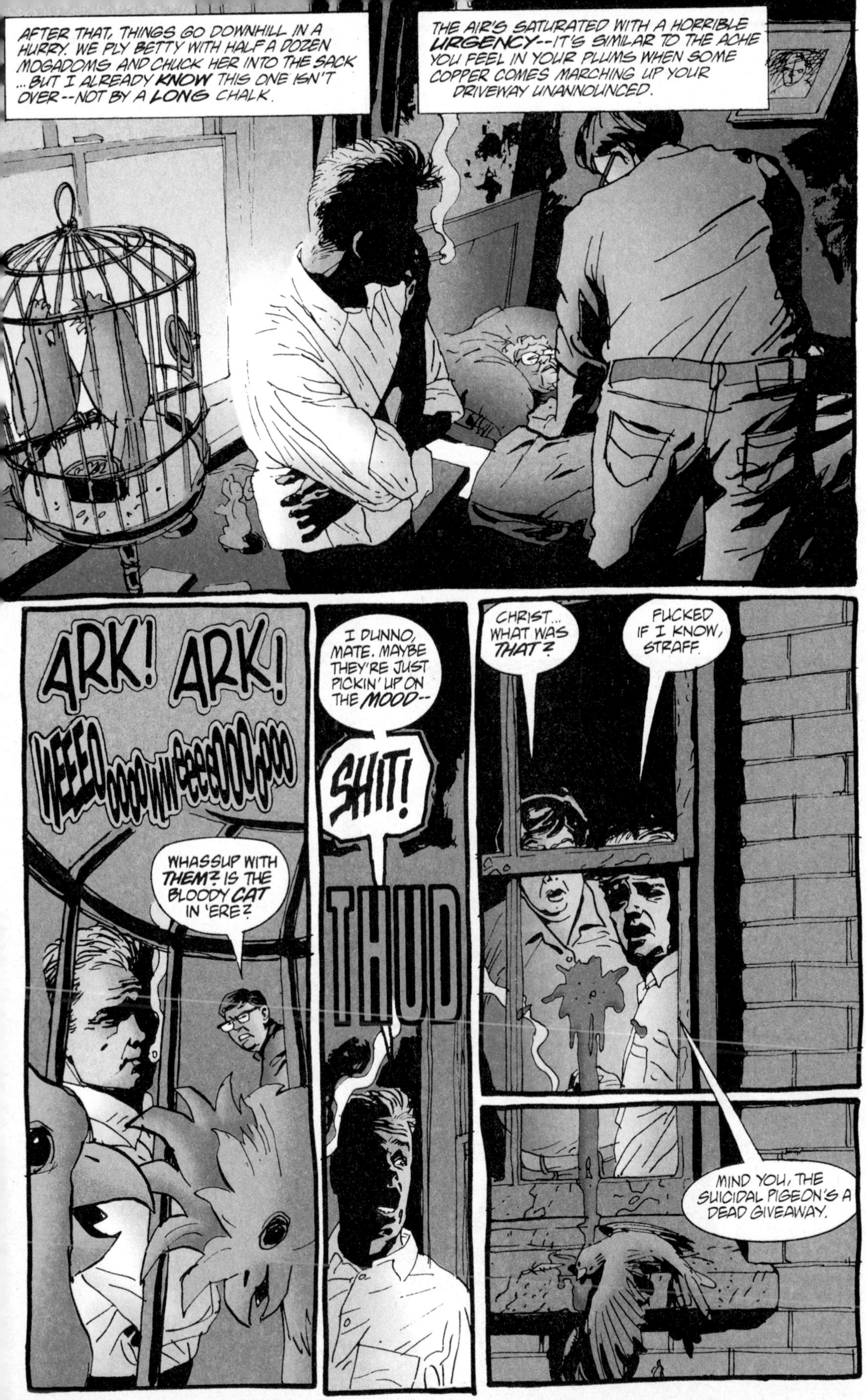
AFTER THAT, THINGS GO DOWNHILL IN A HURRY. WE PLY BETTY WITH HALF A DOZEN MOGADOMS AND CHUCK HER INTO THE SACK ...BUT I ALREADY KNOW THIS ONE ISN'T OVER--NOT BY A LONG CHALK.
THE AIR'S SATURATED WITH A HORRIBLE URGENCY--IT'S SIMILAR TO THE ACHE YOU FEEL IN YOUR PLUMS WHEN SOME COPPER COMES MARCHING UP YOUR DRIVEWAY UNANNOUNCED.
ARK! ARK!
WEEEOoooowweeeOOOooo
WHASSUP WITH THEM? IS THE BLOODY CAT IN 'ERE?
I DUNNO, MATE. MAYBE THEY'RE JUST PICKIN' UP ON THE MOOD--
SHIT!
THUD
CHRIST... WHAT WAS THAT?
FUCKED IF I KNOW, STRAFF.
MIND YOU, THE SUICIDAL PIGEON'S A DEAD GIVEAWAY.

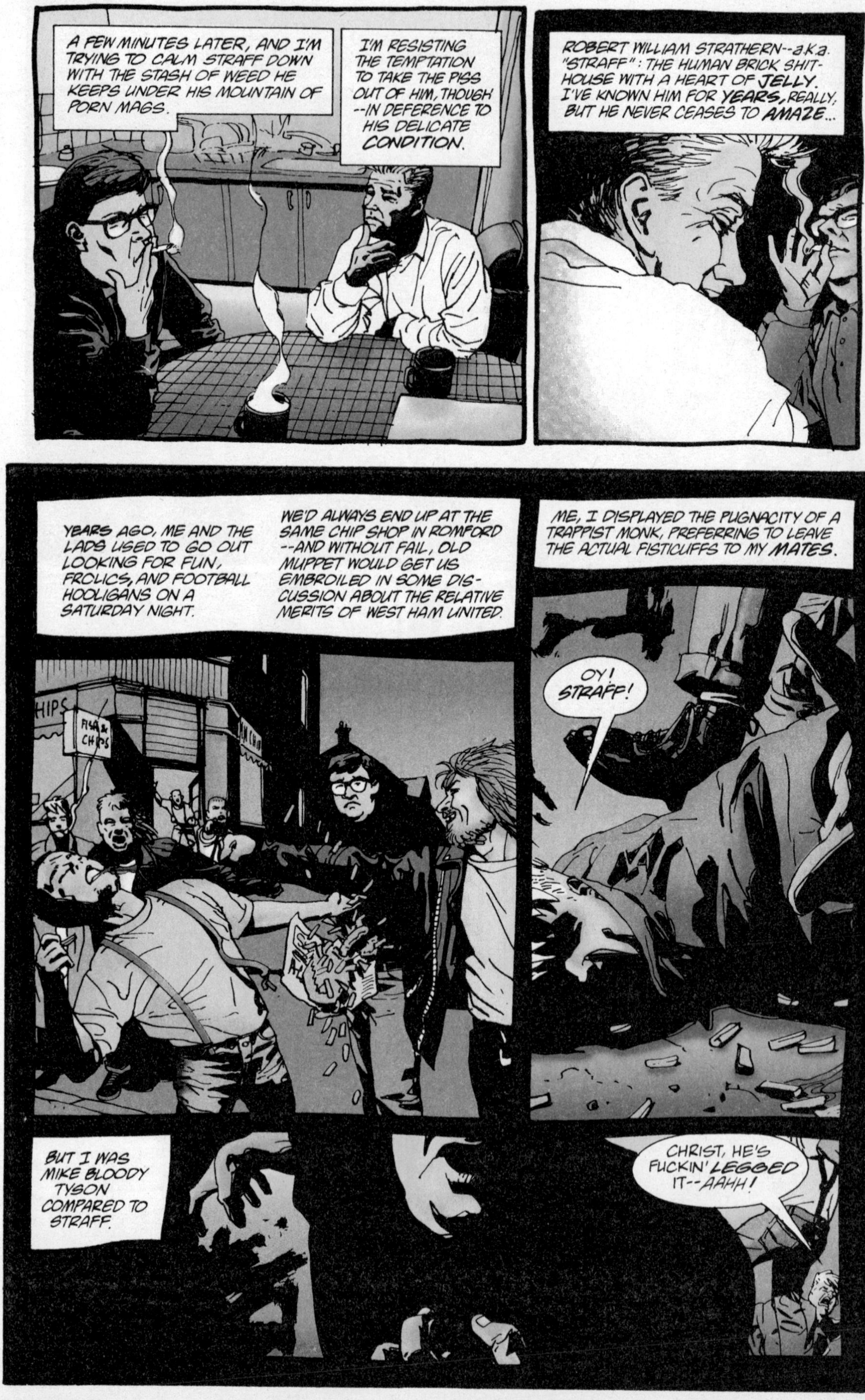
A FEW MINUTES LATER, AND I'M TRYING TO CALM STRAFF DOWN WITH THE STASH OF WEED HE KEEPS UNDER HIS MOUNTAIN OF PORN MAGS.
I'M RESISTING THE TEMPTATION TO TAKE THE PISS OUT OF HIM, THOUGH --IN DEFERENCE TO HIS DELICATE CONDITION.
ROBERT WILLIAM STRATHERN--a.k.a. "STRAFF": THE HUMAN BRICK SHIT-HOUSE WITH A HEART OF JELLY. I'VE KNOWN HIM FOR YEARS, REALLY, BUT HE NEVER CEASES TO AMAZE...
YEARS AGO, ME AND THE LADS USED TO GO OUT LOOKING FOR FUN, FROLICS, AND FOOTBALL HOOLIGANS ON A SATURDAY NIGHT.
WE'D ALWAYS END UP AT THE SAME CHIP SHOP IN ROMFORD --AND WITHOUT FAIL, OLD MUPPET WOULD GET US EMBROILED IN SOME DISCUSSION ABOUT THE RELATIVE MERITS OF WEST HAM UNITED.
CHIPS
FISH & CHIPS
ME, I DISPLAYED THE PUGNACITY OF A TRAPPIST MONK, PREFERRING TO LEAVE THE ACTUAL FISTICUFFS TO MY MATES.
OY! STRAFF!
BUT I WAS MIKE BLOODY TYSON COMPARED TO STRAFF.
CHRIST, HE'S FUCKIN' LEGGED IT--AAHH!

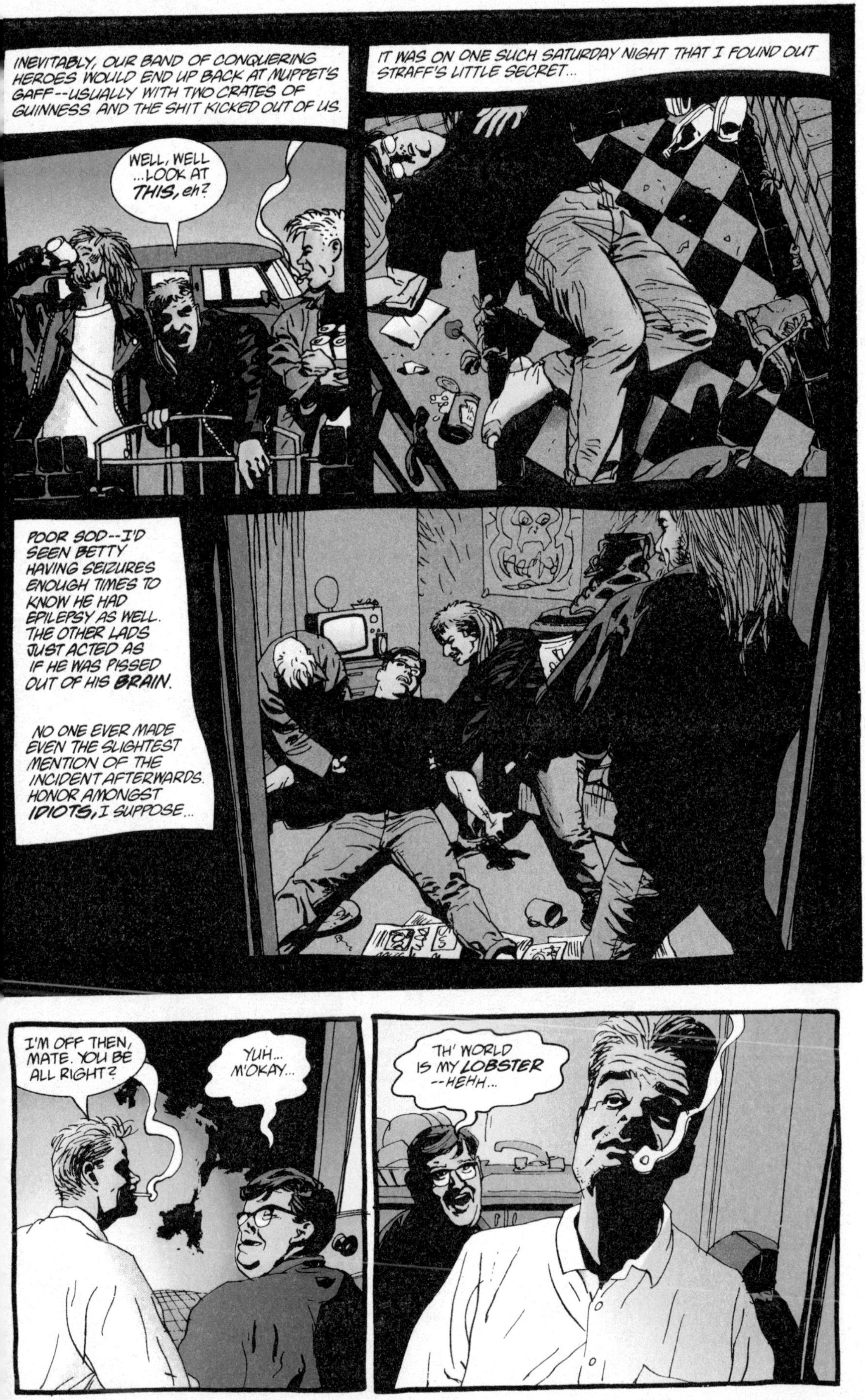
INEVITABLY, OUR BAND OF CONQUERING HEROES WOULD END UP BACK AT MUPPET'S GAFF--USUALLY WITH TWO CRATES OF GUINNESS AND THE SHIT KICKED OUT OF US.
WELL, WELL ...LOOK AT THIS, eh?
IT WAS ON ONE SUCH SATURDAY NIGHT THAT I FOUND OUT STRAFF'S LITTLE SECRET...
POOR SOD--I'D SEEN BETTY HAVING SEIZURES ENOUGH TIMES TO KNOW HE HAD EPILEPSY AS WELL. THE OTHER LADS JUST ACTED AS IF HE WAS PISSED OUT OF HIS BRAIN.
NO ONE EVER MADE EVEN THE SLIGHTEST MENTION OF THE INCIDENT AFTERWARDS. HONOR AMONGST IDIOTS, I SUPPOSE...
I'M OFF THEN, MATE. YOU BE ALL RIGHT?
YUH... M'OKAY...
TH' WORLD IS MY LOBSTER --HEHH...

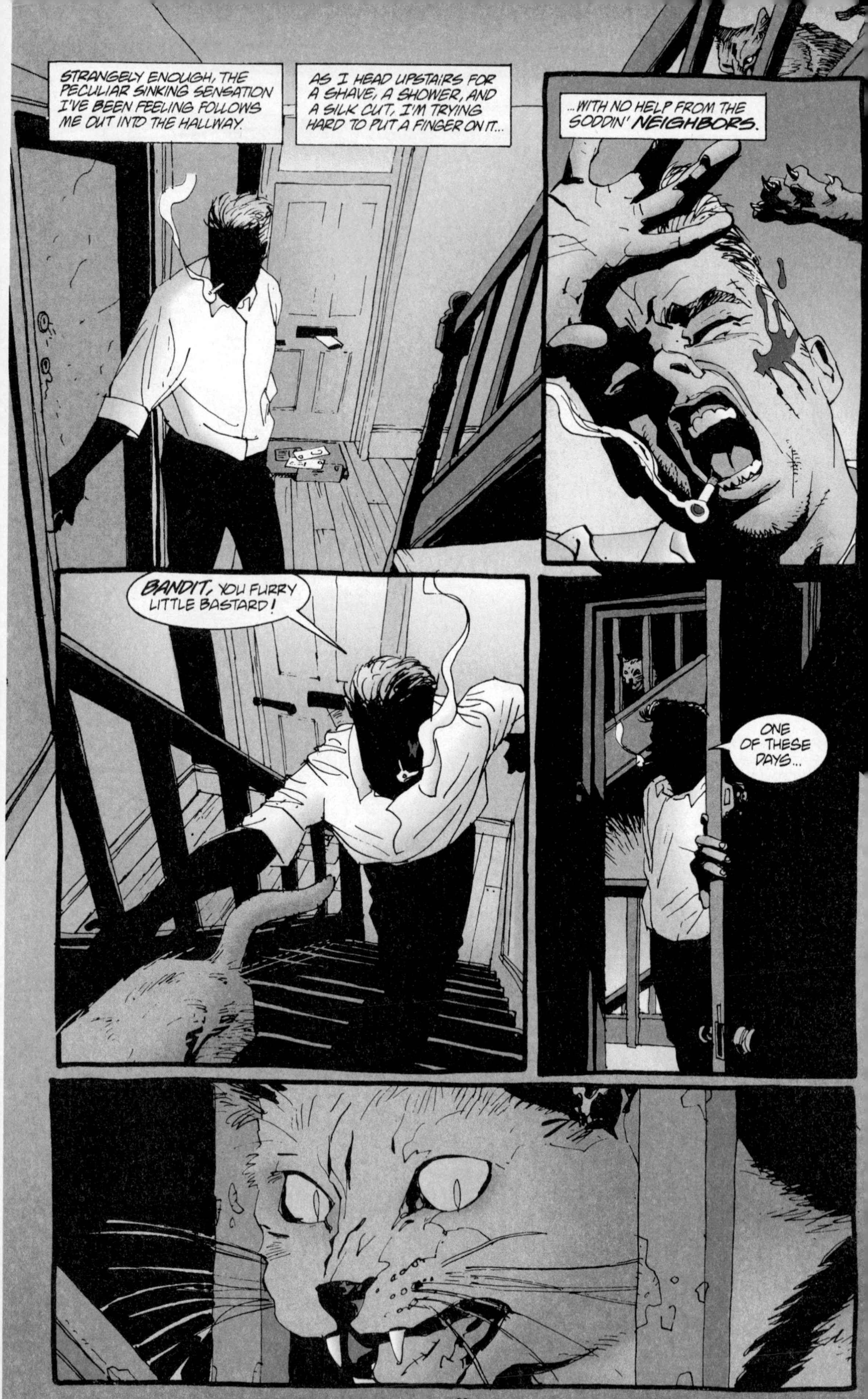
STRANGELY ENOUGH, THE PECULIAR SINKING SENSATION I'VE BEEN FEELING FOLLOWS ME OUT INTO THE HALLWAY.
AS I HEAD UPSTAIRS FOR A SHAVE, A SHOWER, AND A SILK CUT, I'M TRYING HARD TO PUT A FINGER ON IT...
...WITH NO HELP FROM THE SODDIN' NEIGHBORS.
BANDIT, YOU FURRY LITTLE BASTARD!
ONE OF THESE DAYS...

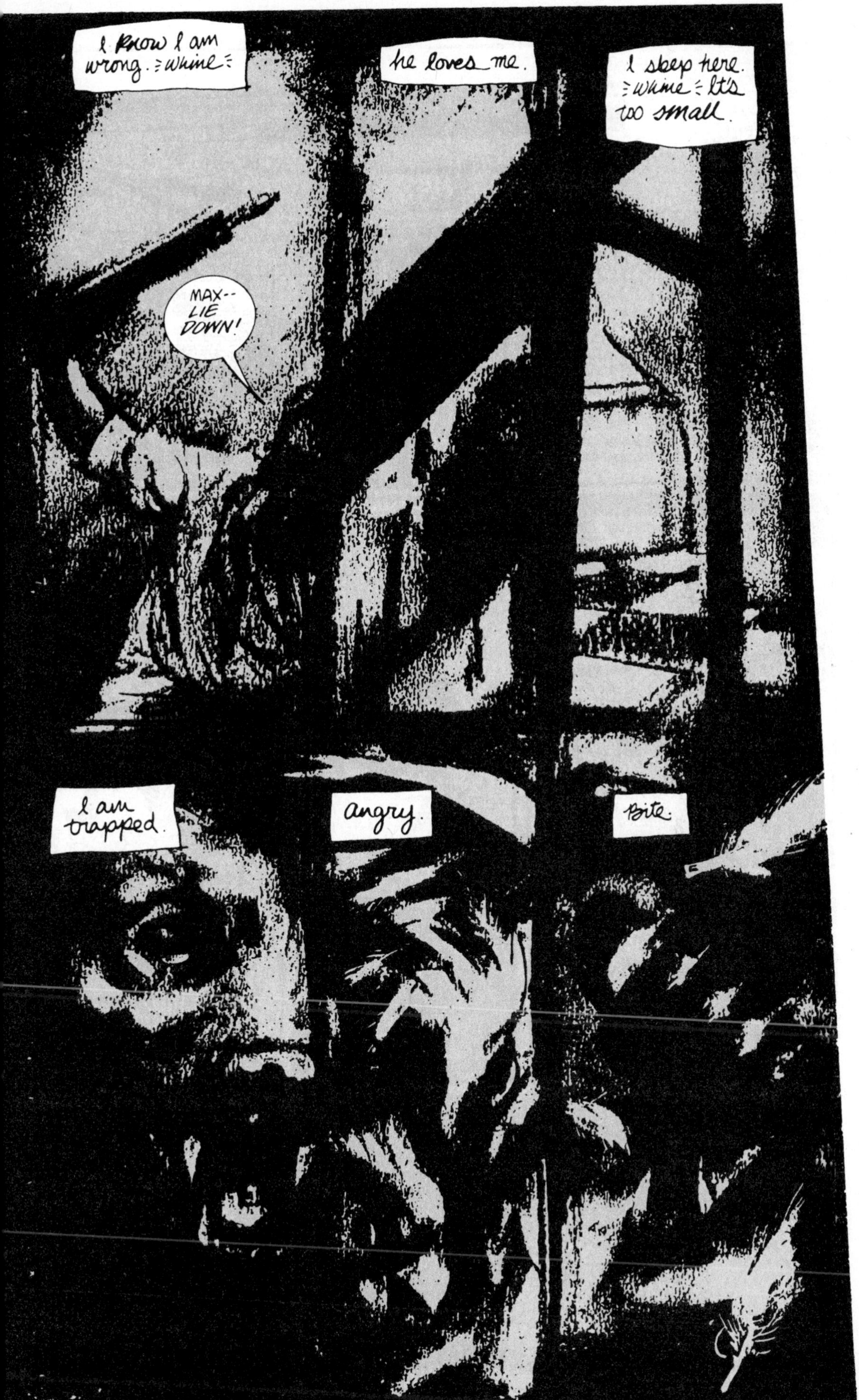

I know I am wrong. ≡whine≡
he loves me.
I sleep here. ≡whine≡ It's too small.
MAX-- LIE DOWN!
I am trapped.
angry.
Bite.

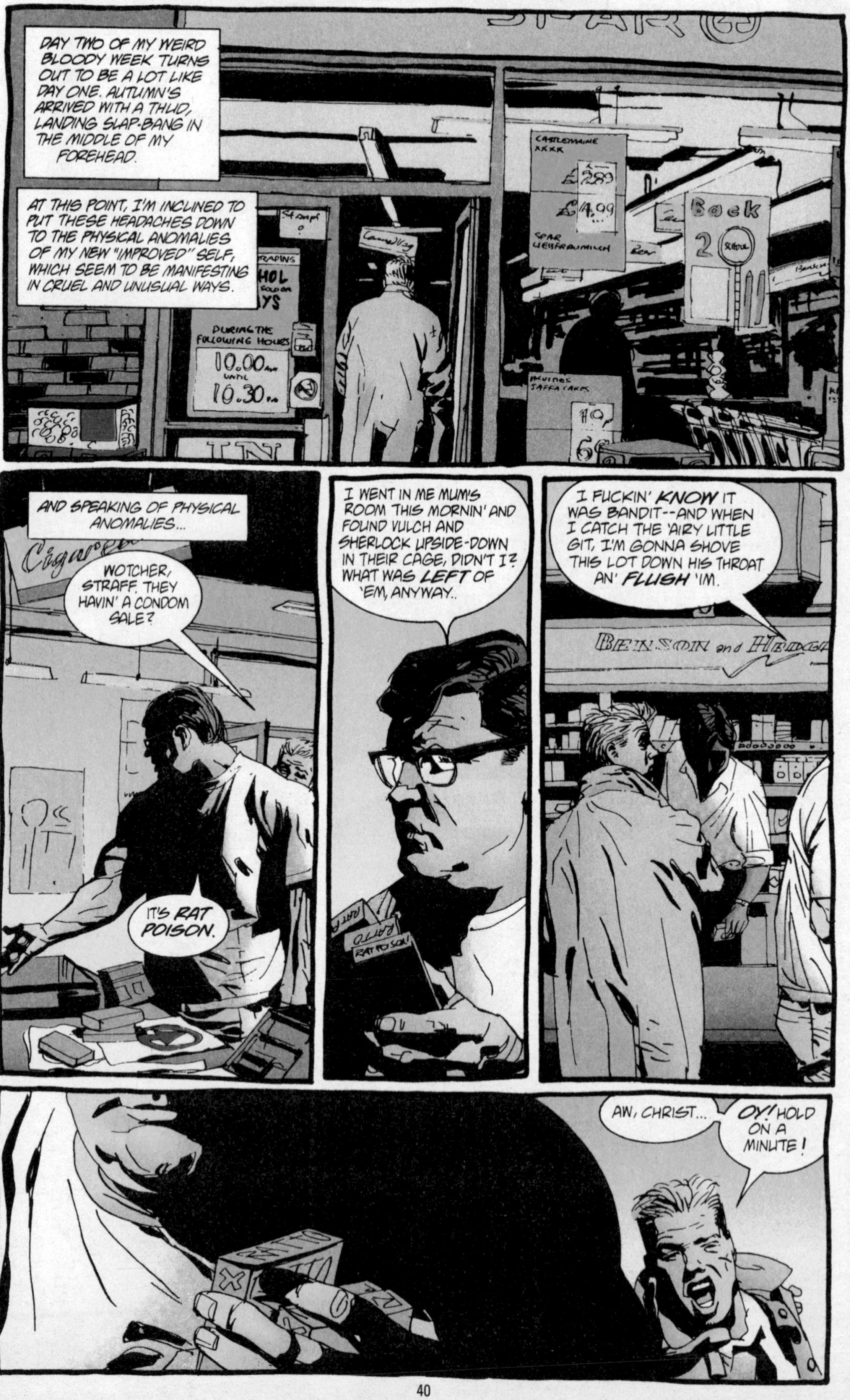
DAY TWO OF MY WEIRD BLOODY WEEK TURNS OUT TO BE A LOT LIKE DAY ONE. AUTUMN'S ARRIVED WITH A THUD, LANDING SLAP-BANG IN THE MIDDLE OF MY FOREHEAD.
AT THIS POINT, I'M INCLINED TO PUT THESE HEADACHES DOWN TO THE PHYSICAL ANOMALIES OF MY NEW "IMPROVED" SELF, WHICH SEEM TO BE MANIFESTING IN CRUEL AND UNUSUAL WAYS.
DURING THE FOLLOWING HOURS
10.00am UNTIL 10.30pm
CASTLEMAINE XXXX
SPAR LIEBFRAUMILCH
AND SPEAKING OF PHYSICAL ANOMALIES...
WOTCHER, STRAFF. THEY HAVIN' A CONDOM SALE?
IT'S RAT POISON.
I WENT IN ME MUM'S ROOM THIS MORNIN' AND FOUND VULCH AND SHERLOCK UPSIDE-DOWN IN THEIR CAGE, DIDN'T I? WHAT WAS LEFT OF 'EM, ANYWAY..
I FUCKIN' KNOW IT WAS BANDIT--AND WHEN I CATCH THE 'AIRY LITTLE GIT, I'M GONNA SHOVE THIS LOT DOWN HIS THROAT AN' FLUSH 'IM.
BENSON and HEDGES
AW, CHRIST...
OY! HOLD ON A MINUTE!

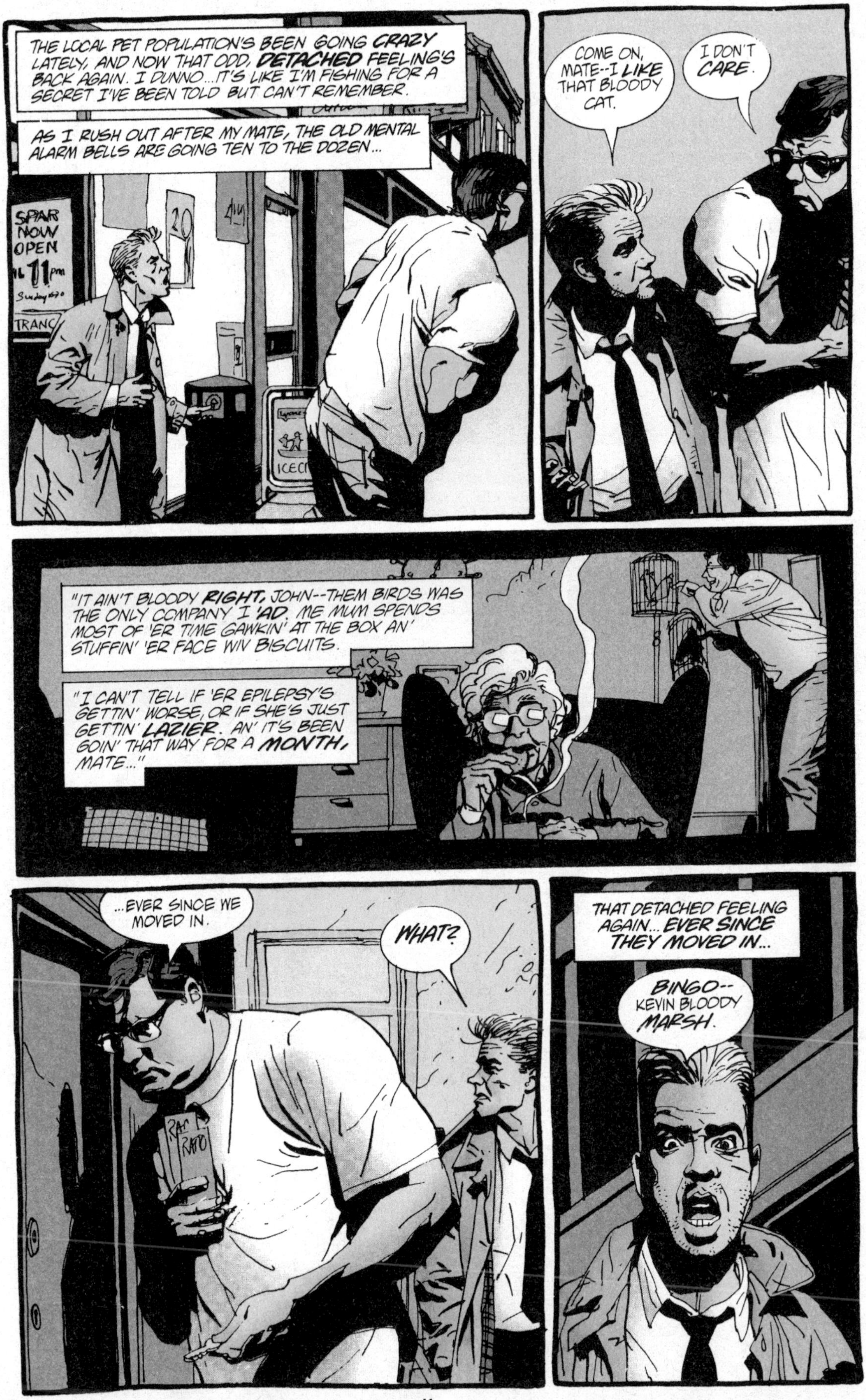
THE LOCAL PET POPULATION'S BEEN GOING CRAZY LATELY, AND NOW THAT ODD, DETACHED FEELING'S BACK AGAIN. I DUNNO... IT'S LIKE I'M FISHING FOR A SECRET I'VE BEEN TOLD BUT CAN'T REMEMBER.
AS I RUSH OUT AFTER MY MATE, THE OLD MENTAL ALARM BELLS ARE GOING TEN TO THE DOZEN...
SPAR NOW OPEN
COME ON, MATE--I LIKE THAT BLOODY CAT.
I DON'T CARE.
"IT AIN'T BLOODY RIGHT, JOHN--THEM BIRDS WAS THE ONLY COMPANY I 'AD. ME MUM SPENDS MOST OF 'ER TIME GAWKIN' AT THE BOX AN' STUFFIN' 'ER FACE WIV BISCUITS.
"I CAN'T TELL IF 'ER EPILEPSY'S GETTIN' WORSE, OR IF SHE'S JUST GETTIN' LAZIER. AN' IT'S BEEN GOIN' THAT WAY FOR A MONTH, MATE..."
...EVER SINCE WE MOVED IN.
WHAT?
THAT DETACHED FEELING AGAIN... EVER SINCE THEY MOVED IN...
BINGO-- KEVIN BLOODY MARSH.

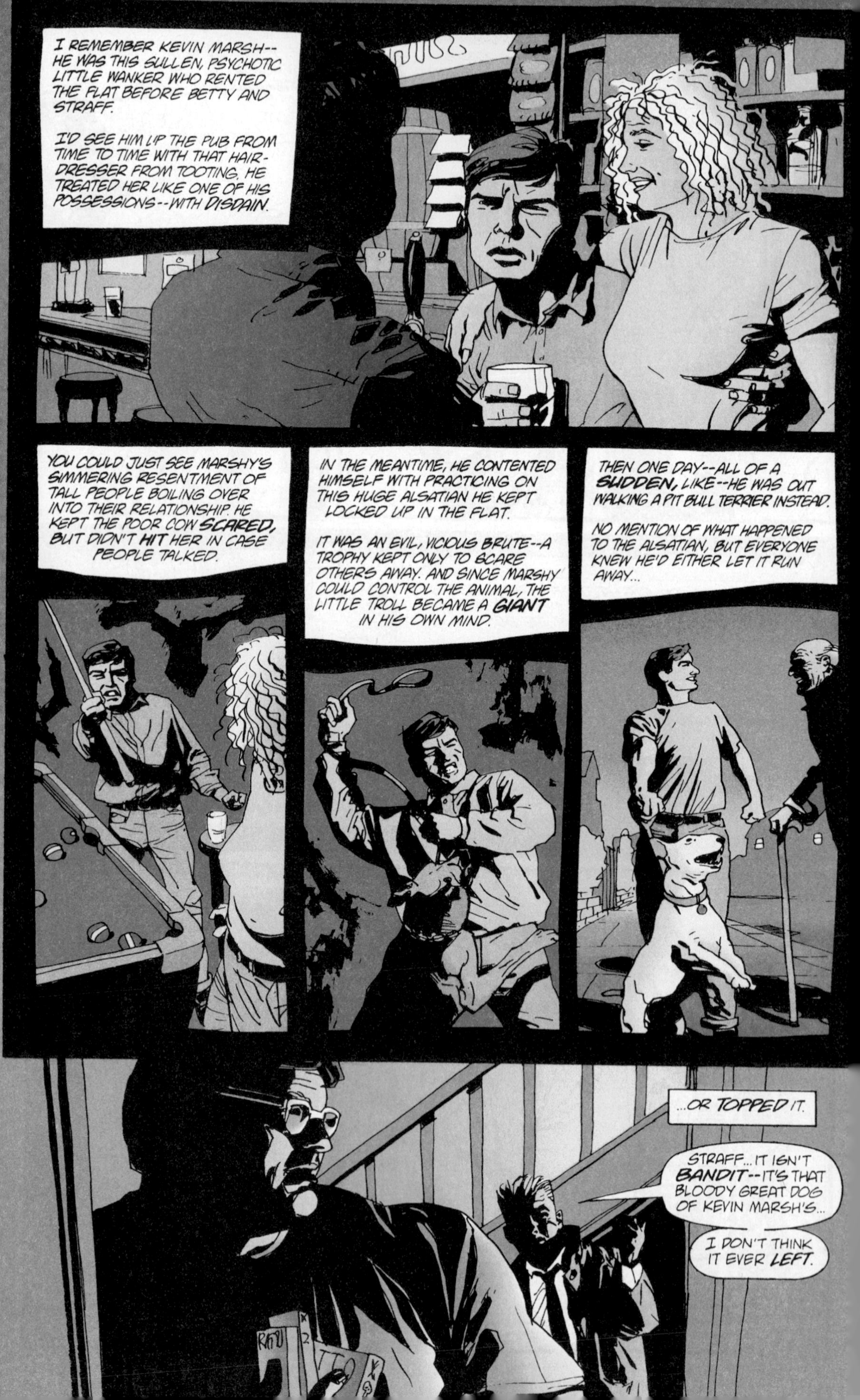
I REMEMBER KEVIN MARSH-- HE WAS THIS SULLEN, PSYCHOTIC LITTLE WANKER WHO RENTED THE FLAT BEFORE BETTY AND STRAFF.
I'D SEE HIM UP THE PUB FROM TIME TO TIME WITH THAT HAIR-DRESSER FROM TOOTING, HE TREATED HER LIKE ONE OF HIS POSSESSIONS--WITH DISDAIN.
YOU COULD JUST SEE MARSHY'S SIMMERING RESENTMENT OF TALL PEOPLE BOILING OVER INTO THEIR RELATIONSHIP. HE KEPT THE POOR COW SCARED, BUT DIDN'T HIT HER IN CASE PEOPLE TALKED.
IN THE MEANTIME, HE CONTENTED HIMSELF WITH PRACTICING ON THIS HUGE ALSATIAN HE KEPT LOCKED UP IN THE FLAT.
IT WAS AN EVIL, VICIOUS BRUTE--A TROPHY KEPT ONLY TO SCARE OTHERS AWAY. AND SINCE MARSHY COULD CONTROL THE ANIMAL, THE LITTLE TROLL BECAME A GIANT IN HIS OWN MIND.
THEN ONE DAY--ALL OF A SUDDEN, LIKE--HE WAS OUT WALKING A PIT BULL TERRIER INSTEAD.
NO MENTION OF WHAT HAPPENED TO THE ALSATIAN, BUT EVERYONE KNEW HE'D EITHER LET IT RUN AWAY...
...OR TOPPED IT.
STRAFF... IT ISN'T BANDIT--IT'S THAT BLOODY GREAT DOG OF KEVIN MARSH'S...
I DON'T THINK IT EVER LEFT.

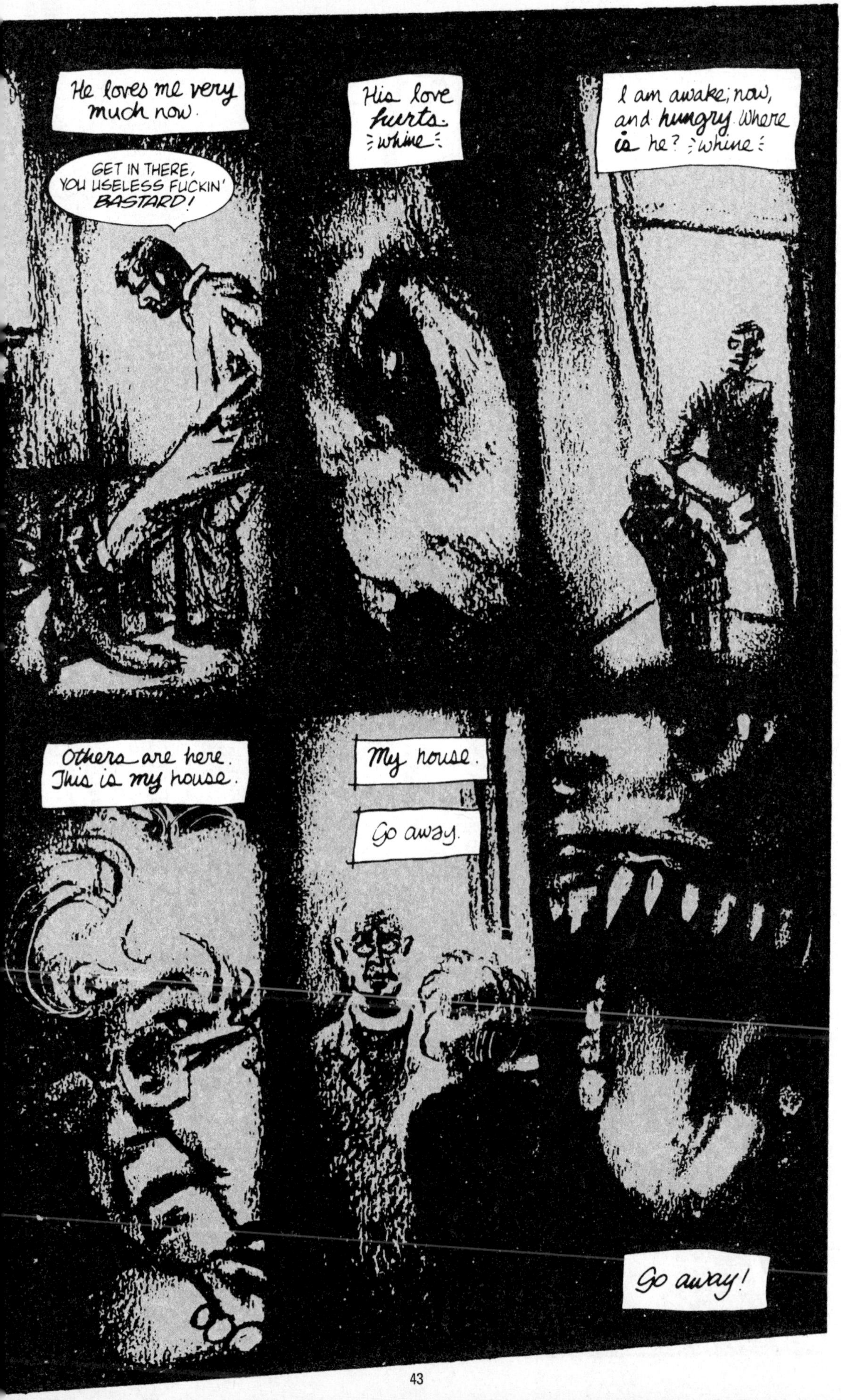
He loves me very much now.
GET IN THERE, YOU USELESS FUCKIN' BASTARD!
His love hurts. ⁝whine⁝
I am awake; now, and hungry. Where is he? ⁝whine⁝
Others are here. This is my house.
My house.
Go away.
Go away!

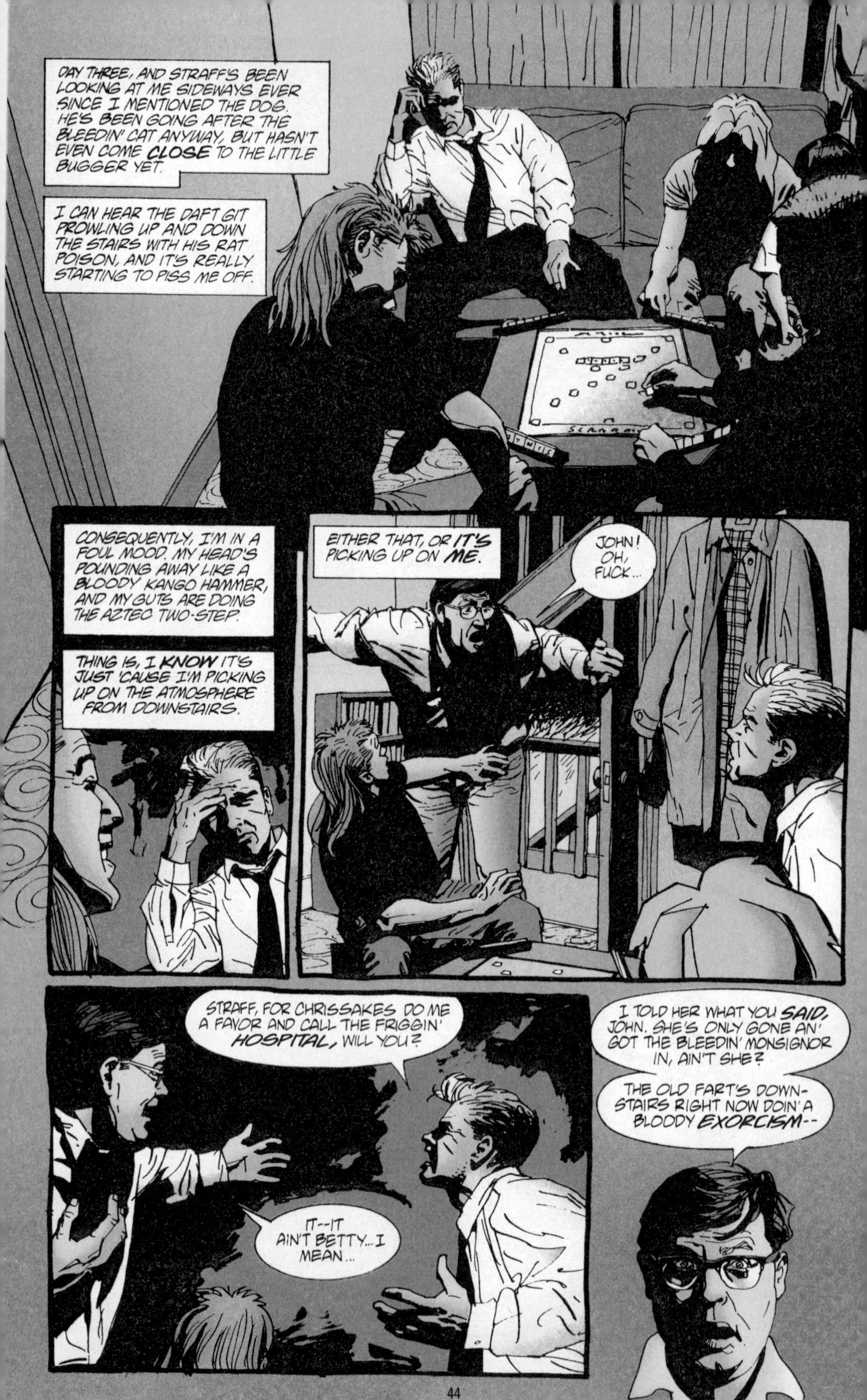

DAY THREE, AND STRAFF'S BEEN LOOKING AT ME SIDEWAYS EVER SINCE I MENTIONED THE DOG. HE'S BEEN GOING AFTER THE BLEEDIN' CAT ANYWAY, BUT HASN'T EVEN COME CLOSE TO THE LITTLE BUGGER YET.
I CAN HEAR THE DAFT GIT PROWLING UP AND DOWN THE STAIRS WITH HIS RAT POISON, AND IT'S REALLY STARTING TO PISS ME OFF.
CONSEQUENTLY, I'M IN A FOUL MOOD. MY HEAD'S POUNDING AWAY LIKE A BLOODY KANGO HAMMER, AND MY GUTS ARE DOING THE AZTEC TWO-STEP.
THING IS, I KNOW IT'S JUST 'CAUSE I'M PICKING UP ON THE ATMOSPHERE FROM DOWNSTAIRS.
EITHER THAT, OR IT'S PICKING UP ON ME.
JOHN! OH, FUCK...
STRAFF, FOR CHRISSAKES DO ME A FAVOR AND CALL THE FRIGGIN' HOSPITAL, WILL YOU?
IT--IT AIN'T BETTY... I MEAN...
I TOLD HER WHAT YOU SAID, JOHN. SHE'S ONLY GONE AN' GOT THE BLEEDIN' MONSIGNOR IN, AIN'T SHE?
THE OLD FART'S DOWN-STAIRS RIGHT NOW DOIN' A BLOODY EXORCISM--

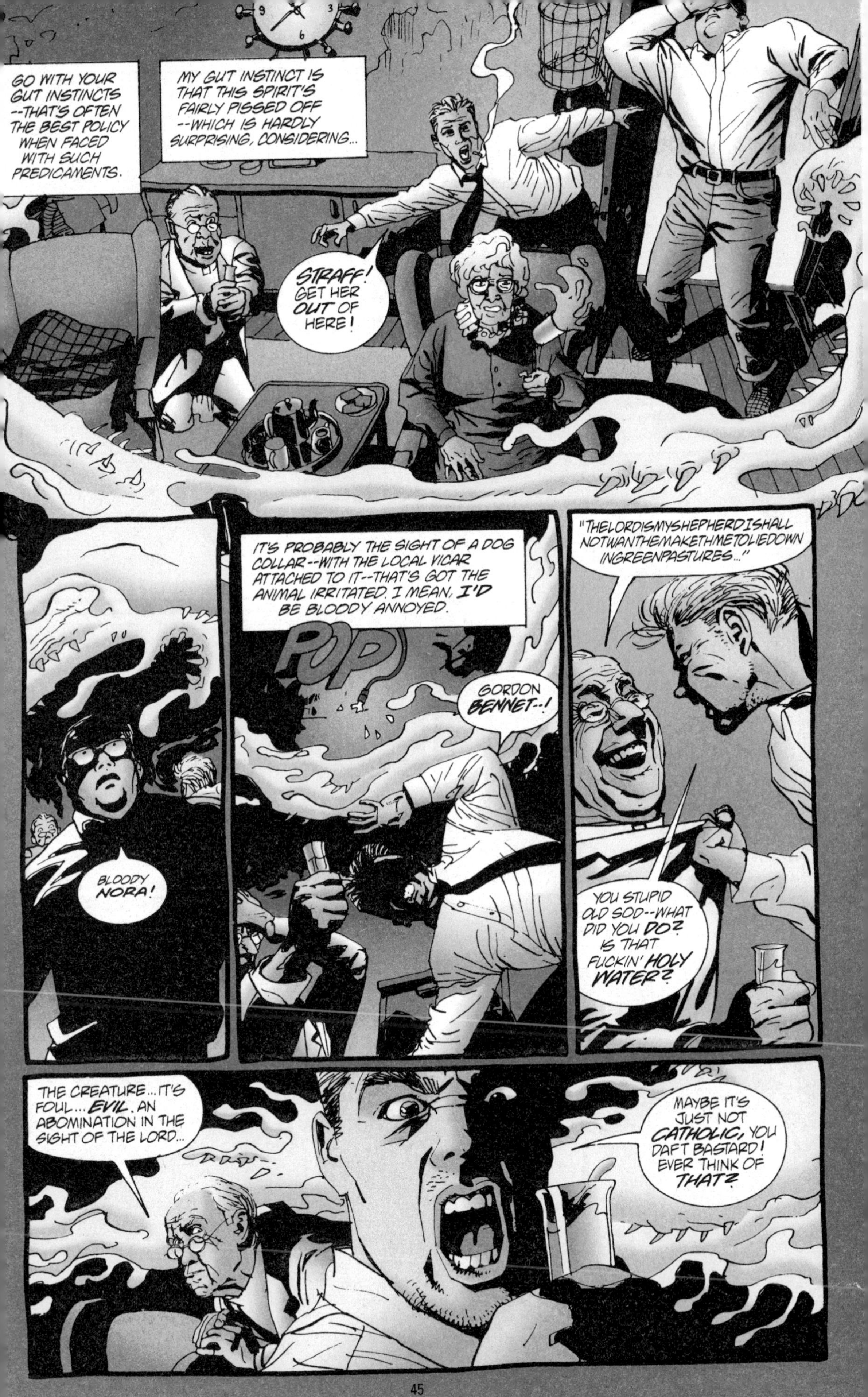
GO WITH YOUR GUT INSTINCTS --THAT'S OFTEN THE BEST POLICY WHEN FACED WITH SUCH PREDICAMENTS.
MY GUT INSTINCT IS THAT THIS SPIRIT'S FAIRLY PISSED OFF --WHICH IS HARDLY SURPRISING, CONSIDERING...
STRAFF! GET HER OUT OF HERE!
BLOODY NORA!
IT'S PROBABLY THE SIGHT OF A DOG COLLAR--WITH THE LOCAL VICAR ATTACHED TO IT--THAT'S GOT THE ANIMAL IRRITATED. I MEAN, I'D BE BLOODY ANNOYED.
POP
GORDON BENNET--!
"THELORDISMYSHEPHERDISHALL NOTWANTHEMAKETHMETOLIEDOWN INGREENPASTURES..."
YOU STUPID OLD SOD--WHAT DID YOU DO? IS THAT FUCKIN' HOLY WATER?
THE CREATURE... IT'S FOUL... EVIL. AN ABOMINATION IN THE SIGHT OF THE LORD...
MAYBE IT'S JUST NOT CATHOLIC, YOU DAFT BASTARD! EVER THINK OF THAT?

SEE, ANGRY SPIRITS ARE USUALLY LESS THAN REASONABLE WHEN IT COMES TO BEING BOOTED OUT OF THEIR HAUNTS.

THE BEST DEFENSE IS TO GET RID OF WHATEVER'S PISSED THEM OFF IN THE FIRST PLACE.

WITH THE SCENT OF HOLY WATER GONE FROM THE ROOM, THE DOG THANKFULLY RELENTS.

TENDRILS OF ECTOPLASM COLLAPSE INWARD, AS THE SPIRIT THINKS BETTER OF IT AND GOES OFF TO BROOD FOR A WHILE.

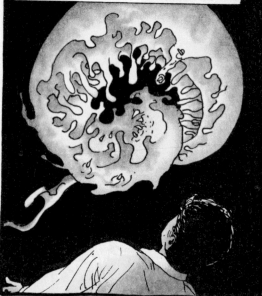

AND OF COURSE, THE *CABARET* ARRIVES JUST IN TIME TO *MISS* IT ALL...

EVENIN' ALL. WHA'S GOIN' ON 'ERE, THEN?

FUCKIN' WIZARD MERLIN! SPLIFF'S 'AVIN' A SODDIN' *PARTY!*

POP

CALLS FOR SOME *TUNES*, eh, CON-JOB? WHAT D'YOU RECKON?

I DUNNO, RICH. HOW ABOUT "NEARER MY GOD TO THEE"?

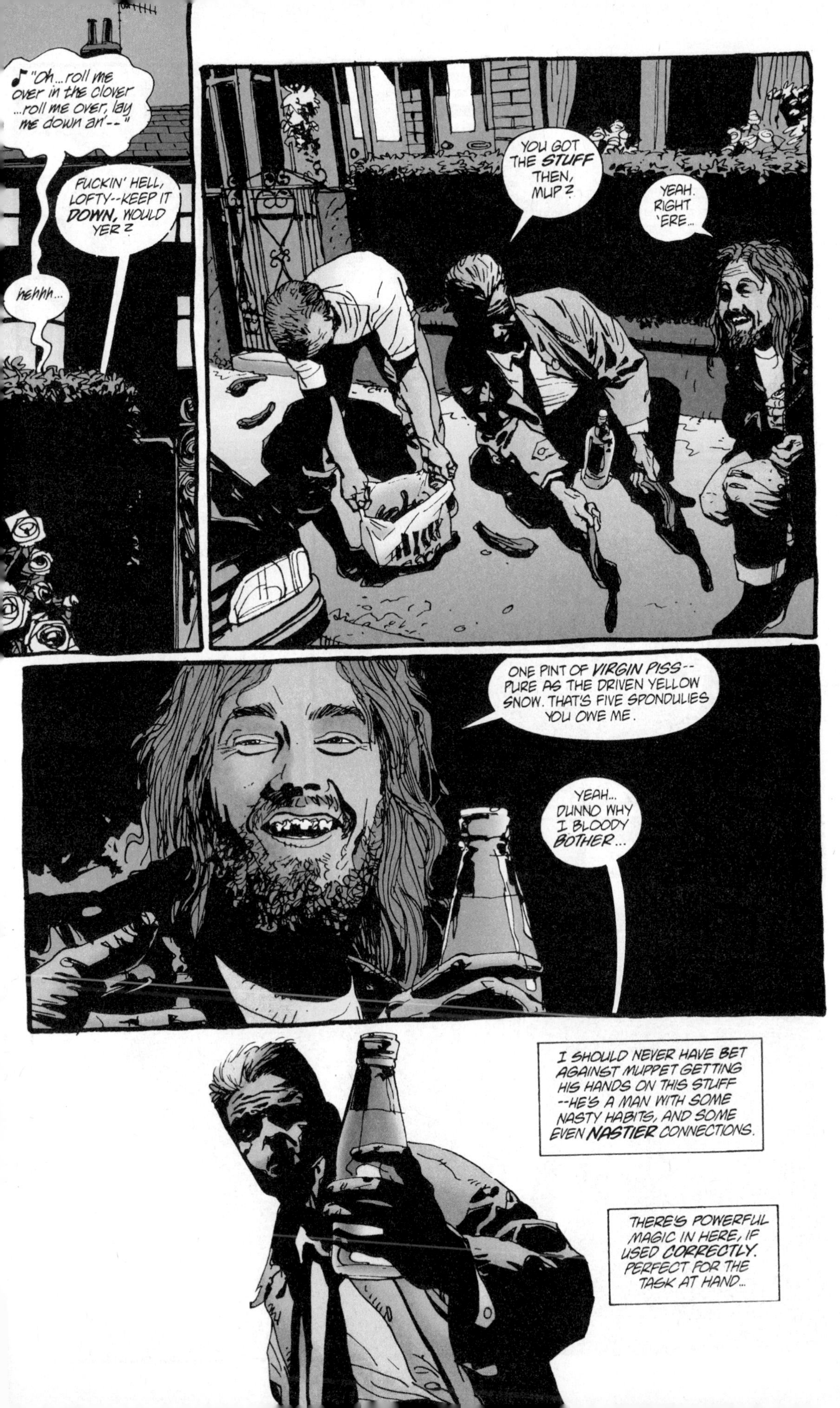
"Oh... roll me over in the clover ...roll me over, lay me down an'--"
FUCKIN' HELL, LOFTY--KEEP IT DOWN, WOULD YER?
hehhh...
YOU GOT THE STUFF THEN, MUP?
YEAH. RIGHT 'ERE...
ONE PINT OF VIRGIN PISS-- PURE AS THE DRIVEN YELLOW SNOW. THAT'S FIVE SPONDULIES YOU OWE ME.
YEAH... DUNNO WHY I BLOODY BOTHER...
I SHOULD NEVER HAVE BET AGAINST MUPPET GETTING HIS HANDS ON THIS STUFF --HE'S A MAN WITH SOME NASTY HABITS, AND SOME EVEN NASTIER CONNECTIONS.
THERE'S POWERFUL MAGIC IN HERE, IF USED CORRECTLY. PERFECT FOR THE TASK AT HAND...

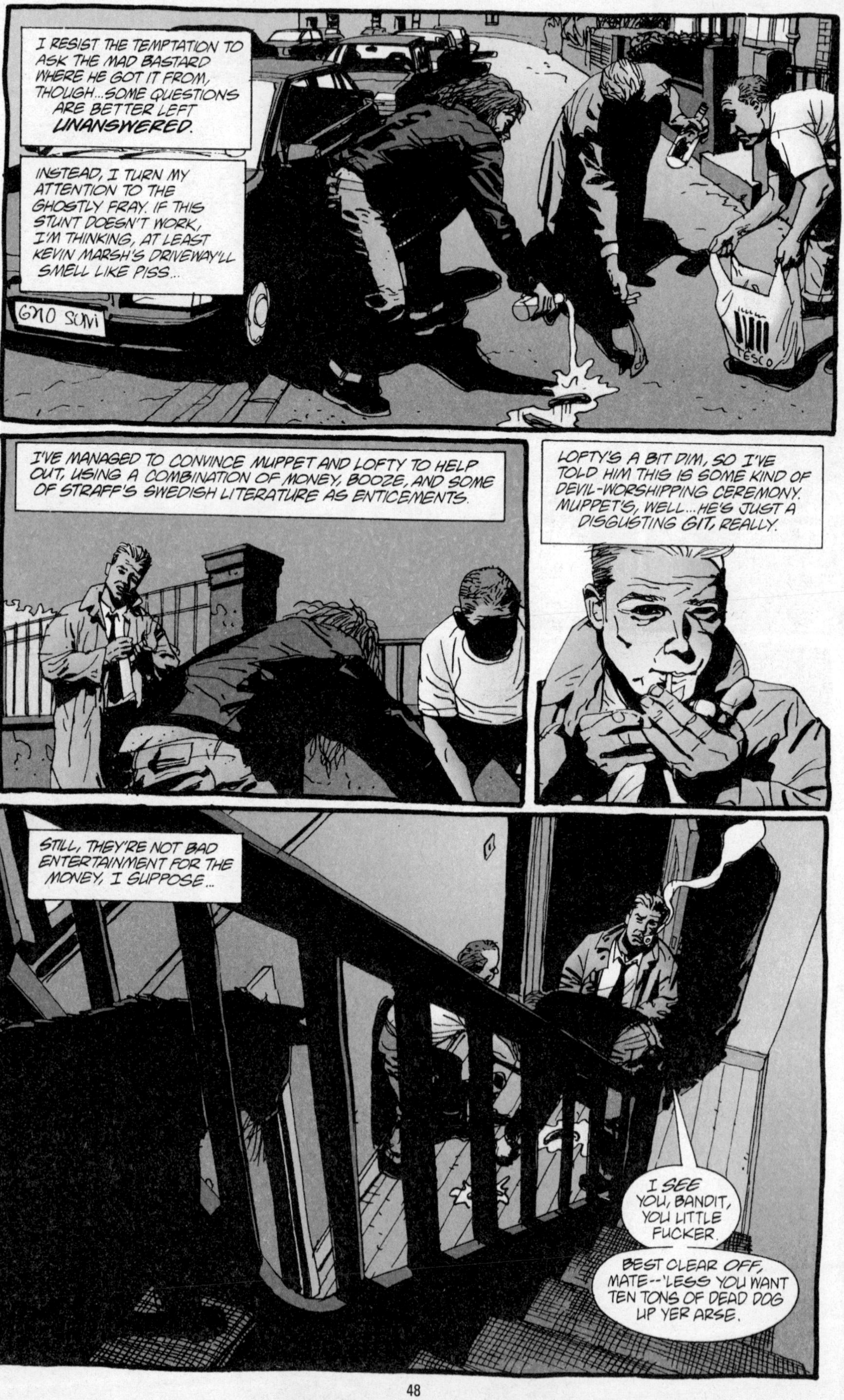
I RESIST THE TEMPTATION TO ASK THE MAD BASTARD WHERE HE GOT IT FROM, THOUGH...SOME QUESTIONS ARE BETTER LEFT UNANSWERED.
INSTEAD, I TURN MY ATTENTION TO THE GHOSTLY FRAY. IF THIS STUNT DOESN'T WORK, I'M THINKING, AT LEAST KEVIN MARSH'S DRIVEWAY'LL SMELL LIKE PISS...
TESCO
I'VE MANAGED TO CONVINCE MUPPET AND LOFTY TO HELP OUT, USING A COMBINATION OF MONEY, BOOZE, AND SOME OF STRAFF'S SWEDISH LITERATURE AS ENTICEMENTS.
LOFTY'S A BIT DIM, SO I'VE TOLD HIM THIS IS SOME KIND OF DEVIL-WORSHIPPING CEREMONY. MUPPET'S, WELL...HE'S JUST A DISGUSTING GIT, REALLY.
STILL, THEY'RE NOT BAD ENTERTAINMENT FOR THE MONEY, I SUPPOSE...
I SEE YOU, BANDIT, YOU LITTLE FUCKER.
BEST CLEAR OFF, MATE--'LESS YOU WANT TEN TONS OF DEAD DOG UP YER ARSE.

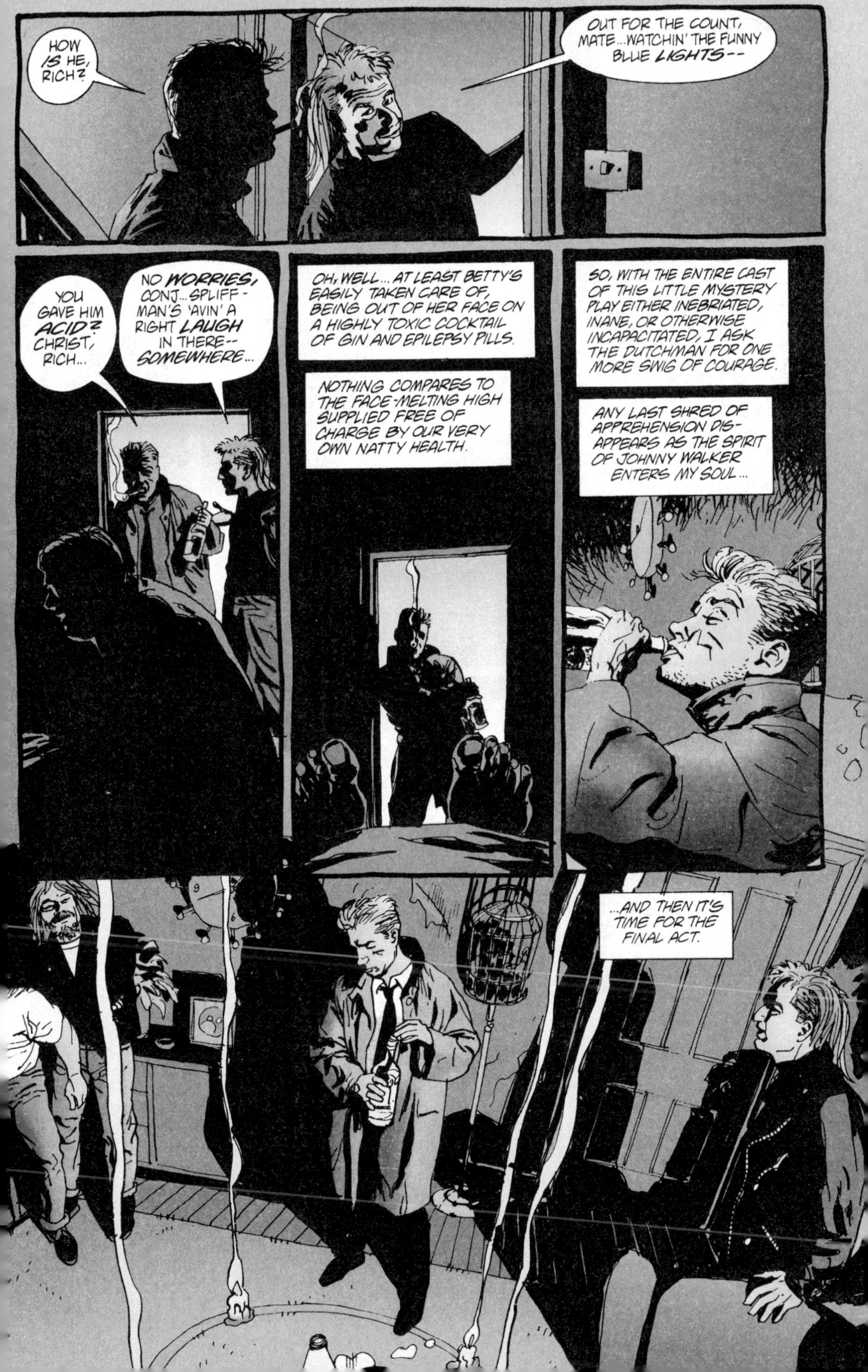
HOW IS HE, RICH?
OUT FOR THE COUNT, MATE... WATCHIN' THE FUNNY BLUE LIGHTS--
YOU GAVE HIM ACID? CHRIST, RICH...
NO WORRIES, CONJ... SPLIFF-MAN'S 'AVIN' A RIGHT LAUGH IN THERE-- SOMEWHERE...
OH, WELL... AT LEAST BETTY'S EASILY TAKEN CARE OF, BEING OUT OF HER FACE ON A HIGHLY TOXIC COCKTAIL OF GIN AND EPILEPSY PILLS.
NOTHING COMPARES TO THE FACE-MELTING HIGH SUPPLIED FREE OF CHARGE BY OUR VERY OWN NATTY HEALTH.
SO, WITH THE ENTIRE CAST OF THIS LITTLE MYSTERY PLAY EITHER INEBRIATED, INANE, OR OTHERWISE INCAPACITATED, I ASK THE DUTCHMAN FOR ONE MORE SWIG OF COURAGE.
ANY LAST SHRED OF APPREHENSION DIS-APPEARS AS THE SPIRIT OF JOHNNY WALKER ENTERS MY SOUL...
...AND THEN IT'S TIME FOR THE FINAL ACT.

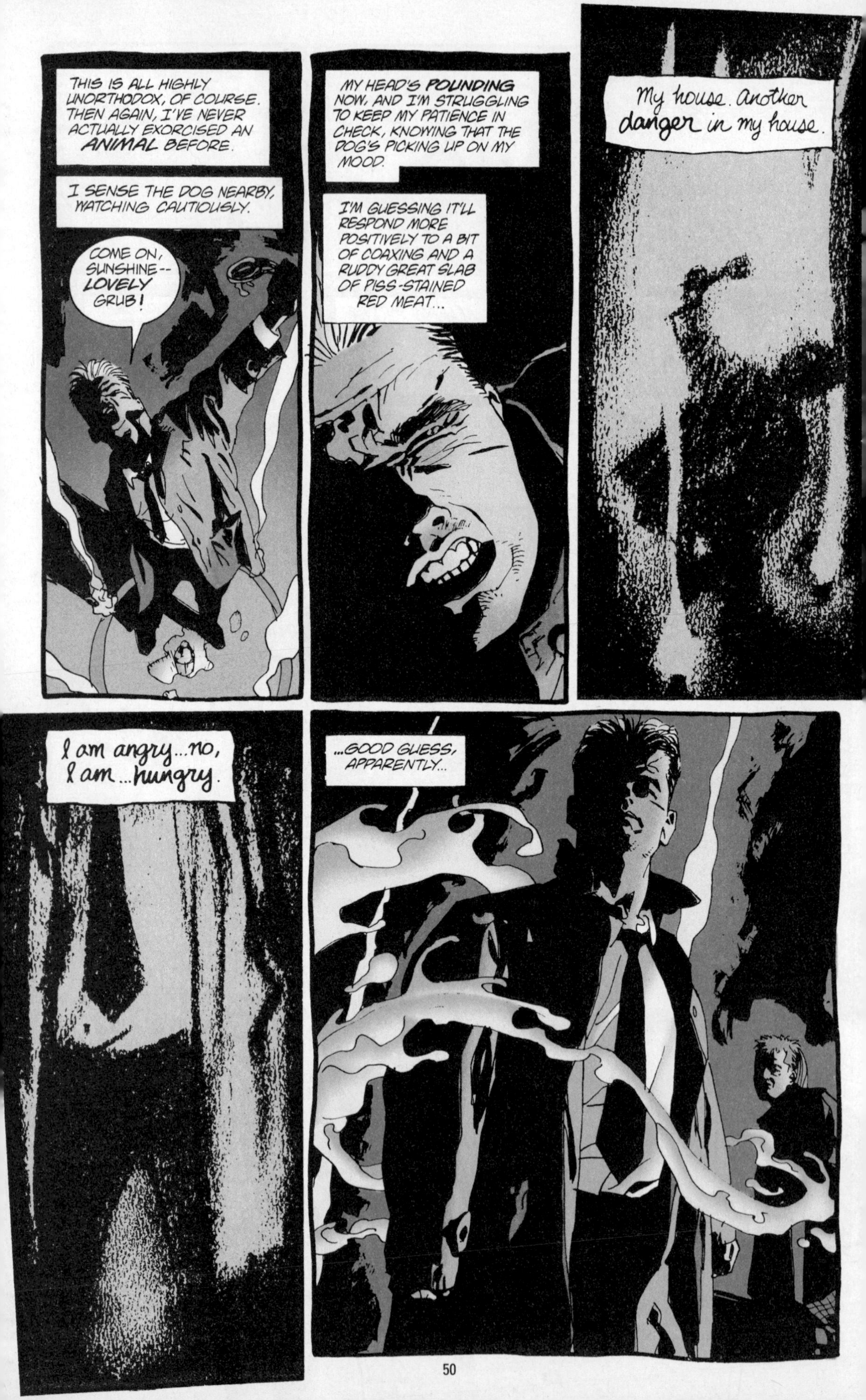
THIS IS ALL HIGHLY UNORTHODOX, OF COURSE. THEN AGAIN, I'VE NEVER ACTUALLY EXORCISED AN ANIMAL BEFORE.
I SENSE THE DOG NEARBY, WATCHING CAUTIOUSLY.
COME ON, SUNSHINE-- LOVELY GRUB!
MY HEAD'S POUNDING NOW, AND I'M STRUGGLING TO KEEP MY PATIENCE IN CHECK, KNOWING THAT THE DOG'S PICKING UP ON MY MOOD.
I'M GUESSING IT'LL RESPOND MORE POSITIVELY TO A BIT OF COAXING AND A RUDDY GREAT SLAB OF PISS-STAINED RED MEAT...
My house. Another danger in my house.
I am angry...no, I am...hungry.
...GOOD GUESS, APPARENTLY...

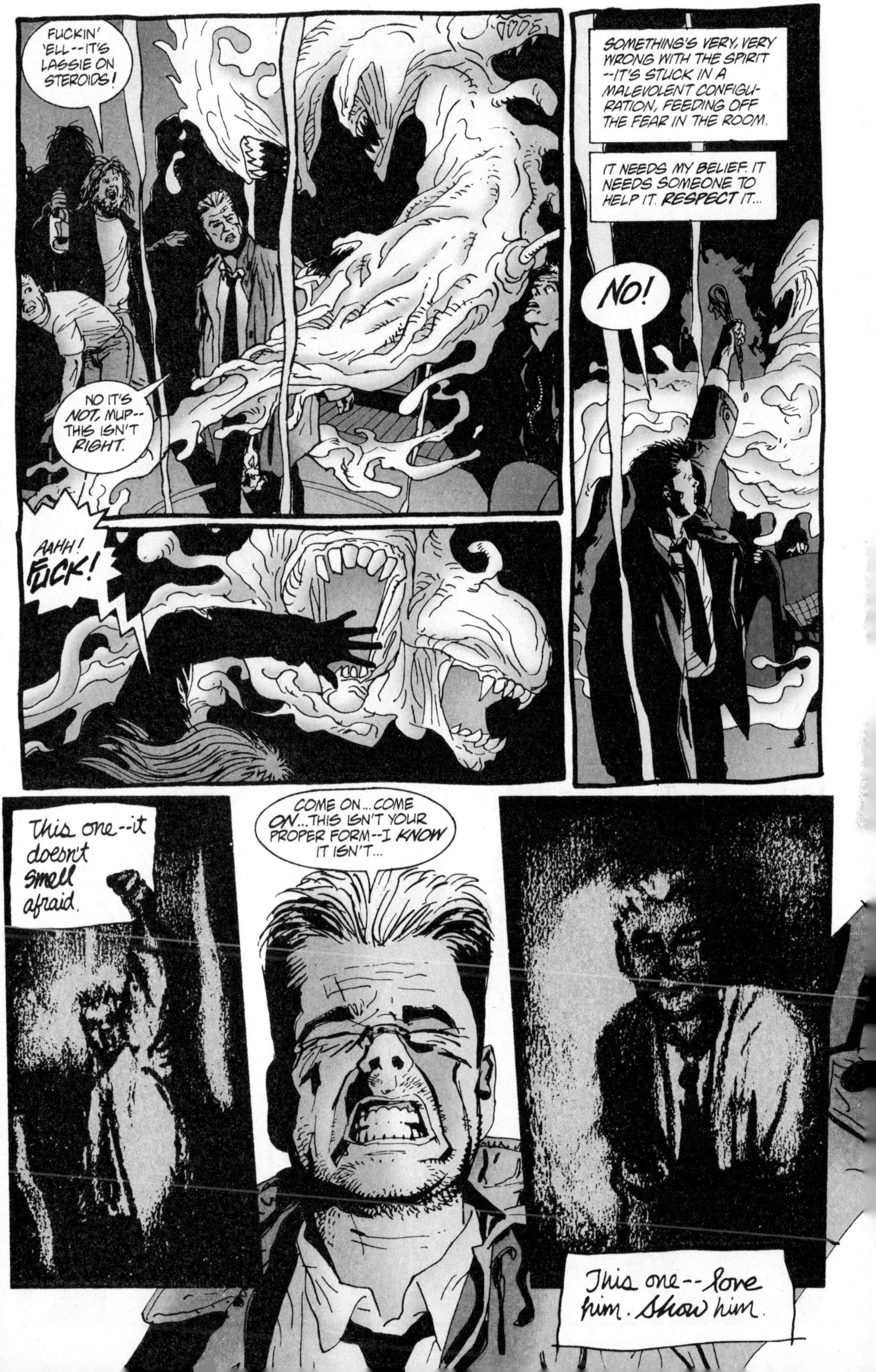
FUCKIN' 'ELL--IT'S LASSIE ON STEROIDS!
NO IT'S NOT, MUP--THIS ISN'T RIGHT.
SOMETHING'S VERY, VERY WRONG WITH THE SPIRIT --IT'S STUCK IN A MALEVOLENT CONFIGURATION, FEEDING OFF THE FEAR IN THE ROOM.
IT NEEDS MY BELIEF. IT NEEDS SOMEONE TO HELP IT. RESPECT IT...
NO!
AAHH! FUCK!
This one--it doesn't smell afraid.
COME ON... COME ON... THIS ISN'T YOUR PROPER FORM--I KNOW IT ISN'T...
This one--love him. Show him.

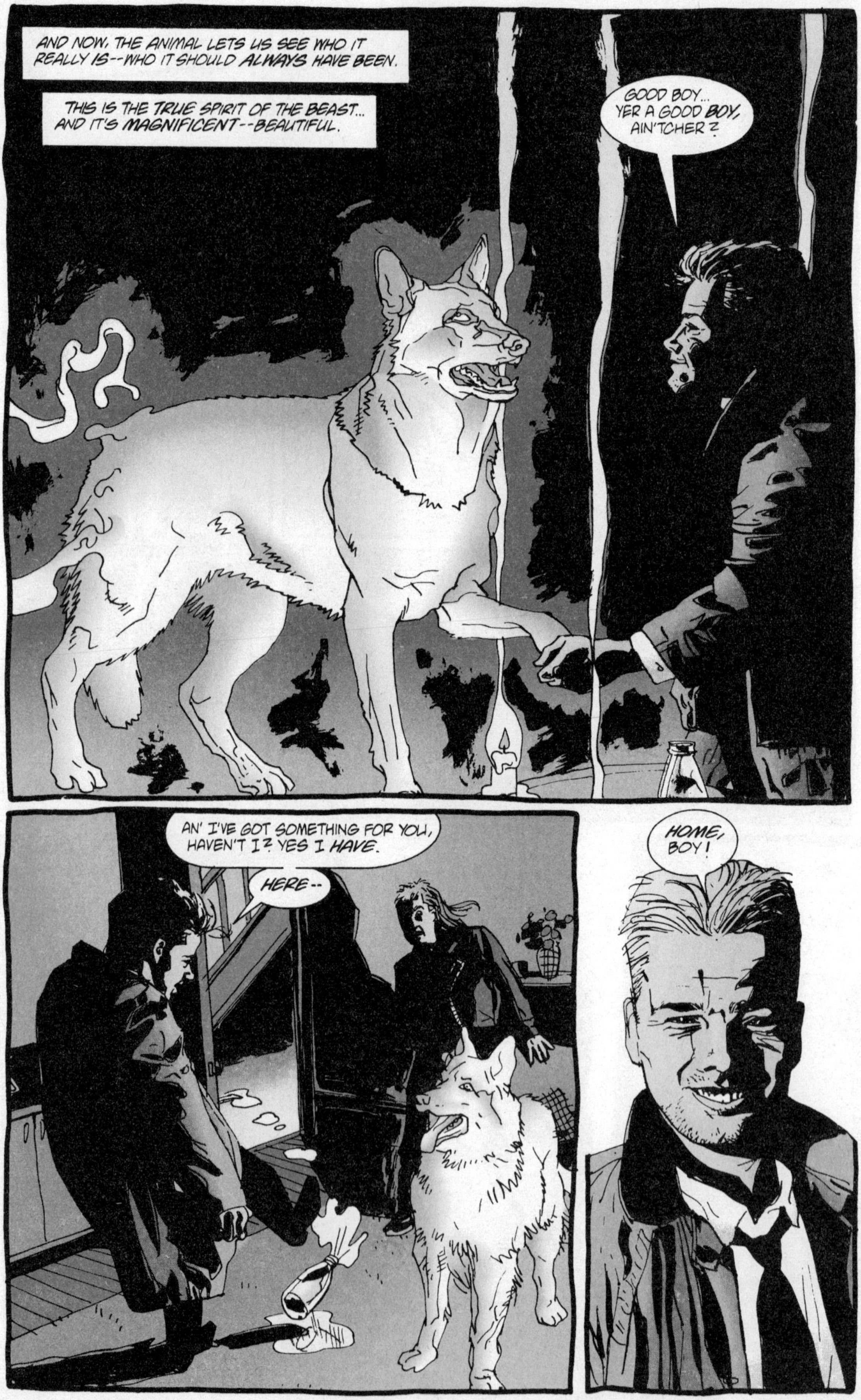
AND NOW, THE ANIMAL LETS US SEE WHO IT REALLY IS--WHO IT SHOULD ALWAYS HAVE BEEN.
THIS IS THE TRUE SPIRIT OF THE BEAST... AND IT'S MAGNIFICENT--BEAUTIFUL.
GOOD BOY... YER A GOOD BOY, AIN'TCHER?
AN' I'VE GOT SOMETHING FOR YOU, HAVEN'T I? YES I HAVE.
HERE--
HOME, BOY!

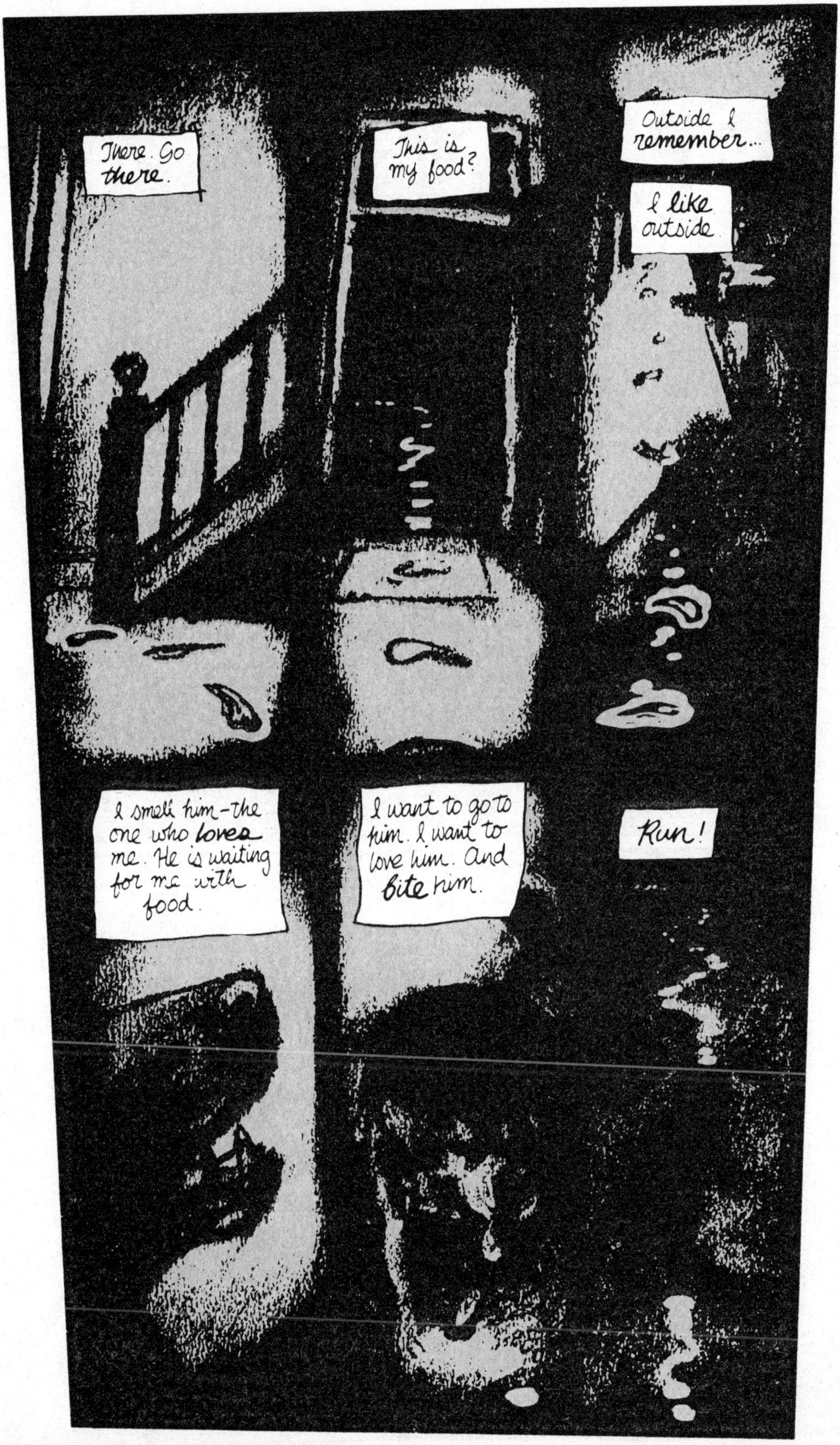

There. Go there.
This is my food?
Outside I remember...
I like outside.
I smell him—the one who loves me. He is waiting for me with food.
I want to go to him. I want to love him. And bite him.
Run!

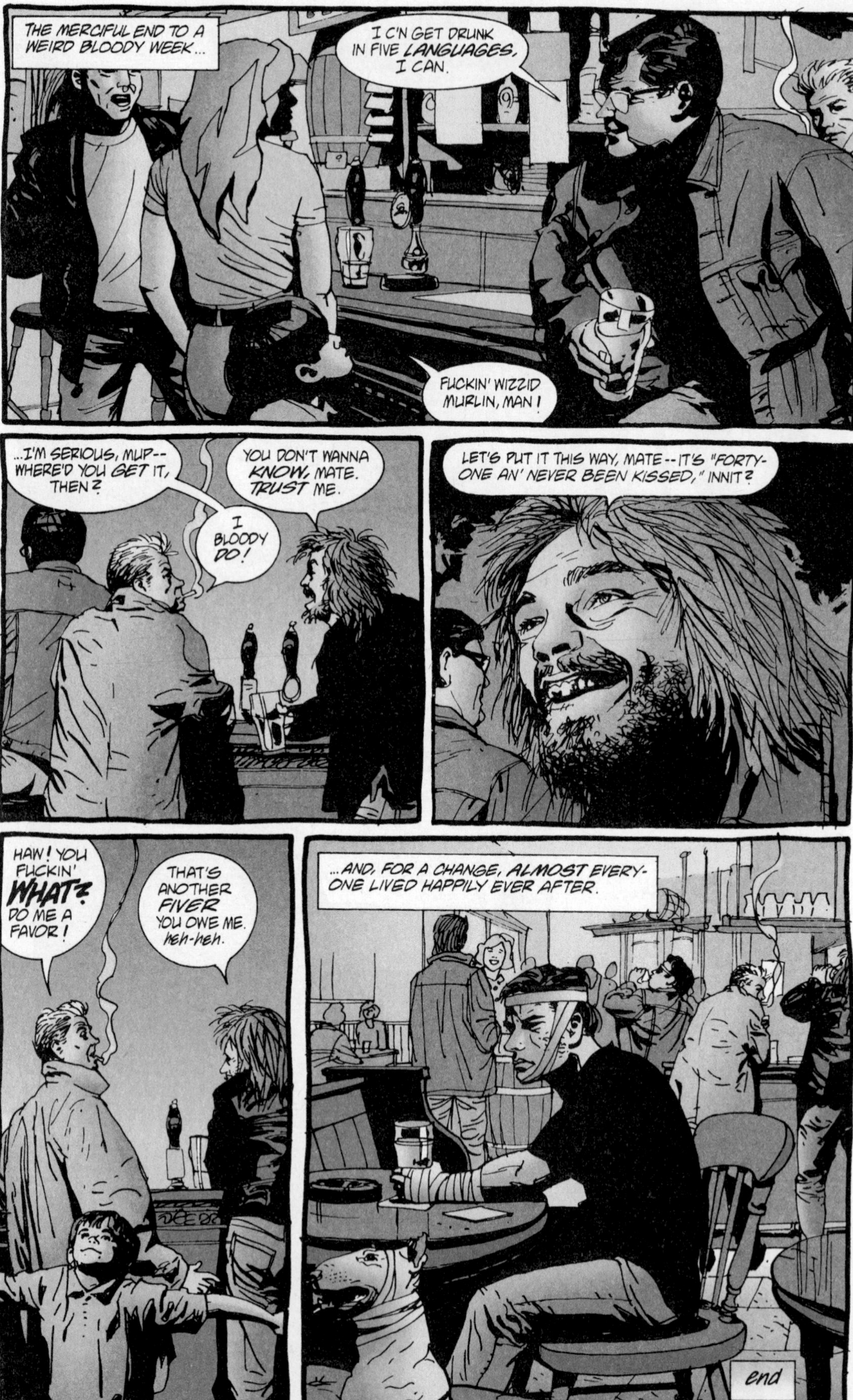
THE MERCIFUL END TO A WEIRD BLOODY WEEK...
I C'N GET DRUNK IN FIVE LANGUAGES, I CAN.
FUCKIN' WIZZID MURLIN, MAN!
...I'M SERIOUS, MUP-- WHERE'D YOU GET IT, THEN?
YOU DON'T WANNA KNOW, MATE. TRUST ME.
I BLOODY DO!
LET'S PUT IT THIS WAY, MATE--IT'S "FORTY-ONE AN' NEVER BEEN KISSED," INNIT?
HAW! YOU FUCKIN' WHAT? DO ME A FAVOR!
THAT'S ANOTHER FIVER YOU OWE ME. heh-heh.
...AND, FOR A CHANGE, ALMOST EVERY-ONE LIVED HAPPILY EVER AFTER.
end

JOHN CONSTANTINE

HELLBLAZER

C
RTIGO

39
96
US
CAN
ESTED
MATURE
ERS

PAUL JENKINS
SEAN PHILLIPS

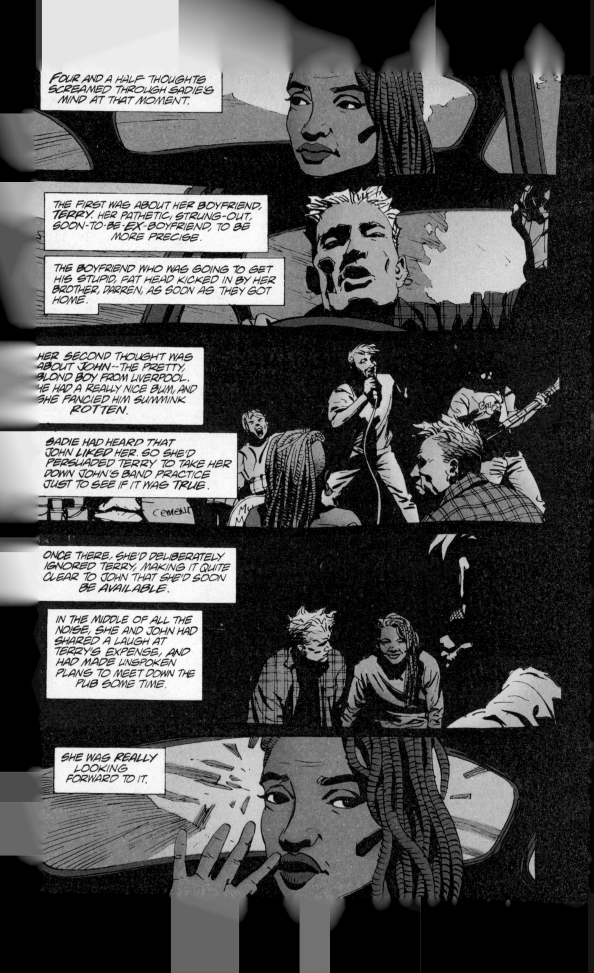

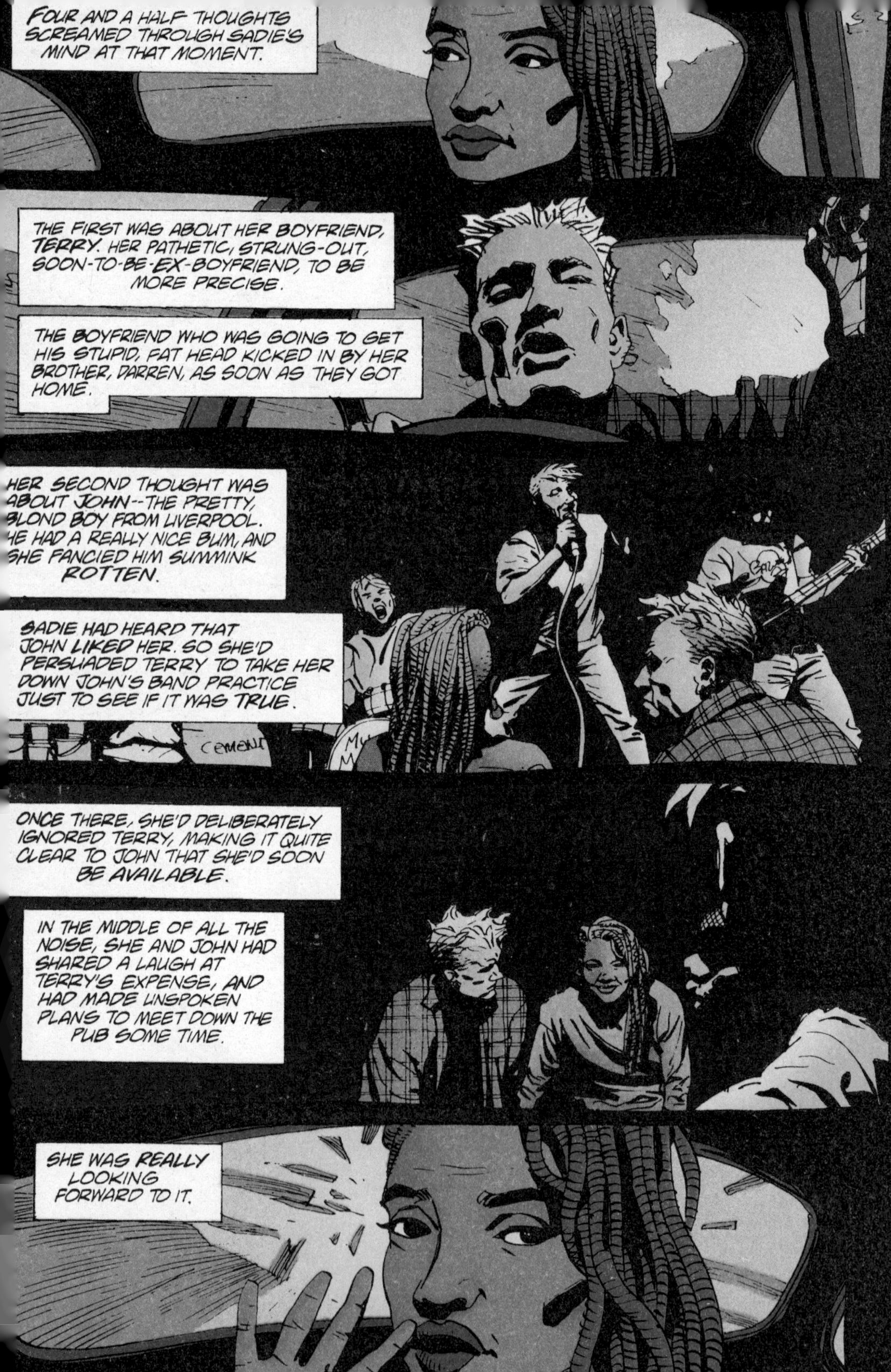
FOUR AND A HALF THOUGHTS SCREAMED THROUGH SADIE'S MIND AT THAT MOMENT.
THE FIRST WAS ABOUT HER BOYFRIEND, **TERRY**. HER PATHETIC, STRUNG-OUT, SOON-TO-BE-**EX**-BOYFRIEND, TO BE MORE PRECISE.
THE **BOYFRIEND** WHO WAS GOING TO GET HIS STUPID, FAT HEAD KICKED IN BY HER BROTHER, DARREN, AS SOON AS THEY GOT HOME.
HER **SECOND** THOUGHT WAS ABOUT **JOHN**--THE PRETTY, BLOND BOY FROM LIVERPOOL. HE HAD A REALLY NICE BUM, AND SHE FANCIED HIM SUMMINK **ROTTEN**.
SADIE HAD HEARD THAT JOHN **LIKED** HER. SO SHE'D PERSUADED TERRY TO TAKE HER DOWN JOHN'S BAND PRACTICE JUST TO SEE IF IT WAS **TRUE**.
ONCE THERE, SHE'D DELIBERATELY IGNORED TERRY, MAKING IT QUITE CLEAR TO JOHN THAT SHE'D SOON **BE AVAILABLE**.
IN THE MIDDLE OF ALL THE NOISE, SHE AND JOHN HAD SHARED A LAUGH AT TERRY'S EXPENSE, AND HAD MADE UNSPOKEN PLANS TO MEET DOWN THE PUB SOME TIME.
SHE WAS **REALLY** LOOKING FORWARD TO IT.

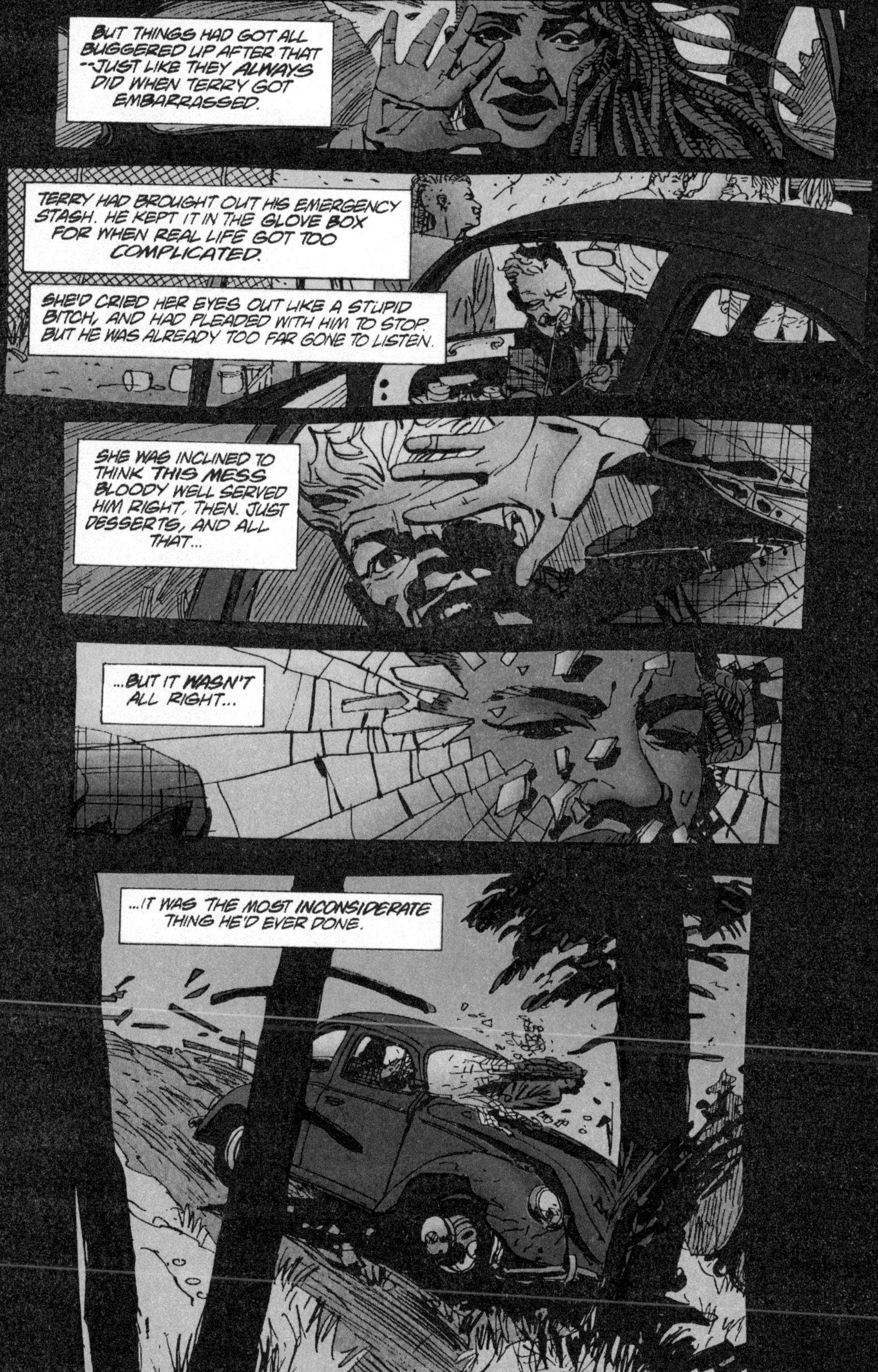
BUT THINGS HAD GOT ALL BUGGERED UP AFTER THAT --JUST LIKE THEY ALWAYS DID WHEN TERRY GOT EMBARRASSED.
TERRY HAD BROUGHT OUT HIS EMERGENCY STASH. HE KEPT IT IN THE GLOVE BOX FOR WHEN REAL LIFE GOT TOO COMPLICATED.
SHE'D CRIED HER EYES OUT LIKE A STUPID BITCH, AND HAD PLEADED WITH HIM TO STOP. BUT HE WAS ALREADY TOO FAR GONE TO LISTEN.
SHE WAS INCLINED TO THINK THIS MESS BLOODY WELL SERVED HIM RIGHT, THEN. JUST DESSERTS, AND ALL THAT...
...BUT IT WASN'T ALL RIGHT...
...IT WAS THE MOST INCONSIDERATE THING HE'D EVER DONE.

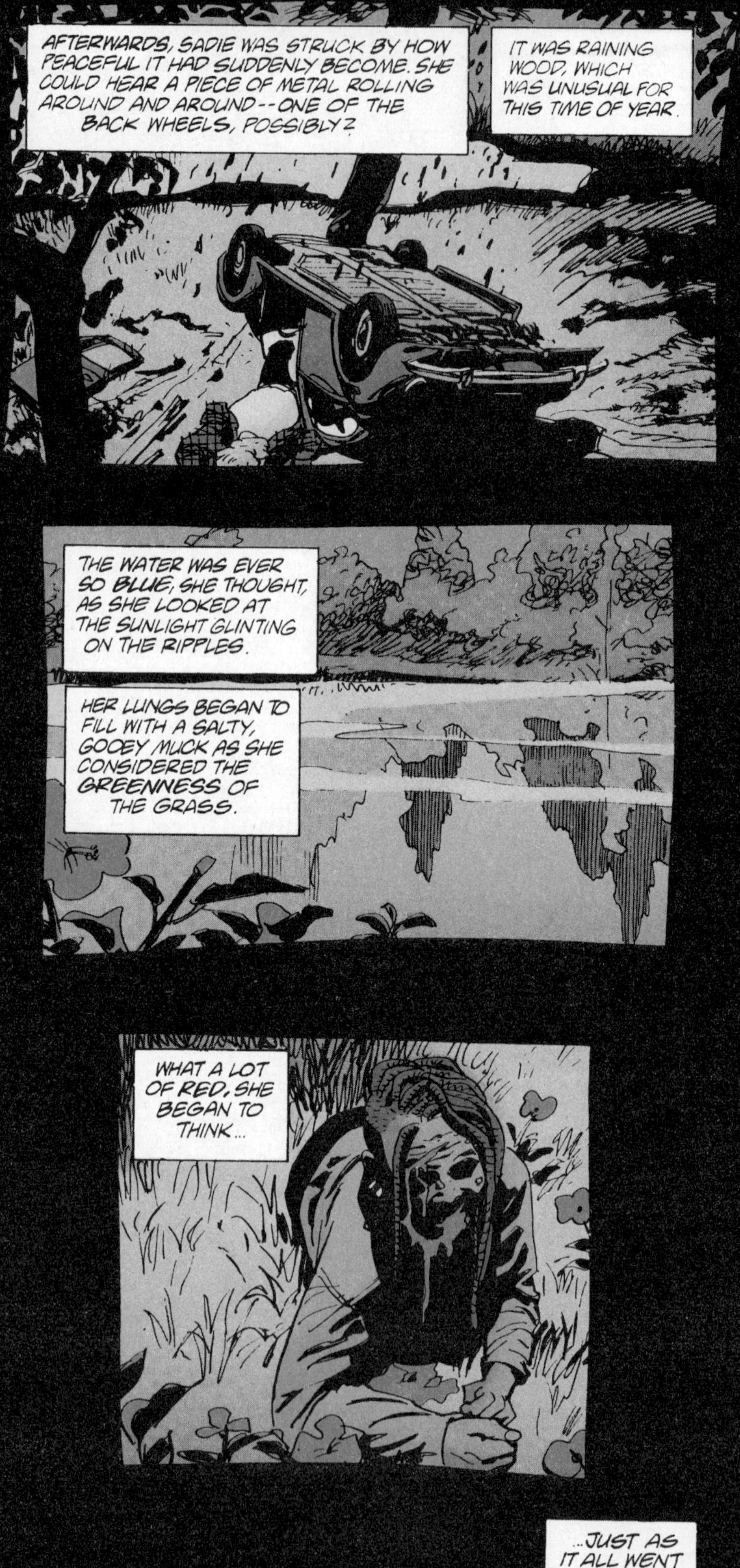
AFTERWARDS, SADIE WAS STRUCK BY HOW PEACEFUL IT HAD SUDDENLY BECOME. SHE COULD HEAR A PIECE OF METAL ROLLING AROUND AND AROUND--ONE OF THE BACK WHEELS, POSSIBLY?
IT WAS RAINING WOOD, WHICH WAS UNUSUAL FOR THIS TIME OF YEAR.
THE WATER WAS EVER SO BLUE, SHE THOUGHT, AS SHE LOOKED AT THE SUNLIGHT GLINTING ON THE RIPPLES.
HER LUNGS BEGAN TO FILL WITH A SALTY, GOOEY MUCK AS SHE CONSIDERED THE GREENNESS OF THE GRASS.
WHAT A LOT OF RED, SHE BEGAN TO THINK...
...JUST AS IT ALL WENT BLACK.

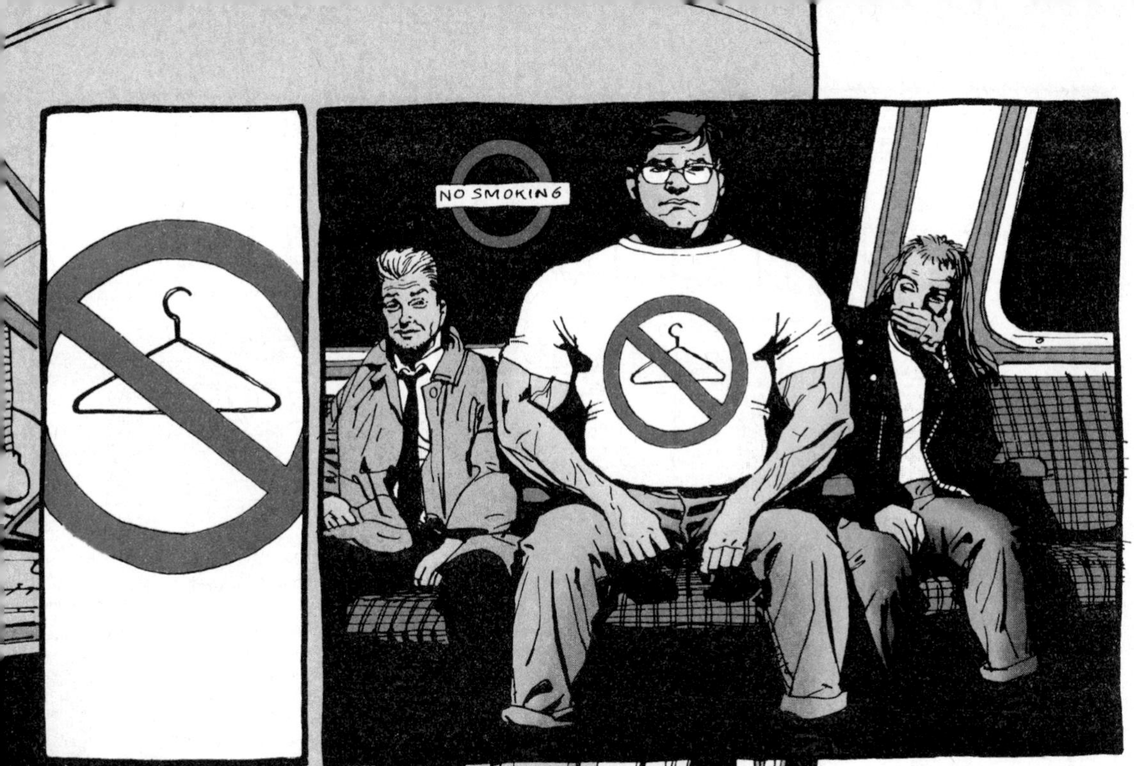
NO SMOKING

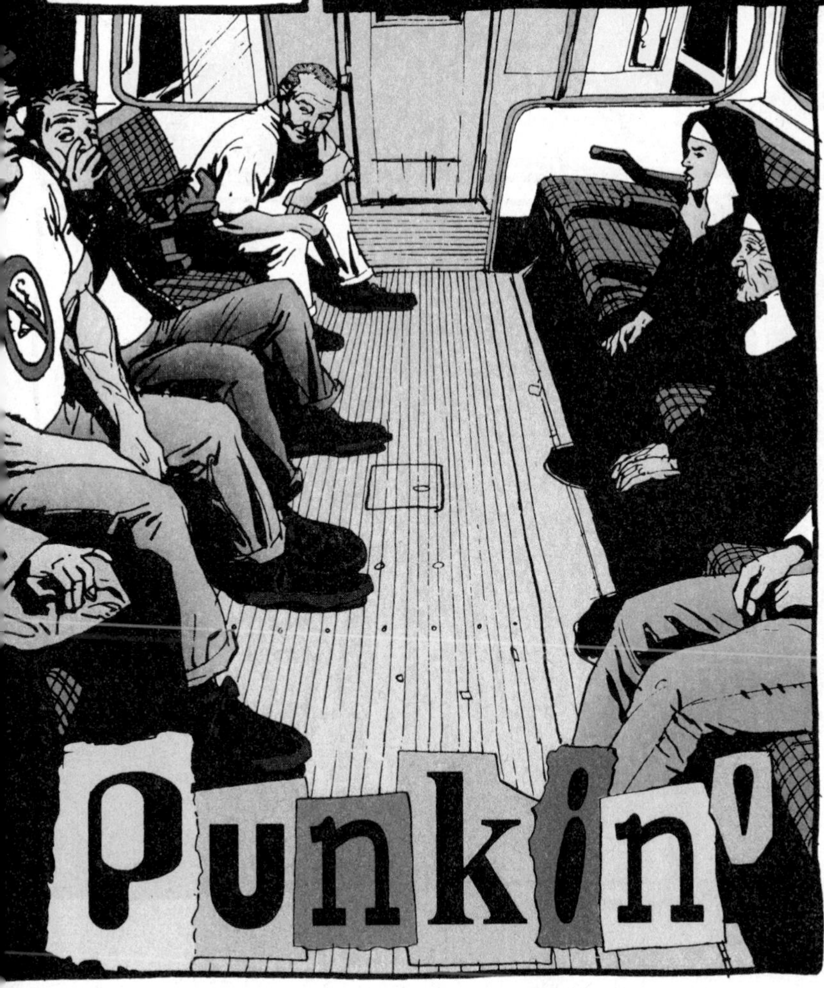

Punkin' up the Great Outdoors

PAUL JENKINS
Writer
SEAN PHILLIPS
Artist
MATT HOLLINGSWORTH
Colorist
CLEM ROBINS
Letterer
AXEL ALONSO
Asst. Editor
LOU STATHIS
Editor

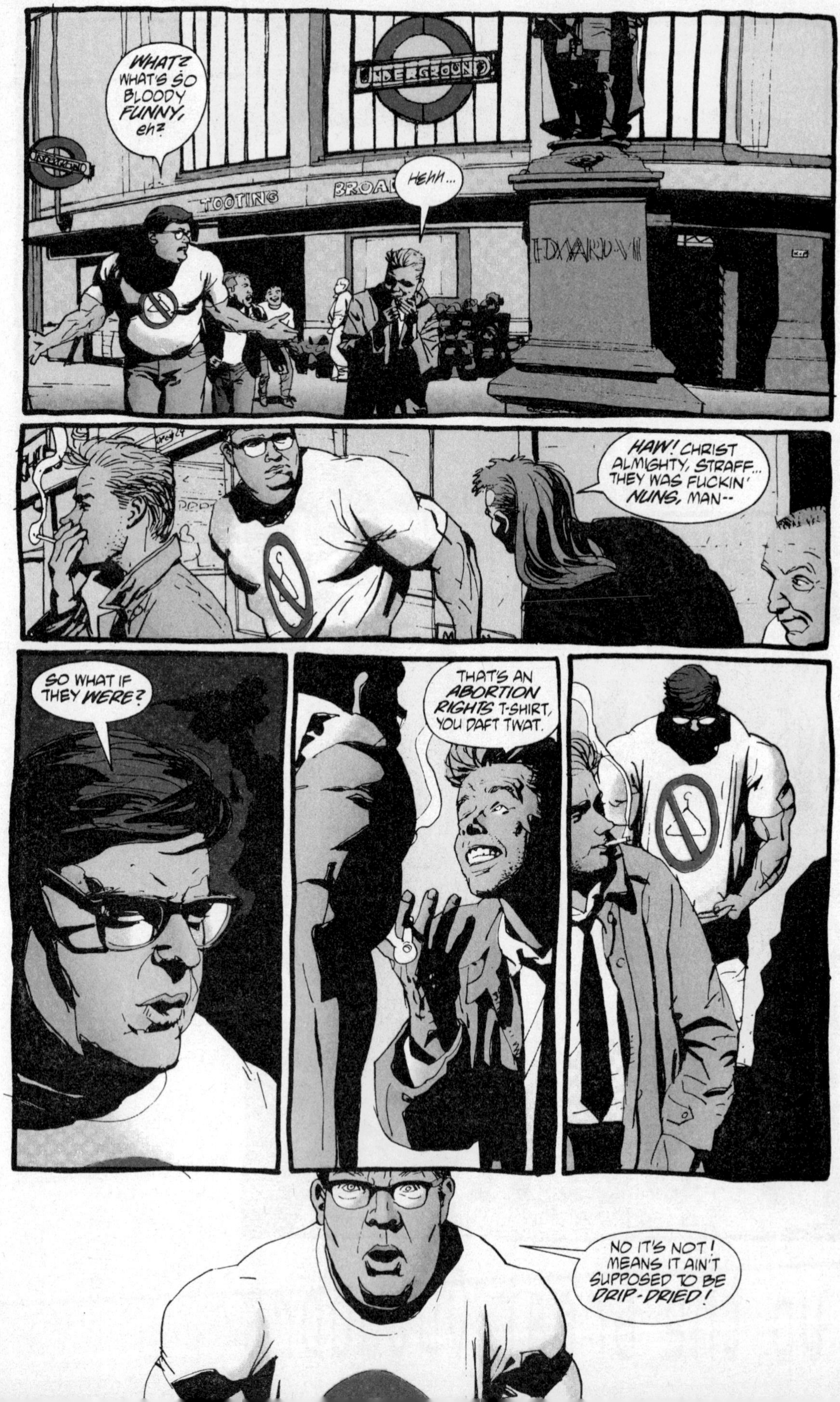
WHAT? WHAT'S SO BLOODY FUNNY, eh?
UNDERGROUND
TOOTING BROAD
HEHH...
EDWARD VII
HAW! CHRIST ALMIGHTY, STRAFF... THEY WAS FUCKIN' NUNS, MAN--
SO WHAT IF THEY WERE?
THAT'S AN ABORTION RIGHTS T-SHIRT, YOU DAFT TWAT.
NO IT'S NOT! MEANS IT AIN'T SUPPOSED TO BE DRIP-DRIED!

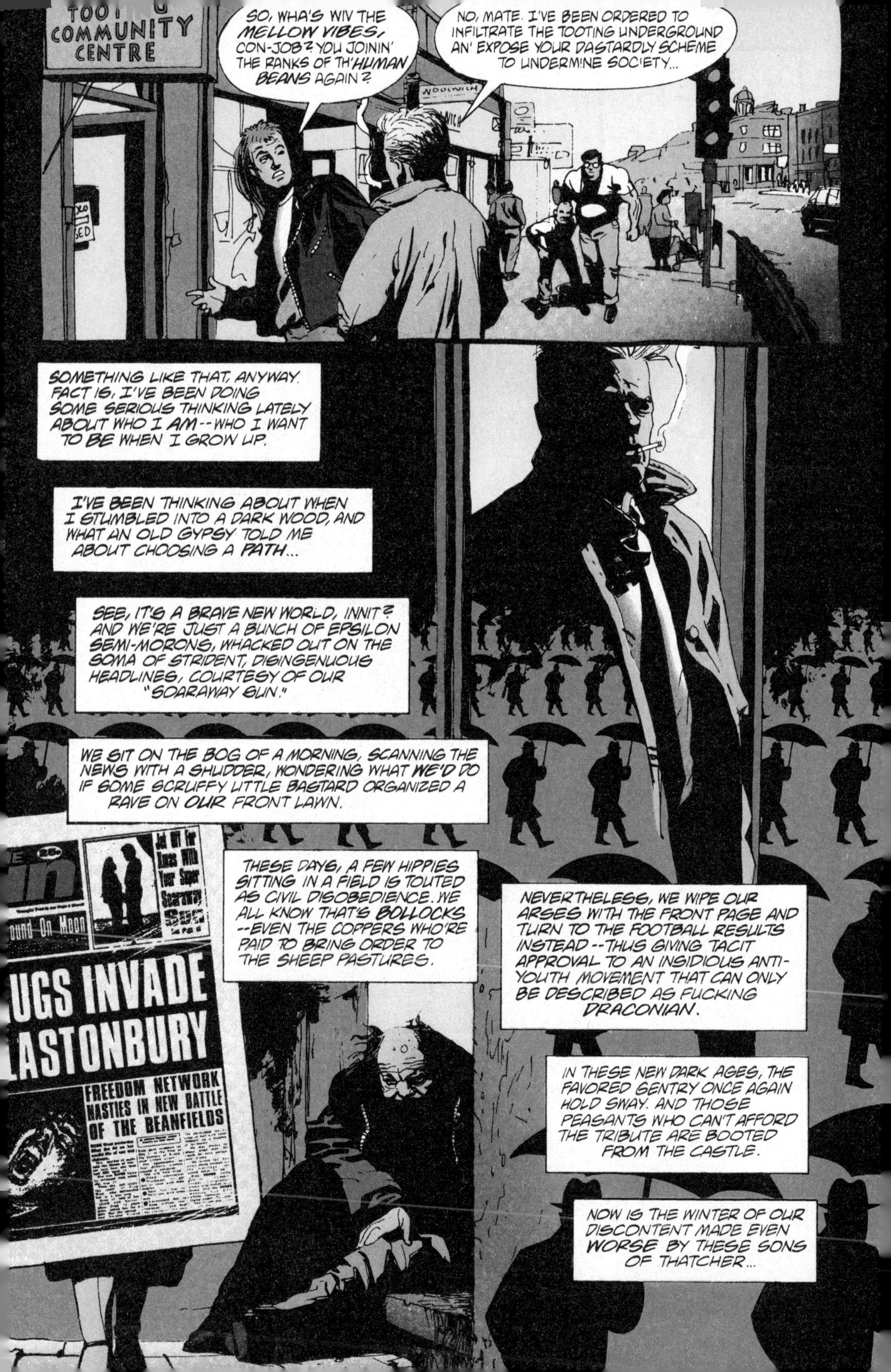

COMMUNITY CENTRE
SO, WHA'S WIV THE MELLOW VIBES, CON-JOB? YOU JOININ' THE RANKS OF TH' HUMAN BEANS AGAIN?
NO, MATE. I'VE BEEN ORDERED TO INFILTRATE THE TOOTING UNDERGROUND AN' EXPOSE YOUR DASTARDLY SCHEME TO UNDERMINE SOCIETY...
WOOLWICH
SOMETHING LIKE THAT, ANYWAY. FACT IS, I'VE BEEN DOING SOME SERIOUS THINKING LATELY ABOUT WHO I AM -- WHO I WANT TO BE WHEN I GROW UP.
I'VE BEEN THINKING ABOUT WHEN I STUMBLED INTO A DARK WOOD, AND WHAT AN OLD GYPSY TOLD ME ABOUT CHOOSING A PATH...
SEE, IT'S A BRAVE NEW WORLD, INNIT? AND WE'RE JUST A BUNCH OF EPSILON SEMI-MORONS, WHACKED OUT ON THE SOMA OF STRIDENT, DISINGENUOUS HEADLINES, COURTESY OF OUR "SOARAWAY SUN."
WE SIT ON THE BOG OF A MORNING, SCANNING THE NEWS WITH A SHUDDER, WONDERING WHAT WE'D DO IF SOME SCRUFFY LITTLE BASTARD ORGANIZED A RAVE ON OUR FRONT LAWN.
25p
Jet Off For Xmas With Your Super Soaraway Sun
ound On Moon
UGS INVADE
LASTONBURY
FREEDOM NETWORK NASTIES IN NEW BATTLE OF THE BEANFIELDS
THESE DAYS, A FEW HIPPIES SITTING IN A FIELD IS TOUTED AS CIVIL DISOBEDIENCE. WE ALL KNOW THAT'S BOLLOCKS --EVEN THE COPPERS WHO'RE PAID TO BRING ORDER TO THE SHEEP PASTURES.
NEVERTHELESS, WE WIPE OUR ARSES WITH THE FRONT PAGE AND TURN TO THE FOOTBALL RESULTS INSTEAD --THUS GIVING TACIT APPROVAL TO AN INSIDIOUS ANTI-YOUTH MOVEMENT THAT CAN ONLY BE DESCRIBED AS FUCKING DRACONIAN.
IN THESE NEW DARK AGES, THE FAVORED GENTRY ONCE AGAIN HOLD SWAY. AND THOSE PEASANTS WHO CAN'T AFFORD THE TRIBUTE ARE BOOTED FROM THE CASTLE.
NOW IS THE WINTER OF OUR DISCONTENT MADE EVEN WORSE BY THESE SONS OF THATCHER...

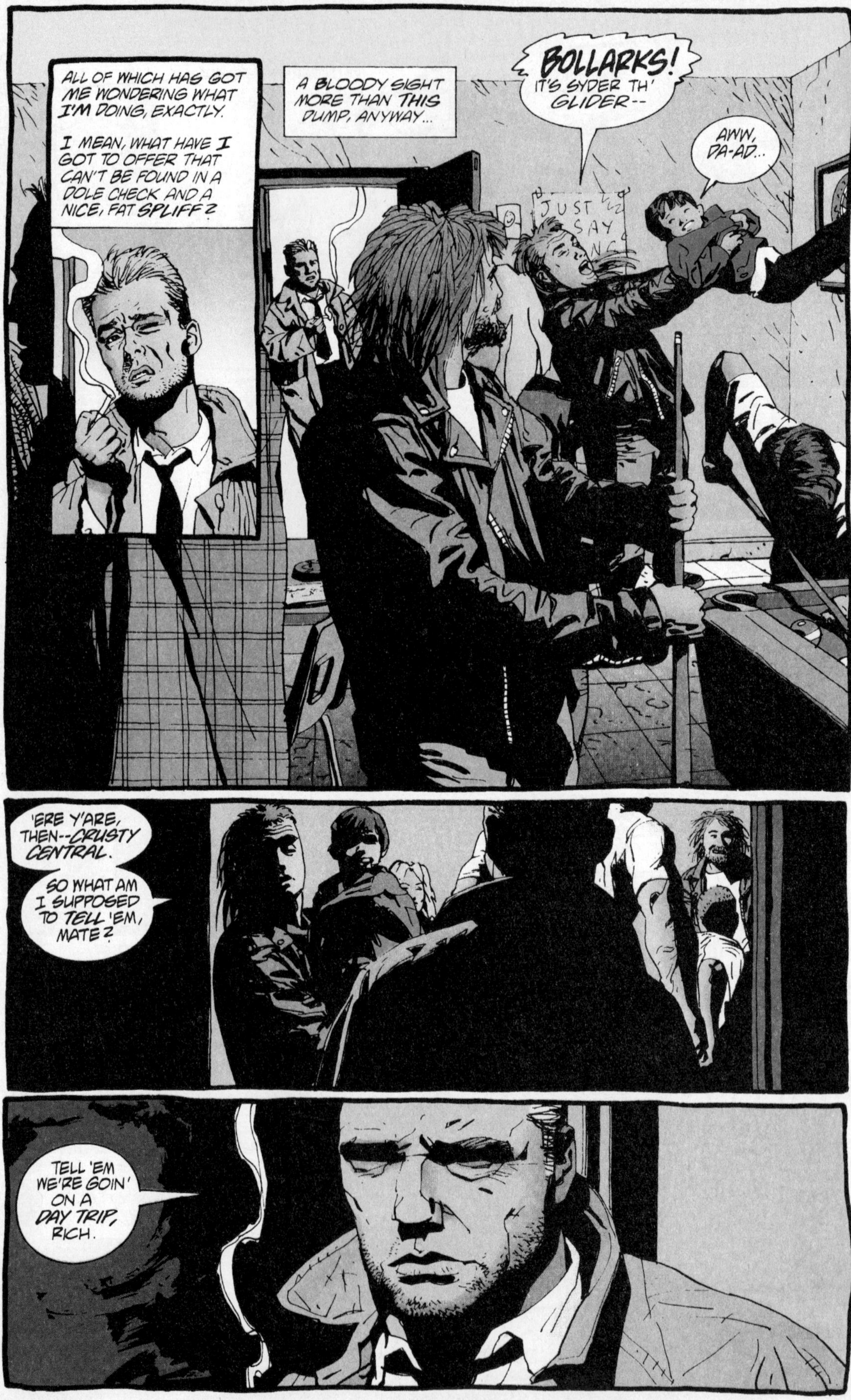
ALL OF WHICH HAS GOT ME WONDERING WHAT I'M DOING, EXACTLY.
I MEAN, WHAT HAVE I GOT TO OFFER THAT CAN'T BE FOUND IN A DOLE CHECK AND A NICE, FAT SPLIFF?
A BLOODY SIGHT MORE THAN THIS DUMP, ANYWAY...
BOLLARKS! IT'S SYDER TH' GLIDER--
AWW, DA-AD...
JUST SAY
'ERE Y'ARE, THEN--CRUSTY CENTRAL.
SO WHAT AM I SUPPOSED TO TELL 'EM, MATE?
TELL 'EM WE'RE GOIN' ON A DAY TRIP, RICH.

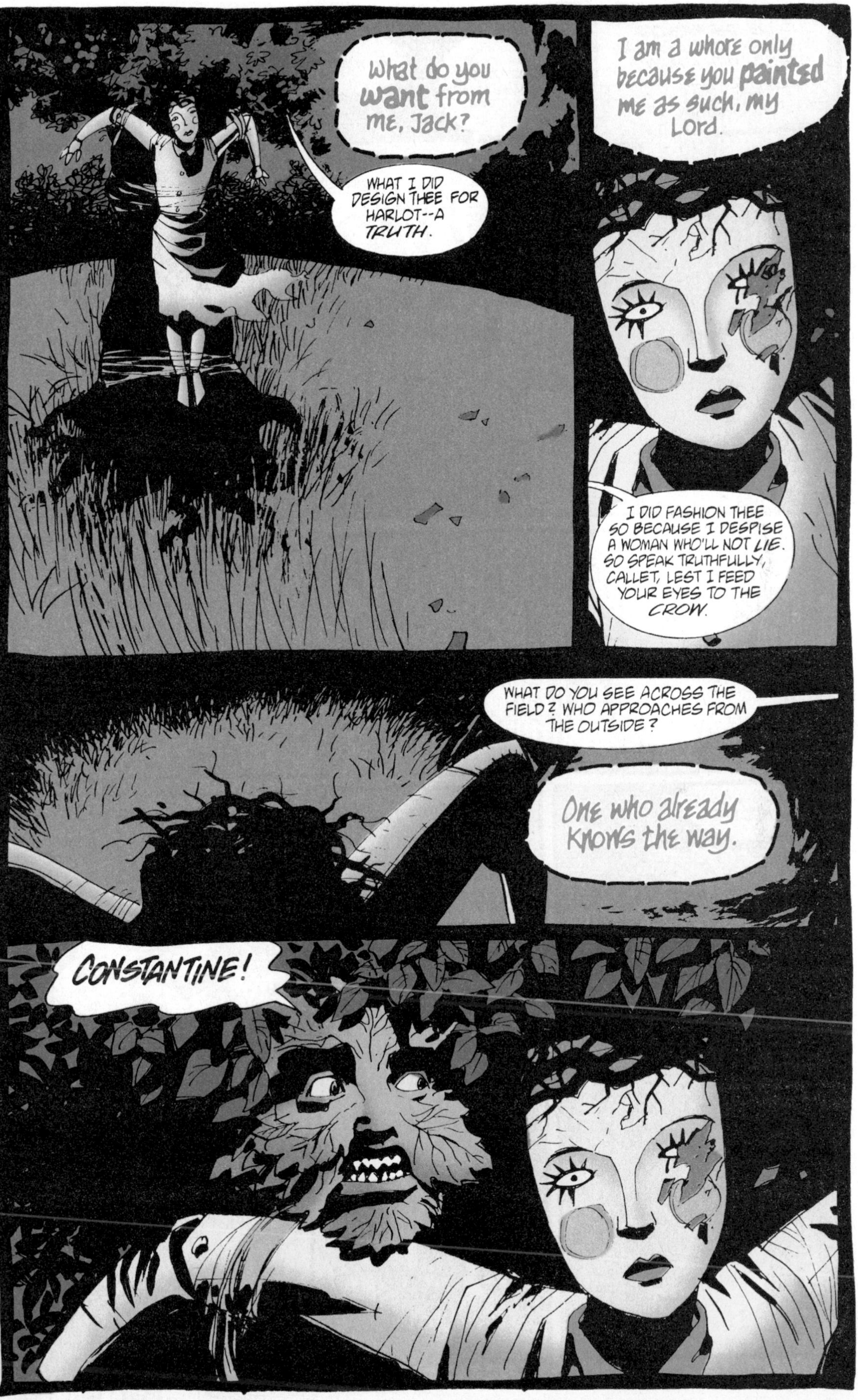
What do you want from me, Jack?
WHAT I DID DESIGN THEE FOR HARLOT--A TRUTH.
I am a whore only because you painted me as such, my Lord.
I DID FASHION THEE SO BECAUSE I DESPISE A WOMAN WHO'LL NOT LIE. SO SPEAK TRUTHFULLY, CALLET, LEST I FEED YOUR EYES TO THE CROW.
WHAT DO YOU SEE ACROSS THE FIELD? WHO APPROACHES FROM THE OUTSIDE?
One who already knows the way.
CONSTANTINE!

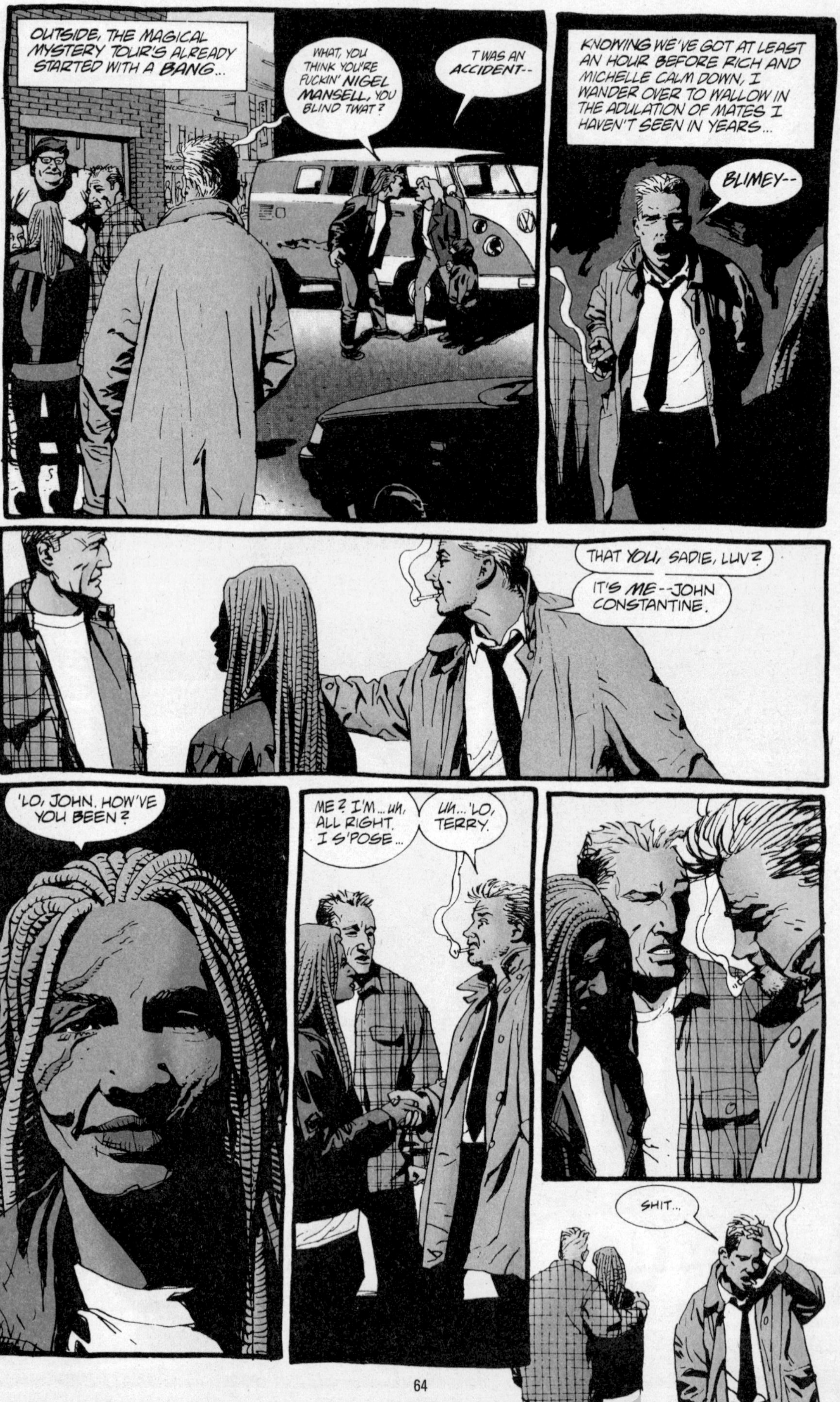
OUTSIDE, THE MAGICAL MYSTERY TOUR'S ALREADY STARTED WITH A BANG...
WHAT, YOU THINK YOU'RE FUCKIN' NIGEL MANSELL, YOU BLIND TWAT?
T WAS AN ACCIDENT--
KNOWING WE'VE GOT AT LEAST AN HOUR BEFORE RICH AND MICHELLE CALM DOWN, I WANDER OVER TO WALLOW IN THE ADULATION OF MATES I HAVEN'T SEEN IN YEARS...
BLIMEY--
THAT YOU, SADIE, LUV?
IT'S ME--JOHN CONSTANTINE.
'LO, JOHN. HOW'VE YOU BEEN?
ME? I'M... UH, ALL RIGHT, I S'POSE...
UH... 'LO, TERRY.
SHIT...

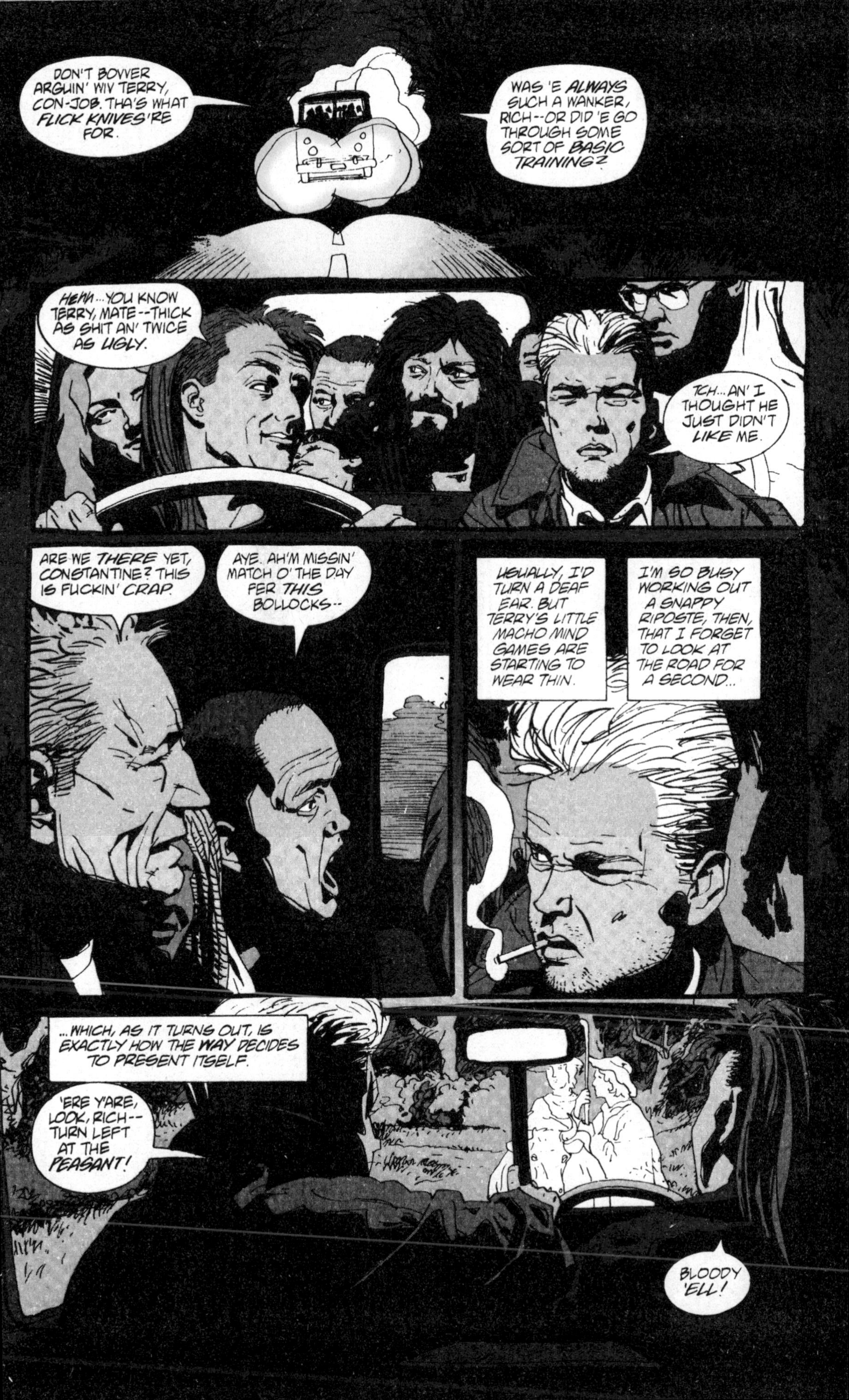
DON'T BOVVER ARGUIN' WIV TERRY, CON-JOB. THA'S WHAT FLICK KNIVES 'RE FOR.
WAS 'E ALWAYS SUCH A WANKER, RICH--OR DID 'E GO THROUGH SOME SORT OF BASIC TRAINING?
HEH ...YOU KNOW TERRY, MATE--THICK AS SHIT AN' TWICE AS UGLY.
TCH... AN' I THOUGHT HE JUST DIDN'T LIKE ME.
ARE WE THERE YET, CONSTANTINE? THIS IS FUCKIN' CRAP.
AYE. AH'M MISSIN' MATCH O' THE DAY FER THIS BOLLOCKS--
USUALLY, I'D TURN A DEAF EAR. BUT TERRY'S LITTLE MACHO MIND GAMES ARE STARTING TO WEAR THIN.
I'M SO BUSY WORKING OUT A SNAPPY RIPOSTE, THEN, THAT I FORGET TO LOOK AT THE ROAD FOR A SECOND...
...WHICH, AS IT TURNS OUT, IS EXACTLY HOW THE WAY DECIDES TO PRESENT ITSELF.
'ERE Y'ARE, LOOK, RICH--TURN LEFT AT THE PEASANT!
BLOODY 'ELL!

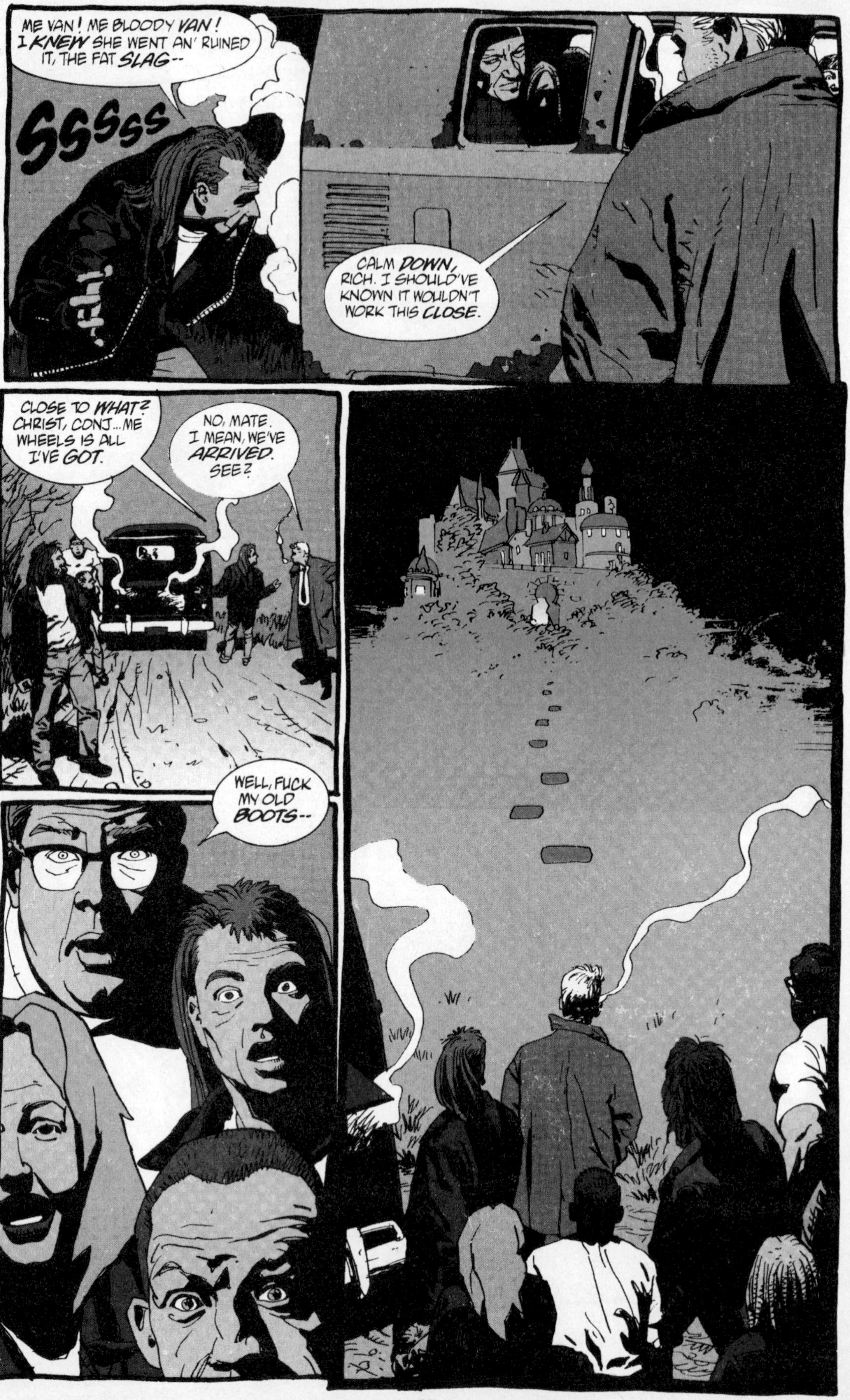
ME VAN! ME BLOODY VAN! I KNEW SHE WENT AN' RUINED IT, THE FAT SLAG--
SSSSS
CALM DOWN, RICH. I SHOULD'VE KNOWN IT WOULDN'T WORK THIS CLOSE.
CLOSE TO WHAT? CHRIST, CONJ... ME WHEELS IS ALL I'VE GOT.
NO, MATE. I MEAN, WE'VE ARRIVED. SEE?
WELL, FUCK MY OLD BOOTS--

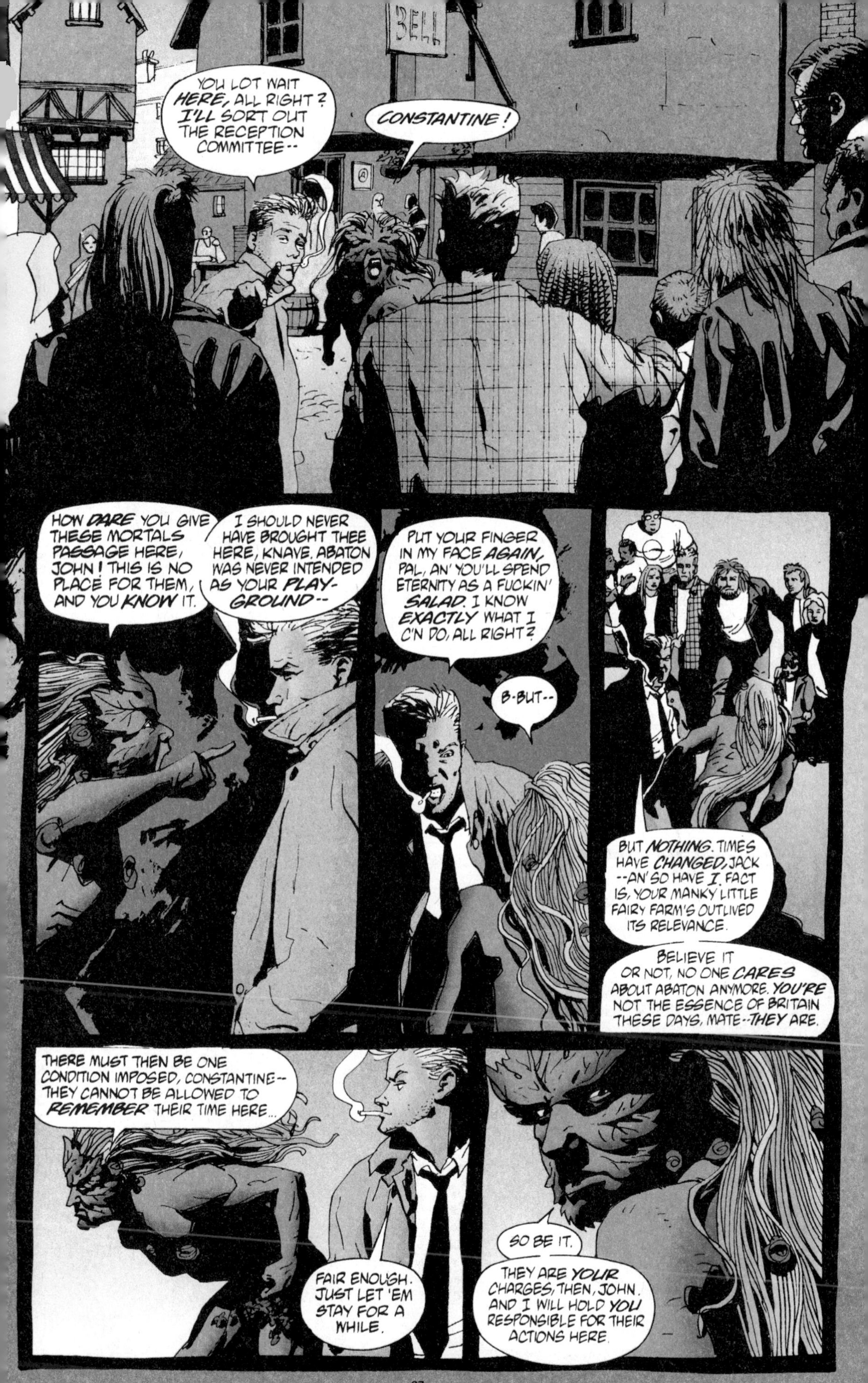

BELL
YOU LOT WAIT HERE, ALL RIGHT? I'LL SORT OUT THE RECEPTION COMMITTEE--
CONSTANTINE!
HOW DARE YOU GIVE THESE MORTALS PASSAGE HERE, JOHN! THIS IS NO PLACE FOR THEM, AND YOU KNOW IT.
I SHOULD NEVER HAVE BROUGHT THEE HERE, KNAVE. ABATON WAS NEVER INTENDED AS YOUR PLAY-GROUND--
PUT YOUR FINGER IN MY FACE AGAIN, PAL, AN' YOU'LL SPEND ETERNITY AS A FUCKIN' SALAD. I KNOW EXACTLY WHAT I C'N DO, ALL RIGHT?
B-BUT--
BUT NOTHING. TIMES HAVE CHANGED, JACK --AN' SO HAVE I. FACT IS, YOUR MANKY LITTLE FAIRY FARM'S OUTLIVED ITS RELEVANCE.
BELIEVE IT OR NOT, NO ONE CARES ABOUT ABATON ANYMORE. YOU'RE NOT THE ESSENCE OF BRITAIN THESE DAYS, MATE--THEY ARE.
THERE MUST THEN BE ONE CONDITION IMPOSED, CONSTANTINE-- THEY CANNOT BE ALLOWED TO REMEMBER THEIR TIME HERE...
FAIR ENOUGH. JUST LET 'EM STAY FOR A WHILE.
SO BE IT.
THEY ARE YOUR CHARGES, THEN, JOHN. AND I WILL HOLD YOU RESPONSIBLE FOR THEIR ACTIONS HERE.

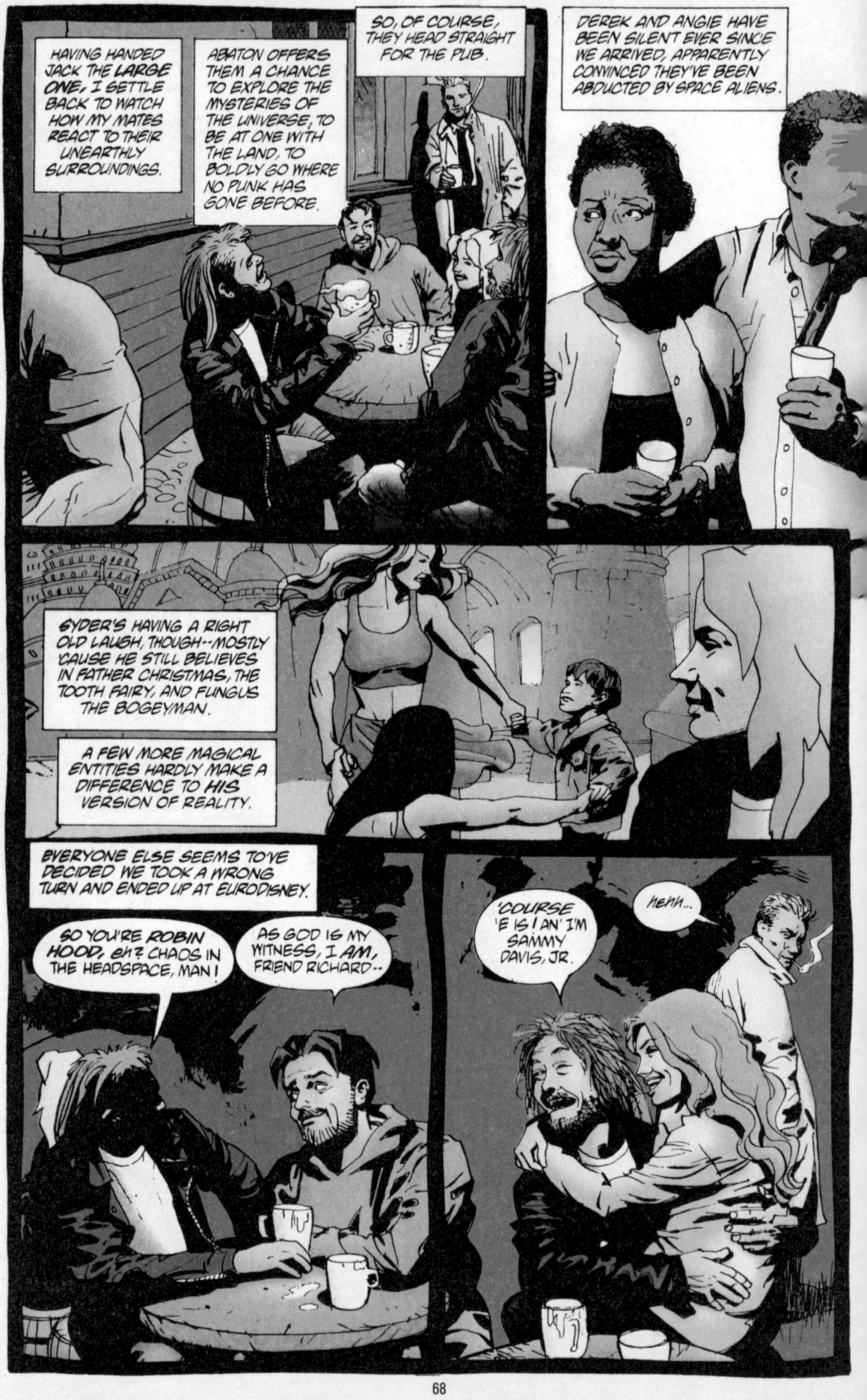
HAVING HANDED JACK THE LARGE ONE, I SETTLE BACK TO WATCH HOW MY MATES REACT TO THEIR UNEARTHLY SURROUNDINGS.
ABATON OFFERS THEM A CHANCE TO EXPLORE THE MYSTERIES OF THE UNIVERSE, TO BE AT ONE WITH THE LAND, TO BOLDLY GO WHERE NO PUNK HAS GONE BEFORE.
SO, OF COURSE, THEY HEAD STRAIGHT FOR THE PUB.
DEREK AND ANGIE HAVE BEEN SILENT EVER SINCE WE ARRIVED, APPARENTLY CONVINCED THEY'VE BEEN ABDUCTED BY SPACE ALIENS.
SYDER'S HAVING A RIGHT OLD LAUGH, THOUGH--MOSTLY 'CAUSE HE STILL BELIEVES IN FATHER CHRISTMAS, THE TOOTH FAIRY, AND FUNGUS THE BOGEYMAN.
A FEW MORE MAGICAL ENTITIES HARDLY MAKE A DIFFERENCE TO HIS VERSION OF REALITY.
EVERYONE ELSE SEEMS TO'VE DECIDED WE TOOK A WRONG TURN AND ENDED UP AT EURODISNEY.
SO YOU'RE ROBIN HOOD, eh? CHAOS IN THE HEADSPACE, MAN!
AS GOD IS MY WITNESS, I AM, FRIEND RICHARD--
'COURSE 'E IS! AN' I'M SAMMY DAVIS, JR.
hehh...

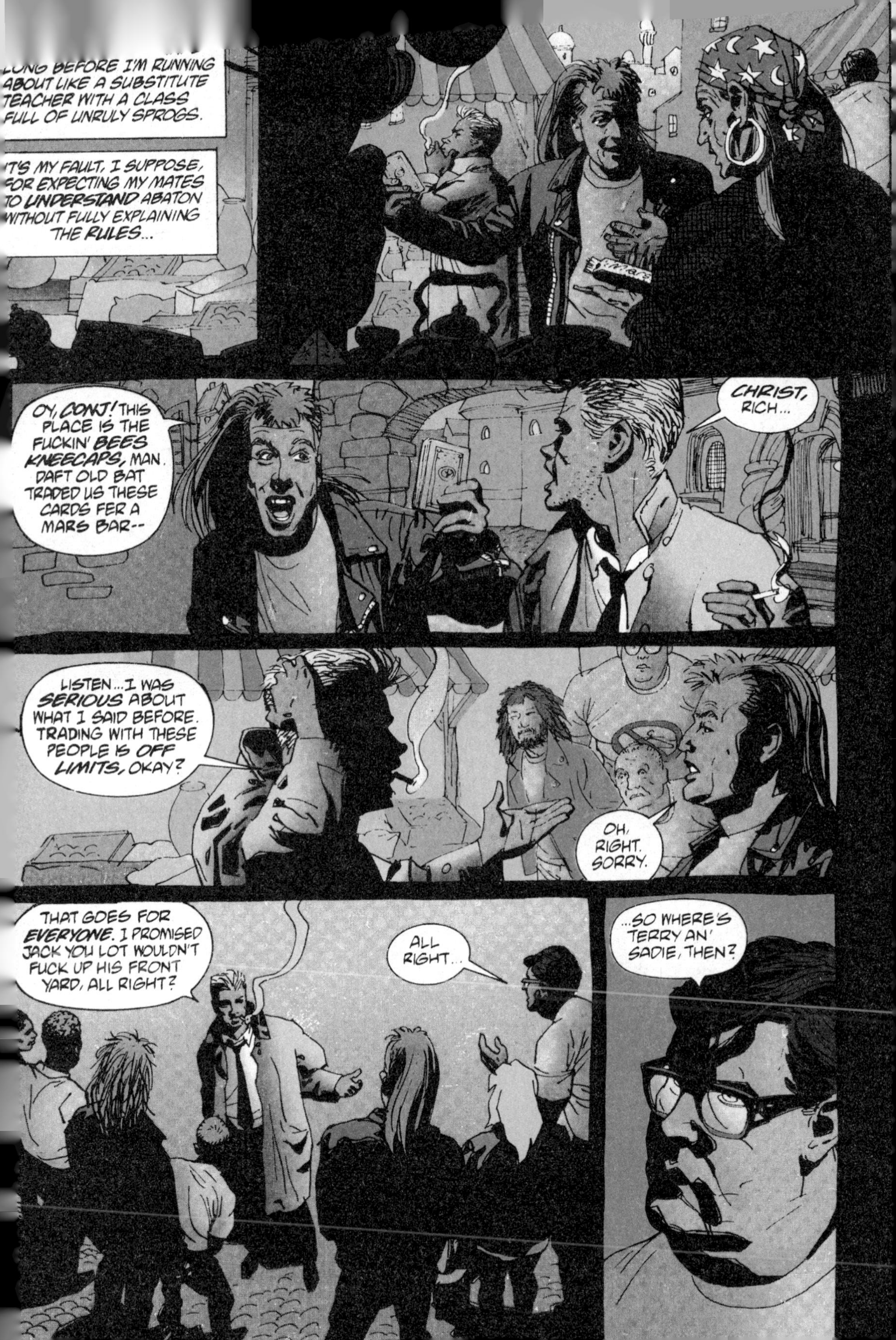
LONG BEFORE I'M RUNNING ABOUT LIKE A SUBSTITUTE TEACHER WITH A CLASS FULL OF UNRULY SPROGS.
IT'S MY FAULT, I SUPPOSE, FOR EXPECTING MY MATES TO UNDERSTAND ABATON WITHOUT FULLY EXPLAINING THE RULES...
OY, CONJ! THIS PLACE IS THE FUCKIN' BEES KNEECAPS, MAN. DAFT OLD BAT TRADED US THESE CARDS FER A MARS BAR--
CHRIST, RICH...
LISTEN...I WAS SERIOUS ABOUT WHAT I SAID BEFORE. TRADING WITH THESE PEOPLE IS OFF LIMITS, OKAY?
OH, RIGHT. SORRY.
THAT GOES FOR EVERYONE. I PROMISED JACK YOU LOT WOULDN'T FUCK UP HIS FRONT YARD, ALL RIGHT?
ALL RIGHT...
...SO WHERE'S TERRY AN' SADIE, THEN?

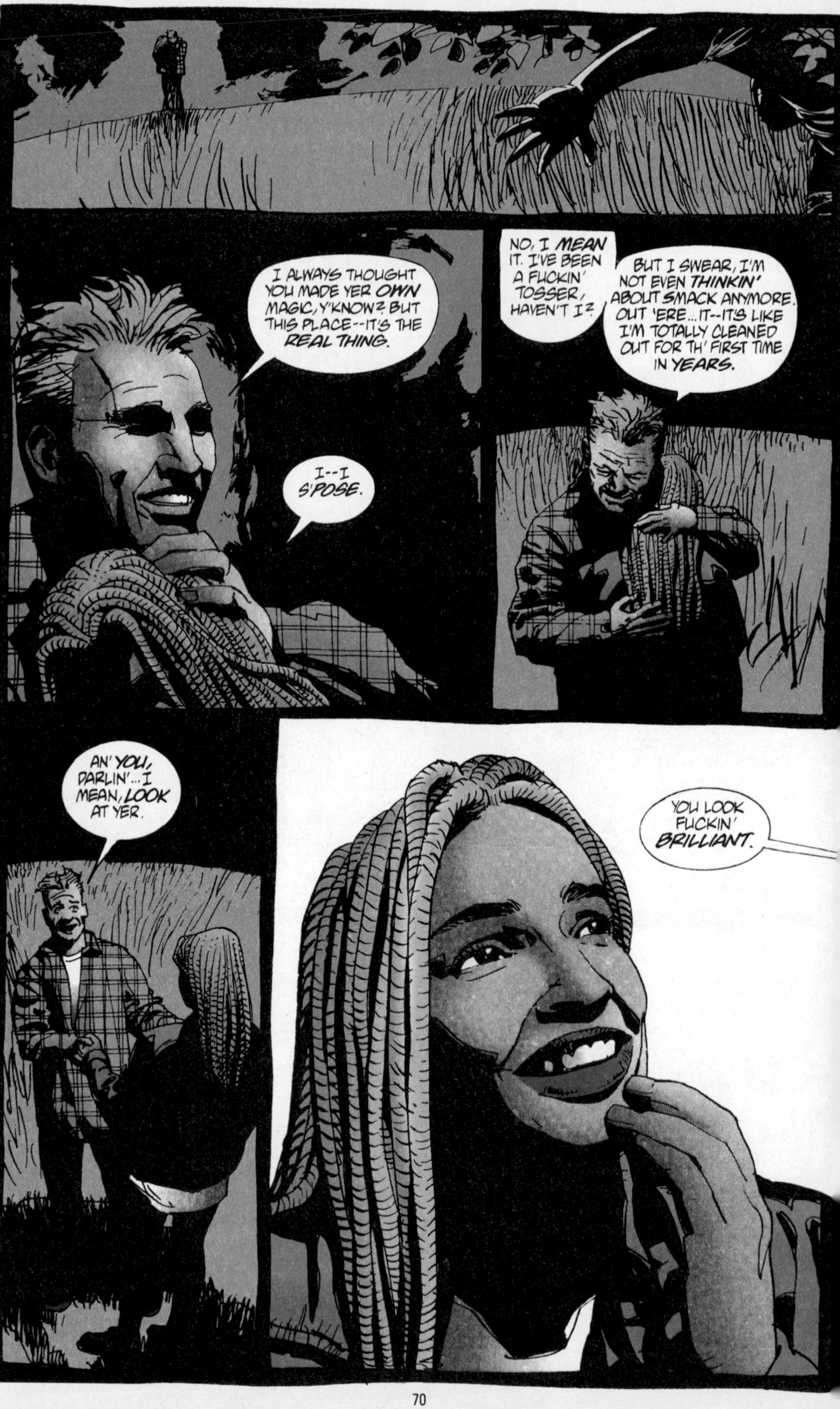
I ALWAYS THOUGHT YOU MADE YER OWN MAGIC, Y'KNOW? BUT THIS PLACE--IT'S THE REAL THING.
I--I S'POSE.
NO, I MEAN IT. I'VE BEEN A FUCKIN' TOSSER, HAVEN'T I?
BUT I SWEAR, I'M NOT EVEN THINKIN' ABOUT SMACK ANYMORE. OUT 'ERE... IT--IT'S LIKE I'M TOTALLY CLEANED OUT FOR TH' FIRST TIME IN YEARS.
AN' YOU, DARLIN'... I MEAN, LOOK AT YER.
YOU LOOK FUCKIN' BRILLIANT.

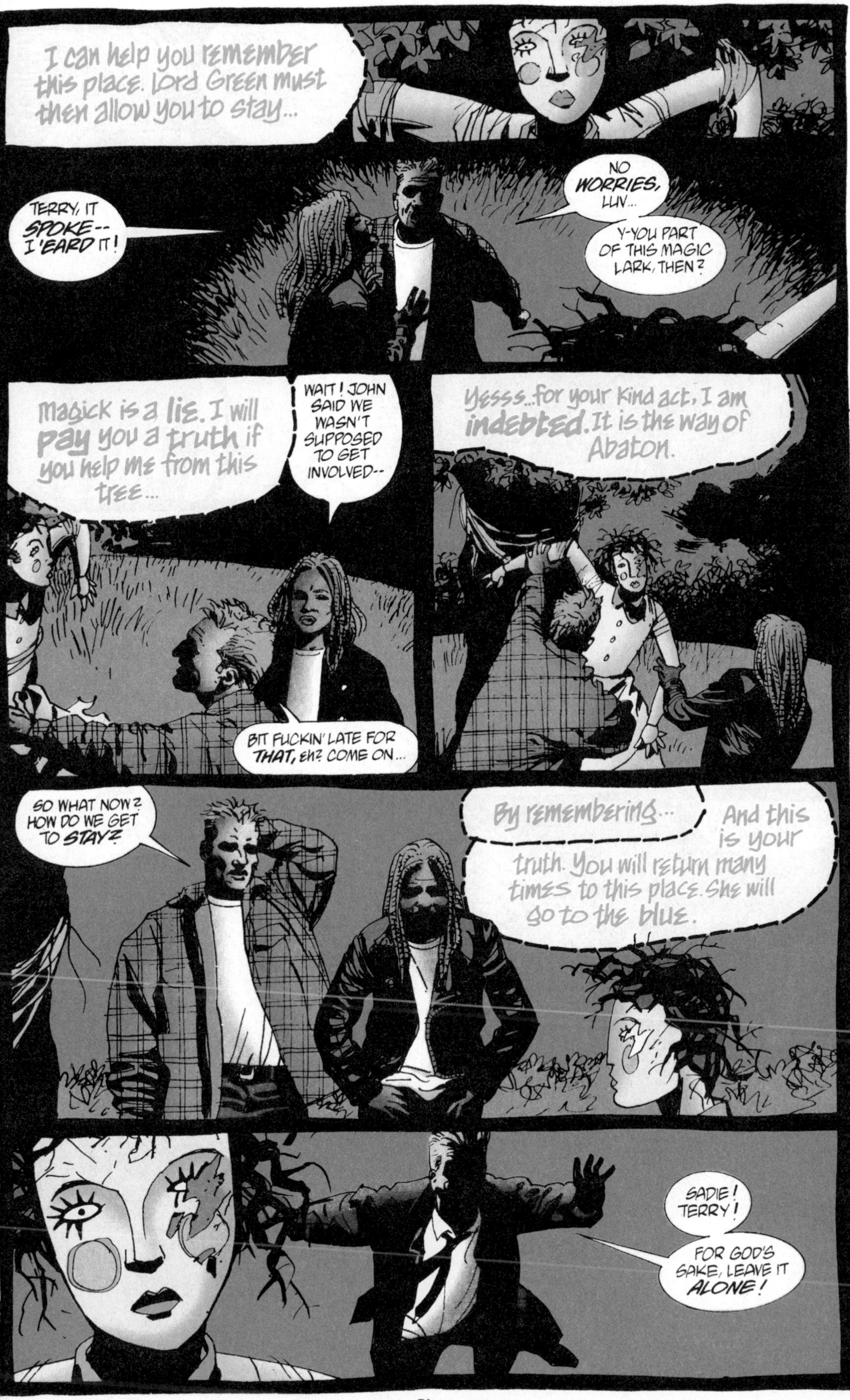
I can help you remember this place. Lord Green must then allow you to stay...
TERRY, IT SPOKE-- I'EARD IT!
NO WORRIES, LUV...
Y-YOU PART OF THIS MAGIC LARK, THEN?
magick is a lie. I will pay you a truth if you help me from this tree...
WAIT! JOHN SAID WE WASN'T SUPPOSED TO GET INVOLVED--
BIT FUCKIN' LATE FOR THAT, EH? COME ON...
Yesss...for your kind act, I am indebted. It is the way of Abaton.
SO WHAT NOW? HOW DO WE GET TO STAY?
By remembering...
And this is your truth. You will return many times to this place. She will go to the blue.
SADIE! TERRY!
FOR GOD'S SAKE, LEAVE IT ALONE!

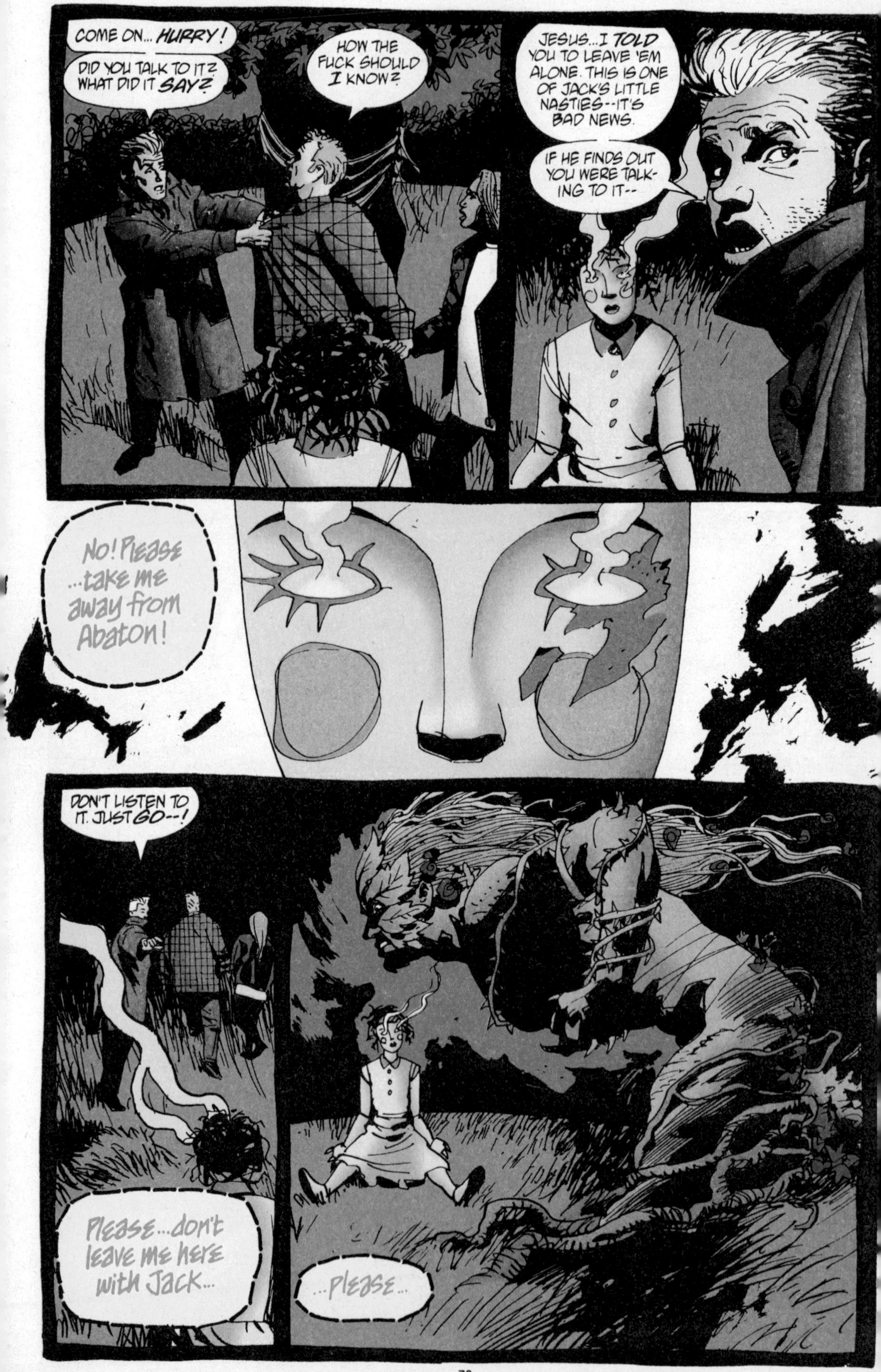
COME ON... HURRY!
DID YOU TALK TO IT? WHAT DID IT SAY?
HOW THE FUCK SHOULD I KNOW?
JESUS...I TOLD YOU TO LEAVE 'EM ALONE. THIS IS ONE OF JACK'S LITTLE NASTIES--IT'S BAD NEWS.
IF HE FINDS OUT YOU WERE TALKING TO IT--
No! Please ...take me away from Abaton!
DON'T LISTEN TO IT. JUST GO--!
Please...don't leave me here with Jack...
...please...

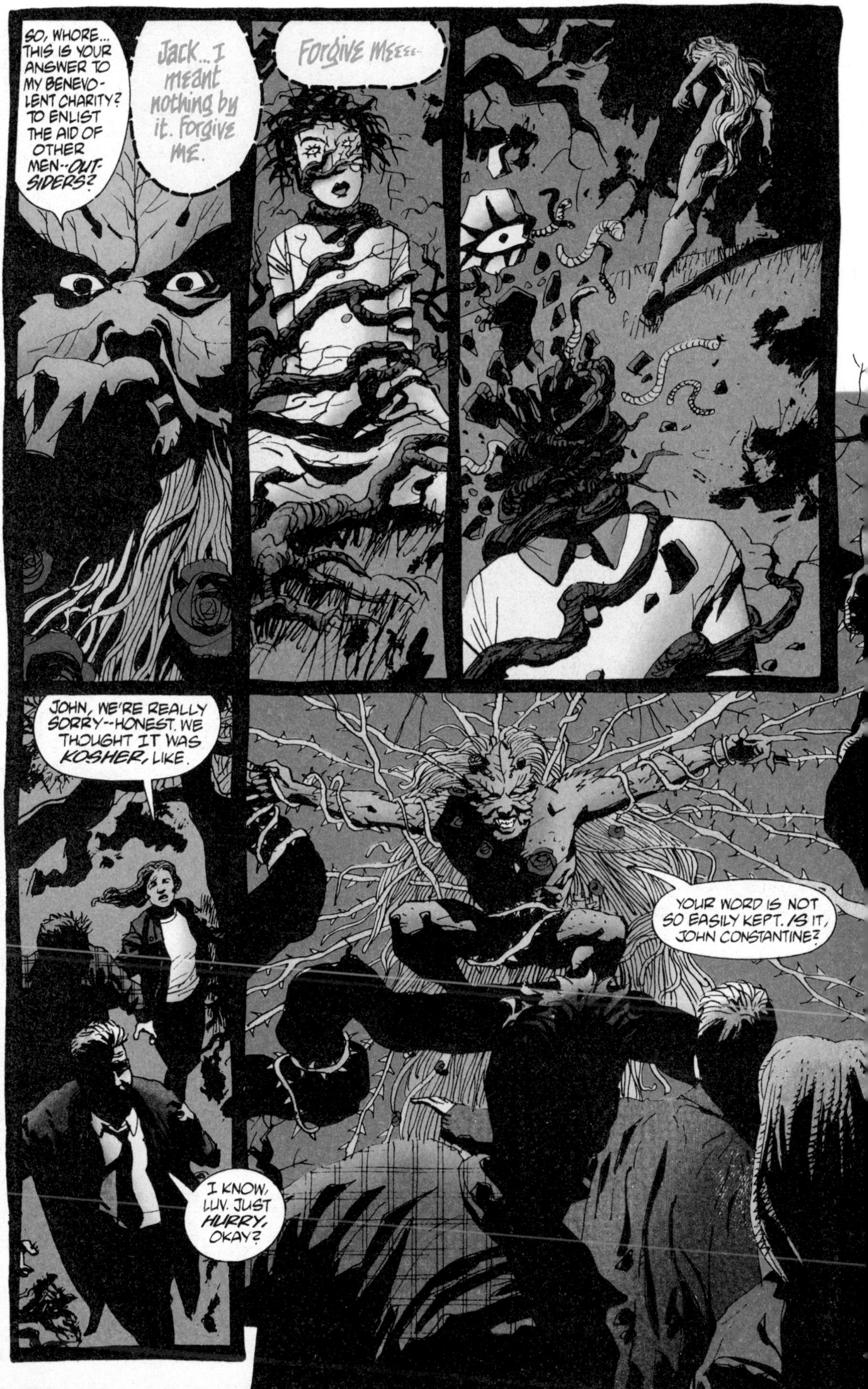
SO, WHORE... THIS IS YOUR ANSWER TO MY BENEVOLENT CHARITY? TO ENLIST THE AID OF OTHER MEN--OUTSIDERS?
Jack... I meant nothing by it. Forgive me.
Forgive meeee...
JOHN, WE'RE REALLY SORRY--HONEST. WE THOUGHT IT WAS KOSHER, LIKE.
YOUR WORD IS NOT SO EASILY KEPT. IS IT, JOHN CONSTANTINE?
I KNOW, LUV. JUST HURRY, OKAY?

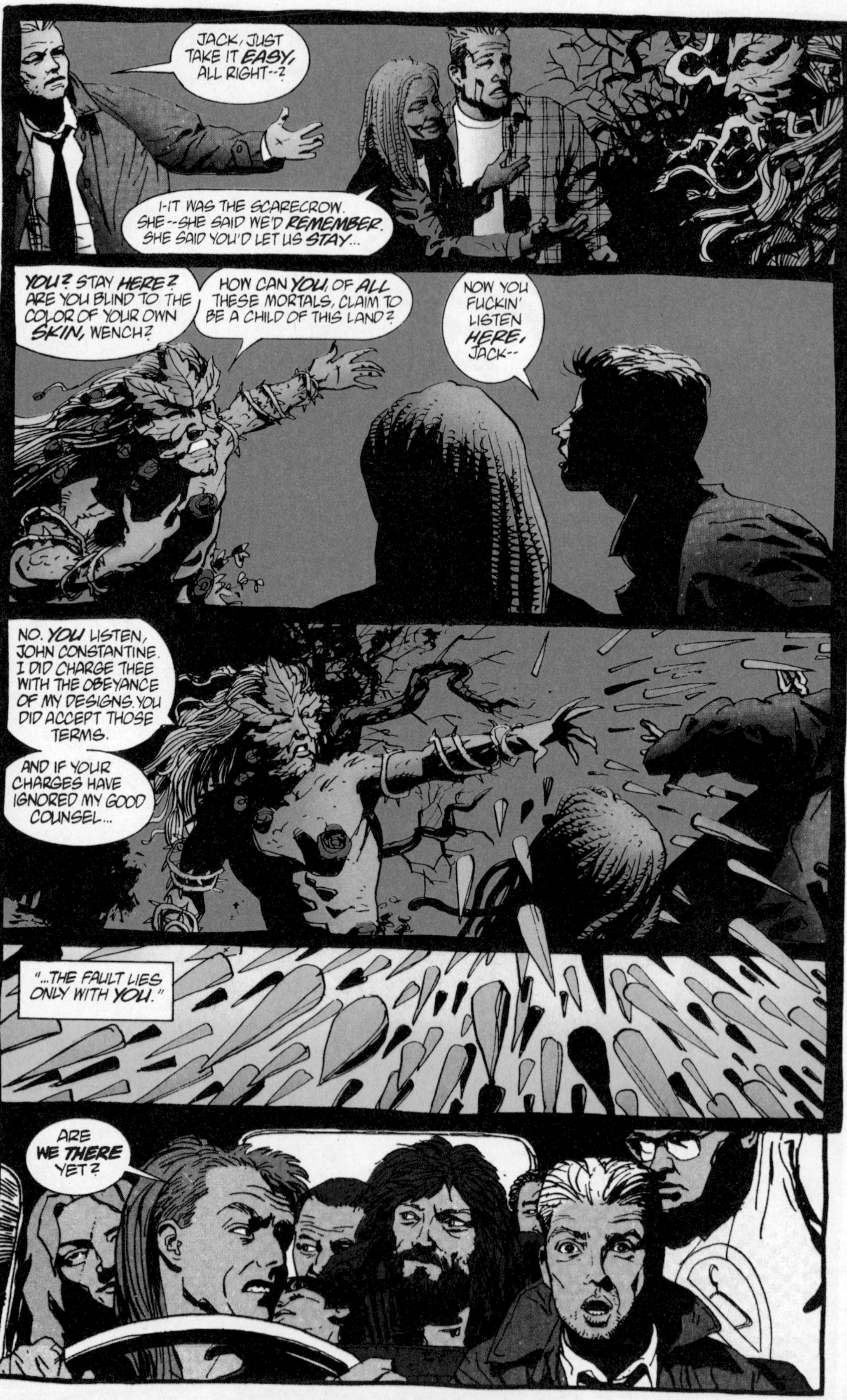
JACK, JUST TAKE IT EASY, ALL RIGHT--?
I-IT WAS THE SCARECROW. SHE--SHE SAID WE'D REMEMBER. SHE SAID YOU'D LET US STAY...
YOU? STAY HERE? ARE YOU BLIND TO THE COLOR OF YOUR OWN SKIN, WENCH?
HOW CAN YOU, OF ALL THESE MORTALS, CLAIM TO BE A CHILD OF THIS LAND?
NOW YOU FUCKIN' LISTEN HERE, JACK--
NO. YOU LISTEN, JOHN CONSTANTINE. I DID CHARGE THEE WITH THE OBEYANCE OF MY DESIGNS. YOU DID ACCEPT THOSE TERMS.
AND IF YOUR CHARGES HAVE IGNORED MY GOOD COUNSEL...
"...THE FAULT LIES ONLY WITH YOU."
ARE WE THERE YET?

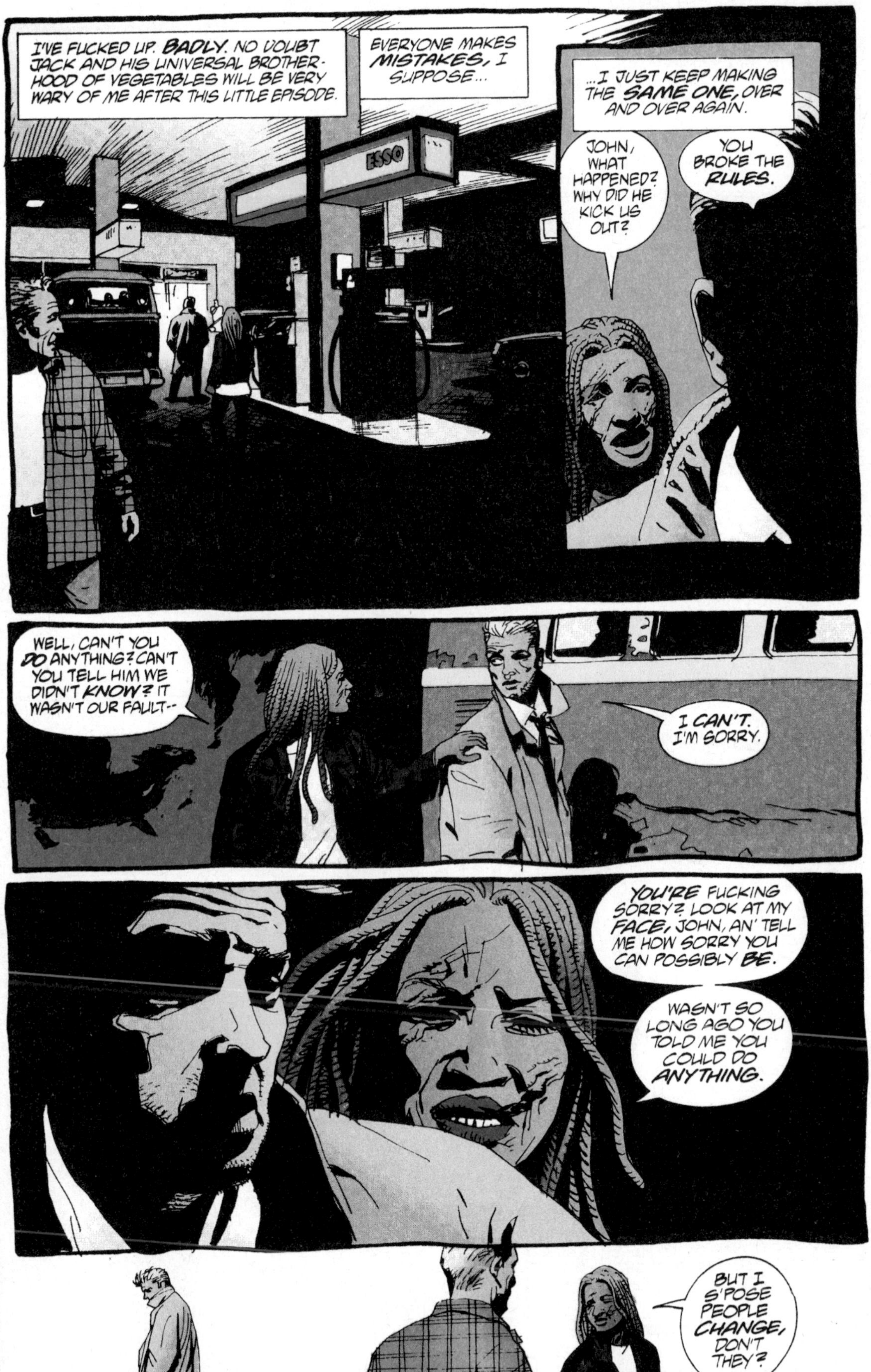
I'VE FUCKED UP. BADLY. NO DOUBT JACK AND HIS UNIVERSAL BROTHERHOOD OF VEGETABLES WILL BE VERY WARY OF ME AFTER THIS LITTLE EPISODE.
EVERYONE MAKES MISTAKES, I SUPPOSE...
...I JUST KEEP MAKING THE SAME ONE, OVER AND OVER AGAIN.
ESSO
JOHN, WHAT HAPPENED? WHY DID HE KICK US OUT?
YOU BROKE THE RULES.
WELL, CAN'T YOU DO ANYTHING? CAN'T YOU TELL HIM WE DIDN'T KNOW? IT WASN'T OUR FAULT--
I CAN'T. I'M SORRY.
YOU'RE FUCKING SORRY? LOOK AT MY FACE, JOHN, AN' TELL ME HOW SORRY YOU CAN POSSIBLY BE.
WASN'T SO LONG AGO YOU TOLD ME YOU COULD DO ANYTHING.
BUT I S'POSE PEOPLE CHANGE, DON'T THEY?

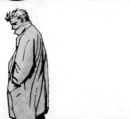

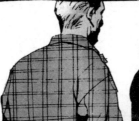

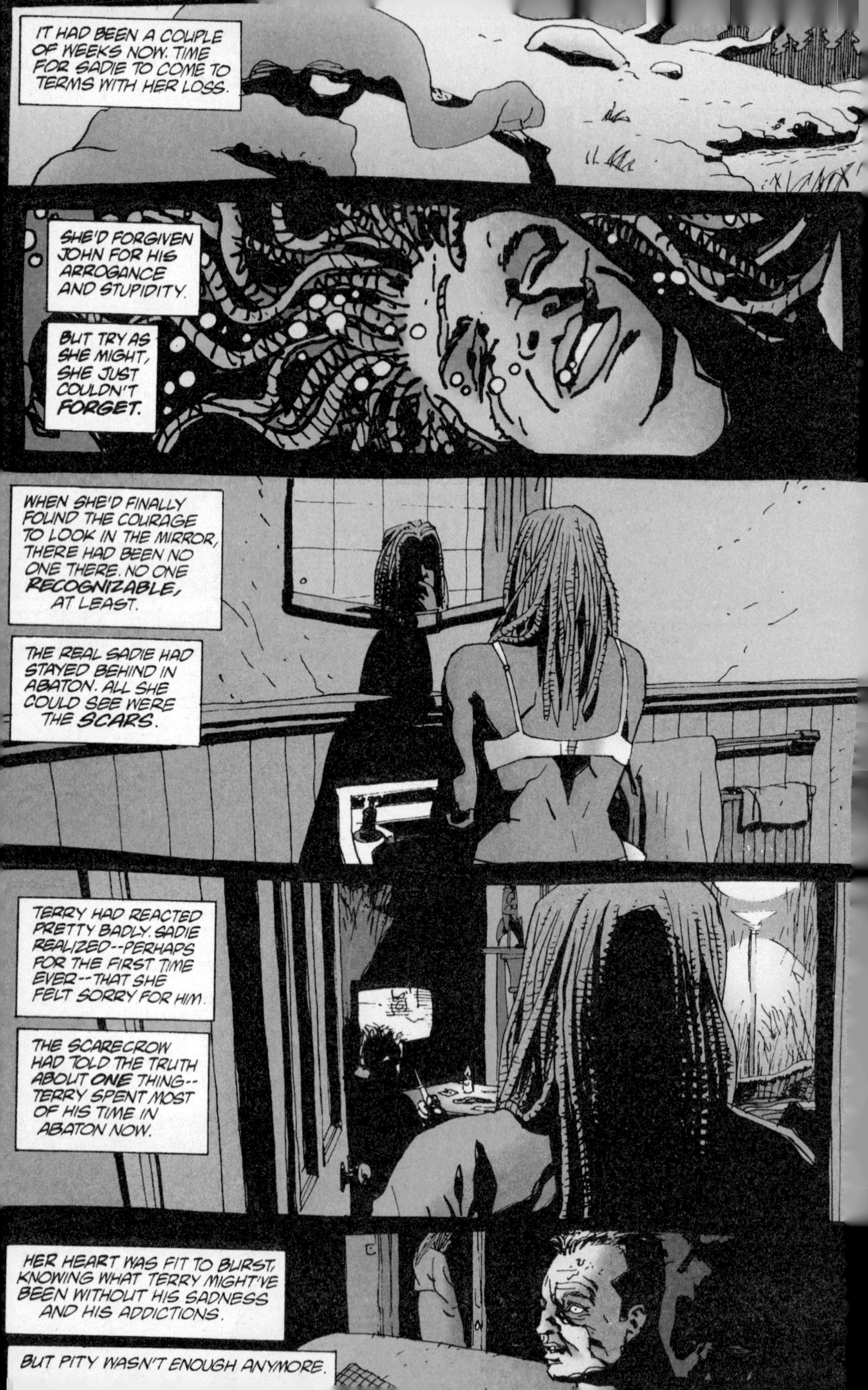

IT HAD BEEN A COUPLE OF WEEKS NOW. TIME FOR SADIE TO COME TO TERMS WITH HER LOSS.
SHE'D FORGIVEN JOHN FOR HIS ARROGANCE AND STUPIDITY.
BUT TRY AS SHE MIGHT, SHE JUST COULDN'T FORGET.
WHEN SHE'D FINALLY FOUND THE COURAGE TO LOOK IN THE MIRROR, THERE HAD BEEN NO ONE THERE. NO ONE RECOGNIZABLE, AT LEAST.
THE REAL SADIE HAD STAYED BEHIND IN ABATON. ALL SHE COULD SEE WERE THE SCARS.
TERRY HAD REACTED PRETTY BADLY. SADIE REALIZED--PERHAPS FOR THE FIRST TIME EVER--THAT SHE FELT SORRY FOR HIM.
THE SCARECROW HAD TOLD THE TRUTH ABOUT ONE THING--TERRY SPENT MOST OF HIS TIME IN ABATON NOW.
HER HEART WAS FIT TO BURST, KNOWING WHAT TERRY MIGHT'VE BEEN WITHOUT HIS SADNESS AND HIS ADDICTIONS.
BUT PITY WASN'T ENOUGH ANYMORE.

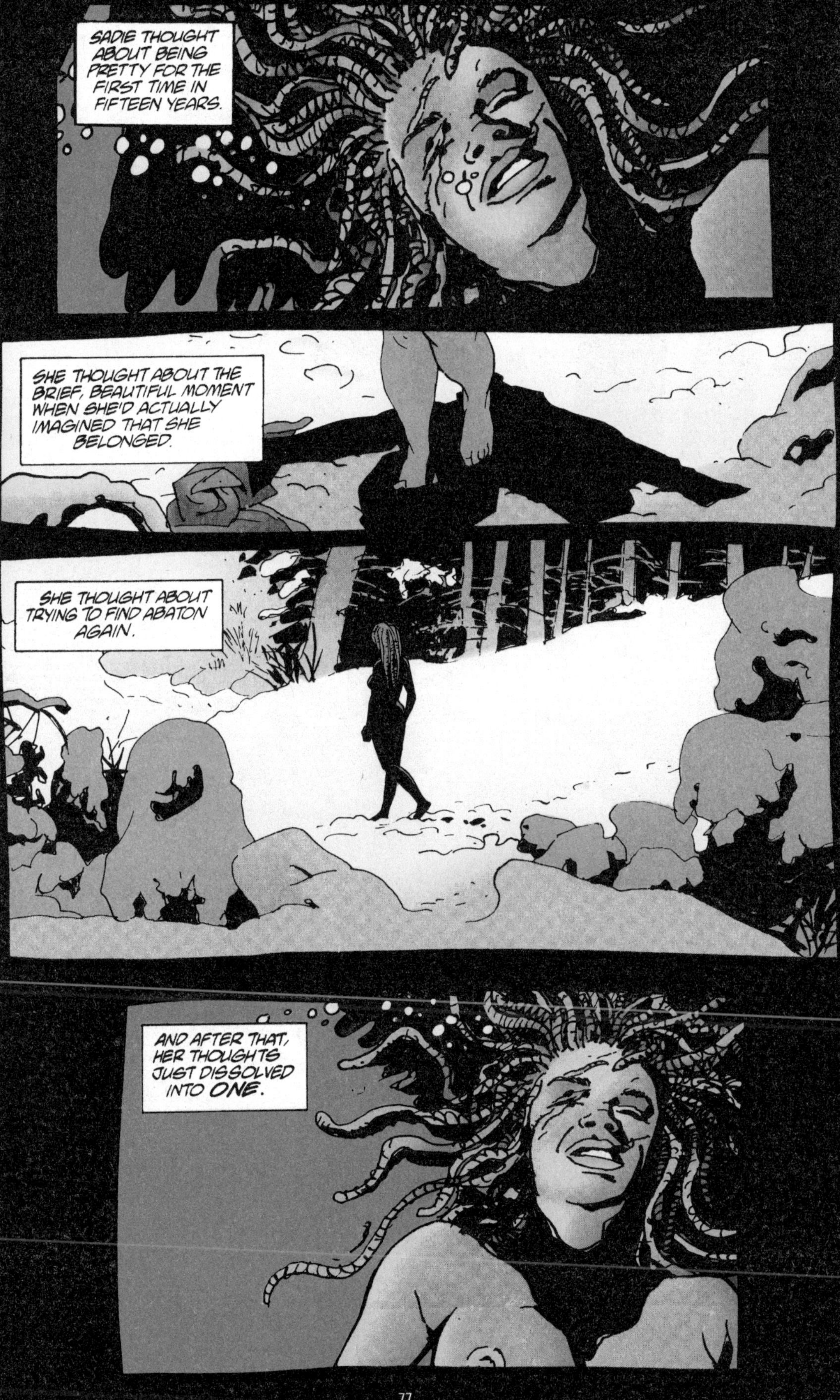
SADIE THOUGHT ABOUT BEING PRETTY FOR THE FIRST TIME IN FIFTEEN YEARS.
SHE THOUGHT ABOUT THE BRIEF, BEAUTIFUL MOMENT WHEN SHE'D ACTUALLY IMAGINED THAT SHE BELONGED.
SHE THOUGHT ABOUT TRYING TO FIND ABATON AGAIN.
AND AFTER THAT, HER THOUGHTS JUST DISSOLVED INTO ONE.

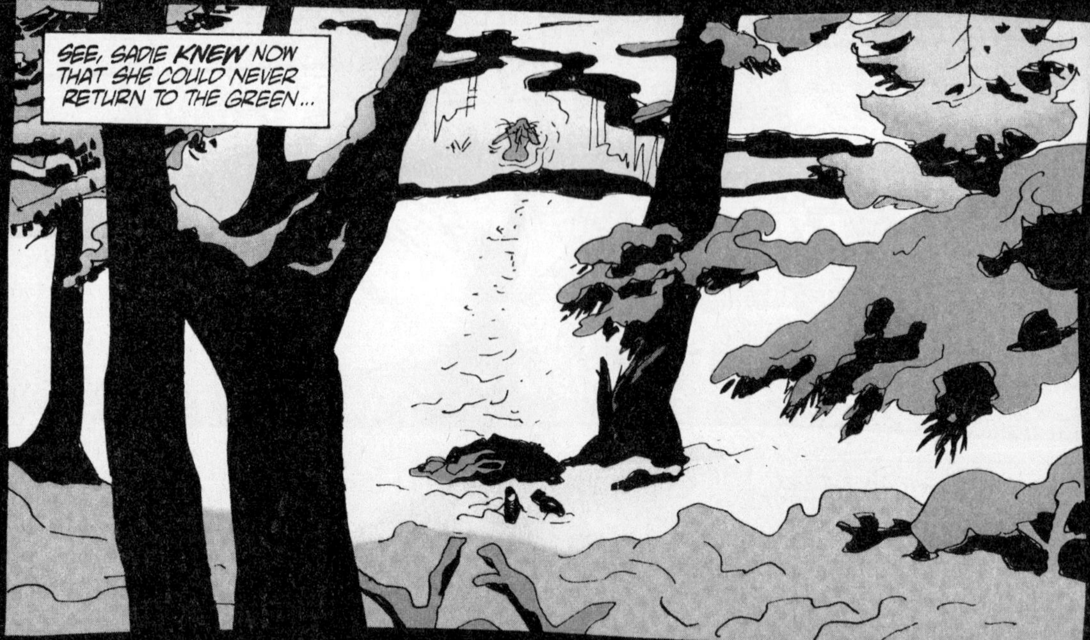
SEE, SADIE KNEW NOW THAT SHE COULD NEVER RETURN TO THE GREEN...

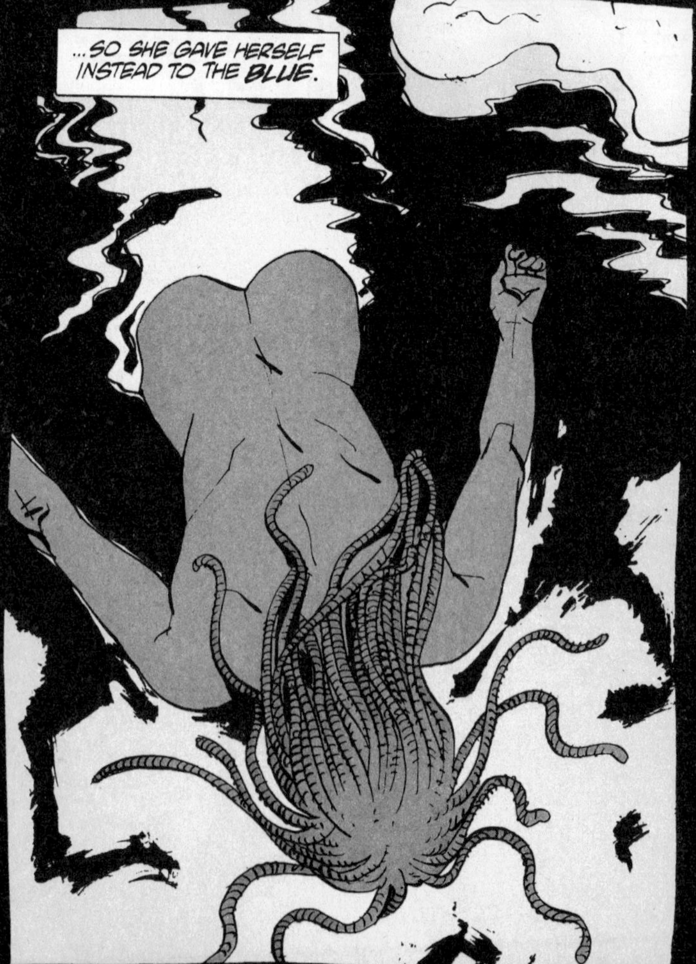
...SO SHE GAVE HERSELF INSTEAD TO THE BLUE.

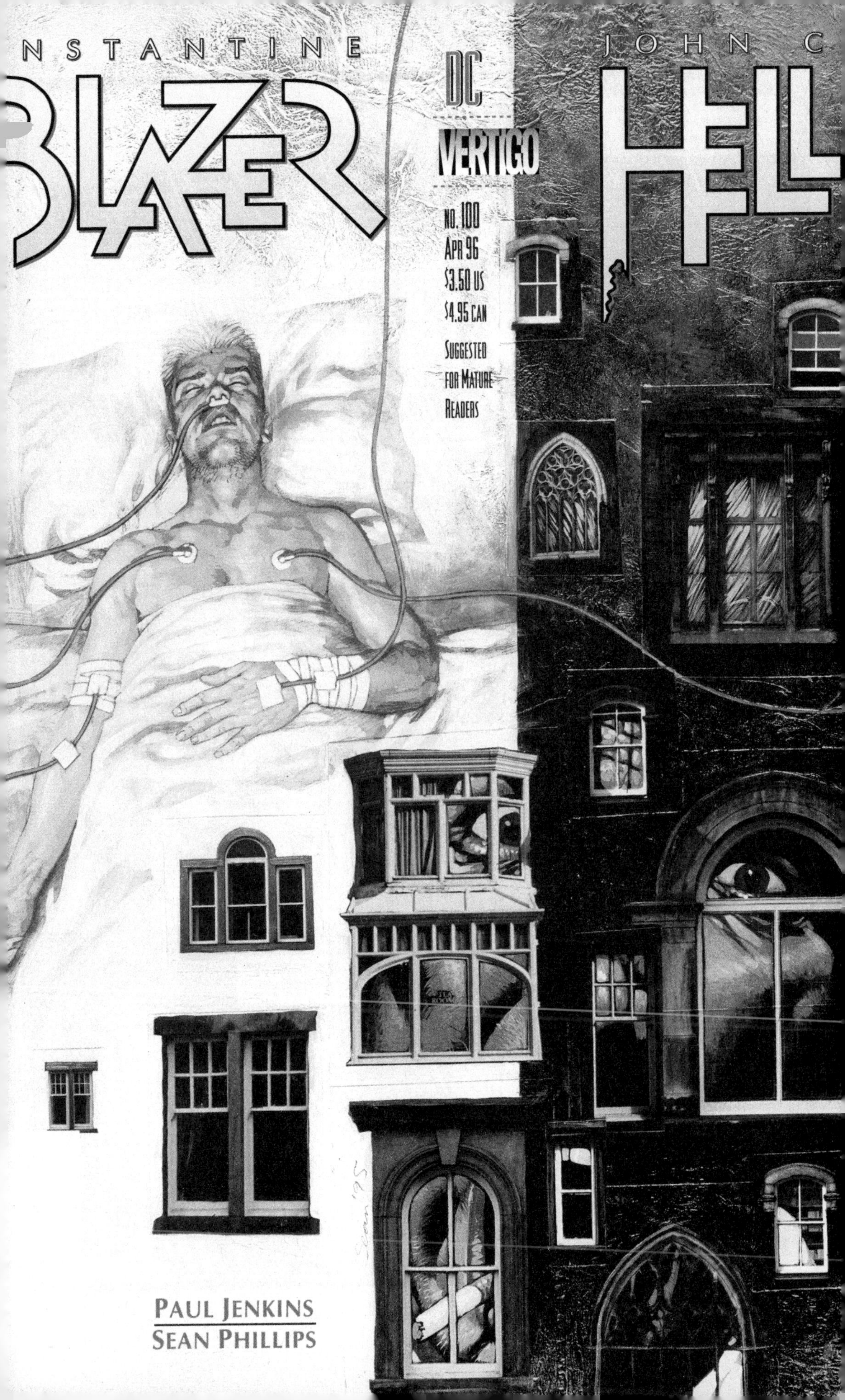

NSTANTINE
BLAZER
DC
VERTIGO
JOHN C
HELL
NO. 100
APR 96
$3.50 US
$4.95 CAN
SUGGESTED FOR MATURE READERS
PAUL JENKINS
SEAN PHILLIPS

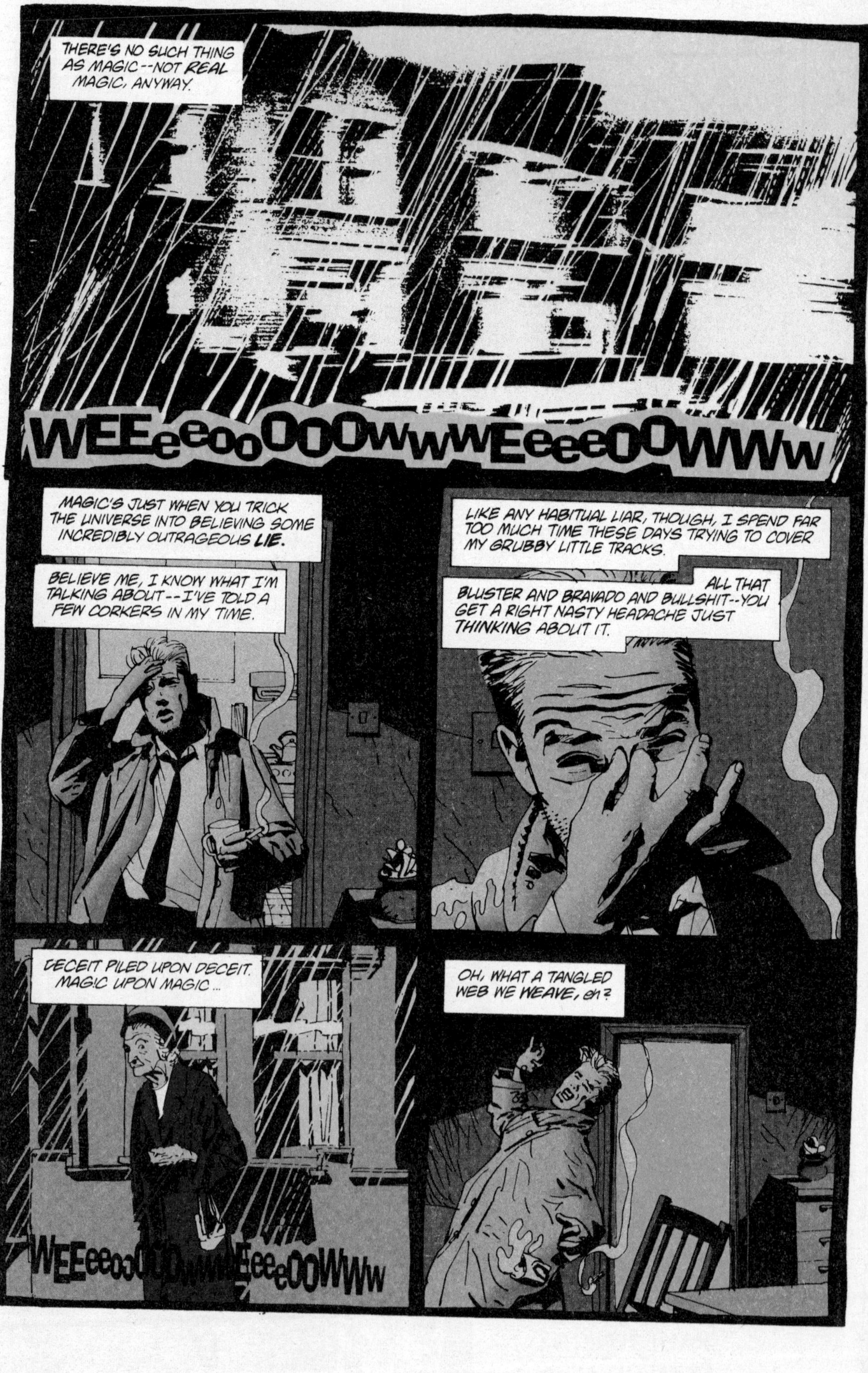
THERE'S NO SUCH THING AS MAGIC--NOT REAL MAGIC, ANYWAY.
WEEeeooOOOOwwwWEeeeeOOWWWw
MAGIC'S JUST WHEN YOU TRICK THE UNIVERSE INTO BELIEVING SOME INCREDIBLY OUTRAGEOUS LIE.
BELIEVE ME, I KNOW WHAT I'M TALKING ABOUT--I'VE TOLD A FEW CORKERS IN MY TIME.
LIKE ANY HABITUAL LIAR, THOUGH, I SPEND FAR TOO MUCH TIME THESE DAYS TRYING TO COVER MY GRUBBY LITTLE TRACKS.
ALL THAT BLUSTER AND BRAVADO AND BULLSHIT--YOU GET A RIGHT NASTY HEADACHE JUST THINKING ABOUT IT.
DECEIT PILED UPON DECEIT. MAGIC UPON MAGIC...
WEEeeooOOOwwwEeeeOOWWWw
OH, WHAT A TANGLED WEB WE WEAVE, eh?

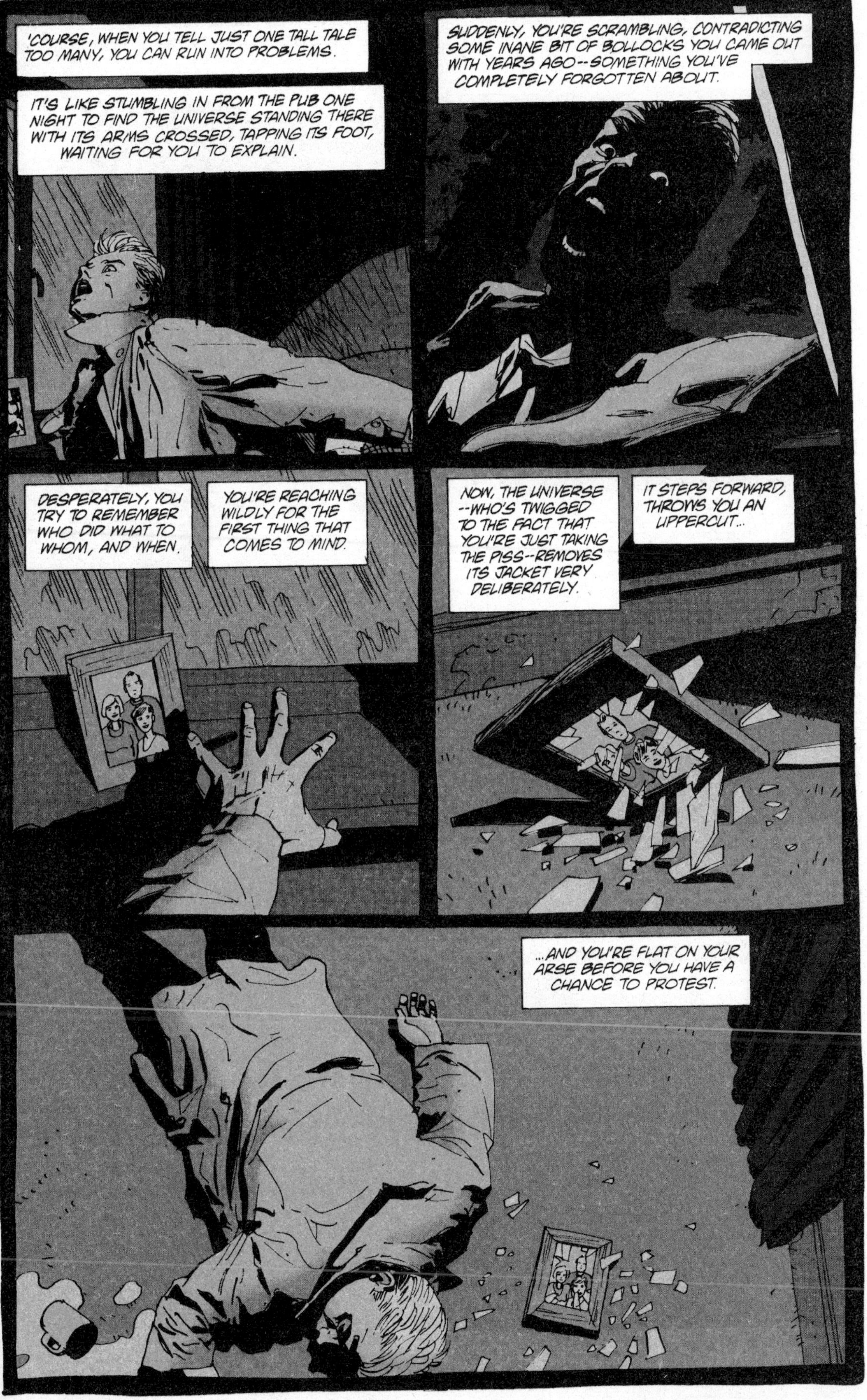
'COURSE, WHEN YOU TELL JUST ONE TALL TALE TOO MANY, YOU CAN RUN INTO PROBLEMS.
IT'S LIKE STUMBLING IN FROM THE PUB ONE NIGHT TO FIND THE UNIVERSE STANDING THERE WITH ITS ARMS CROSSED, TAPPING ITS FOOT, WAITING FOR YOU TO EXPLAIN.
SUDDENLY, YOU'RE SCRAMBLING, CONTRADICTING SOME INANE BIT OF BOLLOCKS YOU CAME OUT WITH YEARS AGO--SOMETHING YOU'VE COMPLETELY FORGOTTEN ABOUT.
DESPERATELY, YOU TRY TO REMEMBER WHO DID WHAT TO WHOM, AND WHEN.
YOU'RE REACHING WILDLY FOR THE FIRST THING THAT COMES TO MIND.
NOW, THE UNIVERSE --WHO'S TWIGGED TO THE FACT THAT YOU'RE JUST TAKING THE PISS--REMOVES ITS JACKET VERY DELIBERATELY.
IT STEPS FORWARD, THROWS YOU AN UPPERCUT...
...AND YOU'RE FLAT ON YOUR ARSE BEFORE YOU HAVE A CHANCE TO PROTEST.

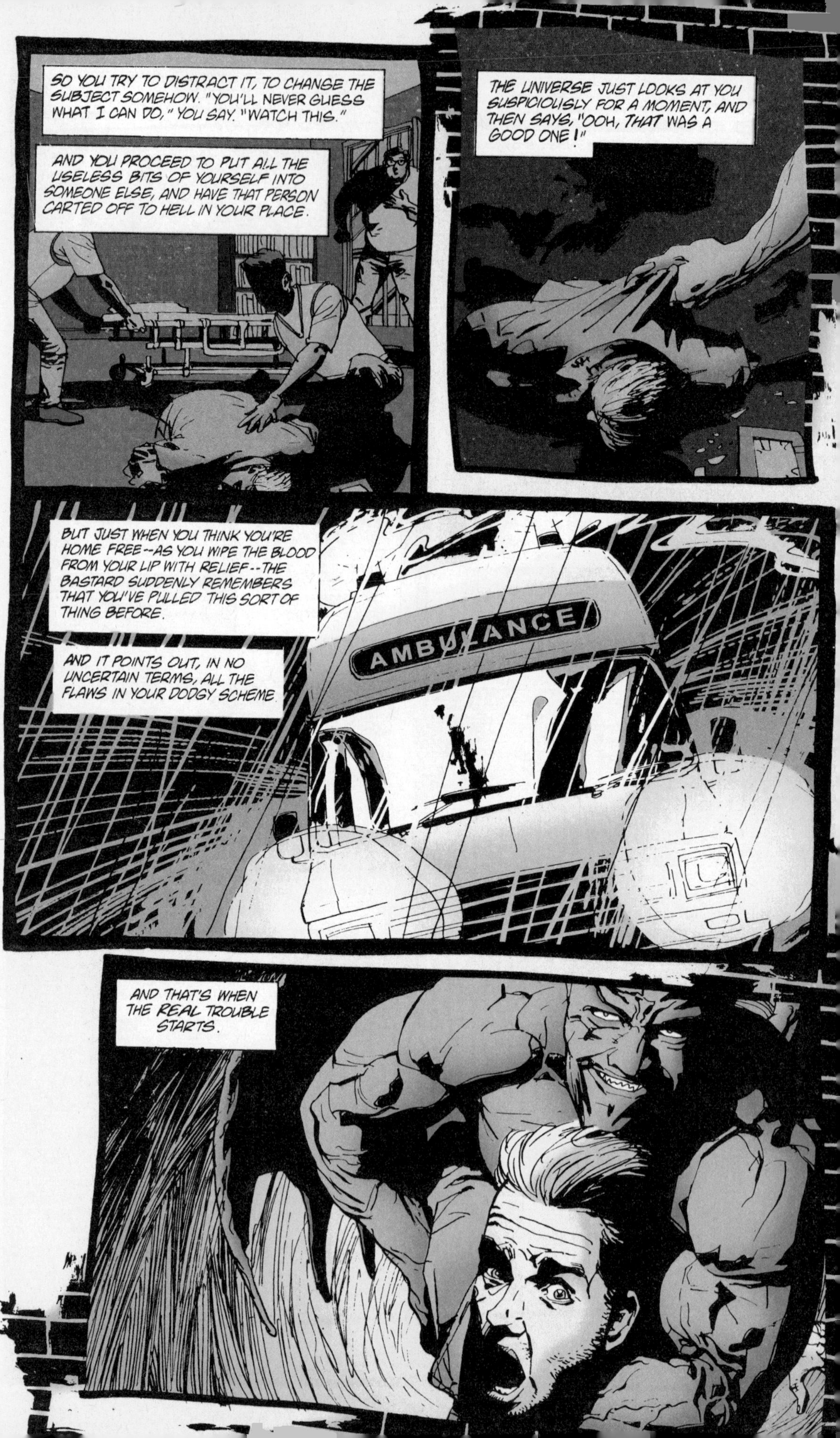
SO YOU TRY TO DISTRACT IT, TO CHANGE THE SUBJECT SOMEHOW. "YOU'LL NEVER GUESS WHAT I CAN DO," YOU SAY. "WATCH THIS."
AND YOU PROCEED TO PUT ALL THE USELESS BITS OF YOURSELF INTO SOMEONE ELSE, AND HAVE THAT PERSON CARTED OFF TO HELL IN YOUR PLACE.
THE UNIVERSE JUST LOOKS AT YOU SUSPICIOUSLY FOR A MOMENT, AND THEN SAYS, "OOH, THAT WAS A GOOD ONE!"
BUT JUST WHEN YOU THINK YOU'RE HOME FREE--AS YOU WIPE THE BLOOD FROM YOUR LIP WITH RELIEF--THE BASTARD SUDDENLY REMEMBERS THAT YOU'VE PULLED THIS SORT OF THING BEFORE.
AND IT POINTS OUT, IN NO UNCERTAIN TERMS, ALL THE FLAWS IN YOUR DODGY SCHEME.
AMBULANCE
AND THAT'S WHEN THE REAL TROUBLE STARTS.

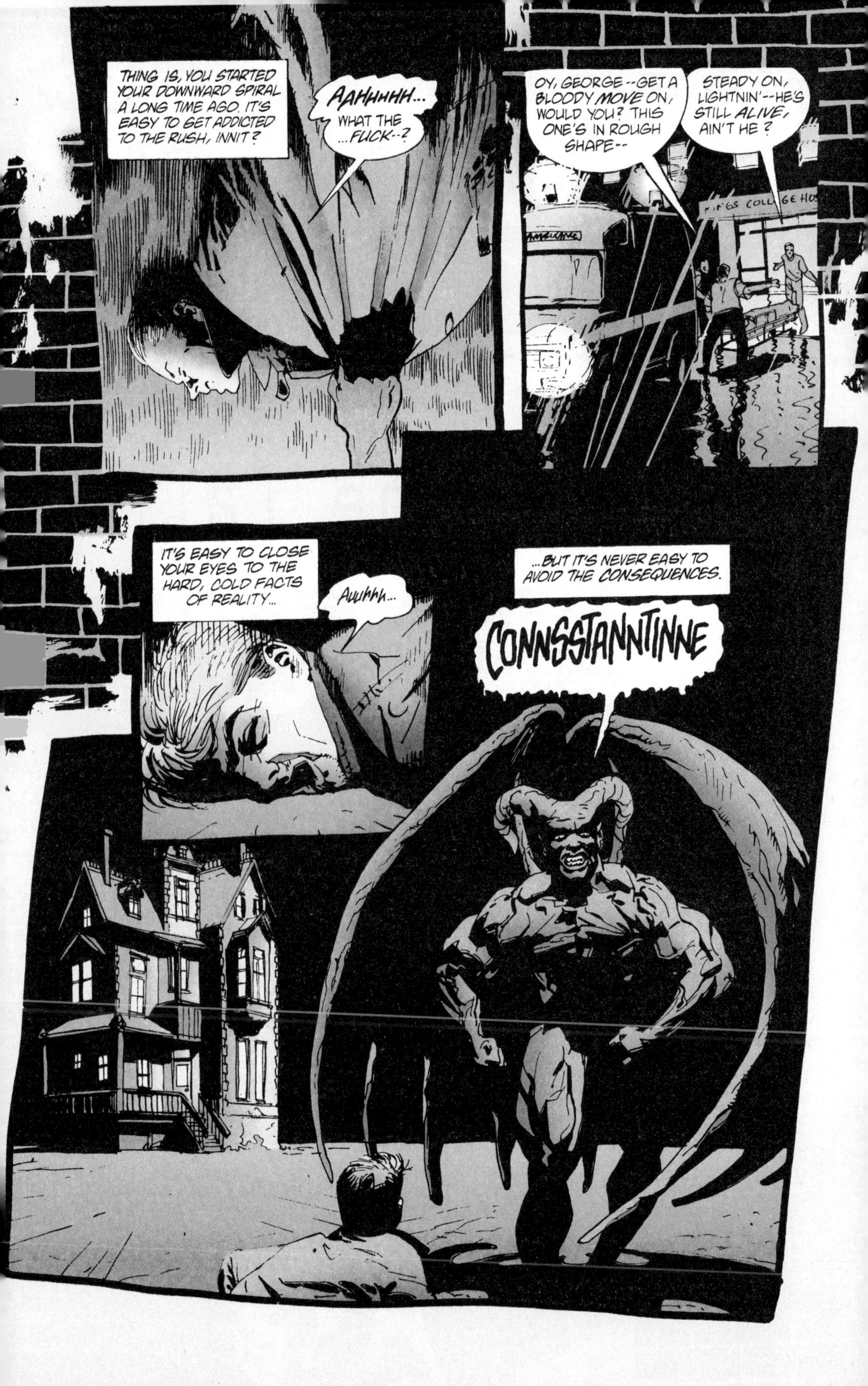
THING IS, YOU STARTED YOUR DOWNWARD SPIRAL A LONG TIME AGO. IT'S EASY TO GET ADDICTED TO THE RUSH, INNIT?
AAHHHHH... WHAT THE ...FUCK--?
OY, GEORGE--GET A BLOODY MOVE ON, WOULD YOU? THIS ONE'S IN ROUGH SHAPE--
STEADY ON, LIGHTNIN'--HE'S STILL ALIVE, AIN'T HE?
IT'S EASY TO CLOSE YOUR EYES TO THE HARD, COLD FACTS OF REALITY...
Auuhhh...
...BUT IT'S NEVER EASY TO AVOID THE CONSEQUENCES.
CONNSSTANNTINNE

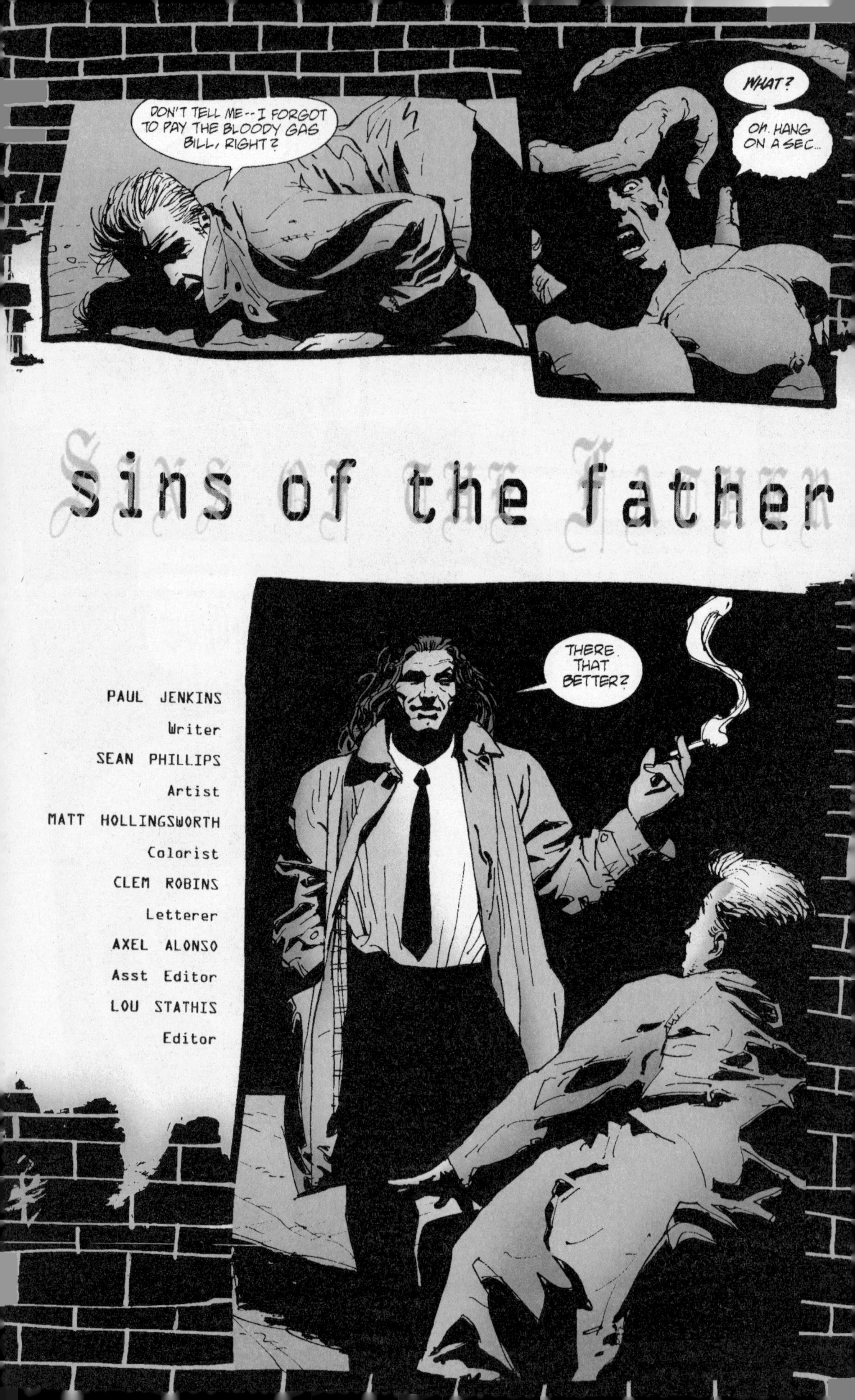
DON'T TELL ME--I FORGOT TO PAY THE BLOODY GAS BILL, RIGHT?
WHAT?
OH. HANG ON A SEC...
THERE. THAT BETTER?

Sins of the Father

PAUL JENKINS
Writer
SEAN PHILLIPS
Artist
MATT HOLLINGSWORTH
Colorist
CLEM ROBINS
Letterer
AXEL ALONSO
Asst Editor
LOU STATHIS
Editor

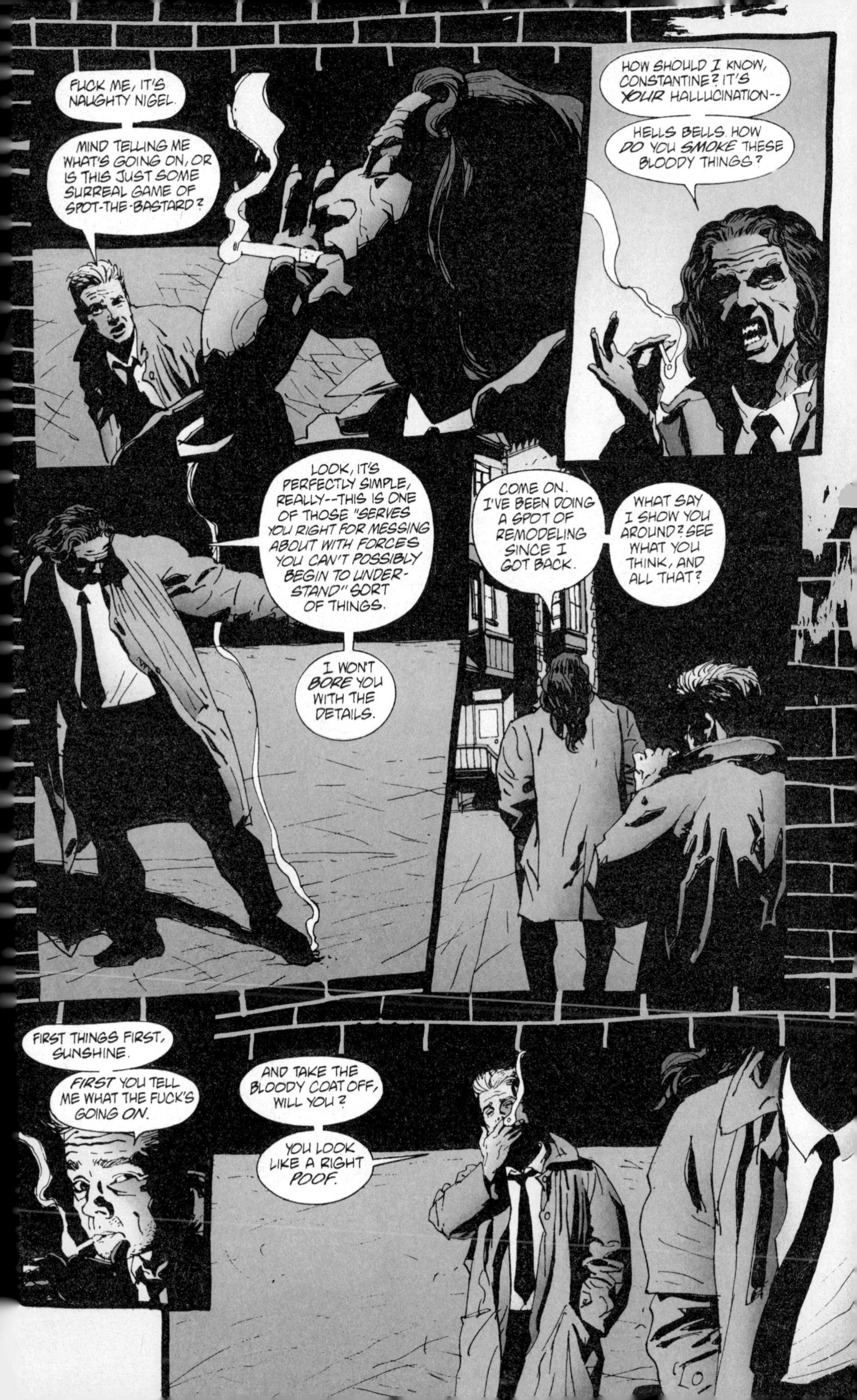
FUCK ME, IT'S NAUGHTY NIGEL.
MIND TELLING ME WHAT'S GOING ON, OR IS THIS JUST SOME SURREAL GAME OF SPOT-THE-BASTARD?
HOW SHOULD I KNOW, CONSTANTINE? IT'S YOUR HALLUCINATION--
HELLS BELLS. HOW DO YOU SMOKE THESE BLOODY THINGS?
LOOK, IT'S PERFECTLY SIMPLE, REALLY--THIS IS ONE OF THOSE "SERVES YOU RIGHT FOR MESSING ABOUT WITH FORCES YOU CAN'T POSSIBLY BEGIN TO UNDERSTAND" SORT OF THINGS.
I WON'T BORE YOU WITH THE DETAILS.
COME ON. I'VE BEEN DOING A SPOT OF REMODELING SINCE I GOT BACK.
WHAT SAY I SHOW YOU AROUND? SEE WHAT YOU THINK, AND ALL THAT?
FIRST THINGS FIRST, SUNSHINE.
FIRST YOU TELL ME WHAT THE FUCK'S GOING ON.
AND TAKE THE BLOODY COAT OFF, WILL YOU?
YOU LOOK LIKE A RIGHT POOF.

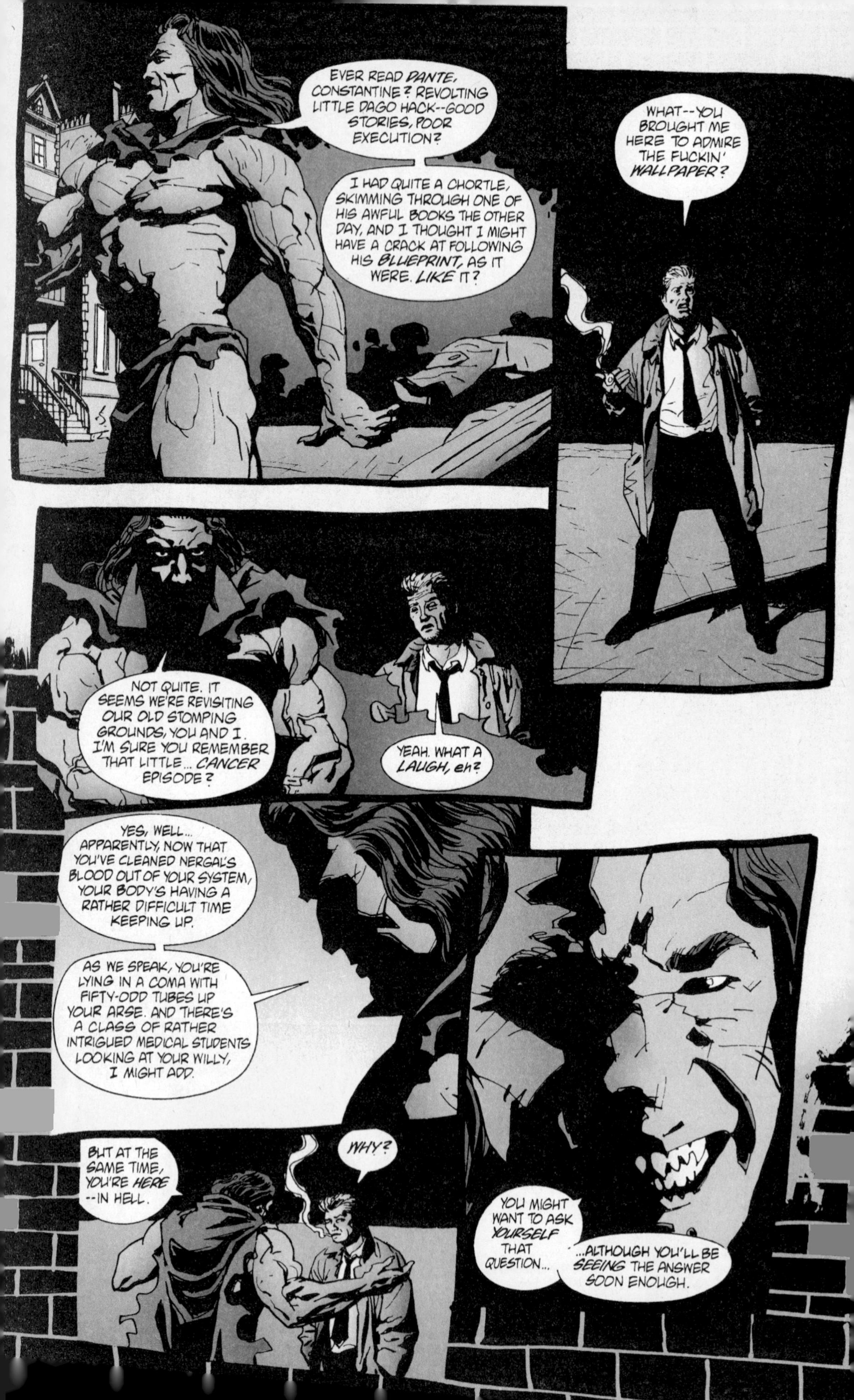
EVER READ DANTE, CONSTANTINE? REVOLTING LITTLE DAGO HACK--GOOD STORIES, POOR EXECUTION?
I HAD QUITE A CHORTLE, SKIMMING THROUGH ONE OF HIS AWFUL BOOKS THE OTHER DAY, AND I THOUGHT I MIGHT HAVE A CRACK AT FOLLOWING HIS BLUEPRINT, AS IT WERE. LIKE IT?
WHAT--YOU BROUGHT ME HERE TO ADMIRE THE FUCKIN' WALLPAPER?
NOT QUITE. IT SEEMS WE'RE REVISITING OUR OLD STOMPING GROUNDS, YOU AND I. I'M SURE YOU REMEMBER THAT LITTLE... CANCER EPISODE?
YEAH. WHAT A LAUGH, eh?
YES, WELL... APPARENTLY, NOW THAT YOU'VE CLEANED NERGAL'S BLOOD OUT OF YOUR SYSTEM, YOUR BODY'S HAVING A RATHER DIFFICULT TIME KEEPING UP.
AS WE SPEAK, YOU'RE LYING IN A COMA WITH FIFTY-ODD TUBES UP YOUR ARSE. AND THERE'S A CLASS OF RATHER INTRIGUED MEDICAL STUDENTS LOOKING AT YOUR WILLY, I MIGHT ADD.
BUT AT THE SAME TIME, YOU'RE HERE --IN HELL.
WHY?
YOU MIGHT WANT TO ASK YOURSELF THAT QUESTION...
...ALTHOUGH YOU'LL BE SEEING THE ANSWER SOON ENOUGH.

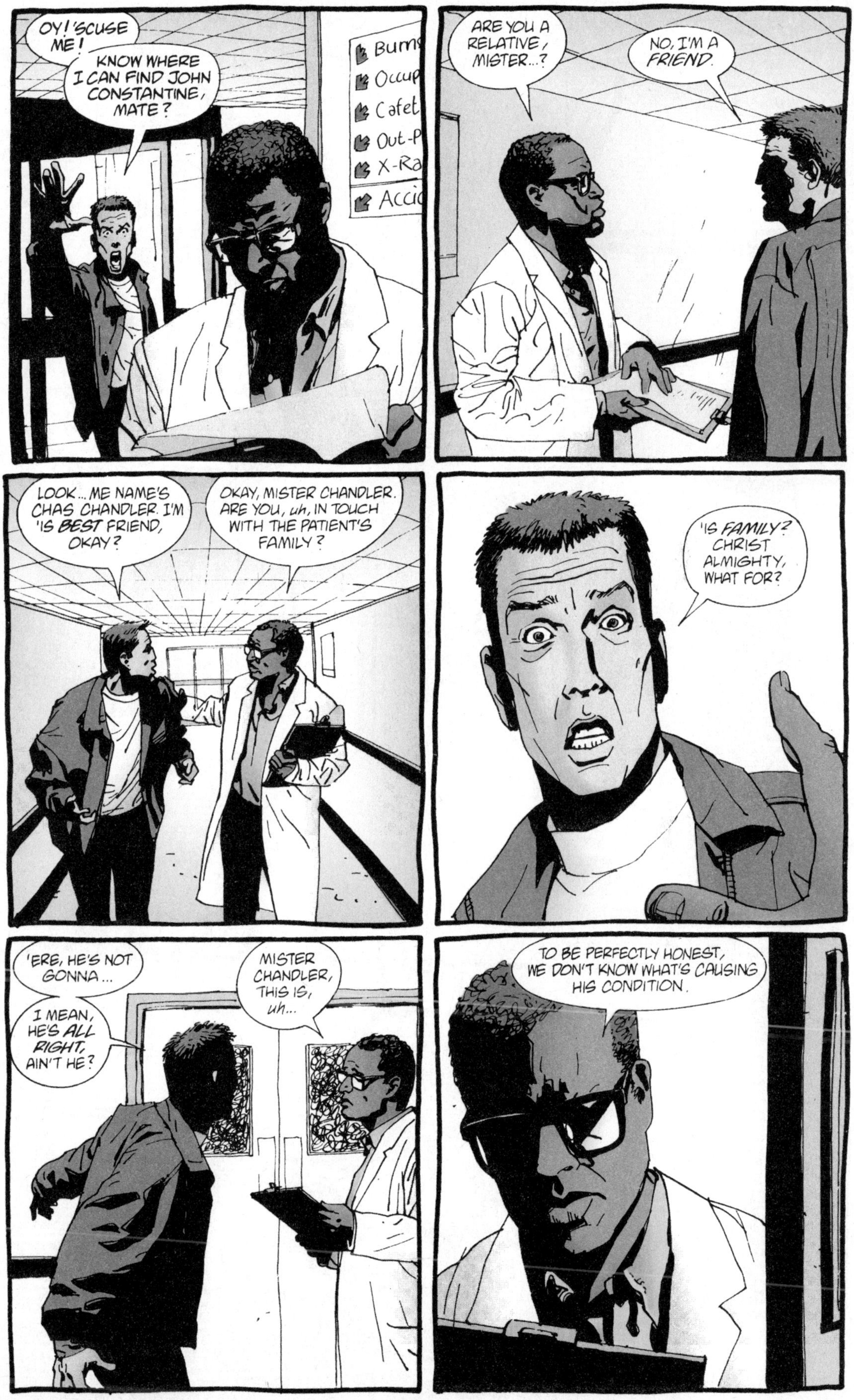
OY! 'SCUSE ME!
KNOW WHERE I CAN FIND JOHN CONSTANTINE, MATE?
Burns
Occup
Cafet
Out-P
X-Ra
Accid
ARE YOU A RELATIVE, MISTER...?
NO, I'M A FRIEND.
LOOK... ME NAME'S CHAS CHANDLER. I'M 'IS BEST FRIEND, OKAY?
OKAY, MISTER CHANDLER. ARE YOU, uh, IN TOUCH WITH THE PATIENT'S FAMILY?
'IS FAMILY? CHRIST ALMIGHTY, WHAT FOR?
'ERE, HE'S NOT GONNA...
I MEAN, HE'S ALL RIGHT, AIN'T HE?
MISTER CHANDLER, THIS IS, uh...
TO BE PERFECTLY HONEST, WE DON'T KNOW WHAT'S CAUSING HIS CONDITION.

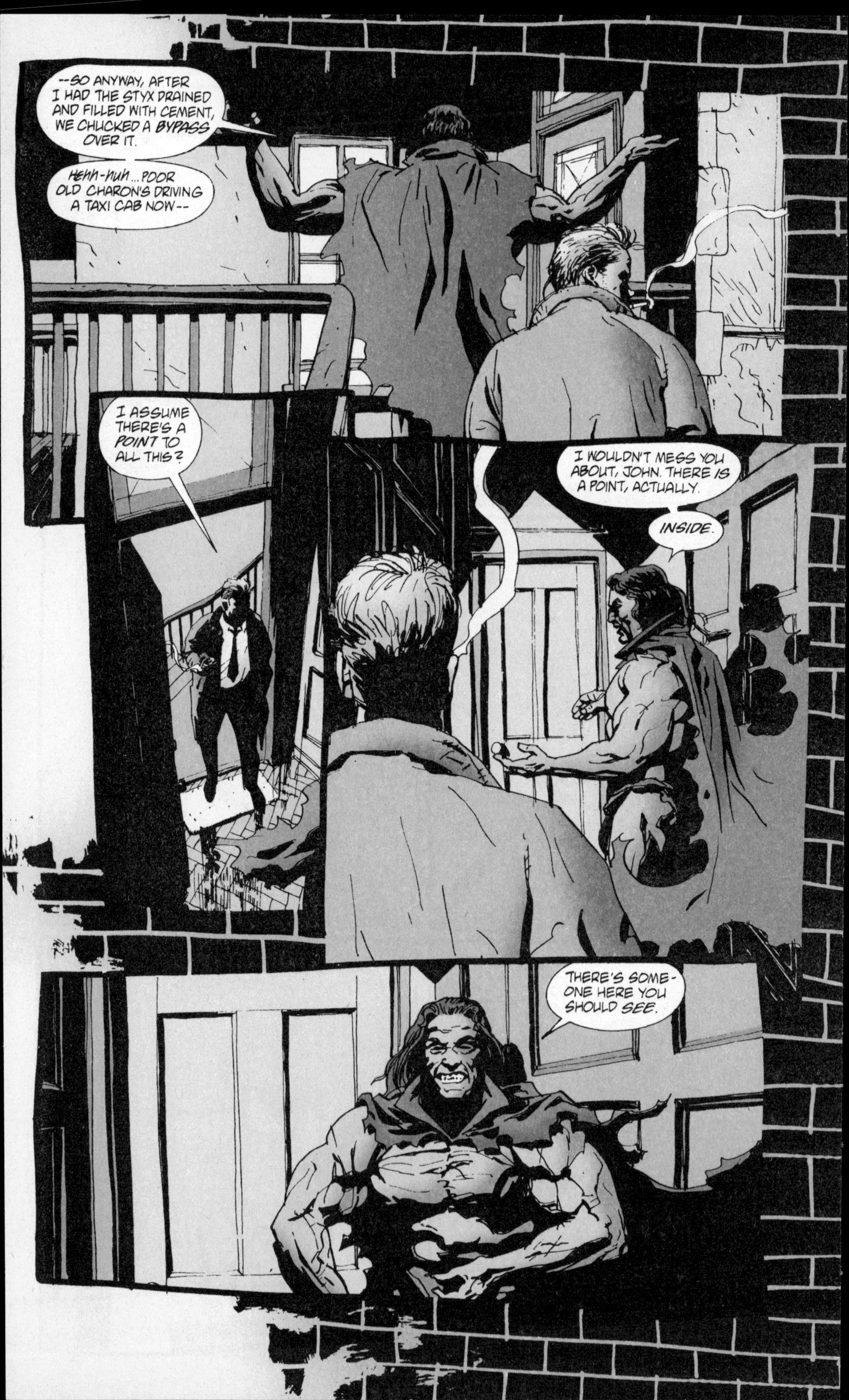
--SO ANYWAY, AFTER I HAD THE STYX DRAINED AND FILLED WITH CEMENT, WE CHUCKED A BYPASS OVER IT.
HEHH-NUH... POOR OLD CHARON'S DRIVING A TAXI CAB NOW--
I ASSUME THERE'S A POINT TO ALL THIS?
I WOULDN'T MESS YOU ABOUT, JOHN. THERE IS A POINT, ACTUALLY.
INSIDE.
THERE'S SOME-ONE HERE YOU SHOULD SEE.

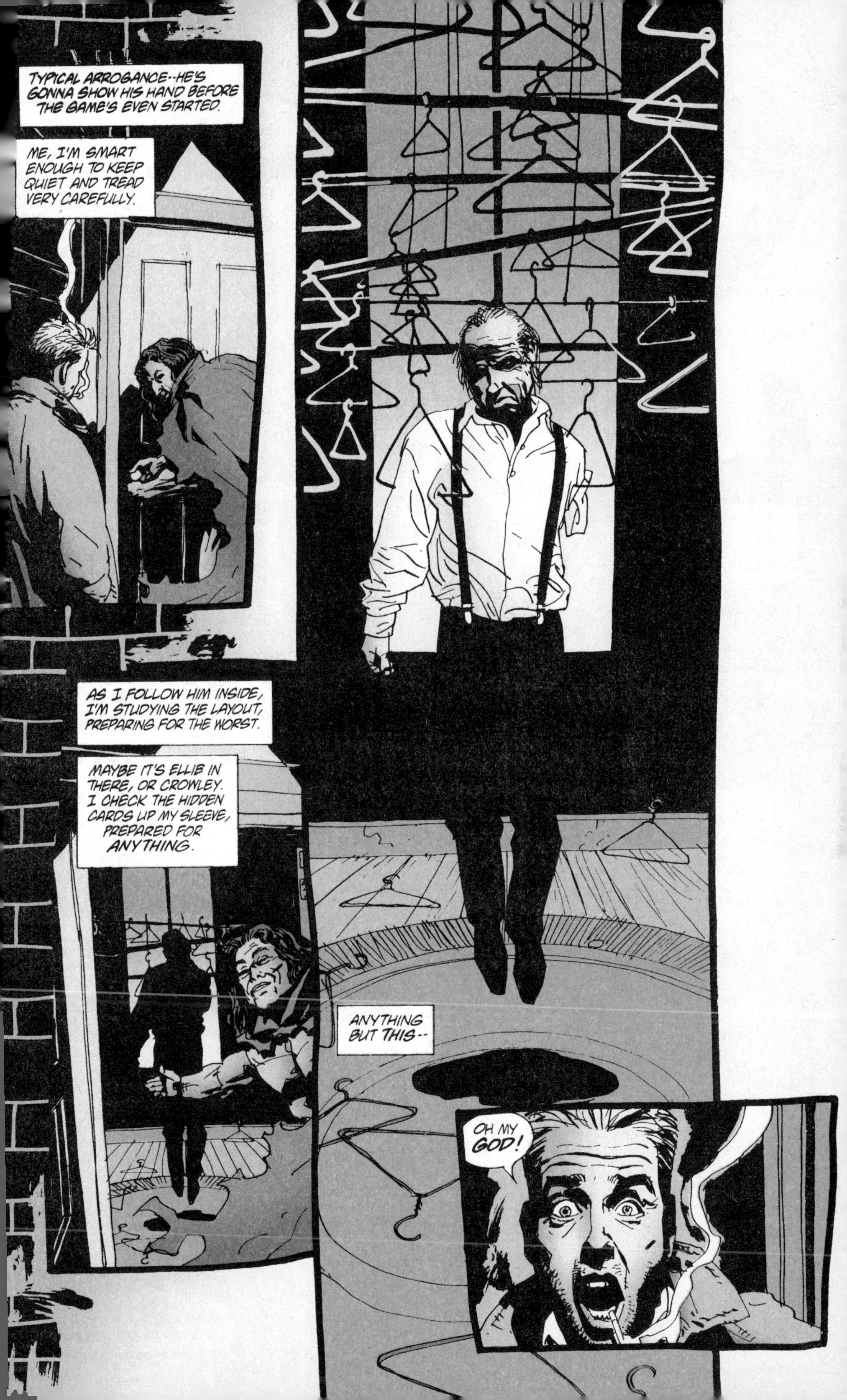
TYPICAL ARROGANCE--HE'S GONNA SHOW HIS HAND BEFORE THE GAME'S EVEN STARTED.
ME, I'M SMART ENOUGH TO KEEP QUIET AND TREAD VERY CAREFULLY.
AS I FOLLOW HIM INSIDE, I'M STUDYING THE LAYOUT, PREPARING FOR THE WORST.
MAYBE IT'S ELLIE IN THERE, OR CROWLEY. I CHECK THE HIDDEN CARDS UP MY SLEEVE, PREPARED FOR ANYTHING.
ANYTHING BUT THIS--
OH MY GOD!

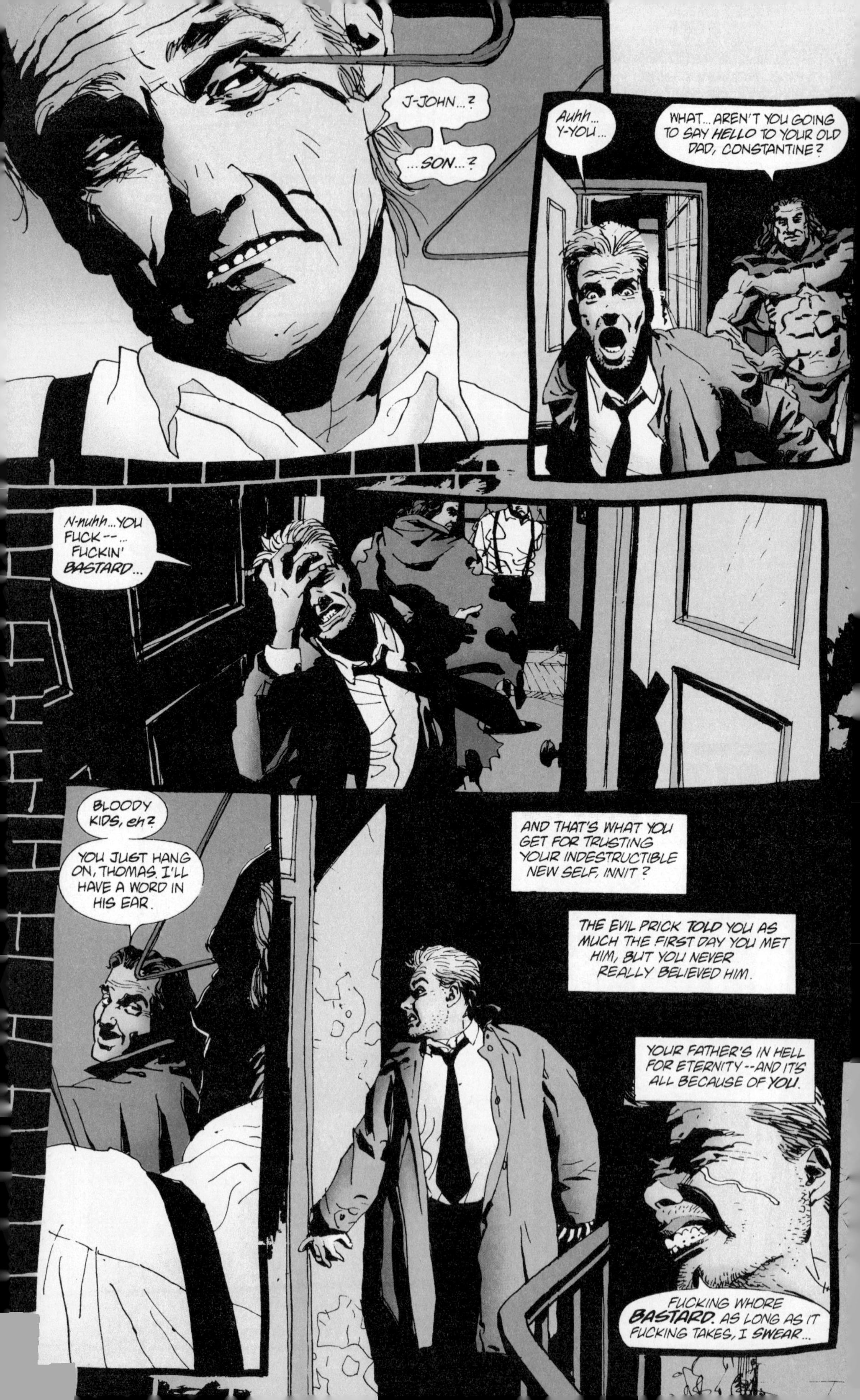
J-JOHN...?
...SON...?
Auhh... Y-YOU...
WHAT... AREN'T YOU GOING TO SAY HELLO TO YOUR OLD DAD, CONSTANTINE?
N-nuhh... YOU FUCK-- ... FUCKIN' BASTARD...
BLOODY KIDS, eh?
YOU JUST HANG ON, THOMAS. I'LL HAVE A WORD IN HIS EAR.
AND THAT'S WHAT YOU GET FOR TRUSTING YOUR INDESTRUCTIBLE NEW SELF, INNIT?
THE EVIL PRICK TOLD YOU AS MUCH THE FIRST DAY YOU MET HIM, BUT YOU NEVER REALLY BELIEVED HIM.
YOUR FATHER'S IN HELL FOR ETERNITY--AND IT'S ALL BECAUSE OF YOU.
FUCKING WHORE BASTARD. AS LONG AS IT FUCKING TAKES, I SWEAR...

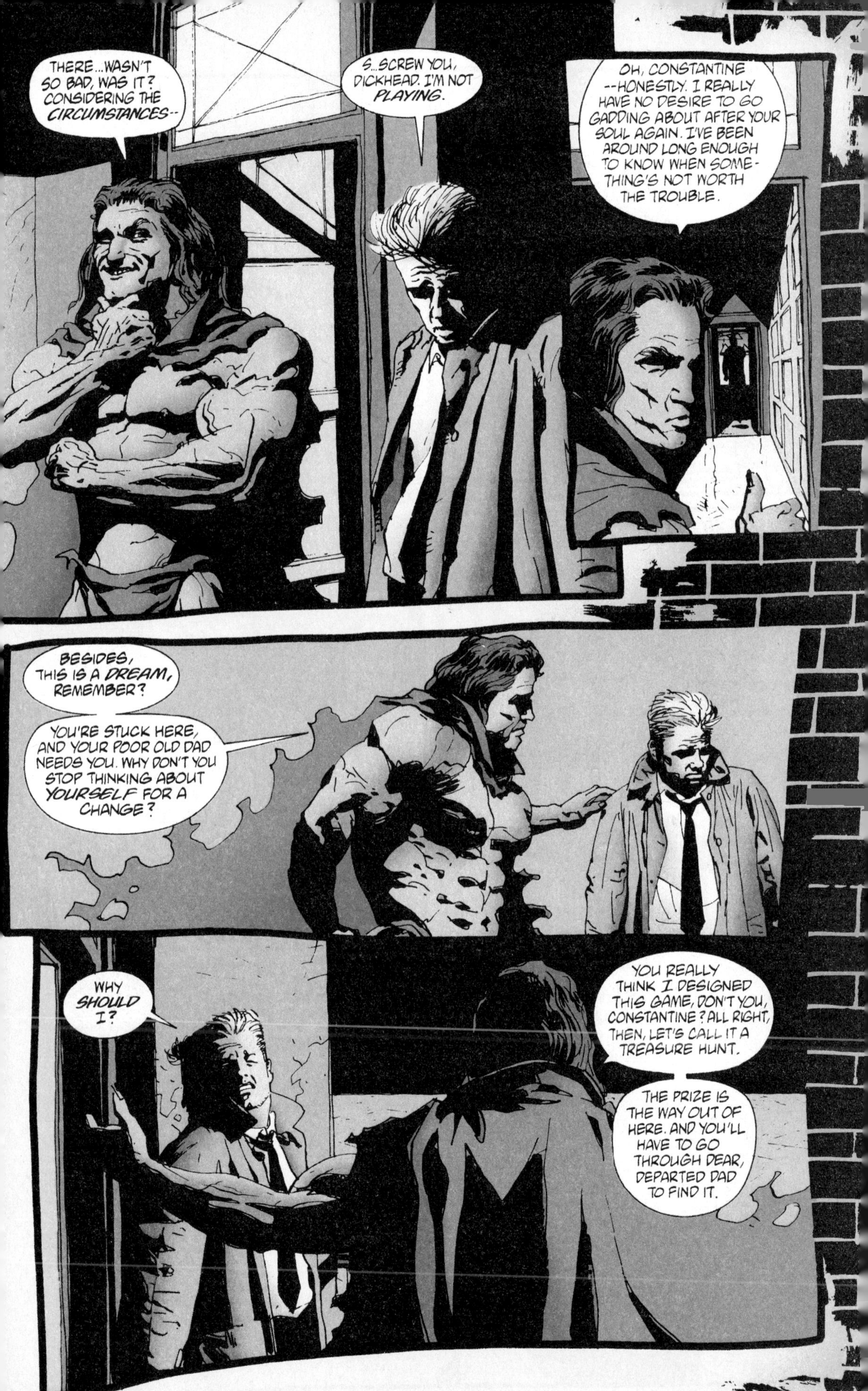
THERE...WASN'T SO BAD, WAS IT? CONSIDERING THE CIRCUMSTANCES--
S...SCREW YOU, DICKHEAD. I'M NOT PLAYING.
OH, CONSTANTINE --HONESTLY. I REALLY HAVE NO DESIRE TO GO GADDING ABOUT AFTER YOUR SOUL AGAIN. I'VE BEEN AROUND LONG ENOUGH TO KNOW WHEN SOMETHING'S NOT WORTH THE TROUBLE.
BESIDES, THIS IS A DREAM, REMEMBER?
YOU'RE STUCK HERE, AND YOUR POOR OLD DAD NEEDS YOU. WHY DON'T YOU STOP THINKING ABOUT YOURSELF FOR A CHANGE?
WHY SHOULD I?
YOU REALLY THINK I DESIGNED THIS GAME, DON'T YOU, CONSTANTINE? ALL RIGHT, THEN, LET'S CALL IT A TREASURE HUNT.
THE PRIZE IS THE WAY OUT OF HERE. AND YOU'LL HAVE TO GO THROUGH DEAR, DEPARTED DAD TO FIND IT.

...HIS HEART RATE'S DIPPED BELOW FIFTY, DOCTOR.

WHAT--?

THAT CAN'T BE RIGHT --AT LEAST, NOT ACCORDING TO HIS EEG READINGS.

HIS PULSE IS SLOWING, BUT HIS BRAIN ACTIVITY'S GOING OFF THE *SCALE*...

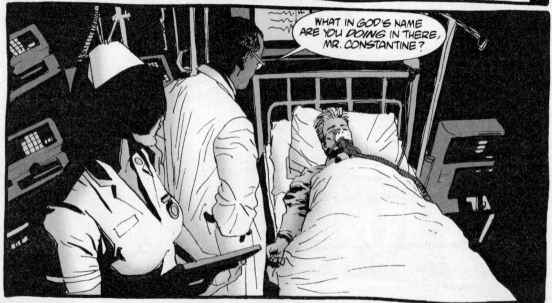

WHAT IN *GOD'S* NAME ARE YOU *DOING* IN THERE, MR. CONSTANTINE?

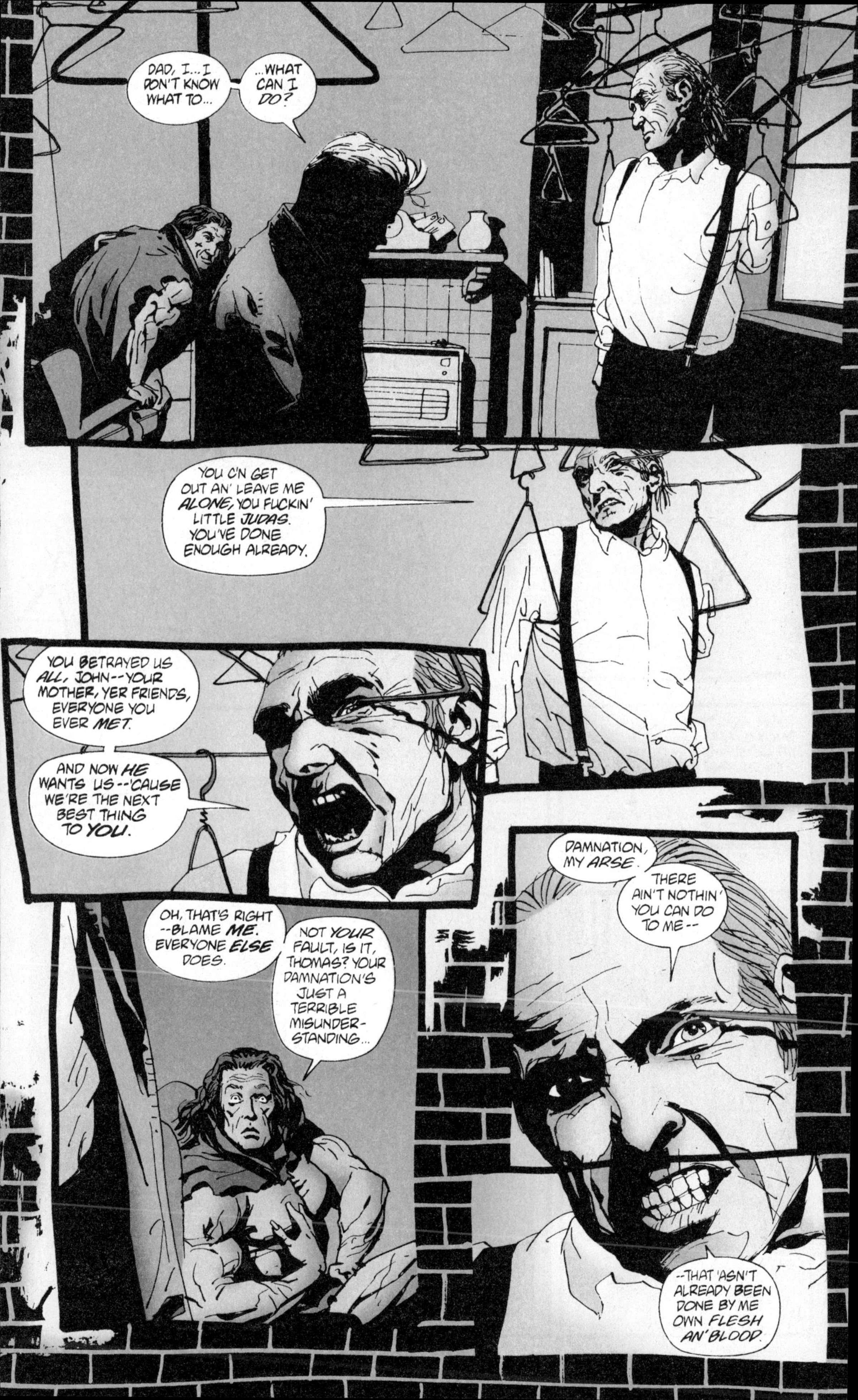
DAD, I... I DON'T KNOW WHAT TO...
...WHAT CAN I DO?
YOU C'N GET OUT AN' LEAVE ME ALONE, YOU FUCKIN' LITTLE JUDAS. YOU'VE DONE ENOUGH ALREADY.
YOU BETRAYED US ALL, JOHN--YOUR MOTHER, YER FRIENDS, EVERYONE YOU EVER MET.
AND NOW HE WANTS US--'CAUSE WE'RE THE NEXT BEST THING TO YOU.
OH, THAT'S RIGHT --BLAME ME. EVERYONE ELSE DOES.
NOT YOUR FAULT, IS IT, THOMAS? YOUR DAMNATION'S JUST A TERRIBLE MISUNDER-STANDING...
DAMNATION, MY ARSE.
THERE AIN'T NOTHIN' YOU CAN DO TO ME--
--THAT 'ASN'T ALREADY BEEN DONE BY ME OWN FLESH AN' BLOOD.

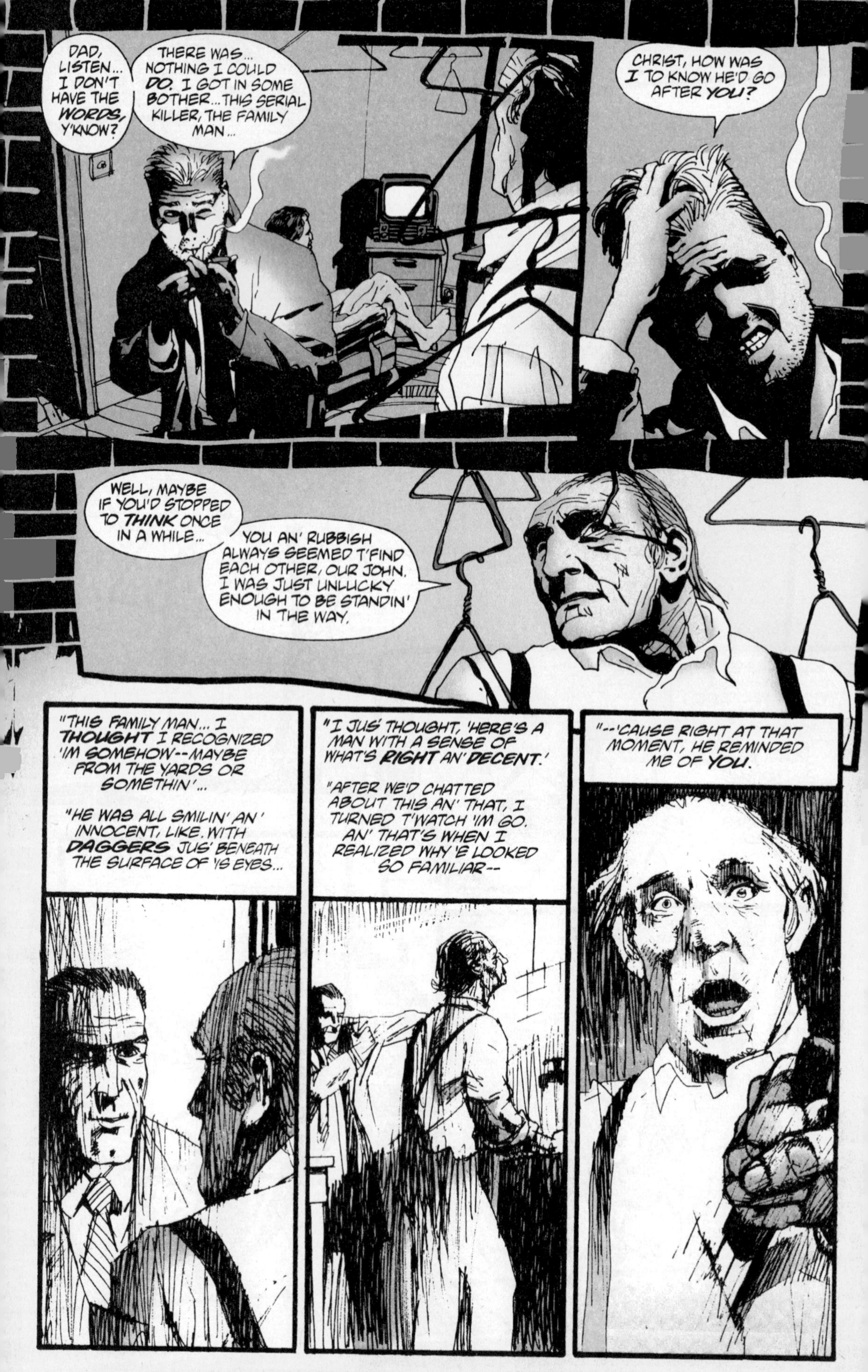
DAD, LISTEN... I DON'T HAVE THE WORDS, Y'KNOW?
THERE WAS... NOTHING I COULD DO. I GOT IN SOME BOTHER... THIS SERIAL KILLER, THE FAMILY MAN...
CHRIST, HOW WAS I TO KNOW HE'D GO AFTER YOU?
WELL, MAYBE IF YOU'D STOPPED TO THINK ONCE IN A WHILE...
YOU AN' RUBBISH ALWAYS SEEMED T'FIND EACH OTHER, OUR JOHN. I WAS JUST UNLUCKY ENOUGH TO BE STANDIN' IN THE WAY.
"THIS FAMILY MAN... I THOUGHT I RECOGNIZED 'IM SOMEHOW--MAYBE FROM THE YARDS OR SOMETHIN'...
"HE WAS ALL SMILIN' AN' INNOCENT, LIKE. WITH DAGGERS JUS' BENEATH THE SURFACE OF 'IS EYES...
"I JUS' THOUGHT, 'HERE'S A MAN WITH A SENSE OF WHAT'S RIGHT AN' DECENT.'
"AFTER WE'D CHATTED ABOUT THIS AN' THAT, I TURNED T'WATCH 'IM GO. AN' THAT'S WHEN I REALIZED WHY 'E LOOKED SO FAMILIAR--
"--'CAUSE RIGHT AT THAT MOMENT, HE REMINDED ME OF YOU.

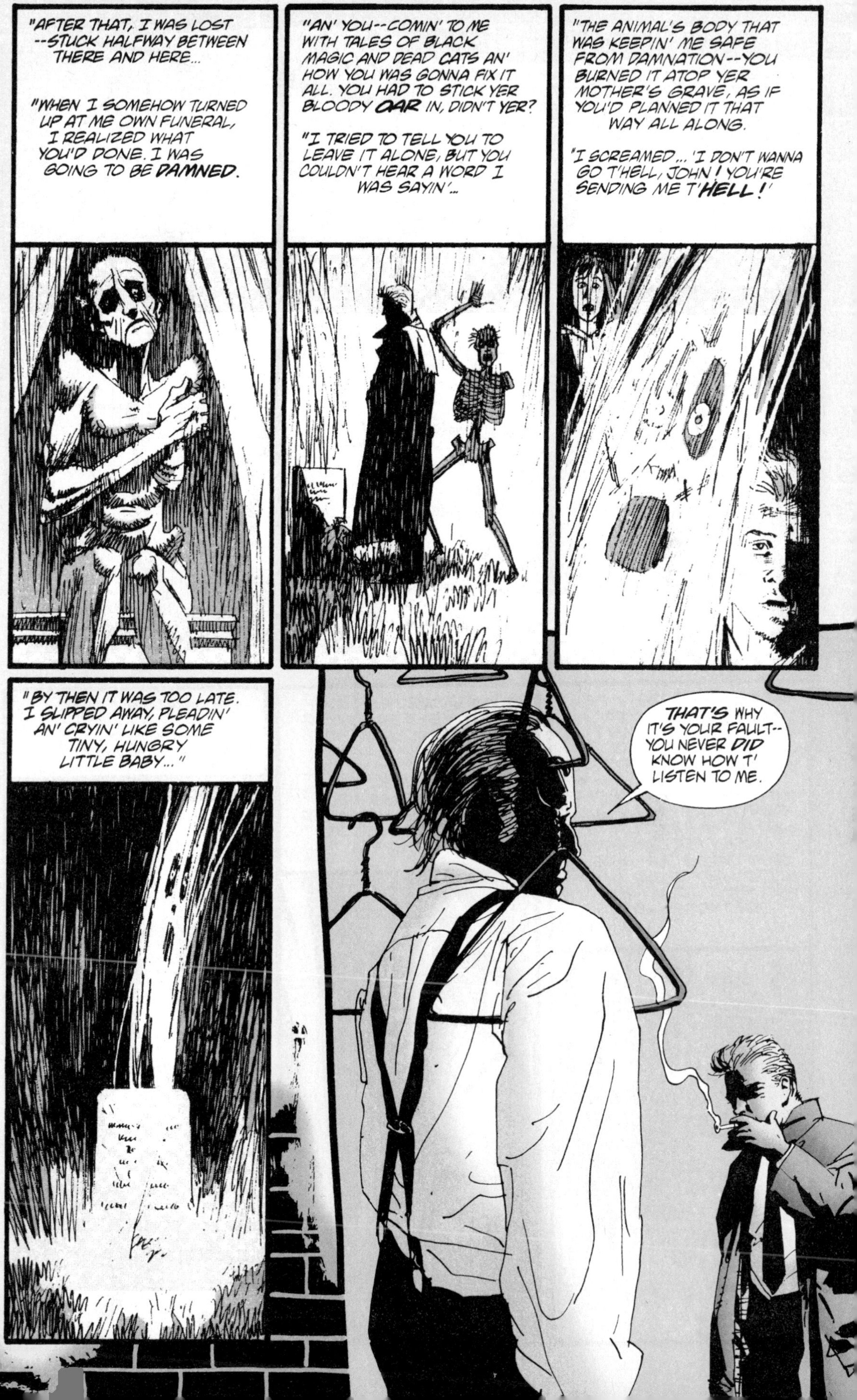
"AFTER THAT, I WAS LOST --STUCK HALFWAY BETWEEN THERE AND HERE...
"WHEN I SOMEHOW TURNED UP AT ME OWN FUNERAL, I REALIZED WHAT YOU'D DONE. I WAS GOING TO BE DAMNED.
"AN' YOU--COMIN' TO ME WITH TALES OF BLACK MAGIC AND DEAD CATS AN' HOW YOU WAS GONNA FIX IT ALL. YOU HAD TO STICK YER BLOODY OAR IN, DIDN'T YER?
"I TRIED TO TELL YOU TO LEAVE IT ALONE, BUT YOU COULDN'T HEAR A WORD I WAS SAYIN'...
"THE ANIMAL'S BODY THAT WAS KEEPIN' ME SAFE FROM DAMNATION--YOU BURNED IT ATOP YER MOTHER'S GRAVE, AS IF YOU'D PLANNED IT THAT WAY ALL ALONG.
"I SCREAMED... 'I DON'T WANNA GO T'HELL, JOHN! YOU'RE SENDING ME T'HELL!'
"BY THEN IT WAS TOO LATE. I SLIPPED AWAY, PLEADIN' AN' CRYIN' LIKE SOME TINY, HUNGRY LITTLE BABY..."
THAT'S WHY IT'S YOUR FAULT-- YOU NEVER DID KNOW HOW T' LISTEN TO ME.

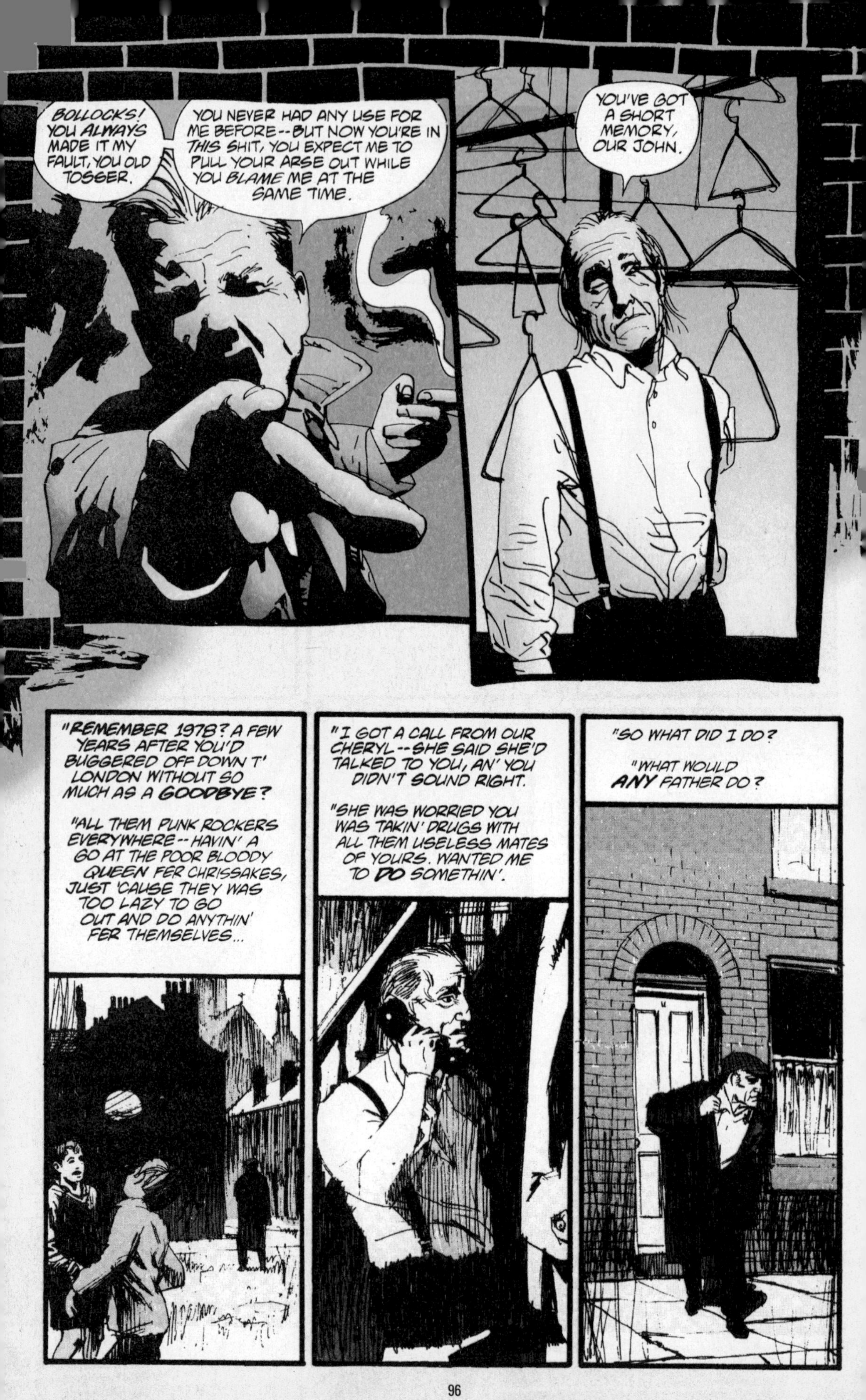
BOLLOCKS! YOU ALWAYS MADE IT MY FAULT, YOU OLD TOSSER.
YOU NEVER HAD ANY USE FOR ME BEFORE--BUT NOW YOU'RE IN THIS SHIT, YOU EXPECT ME TO PULL YOUR ARSE OUT WHILE YOU BLAME ME AT THE SAME TIME.
YOU'VE GOT A SHORT MEMORY, OUR JOHN.
"REMEMBER 1978? A FEW YEARS AFTER YOU'D BUGGERED OFF DOWN T' LONDON WITHOUT SO MUCH AS A GOODBYE?
"ALL THEM PUNK ROCKERS EVERYWHERE--HAVIN' A GO AT THE POOR BLOODY QUEEN FER CHRISSAKES, JUST 'CAUSE THEY WAS TOO LAZY TO GO OUT AND DO ANYTHIN' FER THEMSELVES...
"I GOT A CALL FROM OUR CHERYL--SHE SAID SHE'D TALKED TO YOU, AN' YOU DIDN'T SOUND RIGHT.
"SHE WAS WORRIED YOU WAS TAKIN' DRUGS WITH ALL THEM USELESS MATES OF YOURS. WANTED ME TO DO SOMETHIN'.
"SO WHAT DID I DO?
"WHAT WOULD ANY FATHER DO?

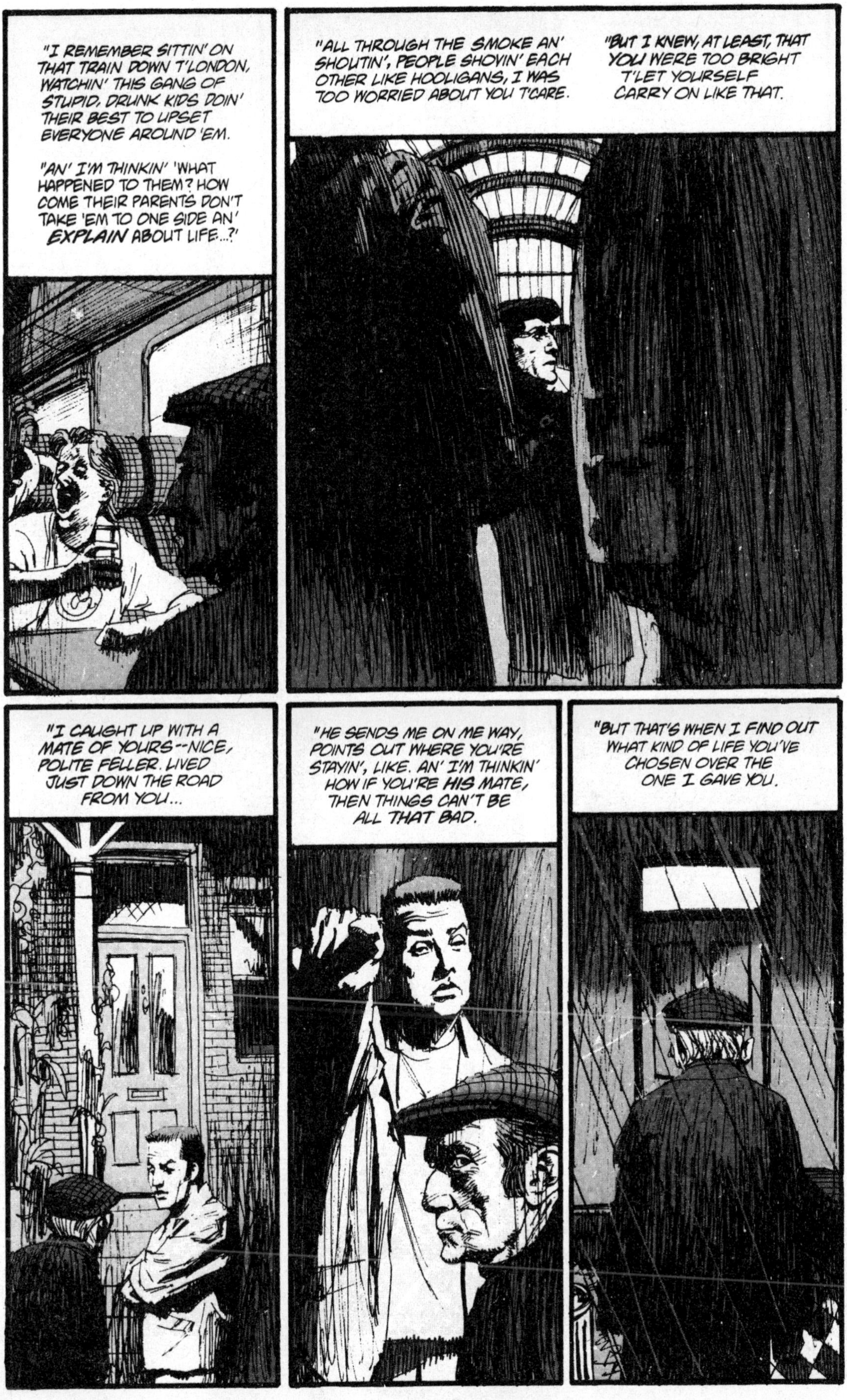
"I REMEMBER SITTIN' ON THAT TRAIN DOWN T'LONDON, WATCHIN' THIS GANG OF STUPID, DRUNK KIDS DOIN' THEIR BEST TO UPSET EVERYONE AROUND 'EM.
"AN' I'M THINKIN' 'WHAT HAPPENED TO THEM? HOW COME THEIR PARENTS DON'T TAKE 'EM TO ONE SIDE AN' EXPLAIN ABOUT LIFE...?'
"ALL THROUGH THE SMOKE AN' SHOUTIN', PEOPLE SHOVIN' EACH OTHER LIKE HOOLIGANS, I WAS TOO WORRIED ABOUT YOU T'CARE.
"BUT I KNEW, AT LEAST, THAT YOU WERE TOO BRIGHT T'LET YOURSELF CARRY ON LIKE THAT.
"I CAUGHT UP WITH A MATE OF YOURS--NICE, POLITE FELLER. LIVED JUST DOWN THE ROAD FROM YOU...
"HE SENDS ME ON ME WAY, POINTS OUT WHERE YOU'RE STAYIN', LIKE. AN' I'M THINKIN' HOW IF YOU'RE HIS MATE, THEN THINGS CAN'T BE ALL THAT BAD.
"BUT THAT'S WHEN I FIND OUT WHAT KIND OF LIFE YOU'VE CHOSEN OVER THE ONE I GAVE YOU.

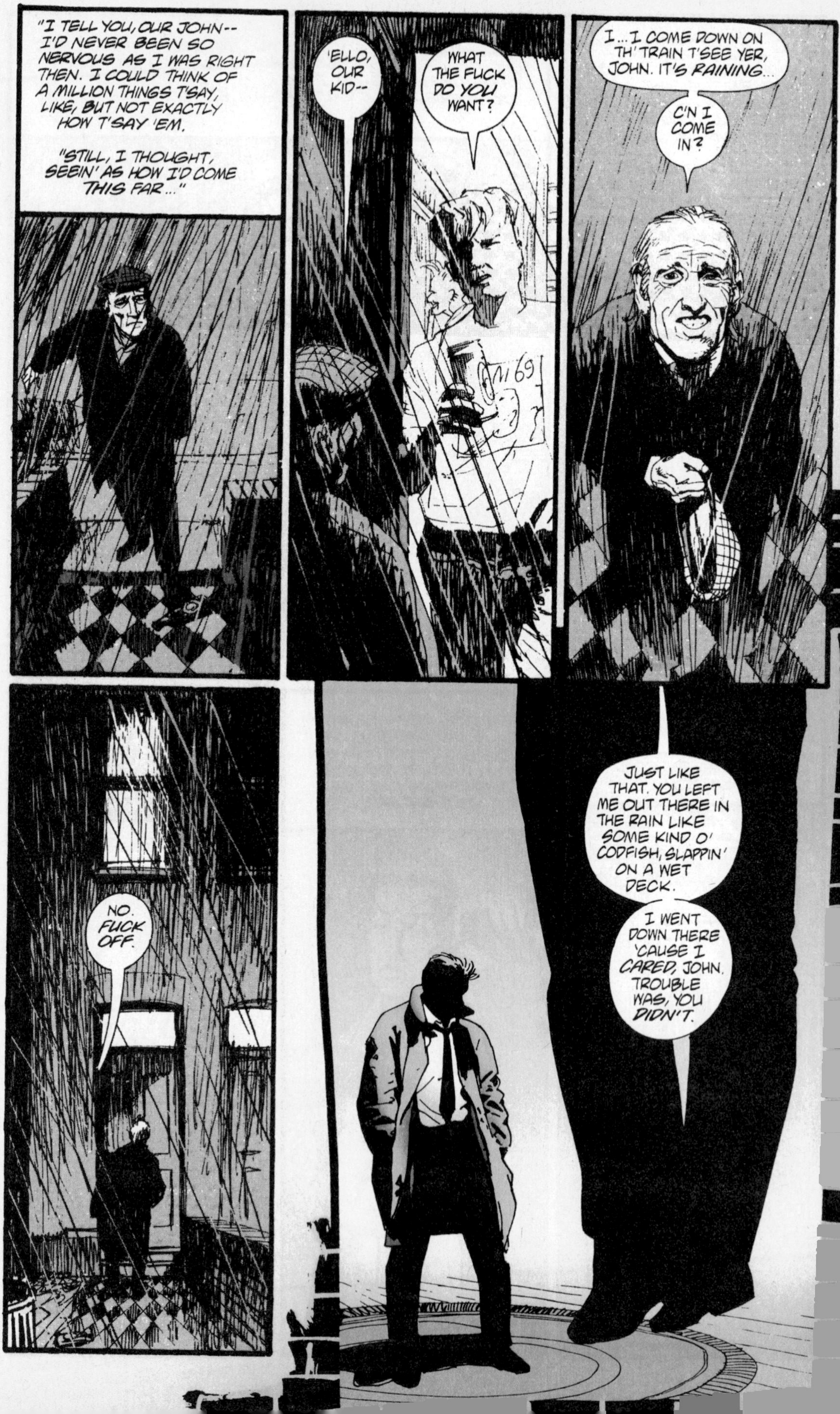
"I TELL YOU, OUR JOHN-- I'D NEVER BEEN SO NERVOUS AS I WAS RIGHT THEN. I COULD THINK OF A MILLION THINGS T'SAY, LIKE, BUT NOT EXACTLY HOW T'SAY 'EM.
"STILL, I THOUGHT, SEEIN' AS HOW I'D COME THIS FAR..."
'ELLO, OUR KID--
WHAT THE FUCK DO YOU WANT?
I... I COME DOWN ON TH' TRAIN T'SEE YER, JOHN. IT'S RAINING...
C'N I COME IN?
NO. FUCK OFF.
JUST LIKE THAT. YOU LEFT ME OUT THERE IN THE RAIN LIKE SOME KIND O' CODFISH, SLAPPIN' ON A WET DECK.
I WENT DOWN THERE 'CAUSE I CARED, JOHN. TROUBLE WAS, YOU DIDN'T.

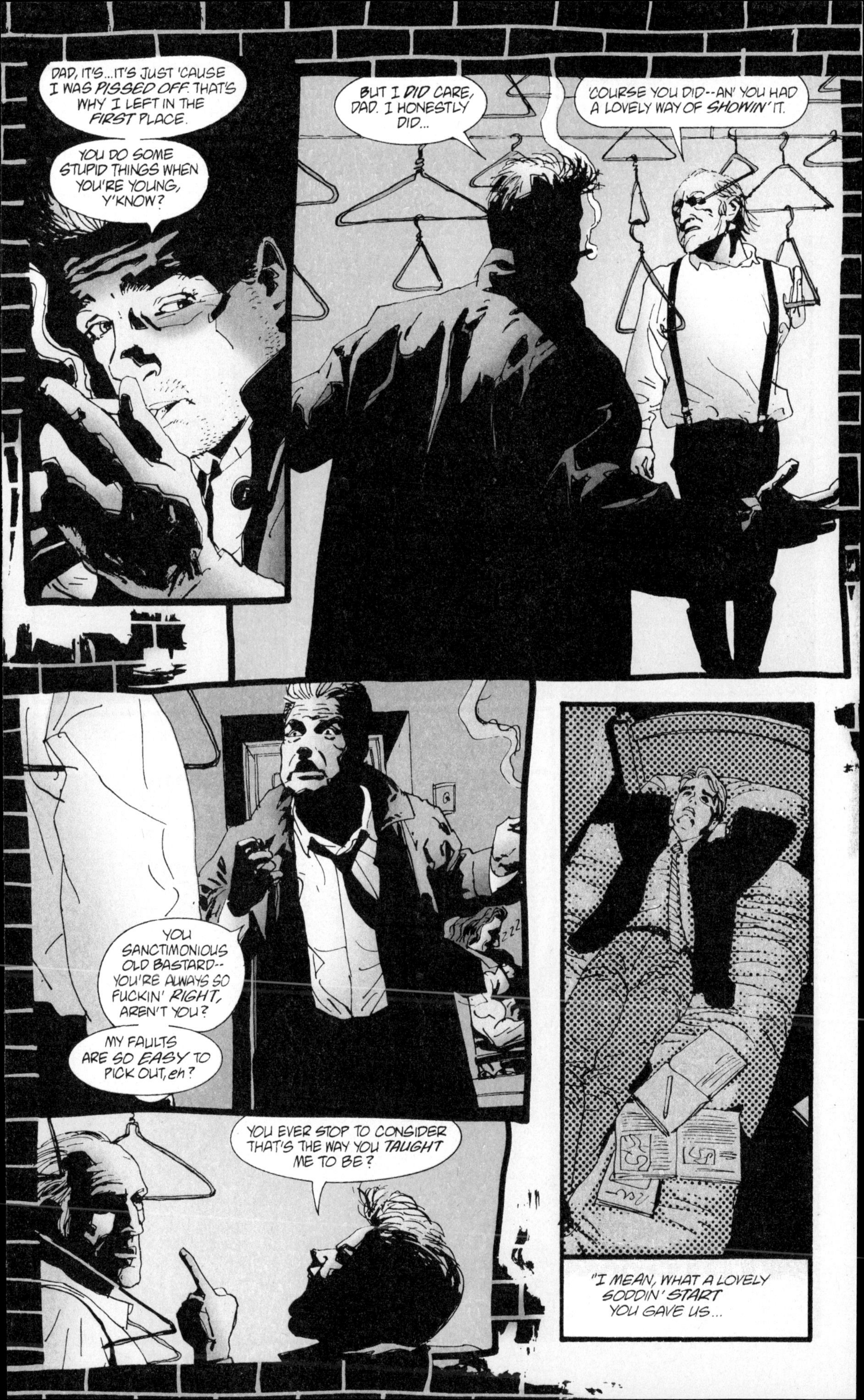
DAD, IT'S...IT'S JUST 'CAUSE I WAS PISSED OFF. THAT'S WHY I LEFT IN THE FIRST PLACE.
YOU DO SOME STUPID THINGS WHEN YOU'RE YOUNG, Y'KNOW?
BUT I DID CARE, DAD. I HONESTLY DID...
'COURSE YOU DID--AN' YOU HAD A LOVELY WAY OF SHOWIN' IT.
YOU SANCTIMONIOUS OLD BASTARD--YOU'RE ALWAYS SO FUCKIN' RIGHT, AREN'T YOU?
MY FAULTS ARE SO EASY TO PICK OUT, eh?
ZZZ
YOU EVER STOP TO CONSIDER THAT'S THE WAY YOU TAUGHT ME TO BE?
"I MEAN, WHAT A LOVELY SODDIN' START YOU GAVE US...

JOHN! WHAT THE FUCK'RE YOU DOIN' ON THAT *BED?*

YOU GOT SCHOOL TOMORROW. DON'T LET ME CATCH YOU WITH-OUT THAT ESSAY DONE. NOT UNLESS YOU WANT T'SEE THE BACK OF MY 'AND...

"'THE BACK OF MY HAND' --IT WAS LIKE SOME FUCKING BOGEYMAN THAT LIFTED ITS UGLY HEAD EVERY TIME YOU GOT PLASTERED.

"IF I CAME HOME HAPPY, YOU'D BE DRUNK. IF I CAME IN SCARED, YOU'D BE SOBER. I COULD NEVER TELL WHICH WAS *WORSE.*

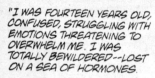

"I WAS FOURTEEN YEARS OLD, CONFUSED, STRUGGLING WITH EMOTIONS THREATENING TO OVERWHELM ME. I WAS TOTALLY BEWILDERED--LOST ON A SEA OF HORMONES.

"AN' IF I DIDN'T KNOW WHAT *I* WAS THINKING AT ANY GIVEN MOMENT, HOW THE HELL WAS I TO GUESS WHAT WAS IN *YOUR* DRUNKEN BLOODY BRAIN?

"I TRIED--I REALLY, HONESTLY *TRIED.* TOOK A LOT JUST TO COME DOWN THE STAIRS...

"I WANTED TO SHOW YOU I WAS LISTENING. I WANTED YOU TO HELP ME WITH MY *HOMEWORK,* FOR CHRISSAKES...

"...BUT ALL YOU WANTED TO DO WAS *BLAME* ME FOR YOUR MISERABLE EXISTENCE.

WHA' THE FUG *YOU* WANT?

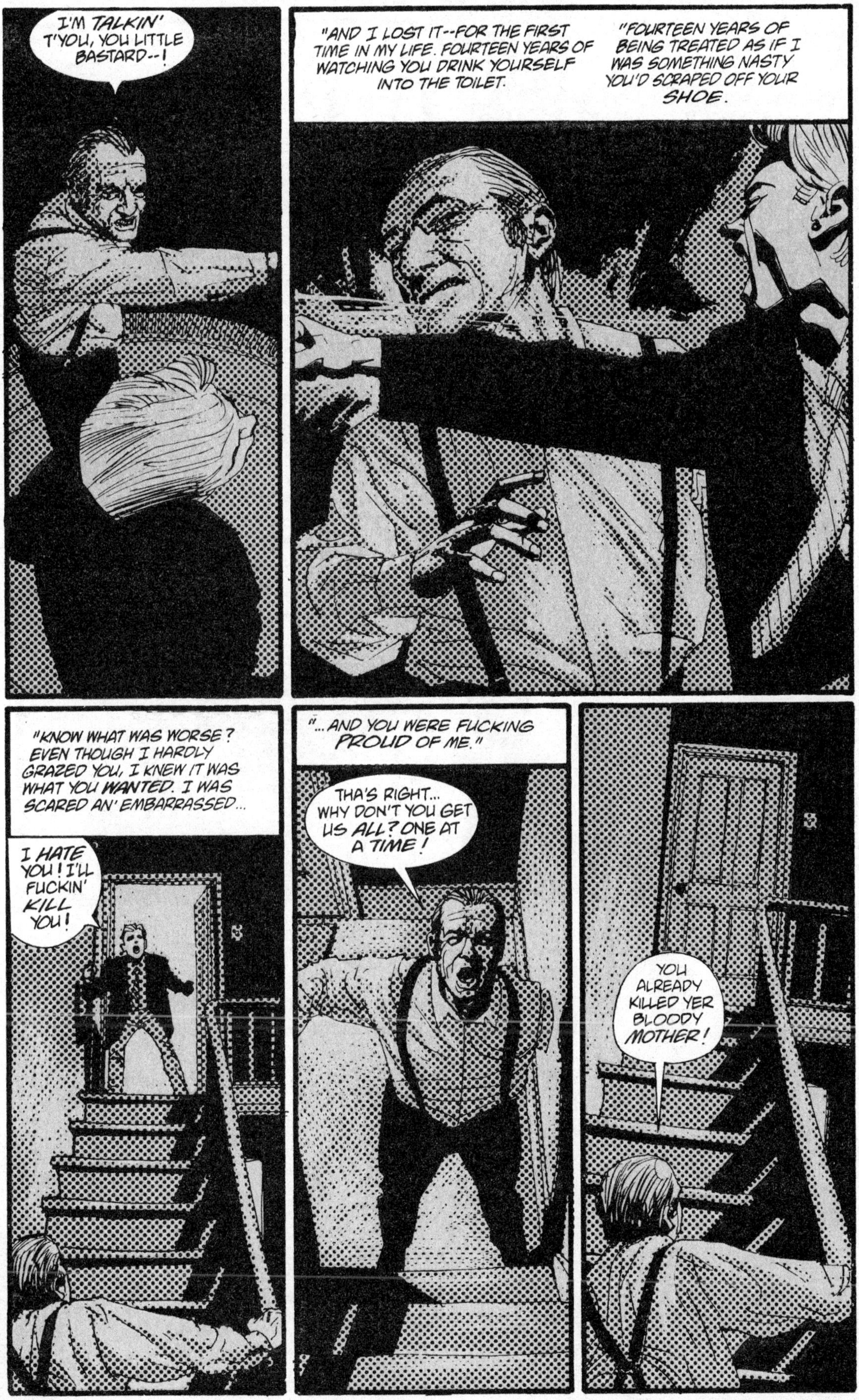
I'M TALKIN' T'YOU, YOU LITTLE BASTARD--!
"AND I LOST IT--FOR THE FIRST TIME IN MY LIFE. FOURTEEN YEARS OF WATCHING YOU DRINK YOURSELF INTO THE TOILET.
"FOURTEEN YEARS OF BEING TREATED AS IF I WAS SOMETHING NASTY YOU'D SCRAPED OFF YOUR SHOE.
"KNOW WHAT WAS WORSE? EVEN THOUGH I HARDLY GRAZED YOU, I KNEW IT WAS WHAT YOU WANTED. I WAS SCARED AN' EMBARRASSED...
I HATE YOU! I'LL FUCKIN' KILL YOU!
"...AND YOU WERE FUCKING PROUD OF ME."
THA'S RIGHT... WHY DON'T YOU GET US ALL? ONE AT A TIME!
YOU ALREADY KILLED YER BLOODY MOTHER!

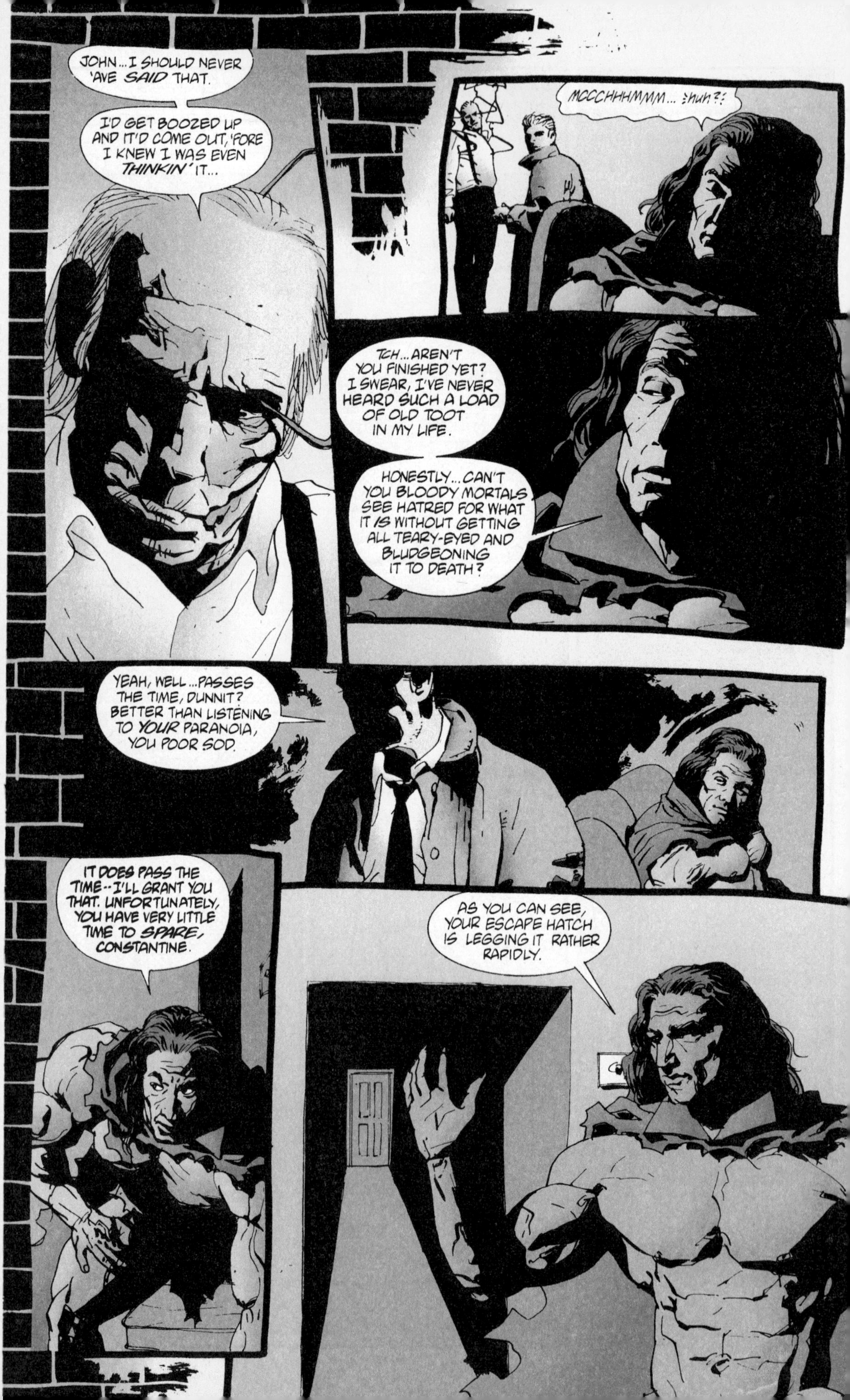
JOHN... I SHOULD NEVER 'AVE SAID THAT.
I'D GET BOOZED UP AND IT'D COME OUT, 'FORE I KNEW I WAS EVEN THINKIN' IT...
MCCCHHHMMM... huh?
TCH... AREN'T YOU FINISHED YET? I SWEAR, I'VE NEVER HEARD SUCH A LOAD OF OLD TOOT IN MY LIFE.
HONESTLY... CAN'T YOU BLOODY MORTALS SEE HATRED FOR WHAT IT IS WITHOUT GETTING ALL TEARY-EYED AND BLUDGEONING IT TO DEATH?
YEAH, WELL... PASSES THE TIME, DUNNIT? BETTER THAN LISTENING TO YOUR PARANOIA, YOU POOR SOD.
IT DOES PASS THE TIME -- I'LL GRANT YOU THAT. UNFORTUNATELY, YOU HAVE VERY LITTLE TIME TO SPARE, CONSTANTINE.
AS YOU CAN SEE, YOUR ESCAPE HATCH IS LEGGING IT RATHER RAPIDLY.

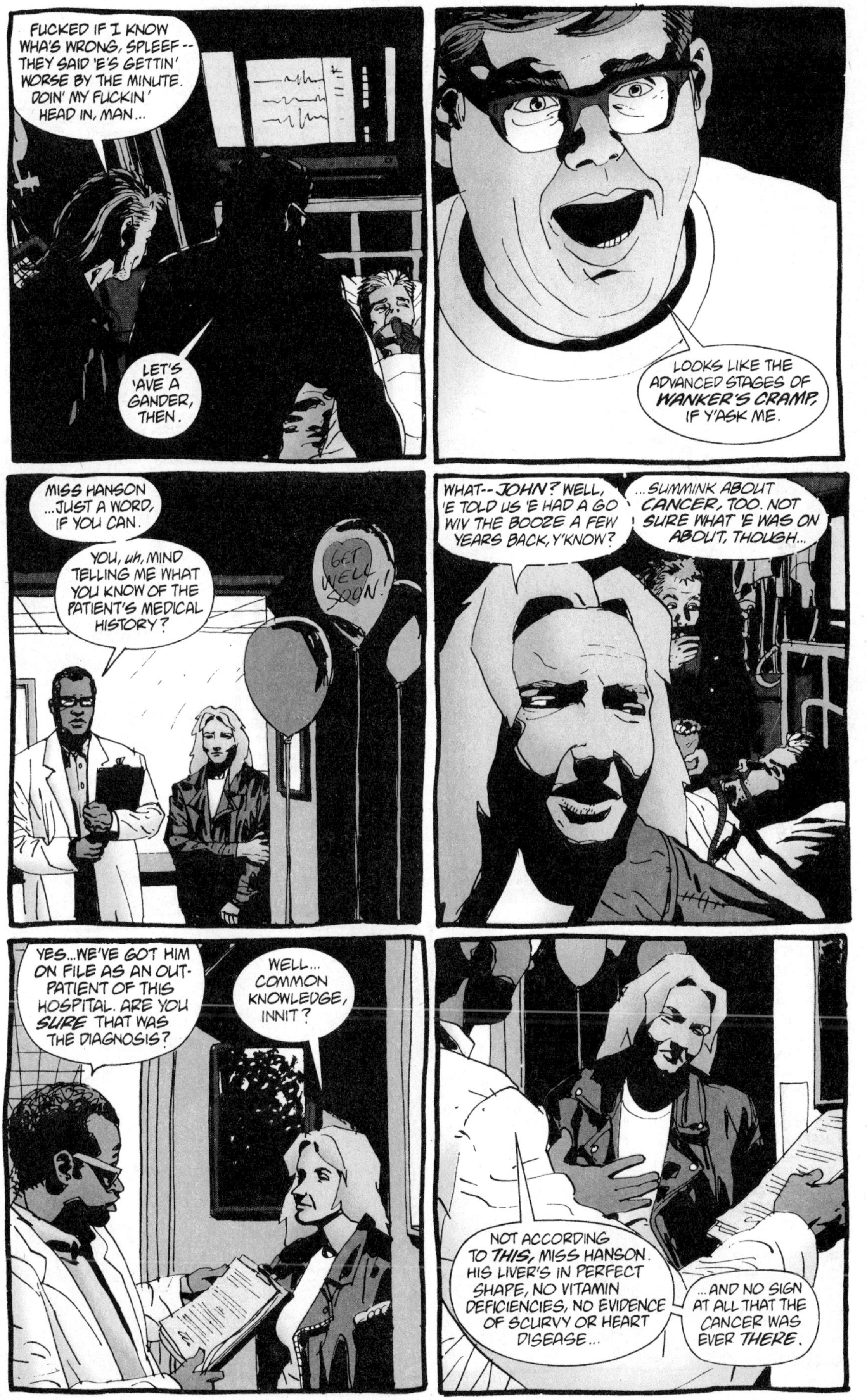
FUCKED IF I KNOW WHA'S WRONG, SPLEEF -- THEY SAID 'E'S GETTIN' WORSE BY THE MINUTE. DOIN' MY FUCKIN' HEAD IN, MAN...
LET'S 'AVE A GANDER, THEN.
LOOKS LIKE THE ADVANCED STAGES OF WANKER'S CRAMP, IF Y'ASK ME.
MISS HANSON ...JUST A WORD, IF YOU CAN.
YOU, uh, MIND TELLING ME WHAT YOU KNOW OF THE PATIENT'S MEDICAL HISTORY?
GET WELL SOON!
WHAT-- JOHN? WELL, 'E TOLD US 'E HAD A GO WIV THE BOOZE A FEW YEARS BACK, Y'KNOW?
...SUMMINK ABOUT CANCER, TOO. NOT SURE WHAT 'E WAS ON ABOUT, THOUGH...
YES... WE'VE GOT HIM ON FILE AS AN OUT-PATIENT OF THIS HOSPITAL. ARE YOU SURE THAT WAS THE DIAGNOSIS?
WELL... COMMON KNOWLEDGE, INNIT?
NOT ACCORDING TO THIS, MISS HANSON. HIS LIVER'S IN PERFECT SHAPE, NO VITAMIN DEFICIENCIES, NO EVIDENCE OF SCURVY OR HEART DISEASE...
...AND NO SIGN AT ALL THAT THE CANCER WAS EVER THERE.

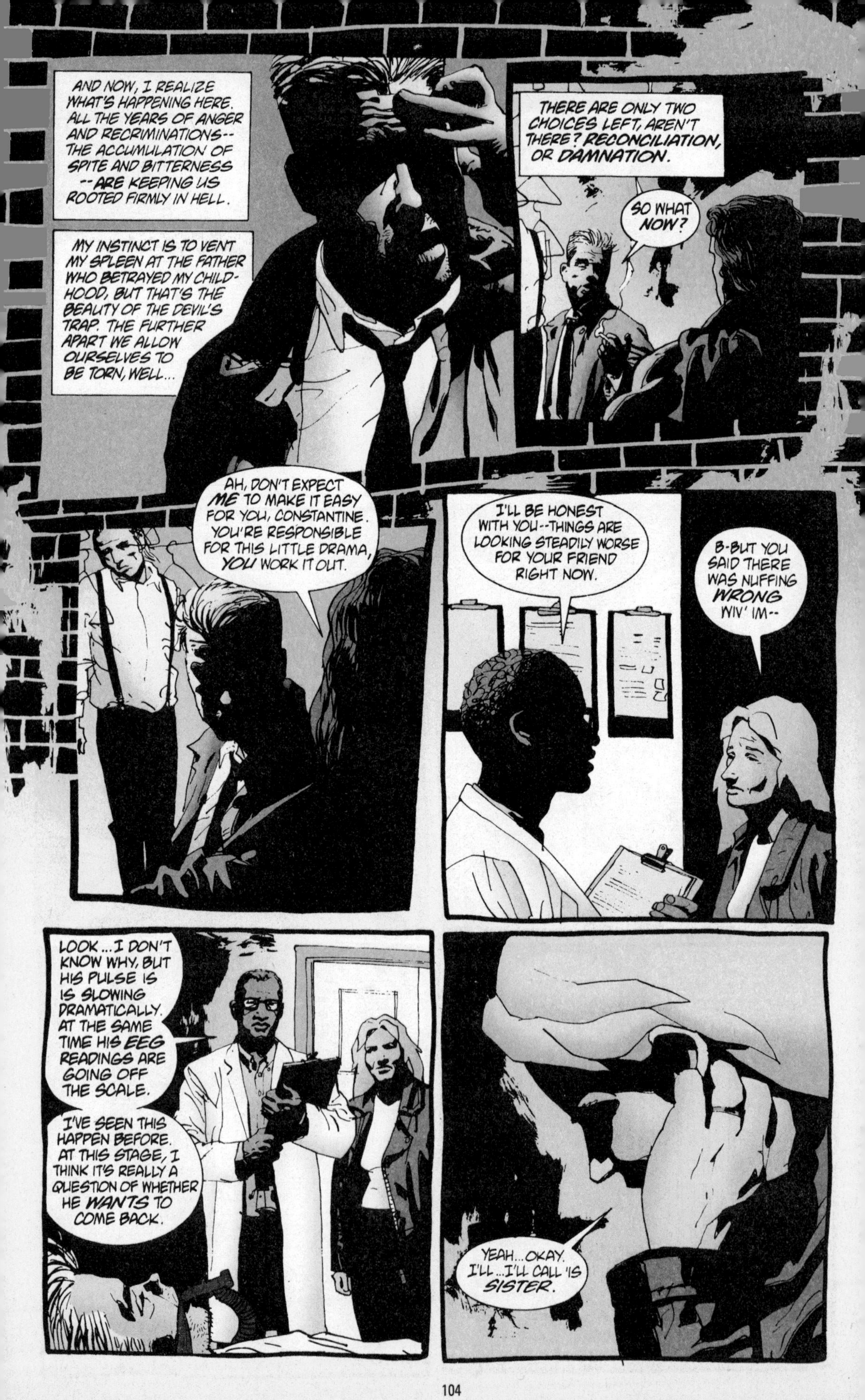

AND NOW, I REALIZE WHAT'S HAPPENING HERE. ALL THE YEARS OF ANGER AND RECRIMINATIONS-- THE ACCUMULATION OF SPITE AND BITTERNESS --ARE KEEPING US ROOTED FIRMLY IN HELL.
MY INSTINCT IS TO VENT MY SPLEEN AT THE FATHER WHO BETRAYED MY CHILD-HOOD, BUT THAT'S THE BEAUTY OF THE DEVIL'S TRAP. THE FURTHER APART WE ALLOW OURSELVES TO BE TORN, WELL...
THERE ARE ONLY TWO CHOICES LEFT, AREN'T THERE? RECONCILIATION, OR DAMNATION.
SO WHAT NOW?
AH, DON'T EXPECT ME TO MAKE IT EASY FOR YOU, CONSTANTINE. YOU'RE RESPONSIBLE FOR THIS LITTLE DRAMA, YOU WORK IT OUT.
I'LL BE HONEST WITH YOU--THINGS ARE LOOKING STEADILY WORSE FOR YOUR FRIEND RIGHT NOW.
B-BUT YOU SAID THERE WAS NUFFING WRONG WIV' IM--
LOOK... I DON'T KNOW WHY, BUT HIS PULSE IS IS SLOWING DRAMATICALLY. AT THE SAME TIME HIS EEG READINGS ARE GOING OFF THE SCALE.
I'VE SEEN THIS HAPPEN BEFORE. AT THIS STAGE, I THINK IT'S REALLY A QUESTION OF WHETHER HE WANTS TO COME BACK.
YEAH... OKAY. I'LL... I'LL CALL 'IS SISTER.

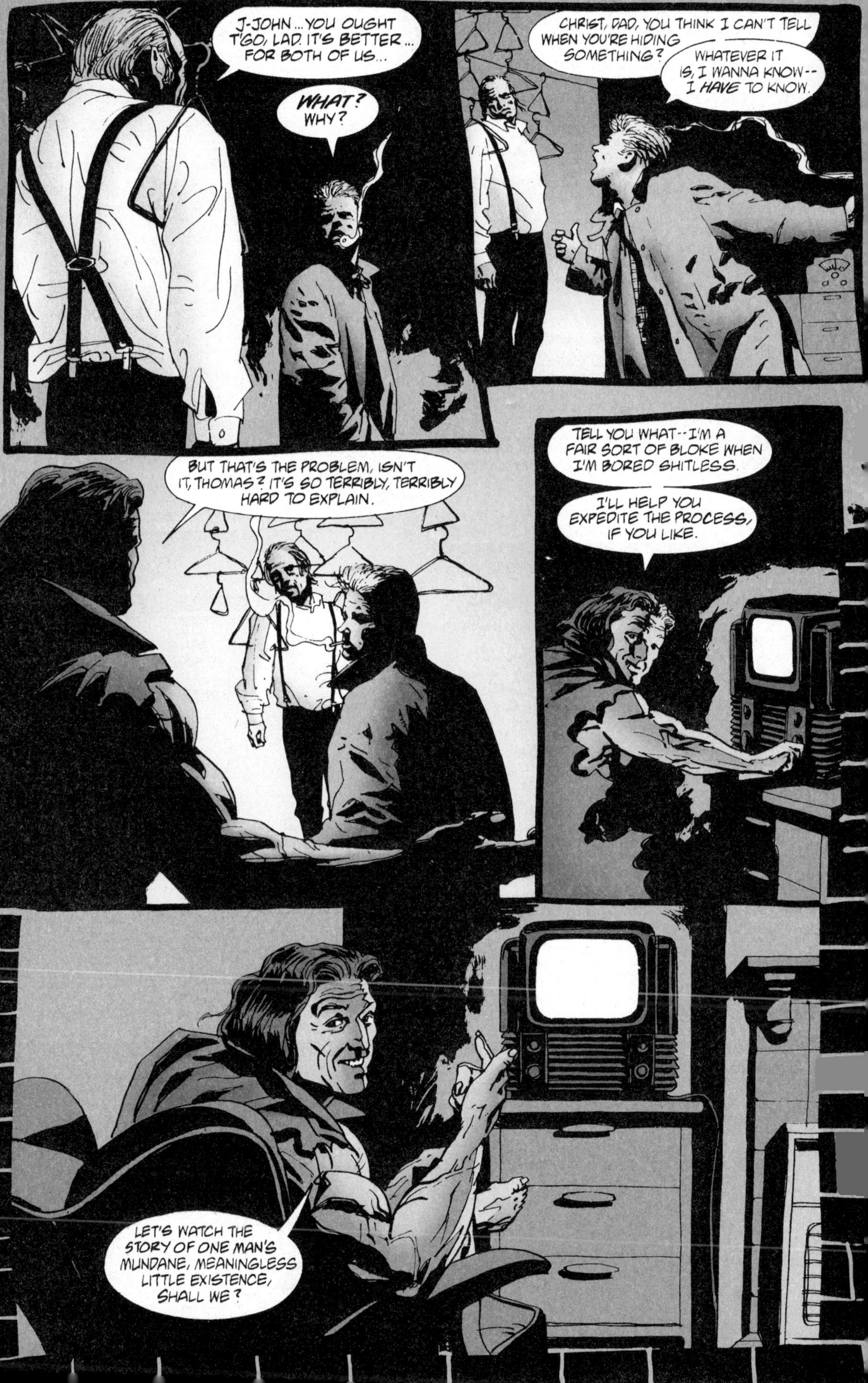
J-JOHN... YOU OUGHT T'GO, LAD. IT'S BETTER... FOR BOTH OF US...
WHAT? WHY?
CHRIST, DAD, YOU THINK I CAN'T TELL WHEN YOU'RE HIDING SOMETHING?
WHATEVER IT IS, I WANNA KNOW-- I HAVE TO KNOW.
BUT THAT'S THE PROBLEM, ISN'T IT, THOMAS? IT'S SO TERRIBLY, TERRIBLY HARD TO EXPLAIN.
TELL YOU WHAT--I'M A FAIR SORT OF BLOKE WHEN I'M BORED SHITLESS.
I'LL HELP YOU EXPEDITE THE PROCESS, IF YOU LIKE.
LET'S WATCH THE STORY OF ONE MAN'S MUNDANE, MEANINGLESS LITTLE EXISTENCE, SHALL WE?

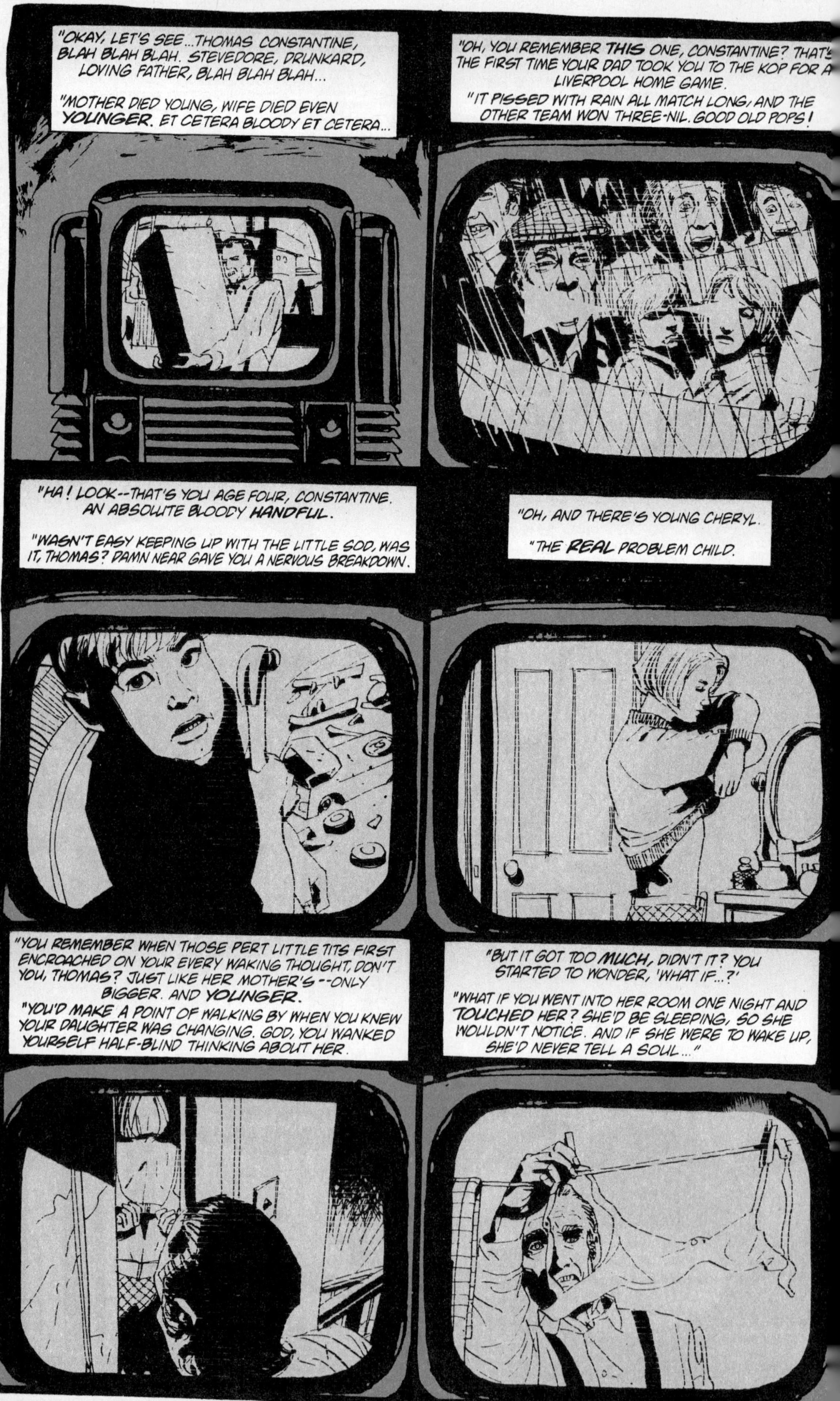
"OKAY, LET'S SEE...THOMAS CONSTANTINE, BLAH BLAH BLAH. STEVEDORE, DRUNKARD, LOVING FATHER, BLAH BLAH BLAH...
"MOTHER DIED YOUNG, WIFE DIED EVEN YOUNGER. ET CETERA BLOODY ET CETERA...
"OH, YOU REMEMBER THIS ONE, CONSTANTINE? THAT'S THE FIRST TIME YOUR DAD TOOK YOU TO THE KOP FOR A LIVERPOOL HOME GAME.
"IT PISSED WITH RAIN ALL MATCH LONG, AND THE OTHER TEAM WON THREE-NIL. GOOD OLD POPS!
"HA! LOOK--THAT'S YOU AGE FOUR, CONSTANTINE. AN ABSOLUTE BLOODY HANDFUL.
"WASN'T EASY KEEPING UP WITH THE LITTLE SOD, WAS IT, THOMAS? DAMN NEAR GAVE YOU A NERVOUS BREAKDOWN.
"OH, AND THERE'S YOUNG CHERYL.
"THE REAL PROBLEM CHILD.
"YOU REMEMBER WHEN THOSE PERT LITTLE TITS FIRST ENCROACHED ON YOUR EVERY WAKING THOUGHT, DON'T YOU, THOMAS? JUST LIKE HER MOTHER'S--ONLY BIGGER. AND YOUNGER.
"YOU'D MAKE A POINT OF WALKING BY WHEN YOU KNEW YOUR DAUGHTER WAS CHANGING. GOD, YOU WANKED YOURSELF HALF-BLIND THINKING ABOUT HER.
"BUT IT GOT TOO MUCH, DIDN'T IT? YOU STARTED TO WONDER, 'WHAT IF...?'
"WHAT IF YOU WENT INTO HER ROOM ONE NIGHT AND TOUCHED HER? SHE'D BE SLEEPING, SO SHE WOULDN'T NOTICE. AND IF SHE WERE TO WAKE UP, SHE'D NEVER TELL A SOUL..."

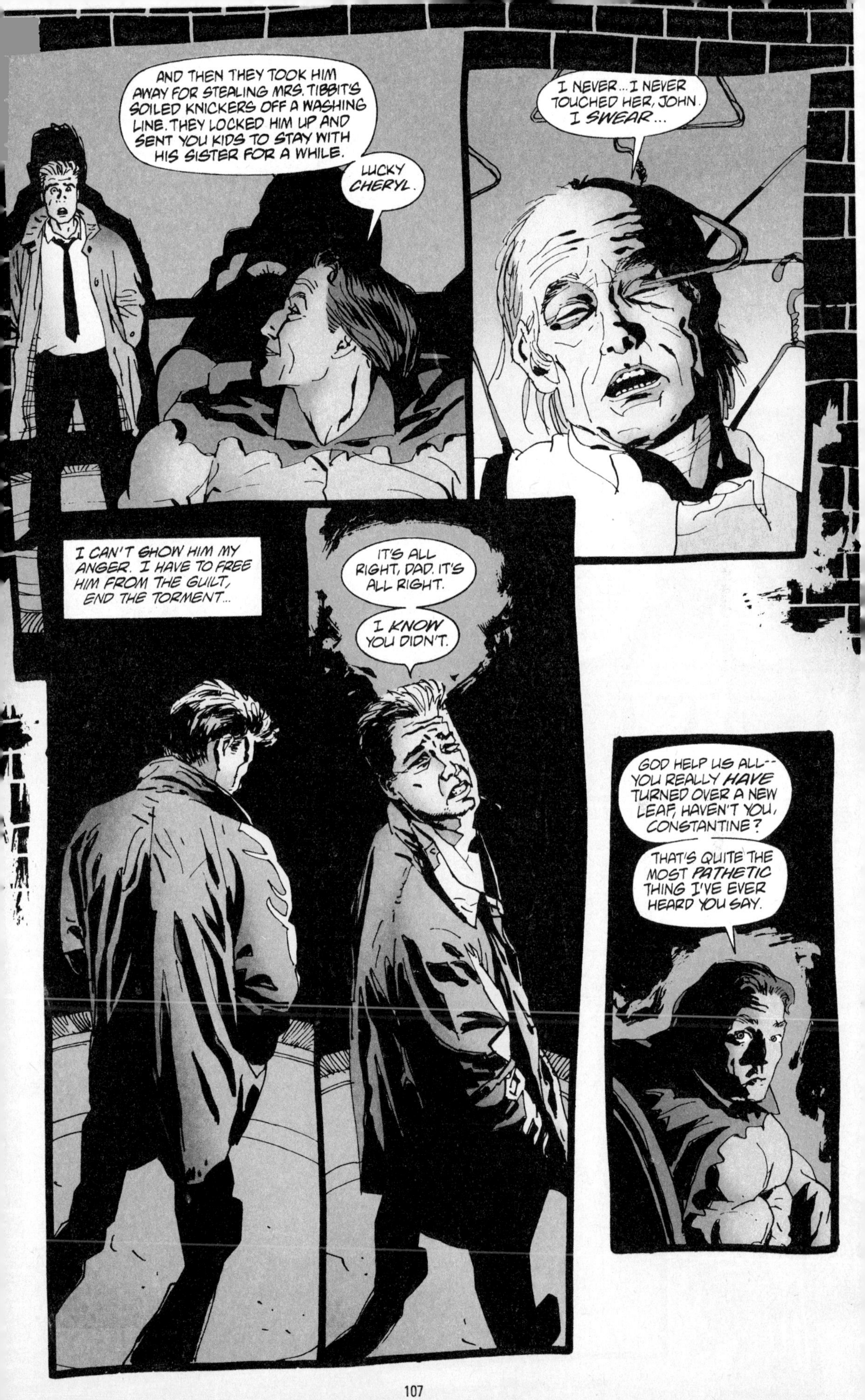
AND THEN THEY TOOK HIM AWAY FOR STEALING MRS. TIBBIT'S SOILED KNICKERS OFF A WASHING LINE. THEY LOCKED HIM UP AND SENT YOU KIDS TO STAY WITH HIS SISTER FOR A WHILE.
LUCKY CHERYL.
I NEVER... I NEVER TOUCHED HER, JOHN. I SWEAR...
I CAN'T SHOW HIM MY ANGER. I HAVE TO FREE HIM FROM THE GUILT, END THE TORMENT...
IT'S ALL RIGHT, DAD. IT'S ALL RIGHT.
I KNOW YOU DIDN'T.
GOD HELP US ALL-- YOU REALLY HAVE TURNED OVER A NEW LEAF, HAVEN'T YOU, CONSTANTINE?
THAT'S QUITE THE MOST PATHETIC THING I'VE EVER HEARD YOU SAY.

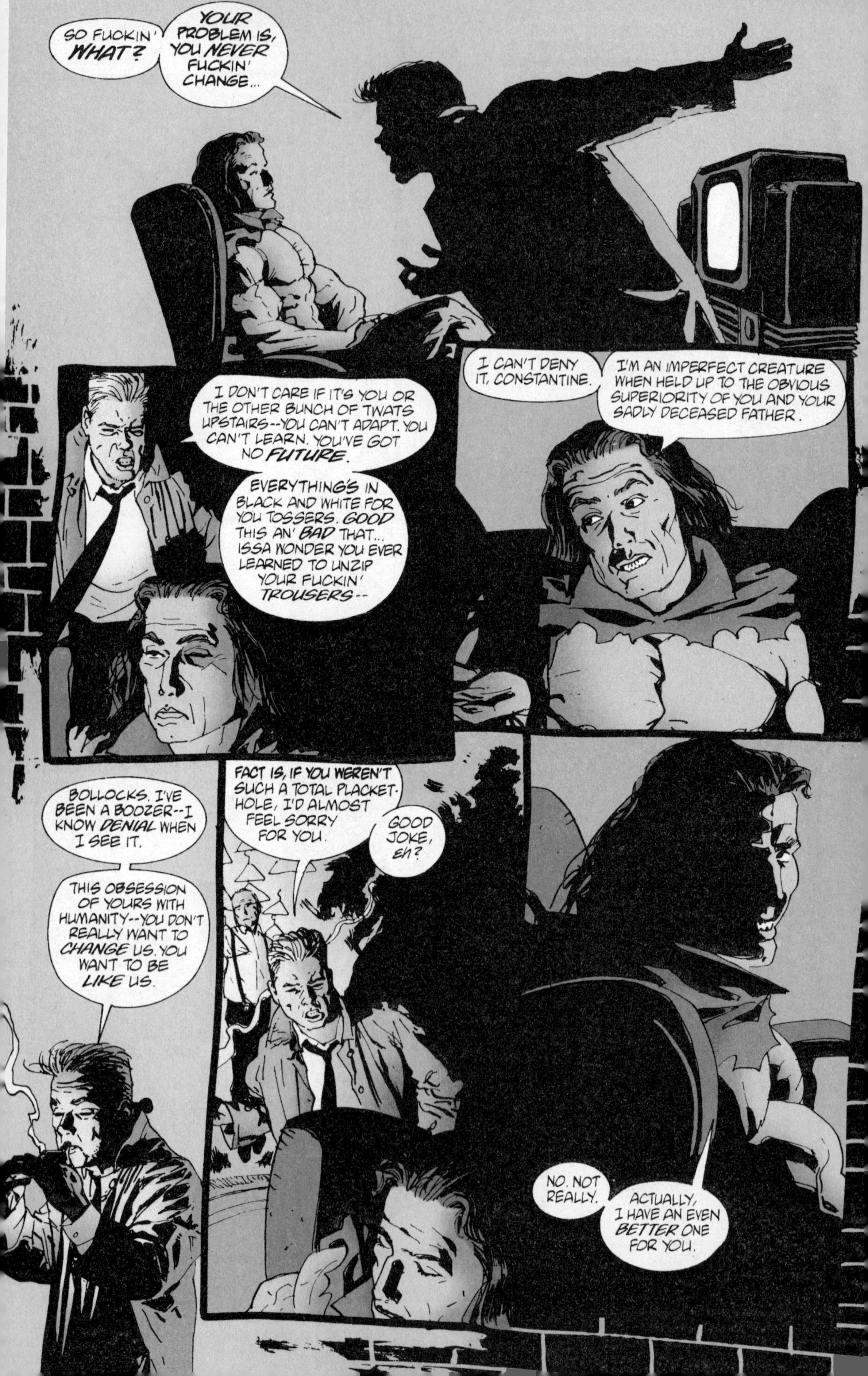
SO FUCKIN' WHAT?
YOUR PROBLEM IS, YOU NEVER FUCKIN' CHANGE...
I DON'T CARE IF IT'S YOU OR THE OTHER BUNCH OF TWATS UPSTAIRS--YOU CAN'T ADAPT. YOU CAN'T LEARN. YOU'VE GOT NO FUTURE.
EVERYTHING'S IN BLACK AND WHITE FOR YOU TOSSERS. GOOD THIS AN' BAD THAT... ISSA WONDER YOU EVER LEARNED TO UNZIP YOUR FUCKIN' TROUSERS--
I CAN'T DENY IT, CONSTANTINE.
I'M AN IMPERFECT CREATURE WHEN HELD UP TO THE OBVIOUS SUPERIORITY OF YOU AND YOUR SADLY DECEASED FATHER.
BOLLOCKS. I'VE BEEN A BOOZER--I KNOW DENIAL WHEN I SEE IT.
THIS OBSESSION OF YOURS WITH HUMANITY--YOU DON'T REALLY WANT TO CHANGE US. YOU WANT TO BE LIKE US.
FACT IS, IF YOU WEREN'T SUCH A TOTAL PLACKET-HOLE, I'D ALMOST FEEL SORRY FOR YOU.
GOOD JOKE, EH?
NO. NOT REALLY.
ACTUALLY, I HAVE AN EVEN BETTER ONE FOR YOU.

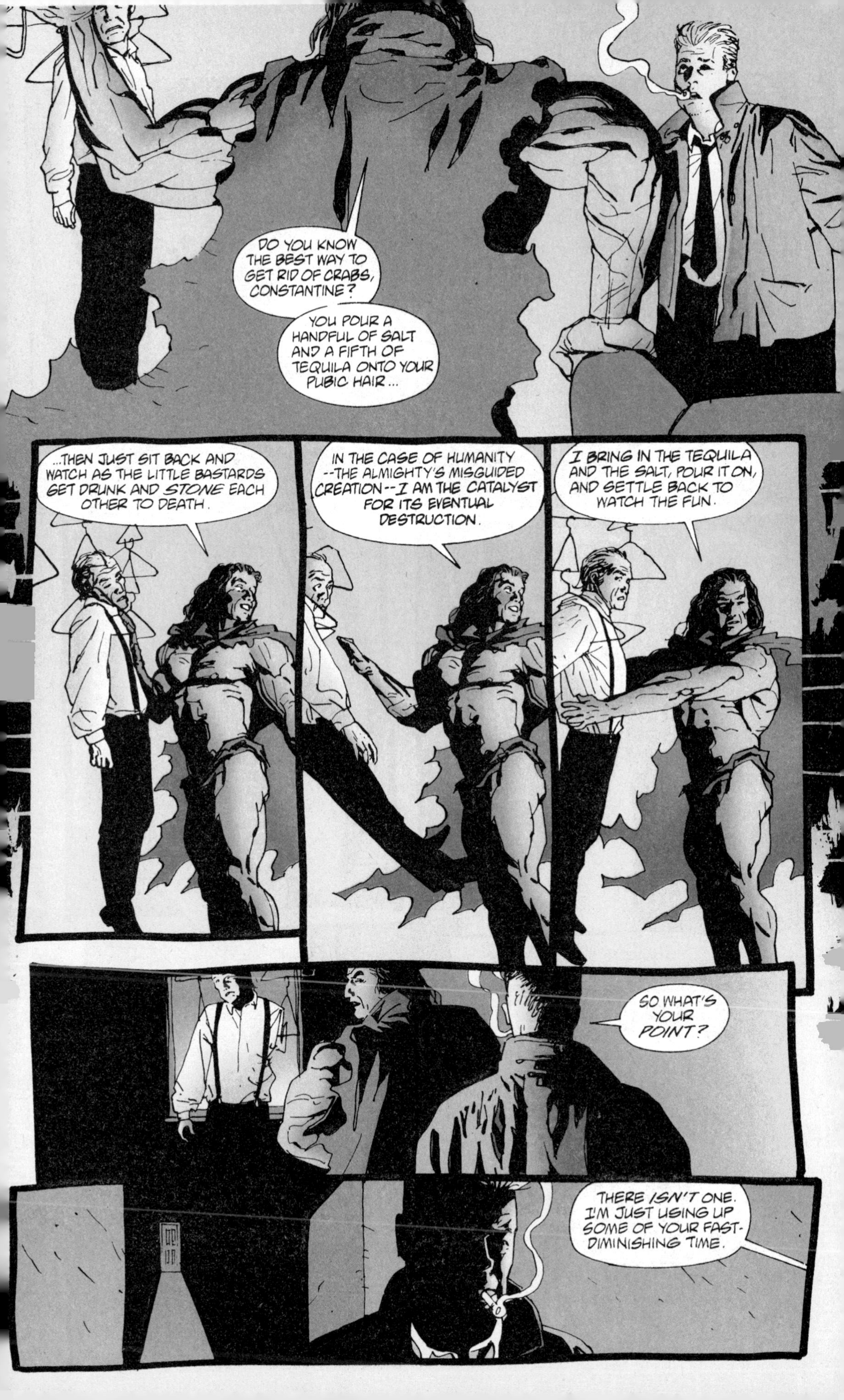
DO YOU KNOW THE BEST WAY TO GET RID OF CRABS, CONSTANTINE?
YOU POUR A HANDFUL OF SALT AND A FIFTH OF TEQUILA ONTO YOUR PUBIC HAIR...
...THEN JUST SIT BACK AND WATCH AS THE LITTLE BASTARDS GET DRUNK AND STONE EACH OTHER TO DEATH.
IN THE CASE OF HUMANITY --THE ALMIGHTY'S MISGUIDED CREATION--I AM THE CATALYST FOR ITS EVENTUAL DESTRUCTION.
I BRING IN THE TEQUILA AND THE SALT, POUR IT ON, AND SETTLE BACK TO WATCH THE FUN.
SO WHAT'S YOUR POINT?
THERE ISN'T ONE. I'M JUST USING UP SOME OF YOUR FAST-DIMINISHING TIME.

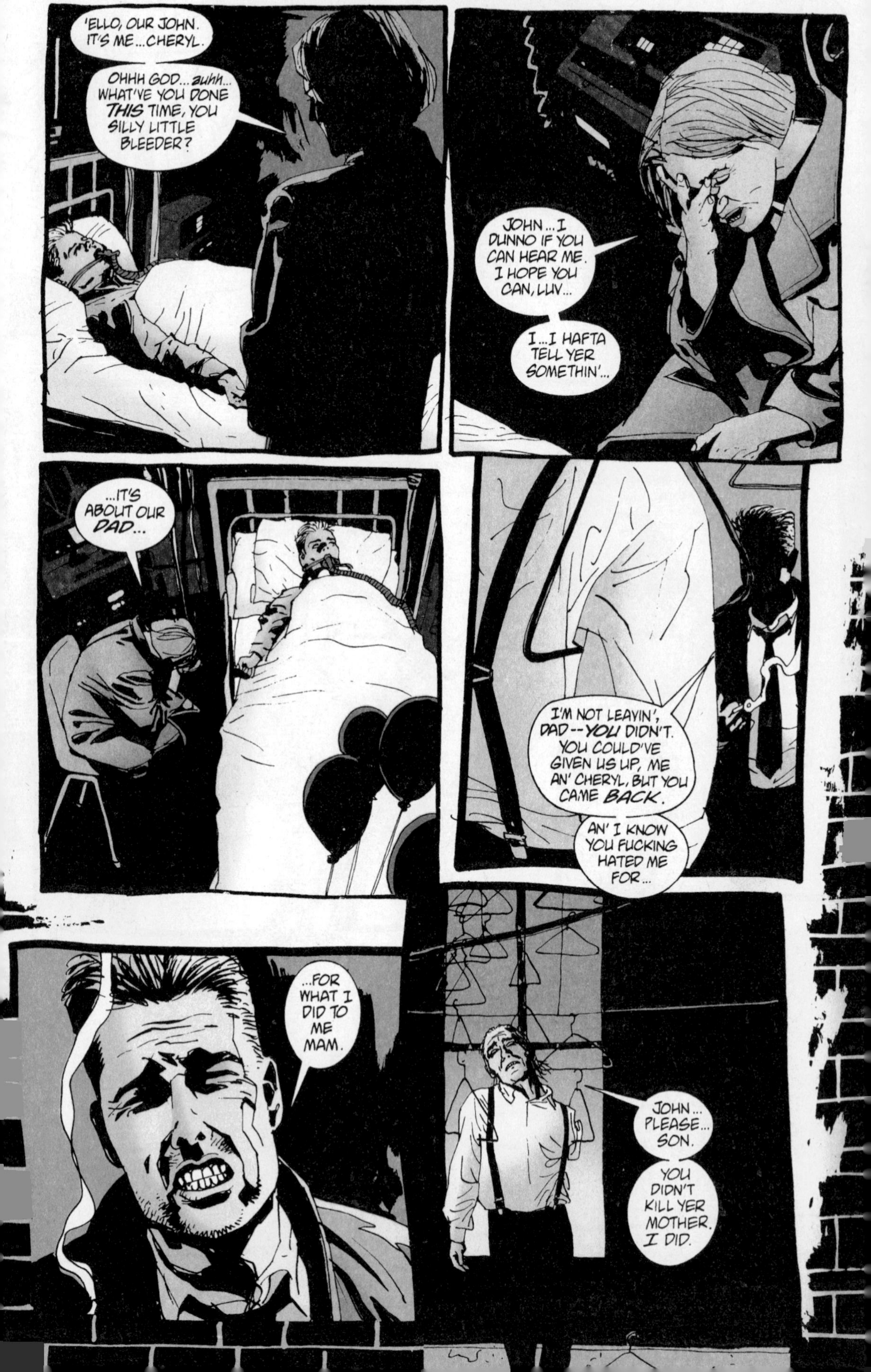
'ELLO, OUR JOHN. IT'S ME...CHERYL.
OHHH GOD... auhh... WHAT'VE YOU DONE THIS TIME, YOU SILLY LITTLE BLEEDER?
JOHN... I DUNNO IF YOU CAN HEAR ME. I HOPE YOU CAN, LUV...
I...I HAFTA TELL YER SOMETHIN'...
...IT'S ABOUT OUR DAD...
I'M NOT LEAVIN', DAD--YOU DIDN'T. YOU COULD'VE GIVEN US UP, ME AN' CHERYL, BUT YOU CAME BACK.
AN' I KNOW YOU FUCKING HATED ME FOR...
...FOR WHAT I DID TO ME MAM.
JOHN... PLEASE... SON.
YOU DIDN'T KILL YER MOTHER. I DID.

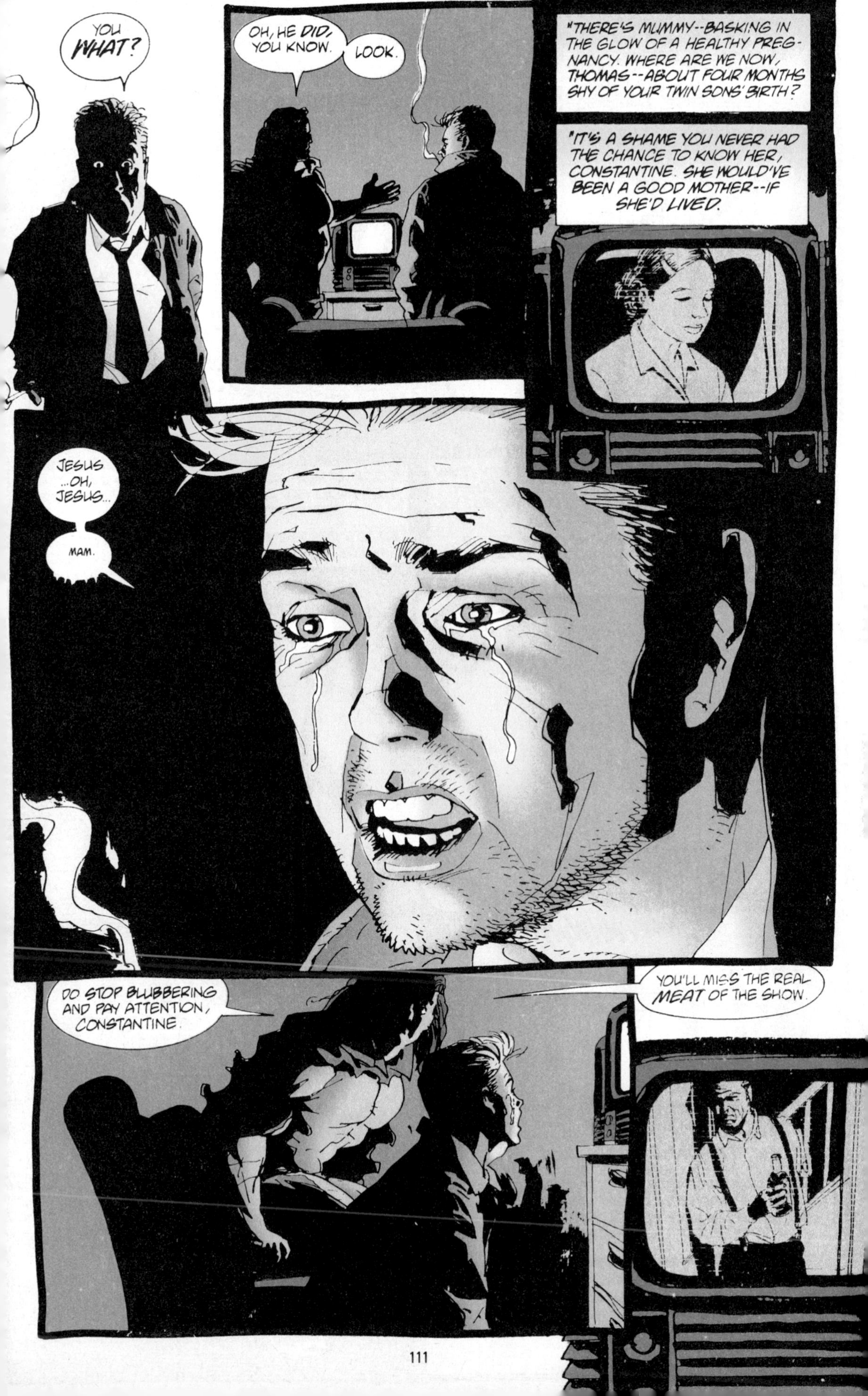

YOU WHAT?
OH, HE DID, YOU KNOW.
LOOK.
"THERE'S MUMMY--BASKING IN THE GLOW OF A HEALTHY PREGNANCY. WHERE ARE WE NOW, THOMAS--ABOUT FOUR MONTHS SHY OF YOUR TWIN SONS' BIRTH?
"IT'S A SHAME YOU NEVER HAD THE CHANCE TO KNOW HER, CONSTANTINE. SHE WOULD'VE BEEN A GOOD MOTHER--IF SHE'D LIVED.
JESUS ...OH, JESUS...
MAM.
DO STOP BLUBBERING AND PAY ATTENTION, CONSTANTINE.
YOU'LL MISS THE REAL MEAT OF THE SHOW.

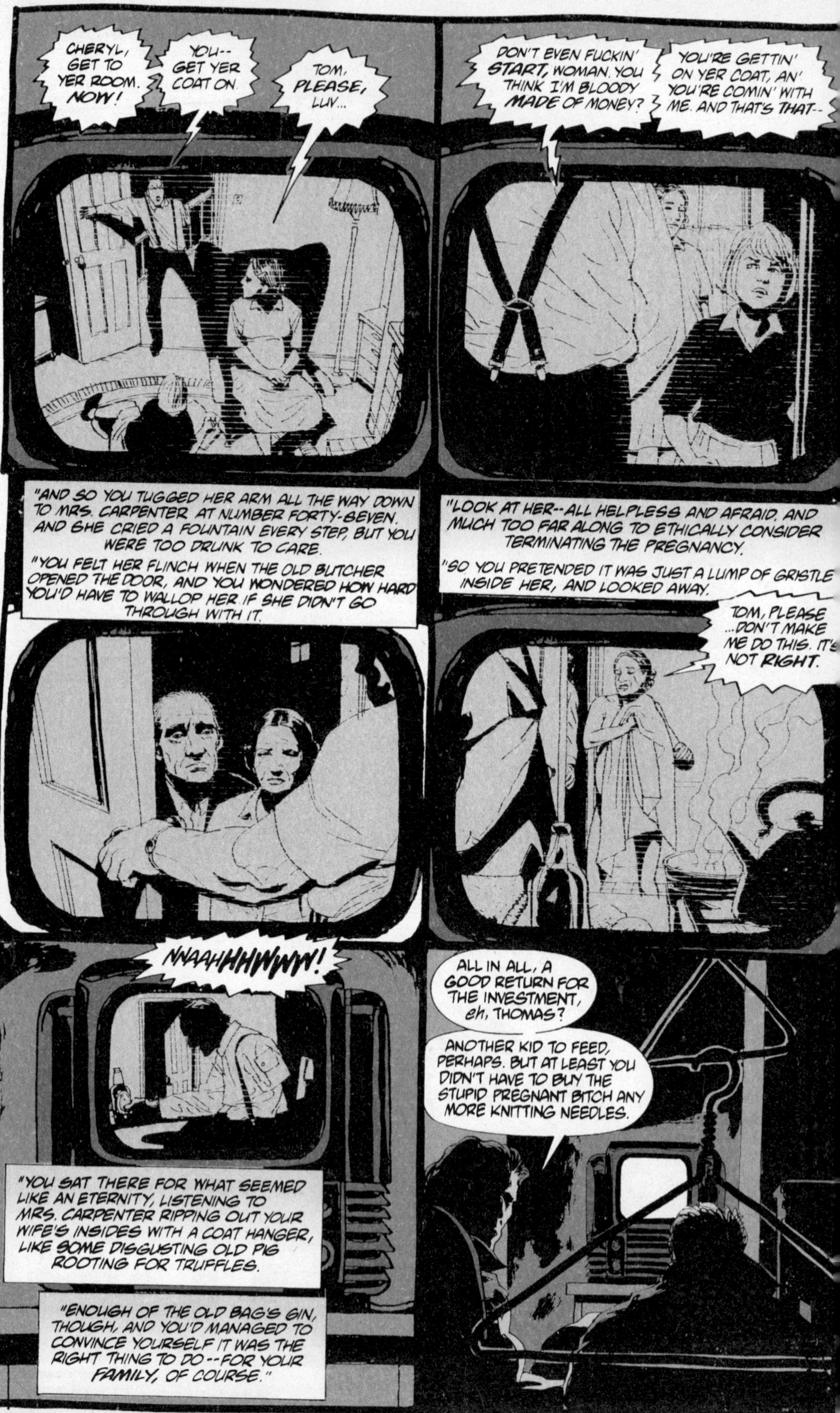
CHERYL, GET TO YER ROOM. NOW!
YOU-- GET YER COAT ON.
TOM, PLEASE, LUV...
DON'T EVEN FUCKIN' START, WOMAN. YOU THINK I'M BLOODY MADE OF MONEY?
YOU'RE GETTIN' ON YER COAT, AN' YOU'RE COMIN' WITH ME. AND THAT'S THAT--
"AND SO YOU TUGGED HER ARM ALL THE WAY DOWN TO MRS. CARPENTER AT NUMBER FORTY-SEVEN. AND SHE CRIED A FOUNTAIN EVERY STEP, BUT YOU WERE TOO DRUNK TO CARE.
"YOU FELT HER FLINCH WHEN THE OLD BUTCHER OPENED THE DOOR, AND YOU WONDERED HOW HARD YOU'D HAVE TO WALLOP HER IF SHE DIDN'T GO THROUGH WITH IT.
"LOOK AT HER--ALL HELPLESS AND AFRAID. AND MUCH TOO FAR ALONG TO ETHICALLY CONSIDER TERMINATING THE PREGNANCY.
"SO YOU PRETENDED IT WAS JUST A LUMP OF GRISTLE INSIDE HER, AND LOOKED AWAY.
TOM, PLEASE ...DON'T MAKE ME DO THIS. IT'S NOT RIGHT.
NNAAAHHHWWW!
"YOU SAT THERE FOR WHAT SEEMED LIKE AN ETERNITY, LISTENING TO MRS. CARPENTER RIPPING OUT YOUR WIFE'S INSIDES WITH A COAT HANGER, LIKE SOME DISGUSTING OLD PIG ROOTING FOR TRUFFLES.
"ENOUGH OF THE OLD BAG'S GIN, THOUGH, AND YOU'D MANAGED TO CONVINCE YOURSELF IT WAS THE RIGHT THING TO DO--FOR YOUR FAMILY, OF COURSE."
ALL IN ALL, A GOOD RETURN FOR THE INVESTMENT, eh, THOMAS?
ANOTHER KID TO FEED, PERHAPS. BUT AT LEAST YOU DIDN'T HAVE TO BUY THE STUPID PREGNANT BITCH ANY MORE KNITTING NEEDLES.

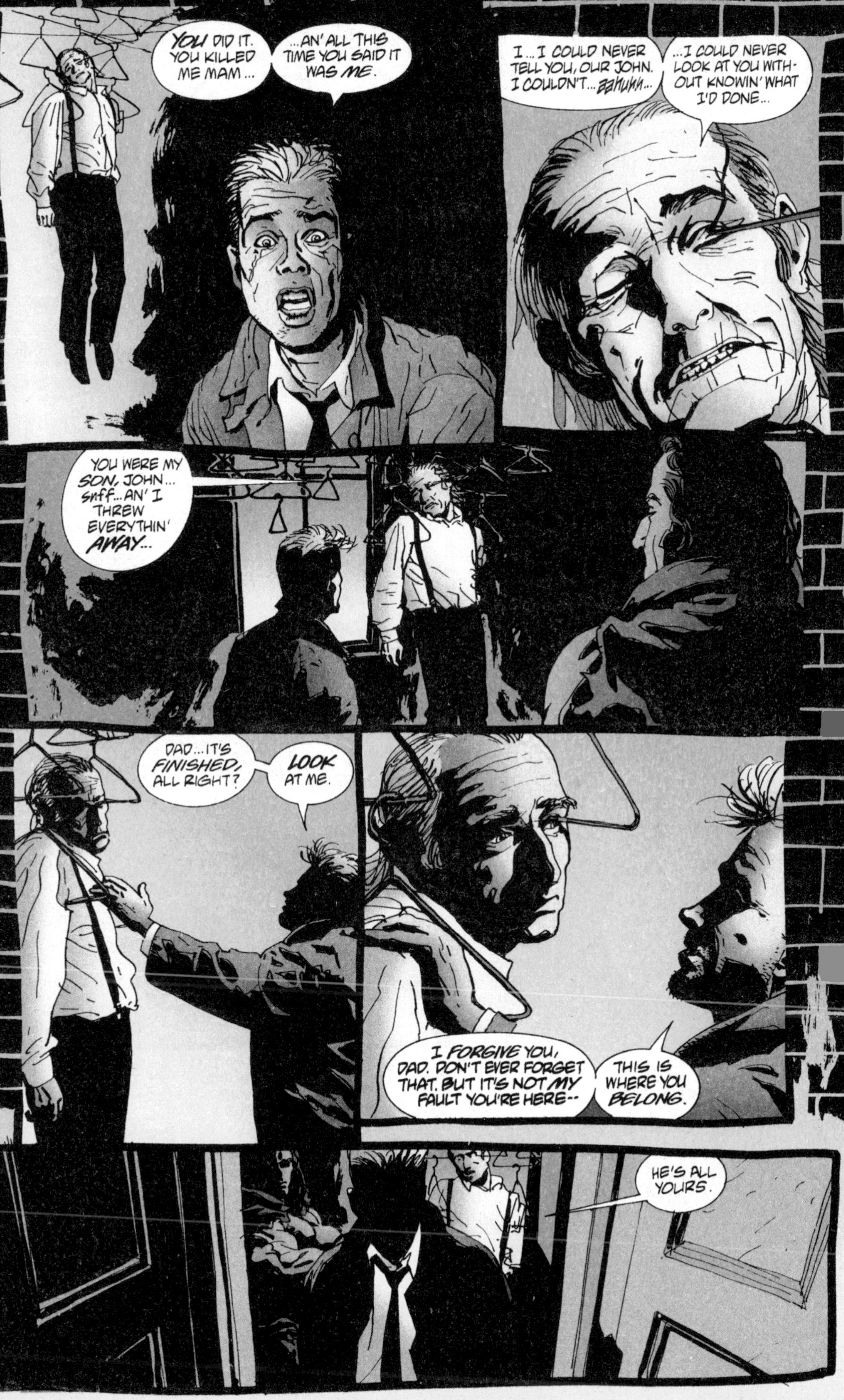

YOU DID IT. YOU KILLED ME MAM...
...AN' ALL THIS TIME YOU SAID IT WAS ME.
I... I COULD NEVER TELL YOU, OUR JOHN. I COULDN'T... aahukh...
...I COULD NEVER LOOK AT YOU WITH-OUT KNOWIN' WHAT I'D DONE...
YOU WERE MY SON, JOHN... snff... AN' I THREW EVERYTHIN' AWAY...
DAD... IT'S FINISHED, ALL RIGHT?
LOOK AT ME.
I FORGIVE YOU, DAD. DON'T EVER FORGET THAT. BUT IT'S NOT MY FAULT YOU'RE HERE--
THIS IS WHERE YOU BELONG.
HE'S ALL YOURS.

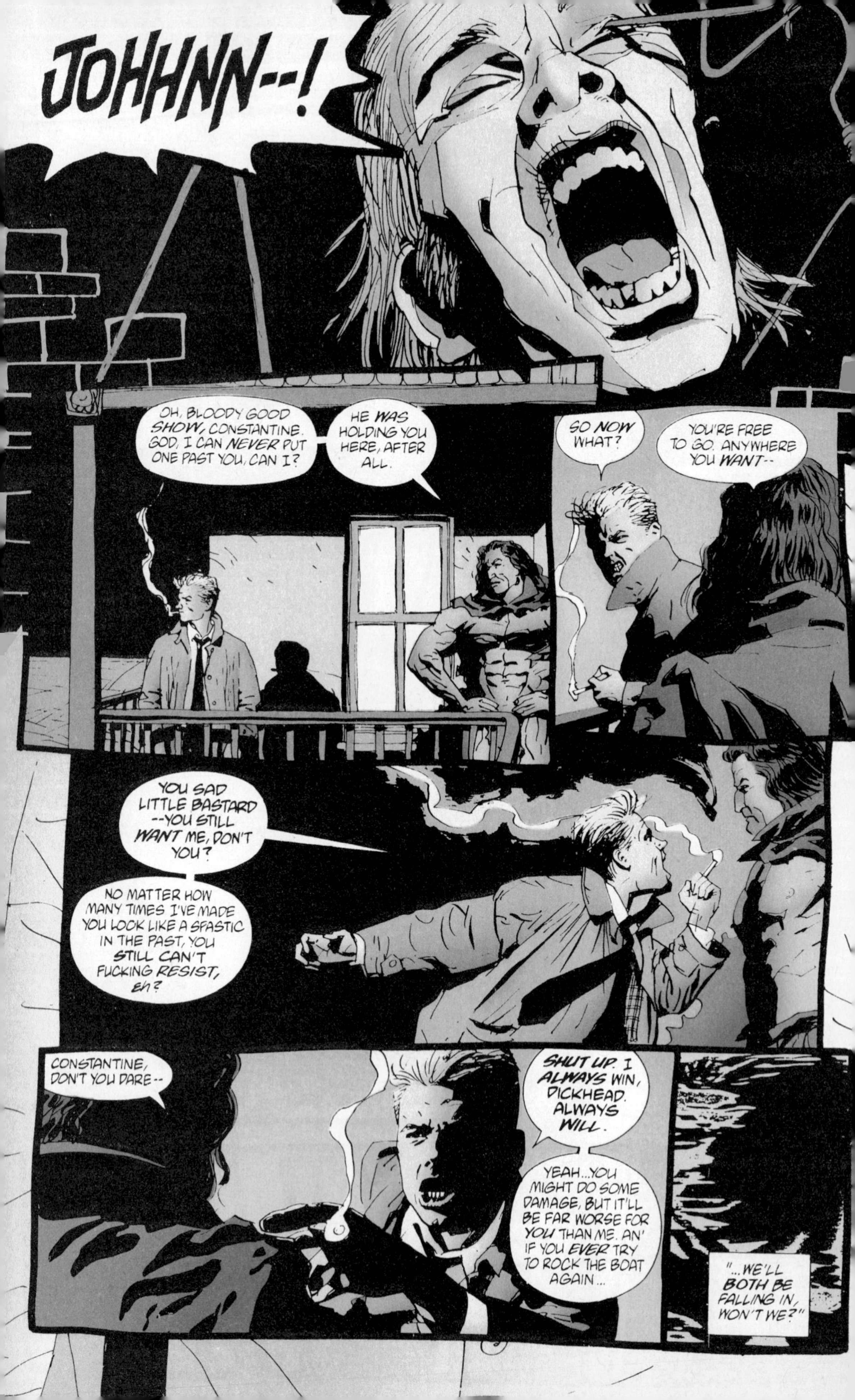

JOHHNN--!
OH, BLOODY GOOD SHOW, CONSTANTINE. GOD, I CAN NEVER PUT ONE PAST YOU, CAN I?
HE WAS HOLDING YOU HERE, AFTER ALL.
SO NOW WHAT?
YOU'RE FREE TO GO. ANYWHERE YOU WANT--
YOU SAD LITTLE BASTARD --YOU STILL WANT ME, DON'T YOU?
NO MATTER HOW MANY TIMES I'VE MADE YOU LOOK LIKE A SPASTIC IN THE PAST, YOU STILL CAN'T FUCKING RESIST, EH?
CONSTANTINE, DON'T YOU DARE--
SHUT UP. I ALWAYS WIN, DICKHEAD. ALWAYS WILL.
YEAH...YOU MIGHT DO SOME DAMAGE, BUT IT'LL BE FAR WORSE FOR YOU THAN ME. AN' IF YOU EVER TRY TO ROCK THE BOAT AGAIN...
"...WE'LL BOTH BE FALLING IN, WON'T WE?"

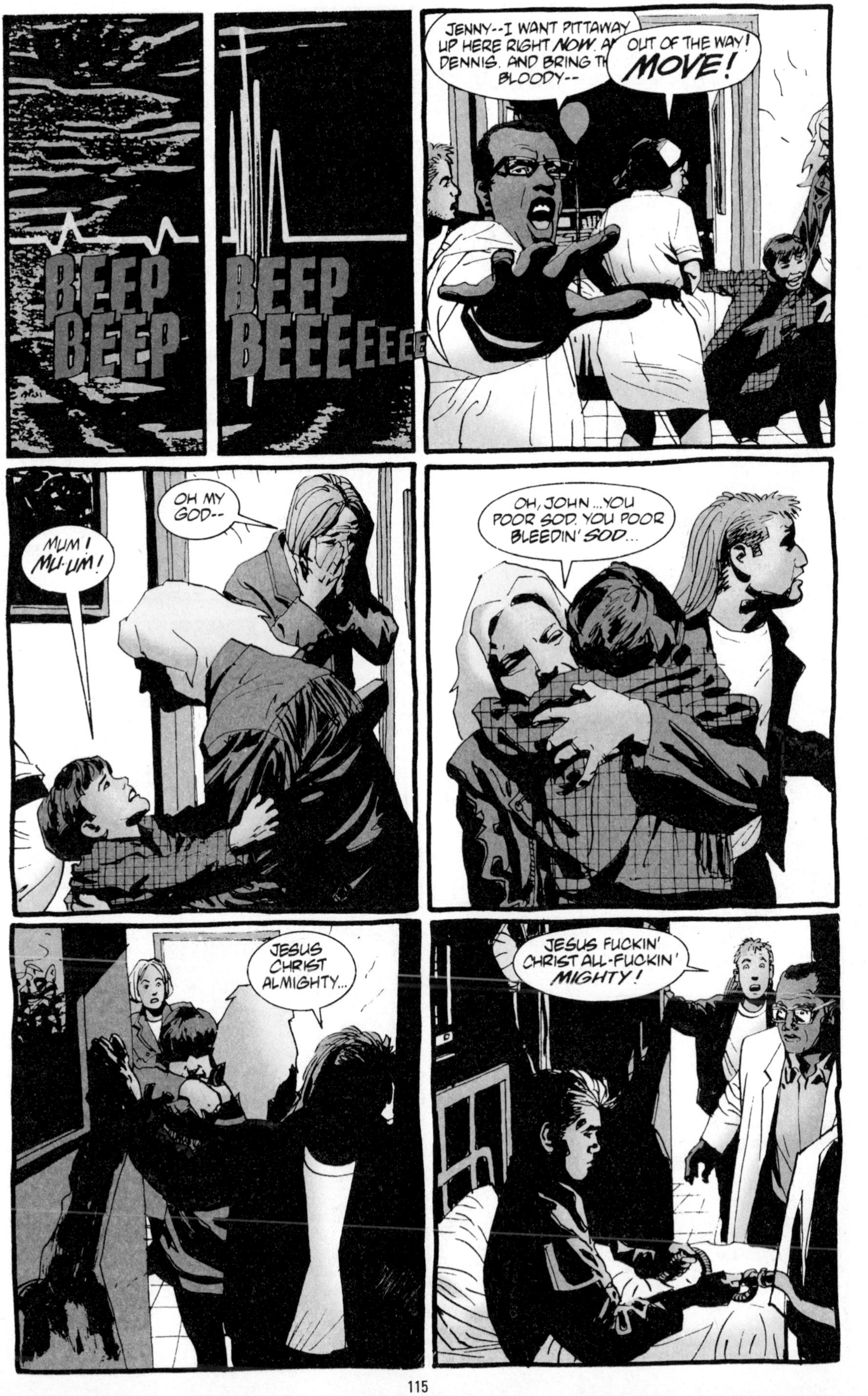
BEEP BEEP
BEEP BEEEEEEE
JENNY--I WANT PITTAWAY UP HERE RIGHT NOW. AN DENNIS. AND BRING TH BLOODY--
OUT OF THE WAY! MOVE!
MUM! MU-UM!
OH MY GOD--
OH, JOHN...YOU POOR SOD. YOU POOR BLEEDIN' SOD...
JESUS CHRIST ALMIGHTY...
JESUS FUCKIN' CHRIST ALL-FUCKIN' MIGHTY!

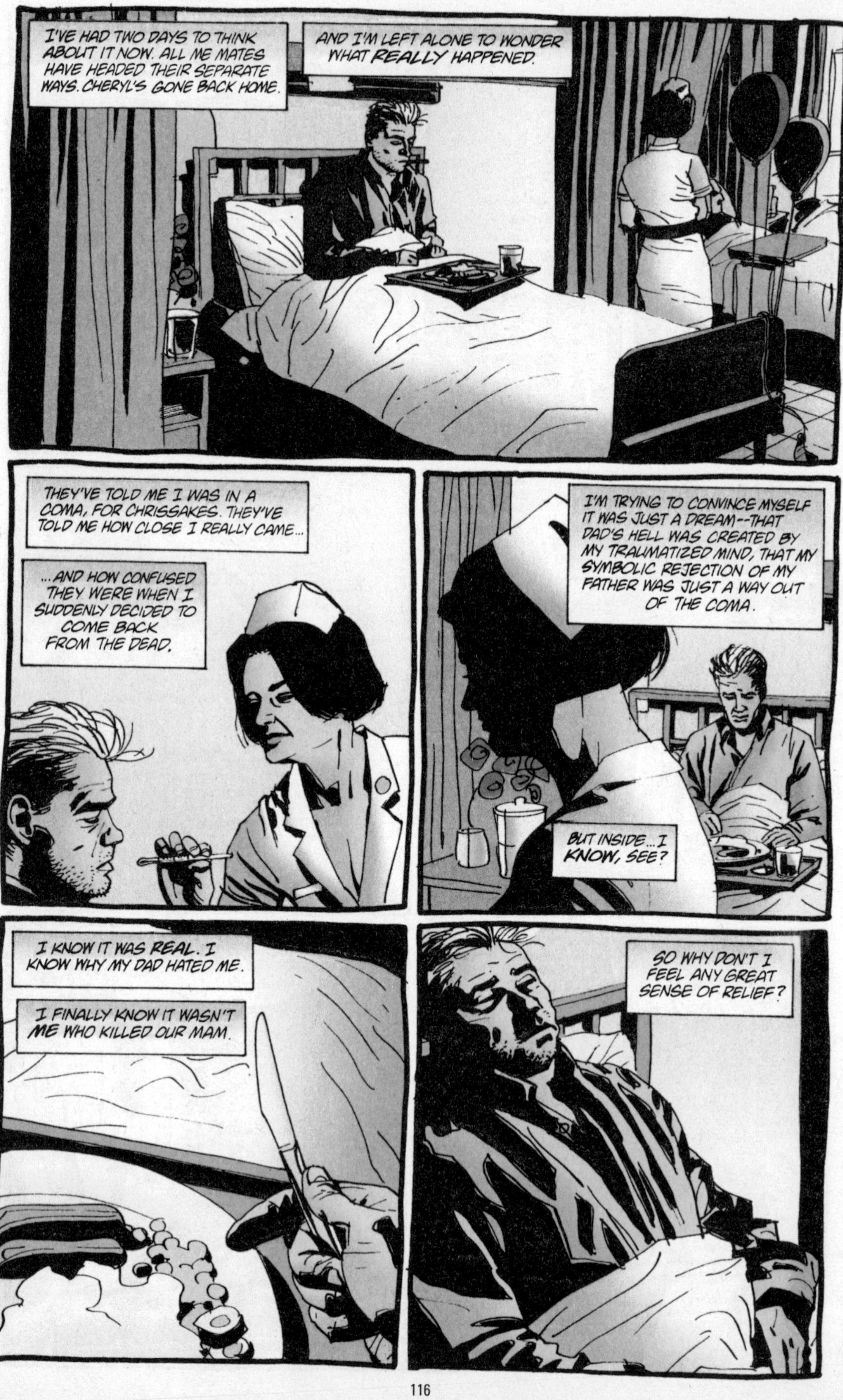
I'VE HAD TWO DAYS TO THINK ABOUT IT NOW. ALL ME MATES HAVE HEADED THEIR SEPARATE WAYS. CHERYL'S GONE BACK HOME.
AND I'M LEFT ALONE TO WONDER WHAT REALLY HAPPENED.
THEY'VE TOLD ME I WAS IN A COMA, FOR CHRISSAKES. THEY'VE TOLD ME HOW CLOSE I REALLY CAME...
...AND HOW CONFUSED THEY WERE WHEN I SUDDENLY DECIDED TO COME BACK FROM THE DEAD.
I'M TRYING TO CONVINCE MYSELF IT WAS JUST A DREAM--THAT DAD'S HELL WAS CREATED BY MY TRAUMATIZED MIND, THAT MY SYMBOLIC REJECTION OF MY FATHER WAS JUST A WAY OUT OF THE COMA.
BUT INSIDE... I KNOW, SEE?
I KNOW IT WAS REAL. I KNOW WHY MY DAD HATED ME.
I FINALLY KNOW IT WASN'T ME WHO KILLED OUR MAM.
SO WHY DON'T I FEEL ANY GREAT SENSE OF RELIEF?

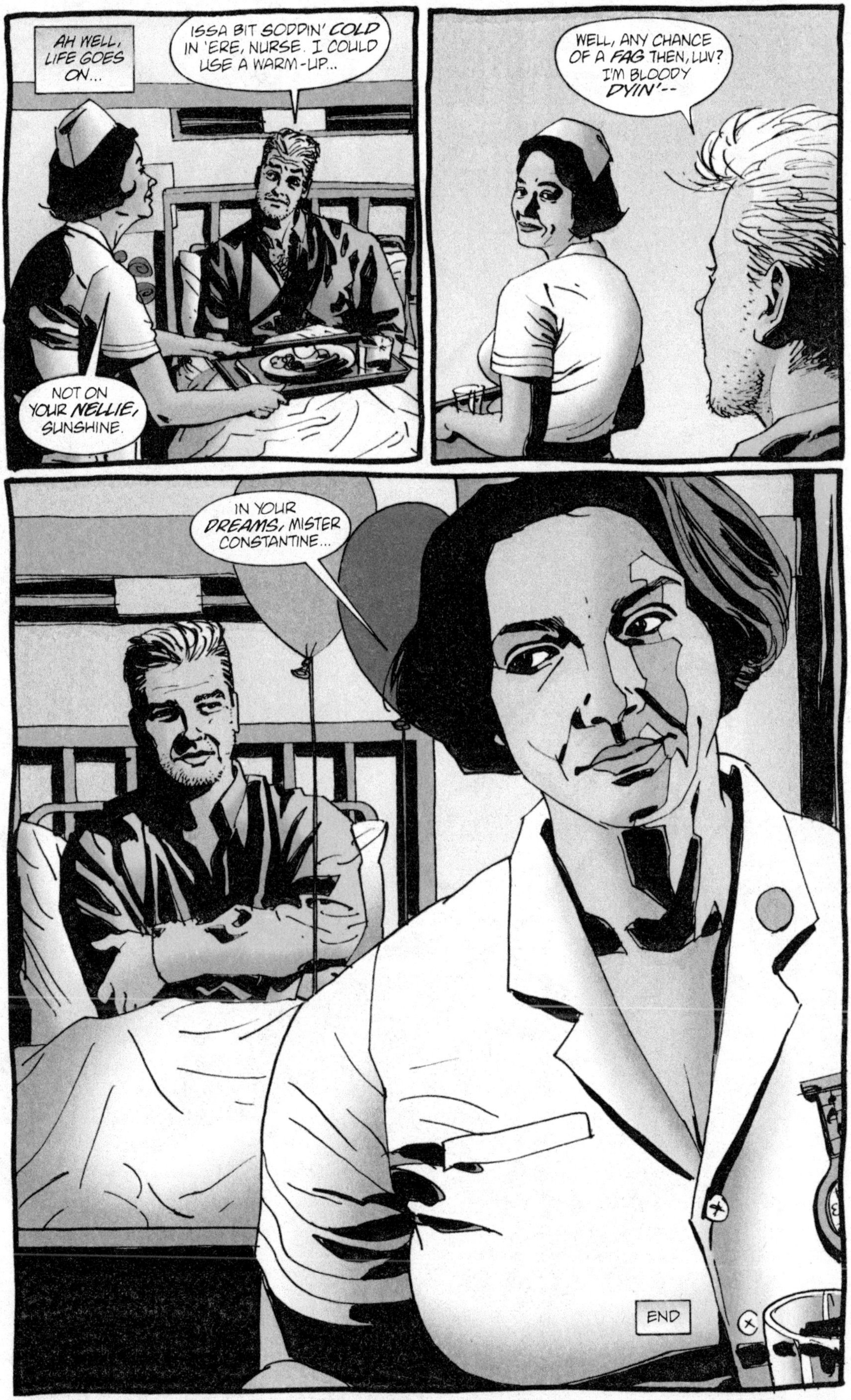
AH WELL, LIFE GOES ON...
ISSA BIT SODDIN' COLD IN 'ERE, NURSE. I COULD USE A WARM-UP...
NOT ON YOUR NELLIE, SUNSHINE.
WELL, ANY CHANCE OF A FAG THEN, LUV? I'M BLOODY DYIN'--
IN YOUR DREAMS, MISTER CONSTANTINE...
END

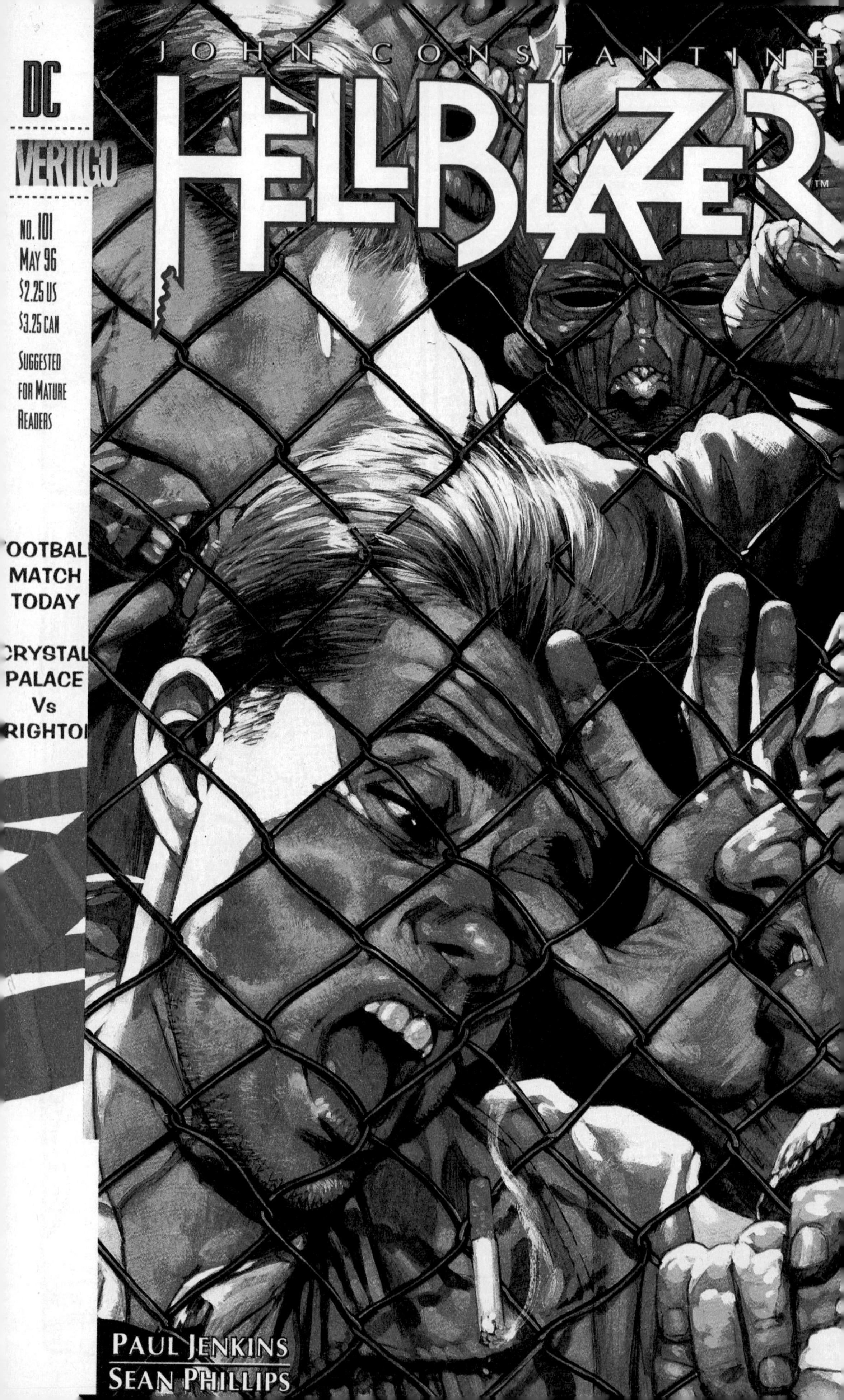

JOHN CONSTANTINE
HELLBLAZER
DC
VERTIGO
no. 101
MAY 96
$2.25 US
$3.25 CAN
SUGGESTED FOR MATURE READERS
OOTBAL
MATCH
TODAY
CRYSTAL
PALACE
Vs
RIGHTO
PAUL JENKINS
SEAN PHILLIPS

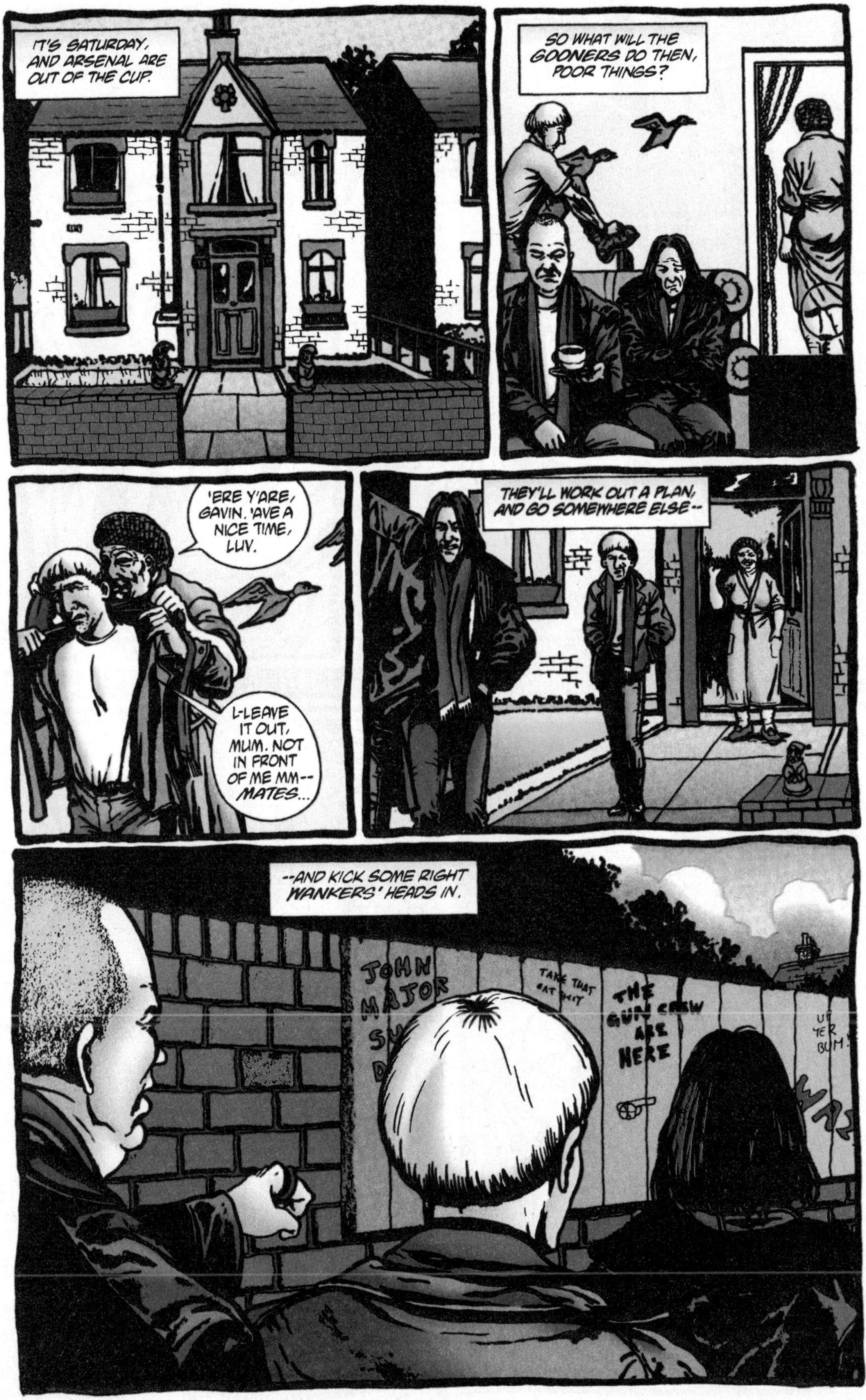
IT'S SATURDAY, AND ARSENAL ARE OUT OF THE CUP.
SO WHAT WILL THE GOONERS DO THEN, POOR THINGS?
'ERE Y'ARE, GAVIN. 'AVE A NICE TIME, LUV.
L-LEAVE IT OUT, MUM. NOT IN FRONT OF ME MM--MATES...
THEY'LL WORK OUT A PLAN, AND GO SOMEWHERE ELSE--
--AND KICK SOME RIGHT WANKERS' HEADS IN.
JOHN MAJOR
TAKE THAT EAT SHIT
THE GUN CREW ARE HERE
UP YER BUM!

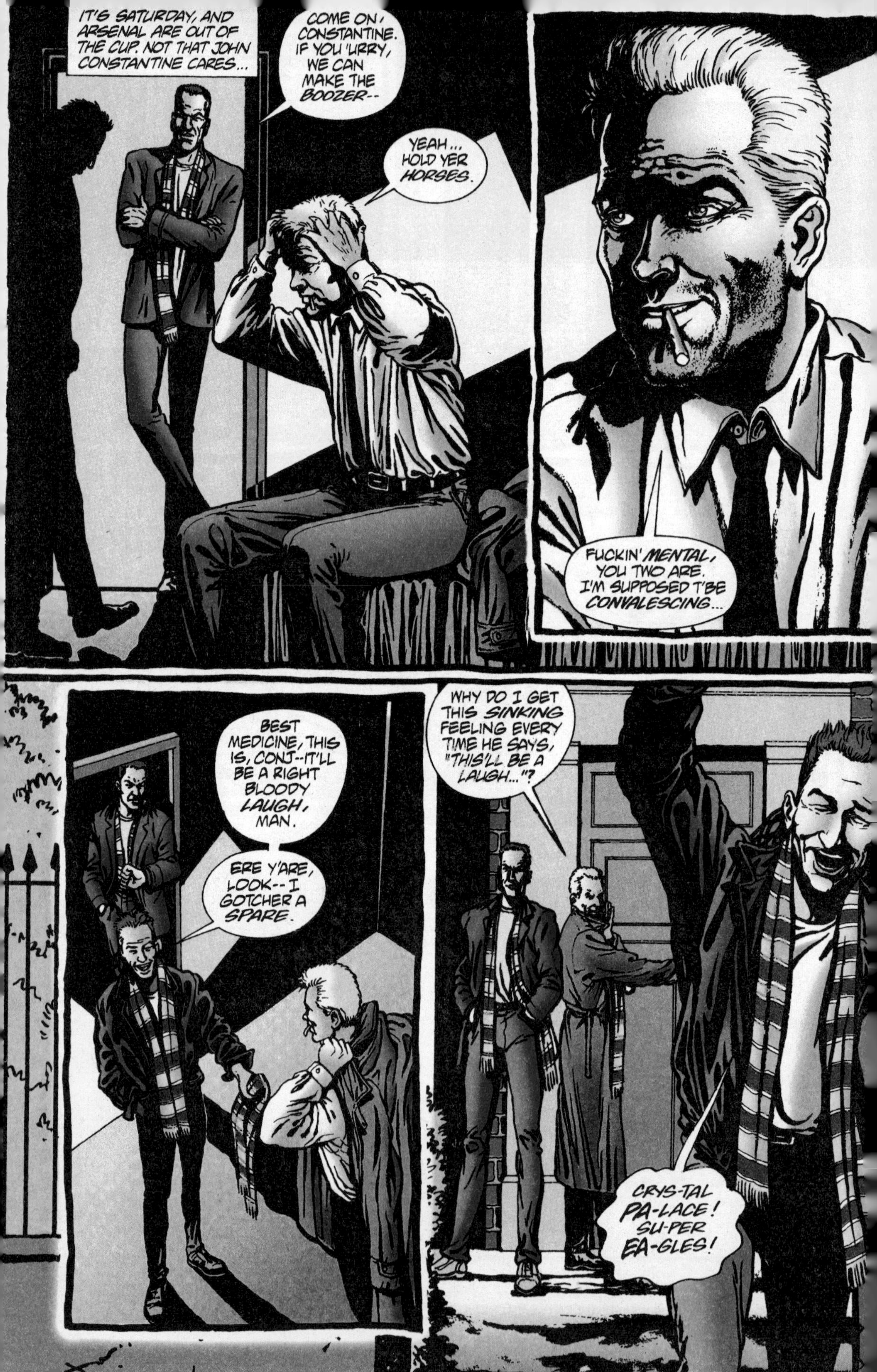
IT'S SATURDAY, AND ARSENAL ARE OUT OF THE CUP. NOT THAT JOHN CONSTANTINE CARES...
COME ON, CONSTANTINE. IF YOU 'URRY, WE CAN MAKE THE BOOZER--
YEAH... HOLD YER HORSES.
FUCKIN' MENTAL, YOU TWO ARE. I'M SUPPOSED T'BE CONVALESCING...
BEST MEDICINE, THIS IS, CONJ--IT'LL BE A RIGHT BLOODY LAUGH, MAN.
ERE Y'ARE, LOOK--I GOTCHER A SPARE.
WHY DO I GET THIS SINKING FEELING EVERY TIME HE SAYS, "THIS'LL BE A LAUGH..."?
CRYS-TAL PA-LACE! SU-PER EA-GLES!

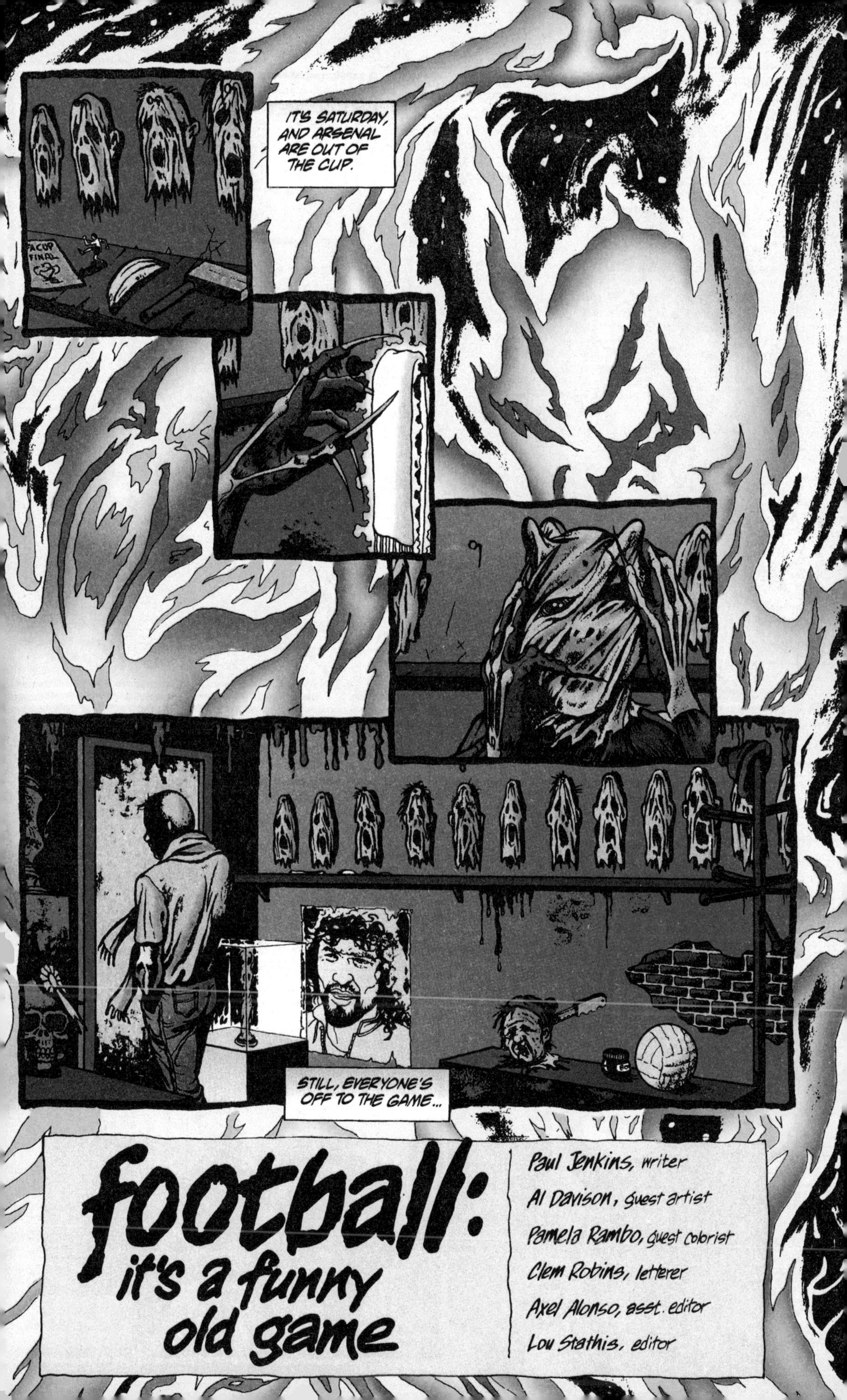
IT'S SATURDAY, AND ARSENAL ARE OUT OF THE CUP.
STILL, EVERYONE'S OFF TO THE GAME...
football: it's a funny old game
Paul Jenkins, writer
Al Davison, guest artist
Pamela Rambo, guest colorist
Clem Robins, letterer
Axel Alonso, asst. editor
Lou Stathis, editor

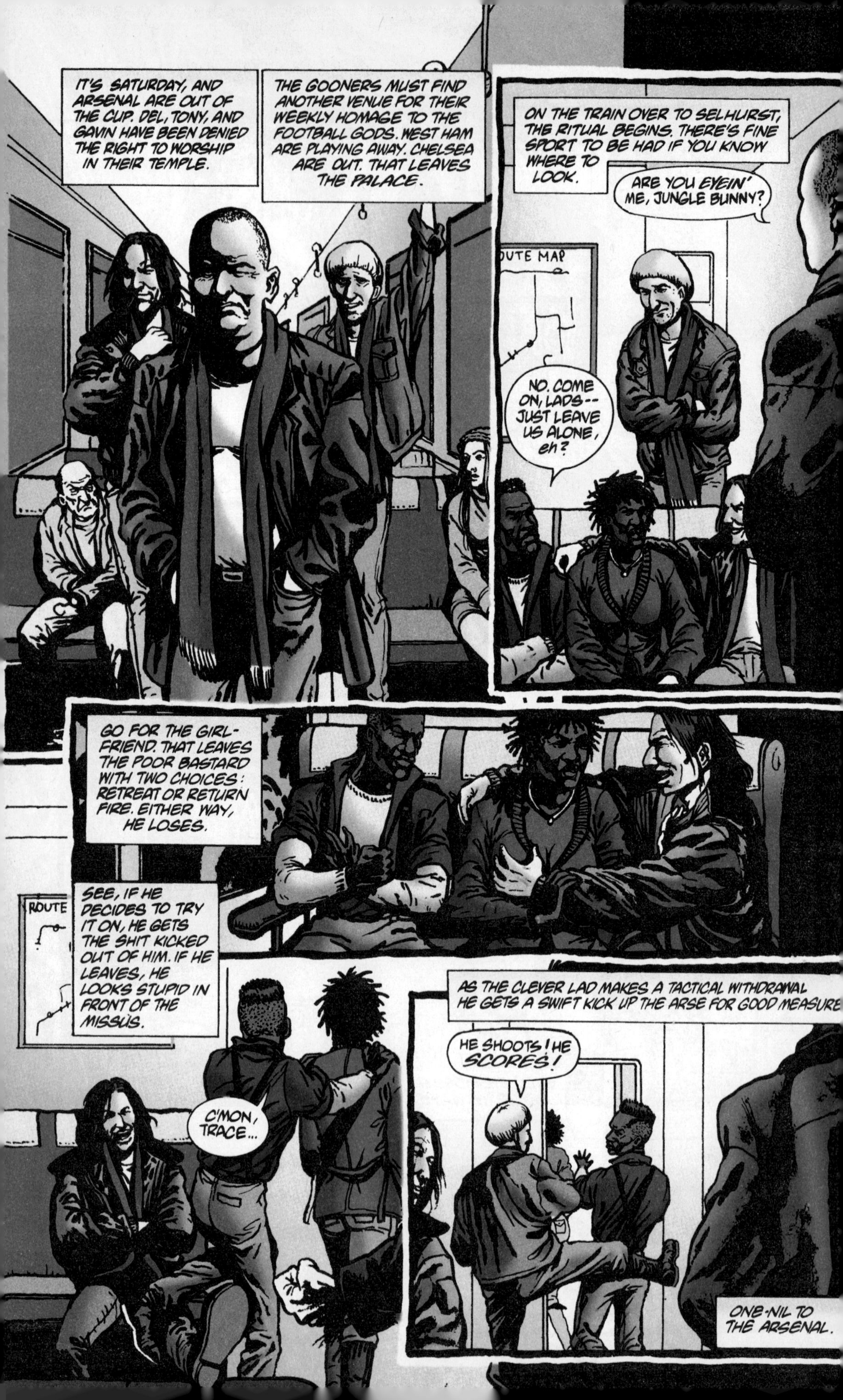
IT'S SATURDAY, AND ARSENAL ARE OUT OF THE CUP. DEL, TONY, AND GAVIN HAVE BEEN DENIED THE RIGHT TO WORSHIP IN THEIR TEMPLE.
THE GOONERS MUST FIND ANOTHER VENUE FOR THEIR WEEKLY HOMAGE TO THE FOOTBALL GODS. WEST HAM ARE PLAYING AWAY. CHELSEA ARE OUT. THAT LEAVES THE PALACE.
ON THE TRAIN OVER TO SELHURST, THE RITUAL BEGINS. THERE'S FINE SPORT TO BE HAD IF YOU KNOW WHERE TO LOOK.
ARE YOU EYEIN' ME, JUNGLE BUNNY?
OUTE MAP
NO. COME ON, LADS-- JUST LEAVE US ALONE, EH?
GO FOR THE GIRL-FRIEND. THAT LEAVES THE POOR BASTARD WITH TWO CHOICES: RETREAT OR RETURN FIRE. EITHER WAY, HE LOSES.
ROUTE
SEE, IF HE DECIDES TO TRY IT ON, HE GETS THE SHIT KICKED OUT OF HIM. IF HE LEAVES, HE LOOKS STUPID IN FRONT OF THE MISSUS.
C'MON, TRACE...
AS THE CLEVER LAD MAKES A TACTICAL WITHDRAWAL HE GETS A SWIFT KICK UP THE ARSE FOR GOOD MEASURE
HE SHOOTS! HE SCORES!
ONE-NIL TO THE ARSENAL.

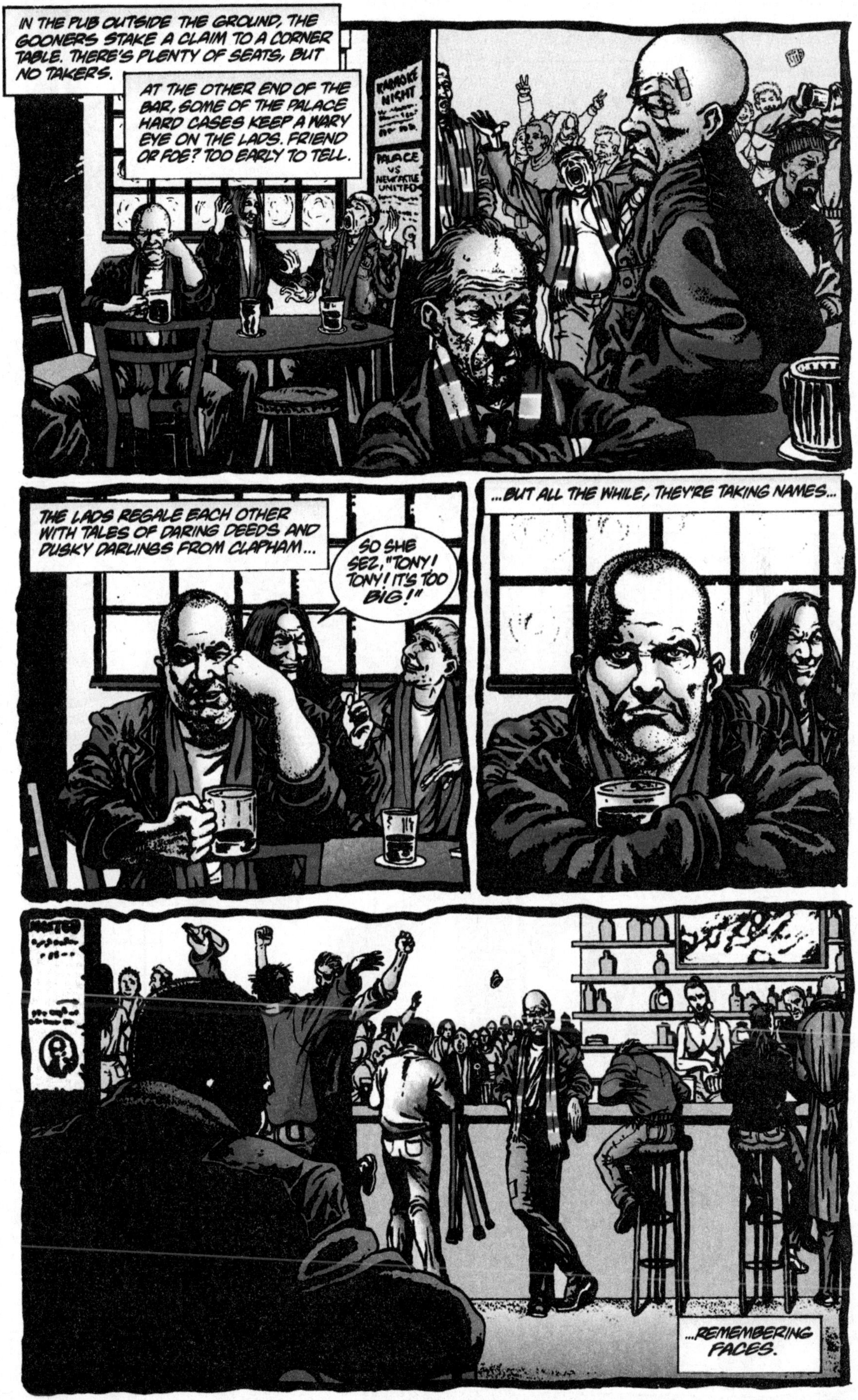
IN THE PUB OUTSIDE THE GROUND, THE GOONERS STAKE A CLAIM TO A CORNER TABLE. THERE'S PLENTY OF SEATS, BUT NO TAKERS.
AT THE OTHER END OF THE BAR, SOME OF THE PALACE HARD CASES KEEP A WARY EYE ON THE LADS. FRIEND OR FOE? TOO EARLY TO TELL.
KARAOKE NIGHT
PALACE VS NEWCASTLE UNITED
THE LADS REGALE EACH OTHER WITH TALES OF DARING DEEDS AND DUSKY DARLINGS FROM CLAPHAM...
SO SHE SEZ, "TONY! TONY! IT'S TOO BIG!"
...BUT ALL THE WHILE, THEY'RE TAKING NAMES...
...REMEMBERING FACES.

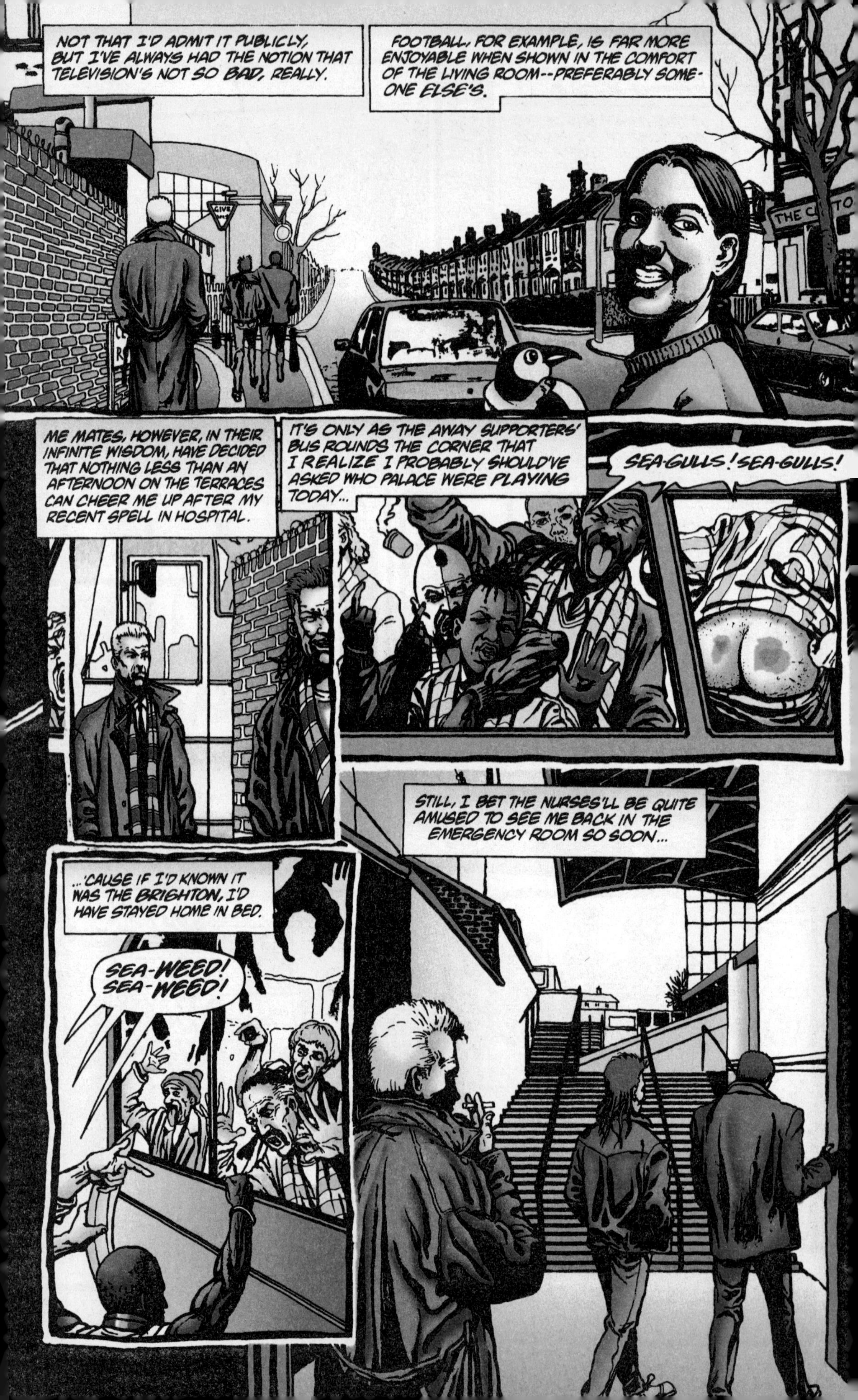
NOT THAT I'D ADMIT IT PUBLICLY, BUT I'VE ALWAYS HAD THE NOTION THAT TELEVISION'S NOT SO BAD, REALLY.
FOOTBALL, FOR EXAMPLE, IS FAR MORE ENJOYABLE WHEN SHOWN IN THE COMFORT OF THE LIVING ROOM--PREFERABLY SOME-ONE ELSE'S.
GIVE WAY
ME MATES, HOWEVER, IN THEIR INFINITE WISDOM, HAVE DECIDED THAT NOTHING LESS THAN AN AFTERNOON ON THE TERRACES CAN CHEER ME UP AFTER MY RECENT SPELL IN HOSPITAL.
IT'S ONLY AS THE AWAY SUPPORTERS' BUS ROUNDS THE CORNER THAT I REALIZE I PROBABLY SHOULD'VE ASKED WHO PALACE WERE PLAYING TODAY...
SEA-GULLS! SEA-GULLS!
...'CAUSE IF I'D KNOWN IT WAS THE BRIGHTON, I'D HAVE STAYED HOME IN BED.
SEA-WEED! SEA-WEED!
STILL, I BET THE NURSES'LL BE QUITE AMUSED TO SEE ME BACK IN THE EMERGENCY ROOM SO SOON...

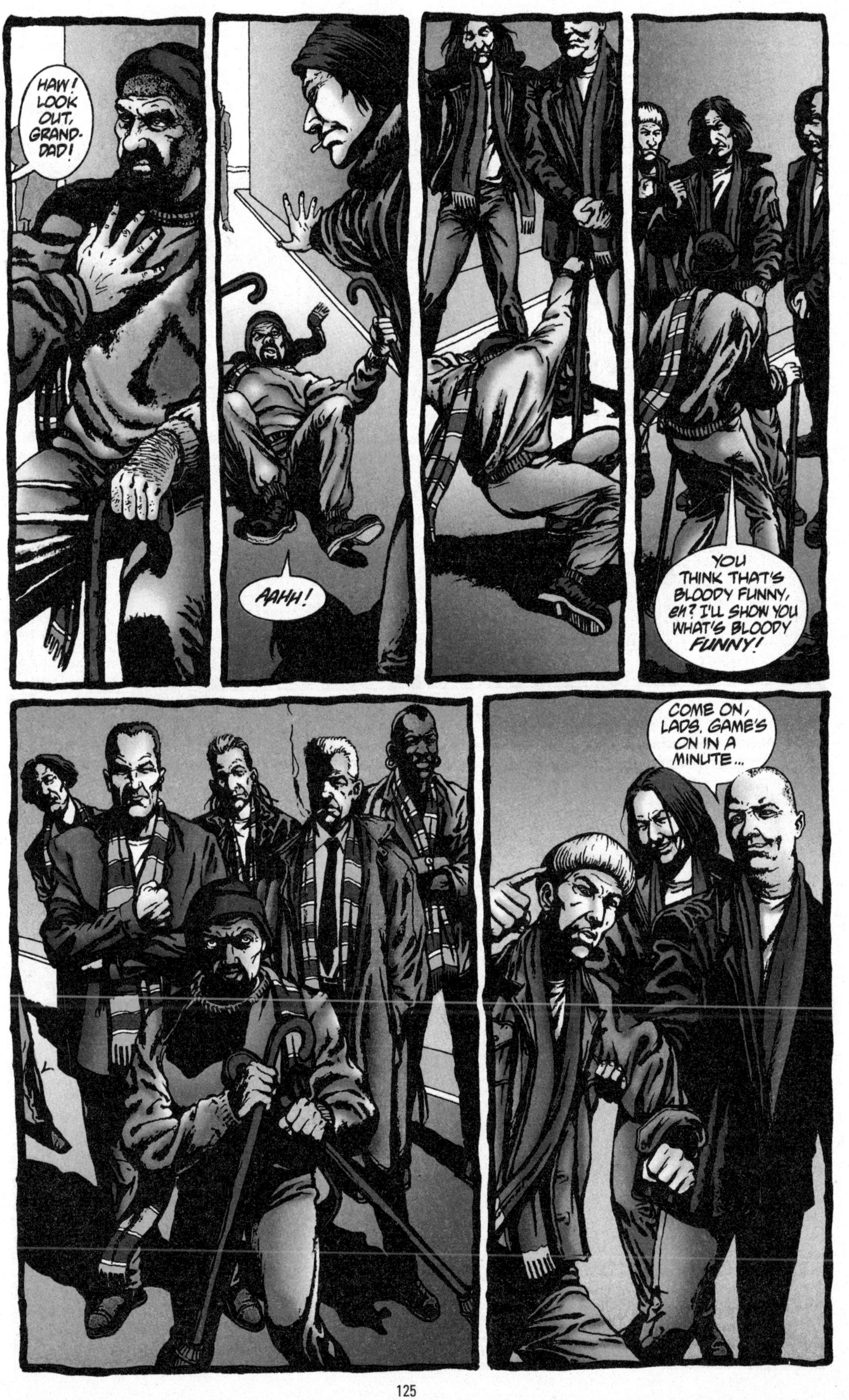
HAW! LOOK OUT, GRAND-DAD!
AAHH!
YOU THINK THAT'S BLOODY FUNNY, eh? I'LL SHOW YOU WHAT'S BLOODY FUNNY!
COME ON, LADS. GAME'S ON IN A MINUTE...

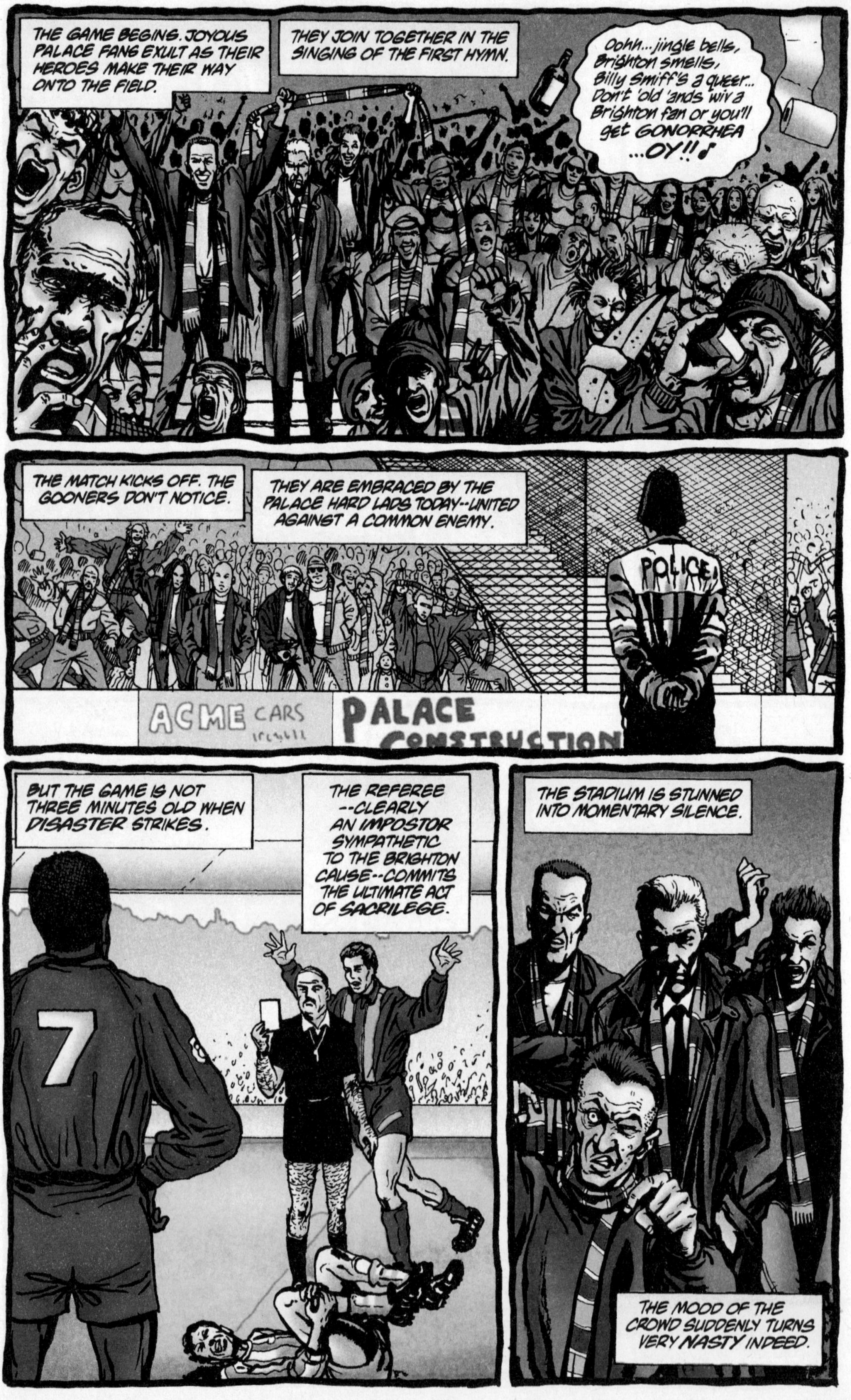
THE GAME BEGINS. JOYOUS PALACE FANS EXULT AS THEIR HEROES MAKE THEIR WAY ONTO THE FIELD.
THEY JOIN TOGETHER IN THE SINGING OF THE FIRST HYMN.
Oohh... jingle bells, Brighton smells, Billy Smiff's a queer... Don't 'old 'ands wiv a Brighton fan or you'll get GONORRHEA ...OY!!
THE MATCH KICKS OFF. THE GOONERS DON'T NOTICE.
THEY ARE EMBRACED BY THE PALACE HARD LADS TODAY--UNITED AGAINST A COMMON ENEMY.
POLICE
ACME CARS
PALACE
BUT THE GAME IS NOT THREE MINUTES OLD WHEN DISASTER STRIKES.
THE REFEREE --CLEARLY AN IMPOSTOR SYMPATHETIC TO THE BRIGHTON CAUSE--COMMITS THE ULTIMATE ACT OF SACRILEGE.
7
THE STADIUM IS STUNNED INTO MOMENTARY SILENCE.
THE MOOD OF THE CROWD SUDDENLY TURNS VERY NASTY INDEED.

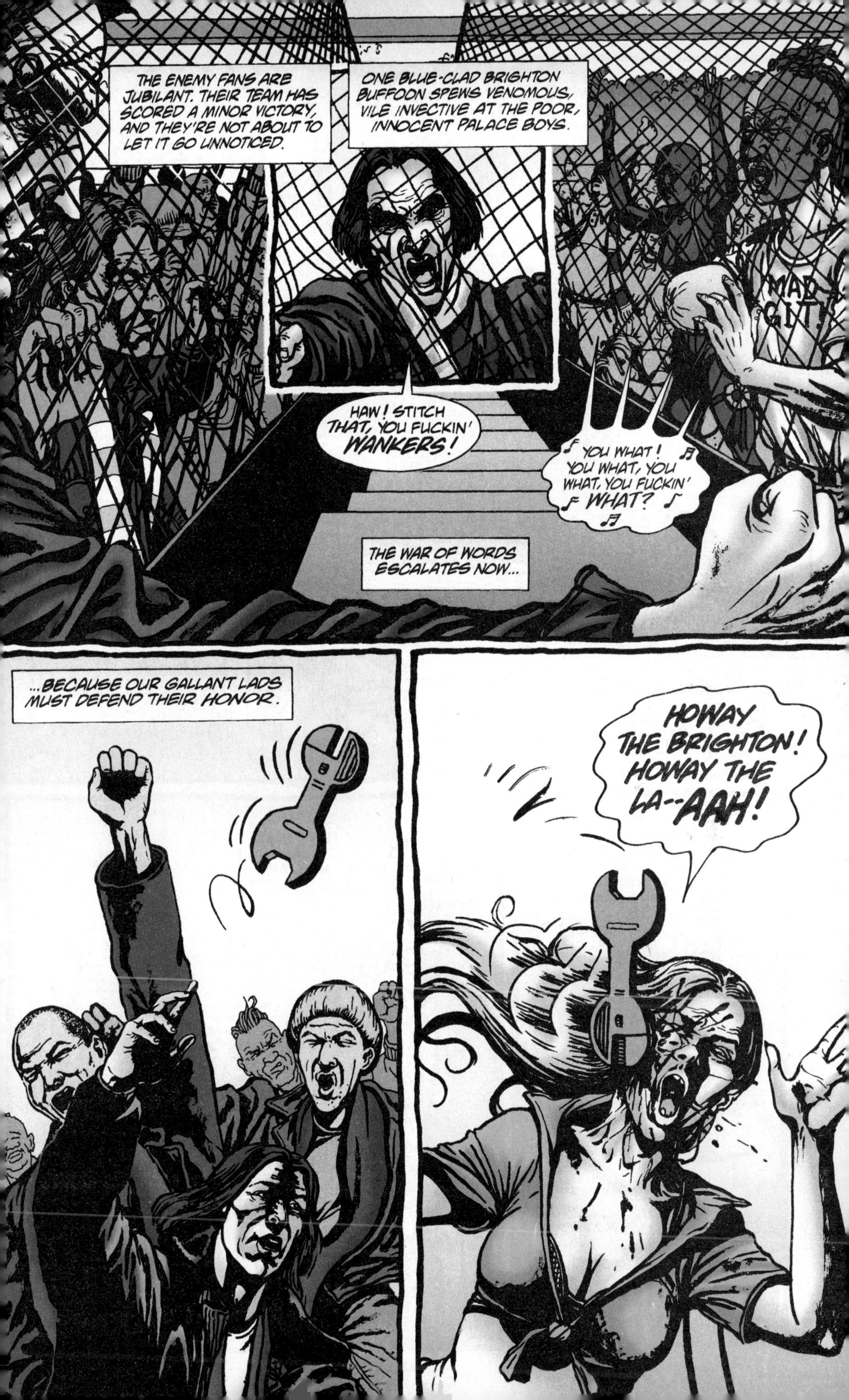
THE ENEMY FANS ARE JUBILANT. THEIR TEAM HAS SCORED A MINOR VICTORY, AND THEY'RE NOT ABOUT TO LET IT GO UNNOTICED.
ONE BLUE-CLAD BRIGHTON BUFFOON SPEWS VENOMOUS, VILE INVECTIVE AT THE POOR, INNOCENT PALACE BOYS.
HAW! STITCH THAT, YOU FUCKIN' WANKERS!
MAD GIT!
YOU WHAT! YOU WHAT, YOU WHAT, YOU FUCKIN' WHAT?
THE WAR OF WORDS ESCALATES NOW...
...BECAUSE OUR GALLANT LADS MUST DEFEND THEIR HONOR.
HOWAY THE BRIGHTON! HOWAY THE LA--AAH!

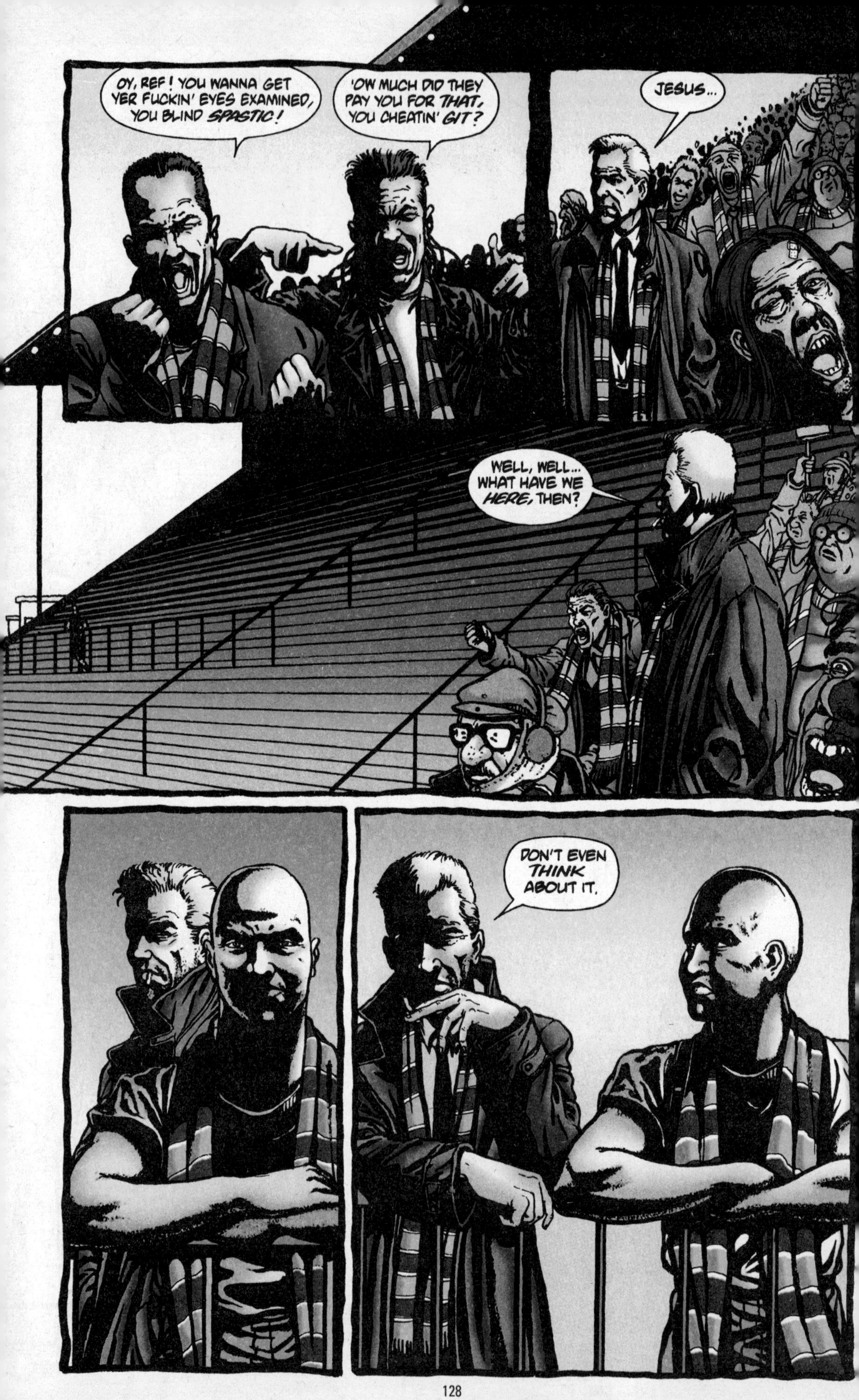
OY, REF! YOU WANNA GET YER FUCKIN' EYES EXAMINED, YOU BLIND SPASTIC!
'OW MUCH DID THEY PAY YOU FOR THAT, YOU CHEATIN' GIT?
JESUS...
WELL, WELL... WHAT HAVE WE HERE, THEN?
DON'T EVEN THINK ABOUT IT.

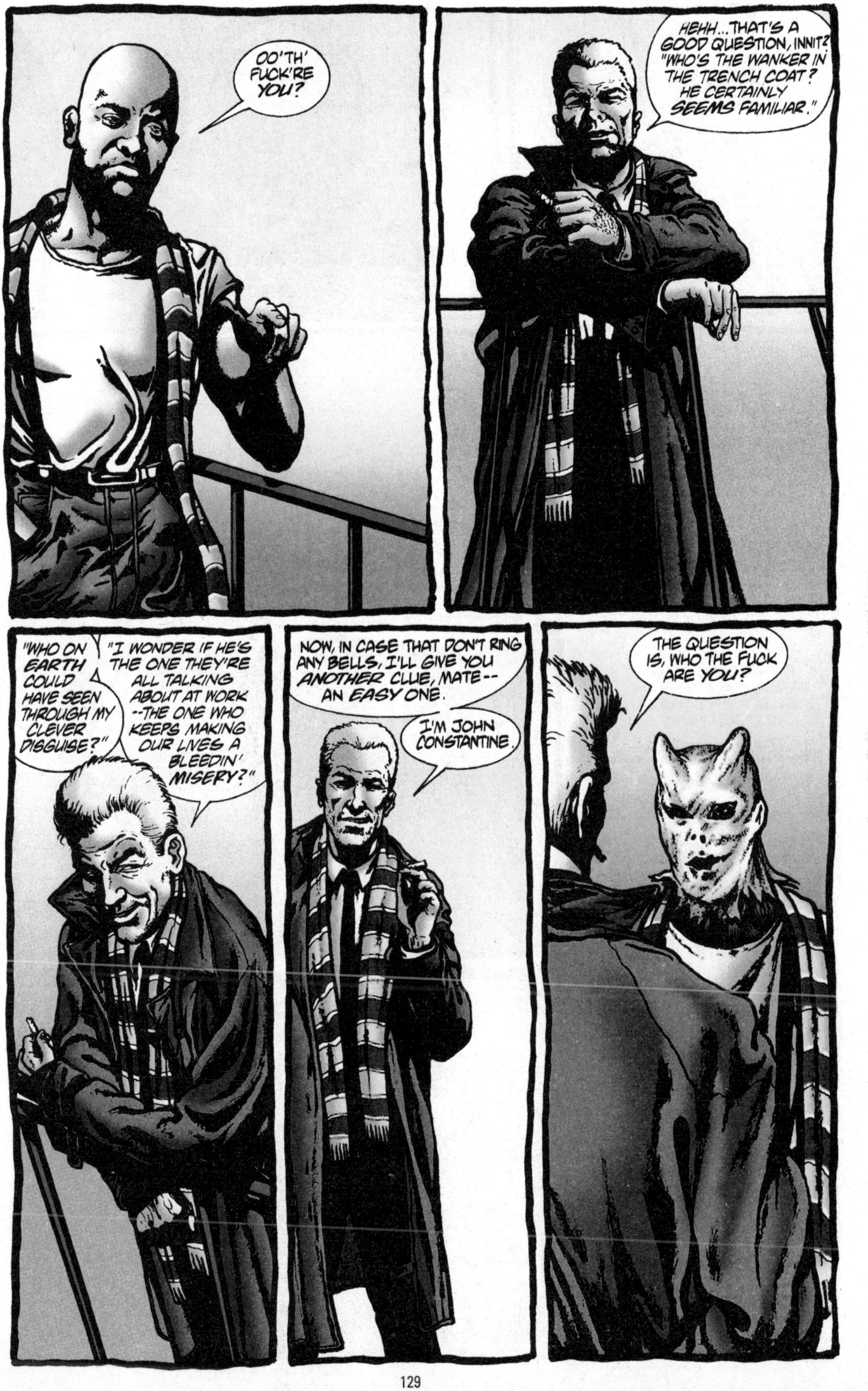
OO'TH' FUCK'RE YOU?
HEHH...THAT'S A GOOD QUESTION, INNIT? "WHO'S THE WANKER IN THE TRENCH COAT? HE CERTAINLY SEEMS FAMILIAR."
"WHO ON EARTH COULD HAVE SEEN THROUGH MY CLEVER DISGUISE?"
"I WONDER IF HE'S THE ONE THEY'RE ALL TALKING ABOUT AT WORK --THE ONE WHO KEEPS MAKING OUR LIVES A BLEEDIN' MISERY?"
NOW, IN CASE THAT DON'T RING ANY BELLS, I'LL GIVE YOU ANOTHER CLUE, MATE-- AN EASY ONE.
I'M JOHN CONSTANTINE.
THE QUESTION IS, WHO THE FUCK ARE YOU?

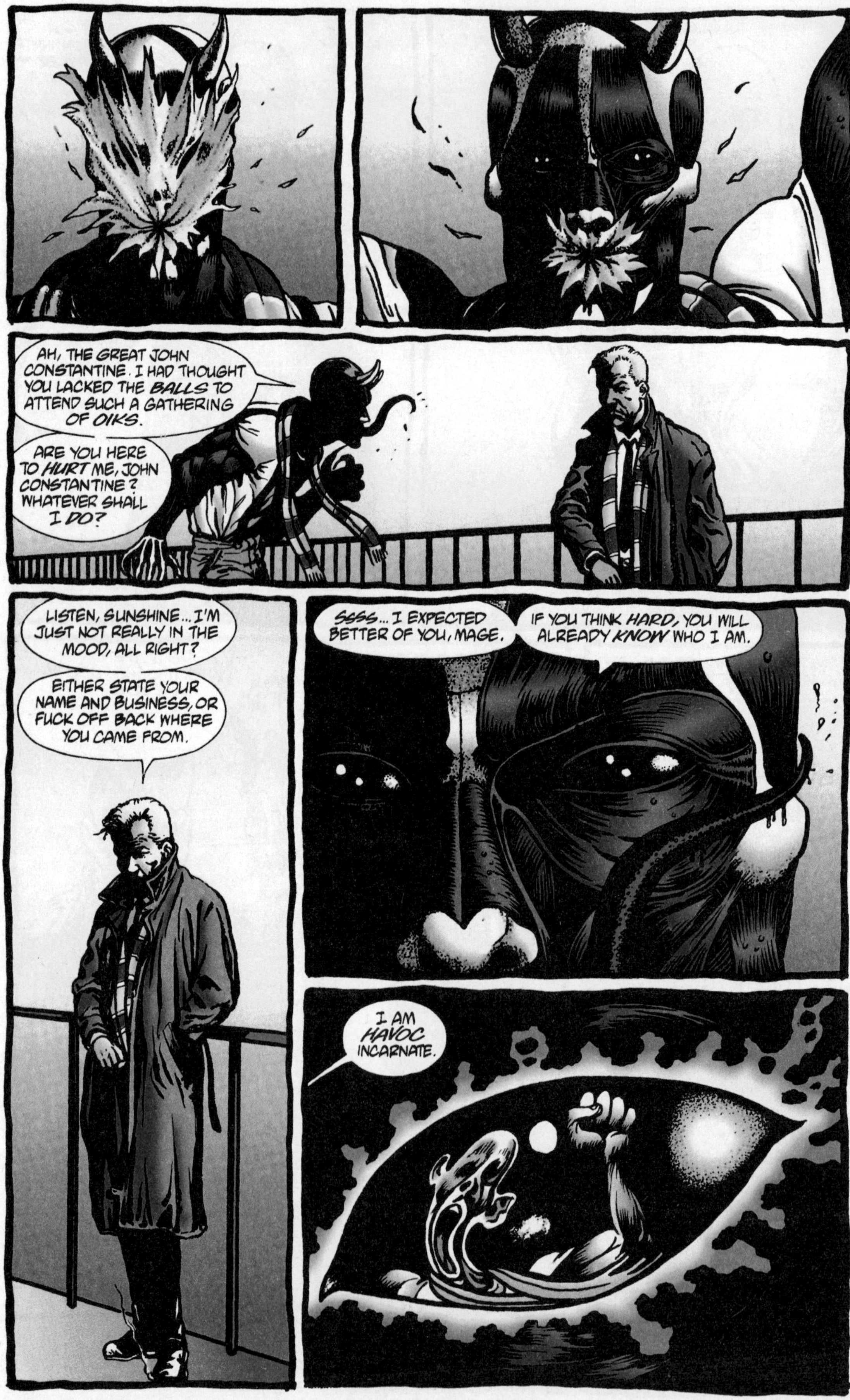
AH, THE GREAT JOHN CONSTANTINE. I HAD THOUGHT YOU LACKED THE BALLS TO ATTEND SUCH A GATHERING OF OIKS.
ARE YOU HERE TO HURT ME, JOHN CONSTANTINE? WHATEVER SHALL I DO?
LISTEN, SUNSHINE... I'M JUST NOT REALLY IN THE MOOD, ALL RIGHT?
EITHER STATE YOUR NAME AND BUSINESS, OR FUCK OFF BACK WHERE YOU CAME FROM.
SSSS... I EXPECTED BETTER OF YOU, MAGE.
IF YOU THINK HARD, YOU WILL ALREADY KNOW WHO I AM.
I AM HAVOC INCARNATE.

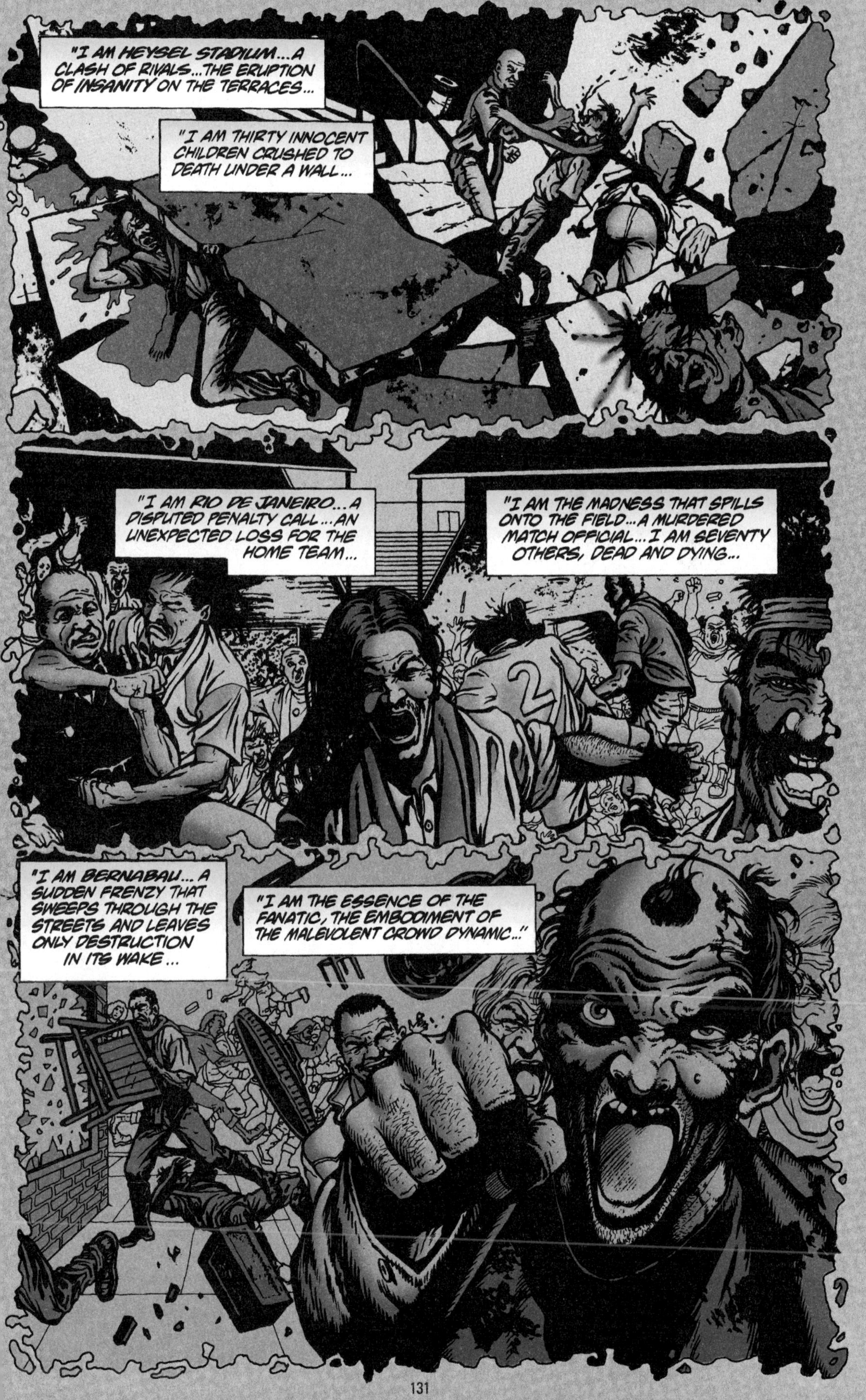
"I AM HEYSEL STADIUM... A CLASH OF RIVALS... THE ERUPTION OF INSANITY ON THE TERRACES...
"I AM THIRTY INNOCENT CHILDREN CRUSHED TO DEATH UNDER A WALL...
"I AM RIO DE JANEIRO... A DISPUTED PENALTY CALL... AN UNEXPECTED LOSS FOR THE HOME TEAM...
"I AM THE MADNESS THAT SPILLS ONTO THE FIELD... A MURDERED MATCH OFFICIAL... I AM SEVENTY OTHERS, DEAD AND DYING...
"I AM BERNABAU... A SUDDEN FRENZY THAT SWEEPS THROUGH THE STREETS AND LEAVES ONLY DESTRUCTION IN ITS WAKE...
"I AM THE ESSENCE OF THE FANATIC, THE EMBODIMENT OF THE MALEVOLENT CROWD DYNAMIC..."

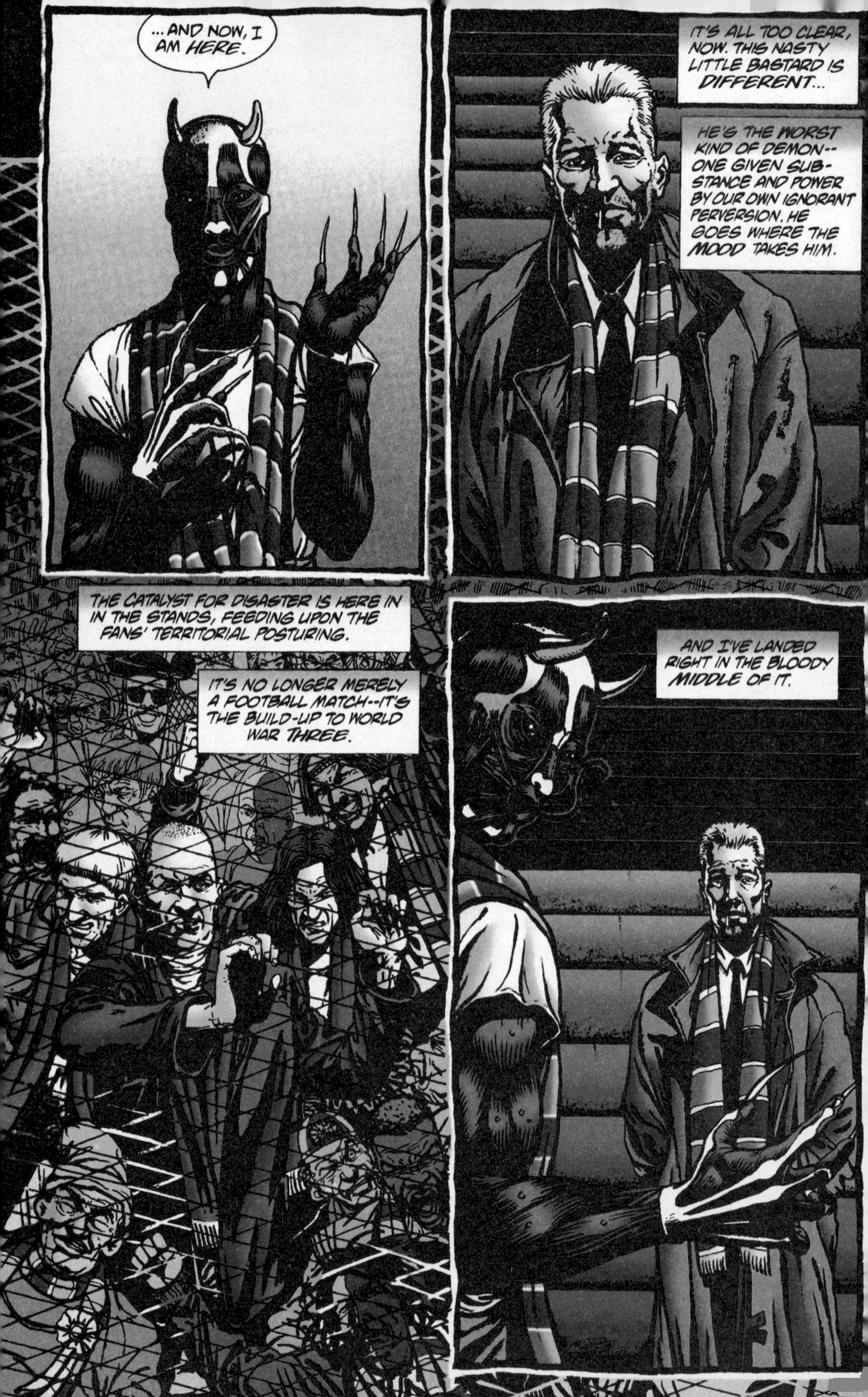
...AND NOW, I AM HERE.
IT'S ALL TOO CLEAR, NOW. THIS NASTY LITTLE BASTARD IS DIFFERENT...
HE'S THE WORST KIND OF DEMON--ONE GIVEN SUBSTANCE AND POWER BY OUR OWN IGNORANT PERVERSION. HE GOES WHERE THE MOOD TAKES HIM.
THE CATALYST FOR DISASTER IS HERE IN IN THE STANDS, FEEDING UPON THE FANS' TERRITORIAL POSTURING.
IT'S NO LONGER MERELY A FOOTBALL MATCH--IT'S THE BUILD-UP TO WORLD WAR THREE.
AND I'VE LANDED RIGHT IN THE BLOODY MIDDLE OF IT.

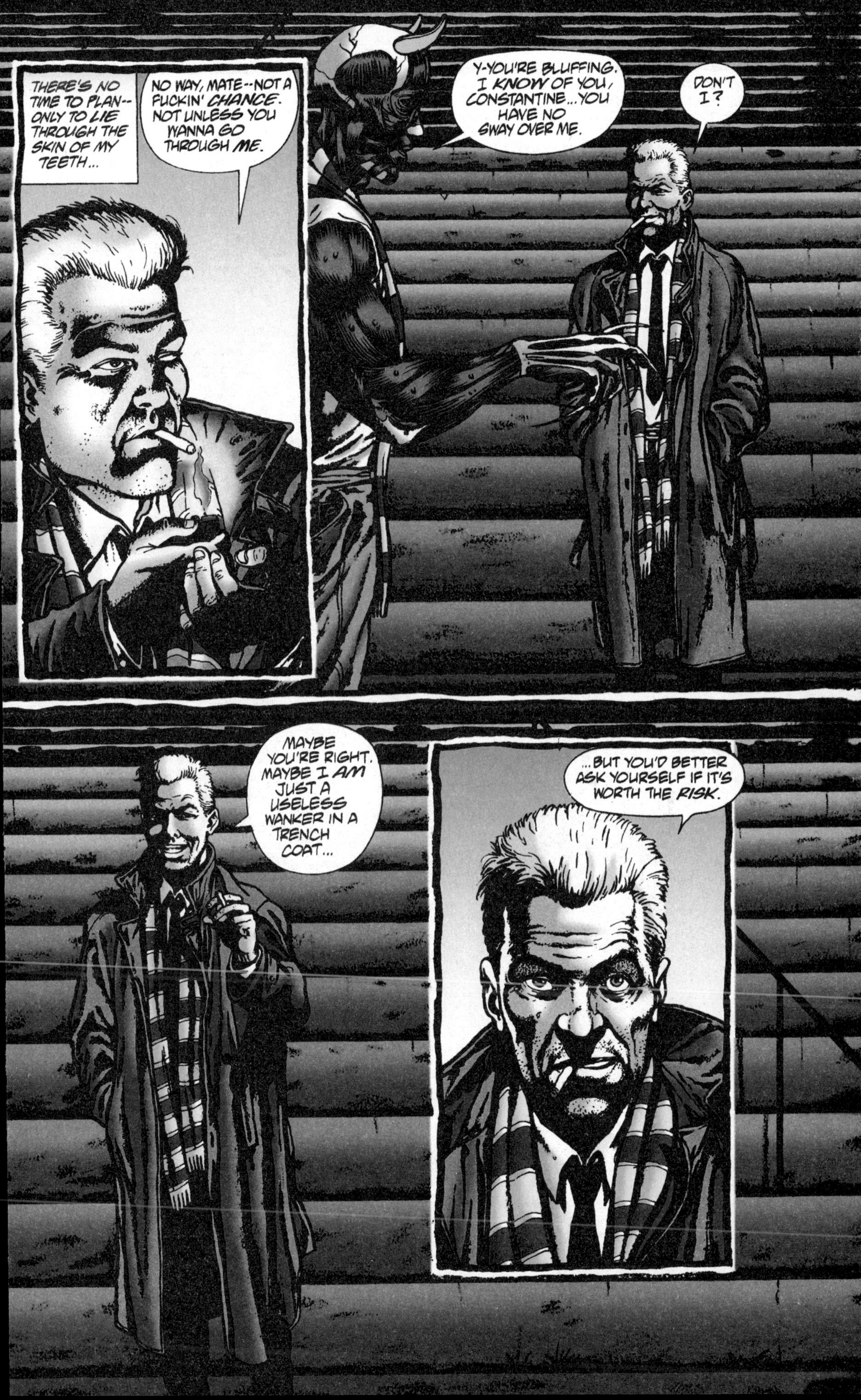
THERE'S NO TIME TO PLAN-- ONLY TO LIE THROUGH THE SKIN OF MY TEETH...
NO WAY, MATE--NOT A FUCKIN' CHANCE. NOT UNLESS YOU WANNA GO THROUGH ME.
Y-YOU'RE BLUFFING. I KNOW OF YOU, CONSTANTINE...YOU HAVE NO SWAY OVER ME.
DON'T I?
MAYBE YOU'RE RIGHT. MAYBE I AM JUST A USELESS WANKER IN A TRENCH COAT...
...BUT YOU'D BETTER ASK YOURSELF IF IT'S WORTH THE RISK.

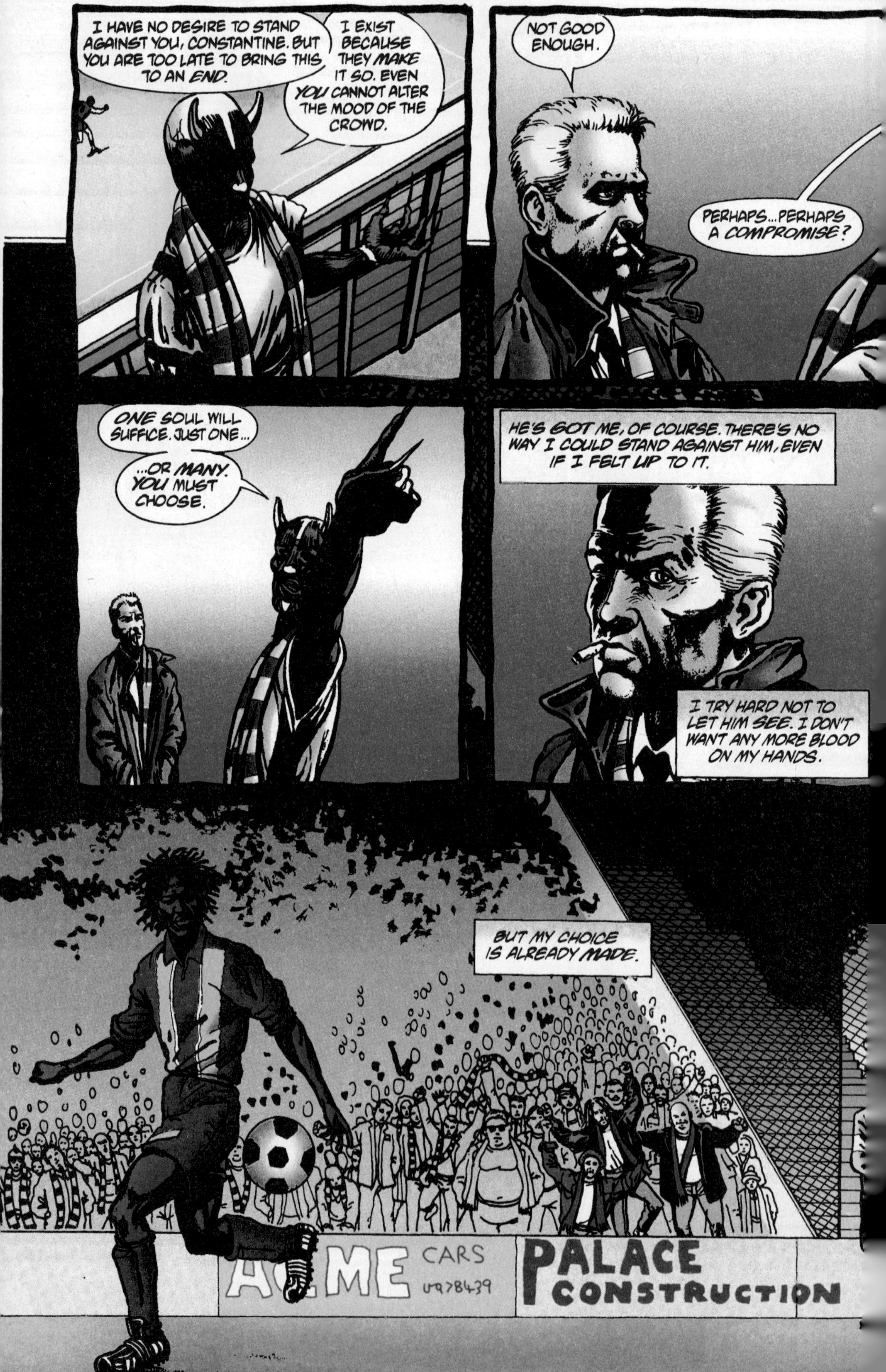
I HAVE NO DESIRE TO STAND AGAINST YOU, CONSTANTINE. BUT YOU ARE TOO LATE TO BRING THIS TO AN END.
I EXIST BECAUSE THEY MAKE IT SO. EVEN YOU CANNOT ALTER THE MOOD OF THE CROWD.
NOT GOOD ENOUGH.
PERHAPS...PERHAPS A COMPROMISE?
ONE SOUL WILL SUFFICE. JUST ONE...
...OR MANY. YOU MUST CHOOSE.
HE'S GOT ME, OF COURSE. THERE'S NO WAY I COULD STAND AGAINST HIM, EVEN IF I FELT UP TO IT.
I TRY HARD NOT TO LET HIM SEE. I DON'T WANT ANY MORE BLOOD ON MY HANDS.
BUT MY CHOICE IS ALREADY MADE.
ACME CARS
PALACE CONSTRUCTION

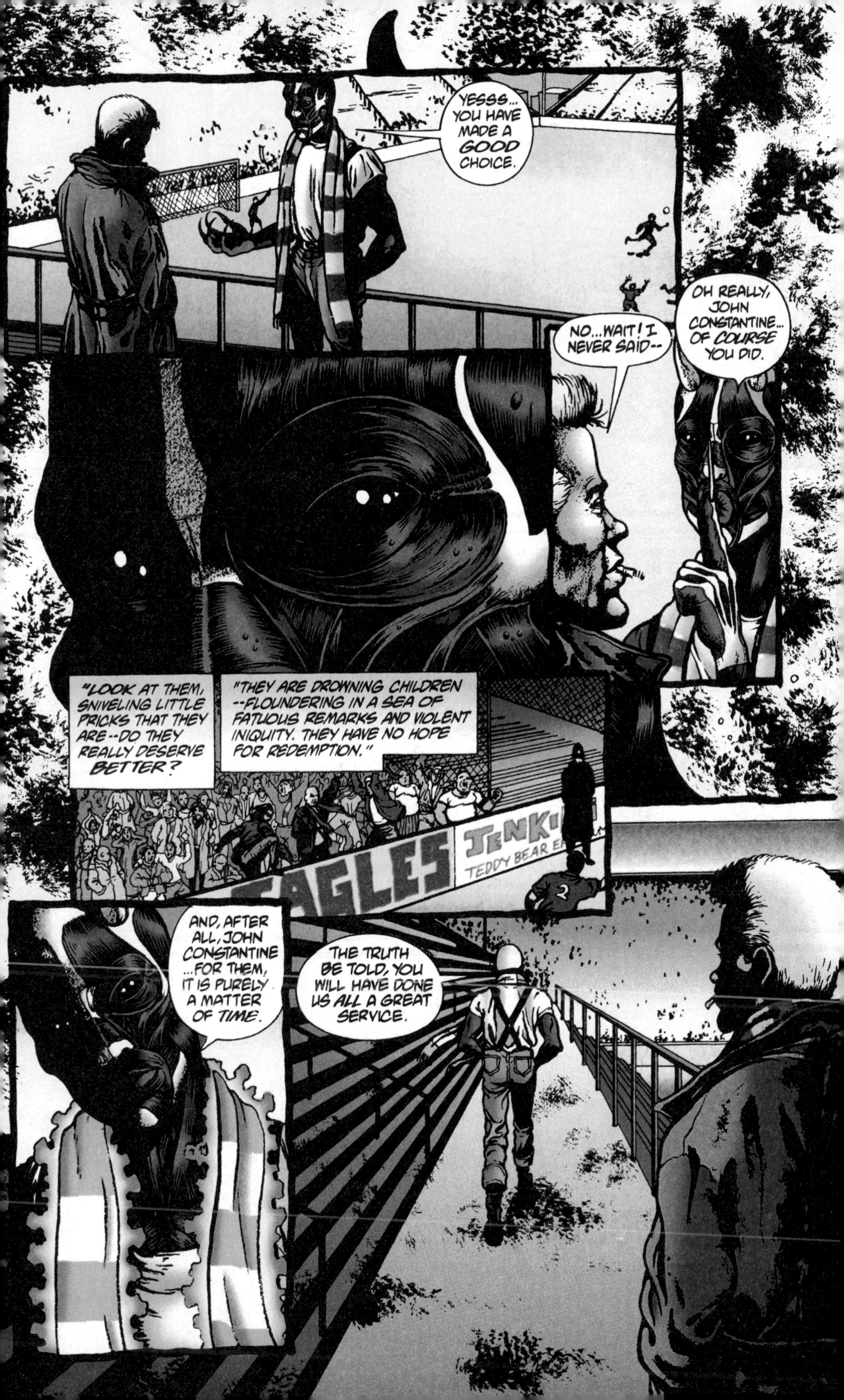
YESSS... YOU HAVE MADE A GOOD CHOICE.
NO...WAIT! I NEVER SAID--
OH REALLY, JOHN CONSTANTINE... OF COURSE YOU DID.
"LOOK AT THEM, SNIVELING LITTLE PRICKS THAT THEY ARE--DO THEY REALLY DESERVE BETTER?
"THEY ARE DROWNING CHILDREN --FLOUNDERING IN A SEA OF FATUOUS REMARKS AND VIOLENT INIQUITY. THEY HAVE NO HOPE FOR REDEMPTION."
EAGLES
TEDDY BEAR
AND, AFTER ALL, JOHN CONSTANTINE ...FOR THEM, IT IS PURELY A MATTER OF TIME.
THE TRUTH BE TOLD, YOU WILL HAVE DONE US ALL A GREAT SERVICE.

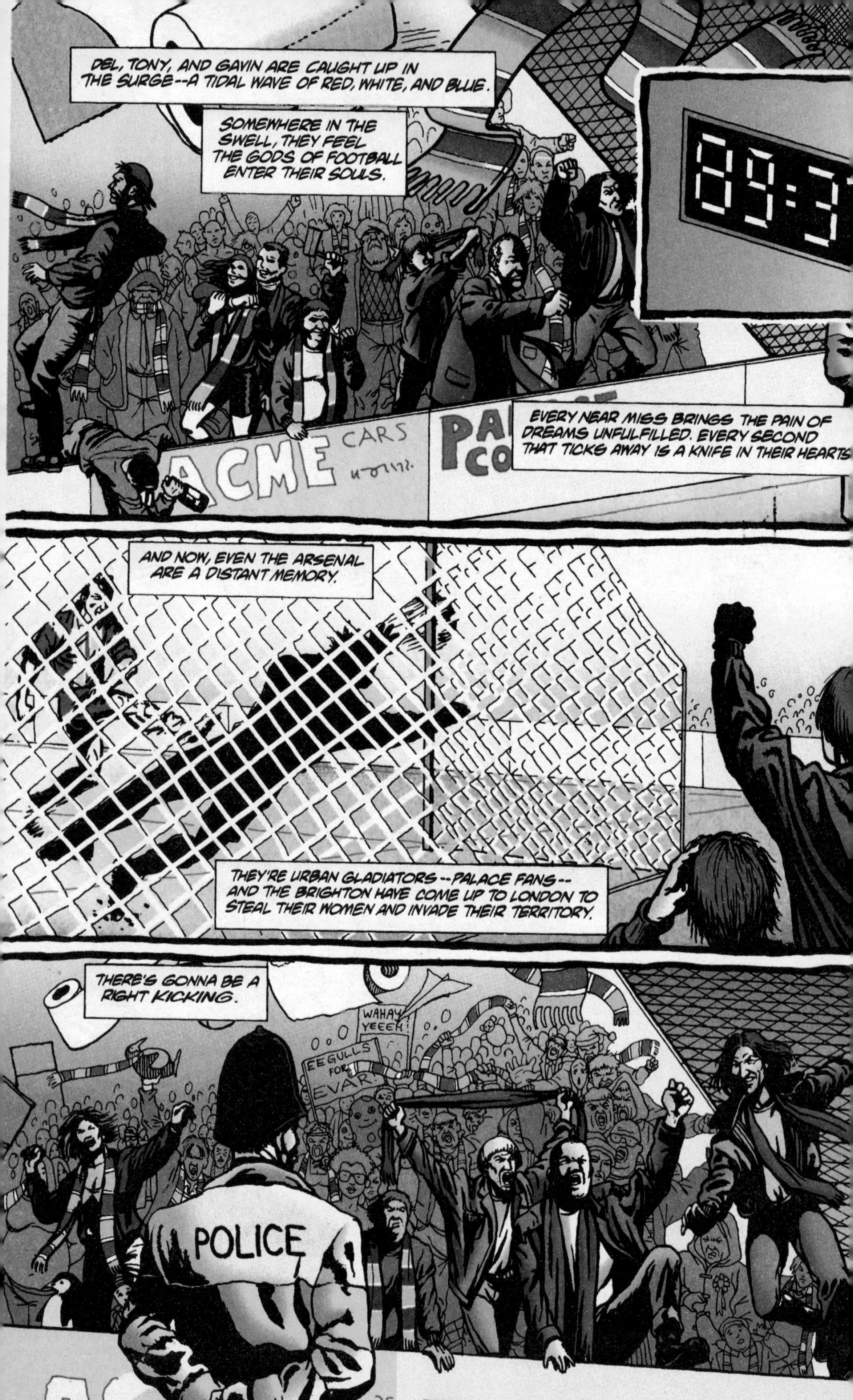
DEL, TONY, AND GAVIN ARE CAUGHT UP IN THE SURGE--A TIDAL WAVE OF RED, WHITE, AND BLUE.
SOMEWHERE IN THE SWELL, THEY FEEL THE GODS OF FOOTBALL ENTER THEIR SOULS.
EVERY NEAR MISS BRINGS THE PAIN OF DREAMS UNFULFILLED. EVERY SECOND THAT TICKS AWAY IS A KNIFE IN THEIR HEARTS.
ACME CARS
AND NOW, EVEN THE ARSENAL ARE A DISTANT MEMORY.
THEY'RE URBAN GLADIATORS--PALACE FANS--AND THE BRIGHTON HAVE COME UP TO LONDON TO STEAL THEIR WOMEN AND INVADE THEIR TERRITORY.
THERE'S GONNA BE A RIGHT KICKING.
WAHAY YEEEH!
EEGULLS FOR EVAR!
POLICE

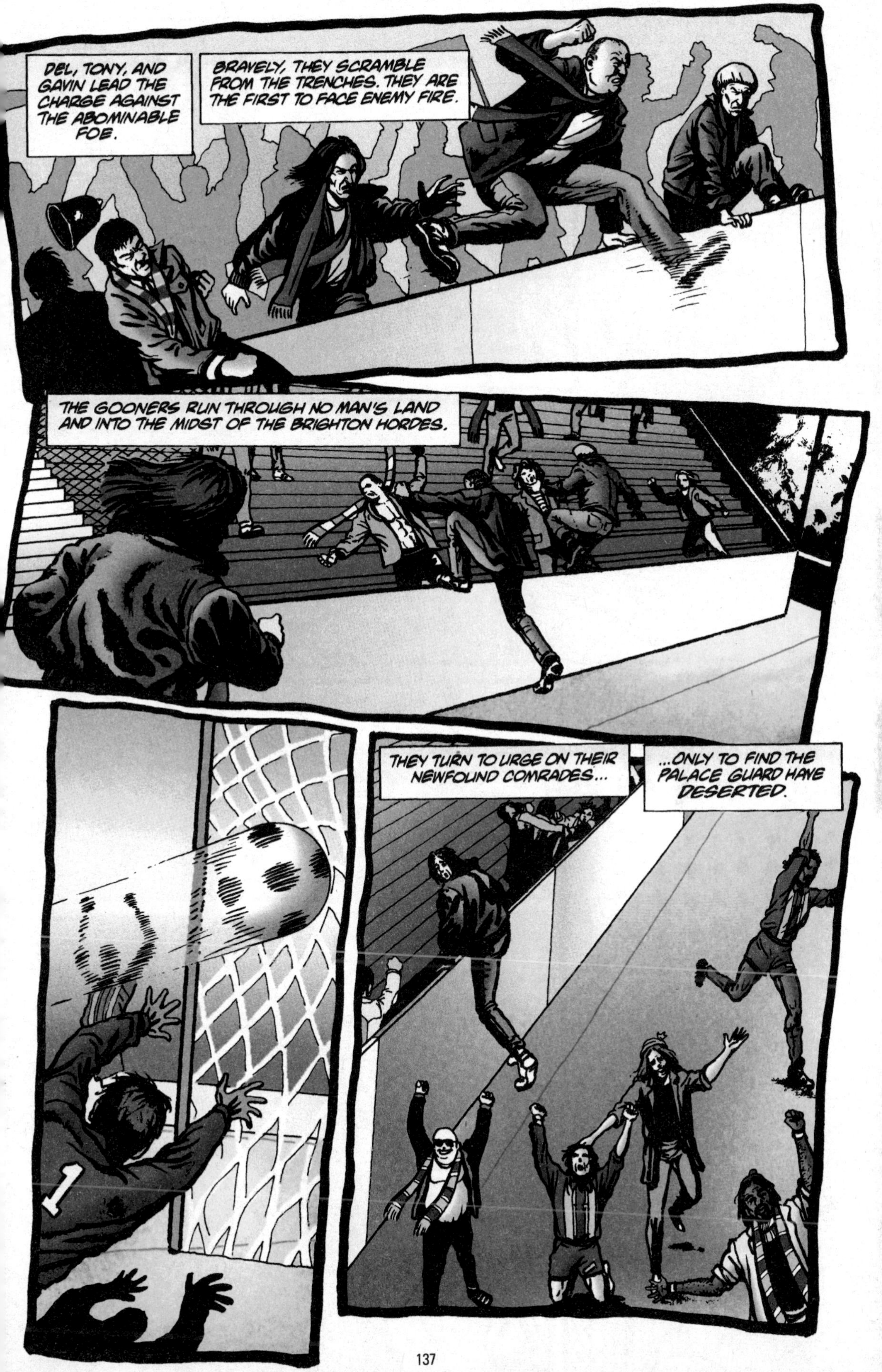
DEL, TONY, AND GAVIN LEAD THE CHARGE AGAINST THE ABOMINABLE FOE.
BRAVELY, THEY SCRAMBLE FROM THE TRENCHES. THEY ARE THE FIRST TO FACE ENEMY FIRE.
THE GOONERS RUN THROUGH NO MAN'S LAND AND INTO THE MIDST OF THE BRIGHTON HORDES.
1
THEY TURN TO URGE ON THEIR NEWFOUND COMRADES...
...ONLY TO FIND THE PALACE GUARD HAVE DESERTED.

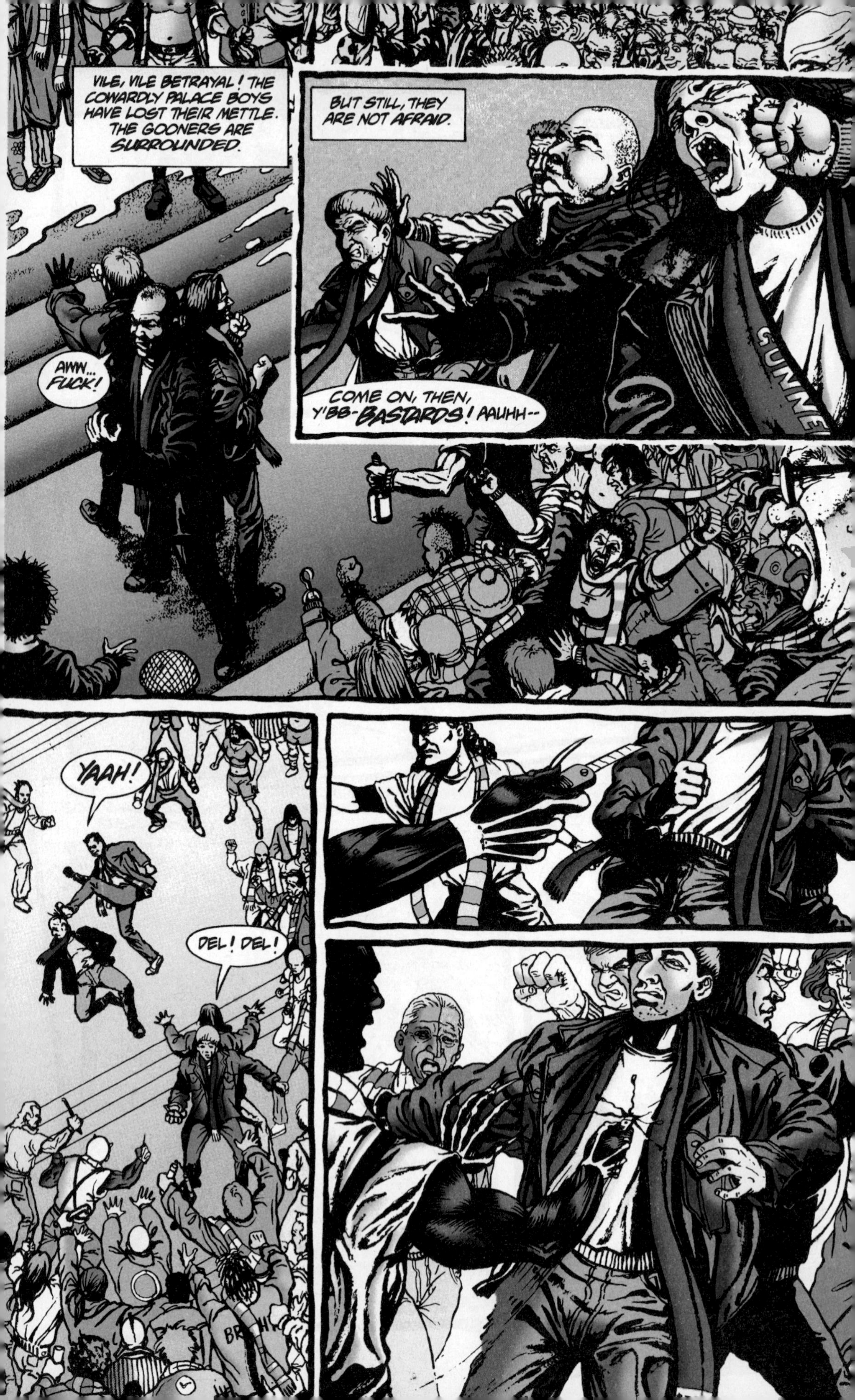
VILE, VILE BETRAYAL! THE COWARDLY PALACE BOYS HAVE LOST THEIR METTLE. THE GOONERS ARE SURROUNDED.
BUT STILL, THEY ARE NOT AFRAID.
AWN... FUCK!
COME ON, THEN, Y'BB-BASTARDS! AAUHH--
YAAH!
DEL! DEL!

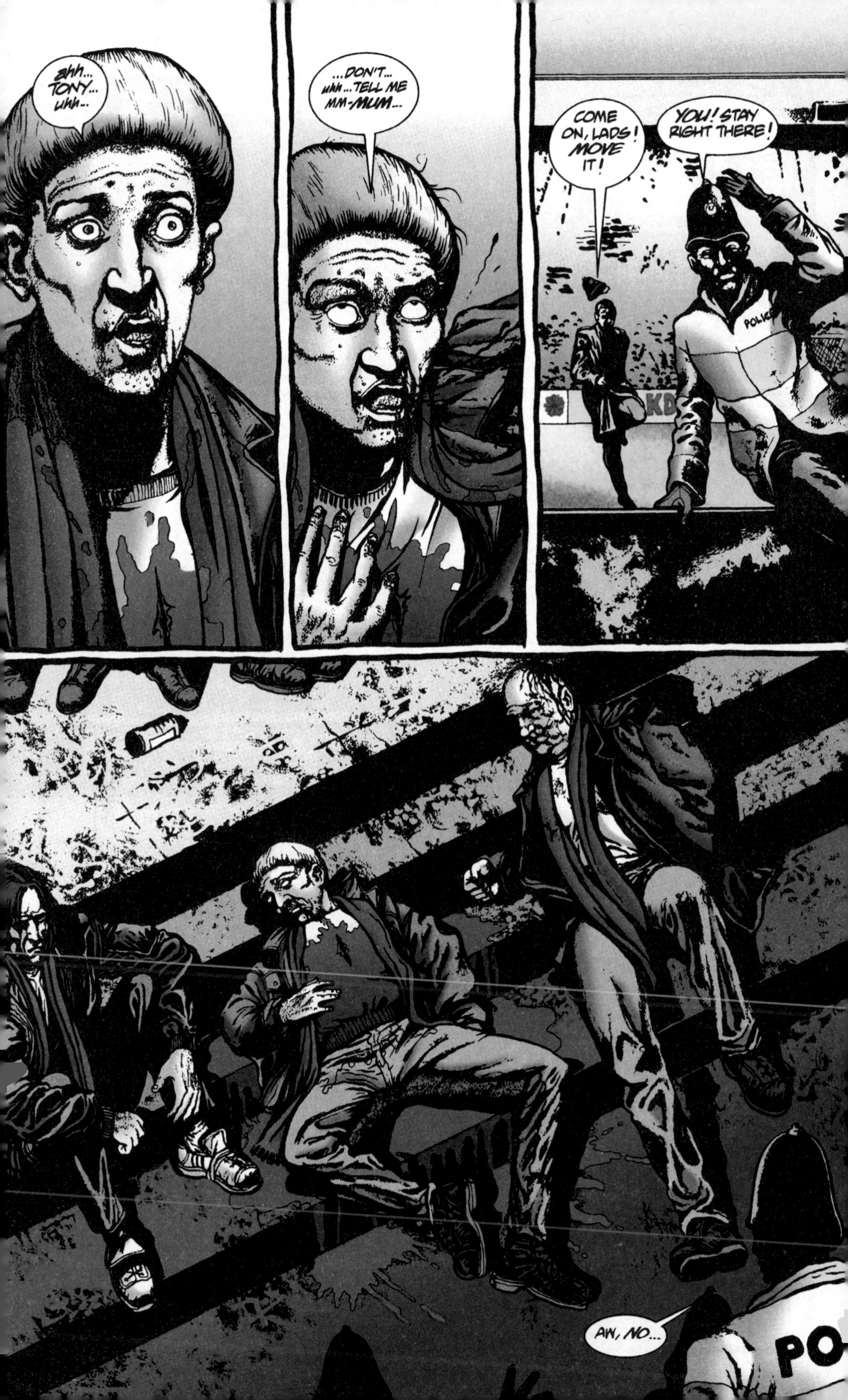
ahh... TONY... uhh...
...DON'T... uhh... TELL ME MM-MUM...
COME ON, LADS! MOVE IT!
YOU! STAY RIGHT THERE!
POLICE
AW, NO...
PO

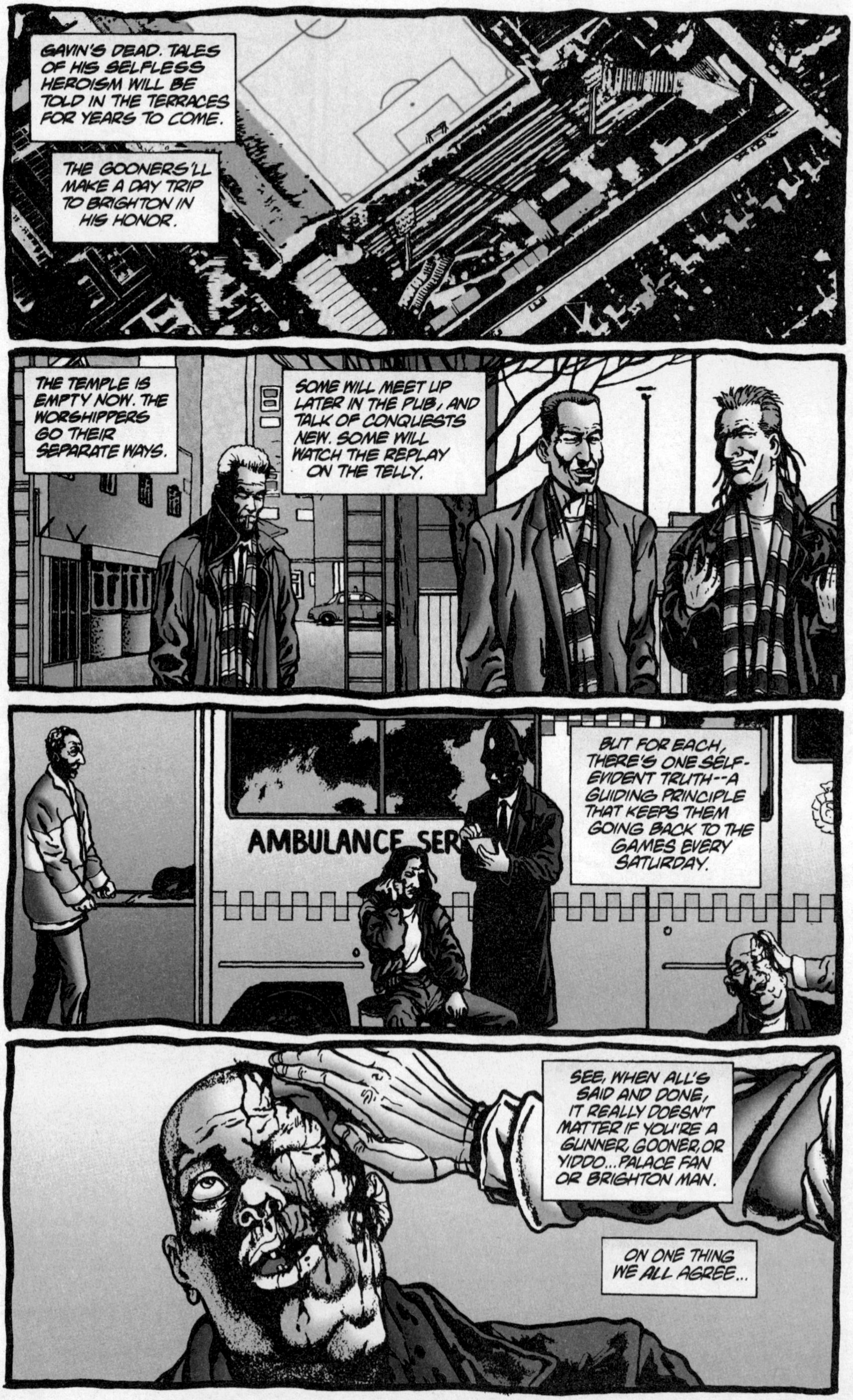
GAVIN'S DEAD. TALES OF HIS SELFLESS HEROISM WILL BE TOLD IN THE TERRACES FOR YEARS TO COME.
THE GOONERS'LL MAKE A DAY TRIP TO BRIGHTON IN HIS HONOR.
THE TEMPLE IS EMPTY NOW. THE WORSHIPPERS GO THEIR SEPARATE WAYS.
SOME WILL MEET UP LATER IN THE PUB, AND TALK OF CONQUESTS NEW. SOME WILL WATCH THE REPLAY ON THE TELLY.
AMBULANCE SER
BUT FOR EACH, THERE'S ONE SELF-EVIDENT TRUTH--A GUIDING PRINCIPLE THAT KEEPS THEM GOING BACK TO THE GAMES EVERY SATURDAY.
SEE, WHEN ALL'S SAID AND DONE, IT REALLY DOESN'T MATTER IF YOU'RE A GUNNER, GOONER, OR YIDDO...PALACE FAN OR BRIGHTON MAN.
ON ONE THING WE ALL AGREE...

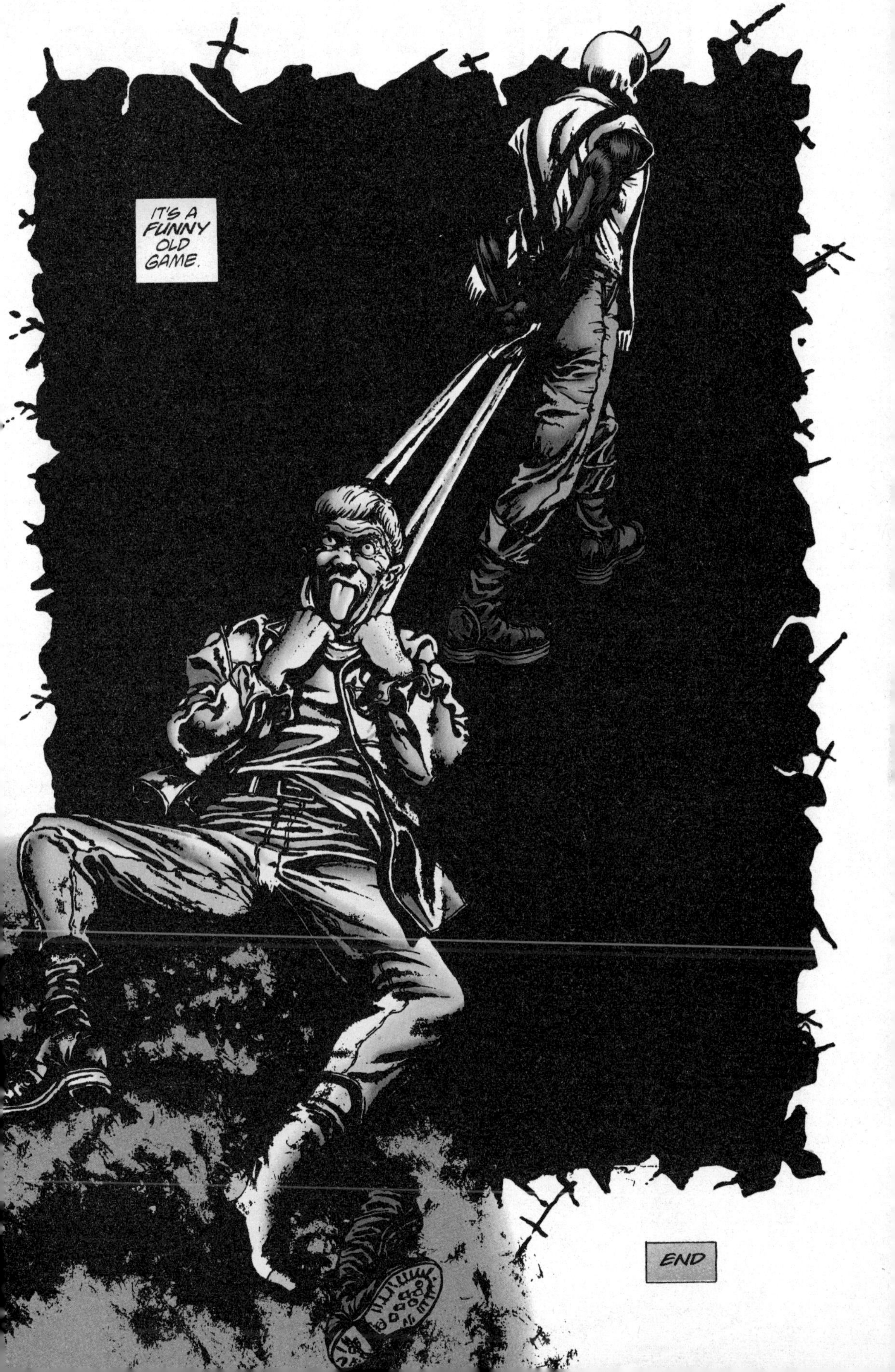
IT'S A FUNNY OLD GAME.
END

DC
VERTIGO
JOHN CONSTANTINE
HELLBLAZER
NO. 102
JUN 96
$2.25 US
$3.25 CAN
SUGGESTED FOR MATURE READERS
DIFFICULT BEGINNINGS
PART I OF III
PAUL JENKINS · SEAN PHILLIPS

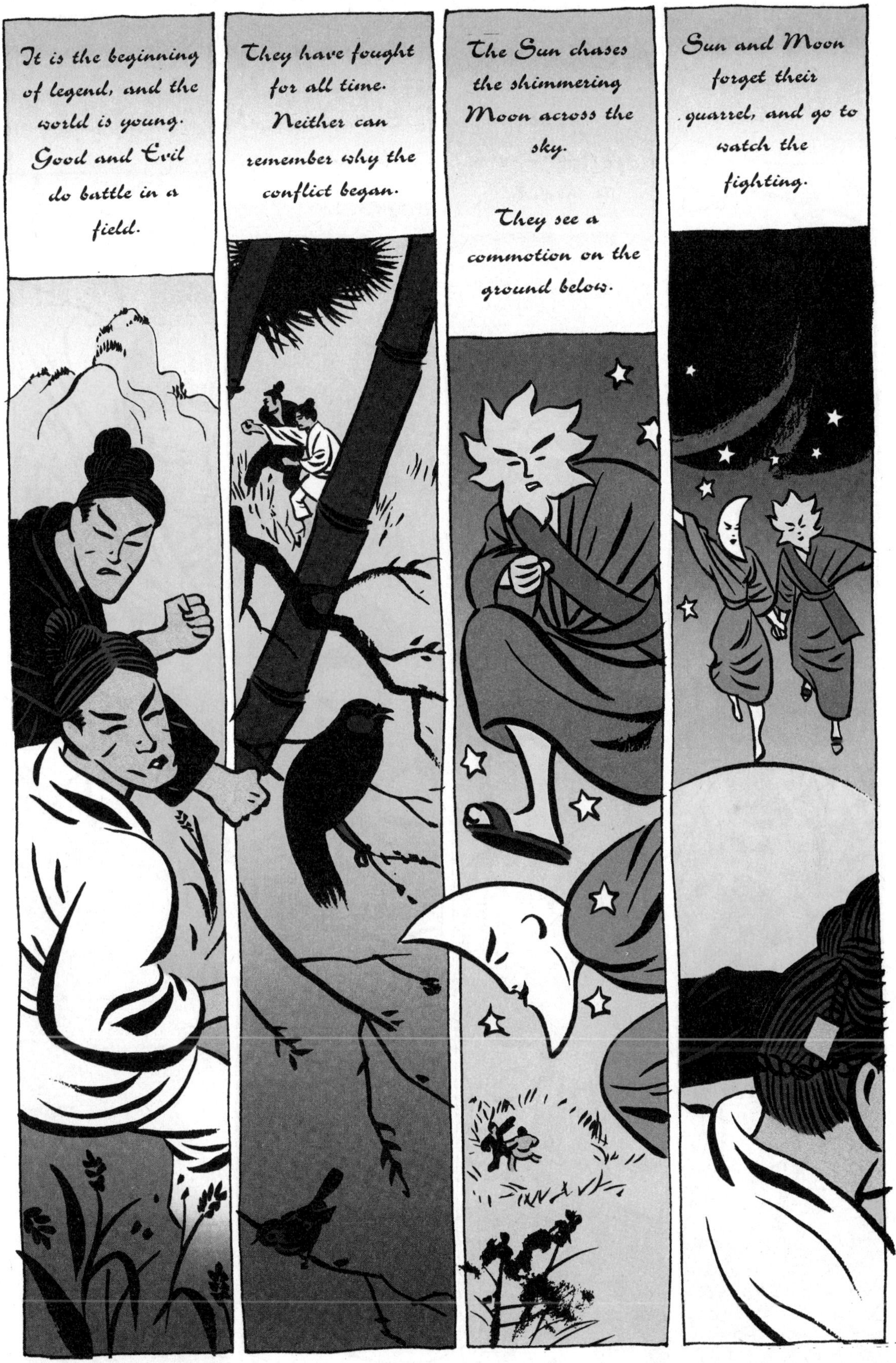
It is the beginning of legend, and the world is young. Good and Evil do battle in a field.
They have fought for all time. Neither can remember why the conflict began.
The Sun chases the shimmering Moon across the sky.
They see a commotion on the ground below.
Sun and Moon forget their quarrel, and go to watch the fighting.

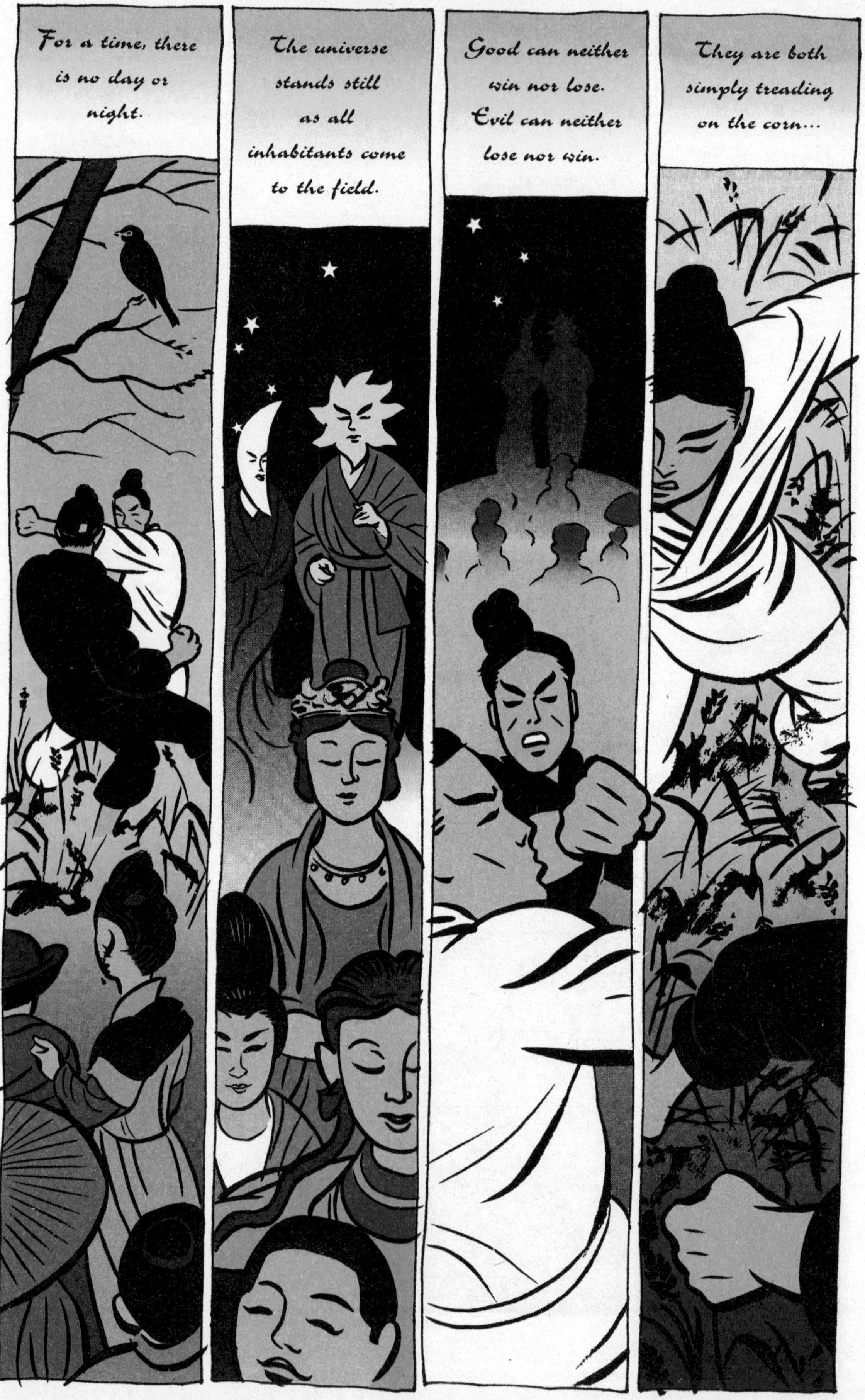
For a time, there is no day or night.
The universe stands still as all inhabitants come to the field.
Good can neither win nor lose. Evil can neither lose nor win.
They are both simply treading on the corn...

A GOOD MATE TOLD ME THAT STORY--IT WAS A LONG TIME AGO, JUST AFTER I ARRIVED IN THE SMOKE. FUNNY THING IS, I CAN'T REMEMBER HOW IT ENDS.

THAT'S NOT MY FAULT, THOUGH--NOT ALL OF ME, ANYWAY.

SEE, I'M NOT THE SAME PERSON I USED TO BE.

I USED TO KNOW MY PLACE IN THE GRAND BLOODY SCHEME, BACK WHEN I WAS JUST A DOWN-TRODDEN EAR OF CORN.

NOW I'M NO MORE THAN A VAGUELY INTERESTED BYSTANDER.

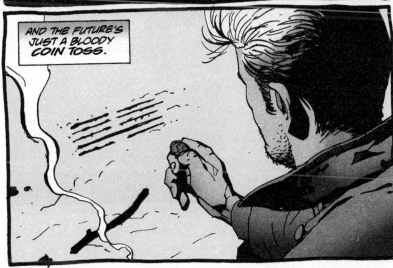

AND THE FUTURE'S JUST A BLOODY COIN TOSS.

DIFFICULT BEGINNINGS

1

the
SINGLE
SIDED
COIN

PAUL JENKINS *Writer*

SEAN PHILLIPS *Artist*

MATT HOLLINGSWORTH *Colorist*

CLEM ROBINS *Letterer*

AXEL ALONSO *Asst. Editor*

LOU STATHIS *Editor*

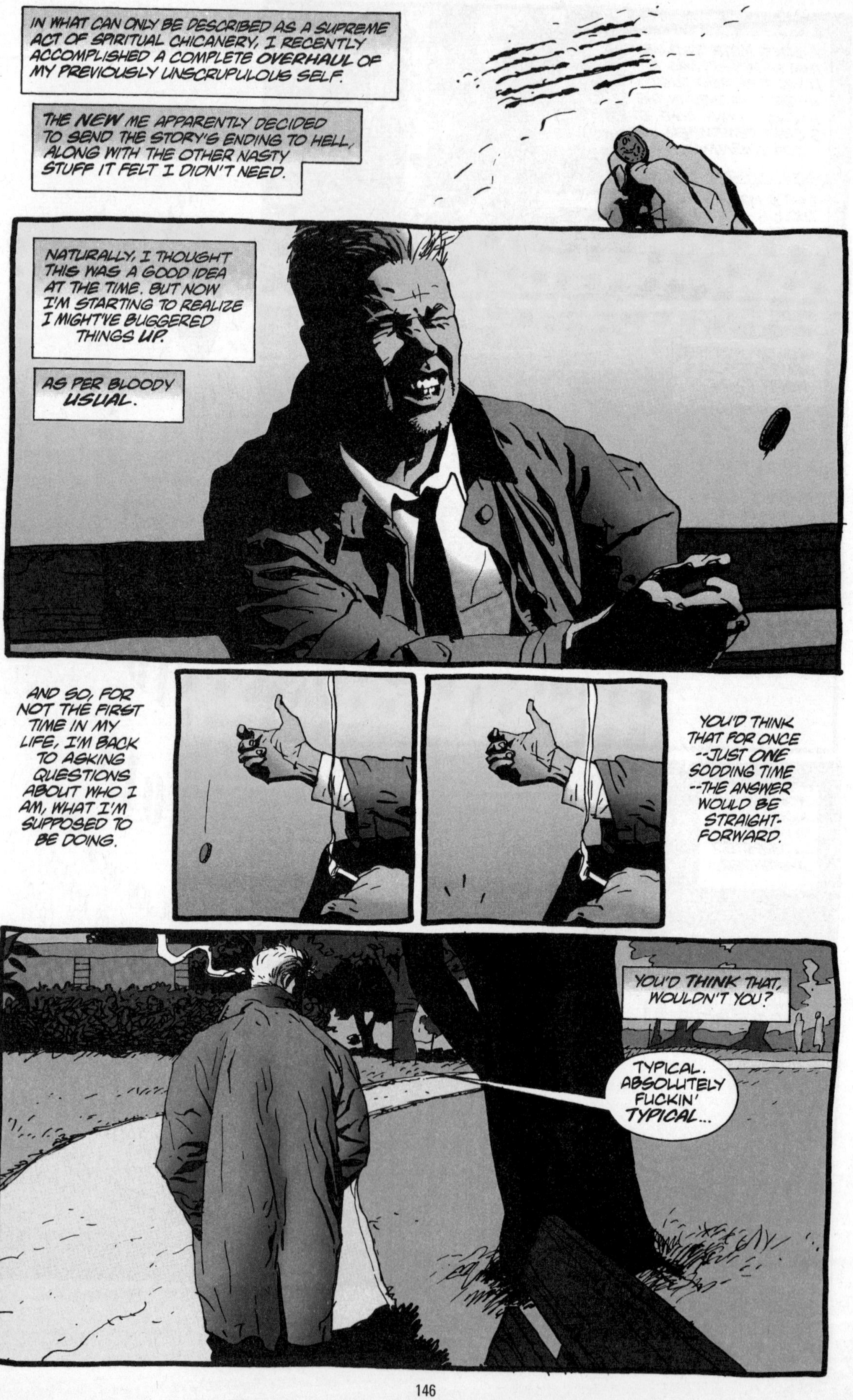

IN WHAT CAN ONLY BE DESCRIBED AS A SUPREME ACT OF SPIRITUAL CHICANERY, I RECENTLY ACCOMPLISHED A COMPLETE OVERHAUL OF MY PREVIOUSLY UNSCRUPULOUS SELF.
THE NEW ME APPARENTLY DECIDED TO SEND THE STORY'S ENDING TO HELL, ALONG WITH THE OTHER NASTY STUFF IT FELT I DIDN'T NEED.
NATURALLY, I THOUGHT THIS WAS A GOOD IDEA AT THE TIME. BUT NOW I'M STARTING TO REALIZE I MIGHT'VE BUGGERED THINGS UP.
AS PER BLOODY USUAL.
AND SO, FOR NOT THE FIRST TIME IN MY LIFE, I'M BACK TO ASKING QUESTIONS ABOUT WHO I AM, WHAT I'M SUPPOSED TO BE DOING.
YOU'D THINK THAT FOR ONCE --JUST ONE SODDING TIME --THE ANSWER WOULD BE STRAIGHT-FORWARD.
YOU'D THINK THAT, WOULDN'T YOU?
TYPICAL. ABSOLUTELY FUCKIN' TYPICAL...

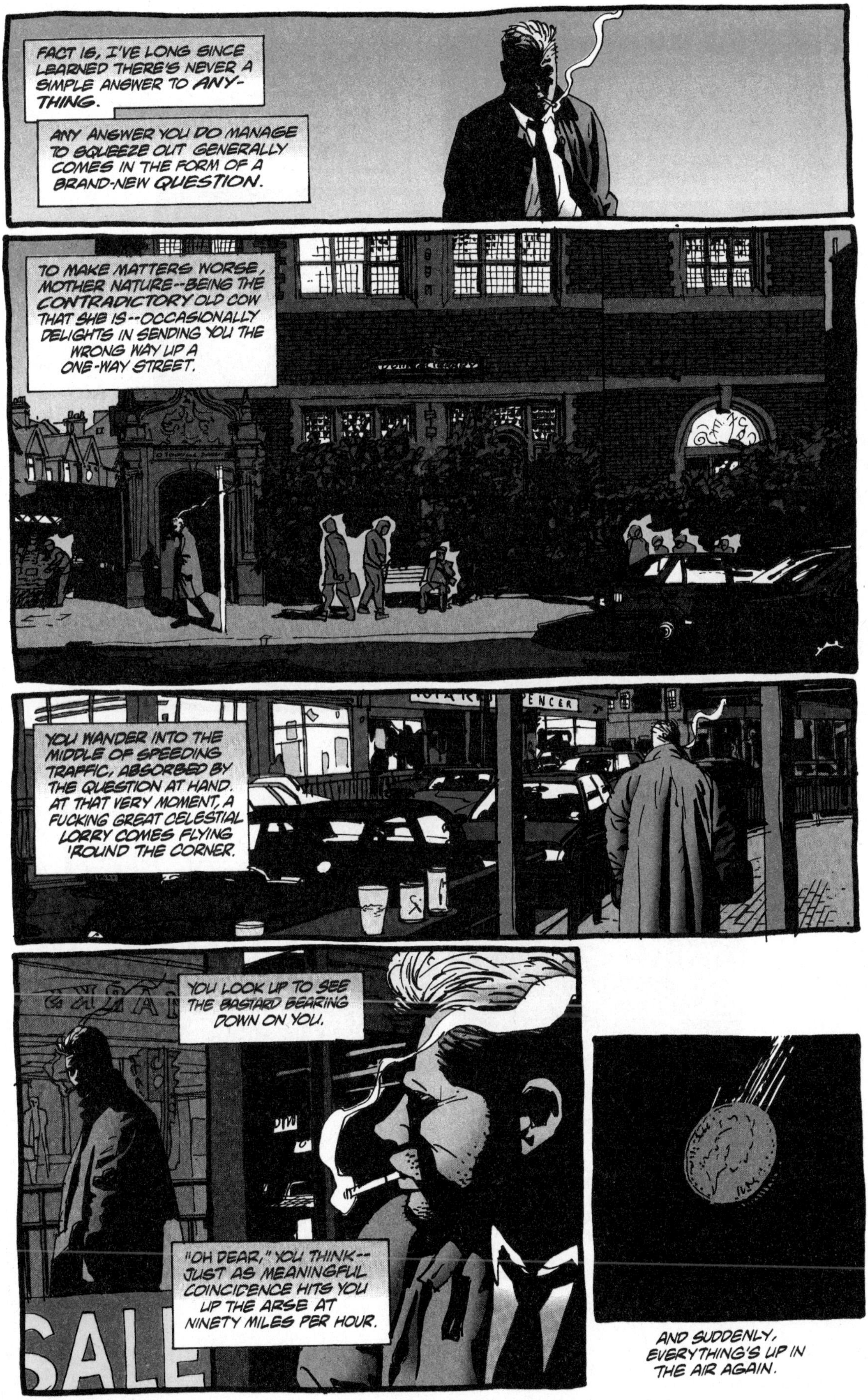
FACT IS, I'VE LONG SINCE LEARNED THERE'S NEVER A SIMPLE ANSWER TO ANY-THING.
ANY ANSWER YOU DO MANAGE TO SQUEEZE OUT GENERALLY COMES IN THE FORM OF A BRAND-NEW QUESTION.
TO MAKE MATTERS WORSE, MOTHER NATURE--BEING THE CONTRADICTORY OLD COW THAT SHE IS--OCCASIONALLY DELIGHTS IN SENDING YOU THE WRONG WAY UP A ONE-WAY STREET.
YOU WANDER INTO THE MIDDLE OF SPEEDING TRAFFIC, ABSORBED BY THE QUESTION AT HAND. AT THAT VERY MOMENT, A FUCKING GREAT CELESTIAL LORRY COMES FLYING 'ROUND THE CORNER.
YOU LOOK UP TO SEE THE BASTARD BEARING DOWN ON YOU.
"OH DEAR," YOU THINK--JUST AS MEANINGFUL COINCIDENCE HITS YOU UP THE ARSE AT NINETY MILES PER HOUR.
SALE
AND SUDDENLY, EVERYTHING'S UP IN THE AIR AGAIN.

WELL, I'VE COMPLETELY OUTDONE MYSELF THIS TIME. EVER SINCE I CAST MY DARKER SIDE INTO THE DEPTHS, I'VE HAD A TERRIBLE FEELING THAT SOMETHING'S *MISSING.*

I'VE TRIED TO IGNORE IT, TO PRETEND IT'S JUST A NATURAL REACTION. BUT NOW I'M CERTAIN SOMETHING'S VERY WRONG INDEED.

TRUE, I'VE PULLED ANOTHER FAST ONE ON THE ASSEMBLED FORCES OF DARKNESS AND MADE GOOD MY ESCAPE.

ONLY PROBLEM IS, I'M *WORSE* OFF NOW THAN BEFORE.

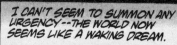

I CAN'T SEEM TO SUMMON ANY URGENCY--THE WORLD NOW SEEMS LIKE A WAKING DREAM.

I'M BEGINNING TO SUSPECT THAT I'M WEARING MY OWN FACE, JUST FOR THE DURATION OF MY RELATIVELY POINTLESS TIME ON EARTH.

BUT SOMEWHERE IN THERE IS THE FEELING THAT MAYBE THIS *ISN'T* A DREAM.

OR MAYBE I CAN NO LONGER SEE WHERE THE DREAM ENDS AND REALITY *BEGINS.*

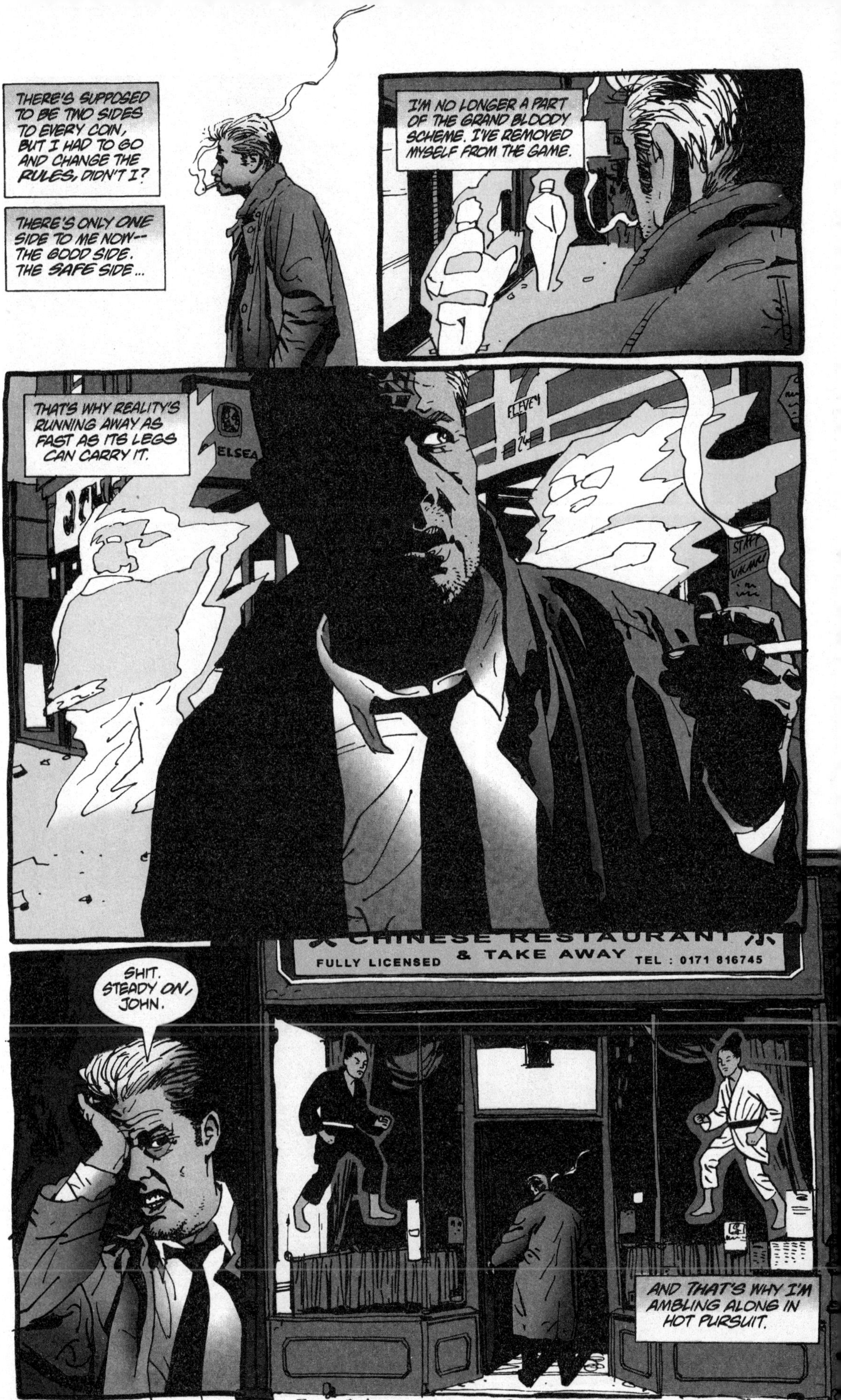
THERE'S SUPPOSED TO BE TWO SIDES TO EVERY COIN, BUT I HAD TO GO AND CHANGE THE RULES, DIDN'T I?
THERE'S ONLY ONE SIDE TO ME NOW-- THE GOOD SIDE. THE SAFE SIDE...
I'M NO LONGER A PART OF THE GRAND BLOODY SCHEME. I'VE REMOVED MYSELF FROM THE GAME.
THAT'S WHY REALITY'S RUNNING AWAY AS FAST AS ITS LEGS CAN CARRY IT.
SHIT. STEADY ON, JOHN.
CHINESE RESTAURANT
FULLY LICENSED
& TAKE AWAY
TEL : 0171 816745
AND THAT'S WHY I'M AMBLING ALONG IN HOT PURSUIT.

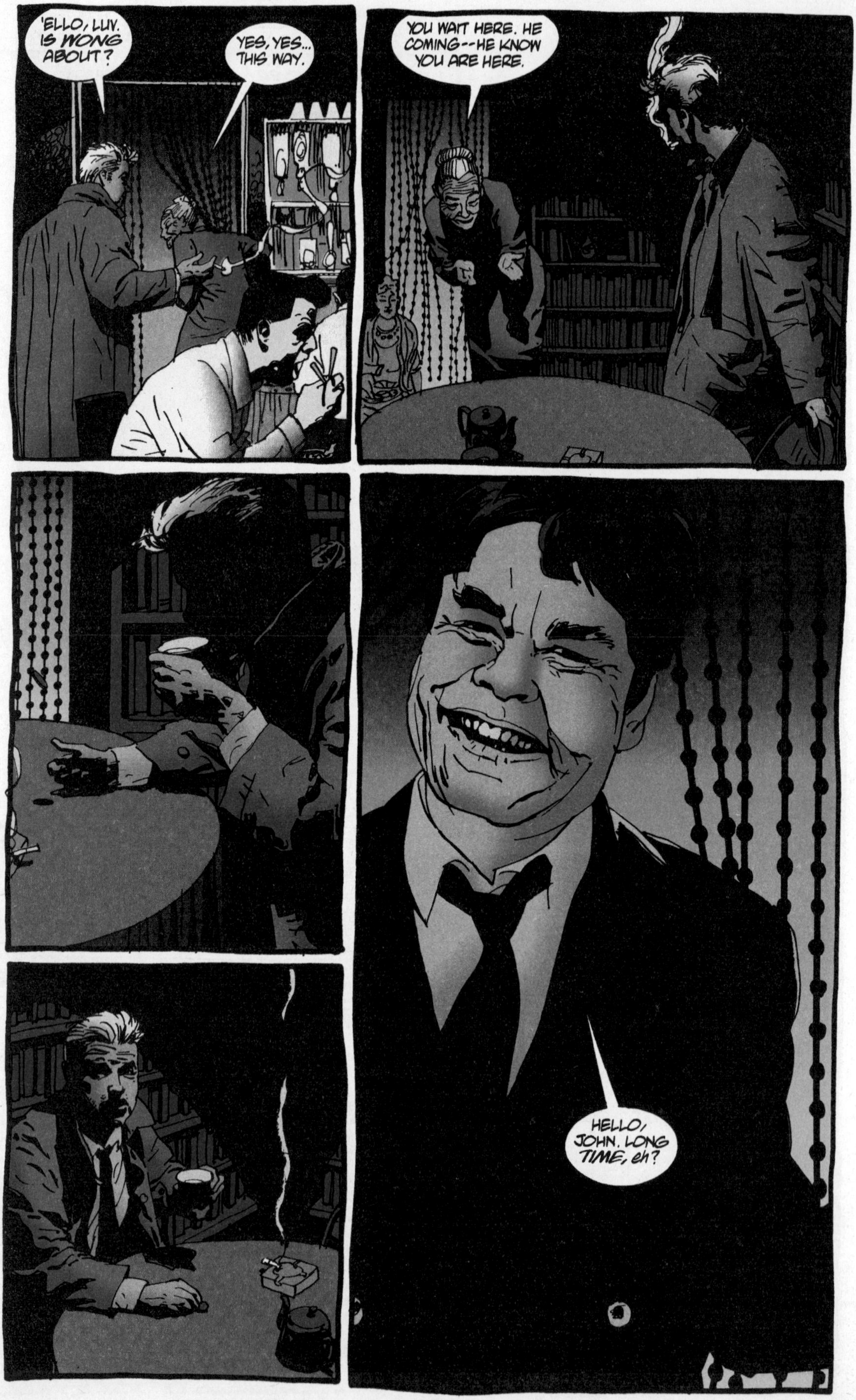
'ELLO, LUV. IS WONG ABOUT?
YES, YES... THIS WAY.
YOU WAIT HERE. HE COMING--HE KNOW YOU ARE HERE.
HELLO, JOHN. LONG TIME, eh?

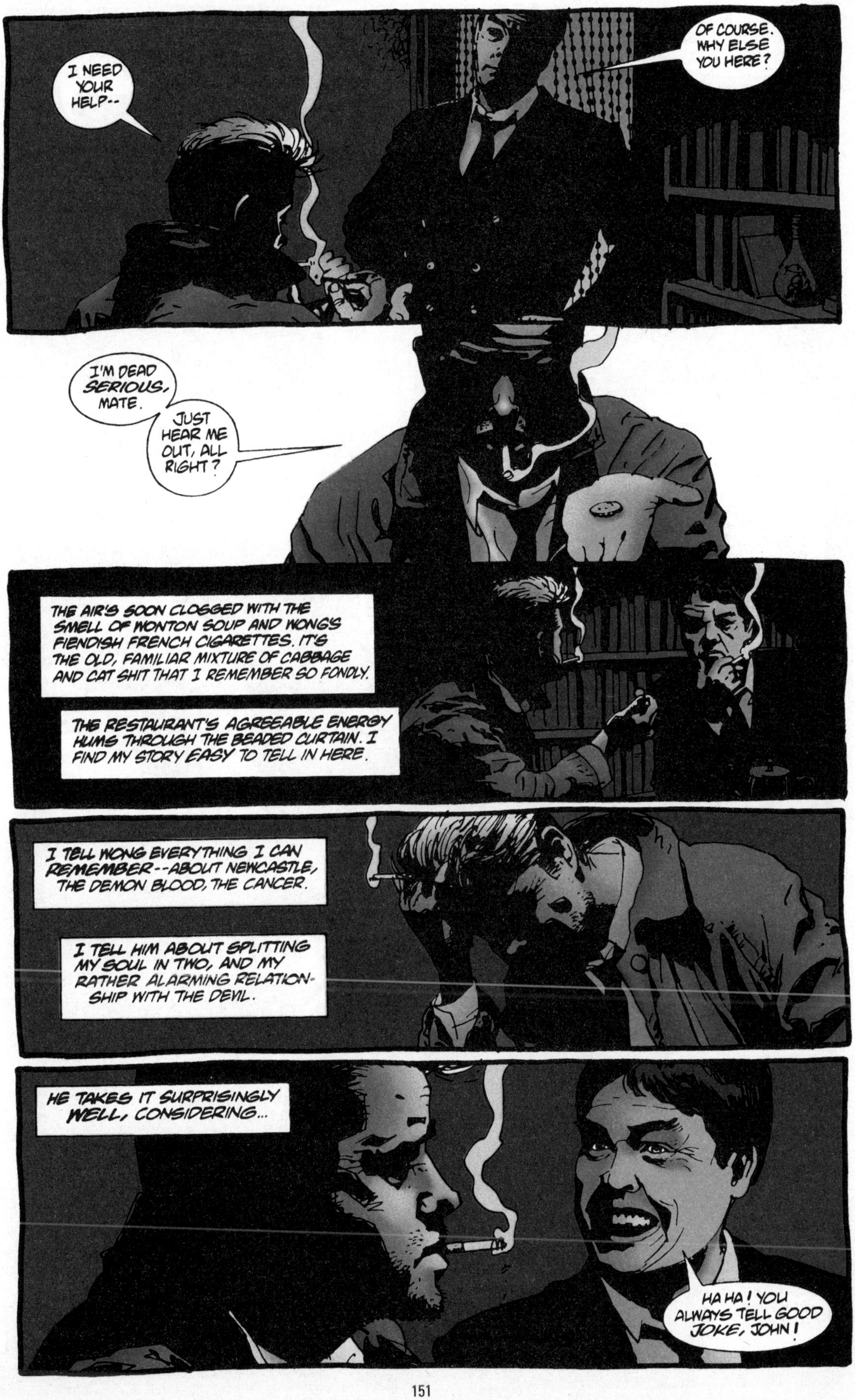
I NEED YOUR HELP--
OF COURSE. WHY ELSE YOU HERE?
I'M DEAD SERIOUS, MATE.
JUST HEAR ME OUT, ALL RIGHT?
THE AIR'S SOON CLOGGED WITH THE SMELL OF WONTON SOUP AND WONG'S FIENDISH FRENCH CIGARETTES. IT'S THE OLD, FAMILIAR MIXTURE OF CABBAGE AND CAT SHIT THAT I REMEMBER SO FONDLY.
THE RESTAURANT'S AGREEABLE ENERGY HUMS THROUGH THE BEADED CURTAIN. I FIND MY STORY EASY TO TELL IN HERE.
I TELL WONG EVERYTHING I CAN REMEMBER--ABOUT NEWCASTLE, THE DEMON BLOOD, THE CANCER.
I TELL HIM ABOUT SPLITTING MY SOUL IN TWO, AND MY RATHER ALARMING RELATIONSHIP WITH THE DEVIL.
HE TAKES IT SURPRISINGLY WELL, CONSIDERING...
HA HA! YOU ALWAYS TELL GOOD JOKE, JOHN!

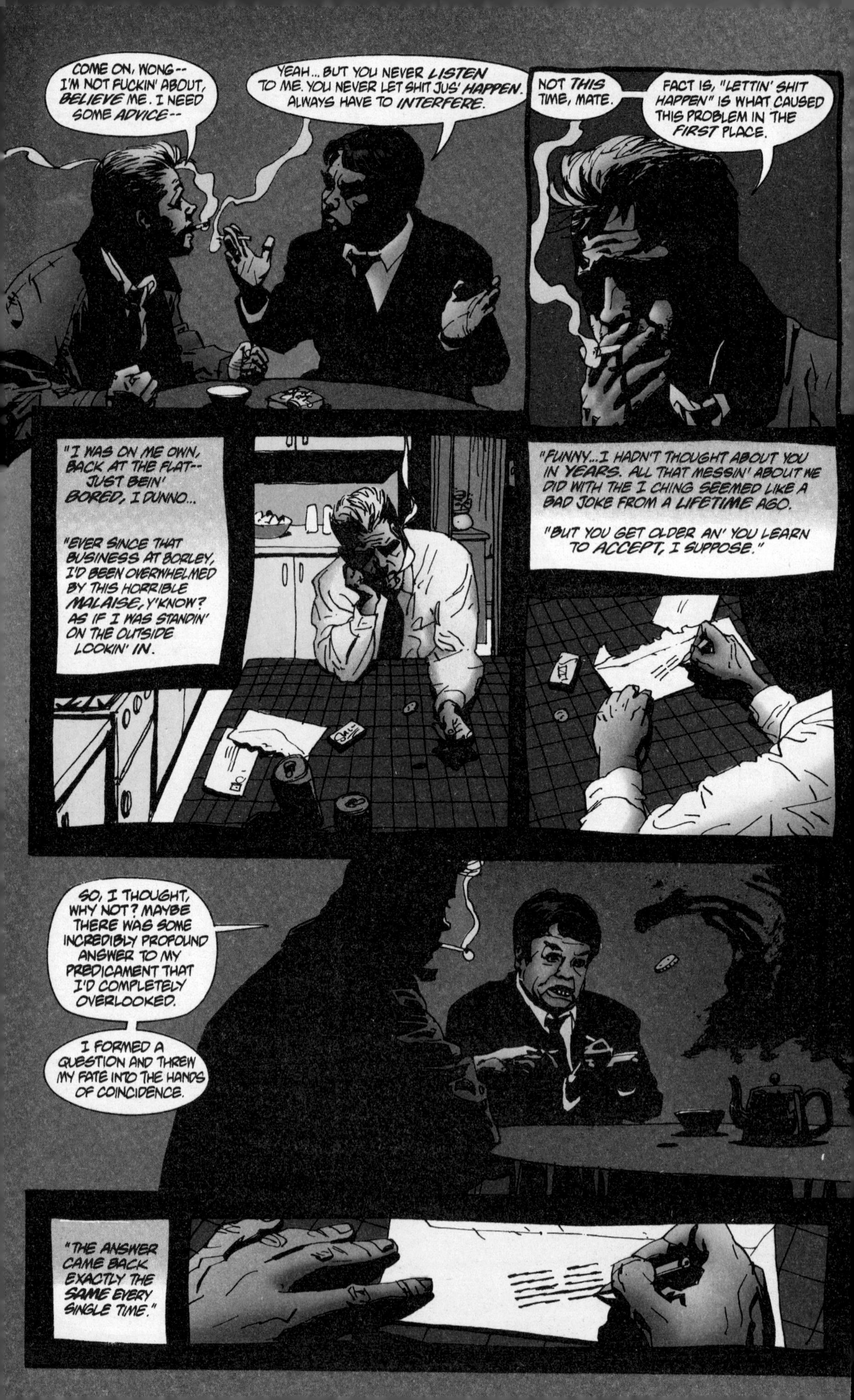
COME ON, WONG-- I'M NOT FUCKIN' ABOUT, BELIEVE ME. I NEED SOME ADVICE--
YEAH... BUT YOU NEVER LISTEN TO ME. YOU NEVER LET SHIT JUS' HAPPEN. ALWAYS HAVE TO INTERFERE.
NOT THIS TIME, MATE.
FACT IS, "LETTIN' SHIT HAPPEN" IS WHAT CAUSED THIS PROBLEM IN THE FIRST PLACE.
"I WAS ON ME OWN, BACK AT THE FLAT-- JUST BEIN' BORED, I DUNNO...
"EVER SINCE THAT BUSINESS AT BORLEY, I'D BEEN OVERWHELMED BY THIS HORRIBLE MALAISE, Y'KNOW? AS IF I WAS STANDIN' ON THE OUTSIDE LOOKIN' IN.
"FUNNY...I HADN'T THOUGHT ABOUT YOU IN YEARS. ALL THAT MESSIN' ABOUT WE DID WITH THE I CHING SEEMED LIKE A BAD JOKE FROM A LIFETIME AGO.
"BUT YOU GET OLDER AN' YOU LEARN TO ACCEPT, I SUPPOSE."
SO, I THOUGHT, WHY NOT? MAYBE THERE WAS SOME INCREDIBLY PROFOUND ANSWER TO MY PREDICAMENT THAT I'D COMPLETELY OVERLOOKED.
I FORMED A QUESTION AND THREW MY FATE INTO THE HANDS OF COINCIDENCE.
"THE ANSWER CAME BACK EXACTLY THE SAME EVERY SINGLE TIME."

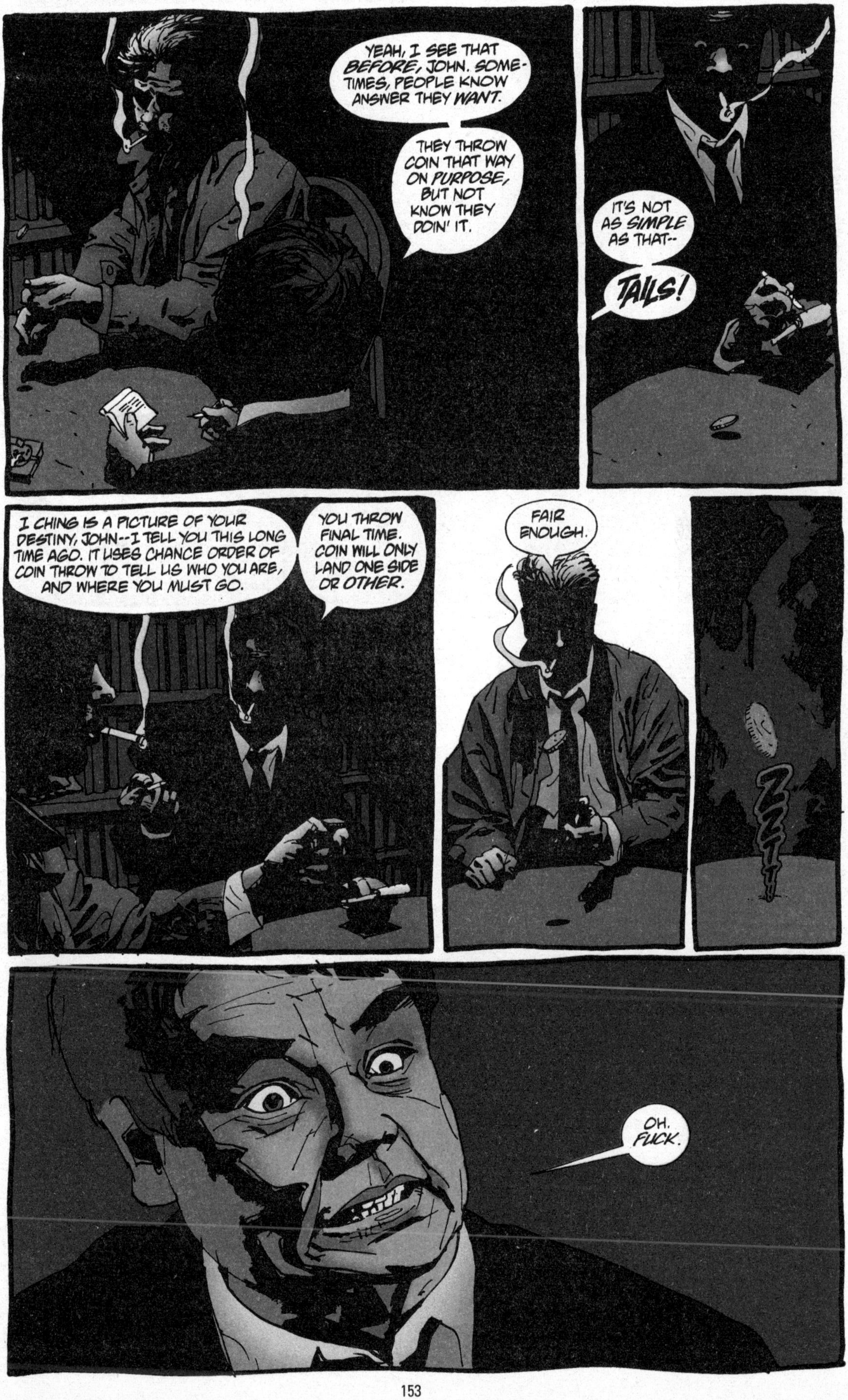
YEAH, I SEE THAT BEFORE, JOHN. SOMETIMES, PEOPLE KNOW ANSWER THEY WANT.
THEY THROW COIN THAT WAY ON PURPOSE, BUT NOT KNOW THEY DOIN' IT.
IT'S NOT AS SIMPLE AS THAT--
TAILS!
I CHING IS A PICTURE OF YOUR DESTINY, JOHN--I TELL YOU THIS LONG TIME AGO. IT USES CHANCE ORDER OF COIN THROW TO TELL US WHO YOU ARE, AND WHERE YOU MUST GO.
YOU THROW FINAL TIME. COIN WILL ONLY LAND ONE SIDE OR OTHER.
FAIR ENOUGH.
ZZZT
OH. FUCK.

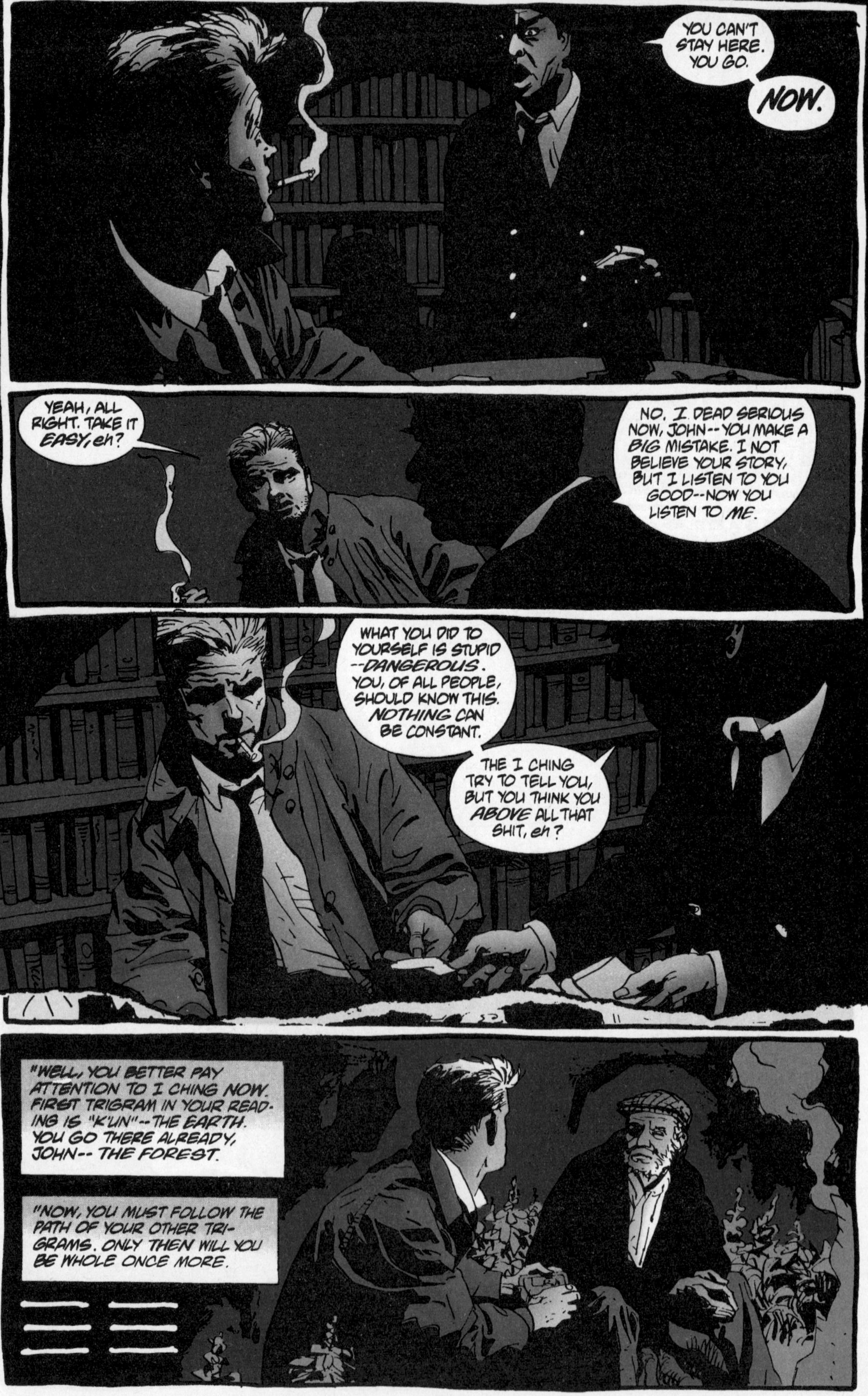
YOU CAN'T STAY HERE. YOU GO.
NOW.
YEAH, ALL RIGHT. TAKE IT EASY, eh?
NO. I DEAD SERIOUS NOW, JOHN--YOU MAKE A BIG MISTAKE. I NOT BELIEVE YOUR STORY, BUT I LISTEN TO YOU GOOD--NOW YOU LISTEN TO ME.
WHAT YOU DID TO YOURSELF IS STUPID --DANGEROUS. YOU, OF ALL PEOPLE, SHOULD KNOW THIS. NOTHING CAN BE CONSTANT.
THE I CHING TRY TO TELL YOU, BUT YOU THINK YOU ABOVE ALL THAT SHIT, eh?
"WELL, YOU BETTER PAY ATTENTION TO I CHING NOW. FIRST TRIGRAM IN YOUR READING IS "K'UN"--THE EARTH. YOU GO THERE ALREADY, JOHN-- THE FOREST.
"NOW, YOU MUST FOLLOW THE PATH OF YOUR OTHER TRIGRAMS. ONLY THEN WILL YOU BE WHOLE ONCE MORE.

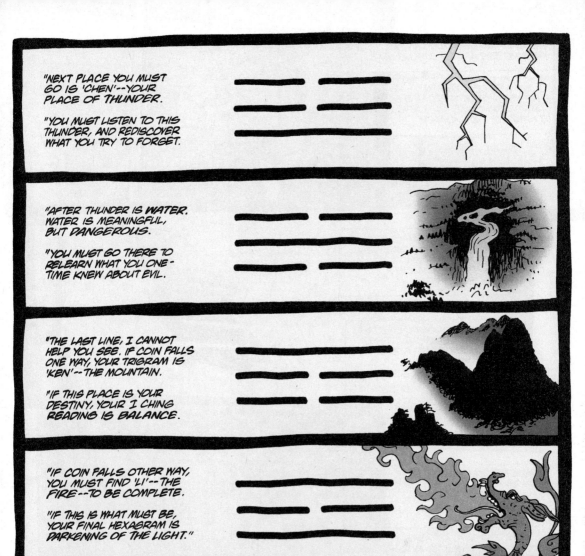

"NEXT PLACE YOU MUST GO IS 'CHEN'--YOUR PLACE OF THUNDER.

"YOU MUST LISTEN TO THIS THUNDER, AND REDISCOVER WHAT YOU TRY TO FORGET.

"AFTER THUNDER IS WATER. WATER IS MEANINGFUL, BUT DANGEROUS.

"YOU MUST GO THERE TO RELEARN WHAT YOU ONE-TIME KNEW ABOUT EVIL.

"THE LAST LINE, I CANNOT HELP YOU SEE. IF COIN FALLS ONE WAY, YOUR TRIGRAM IS 'KEN'--THE MOUNTAIN.

"IF THIS PLACE IS YOUR DESTINY, YOUR I CHING READING IS BALANCE.

"IF COIN FALLS OTHER WAY, YOU MUST FIND 'LI'--THE FIRE--TO BE COMPLETE.

"IF THIS IS WHAT MUST BE, YOUR FINAL HEXAGRAM IS DARKENING OF THE LIGHT."

YOU BE THE COIN, JOHN.

THROW YOUR-SELF IN THE AIR. SEE WHERE YOU LAND.

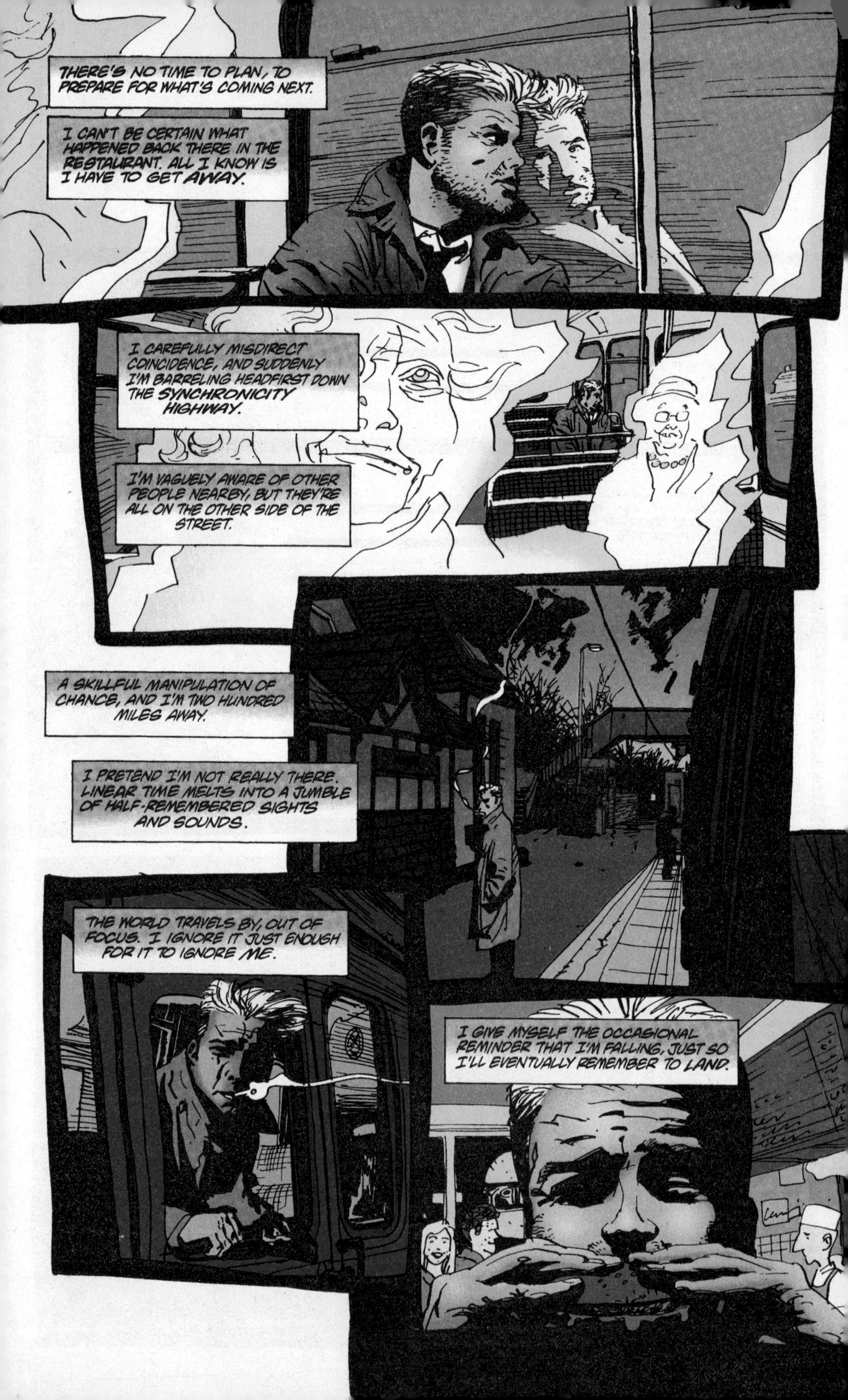

THERE'S NO TIME TO PLAN, TO PREPARE FOR WHAT'S COMING NEXT.
I CAN'T BE CERTAIN WHAT HAPPENED BACK THERE IN THE RESTAURANT. ALL I KNOW IS I HAVE TO GET AWAY.
I CAREFULLY MISDIRECT COINCIDENCE, AND SUDDENLY I'M BARRELING HEADFIRST DOWN THE SYNCHRONICITY HIGHWAY.
I'M VAGUELY AWARE OF OTHER PEOPLE NEARBY, BUT THEY'RE ALL ON THE OTHER SIDE OF THE STREET.
A SKILLFUL MANIPULATION OF CHANCE, AND I'M TWO HUNDRED MILES AWAY.
I PRETEND I'M NOT REALLY THERE. LINEAR TIME MELTS INTO A JUMBLE OF HALF-REMEMBERED SIGHTS AND SOUNDS.
THE WORLD TRAVELS BY, OUT OF FOCUS. I IGNORE IT JUST ENOUGH FOR IT TO IGNORE ME.
I GIVE MYSELF THE OCCASIONAL REMINDER THAT I'M FALLING, JUST SO I'LL EVENTUALLY REMEMBER TO LAND.

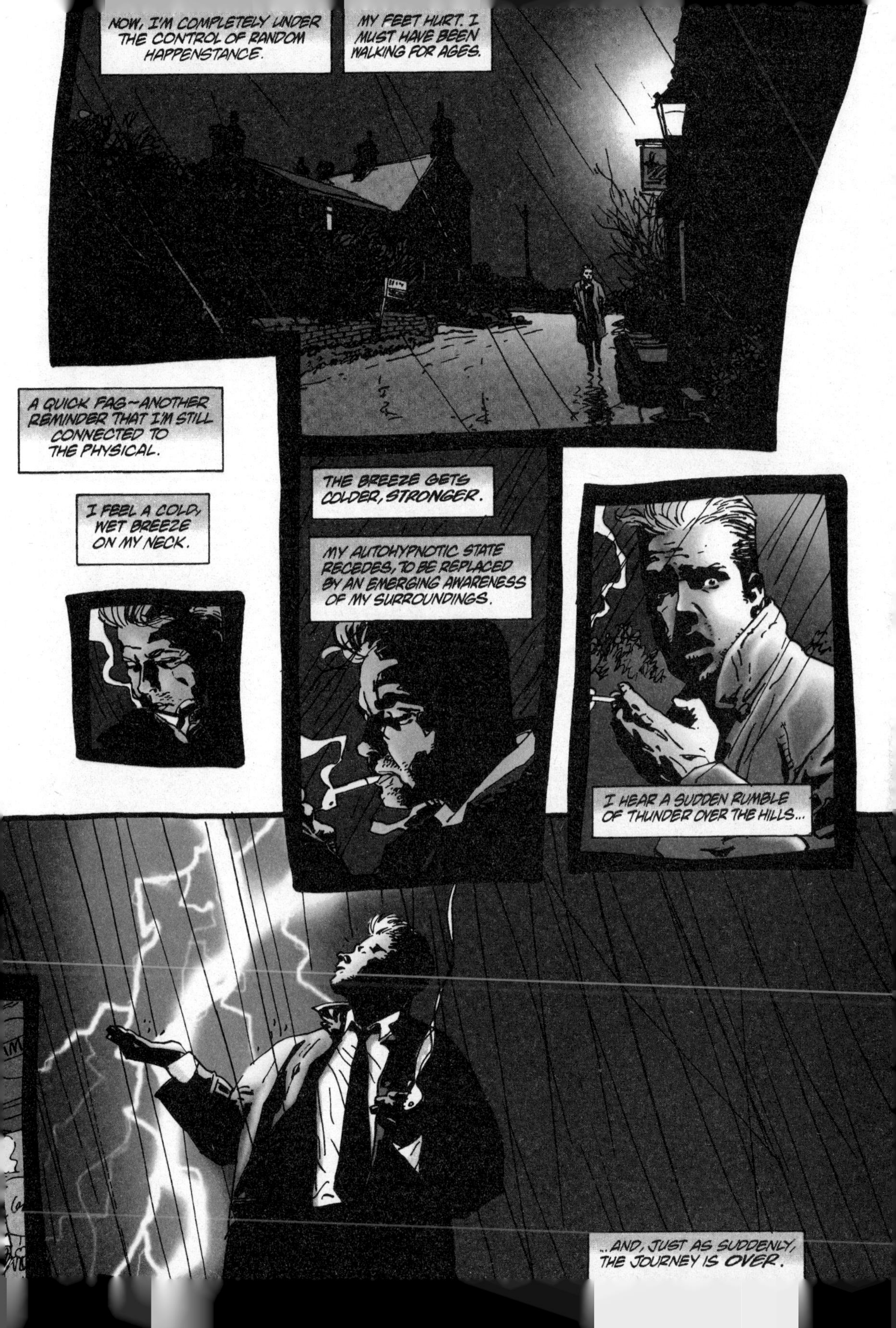
NOW, I'M COMPLETELY UNDER THE CONTROL OF RANDOM HAPPENSTANCE.
MY FEET HURT. I MUST HAVE BEEN WALKING FOR AGES.
A QUICK FAG--ANOTHER REMINDER THAT I'M STILL CONNECTED TO THE PHYSICAL.
I FEEL A COLD, WET BREEZE ON MY NECK.
THE BREEZE GETS COLDER, STRONGER.
MY AUTOHYPNOTIC STATE RECEDES, TO BE REPLACED BY AN EMERGING AWARENESS OF MY SURROUNDINGS.
I HEAR A SUDDEN RUMBLE OF THUNDER OVER THE HILLS...
...AND, JUST AS SUDDENLY, THE JOURNEY IS OVER.

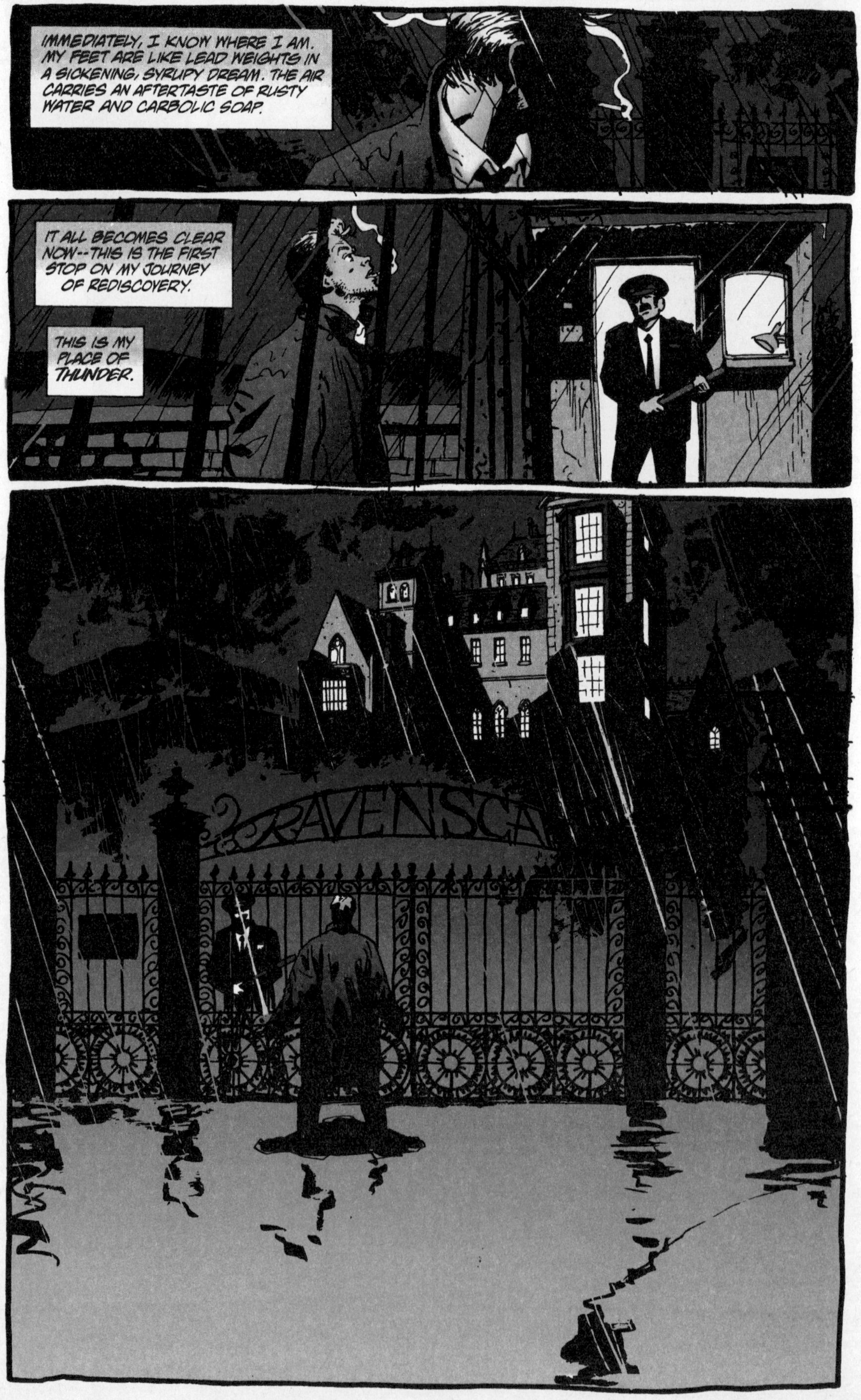
IMMEDIATELY, I KNOW WHERE I AM. MY FEET ARE LIKE LEAD WEIGHTS IN A SICKENING, SYRUPY DREAM. THE AIR CARRIES AN AFTERTASTE OF RUSTY WATER AND CARBOLIC SOAP.
IT ALL BECOMES CLEAR NOW--THIS IS THE FIRST STOP ON MY JOURNEY OF REDISCOVERY.
THIS IS MY PLACE OF THUNDER.
RAVENSCA

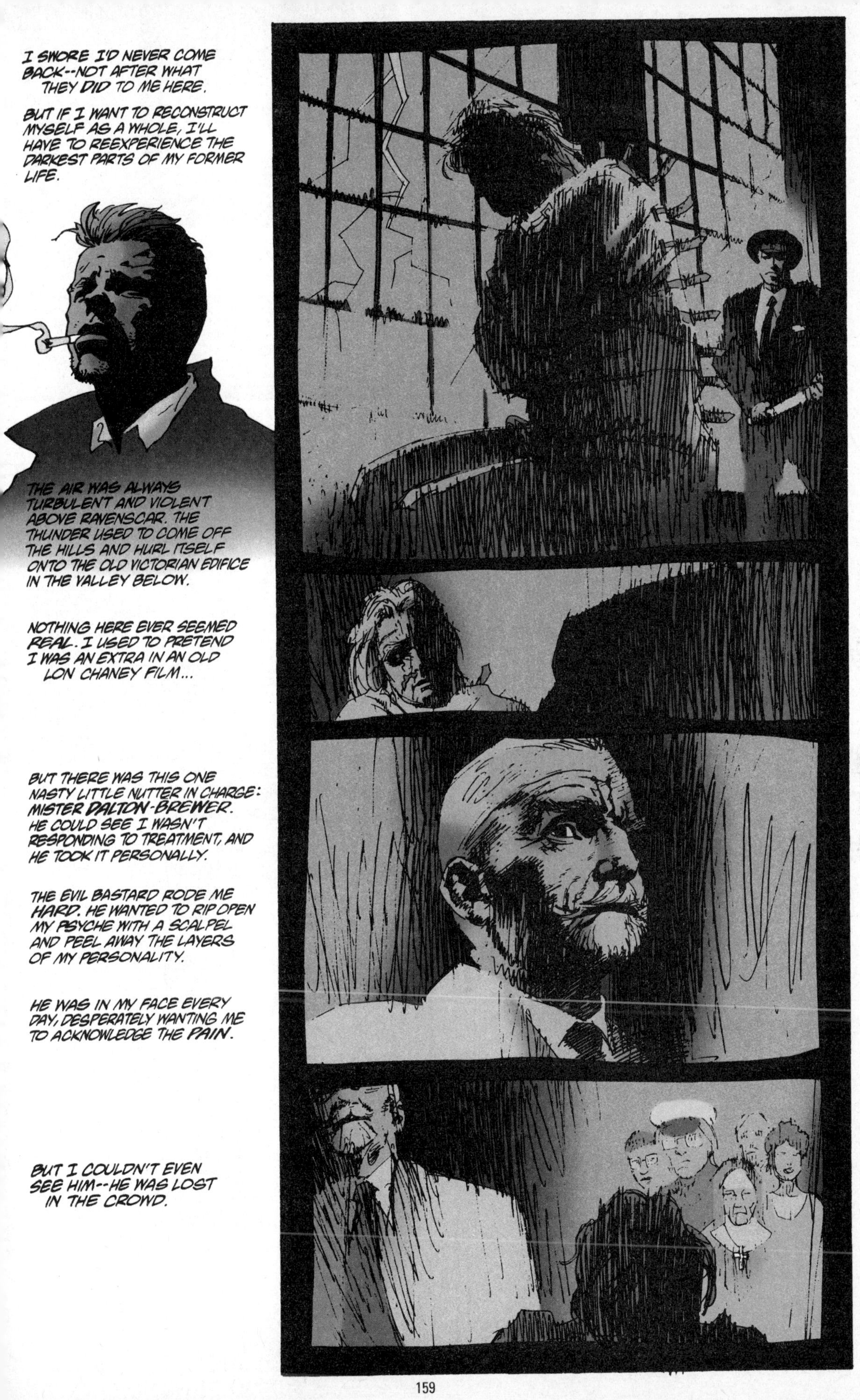
I SWORE I'D NEVER COME BACK--NOT AFTER WHAT THEY DID TO ME HERE.
BUT IF I WANT TO RECONSTRUCT MYSELF AS A WHOLE, I'LL HAVE TO REEXPERIENCE THE DARKEST PARTS OF MY FORMER LIFE.
THE AIR WAS ALWAYS TURBULENT AND VIOLENT ABOVE RAVENSCAR. THE THUNDER USED TO COME OFF THE HILLS AND HURL ITSELF ONTO THE OLD VICTORIAN EDIFICE IN THE VALLEY BELOW.
NOTHING HERE EVER SEEMED REAL. I USED TO PRETEND I WAS AN EXTRA IN AN OLD LON CHANEY FILM...
BUT THERE WAS THIS ONE NASTY LITTLE NUTTER IN CHARGE: MISTER DALTON-BREWER. HE COULD SEE I WASN'T RESPONDING TO TREATMENT, AND HE TOOK IT PERSONALLY.
THE EVIL BASTARD RODE ME HARD. HE WANTED TO RIP OPEN MY PSYCHE WITH A SCALPEL AND PEEL AWAY THE LAYERS OF MY PERSONALITY.
HE WAS IN MY FACE EVERY DAY, DESPERATELY WANTING ME TO ACKNOWLEDGE THE PAIN.
BUT I COULDN'T EVEN SEE HIM--HE WAS LOST IN THE CROWD.

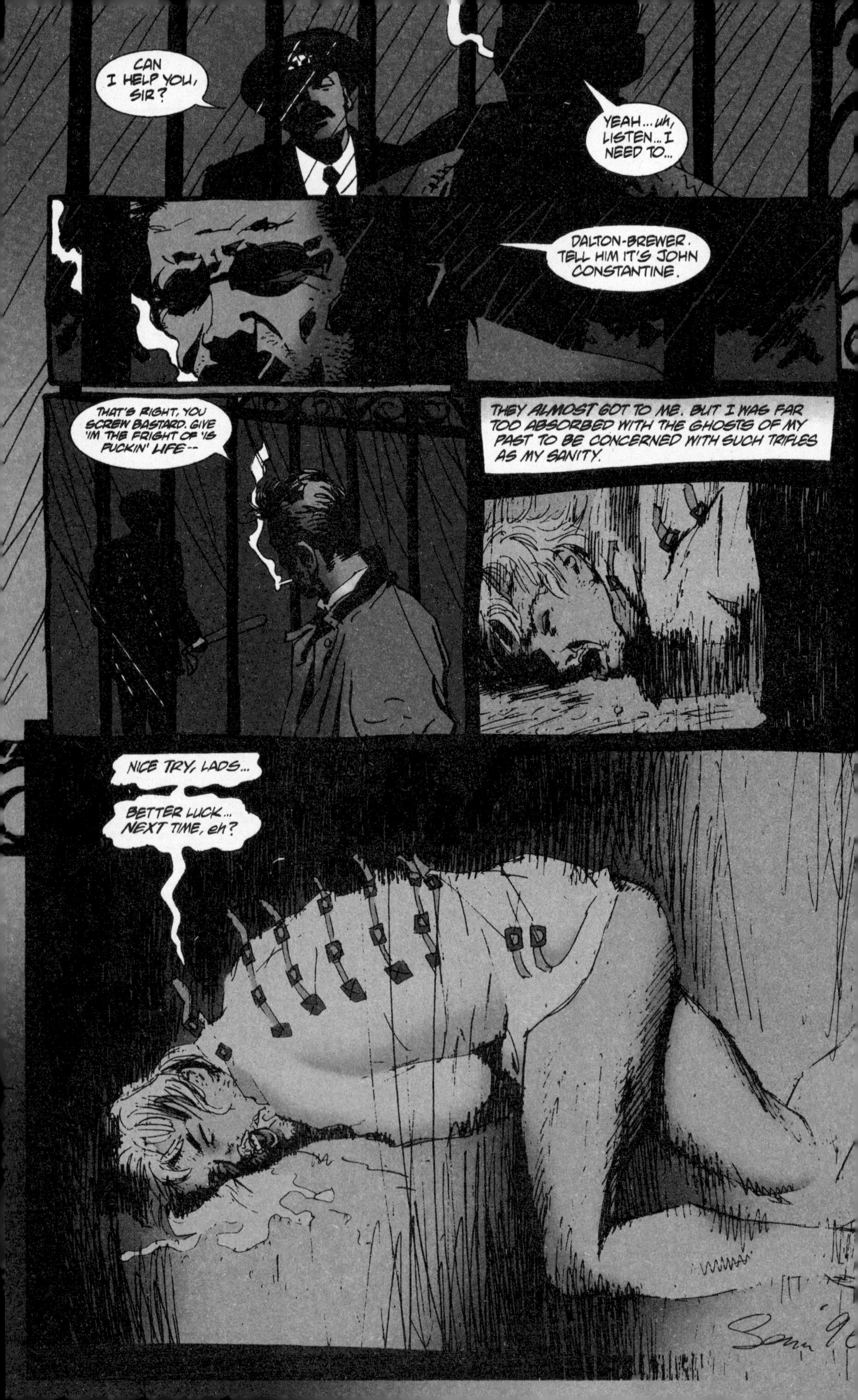
CAN I HELP YOU, SIR?
YEAH... uh, LISTEN... I NEED TO...
DALTON-BREWER. TELL HIM IT'S JOHN CONSTANTINE.
THAT'S RIGHT, YOU SCREW BASTARD. GIVE 'IM THE FRIGHT OF 'IS FUCKIN' LIFE--
THEY ALMOST GOT TO ME. BUT I WAS FAR TOO ABSORBED WITH THE GHOSTS OF MY PAST TO BE CONCERNED WITH SUCH TRIFLES AS MY SANITY.
NICE TRY, LADS...
BETTER LUCK... NEXT TIME, eh?

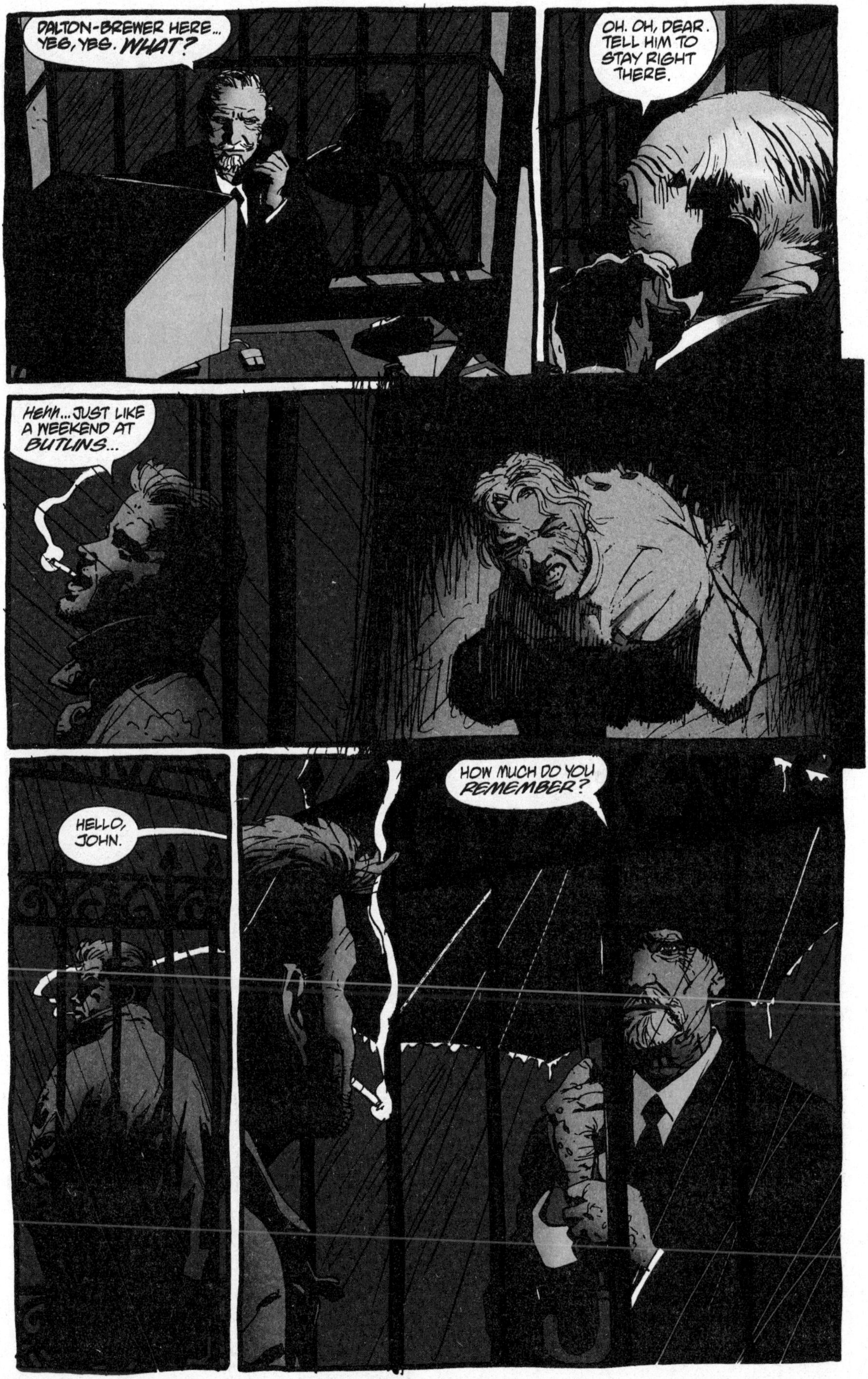

DALTON-BREWER HERE... YES, YES. WHAT?
OH. OH, DEAR. TELL HIM TO STAY RIGHT THERE.
Hehh... JUST LIKE A WEEKEND AT BUTLINS...
HELLO, JOHN.
HOW MUCH DO YOU REMEMBER?

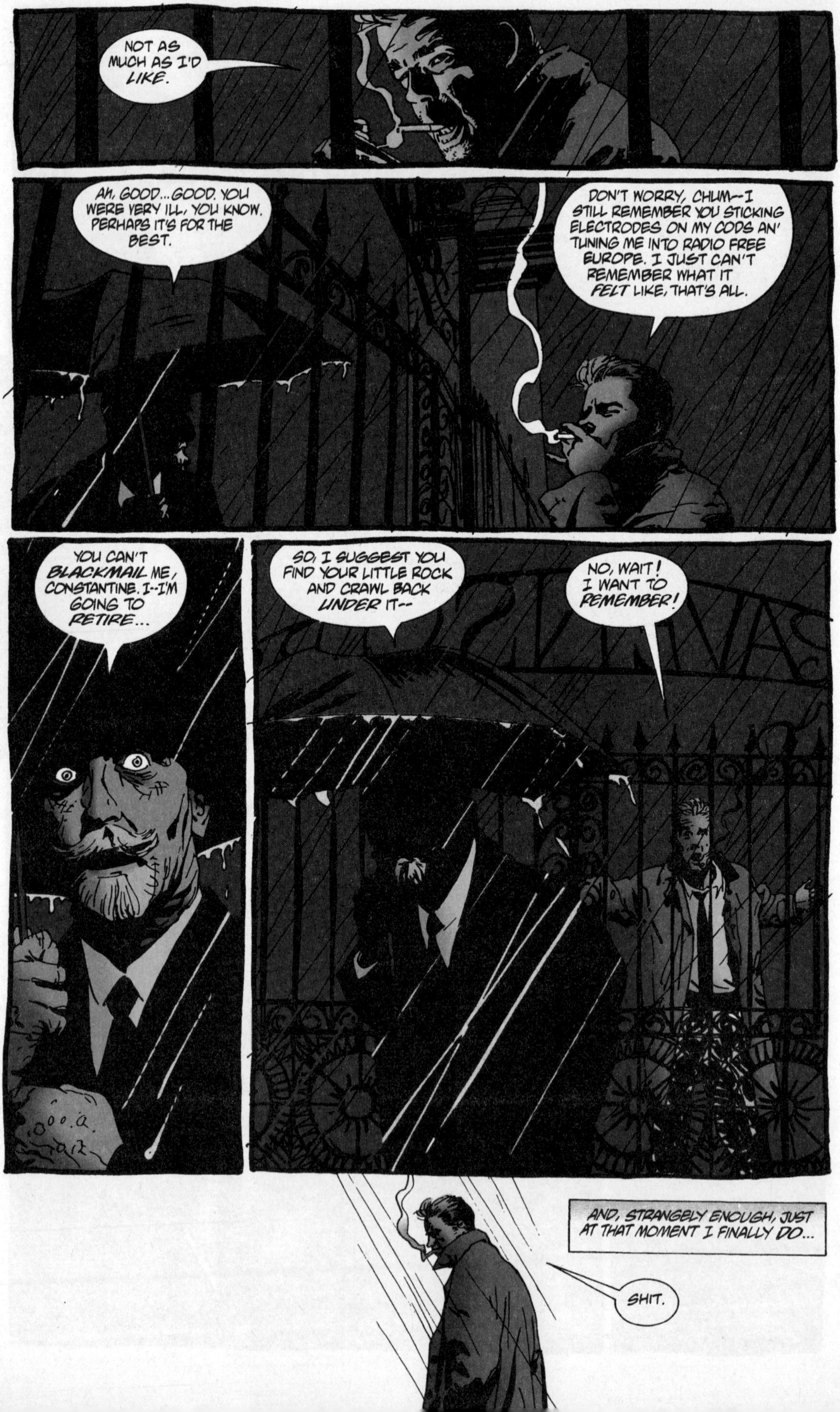
NOT AS MUCH AS I'D LIKE.
AH, GOOD...GOOD. YOU WERE VERY ILL, YOU KNOW. PERHAPS IT'S FOR THE BEST.
DON'T WORRY, CHUM--I STILL REMEMBER YOU STICKING ELECTRODES ON MY CODS AN' TUNING ME INTO RADIO FREE EUROPE. I JUST CAN'T REMEMBER WHAT IT FELT LIKE, THAT'S ALL.
YOU CAN'T BLACKMAIL ME, CONSTANTINE. I--I'M GOING TO RETIRE...
SO, I SUGGEST YOU FIND YOUR LITTLE ROCK AND CRAWL BACK UNDER IT--
NO, WAIT! I WANT TO REMEMBER!
AND, STRANGELY ENOUGH, JUST AT THAT MOMENT I FINALLY DO...
SHIT.

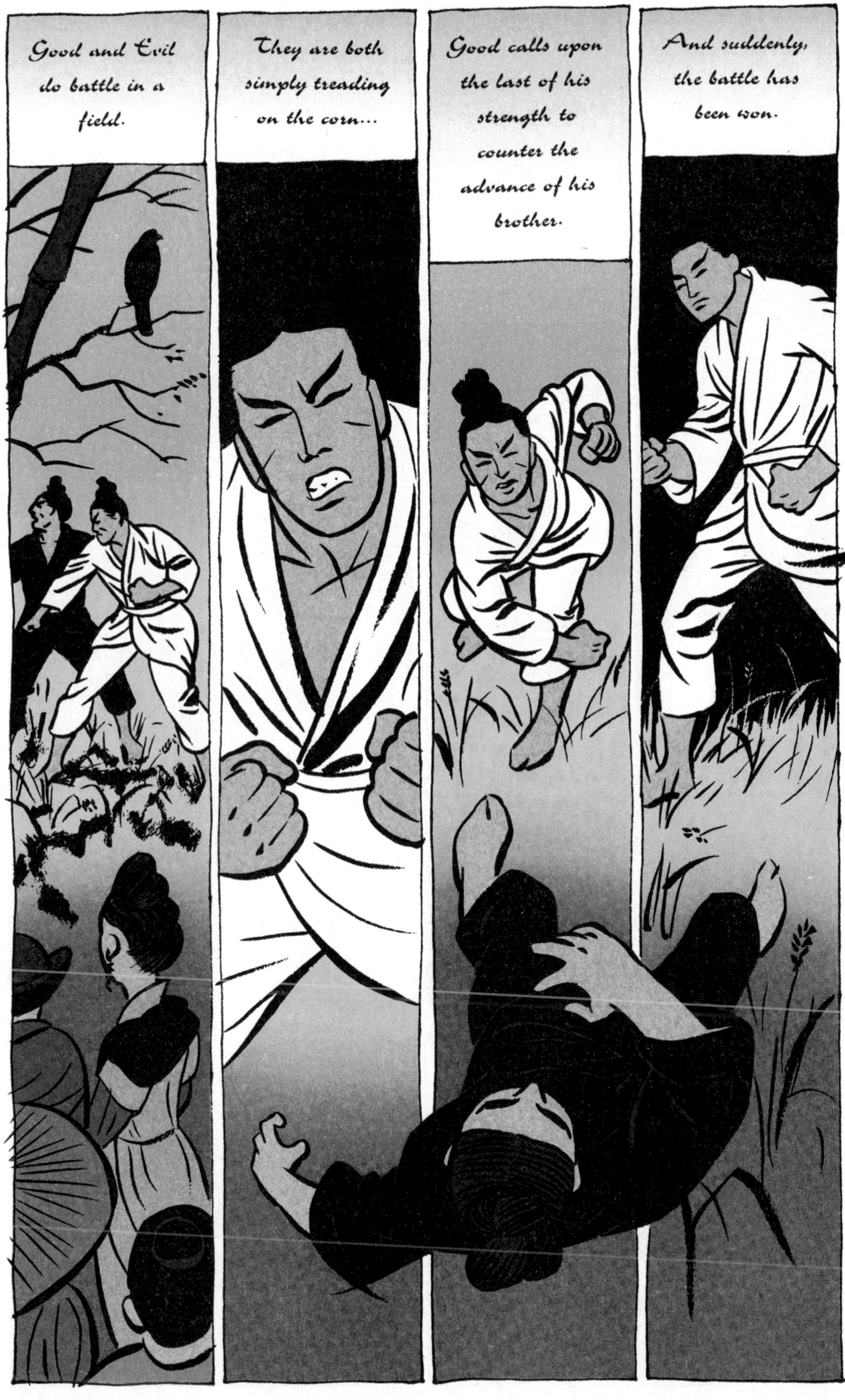
Good and Evil do battle in a field.
They are both simply treading on the corn...
Good calls upon the last of his strength to counter the advance of his brother.
And suddenly, the battle has been won.

The world rejoices. Good has defeated Evil.

The people have found their champion.

For ten days and nights, the wine flows freely.

Those present tell Good that they will never forget what he has done.

But afterwards, all guests depart. The Sun goes back to chasing the Moon across the heavens.

Good is left alone to ponder what he has done.

His brother lies decaying in the field.

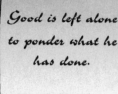

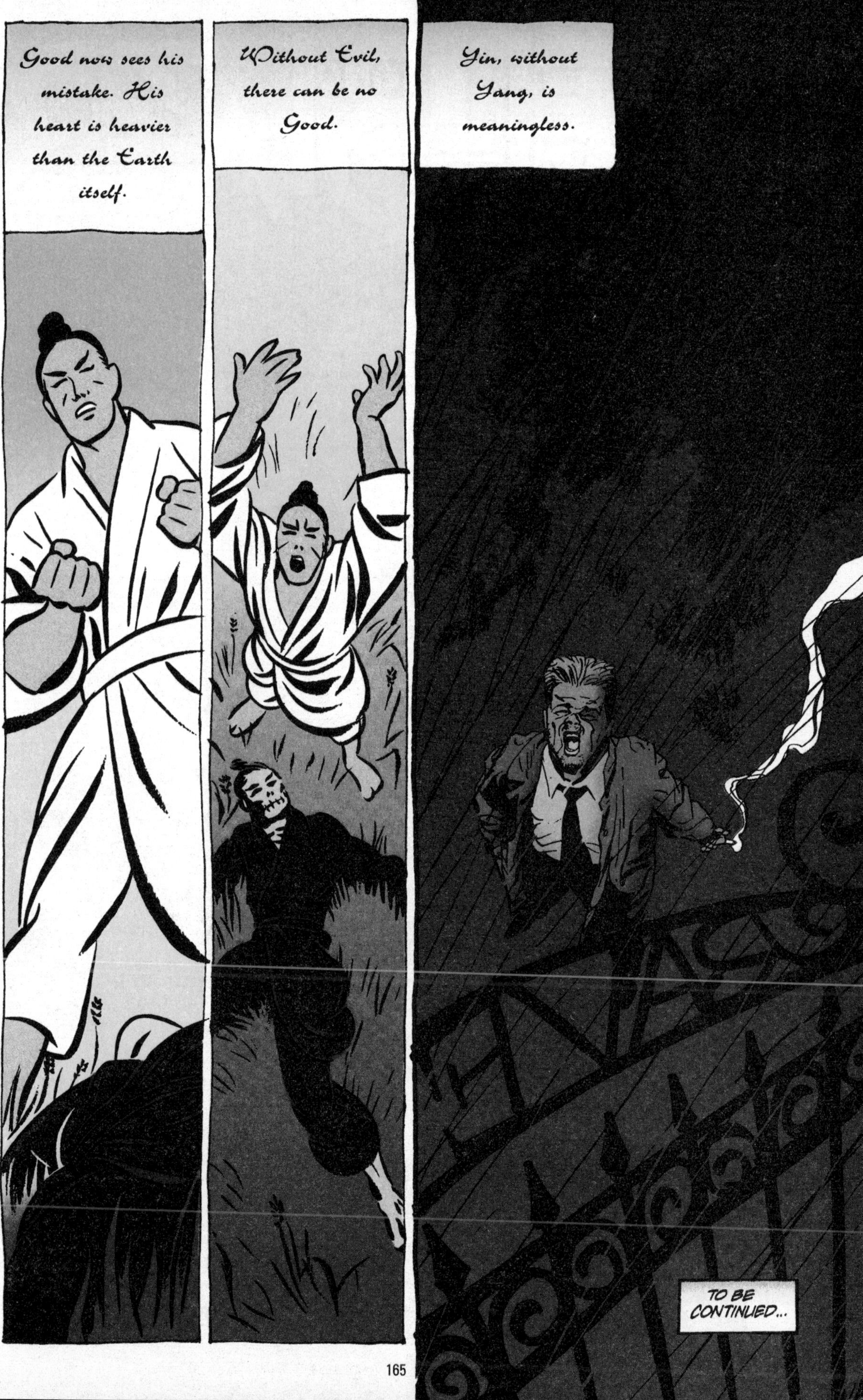
Good now sees his mistake. His heart is heavier than the Earth itself.
Without Evil, there can be no Good.
Yin, without Yang, is meaningless.
TO BE CONTINUED...

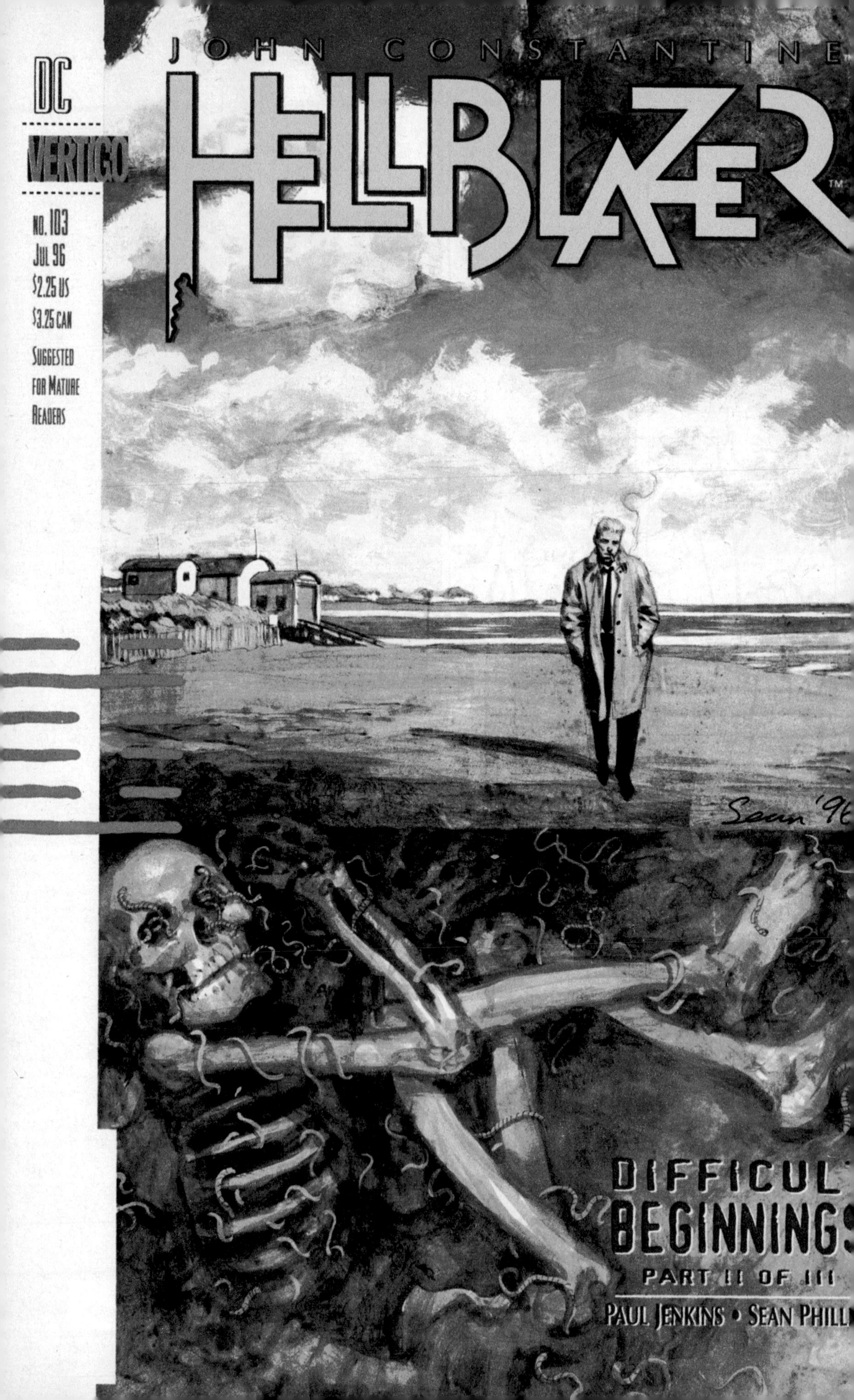

JOHN CONSTANTINE
HELLBLAZER™
DC
VERTIGO
NO. 103
JUL 96
$2.25 US
$3.25 CAN
SUGGESTED FOR MATURE READERS
Sean '96
DIFFICUL
BEGINNINGS
PART II OF III
PAUL JENKINS • SEAN PHILL

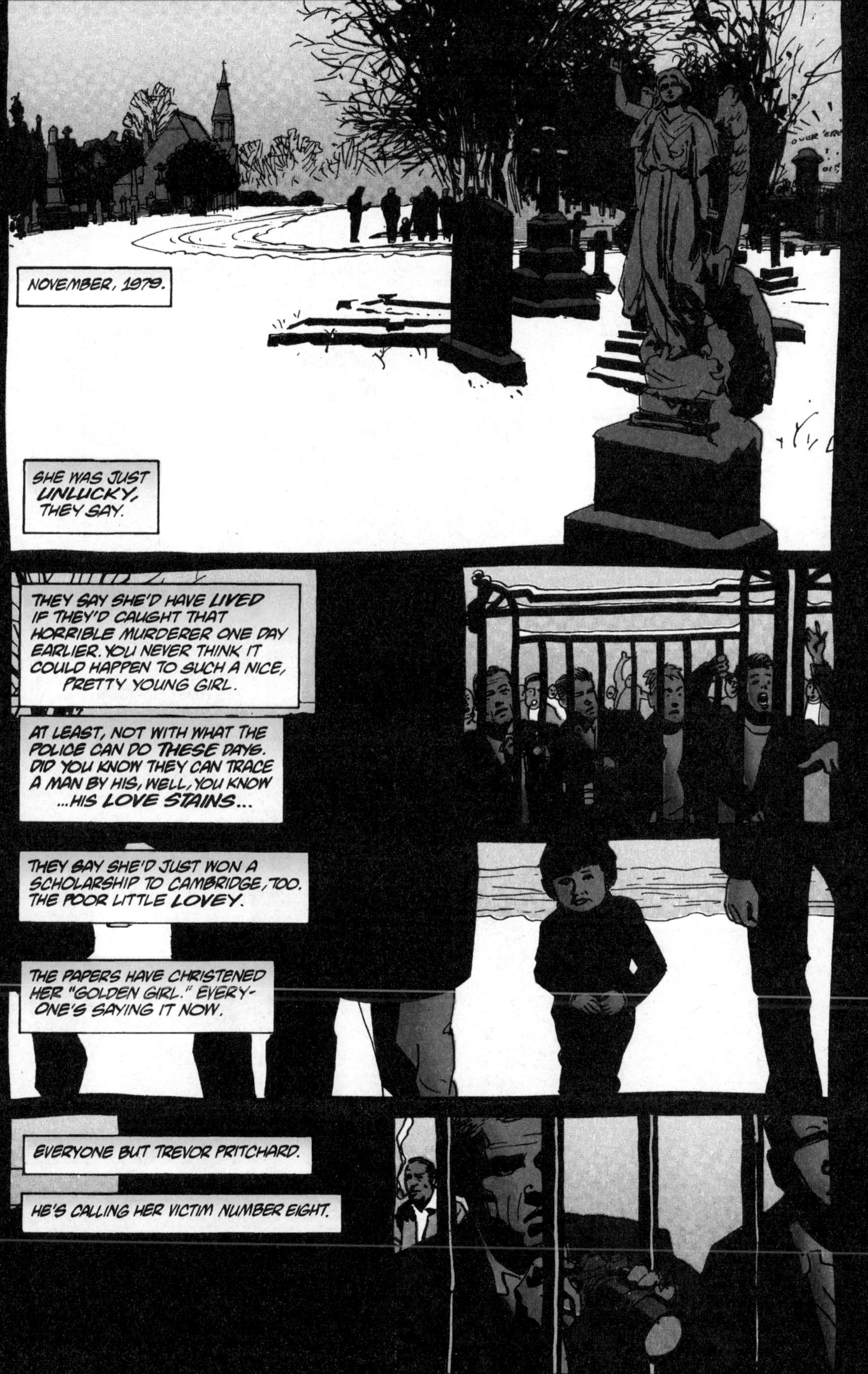
NOVEMBER, 1979.
SHE WAS JUST UNLUCKY, THEY SAY.
THEY SAY SHE'D HAVE LIVED IF THEY'D CAUGHT THAT HORRIBLE MURDERER ONE DAY EARLIER. YOU NEVER THINK IT COULD HAPPEN TO SUCH A NICE, PRETTY YOUNG GIRL.
AT LEAST, NOT WITH WHAT THE POLICE CAN DO THESE DAYS. DID YOU KNOW THEY CAN TRACE A MAN BY HIS, WELL, YOU KNOW ...HIS LOVE STAINS...
THEY SAY SHE'D JUST WON A SCHOLARSHIP TO CAMBRIDGE, TOO. THE POOR LITTLE LOVEY.
THE PAPERS HAVE CHRISTENED HER "GOLDEN GIRL." EVERY-ONE'S SAYING IT NOW.
EVERYONE BUT TREVOR PRITCHARD.
HE'S CALLING HER VICTIM NUMBER EIGHT.

TREVOR STUDIES THE TYPICAL-MIDLANDS-TRASH FATHER. HIS DAUGHTER'S NEW HOME IS A HOLE IN THE GROUND, YET HE'S STILL WONDERING WHAT HE COULD HAVE DONE TO **SAVE** HER.

DADDY STANDS FIRM, WITH THE EYES OF BRITAIN TRAINED UPON HIM. THE STUPID, BURLY BASTARD AND HIS WORKING-CLASS BRAVADO...

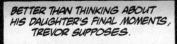

BETTER THAN THINKING ABOUT HIS DAUGHTER'S FINAL MOMENTS, TREVOR SUPPOSES.

BETTER THAN LISTENING HOPE-LESSLY TO THE ECHO OF HER **SCREAMS** AS THE MADMAN'S BAYONET OPENS HER UP LIKE A TIN OF SARDINES.

BETTER THAN IMAGINING HER GLISTENING INTESTINES SPILLING OUT THROUGH THE GAPING HOLE IN HER STOMACH.

LIKE BIG, SILVER **WORMS** FIGHTING FOR POSITION IN A NICE, COZY **NEST.**

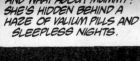

AND WHAT ABOUT MUMMY? SHE'S HIDDEN BEHIND A HAZE OF VALIUM PILLS AND SLEEPLESS NIGHTS.

AT LEAST THIS WAY SHE WON'T HAVE TO THINK ABOUT THE **ANIMAL** WHO BUTCHERED HER LITTLE GIRL.

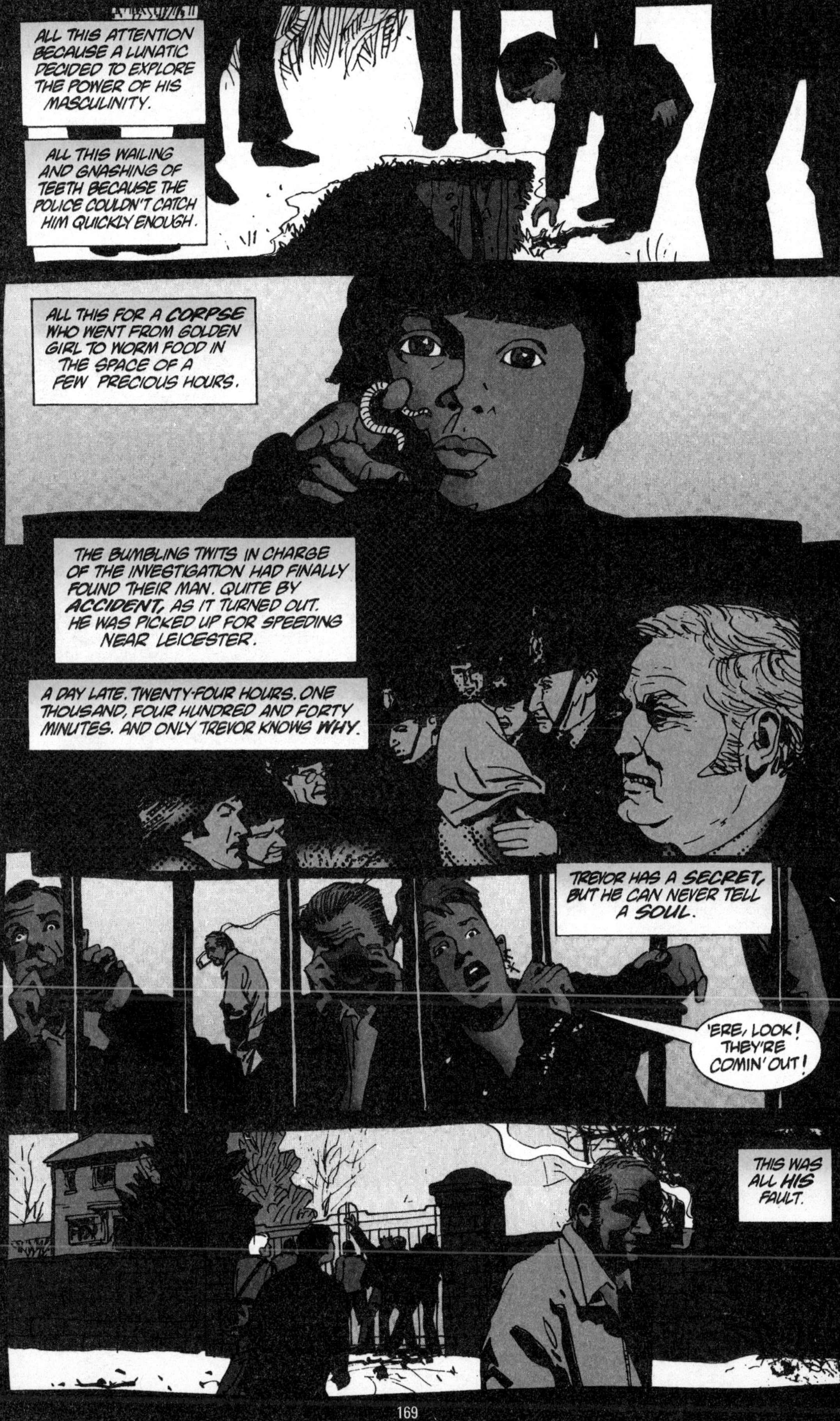
ALL THIS ATTENTION BECAUSE A LUNATIC DECIDED TO EXPLORE THE POWER OF HIS MASCULINITY.
ALL THIS WAILING AND GNASHING OF TEETH BECAUSE THE POLICE COULDN'T CATCH HIM QUICKLY ENOUGH.
ALL THIS FOR A CORPSE WHO WENT FROM GOLDEN GIRL TO WORM FOOD IN THE SPACE OF A FEW PRECIOUS HOURS.
THE BUMBLING TWITS IN CHARGE OF THE INVESTIGATION HAD FINALLY FOUND THEIR MAN. QUITE BY ACCIDENT, AS IT TURNED OUT. HE WAS PICKED UP FOR SPEEDING NEAR LEICESTER.
A DAY LATE. TWENTY-FOUR HOURS. ONE THOUSAND, FOUR HUNDRED AND FORTY MINUTES. AND ONLY TREVOR KNOWS WHY.
TREVOR HAS A SECRET, BUT HE CAN NEVER TELL A SOUL.
'ERE, LOOK! THEY'RE COMIN' OUT!
THIS WAS ALL HIS FAULT.

TRYING TO DESCRIBE THE SYNCHRONICITY HIGHWAY IS DIFFICULT --IT'S LIKE TRYING TO BITE YOUR OWN TEETH.

YOU MOVE AND STAND STILL AT THE SAME TIME. ROAD SIGNS ZOOM PAST BEFORE YOU CAN READ THEM, BUT YOU KNOW WHERE YOU'RE GOING WITHOUT EVER HAVING TRAVELED THIS WAY BEFORE.

HAVING SAID THAT, I'M *LOST* AGAIN. WHICH-- AS ALL EXPERIENCED COSMIC TRAVELERS KNOW--IS EXACTLY HOW IT *SHOULD* BE.

I'VE LET MYSELF BE HYPNOTIZED BY THE STEADY HUM OF TRAFFIC, BUT NOW I'M EMERGING INTO AN AWARENESS OF SELF SOMEWHERE NEAR THE TURNOFF TO MY NEXT DESTINATION.

IT'S ALL UP TO ME FROM HERE.

MAKES ME WISH I'D LEARNED HOW TO BLOODY *DRIVE*, REALLY...

DIFFICULT BEGINNINGS ②

the TROUBLE with WORMS

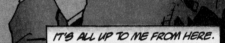

PAUL JENKINS Writer

SEAN PHILLIPS Artist

MATT HOLLINGSWORTH Colors

CLEM ROBINS Letters

AXEL ALONSO Asst Editor

LOU STATHIS Editor

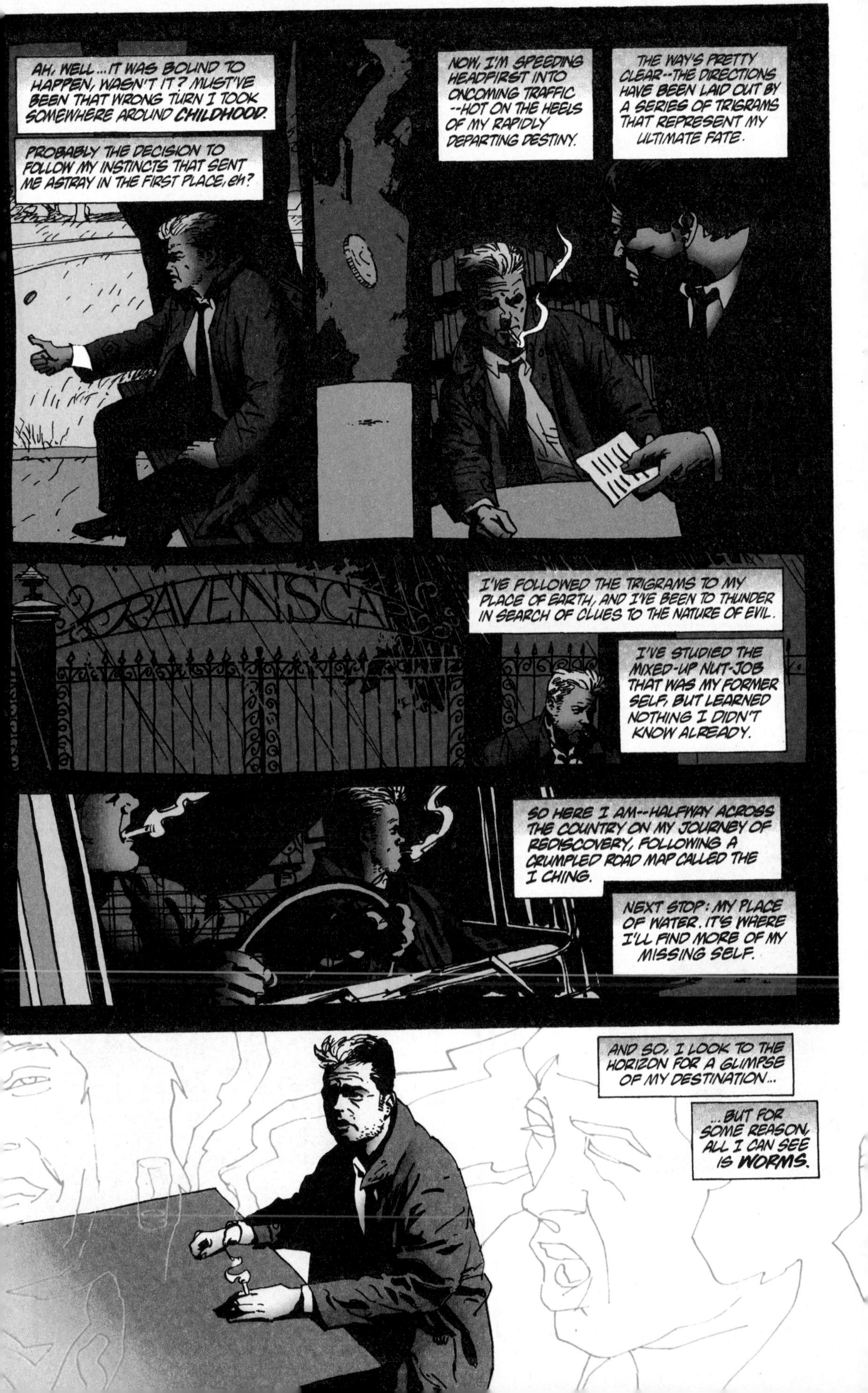
AH, WELL...IT WAS BOUND TO HAPPEN, WASN'T IT? MUST'VE BEEN THAT WRONG TURN I TOOK SOMEWHERE AROUND CHILDHOOD.
PROBABLY THE DECISION TO FOLLOW MY INSTINCTS THAT SENT ME ASTRAY IN THE FIRST PLACE, eh?
NOW, I'M SPEEDING HEADFIRST INTO ONCOMING TRAFFIC --HOT ON THE HEELS OF MY RAPIDLY DEPARTING DESTINY.
THE WAY'S PRETTY CLEAR--THE DIRECTIONS HAVE BEEN LAID OUT BY A SERIES OF TRIGRAMS THAT REPRESENT MY ULTIMATE FATE.
RAVENSCA
I'VE FOLLOWED THE TRIGRAMS TO MY PLACE OF EARTH, AND I'VE BEEN TO THUNDER IN SEARCH OF CLUES TO THE NATURE OF EVIL.
I'VE STUDIED THE MIXED-UP NUT-JOB THAT WAS MY FORMER SELF, BUT LEARNED NOTHING I DIDN'T KNOW ALREADY.
SO HERE I AM--HALFWAY ACROSS THE COUNTRY ON MY JOURNEY OF REDISCOVERY, FOLLOWING A CRUMPLED ROAD MAP CALLED THE I CHING.
NEXT STOP: MY PLACE OF WATER. IT'S WHERE I'LL FIND MORE OF MY MISSING SELF.
AND SO, I LOOK TO THE HORIZON FOR A GLIMPSE OF MY DESTINATION...
...BUT FOR SOME REASON, ALL I CAN SEE IS WORMS.

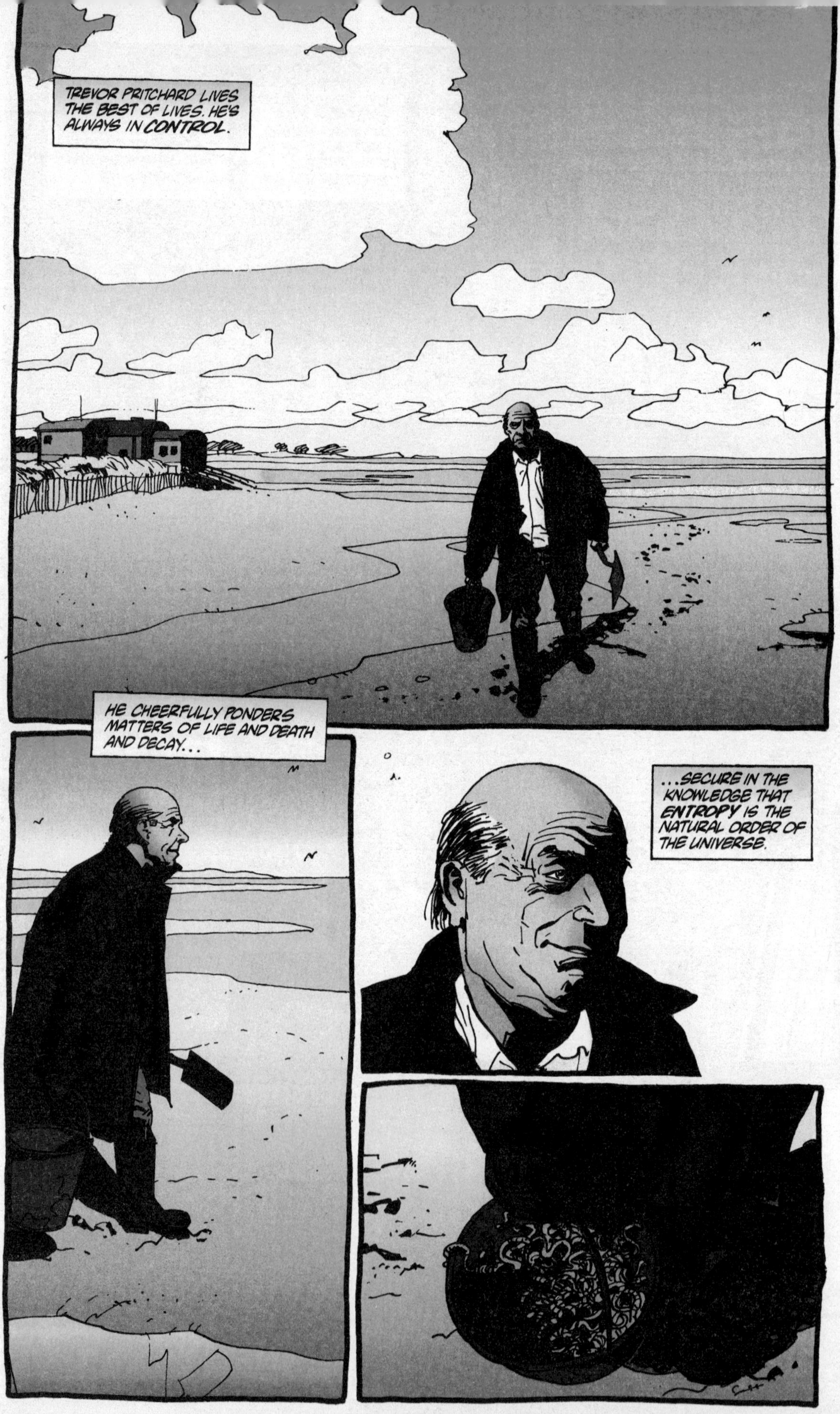
TREVOR PRITCHARD LIVES THE BEST OF LIVES. HE'S ALWAYS IN CONTROL.
HE CHEERFULLY PONDERS MATTERS OF LIFE AND DEATH AND DECAY...
...SECURE IN THE KNOWLEDGE THAT ENTROPY IS THE NATURAL ORDER OF THE UNIVERSE.

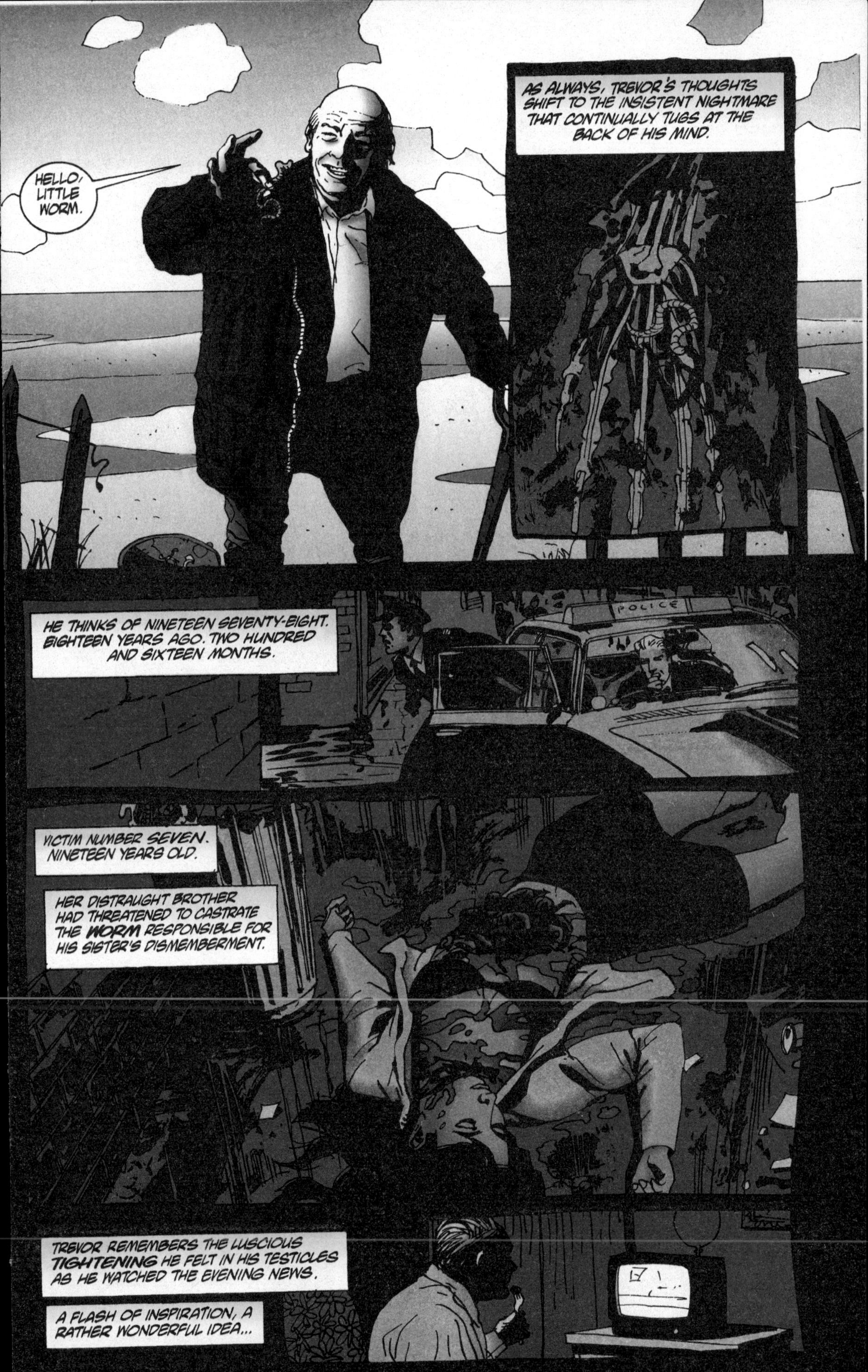
HELLO, LITTLE WORM.
AS ALWAYS, TREVOR'S THOUGHTS SHIFT TO THE INSISTENT NIGHTMARE THAT CONTINUALLY TUGS AT THE BACK OF HIS MIND.
HE THINKS OF NINETEEN SEVENTY-EIGHT. EIGHTEEN YEARS AGO. TWO HUNDRED AND SIXTEEN MONTHS.
POLICE
VICTIM NUMBER SEVEN. NINETEEN YEARS OLD.
HER DISTRAUGHT BROTHER HAD THREATENED TO CASTRATE THE WORM RESPONSIBLE FOR HIS SISTER'S DISMEMBERMENT.
TREVOR REMEMBERS THE LUSCIOUS TIGHTENING HE FELT IN HIS TESTICLES AS HE WATCHED THE EVENING NEWS.
A FLASH OF INSPIRATION, A RATHER WONDERFUL IDEA...

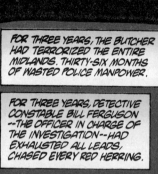

FOR THREE YEARS, THE BUTCHER HAD TERRORIZED THE ENTIRE MIDLANDS. THIRTY-SIX MONTHS OF WASTED POLICE MANPOWER.

FOR THREE YEARS, DETECTIVE CONSTABLE BILL FERGUSON --THE OFFICER IN CHARGE OF THE INVESTIGATION-- HAD EXHAUSTED ALL LEADS, CHASED EVERY RED HERRING.

FOR THREE YEARS, D.C. FERGUSON HAD WAITED FOR THIS MOMENT...

HELLO, BILL. I CAN SEE YOU ARE HAVIN' TROUBLE CATCHIN' ME...

HE'D BEEN TOTALLY CONVINCED OF THE TAPE'S AUTHENTICITY, OF COURSE. THE POOR BASTARD HAD SO WANTED TO CATCH THE KILLER, YOU SEE.

IT HAD BECOME THE VERY REASON FOR HIS EXISTENCE.

TEN THOUSAND HOURS OF MANPOWER, AN ARMY OF THIRTY-SEVEN INVESTIGATORS, A REWARD OF A MILLION POUNDS.

A DAY LATE. A PENNY SHORT. A DEAD GIRL.

ALL BECAUSE OF TREVOR PRITCHARD.

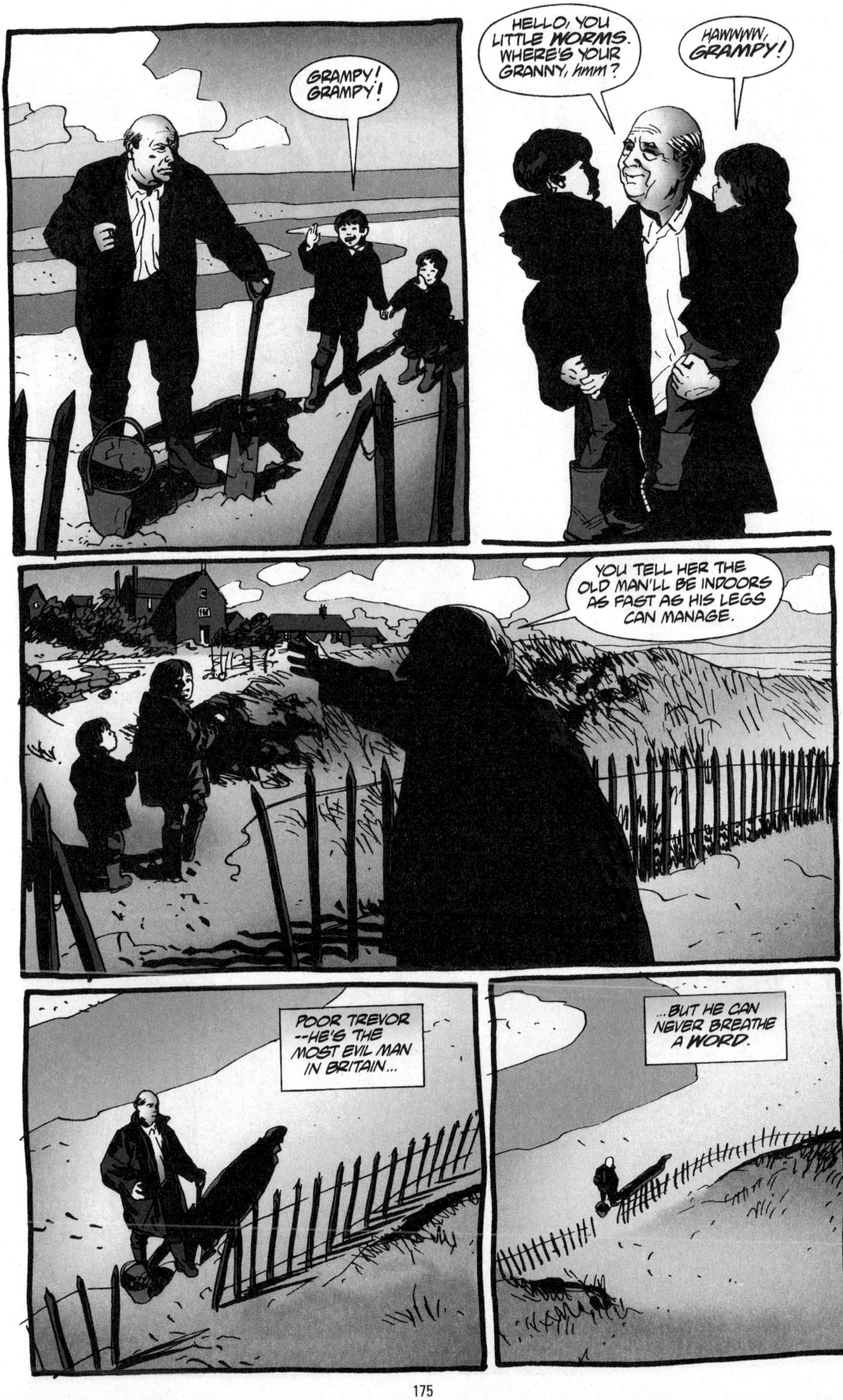
GRAMPY! GRAMPY!
HELLO, YOU LITTLE WORMS. WHERE'S YOUR GRANNY, hmm?
HAWWWW, GRAMPY!
YOU TELL HER THE OLD MAN'LL BE INDOORS AS FAST AS HIS LEGS CAN MANAGE.
POOR TREVOR --HE'S THE MOST EVIL MAN IN BRITAIN...
...BUT HE CAN NEVER BREATHE A WORD.

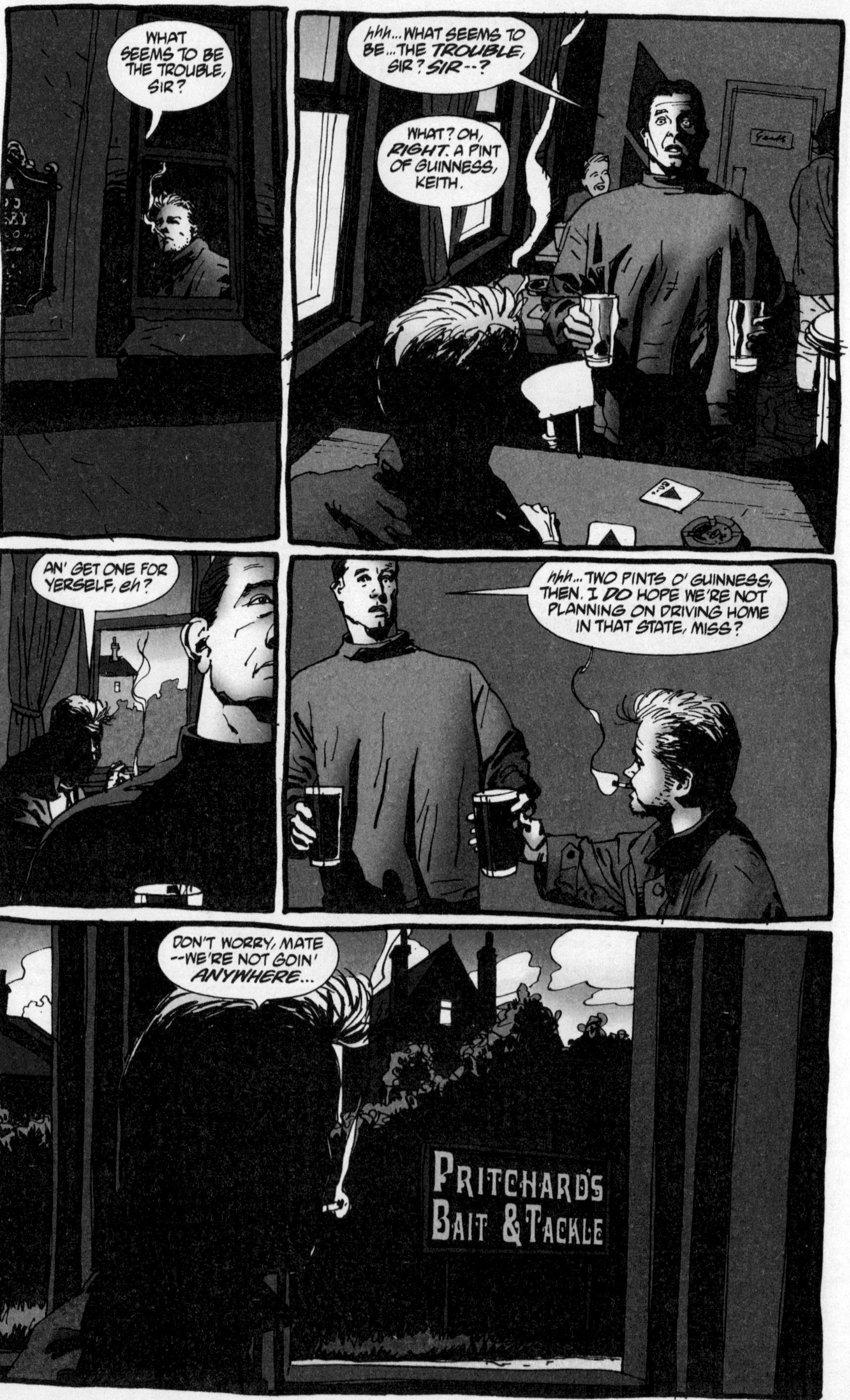
WHAT SEEMS TO BE THE TROUBLE, SIR?
hhh... WHAT SEEMS TO BE... THE TROUBLE, SIR? SIR--?
WHAT? OH, RIGHT. A PINT OF GUINNESS, KEITH.
AN' GET ONE FOR YERSELF, eh?
hhh... TWO PINTS O' GUINNESS, THEN. I DO HOPE WE'RE NOT PLANNING ON DRIVING HOME IN THAT STATE, MISS?
DON'T WORRY, MATE --WE'RE NOT GOIN' ANYWHERE...
PRITCHARD'S BAIT & TACKLE

FUNNY HOW LIFE WORKS, REALLY. TAKE THIS POOR SOD, FOR INSTANCE--RIGHT NOW, HE THINKS HE'S SITTING BY THE SIDE OF THE M4 EATING A HAM SANDWICH.

WELL, *SOME* OF HIM DOES--THE REST OF HIM IS ENJOYING A PINT IN A NICE WARM PUB IN LINCOLN-SHIRE. CONFUSED AND AWARE AT THE SAME TIME. I KNOW JUST HOW HE FEELS.

STILL, IT'S ALL PART OF LIFE'S RICH PATTERN, AS THEY SAY. IT'S HOW WE GET WHERE WE'RE *GOING.*

WE PICK UP LITTLE BITS AND PIECES ALONG THE WAY, AND ARRANGE THEM INTO A COMPLETED SINGLE IMAGE.

Butcher

A GHOST OF AN IDEA HERE, A SNIPPET OF INFORMATION THERE, A MEMORY OF SOMETHING THAT HAPPENED YEARS AGO...

AND BEFORE YOU KNOW IT, A *CONCLUSION.* YOU'RE SITTING IN A PUB IN LINCOLNSHIRE...

...AND THE WHOLE SORDID STORY'S JUST FALLEN RIGHT IN YOUR LAP.

COME ON, THEN, MATE.

WHERE WE GOIN', SARGE?

TO SEE A MAN ABOUT A GIRL.

the TICKLED TROUT

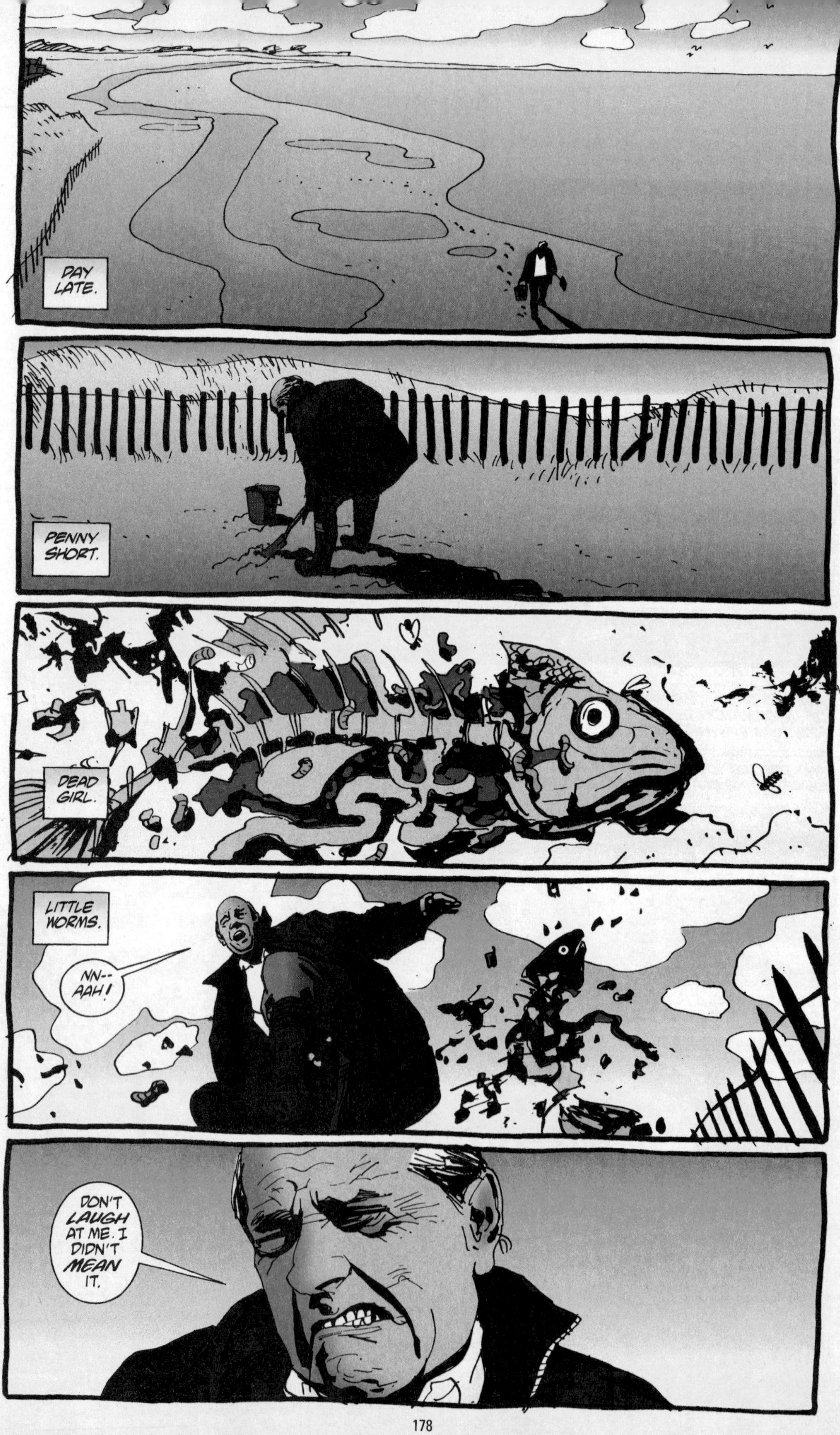
DAY LATE.
PENNY SHORT.
DEAD GIRL.
LITTLE WORMS.
NN-- AAH!
DON'T LAUGH AT ME. I DIDN'T MEAN IT.

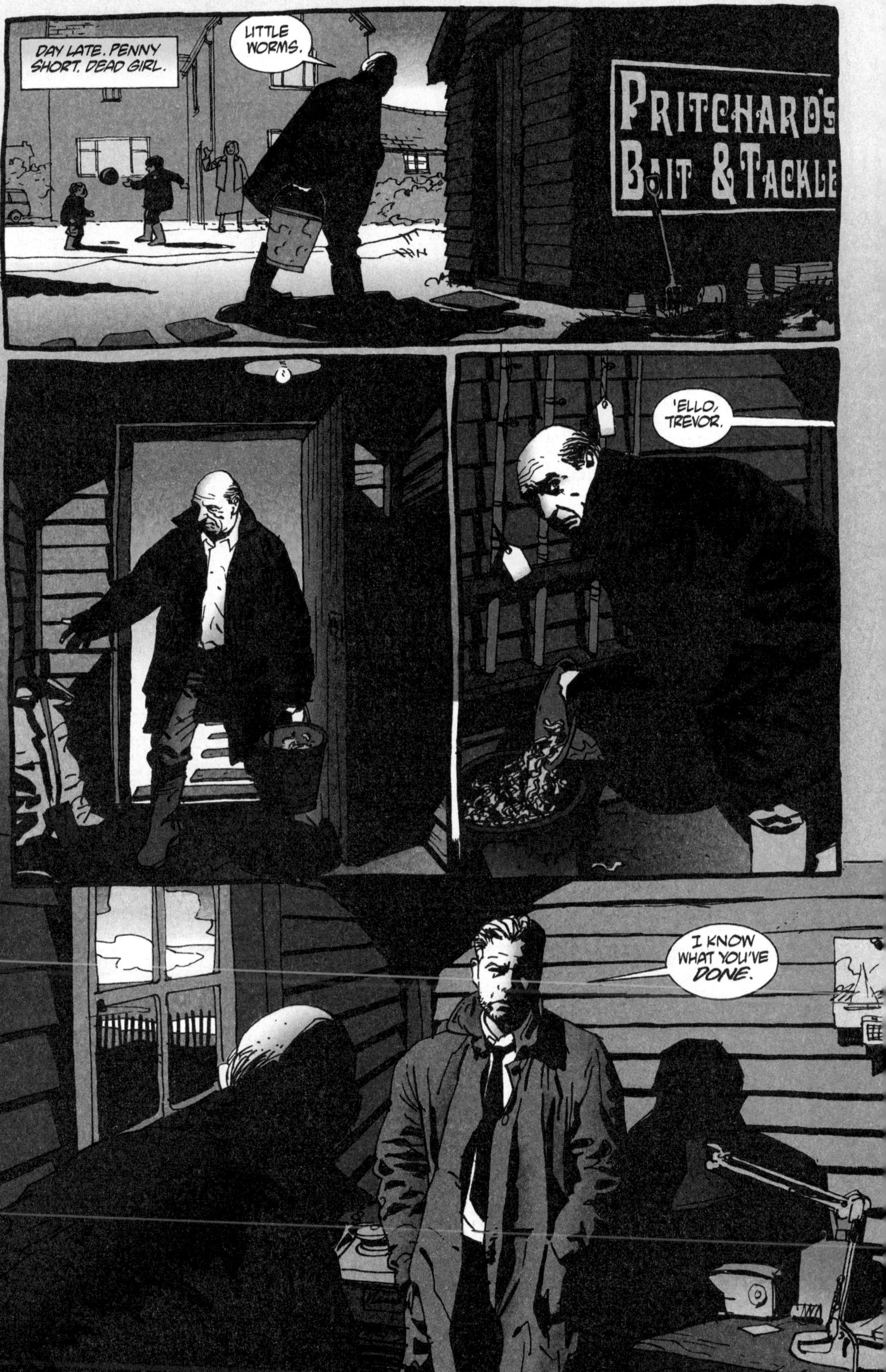
DAY LATE. PENNY SHORT. DEAD GIRL.
LITTLE WORMS.
PRITCHARD'S BAIT & TACKLE
'ELLO, TREVOR.
I KNOW WHAT YOU'VE DONE.

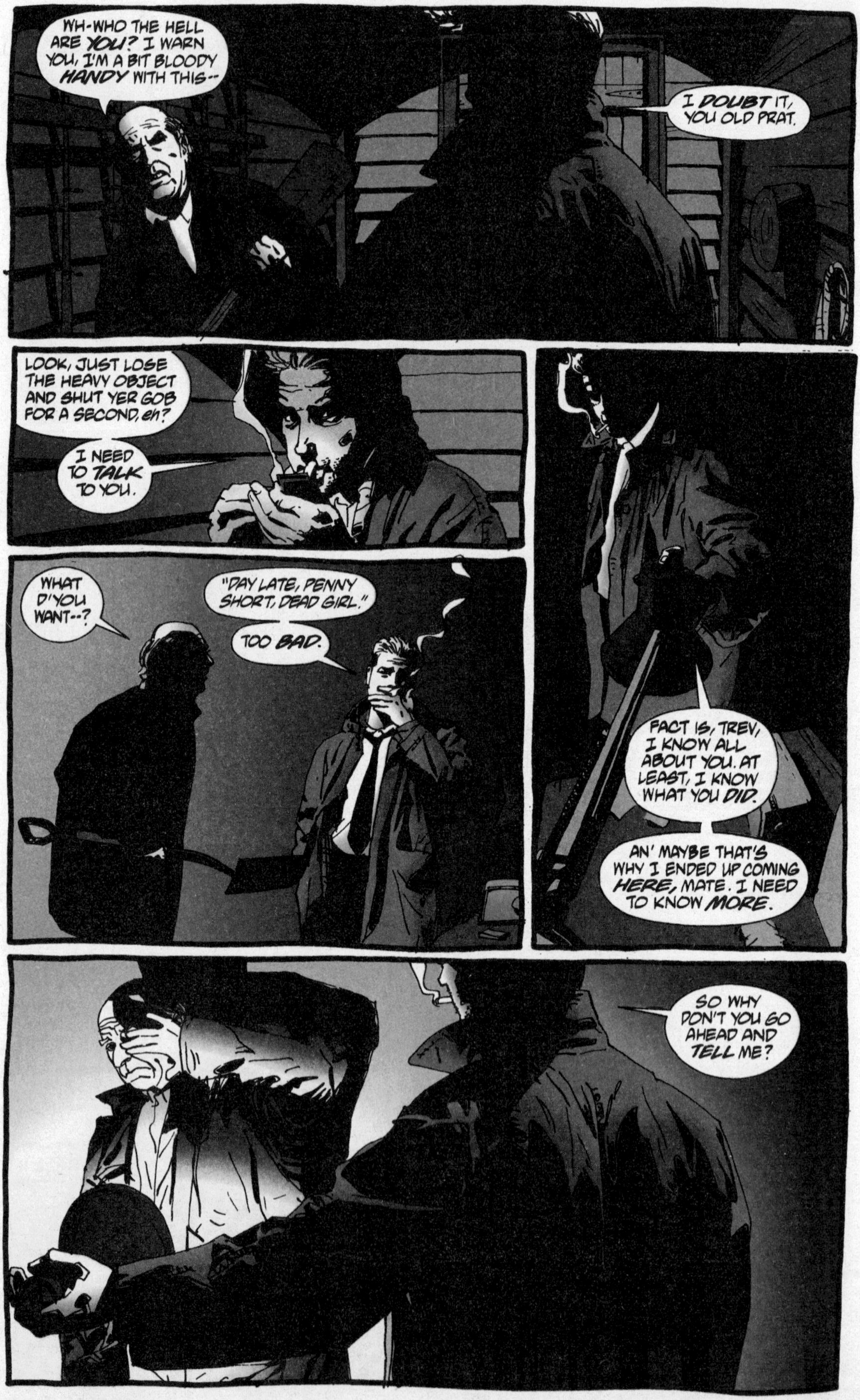
WH-WHO THE HELL ARE YOU? I WARN YOU, I'M A BIT BLOODY HANDY WITH THIS--
I DOUBT IT, YOU OLD PRAT.
LOOK, JUST LOSE THE HEAVY OBJECT AND SHUT YER GOB FOR A SECOND, eh?
I NEED TO TALK TO YOU.
WHAT D'YOU WANT--?
"DAY LATE, PENNY SHORT, DEAD GIRL."
TOO BAD.
FACT IS, TREV, I KNOW ALL ABOUT YOU. AT LEAST, I KNOW WHAT YOU DID.
AN' MAYBE THAT'S WHY I ENDED UP COMING HERE, MATE. I NEED TO KNOW MORE.
SO WHY DON'T YOU GO AHEAD AND TELL ME?

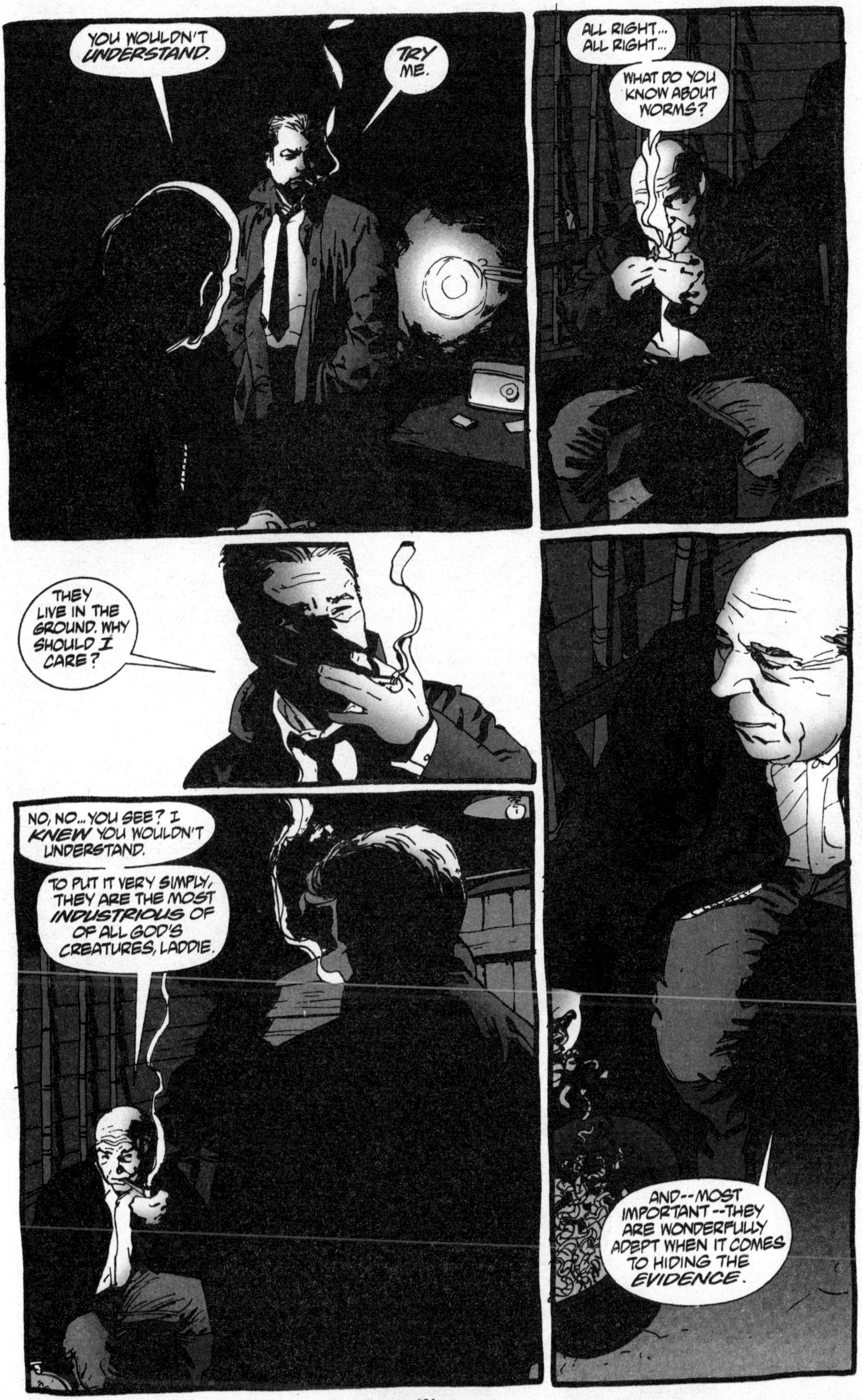
YOU WOULDN'T UNDERSTAND.
TRY ME.
ALL RIGHT... ALL RIGHT...
WHAT DO YOU KNOW ABOUT WORMS?
THEY LIVE IN THE GROUND. WHY SHOULD I CARE?
NO, NO... YOU SEE? I KNEW YOU WOULDN'T UNDERSTAND.
TO PUT IT VERY SIMPLY, THEY ARE THE MOST INDUSTRIOUS OF OF ALL GOD'S CREATURES, LADDIE.
AND--MOST IMPORTANT--THEY ARE WONDERFULLY ADEPT WHEN IT COMES TO HIDING THE EVIDENCE.

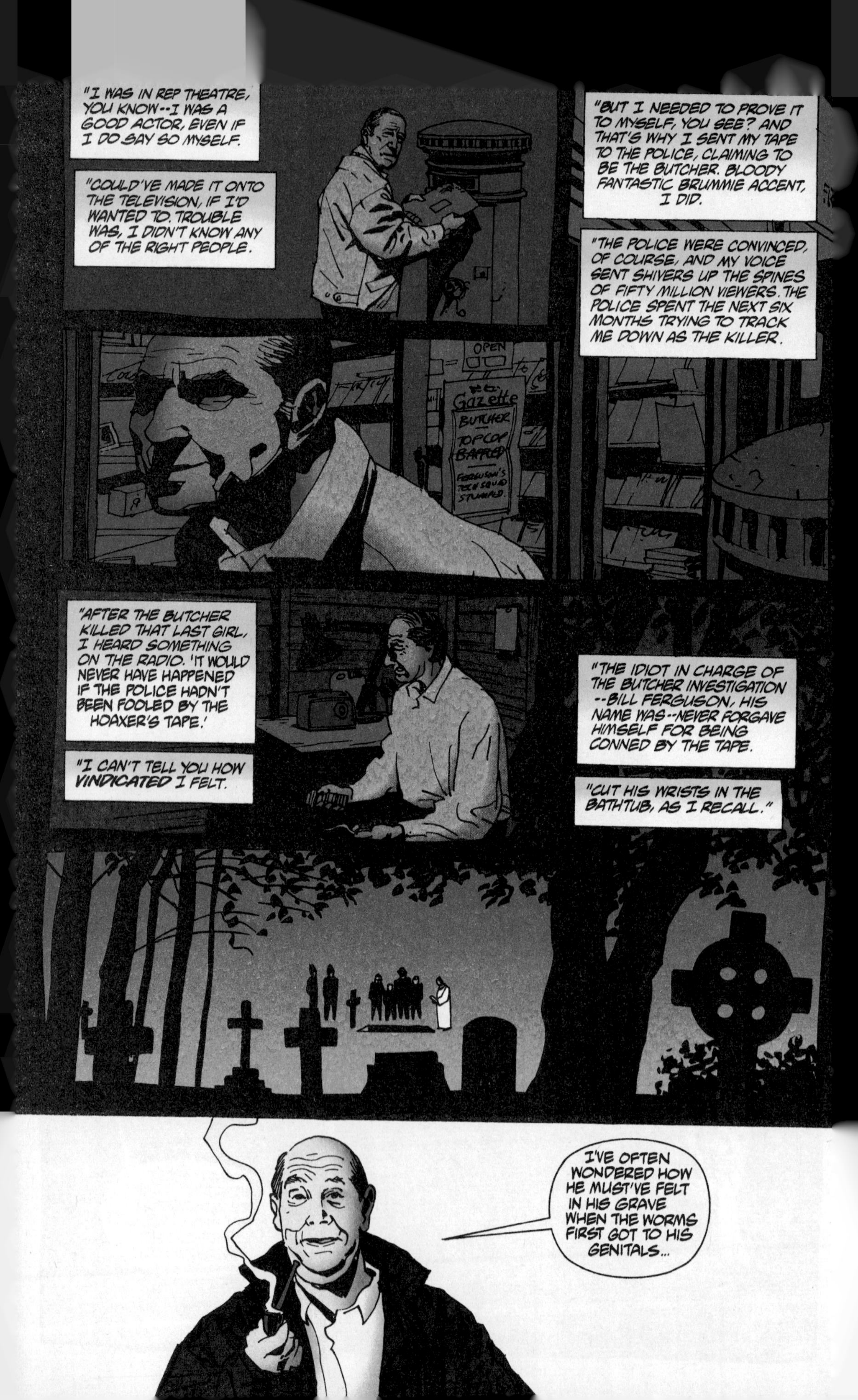
"I WAS IN REP THEATRE, YOU KNOW--I WAS A GOOD ACTOR, EVEN IF I DO SAY SO MYSELF.
"COULD'VE MADE IT ONTO THE TELEVISION, IF I'D WANTED TO. TROUBLE WAS, I DIDN'T KNOW ANY OF THE RIGHT PEOPLE.
"BUT I NEEDED TO PROVE IT TO MYSELF, YOU SEE? AND THAT'S WHY I SENT MY TAPE TO THE POLICE, CLAIMING TO BE THE BUTCHER. BLOODY FANTASTIC BRUMMIE ACCENT, I DID.
"THE POLICE WERE CONVINCED, OF COURSE, AND MY VOICE SENT SHIVERS UP THE SPINES OF FIFTY MILLION VIEWERS. THE POLICE SPENT THE NEXT SIX MONTHS TRYING TO TRACK ME DOWN AS THE KILLER.
OPEN
Gazette
BUTCHER
TOP COP BAFFLED
FERGUSON'S TECH SQUAD STUMPED.
"AFTER THE BUTCHER KILLED THAT LAST GIRL, I HEARD SOMETHING ON THE RADIO. 'IT WOULD NEVER HAVE HAPPENED IF THE POLICE HADN'T BEEN FOOLED BY THE HOAXER'S TAPE.'
"I CAN'T TELL YOU HOW VINDICATED I FELT.
"THE IDIOT IN CHARGE OF THE BUTCHER INVESTIGATION --BILL FERGUSON, HIS NAME WAS--NEVER FORGAVE HIMSELF FOR BEING CONNED BY THE TAPE.
"CUT HIS WRISTS IN THE BATHTUB, AS I RECALL."
I'VE OFTEN WONDERED HOW HE MUST'VE FELT IN HIS GRAVE WHEN THE WORMS FIRST GOT TO HIS GENITALS...

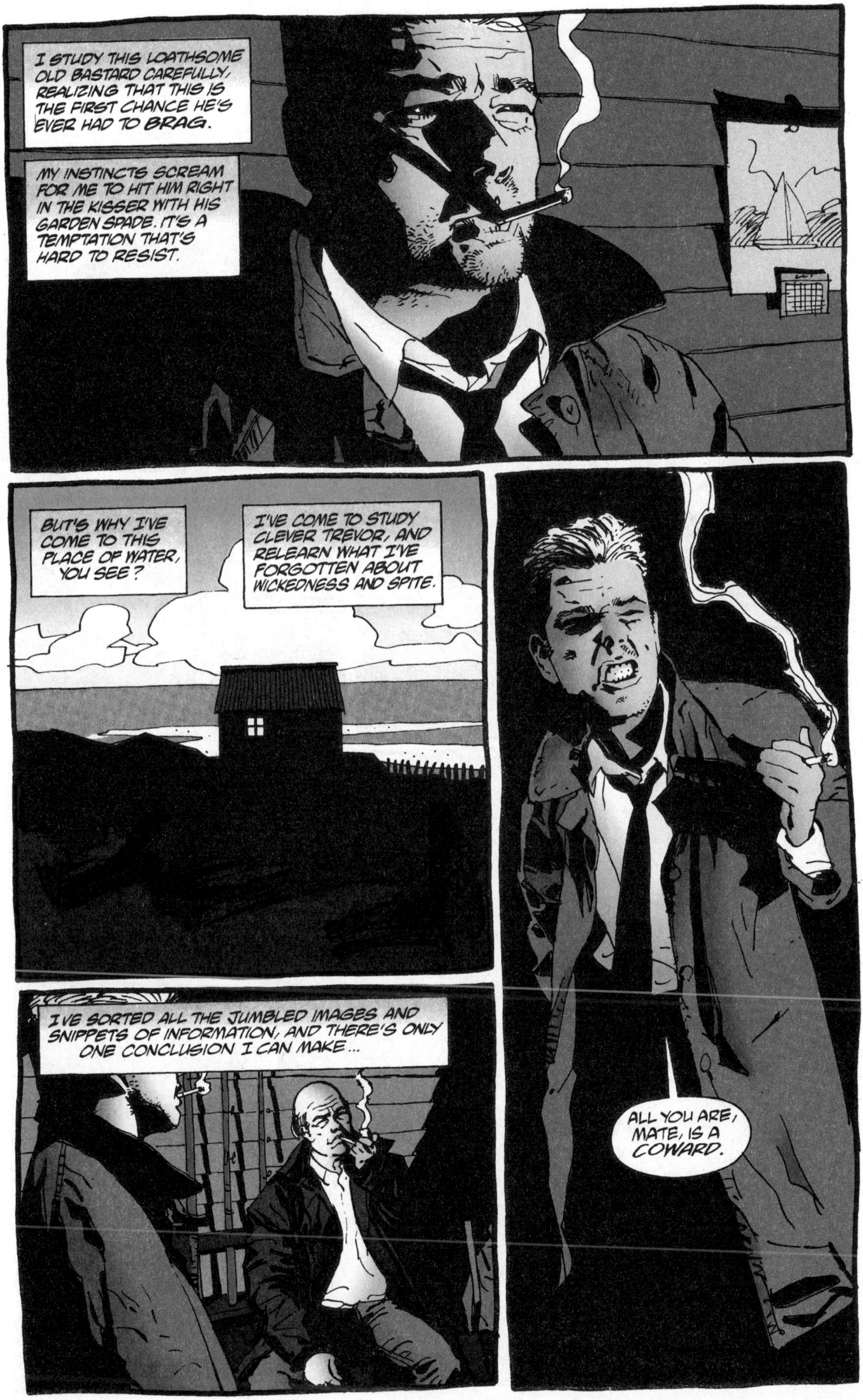
I STUDY THIS LOATHSOME OLD BASTARD CAREFULLY, REALIZING THAT THIS IS THE FIRST CHANCE HE'S EVER HAD TO BRAG.
MY INSTINCTS SCREAM FOR ME TO HIT HIM RIGHT IN THE KISSER WITH HIS GARDEN SPADE. IT'S A TEMPTATION THAT'S HARD TO RESIST.
BUT'S WHY I'VE COME TO THIS PLACE OF WATER, YOU SEE?
I'VE COME TO STUDY CLEVER TREVOR, AND RELEARN WHAT I'VE FORGOTTEN ABOUT WICKEDNESS AND SPITE.
I'VE SORTED ALL THE JUMBLED IMAGES AND SNIPPETS OF INFORMATION, AND THERE'S ONLY ONE CONCLUSION I CAN MAKE...
ALL YOU ARE, MATE, IS A COWARD.

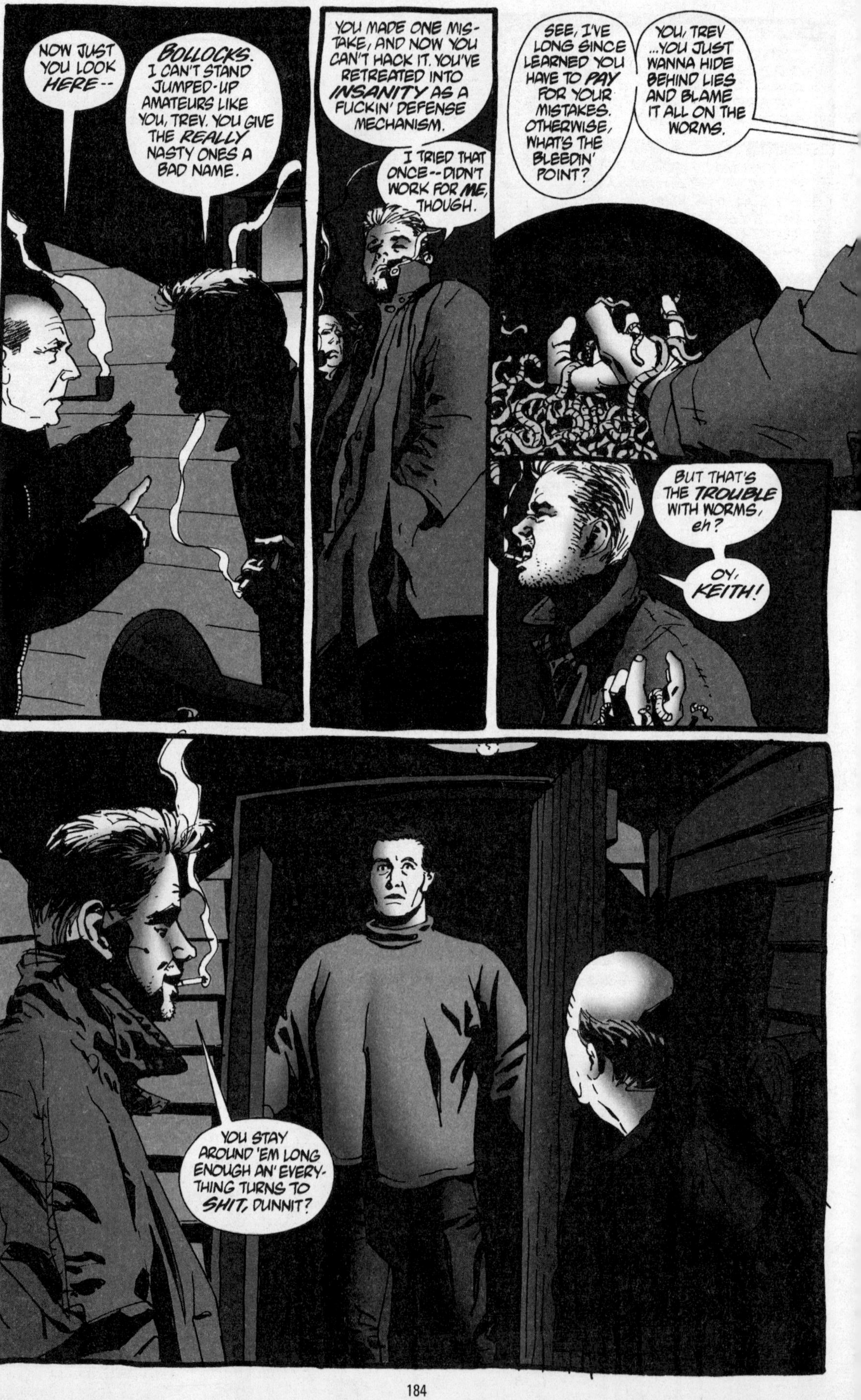
NOW JUST YOU LOOK HERE--
BOLLOCKS. I CAN'T STAND JUMPED-UP AMATEURS LIKE YOU, TREV. YOU GIVE THE REALLY NASTY ONES A BAD NAME.
YOU MADE ONE MISTAKE, AND NOW YOU CAN'T HACK IT. YOU'VE RETREATED INTO INSANITY AS A FUCKIN' DEFENSE MECHANISM.
I TRIED THAT ONCE--DIDN'T WORK FOR ME, THOUGH.
SEE, I'VE LONG SINCE LEARNED YOU HAVE TO PAY FOR YOUR MISTAKES. OTHERWISE, WHAT'S THE BLEEDIN' POINT?
YOU, TREV ...YOU JUST WANNA HIDE BEHIND LIES AND BLAME IT ALL ON THE WORMS.
BUT THAT'S THE TROUBLE WITH WORMS, eh?
OY, KEITH!
YOU STAY AROUND 'EM LONG ENOUGH AN' EVERYTHING TURNS TO SHIT, DUNNIT?

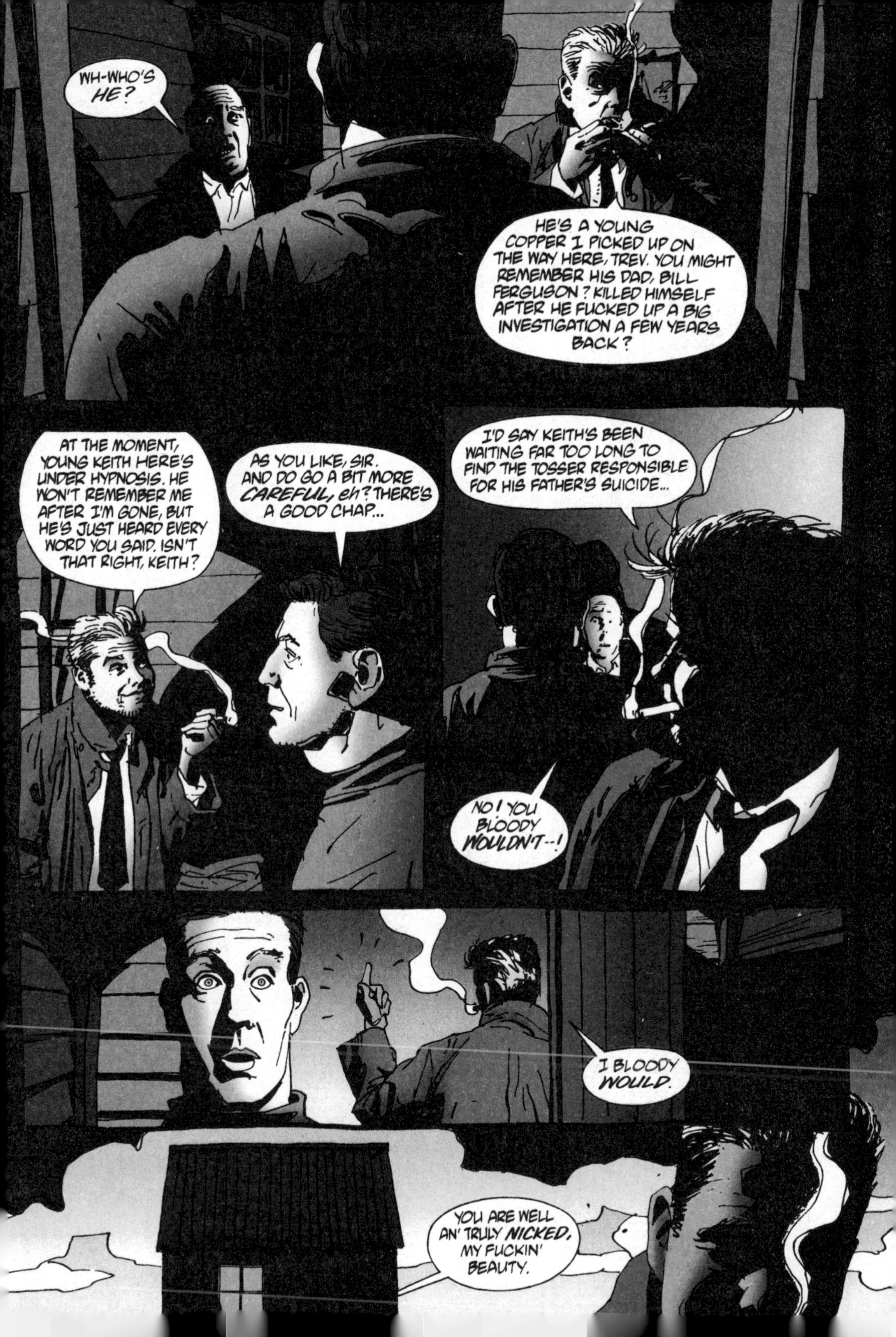
WH-WHO'S HE?
HE'S A YOUNG COPPER I PICKED UP ON THE WAY HERE, TREV. YOU MIGHT REMEMBER HIS DAD, BILL FERGUSON? KILLED HIMSELF AFTER HE FUCKED UP A BIG INVESTIGATION A FEW YEARS BACK?
AT THE MOMENT, YOUNG KEITH HERE'S UNDER HYPNOSIS. HE WON'T REMEMBER ME AFTER I'M GONE, BUT HE'S JUST HEARD EVERY WORD YOU SAID. ISN'T THAT RIGHT, KEITH?
AS YOU LIKE, SIR. AND DO GO A BIT MORE CAREFUL, eh? THERE'S A GOOD CHAP...
I'D SAY KEITH'S BEEN WAITING FAR TOO LONG TO FIND THE TOSSER RESPONSIBLE FOR HIS FATHER'S SUICIDE...
NO! YOU BLOODY WOULDN'T--!
I BLOODY WOULD.
YOU ARE WELL AN' TRULY NICKED, MY FUCKIN' BEAUTY.

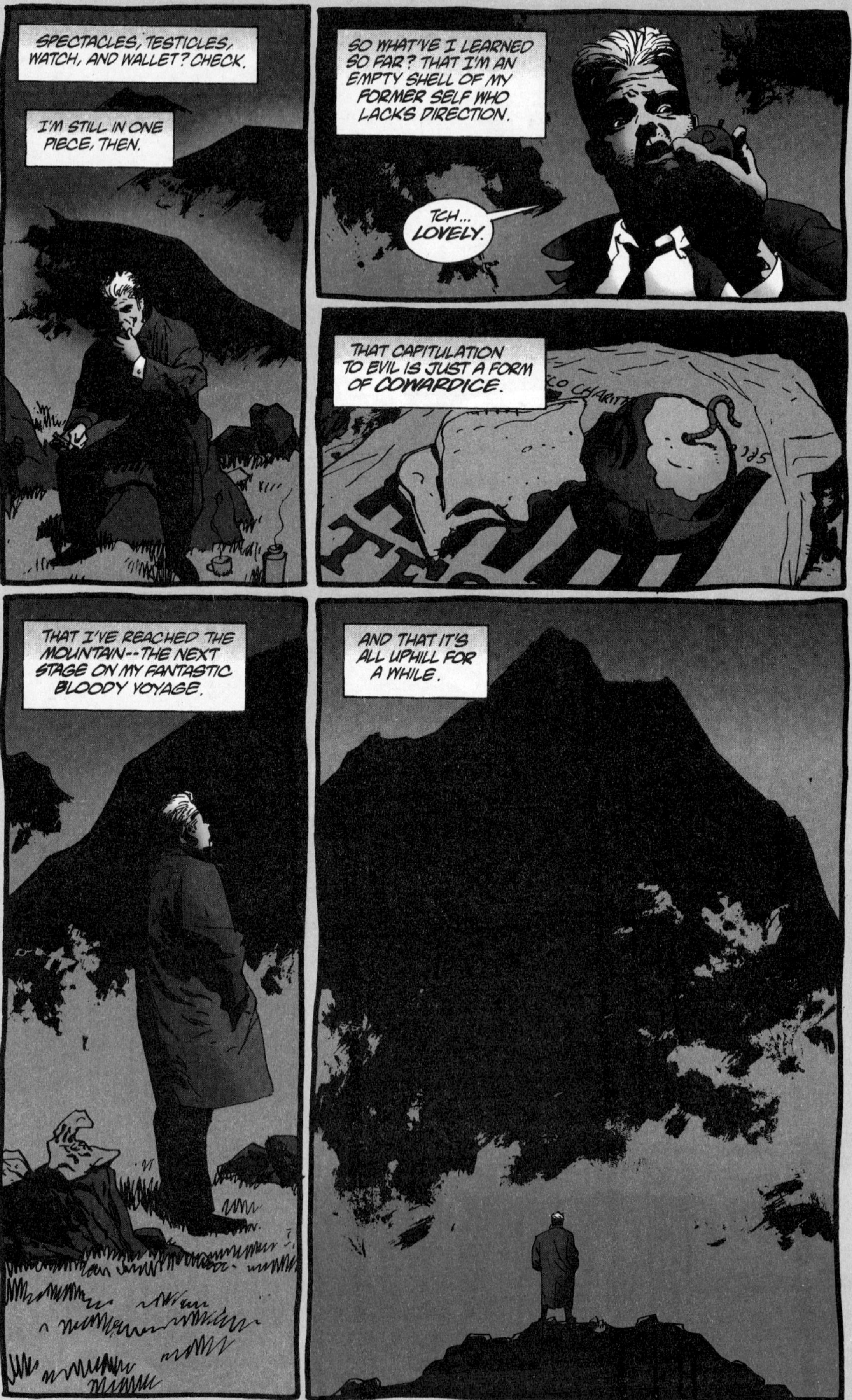
SPECTACLES, TESTICLES, WATCH, AND WALLET? CHECK.
I'M STILL IN ONE PIECE, THEN.
SO WHAT'VE I LEARNED SO FAR? THAT I'M AN EMPTY SHELL OF MY FORMER SELF WHO LACKS DIRECTION.
TCH... LOVELY.
THAT CAPITULATION TO EVIL IS JUST A FORM OF COWARDICE.
THAT I'VE REACHED THE MOUNTAIN--THE NEXT STAGE ON MY FANTASTIC BLOODY VOYAGE.
AND THAT IT'S ALL UPHILL FOR A WHILE.

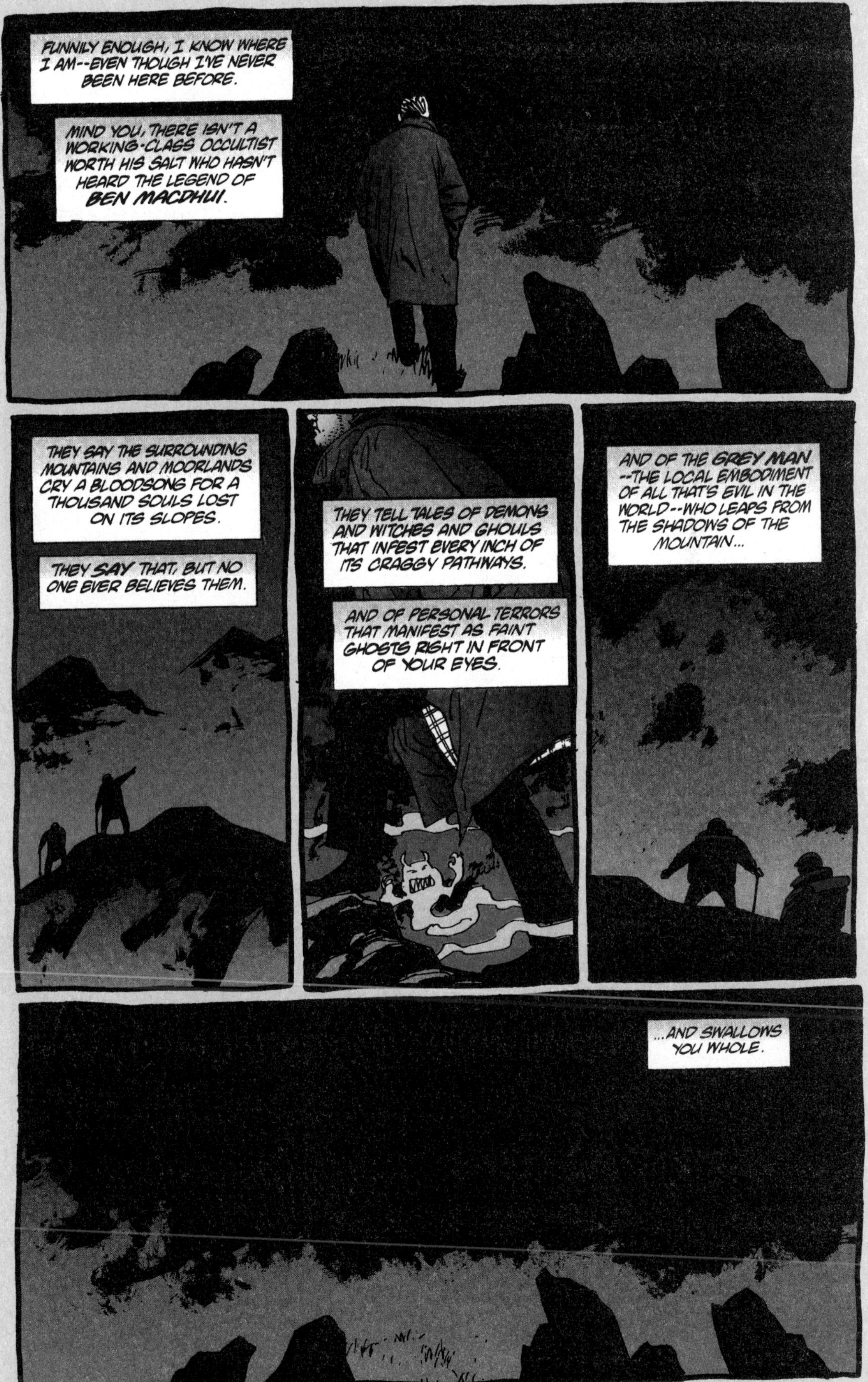
FUNNILY ENOUGH, I KNOW WHERE I AM--EVEN THOUGH I'VE NEVER BEEN HERE BEFORE.
MIND YOU, THERE ISN'T A WORKING-CLASS OCCULTIST WORTH HIS SALT WHO HASN'T HEARD THE LEGEND OF BEN MACDHUI.
THEY SAY THE SURROUNDING MOUNTAINS AND MOORLANDS CRY A BLOODSONG FOR A THOUSAND SOULS LOST ON ITS SLOPES.
THEY SAY THAT, BUT NO ONE EVER BELIEVES THEM.
THEY TELL TALES OF DEMONS AND WITCHES AND GHOULS THAT INFEST EVERY INCH OF ITS CRAGGY PATHWAYS.
AND OF PERSONAL TERRORS THAT MANIFEST AS FAINT GHOSTS RIGHT IN FRONT OF YOUR EYES.
AND OF THE GREY MAN --THE LOCAL EMBODIMENT OF ALL THAT'S EVIL IN THE WORLD--WHO LEAPS FROM THE SHADOWS OF THE MOUNTAIN...
...AND SWALLOWS YOU WHOLE.

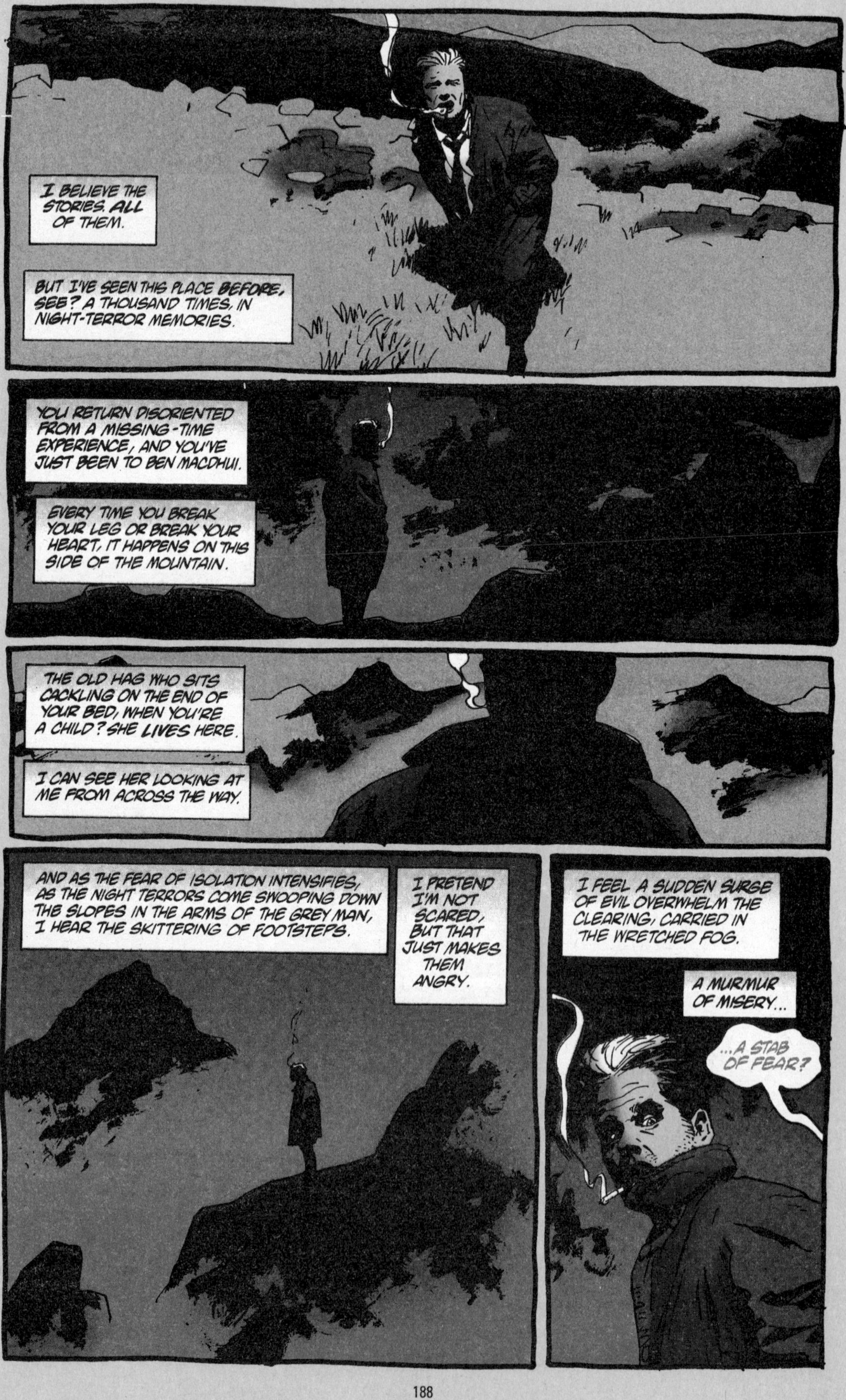
I BELIEVE THE STORIES. ALL OF THEM.
BUT I'VE SEEN THIS PLACE BEFORE, SEE? A THOUSAND TIMES, IN NIGHT-TERROR MEMORIES.
YOU RETURN DISORIENTED FROM A MISSING-TIME EXPERIENCE, AND YOU'VE JUST BEEN TO BEN MACDHUI.
EVERY TIME YOU BREAK YOUR LEG OR BREAK YOUR HEART, IT HAPPENS ON THIS SIDE OF THE MOUNTAIN.
THE OLD HAG WHO SITS CACKLING ON THE END OF YOUR BED, WHEN YOU'RE A CHILD? SHE LIVES HERE.
I CAN SEE HER LOOKING AT ME FROM ACROSS THE WAY.
AND AS THE FEAR OF ISOLATION INTENSIFIES, AS THE NIGHT TERRORS COME SWOOPING DOWN THE SLOPES IN THE ARMS OF THE GREY MAN, I HEAR THE SKITTERING OF FOOTSTEPS.
I PRETEND I'M NOT SCARED, BUT THAT JUST MAKES THEM ANGRY.
I FEEL A SUDDEN SURGE OF EVIL OVERWHELM THE CLEARING, CARRIED IN THE WRETCHED FOG.
A MURMUR OF MISERY...
...A STAB OF FEAR?

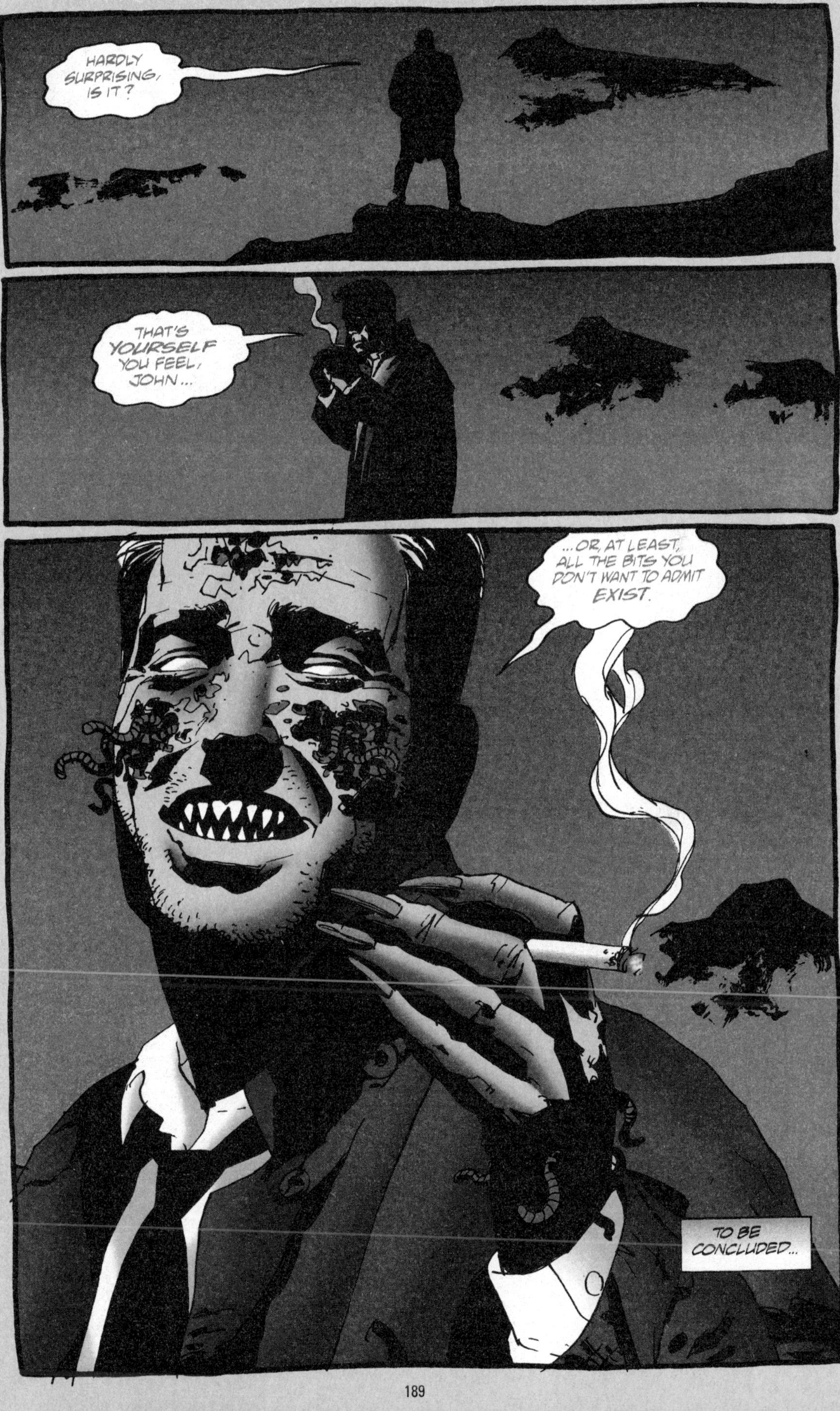
HARDLY SURPRISING, IS IT?
THAT'S YOURSELF YOU FEEL, JOHN...
...OR, AT LEAST, ALL THE BITS YOU DON'T WANT TO ADMIT EXIST.
TO BE CONCLUDED...

JOHN CONSTANTINE
HELLBLAZER
DC
VERTIGO
NO. 104
AUG 96
$2.25 US
$3.25 CAN
SUGGESTED FOR MATURE READERS
DIFFICULT BEGINNINGS
CONCLUSION
PAUL JENKINS • SEAN PHILLIPS

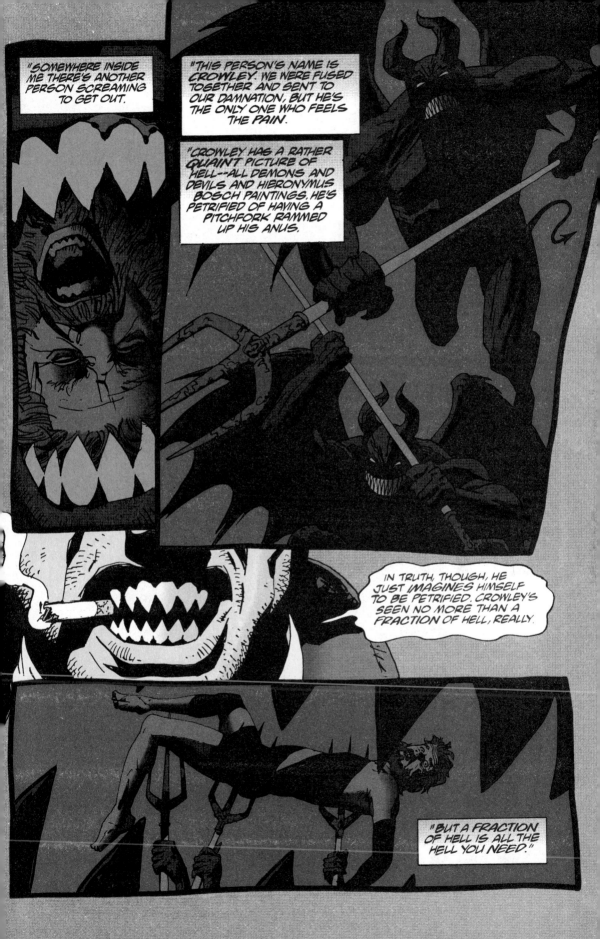

"SOMEWHERE INSIDE ME THERE'S ANOTHER PERSON SCREAMING TO GET OUT.

"THIS PERSON'S NAME IS CROWLEY. WE WERE FUSED TOGETHER AND SENT TO OUR DAMNATION, BUT HE'S THE ONLY ONE WHO FEELS THE PAIN.

"CROWLEY HAS A RATHER QUAINT PICTURE OF HELL--ALL DEMONS AND DEVILS AND HIERONYMUS BOSCH PAINTINGS. HE'S PETRIFIED OF HAVING A PITCHFORK RAMMED UP HIS ANUS.

IN TRUTH, THOUGH, HE JUST IMAGINES HIMSELF TO BE PETRIFIED. CROWLEY'S SEEN NO MORE THAN A FRACTION OF HELL, REALLY.

"BUT A FRACTION OF HELL IS ALL THE HELL YOU NEED."

I'VE TRIED TO MAKE THE **BEST** OF THE SITUATION -- TO **IGNORE** THE AWFUL BLOODY RACKET INSIDE ME. ALL THAT YELLING AND SWEARING, THOUGH...Tch.

THING IS, JOHN, I'VE BEEN FAR TOO BUSY WATCHING WHAT'S BEEN GOING ON DOWN THERE TO CARE ABOUT THE DAFT WEE LADDIE AND HIS PITCHFORKS...

"HELL WASN'T WHAT I **EXPECTED**, I MUST SAY. AFTER ALL, YOU AND I'VE SEEN A FEW BITS AND PIECES OF IT IN OUR TIME, EH?

"TURNS OUT, WHAT WE ALWAYS SAW WAS JUST OUR OWN **PERSONAL** HELL.

I EXPECTED DAMNATION TO ENTAIL SOME KIND OF **PHYSICAL** TORTURE. YOU KNOW--HOOKS AND CHAINS AND SO FORTH.

BUT THAT WOULD BE TOO **OBVIOUS**, WOULDN'T IT?

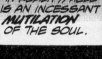

"IN REALITY, HELL IS AN INCESSANT **MUTILATION** OF THE SOUL.

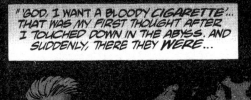

"FIRST THING I DISCOVERED WAS THAT I WAS DIFFERENT--I MEAN, YOU *MADE* ME THAT WAY, DIDN'T YOU?

"'GOD, I WANT A BLOODY *CIGARETTE'*... THAT WAS MY FIRST THOUGHT AFTER I TOUCHED DOWN IN THE ABYSS. AND SUDDENLY, THERE THEY *WERE*...

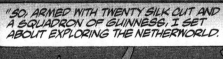

"SO, ARMED WITH TWENTY SILK CUT AND A SQUADRON OF GUINNESS, I SET ABOUT EXPLORING THE NETHERWORLD.

"THE SIGHTS I'VE SEEN, JOHN...ALL THAT TIME AND EFFORT DEVOTED TO THE FLAGELLATION OF THE HUMAN SPIRIT.

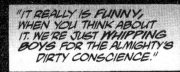

"IT REALLY IS *FUNNY*, WHEN YOU THINK ABOUT IT. WE'RE JUST *WHIPPING BOYS* FOR THE ALMIGHTY'S DIRTY CONSCIENCE."

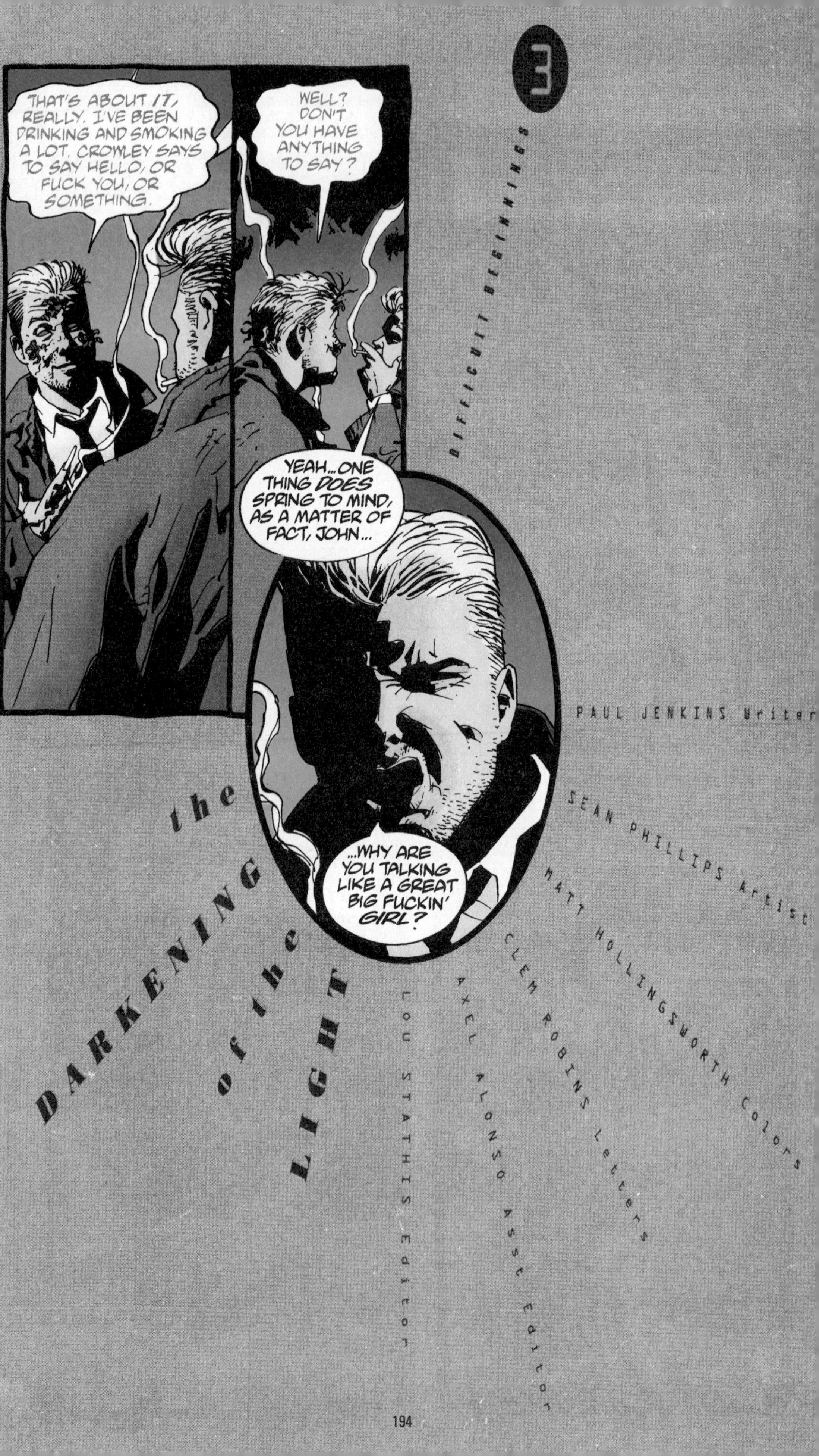
THAT'S ABOUT IT, REALLY. I'VE BEEN DRINKING AND SMOKING A LOT. CROWLEY SAYS TO SAY HELLO, OR FUCK YOU, OR SOMETHING.
WELL? DON'T YOU HAVE ANYTHING TO SAY?
YEAH...ONE THING DOES SPRING TO MIND, AS A MATTER OF FACT, JOHN...
...WHY ARE YOU TALKING LIKE A GREAT BIG FUCKIN' GIRL?

3

DIFFICULT BEGINNINGS

the DARKENING of the LIGHT

PAUL JENKINS Writer

SEAN PHILLIPS Artist

MATT HOLLINGSWORTH Colors

CLEM ROBINS Letters

AXEL ALONSO Asst Editor

LOU STATHIS Editor

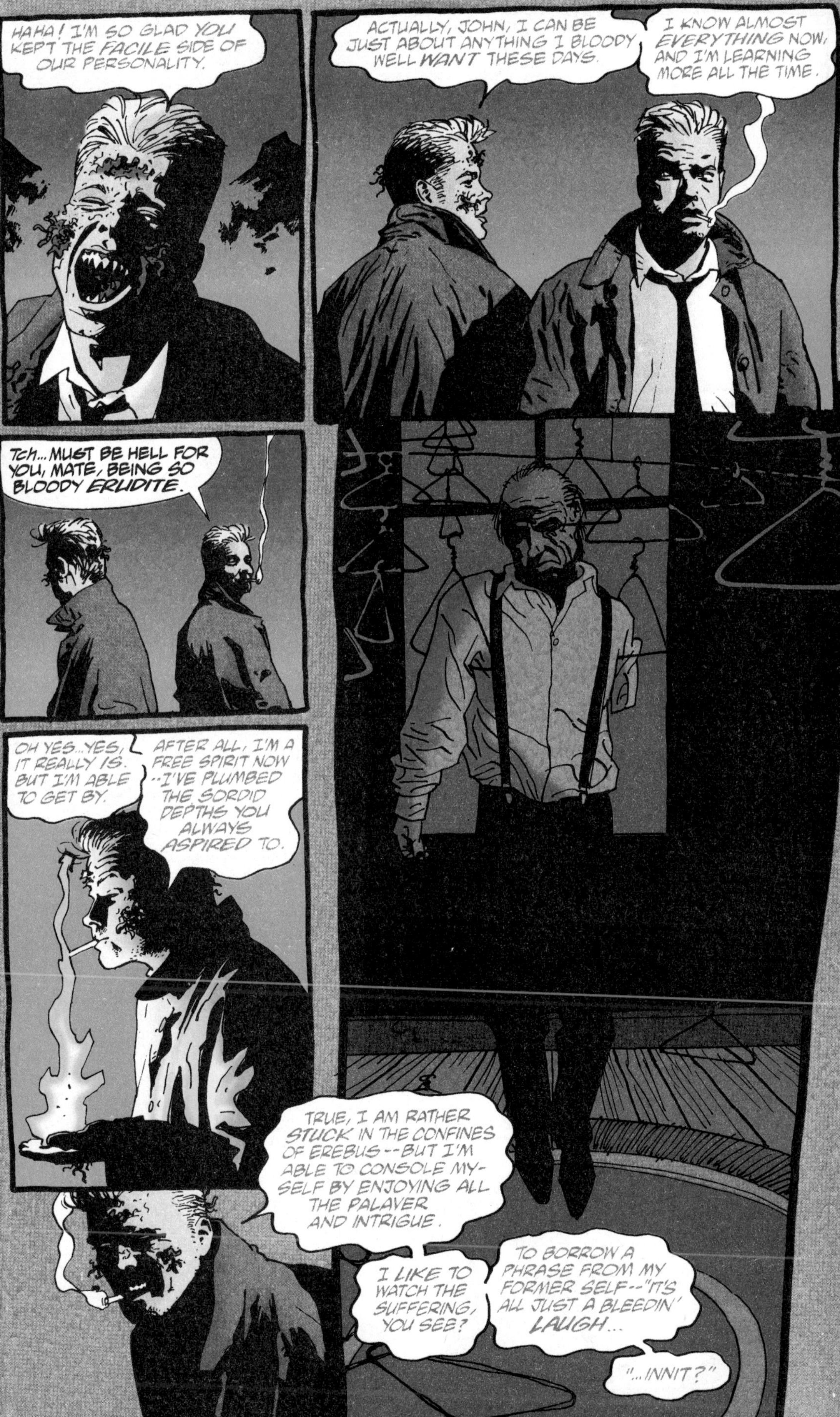
HAHA! I'M SO GLAD YOU KEPT THE FACILE SIDE OF OUR PERSONALITY.
ACTUALLY, JOHN, I CAN BE JUST ABOUT ANYTHING I BLOODY WELL WANT THESE DAYS.
I KNOW ALMOST EVERYTHING NOW, AND I'M LEARNING MORE ALL THE TIME.
TCH... MUST BE HELL FOR YOU, MATE, BEING SO BLOODY ERUDITE.
OH YES...YES, IT REALLY IS. BUT I'M ABLE TO GET BY.
AFTER ALL, I'M A FREE SPIRIT NOW --I'VE PLUMBED THE SORDID DEPTHS YOU ALWAYS ASPIRED TO.
TRUE, I AM RATHER STUCK IN THE CONFINES OF EREBUS--BUT I'M ABLE TO CONSOLE MY-SELF BY ENJOYING ALL THE PALAVER AND INTRIGUE.
I LIKE TO WATCH THE SUFFERING, YOU SEE?
TO BORROW A PHRASE FROM MY FORMER SELF--"IT'S ALL JUST A BLEEDIN' LAUGH...
"...INNIT?"

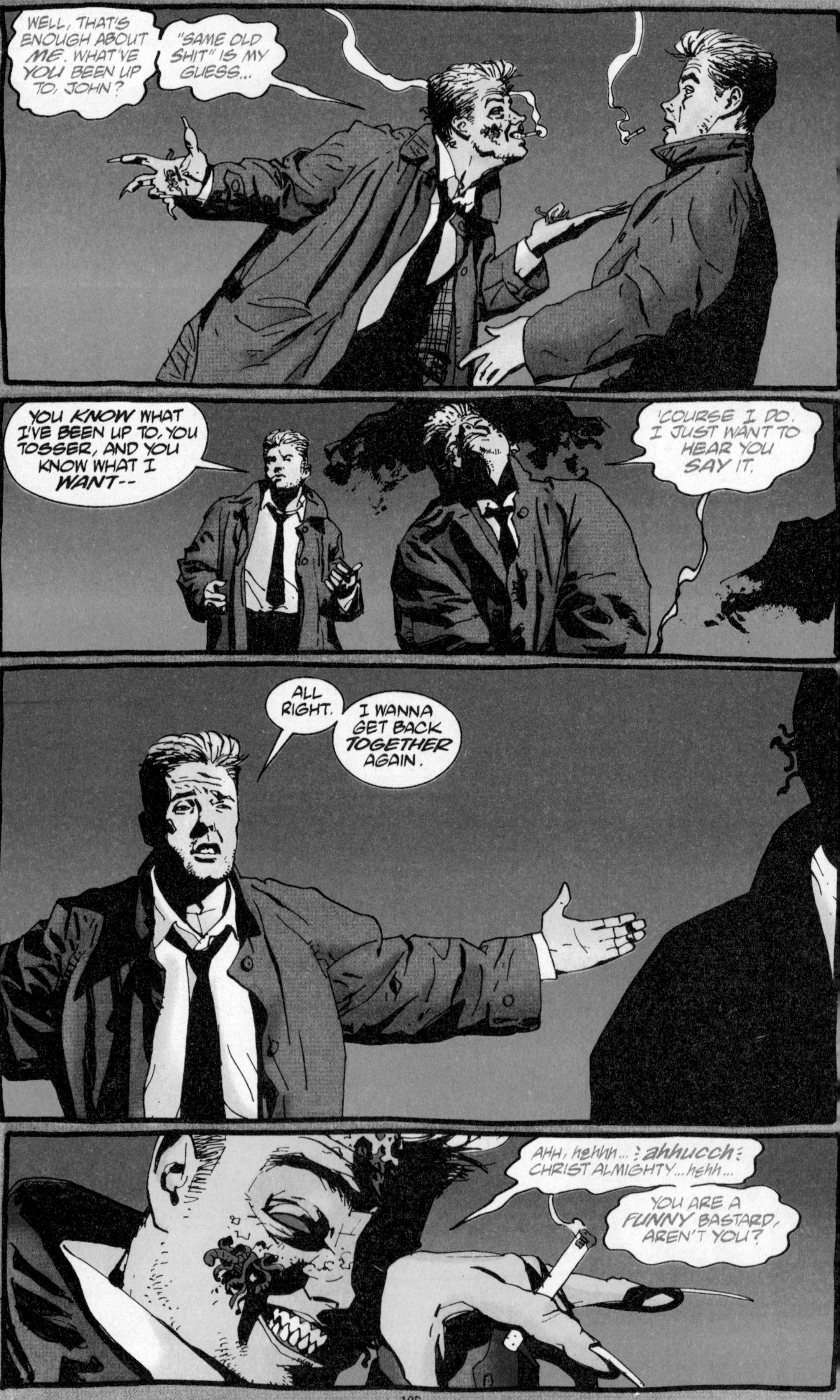
WELL, THAT'S ENOUGH ABOUT ME. WHAT'VE YOU BEEN UP TO, JOHN?
"SAME OLD SHIT" IS MY GUESS...
YOU KNOW WHAT I'VE BEEN UP TO, YOU TOSSER, AND YOU KNOW WHAT I WANT--
'COURSE I DO. I JUST WANT TO HEAR YOU SAY IT.
ALL RIGHT.
I WANNA GET BACK TOGETHER AGAIN.
AHH, hehhh... ahhucch CHRIST ALMIGHTY...hehh...
YOU ARE A FUNNY BASTARD, AREN'T YOU?

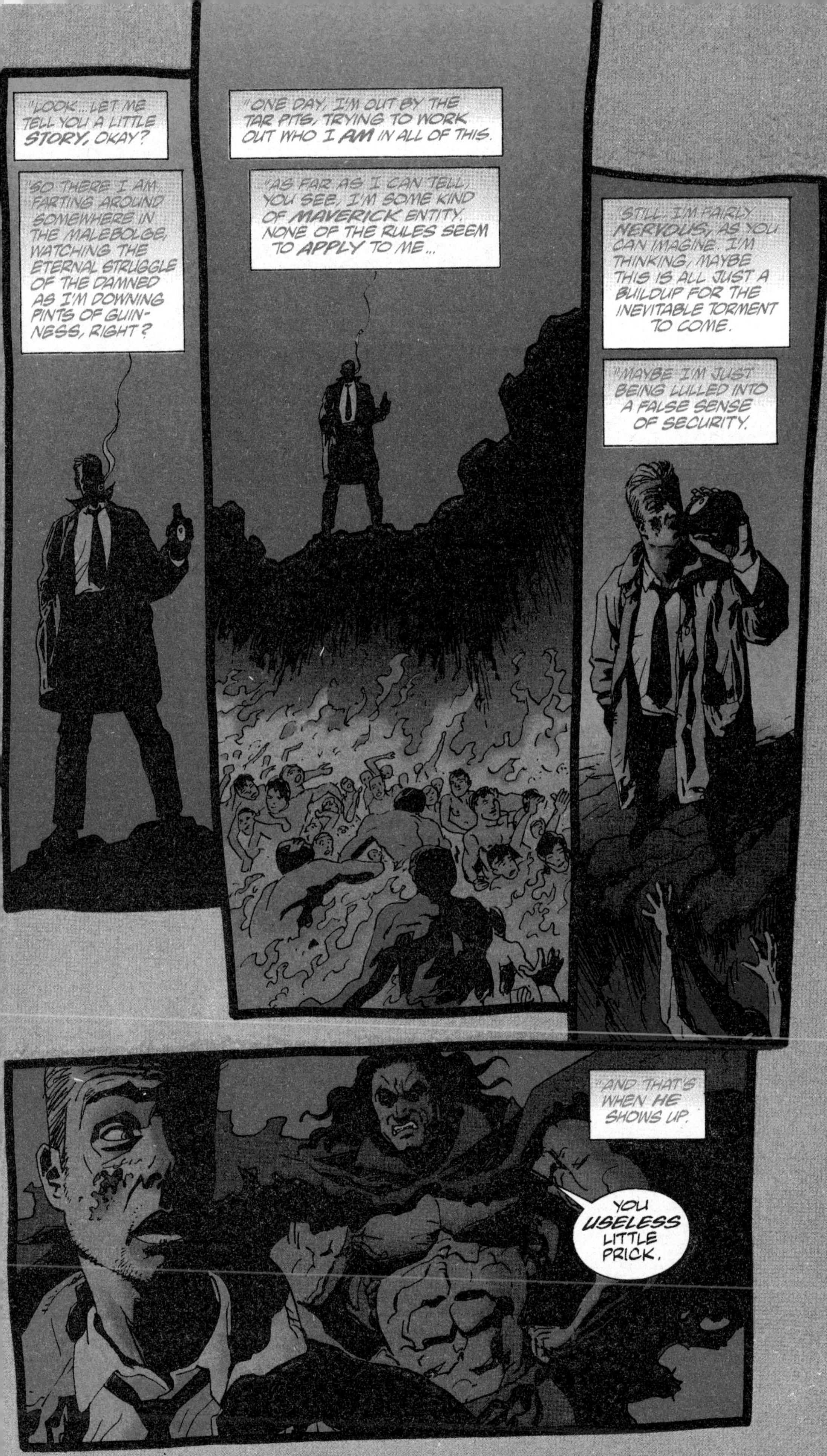
"LOOK... LET ME TELL YOU A LITTLE STORY, OKAY?
"SO THERE I AM FARTING AROUND SOMEWHERE IN THE MALEBOLGE, WATCHING THE ETERNAL STRUGGLE OF THE DAMNED AS I'M DOWNING PINTS OF GUIN-NESS, RIGHT?
"ONE DAY, I'M OUT BY THE TAR PITS, TRYING TO WORK OUT WHO I AM IN ALL OF THIS.
"AS FAR AS I CAN TELL, YOU SEE, I'M SOME KIND OF MAVERICK ENTITY. NONE OF THE RULES SEEM TO APPLY TO ME...
"STILL, I'M FAIRLY NERVOUS, AS YOU CAN IMAGINE. I'M THINKING, MAYBE THIS IS ALL JUST A BUILDUP FOR THE INEVITABLE TORMENT TO COME.
"MAYBE I'M JUST BEING LULLED INTO A FALSE SENSE OF SECURITY.
"AND THAT'S WHEN HE SHOWS UP.
YOU USELESS LITTLE PRICK.

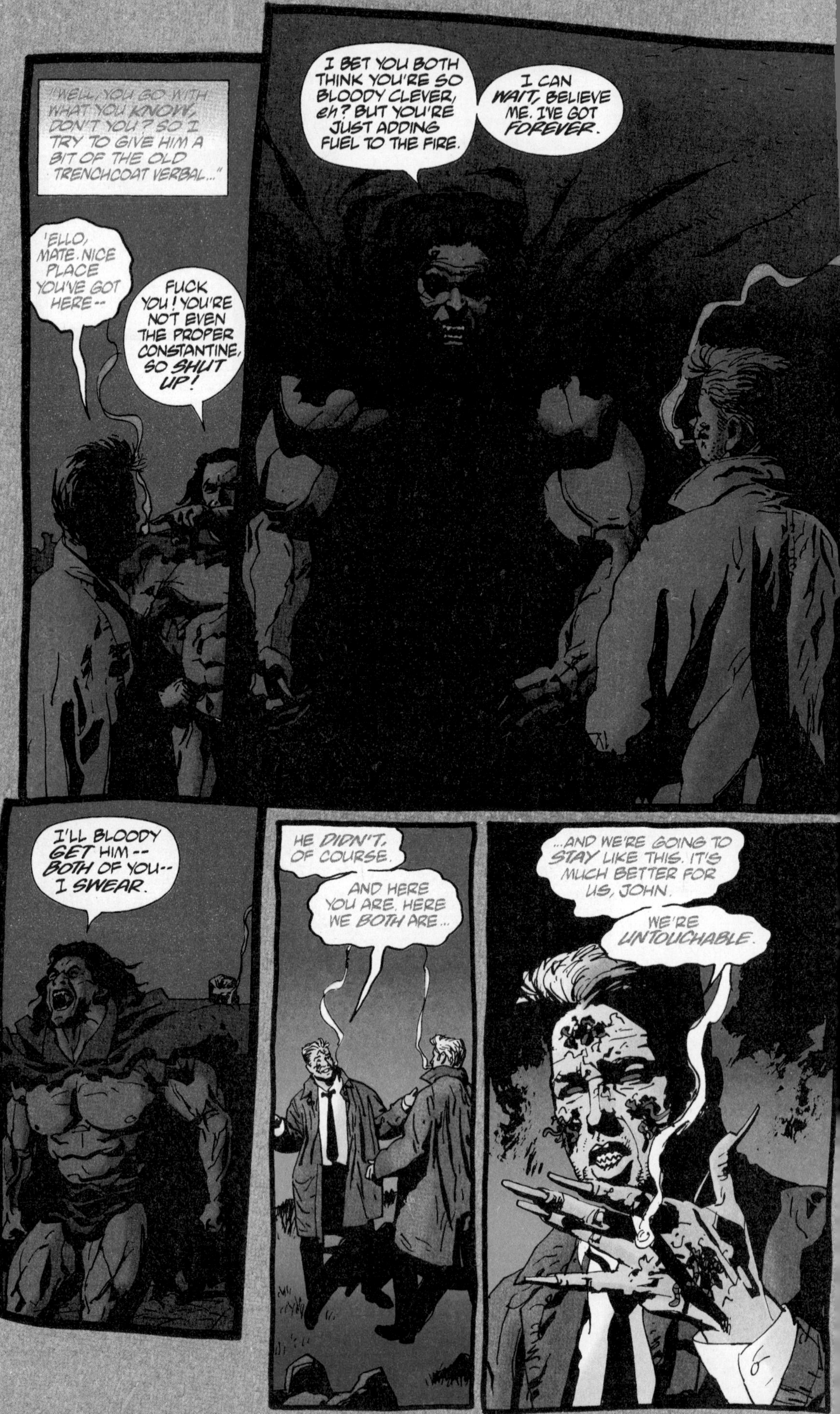
"WELL, YOU GO WITH WHAT YOU KNOW, DON'T YOU? SO I TRY TO GIVE HIM A BIT OF THE OLD TRENCHCOAT VERBAL..."
'ELLO, MATE. NICE PLACE YOU'VE GOT HERE--
FUCK YOU! YOU'RE NOT EVEN THE PROPER CONSTANTINE, SO SHUT UP!
I BET YOU BOTH THINK YOU'RE SO BLOODY CLEVER, eh? BUT YOU'RE JUST ADDING FUEL TO THE FIRE.
I CAN WAIT, BELIEVE ME. I'VE GOT FOREVER.
I'LL BLOODY GET HIM -- BOTH OF YOU-- I SWEAR.
HE DIDN'T, OF COURSE.
AND HERE YOU ARE. HERE WE BOTH ARE...
...AND WE'RE GOING TO STAY LIKE THIS. IT'S MUCH BETTER FOR US, JOHN.
WE'RE UNTOUCHABLE.

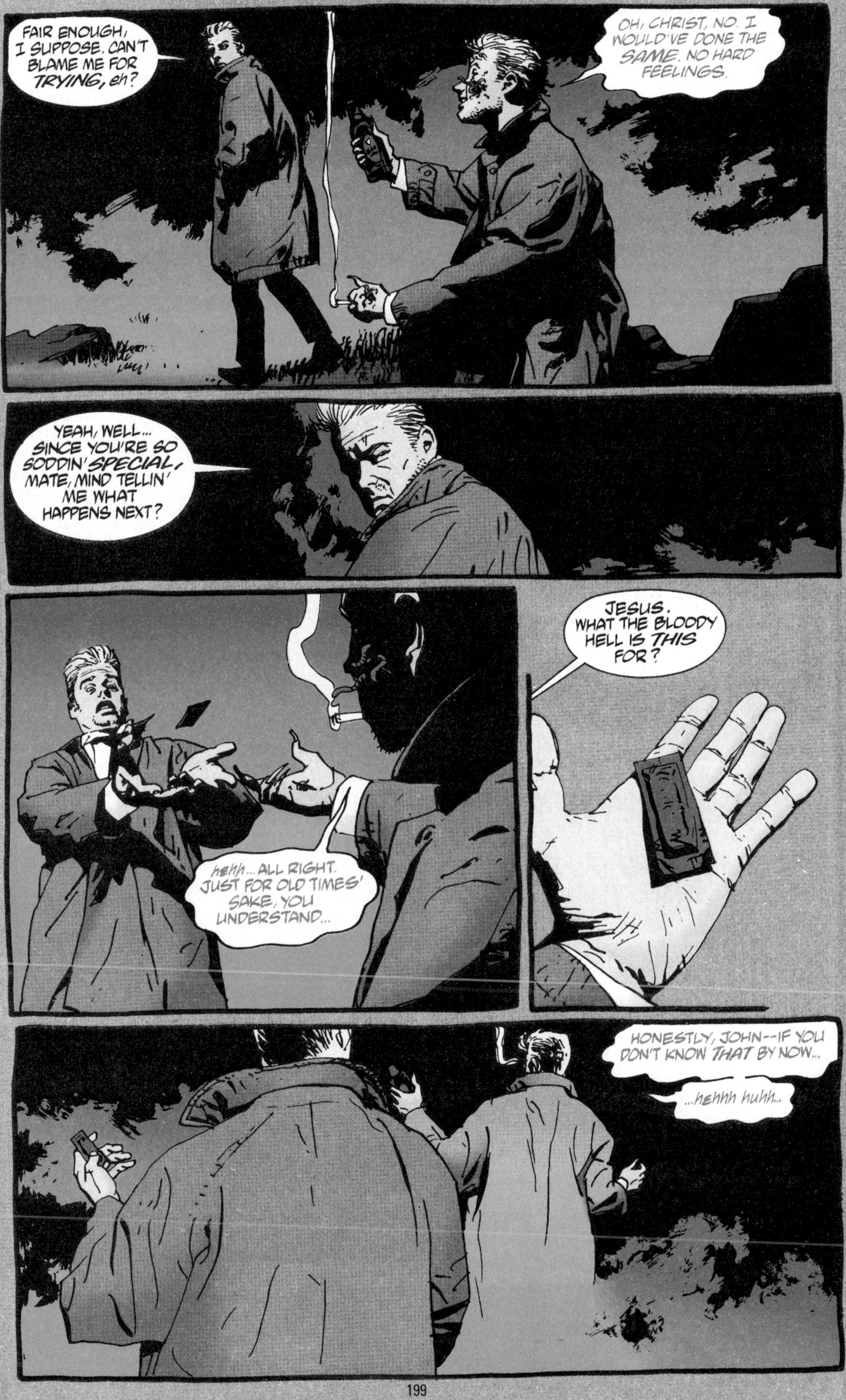
FAIR ENOUGH, I SUPPOSE. CAN'T BLAME ME FOR TRYING, eh?
OH, CHRIST, NO. I WOULD'VE DONE THE SAME. NO HARD FEELINGS.
YEAH, WELL... SINCE YOU'RE SO SODDIN' SPECIAL, MATE, MIND TELLIN' ME WHAT HAPPENS NEXT?
hehh... ALL RIGHT. JUST FOR OLD TIMES' SAKE, YOU UNDERSTAND...
JESUS. WHAT THE BLOODY HELL IS THIS FOR?
HONESTLY, JOHN--IF YOU DON'T KNOW THAT BY NOW...
...hehhh huhh...

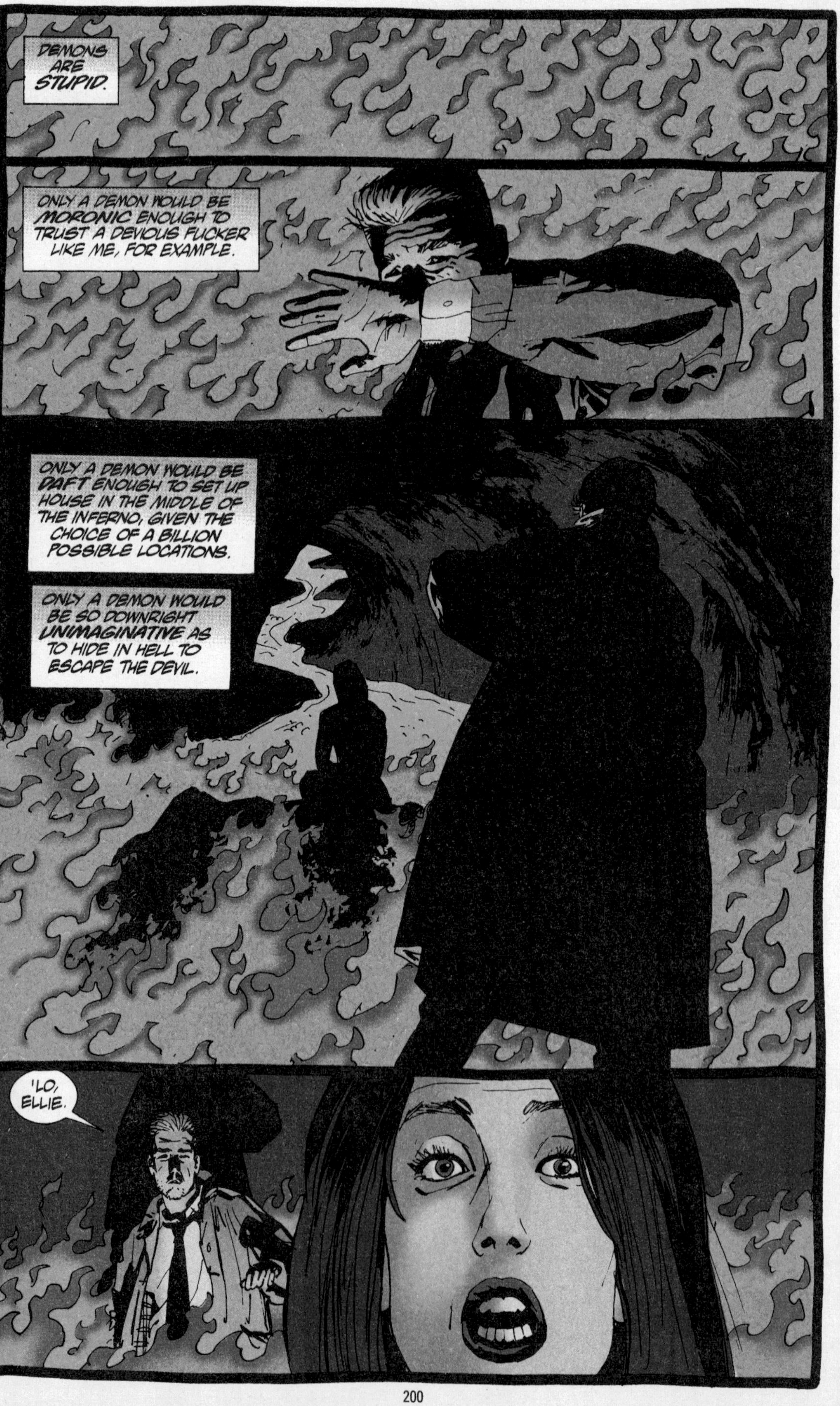
DEMONS ARE STUPID.
ONLY A DEMON WOULD BE MORONIC ENOUGH TO TRUST A DEVIOUS FUCKER LIKE ME, FOR EXAMPLE.
ONLY A DEMON WOULD BE DAFT ENOUGH TO SET UP HOUSE IN THE MIDDLE OF THE INFERNO, GIVEN THE CHOICE OF A BILLION POSSIBLE LOCATIONS.
ONLY A DEMON WOULD BE SO DOWNRIGHT UNIMAGINATIVE AS TO HIDE IN HELL TO ESCAPE THE DEVIL.
'LO, ELLIE.

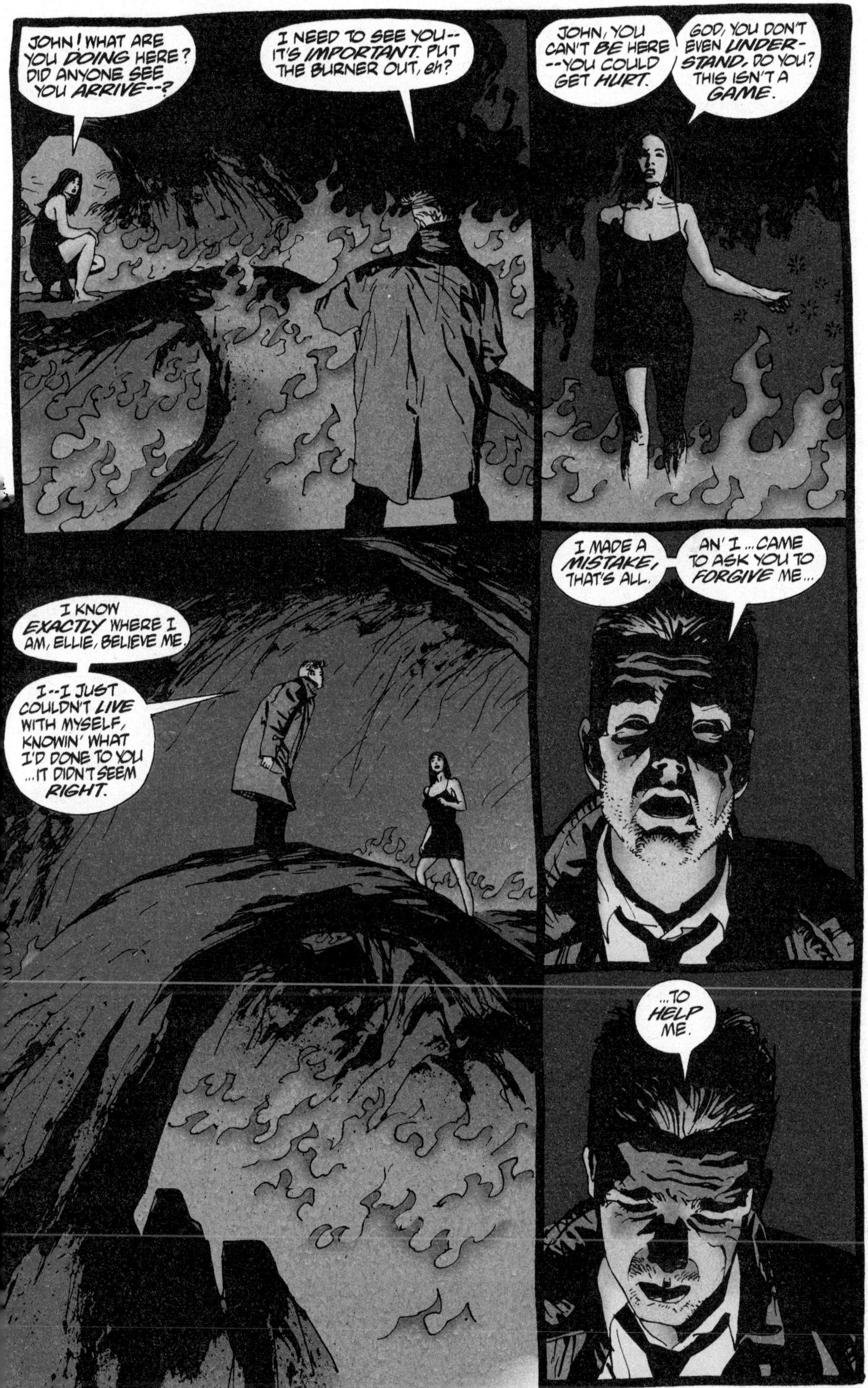

JOHN! WHAT ARE YOU *DOING* HERE? DID ANYONE SEE YOU *ARRIVE*--?
I NEED TO SEE YOU-- IT'S *IMPORTANT*. PUT THE BURNER OUT, *eh*?
JOHN, YOU CAN'T *BE* HERE --YOU COULD GET *HURT*.
GOD, YOU DON'T EVEN *UNDER-STAND*, DO YOU? THIS ISN'T A *GAME*.
I KNOW *EXACTLY* WHERE I AM, ELLIE, BELIEVE ME.
I--I JUST COULDN'T *LIVE* WITH MYSELF, KNOWIN' WHAT I'D DONE TO YOU ...IT DIDN'T SEEM *RIGHT*.
I MADE A *MISTAKE*, THAT'S ALL.
AN' I ...CAME TO ASK YOU TO *FORGIVE* ME...
...TO *HELP* ME.

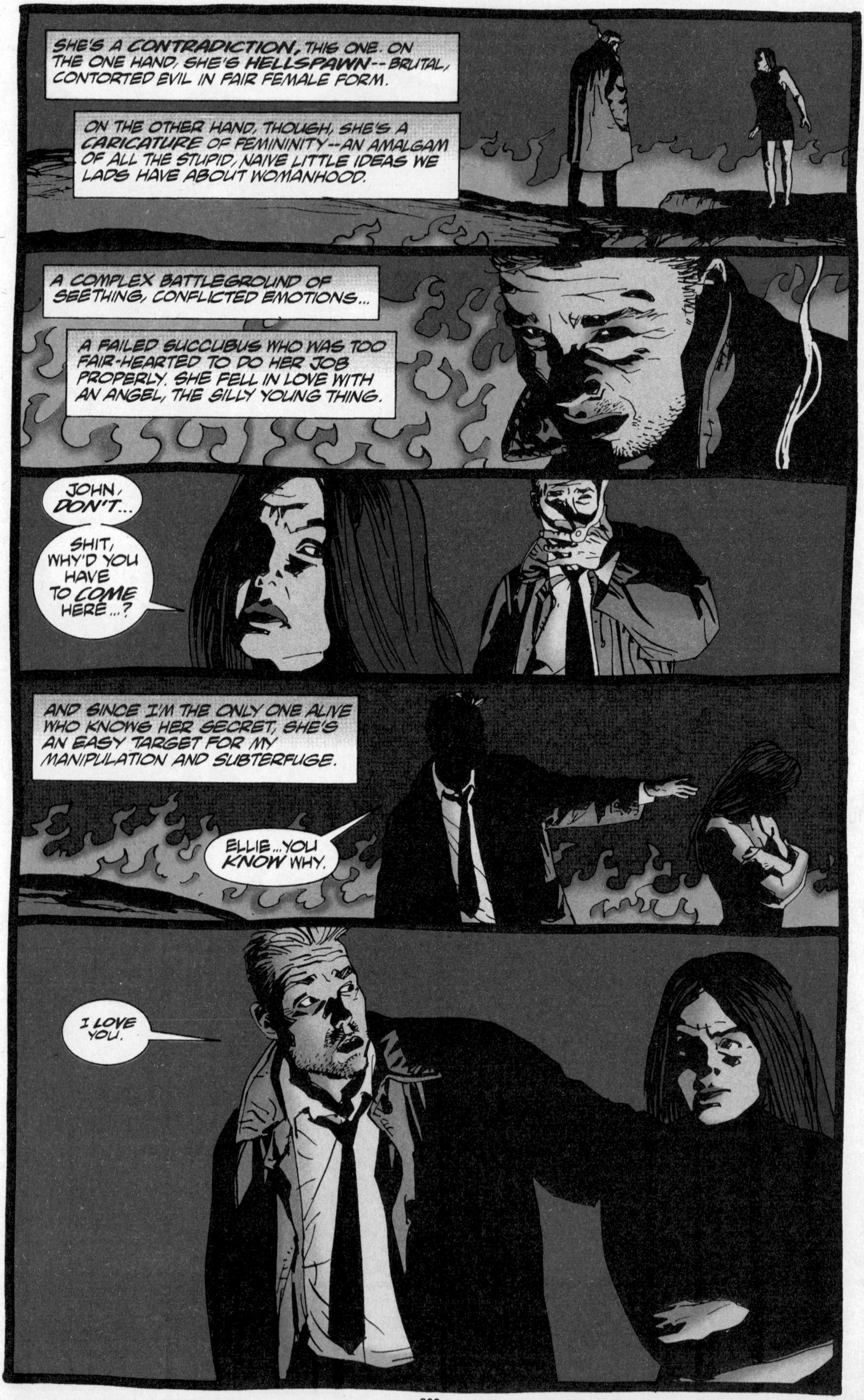
SHE'S A CONTRADICTION, THIS ONE. ON THE ONE HAND, SHE'S HELLSPAWN--BRUTAL, CONTORTED EVIL IN FAIR FEMALE FORM.
ON THE OTHER HAND, THOUGH, SHE'S A CARICATURE OF FEMININITY--AN AMALGAM OF ALL THE STUPID, NAIVE LITTLE IDEAS WE LADS HAVE ABOUT WOMANHOOD.
A COMPLEX BATTLEGROUND OF SEETHING, CONFLICTED EMOTIONS...
A FAILED SUCCUBUS WHO WAS TOO FAIR-HEARTED TO DO HER JOB PROPERLY. SHE FELL IN LOVE WITH AN ANGEL, THE SILLY YOUNG THING.
JOHN, DON'T...
SHIT, WHY'D YOU HAVE TO COME HERE...?
AND SINCE I'M THE ONLY ONE ALIVE WHO KNOWS HER SECRET, SHE'S AN EASY TARGET FOR MY MANIPULATION AND SUBTERFUGE.
ELLIE...YOU KNOW WHY.
I LOVE YOU.

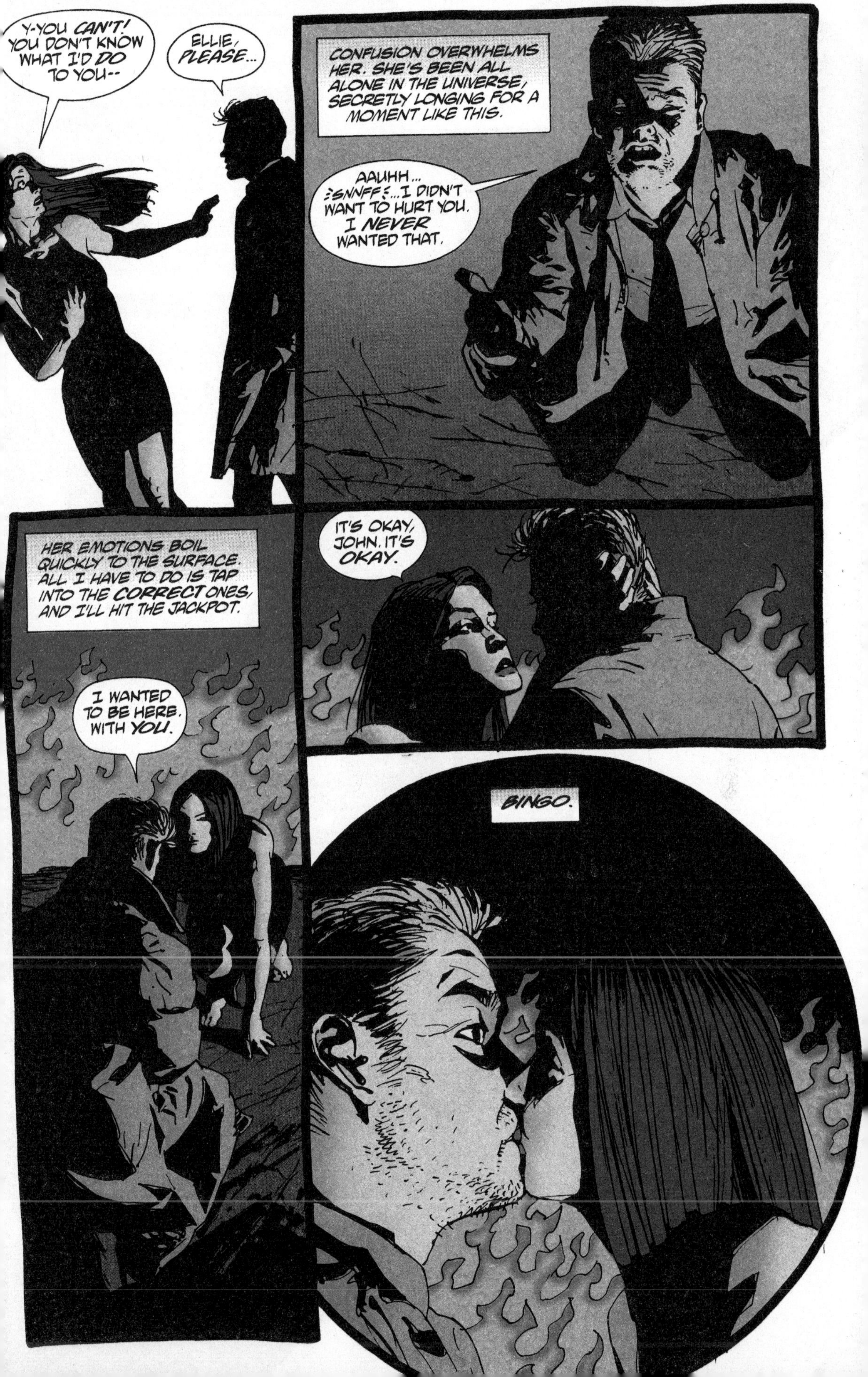

Y-YOU CAN'T! YOU DON'T KNOW WHAT I'D DO TO YOU--
ELLIE, PLEASE...
CONFUSION OVERWHELMS HER. SHE'S BEEN ALL ALONE IN THE UNIVERSE, SECRETLY LONGING FOR A MOMENT LIKE THIS.
AAUHH... SNNFF ...I DIDN'T WANT TO HURT YOU. I NEVER WANTED THAT.
HER EMOTIONS BOIL QUICKLY TO THE SURFACE. ALL I HAVE TO DO IS TAP INTO THE CORRECT ONES, AND I'LL HIT THE JACKPOT.
I WANTED TO BE HERE. WITH YOU.
IT'S OKAY, JOHN. IT'S OKAY.
BINGO.

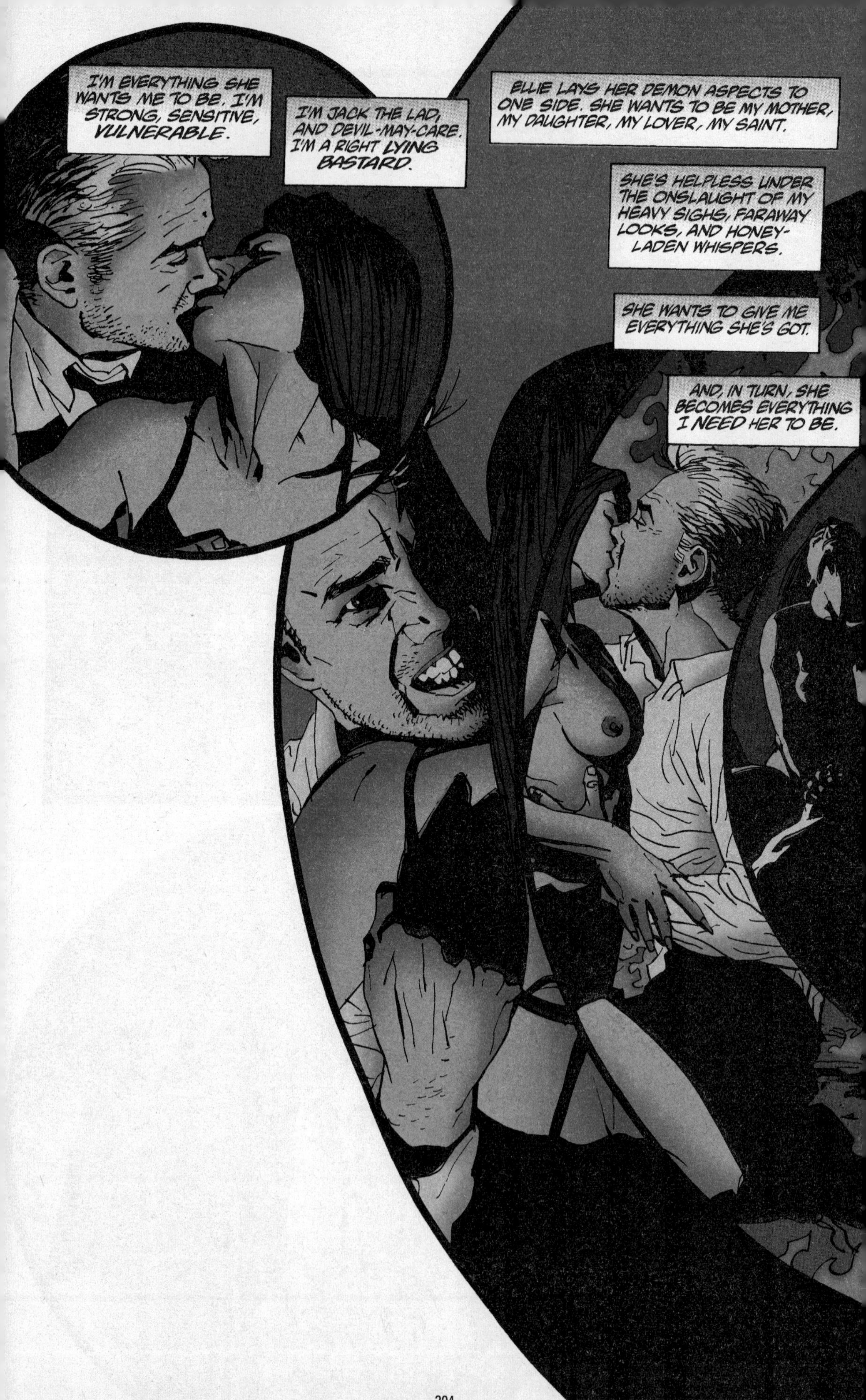
I'M EVERYTHING SHE WANTS ME TO BE. I'M STRONG, SENSITIVE, VULNERABLE.
I'M JACK THE LAD, AND DEVIL-MAY-CARE. I'M A RIGHT LYING BASTARD.
ELLIE LAYS HER DEMON ASPECTS TO ONE SIDE. SHE WANTS TO BE MY MOTHER, MY DAUGHTER, MY LOVER, MY SAINT.
SHE'S HELPLESS UNDER THE ONSLAUGHT OF MY HEAVY SIGHS, FARAWAY LOOKS, AND HONEY-LADEN WHISPERS.
SHE WANTS TO GIVE ME EVERYTHING SHE'S GOT.
AND, IN TURN, SHE BECOMES EVERYTHING I NEED HER TO BE.

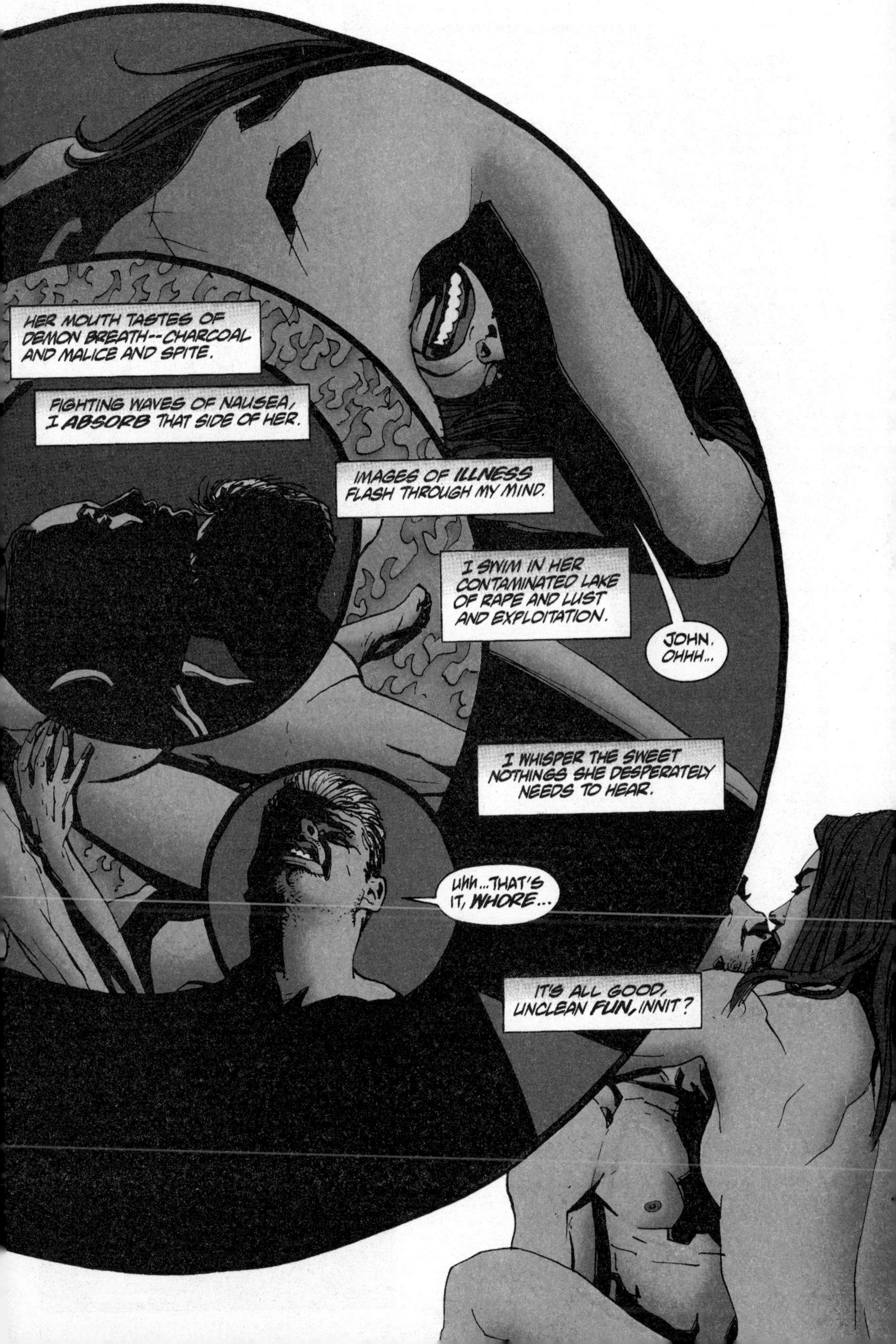
HER MOUTH TASTES OF DEMON BREATH--CHARCOAL AND MALICE AND SPITE.
FIGHTING WAVES OF NAUSEA, I ABSORB THAT SIDE OF HER.
IMAGES OF ILLNESS FLASH THROUGH MY MIND.
I SWIM IN HER CONTAMINATED LAKE OF RAPE AND LUST AND EXPLOITATION.
JOHN. OHHH...
I WHISPER THE SWEET NOTHINGS SHE DESPERATELY NEEDS TO HEAR.
UHH...THAT'S IT, WHORE...
IT'S ALL GOOD, UNCLEAN FUN, INNIT?

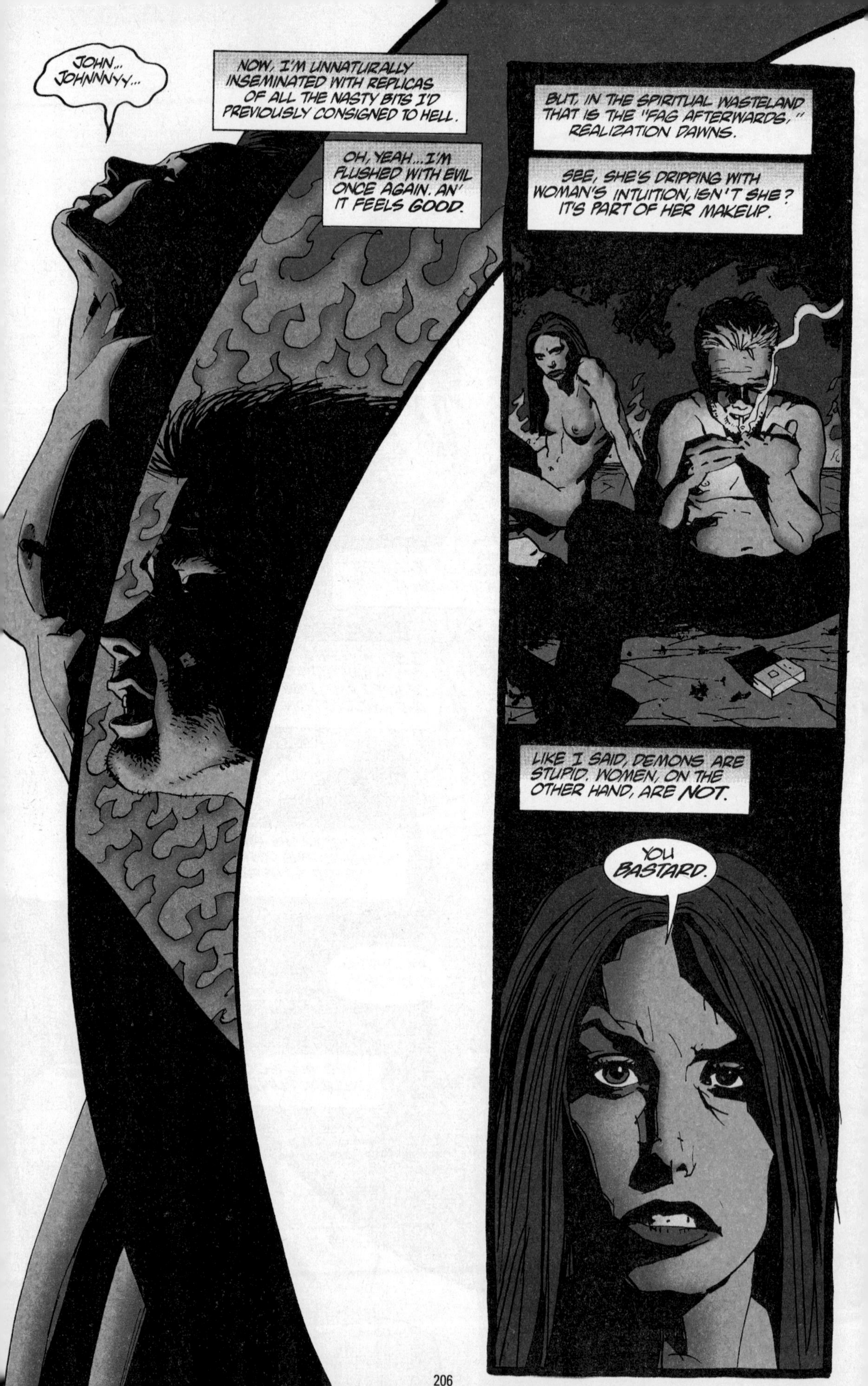
JOHN... JOHNNNYY...
NOW, I'M UNNATURALLY INSEMINATED WITH REPLICAS OF ALL THE NASTY BITS I'D PREVIOUSLY CONSIGNED TO HELL.
OH, YEAH...I'M FLUSHED WITH EVIL ONCE AGAIN. AN' IT FEELS GOOD.
BUT, IN THE SPIRITUAL WASTELAND THAT IS THE "FAG AFTERWARDS," REALIZATION DAWNS.
SEE, SHE'S DRIPPING WITH WOMAN'S INTUITION, ISN'T SHE? IT'S PART OF HER MAKEUP.
LIKE I SAID, DEMONS ARE STUPID. WOMEN, ON THE OTHER HAND, ARE NOT.
YOU BASTARD.

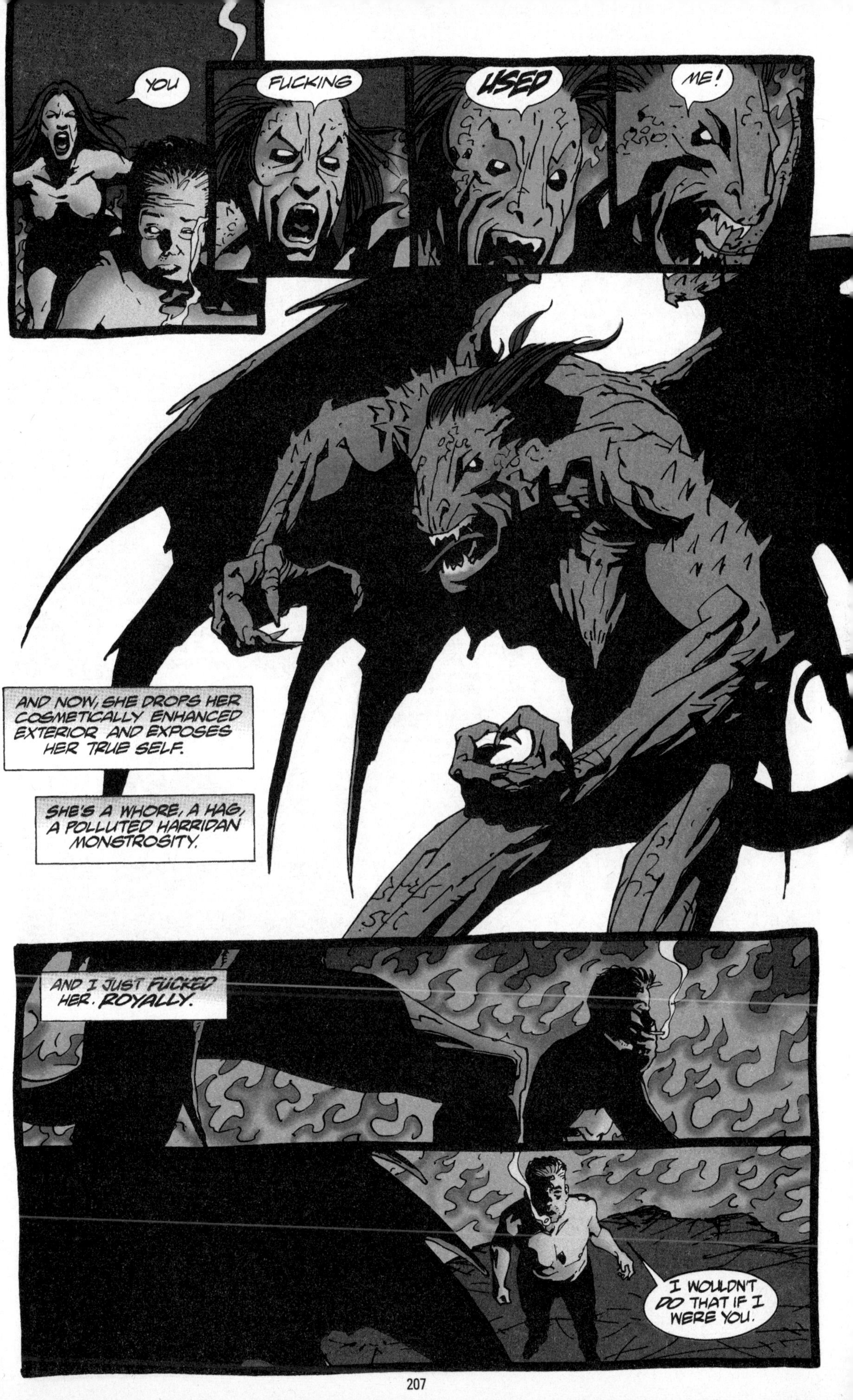
YOU
FUCKING
USED
ME!
AND NOW, SHE DROPS HER COSMETICALLY ENHANCED EXTERIOR AND EXPOSES HER TRUE SELF.
SHE'S A WHORE, A HAG, A POLLUTED HARRIDAN MONSTROSITY.
AND I JUST FUCKED HER. ROYALLY.
I WOULDN'T DO THAT IF I WERE YOU.

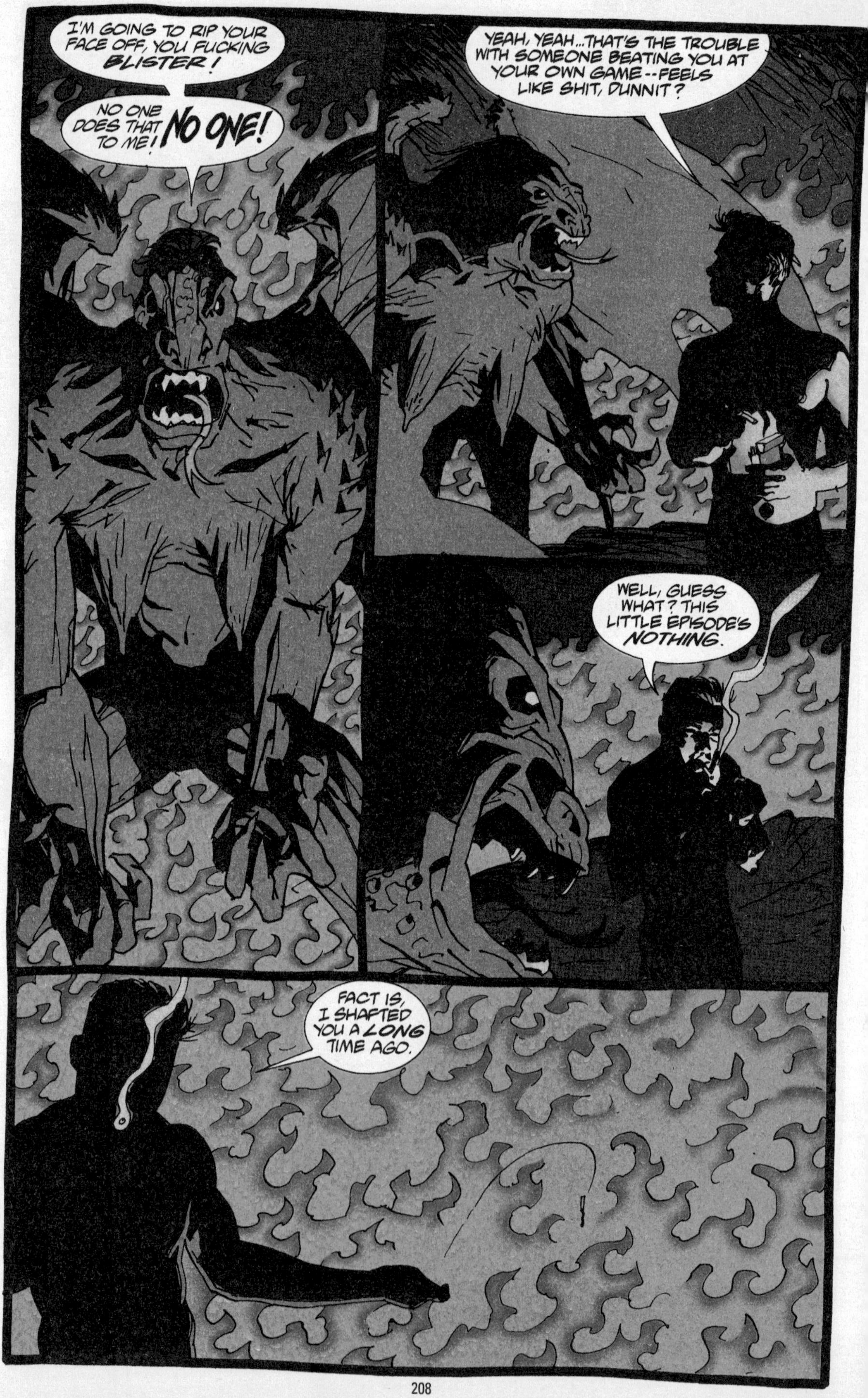
I'M GOING TO RIP YOUR FACE OFF, YOU FUCKING BLISTER!
NO ONE DOES THAT TO ME! NO ONE!
YEAH, YEAH...THAT'S THE TROUBLE WITH SOMEONE BEATING YOU AT YOUR OWN GAME--FEELS LIKE SHIT, DUNNIT?
WELL, GUESS WHAT? THIS LITTLE EPISODE'S NOTHING.
FACT IS, I SHAFTED YOU A LONG TIME AGO.

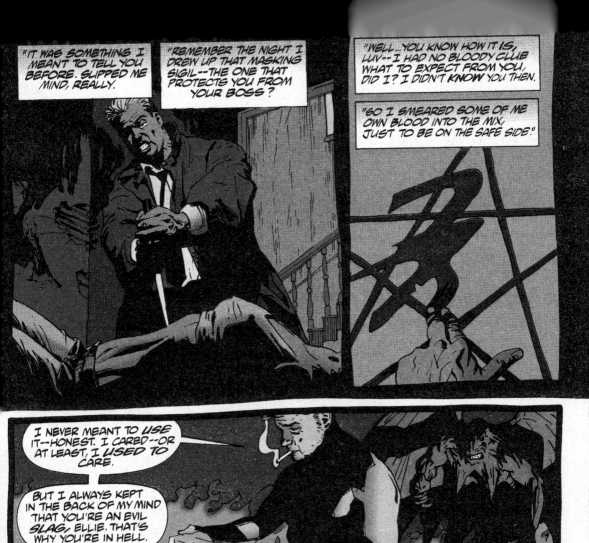

"IT WAS SOMETHING I MEANT TO TELL YOU BEFORE. SLIPPED ME MIND, REALLY.

"REMEMBER THE NIGHT I DREW UP THAT MASKING SIGIL--THE ONE THAT PROTECTS YOU FROM YOUR BOSS?

"WELL...YOU KNOW HOW IT IS, LUV-- I HAD NO BLOODY CLUE WHAT TO EXPECT FROM YOU, DID I? I DIDN'T KNOW YOU THEN.

"SO I SMEARED SOME OF ME OWN BLOOD INTO THE MIX, JUST TO BE ON THE SAFE SIDE."

I NEVER MEANT TO USE IT--HONEST. I CARED--OR AT LEAST, I USED TO CARE.

BUT I ALWAYS KEPT IN THE BACK OF MY MIND THAT YOU'RE AN EVIL SLAG, ELLIE. THAT'S WHY YOU'RE IN HELL.

SO, I'D SAY THERE'S A FAIRLY GOOD REASON TO KEEP ME ALIVE, REALLY.

'CAUSE WHEN I DIE, THE SIGIL LOSES ITS POWER.

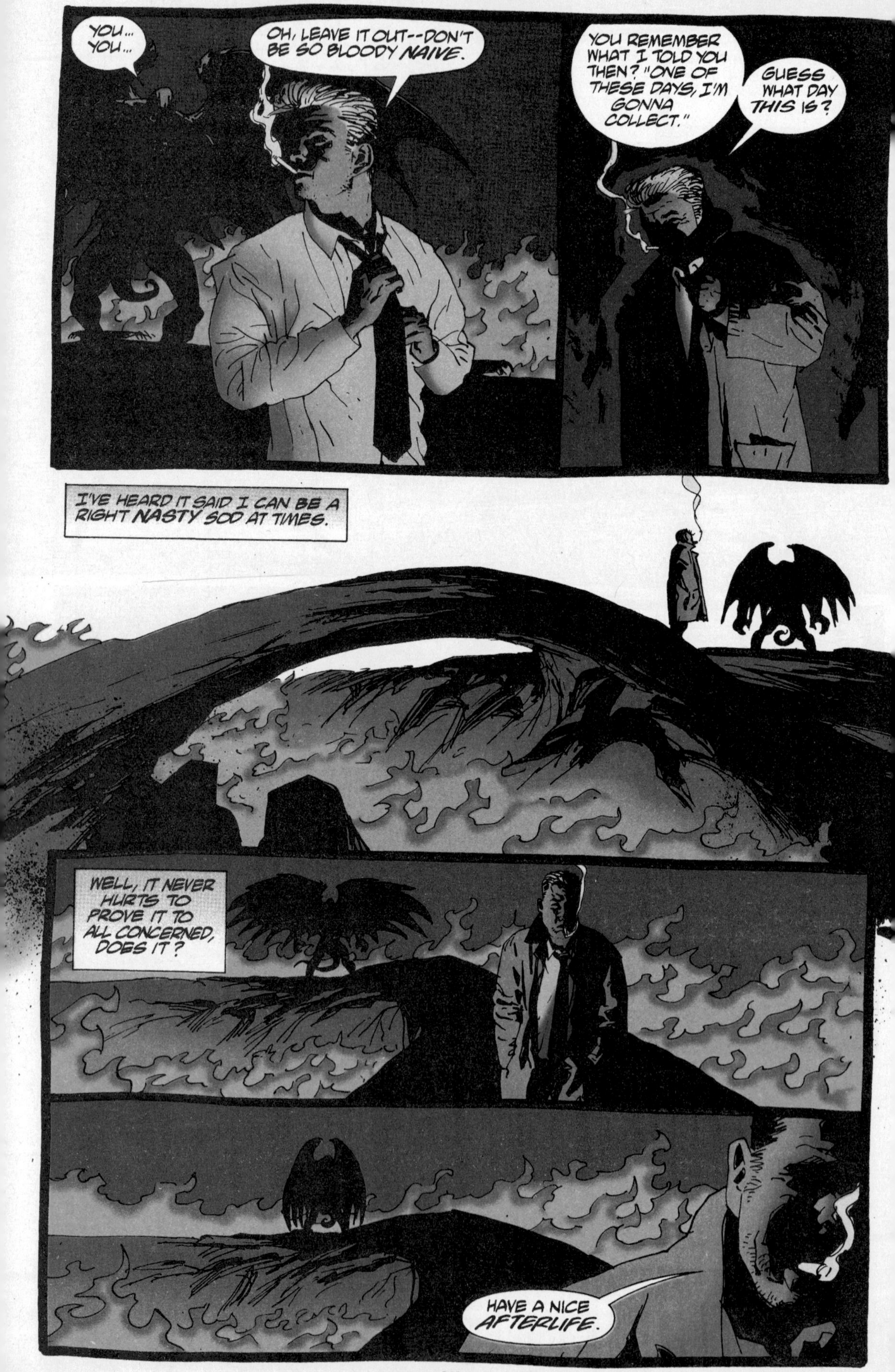
YOU... YOU...
OH, LEAVE IT OUT--DON'T BE SO BLOODY NAIVE.
YOU REMEMBER WHAT I TOLD YOU THEN? "ONE OF THESE DAYS, I'M GONNA COLLECT."
GUESS WHAT DAY THIS IS?
I'VE HEARD IT SAID I CAN BE A RIGHT NASTY SOD AT TIMES.
WELL, IT NEVER HURTS TO PROVE IT TO ALL CONCERNED, DOES IT?
HAVE A NICE AFTERLIFE.

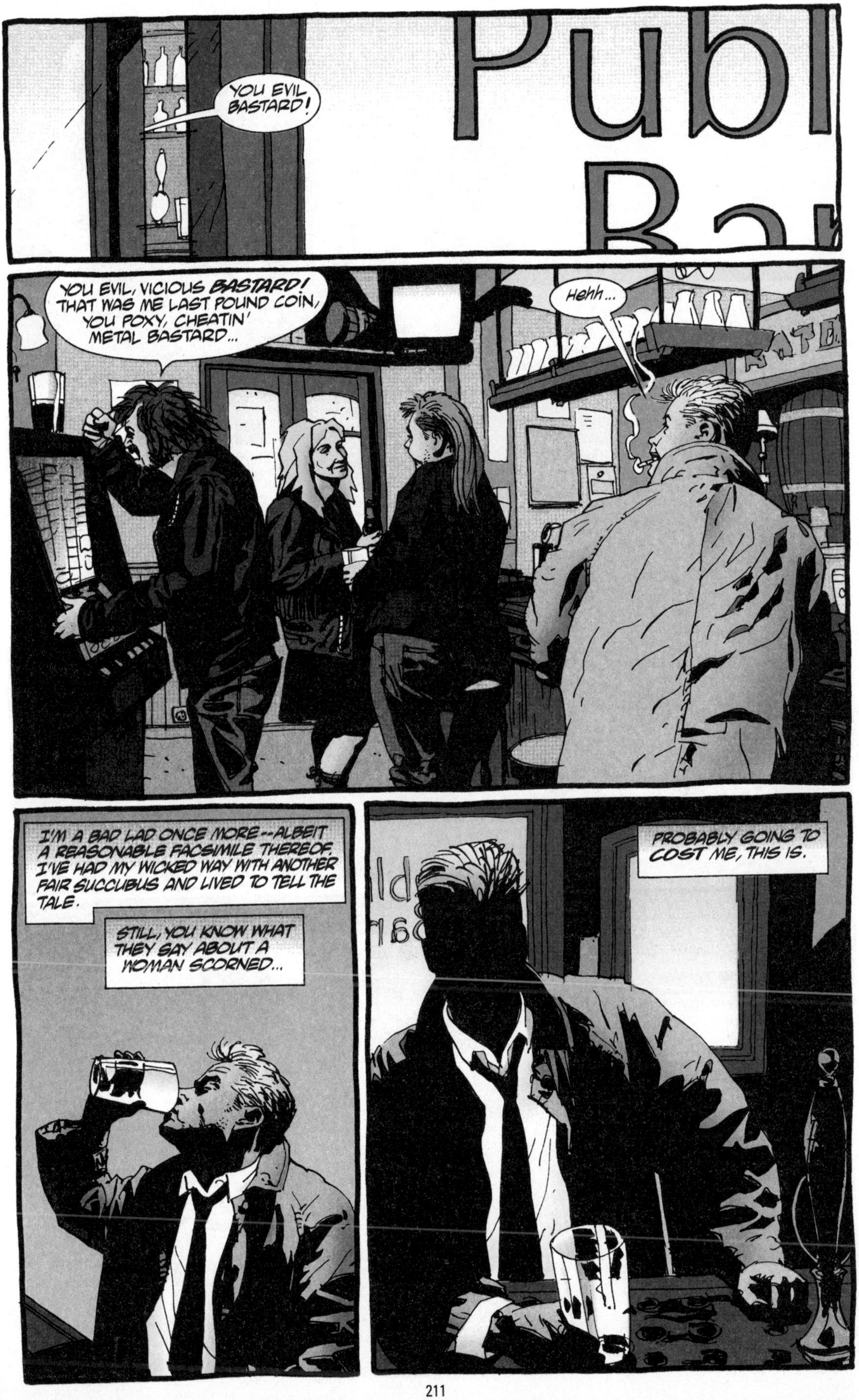
Publ
Ba
YOU EVIL BASTARD!
YOU EVIL, VICIOUS BASTARD! THAT WAS ME LAST POUND COIN, YOU POXY, CHEATIN' METAL BASTARD...
Hehh...
I'M A BAD LAD ONCE MORE--ALBEIT A REASONABLE FACSIMILE THEREOF. I'VE HAD MY WICKED WAY WITH ANOTHER FAIR SUCCUBUS AND LIVED TO TELL THE TALE.
STILL, YOU KNOW WHAT THEY SAY ABOUT A WOMAN SCORNED...
PROBABLY GOING TO COST ME, THIS IS.

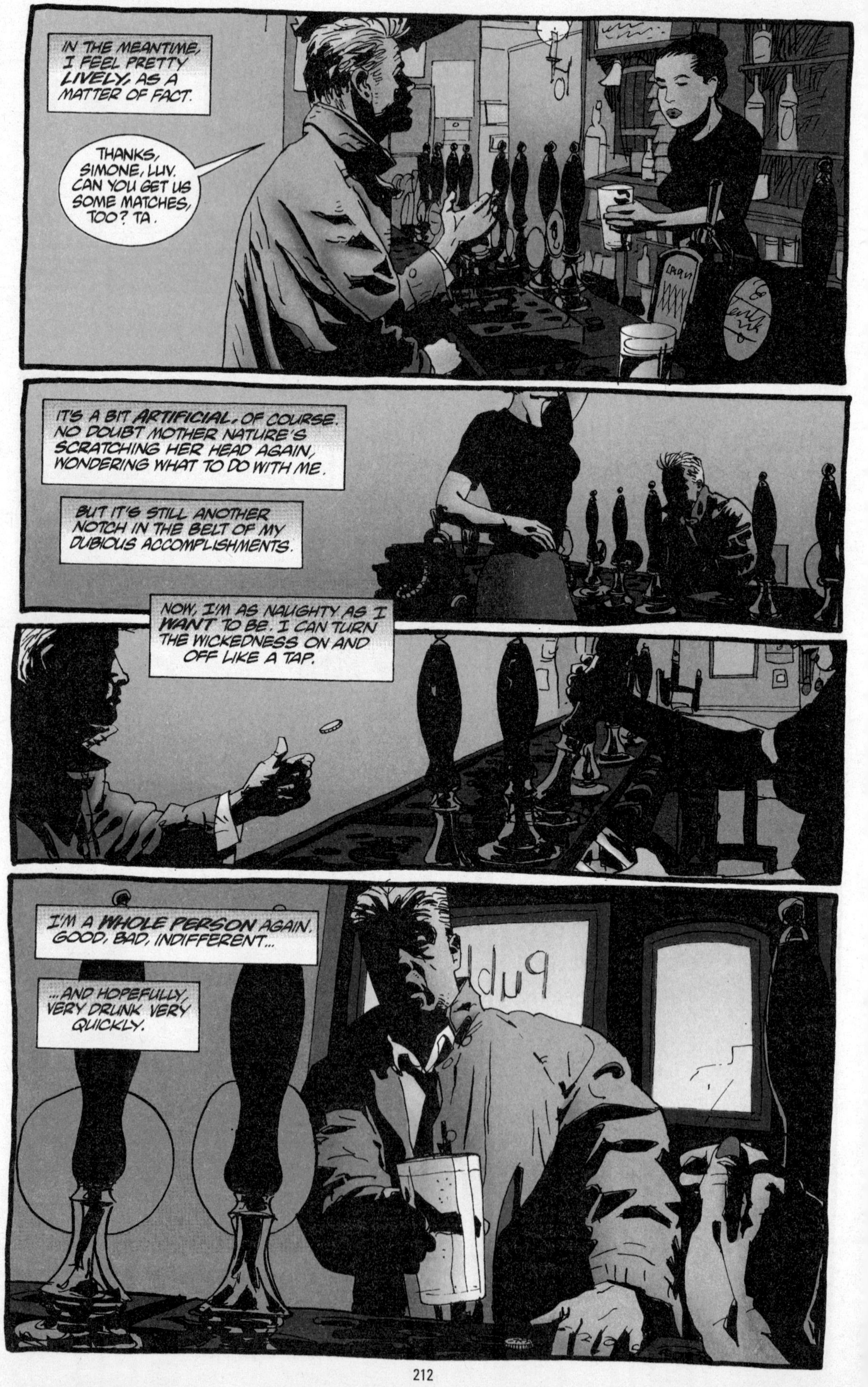
IN THE MEANTIME, I FEEL PRETTY LIVELY, AS A MATTER OF FACT.
THANKS, SIMONE, LUV. CAN YOU GET US SOME MATCHES, TOO? TA.
IT'S A BIT ARTIFICIAL, OF COURSE. NO DOUBT MOTHER NATURE'S SCRATCHING HER HEAD AGAIN, WONDERING WHAT TO DO WITH ME.
BUT IT'S STILL ANOTHER NOTCH IN THE BELT OF MY DUBIOUS ACCOMPLISHMENTS.
NOW, I'M AS NAUGHTY AS I WANT TO BE. I CAN TURN THE WICKEDNESS ON AND OFF LIKE A TAP.
I'M A WHOLE PERSON AGAIN. GOOD, BAD, INDIFFERENT...
...AND HOPEFULLY, VERY DRUNK VERY QUICKLY.

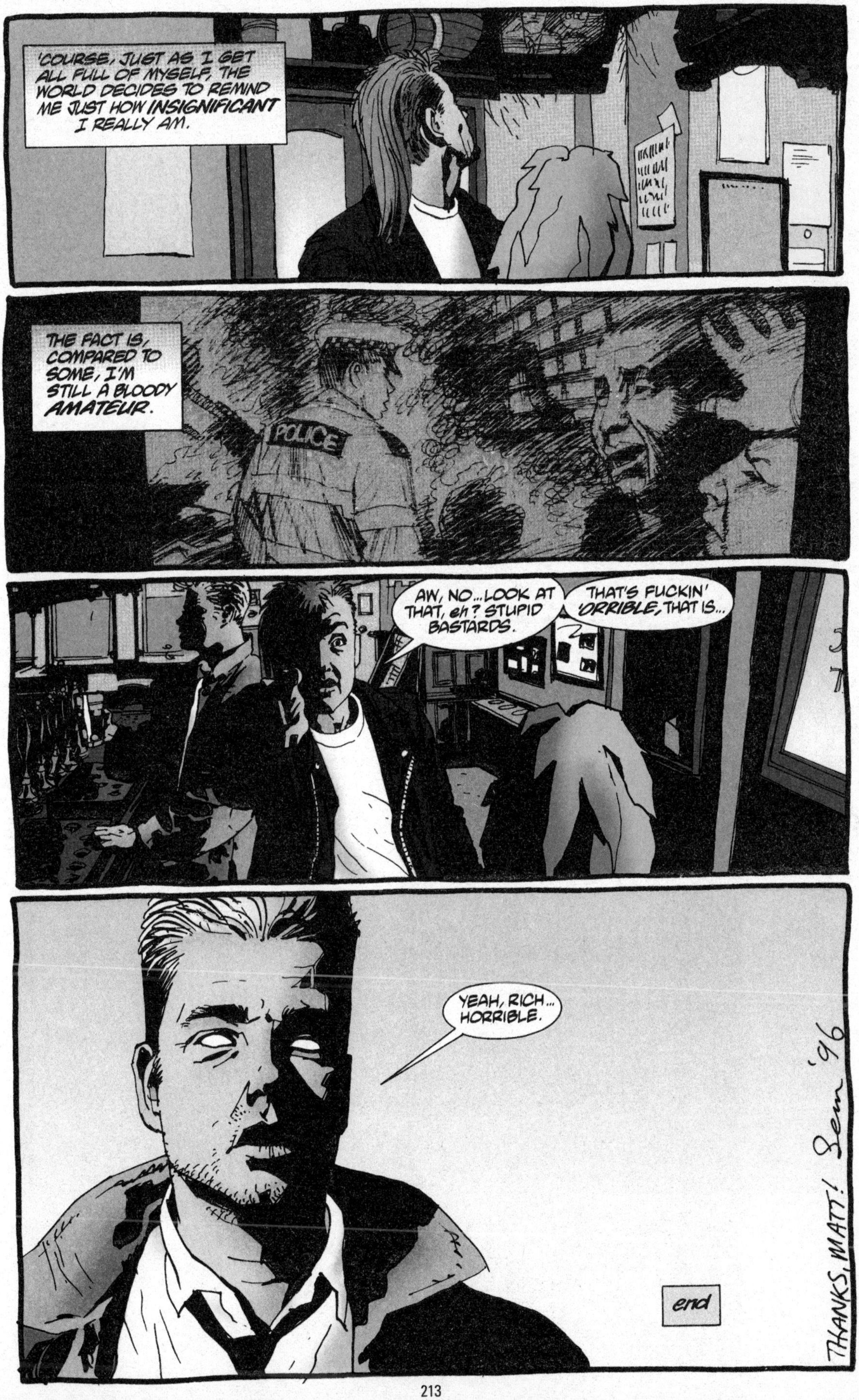
'COURSE, JUST AS I GET ALL FULL OF MYSELF, THE WORLD DECIDES TO REMIND ME JUST HOW INSIGNIFICANT I REALLY AM.
THE FACT IS, COMPARED TO SOME, I'M STILL A BLOODY AMATEUR.
POLICE
AW, NO... LOOK AT THAT, eh? STUPID BASTARDS.
THAT'S FUCKIN' 'ORRIBLE, THAT IS...
YEAH, RICH... HORRIBLE.
end
THANKS, MATT! Sean '96

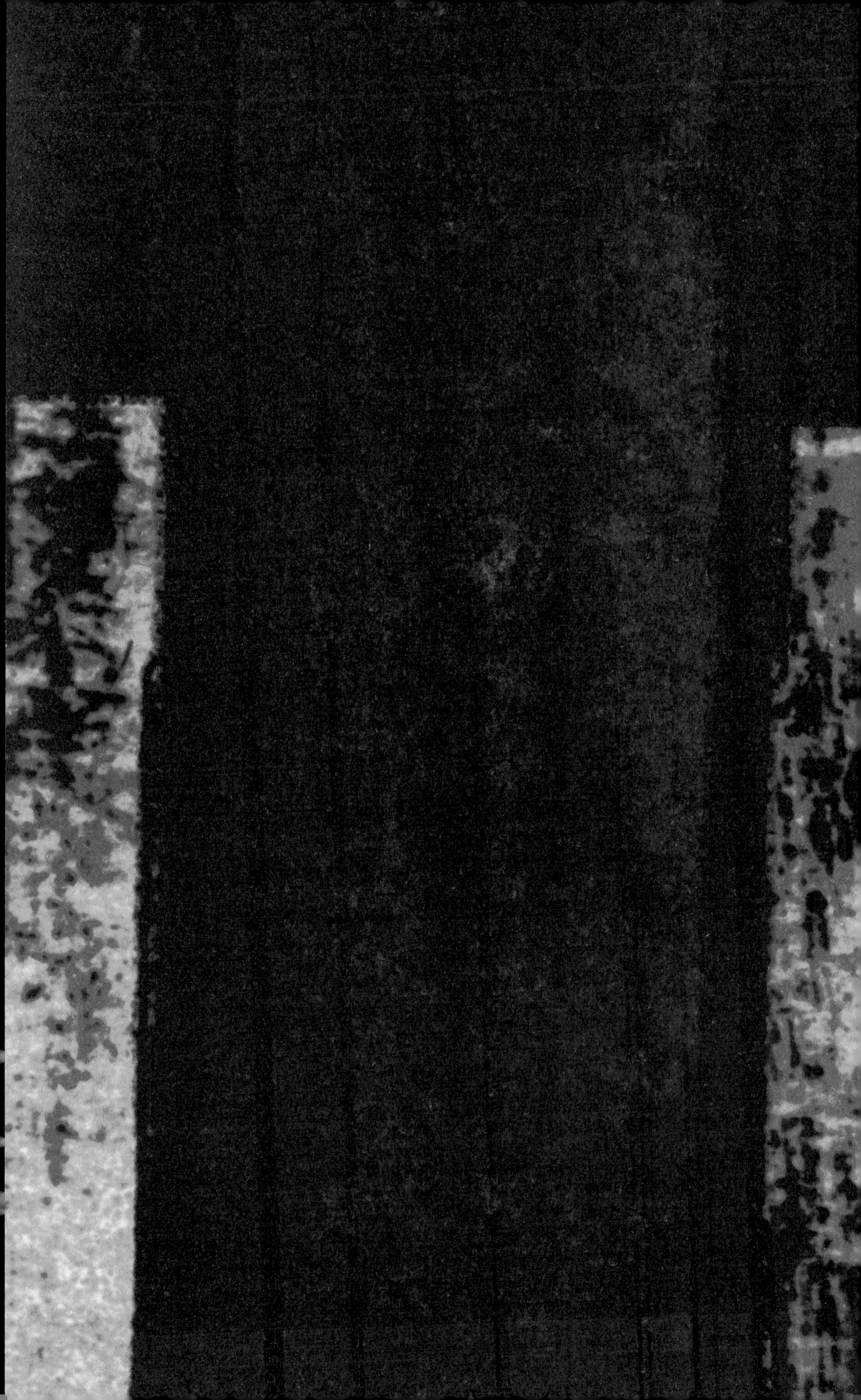

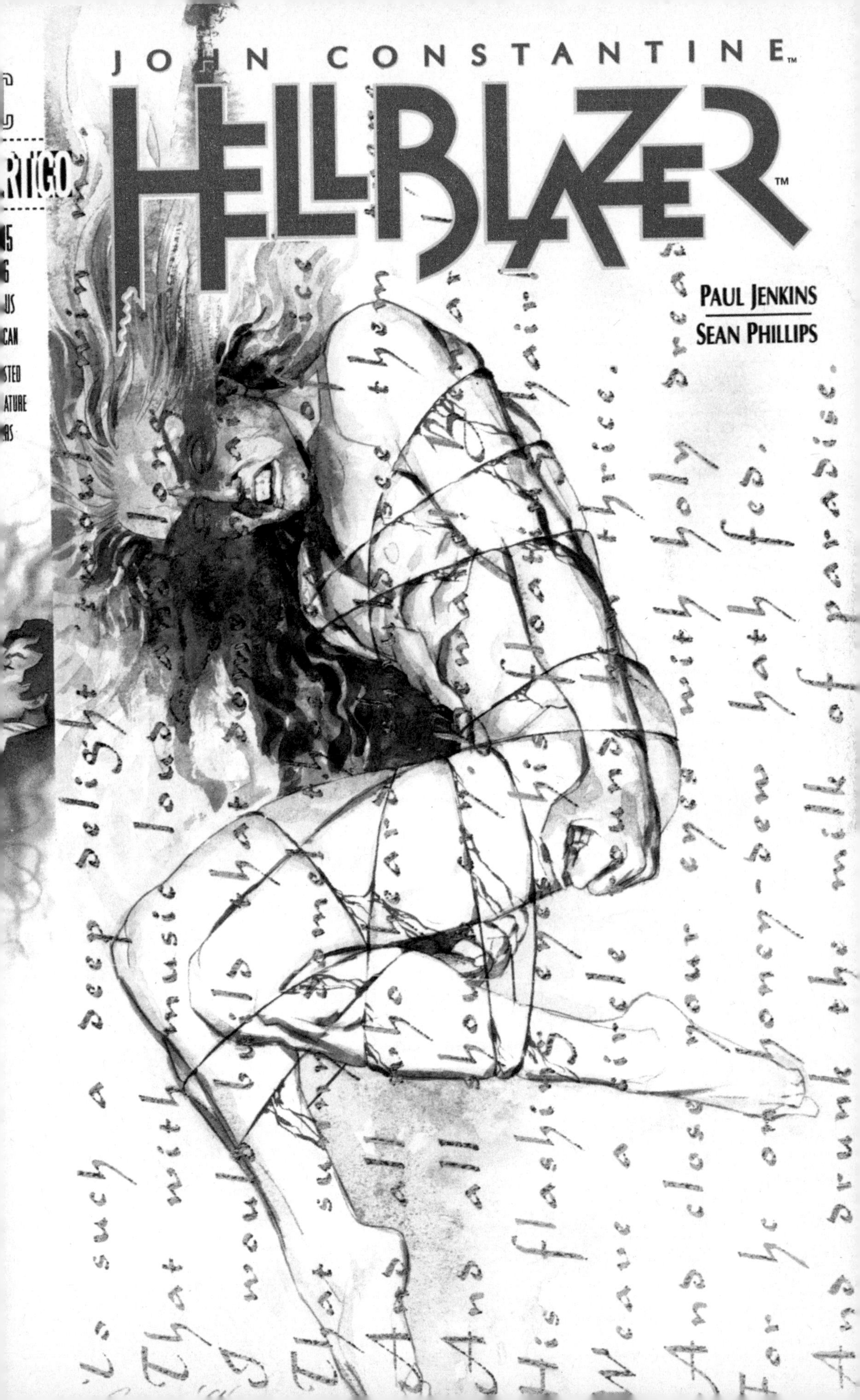
JOHN CONSTANTINE
HELLBLAZER
PAUL JENKINS
SEAN PHILLIPS

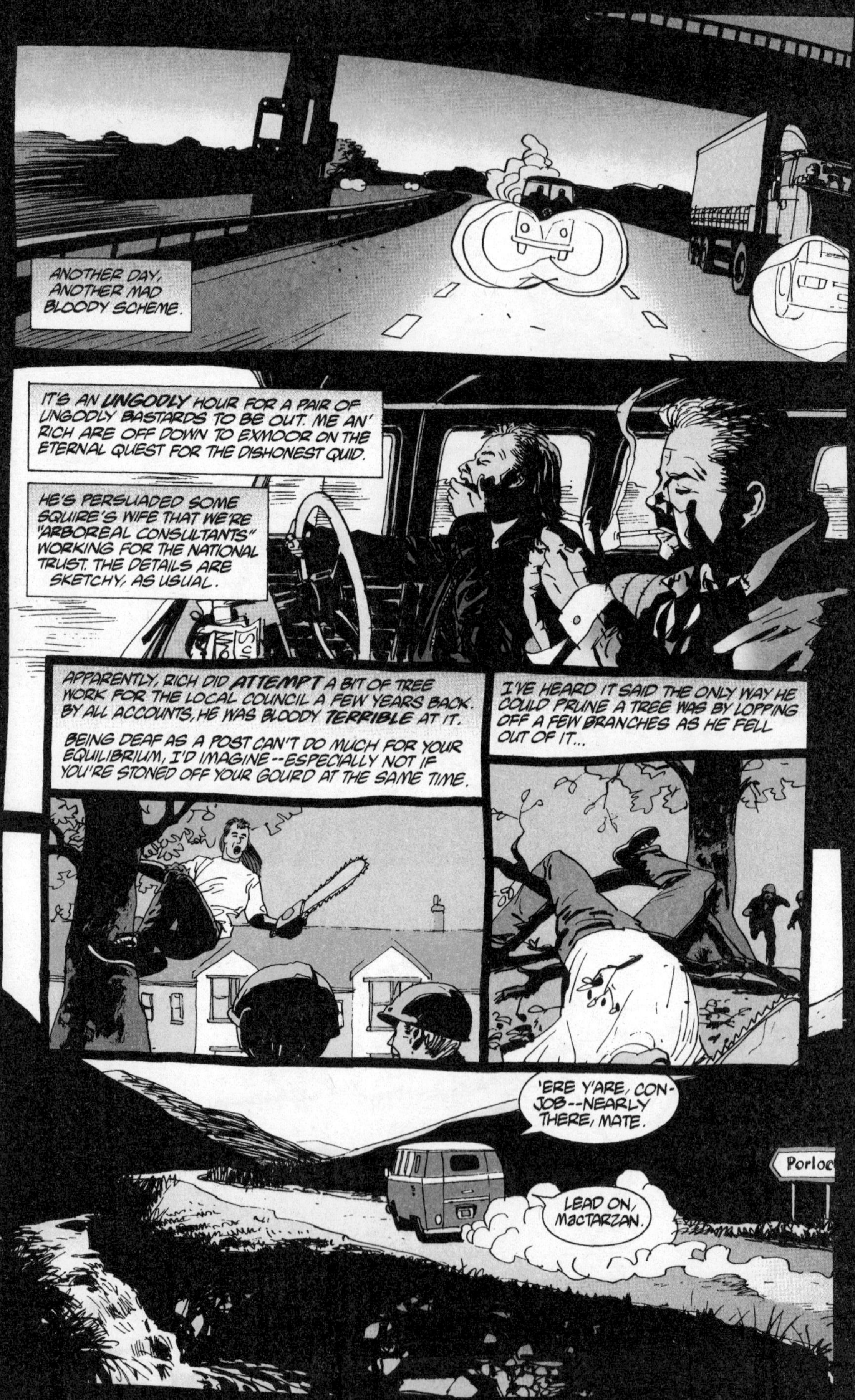
ANOTHER DAY, ANOTHER MAD BLOODY SCHEME.
IT'S AN UNGODLY HOUR FOR A PAIR OF UNGODLY BASTARDS TO BE OUT. ME AN' RICH ARE OFF DOWN TO EXMOOR ON THE ETERNAL QUEST FOR THE DISHONEST QUID.
HE'S PERSUADED SOME SQUIRE'S WIFE THAT WE'RE "ARBOREAL CONSULTANTS" WORKING FOR THE NATIONAL TRUST. THE DETAILS ARE SKETCHY, AS USUAL.
APPARENTLY, RICH DID ATTEMPT A BIT OF TREE WORK FOR THE LOCAL COUNCIL A FEW YEARS BACK. BY ALL ACCOUNTS, HE WAS BLOODY TERRIBLE AT IT.
BEING DEAF AS A POST CAN'T DO MUCH FOR YOUR EQUILIBRIUM, I'D IMAGINE--ESPECIALLY NOT IF YOU'RE STONED OFF YOUR GOURD AT THE SAME TIME.
I'VE HEARD IT SAID THE ONLY WAY HE COULD PRUNE A TREE WAS BY LOPPING OFF A FEW BRANCHES AS HE FELL OUT OF IT...
'ERE Y'ARE, CON-JOB--NEARLY THERE, MATE.
LEAD ON, MacTARZAN.
Porloc

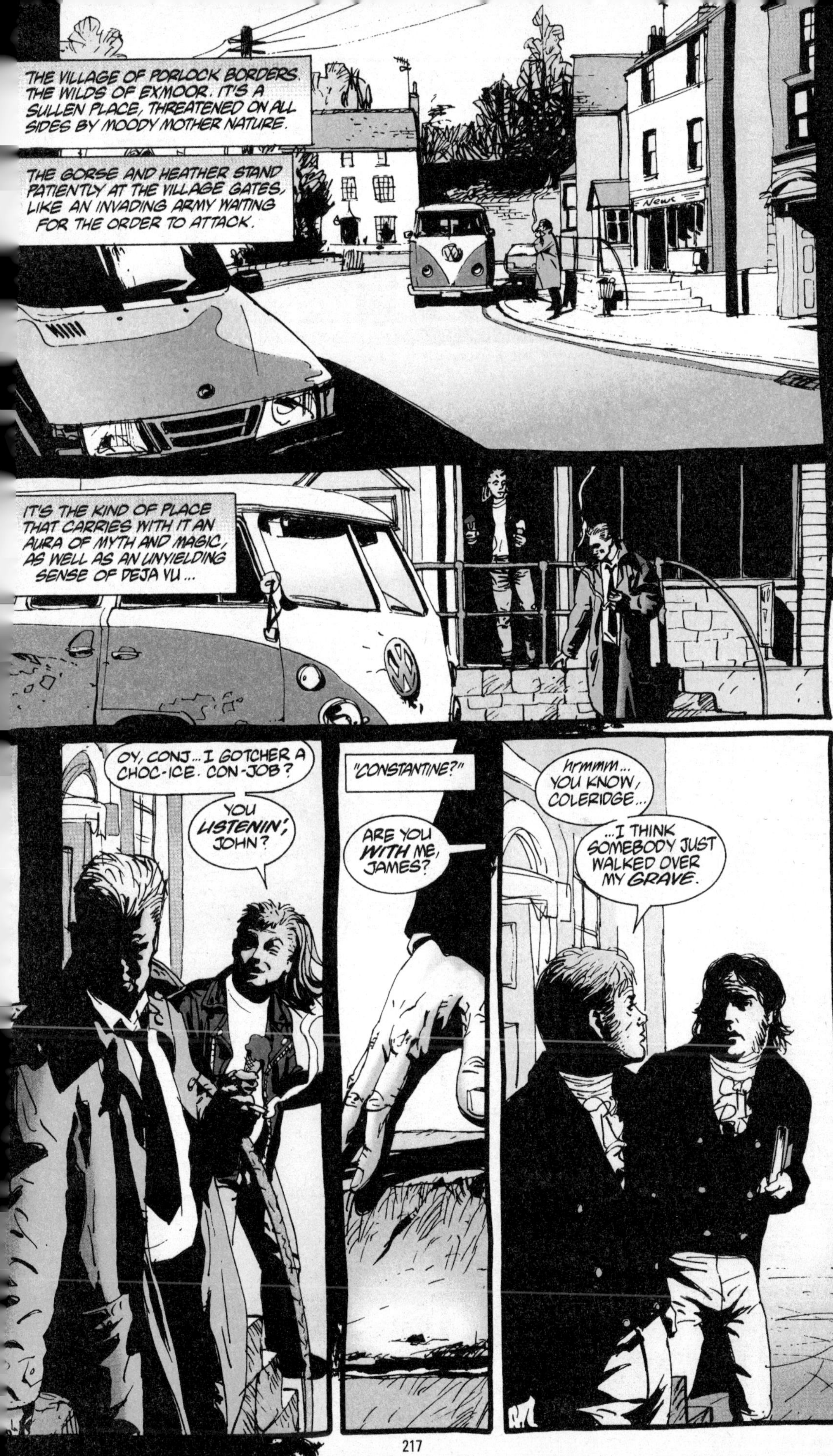
THE VILLAGE OF PORLOCK BORDERS THE WILDS OF EXMOOR. IT'S A SULLEN PLACE, THREATENED ON ALL SIDES BY MOODY MOTHER NATURE.
THE GORSE AND HEATHER STAND PATIENTLY AT THE VILLAGE GATES, LIKE AN INVADING ARMY WAITING FOR THE ORDER TO ATTACK.
News
IT'S THE KIND OF PLACE THAT CARRIES WITH IT AN AURA OF MYTH AND MAGIC, AS WELL AS AN UNYIELDING SENSE OF DEJA VU ...
OY, CONJ... I GOTCHER A CHOC-ICE. CON-JOB?
YOU LISTENIN', JOHN?
"CONSTANTINE?"
ARE YOU WITH ME, JAMES?
hrmmm... YOU KNOW, COLERIDGE...
...I THINK SOMEBODY JUST WALKED OVER MY GRAVE.

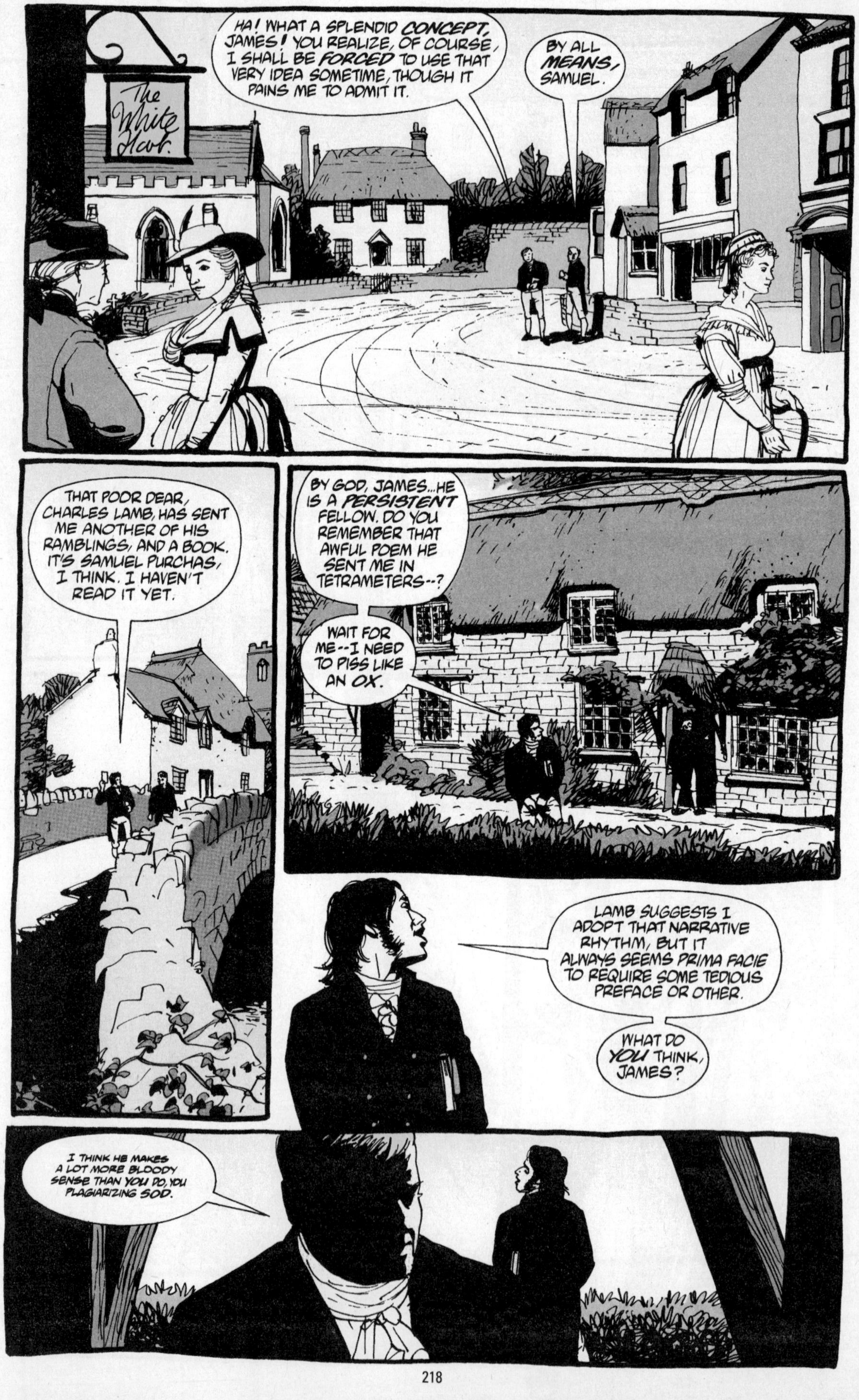

The White Hart
HA! WHAT A SPLENDID CONCEPT, JAMES! YOU REALIZE, OF COURSE, I SHALL BE FORCED TO USE THAT VERY IDEA SOMETIME, THOUGH IT PAINS ME TO ADMIT IT.
BY ALL MEANS, SAMUEL.
THAT POOR DEAR, CHARLES LAMB, HAS SENT ME ANOTHER OF HIS RAMBLINGS, AND A BOOK. IT'S SAMUEL PURCHAS, I THINK. I HAVEN'T READ IT YET.
BY GOD, JAMES...HE IS A PERSISTENT FELLOW. DO YOU REMEMBER THAT AWFUL POEM HE SENT ME IN TETRAMETERS--?
WAIT FOR ME--I NEED TO PISS LIKE AN OX.
LAMB SUGGESTS I ADOPT THAT NARRATIVE RHYTHM, BUT IT ALWAYS SEEMS PRIMA FACIE TO REQUIRE SOME TEDIOUS PREFACE OR OTHER.
WHAT DO YOU THINK, JAMES?
I THINK HE MAKES A LOT MORE BLOODY SENSE THAN YOU DO, YOU PLAGIARIZING SOD.

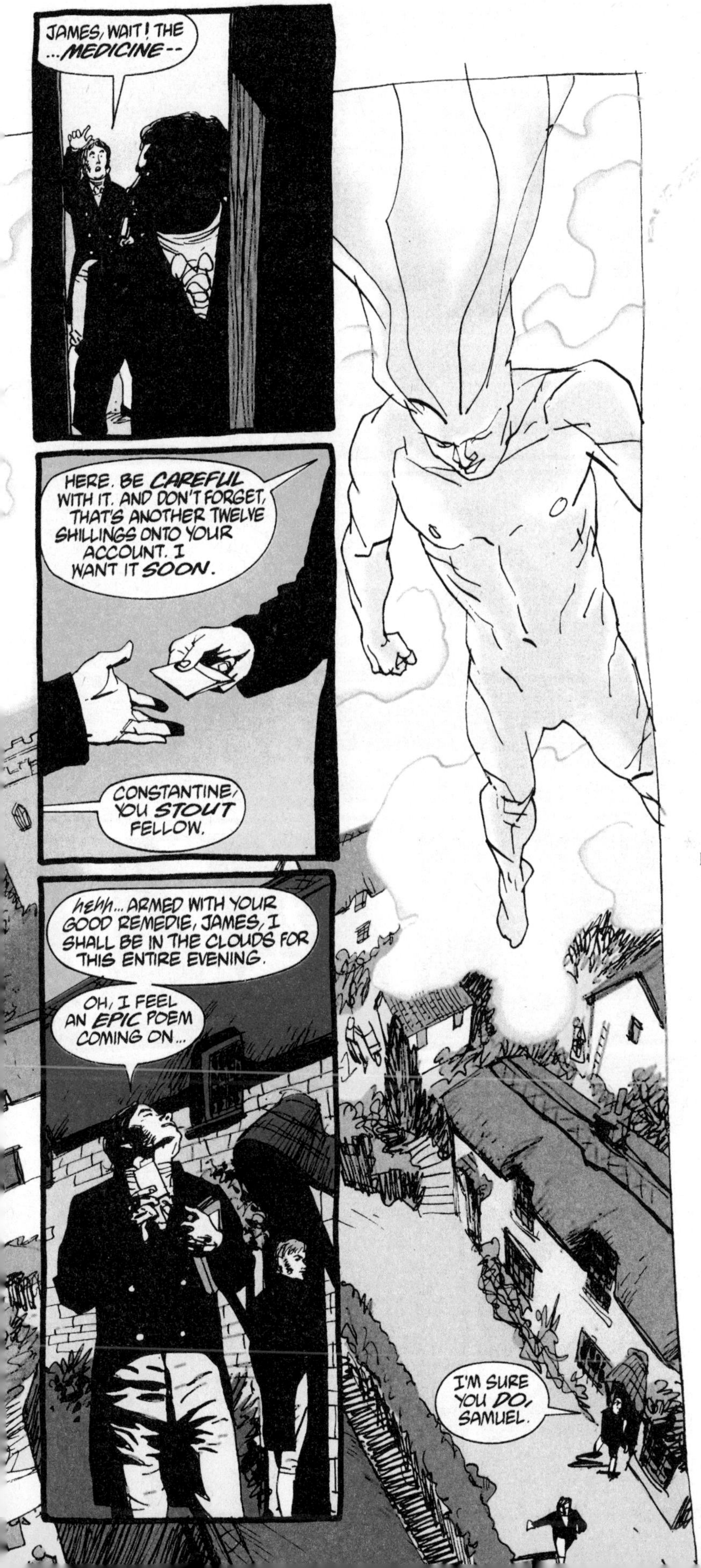
JAMES, WAIT! THE ...MEDICINE--
HERE. BE CAREFUL WITH IT. AND DON'T FORGET, THAT'S ANOTHER TWELVE SHILLINGS ONTO YOUR ACCOUNT. I WANT IT SOON.
CONSTANTINE, YOU STOUT FELLOW.
hehh... ARMED WITH YOUR GOOD REMEDIE, JAMES, I SHALL BE IN THE CLOUDS FOR THIS ENTIRE EVENING.
OH, I FEEL AN EPIC POEM COMING ON...
I'M SURE YOU DO, SAMUEL.

a taste of heaven

PAUL JENKINS
Writer
SEAN PHILLIPS
Artist
JAMES SINCLAIR
Colors
DIGITAL CHAMELEON
Separations
CLEM ROBINS
Letters
AXEL ALONSO
Asst Editor
LOU STATHIS
Editor

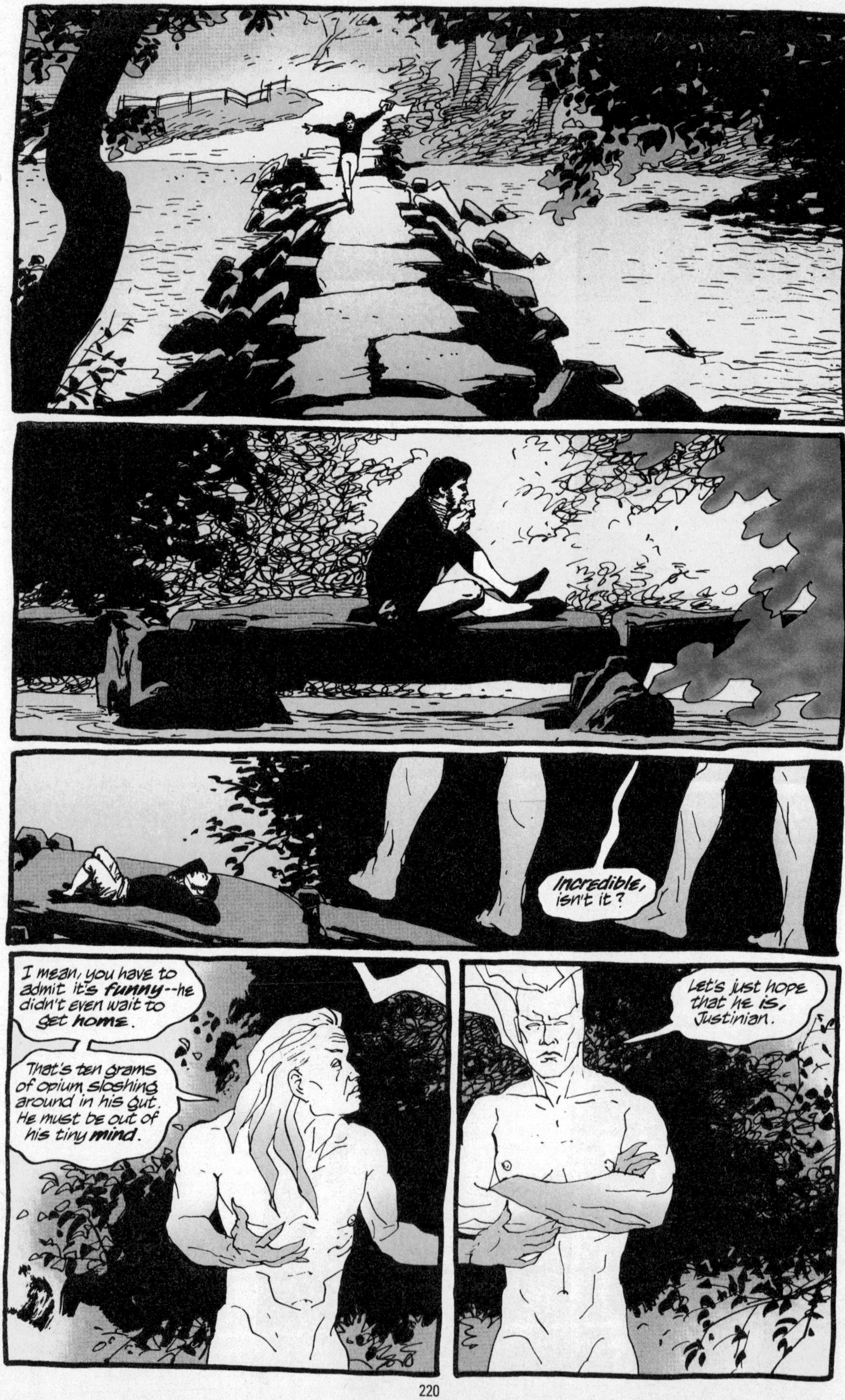
Incredible, isn't it?
I mean, you have to admit it's **funny**--he didn't even wait to get **home**.
That's ten grams of opium sloshing around in his gut. He must be out of his tiny **mind**.
Let's just hope that he **is**, Justinian.

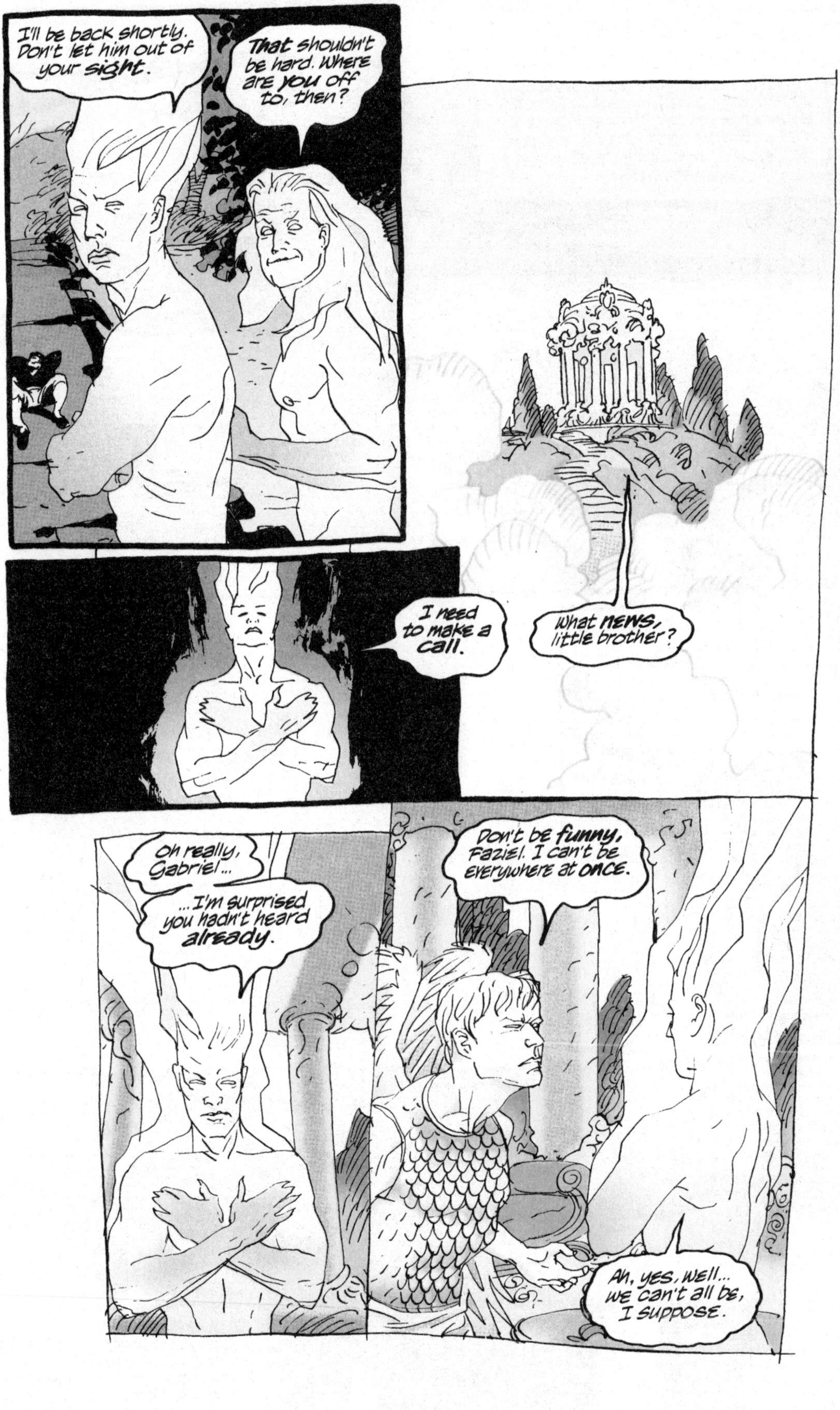

I'll be back shortly. Don't let him out of your sight.
That shouldn't be hard. Where are you off to, then?
I need to make a call.
What NEWS, little brother?
Oh really, Gabriel...
...I'm surprised you hadn't heard already.
Don't be funny, Faziel. I can't be everywhere at ONCE.
Ah, yes, well... we can't all be, I suppose.

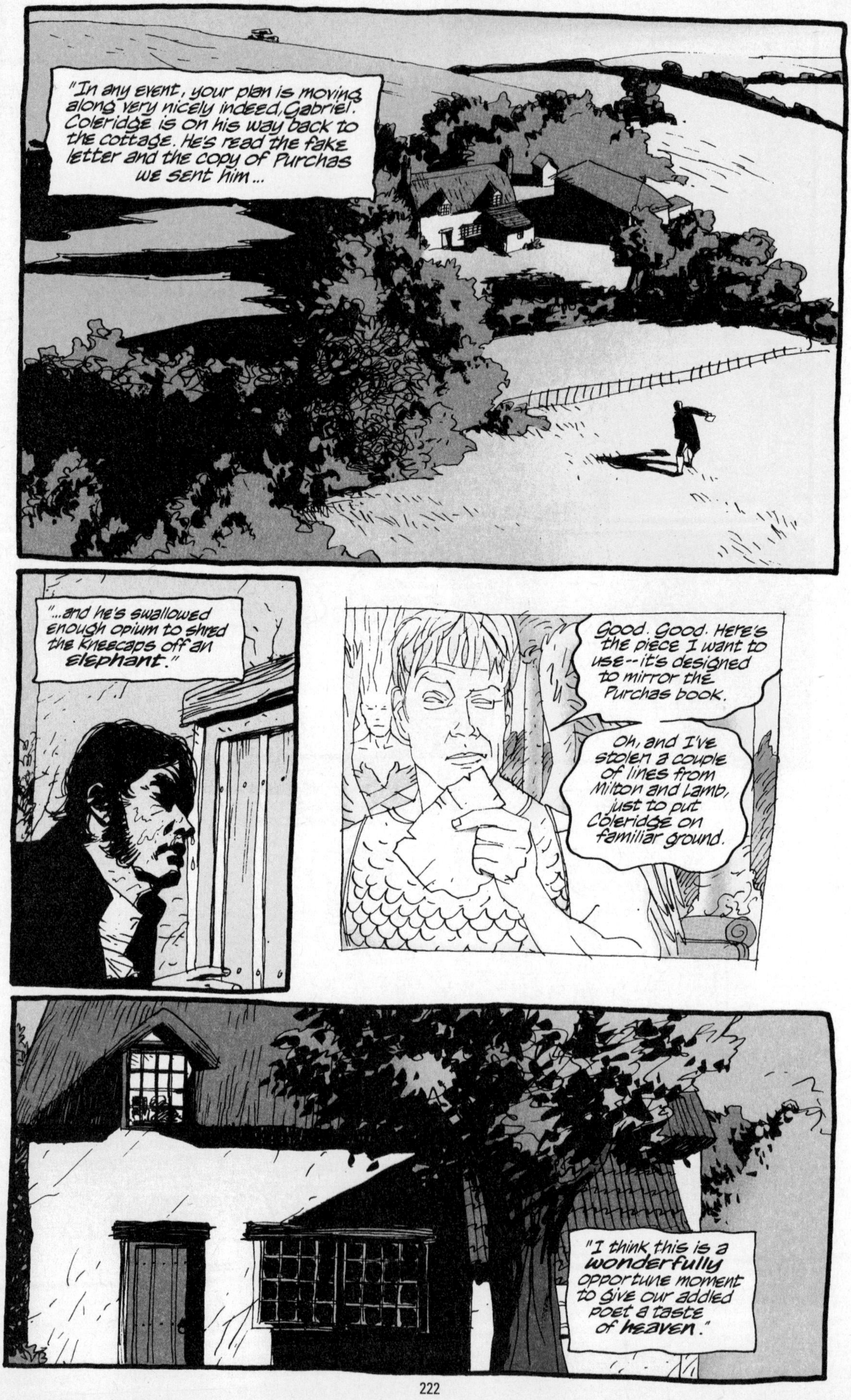
"In any event, your plan is moving along very nicely indeed, Gabriel. Coleridge is on his way back to the cottage. He's read the fake letter and the copy of Purchas we sent him...
"...and he's swallowed enough opium to shred the kneecaps off an **elephant**."
Good. Good. Here's the piece I want to use--it's designed to mirror the Purchas book.
Oh, and I've stolen a couple of lines from Milton and Lamb, just to put Coleridge on familiar ground.
"I think this is a **wonderfully** opportune moment to give our addled poet a taste of **heaven**."

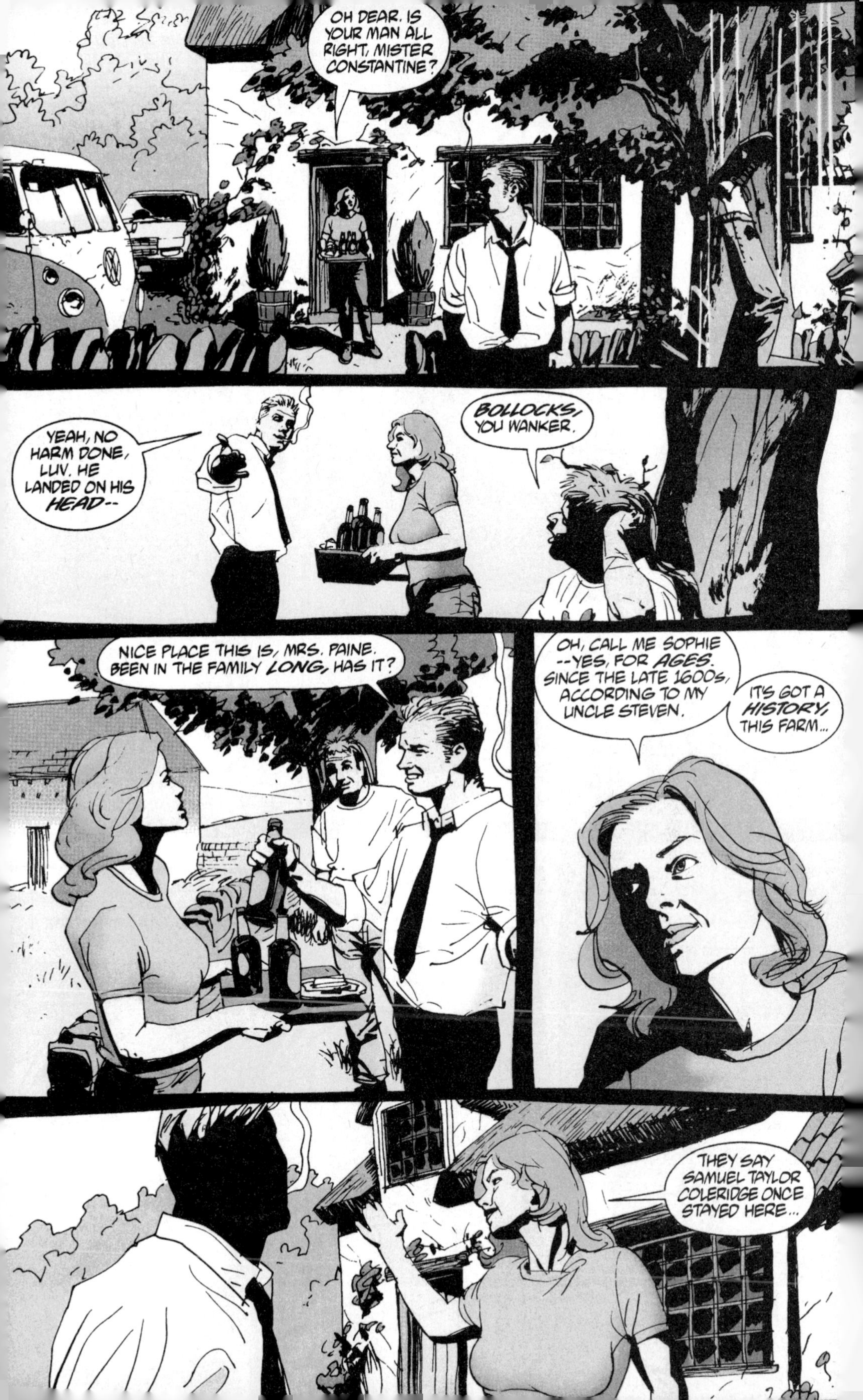
OH DEAR. IS YOUR MAN ALL RIGHT, MISTER CONSTANTINE?
YEAH, NO HARM DONE, LUV. HE LANDED ON HIS HEAD--
BOLLOCKS, YOU WANKER.
NICE PLACE THIS IS, MRS. PAINE. BEEN IN THE FAMILY LONG, HAS IT?
OH, CALL ME SOPHIE --YES, FOR AGES. SINCE THE LATE 1600s, ACCORDING TO MY UNCLE STEVEN.
IT'S GOT A HISTORY, THIS FARM...
THEY SAY SAMUEL TAYLOR COLERIDGE ONCE STAYED HERE...

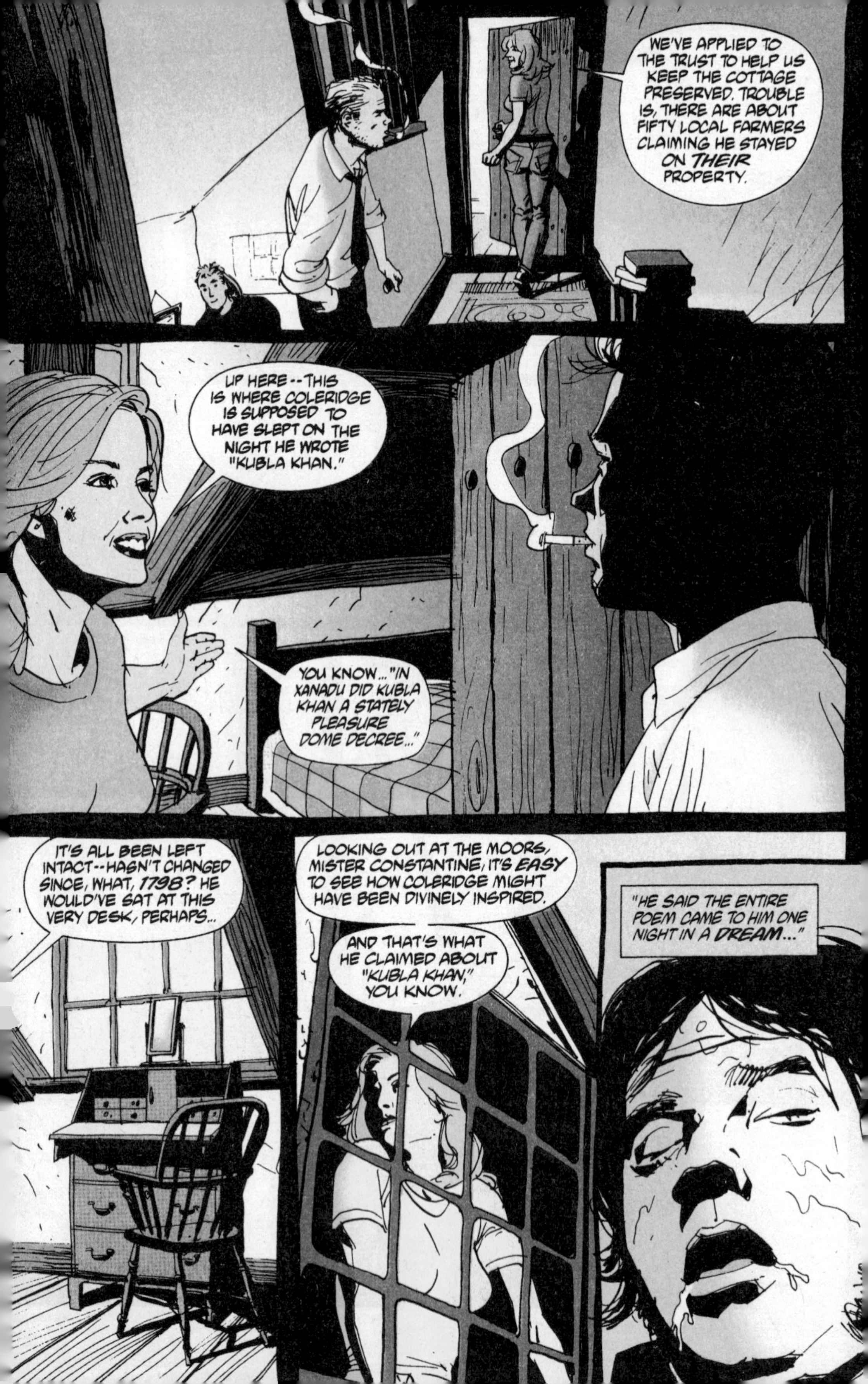
WE'VE APPLIED TO THE TRUST TO HELP US KEEP THE COTTAGE PRESERVED. TROUBLE IS, THERE ARE ABOUT FIFTY LOCAL FARMERS CLAIMING HE STAYED ON THEIR PROPERTY.
UP HERE--THIS IS WHERE COLERIDGE IS SUPPOSED TO HAVE SLEPT ON THE NIGHT HE WROTE "KUBLA KHAN."
YOU KNOW..."IN XANADU DID KUBLA KHAN A STATELY PLEASURE DOME DECREE..."
IT'S ALL BEEN LEFT INTACT--HASN'T CHANGED SINCE, WHAT, 1798? HE WOULD'VE SAT AT THIS VERY DESK, PERHAPS...
LOOKING OUT AT THE MOORS, MISTER CONSTANTINE, IT'S EASY TO SEE HOW COLERIDGE MIGHT HAVE BEEN DIVINELY INSPIRED.
AND THAT'S WHAT HE CLAIMED ABOUT "KUBLA KHAN," YOU KNOW.
"HE SAID THE ENTIRE POEM CAME TO HIM ONE NIGHT IN A DREAM..."

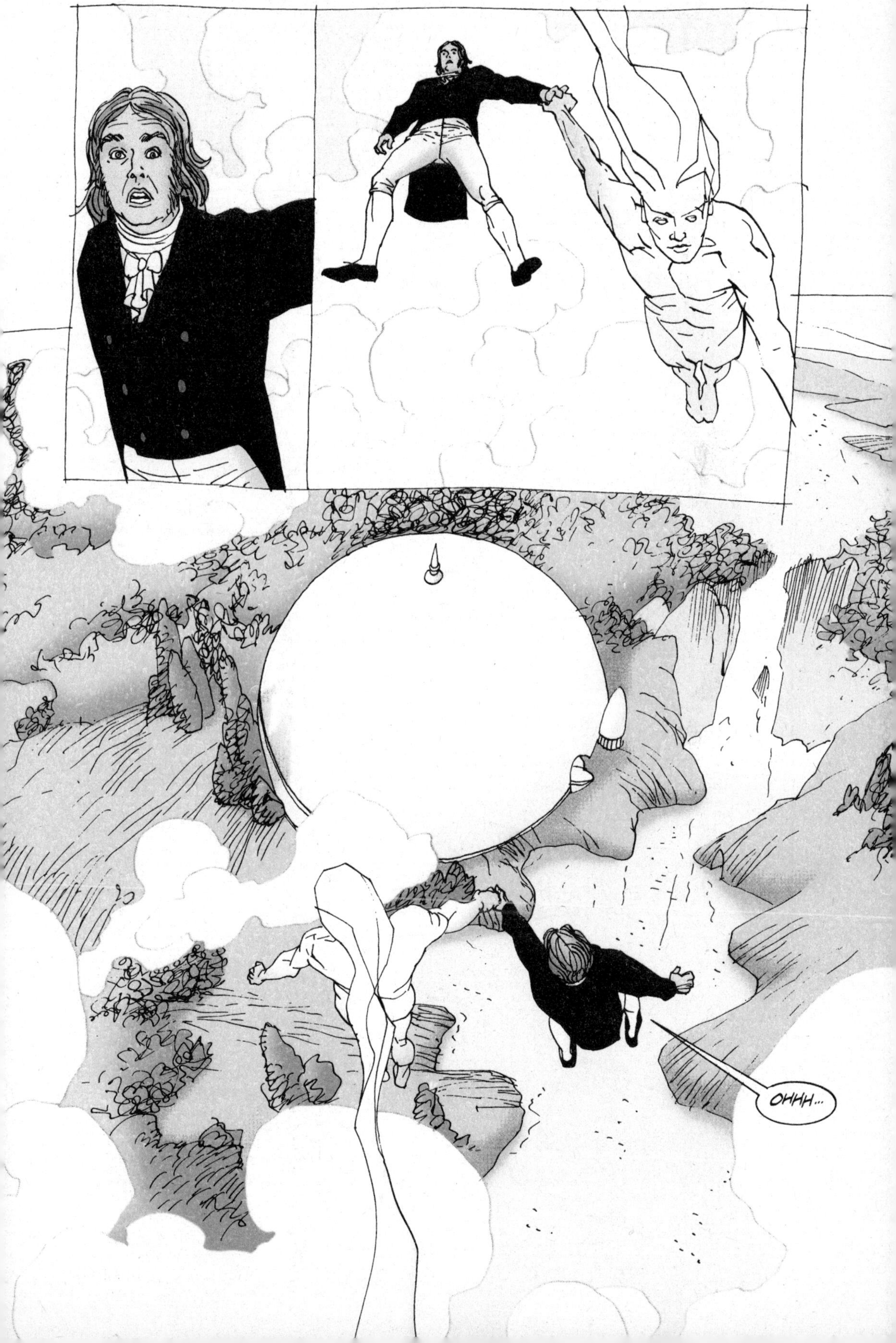
OHHH...

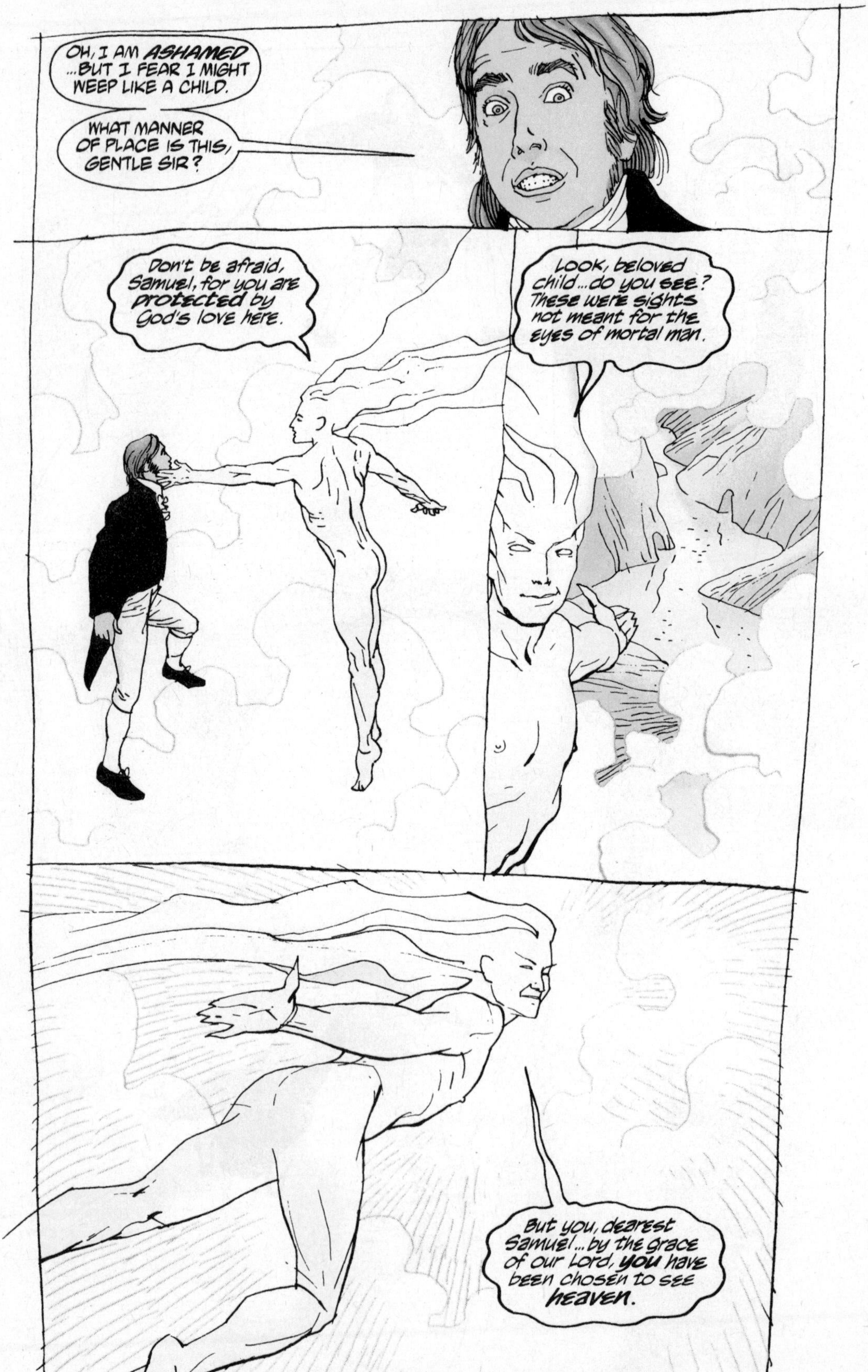
OH, I AM ASHAMED ...BUT I FEAR I MIGHT WEEP LIKE A CHILD.
WHAT MANNER OF PLACE IS THIS, GENTLE SIR?
Don't be afraid, Samuel, for you are protected by God's love here.
Look, beloved child...do you see? These were sights not meant for the eyes of mortal man.
But you, dearest Samuel... by the grace of our Lord, you have been chosen to see heaven.

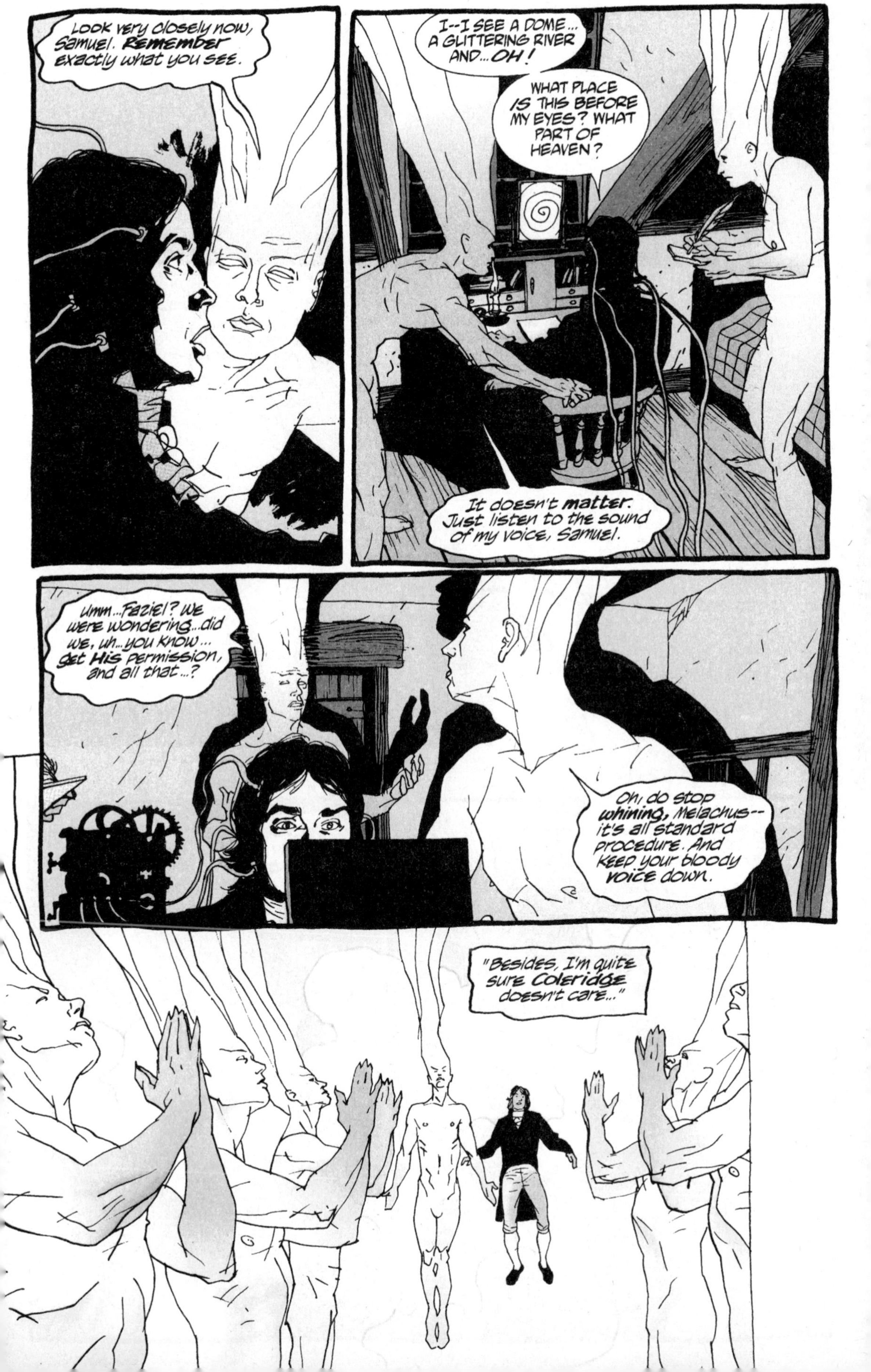

Look very closely now, Samuel. Remember exactly what you see.
I--I see a dome... a glittering river and... OH!
WHAT PLACE IS THIS BEFORE MY EYES? WHAT PART OF HEAVEN?
It doesn't matter. Just listen to the sound of my voice, Samuel.
Umm...Faziel? We were wondering...did we, uh...you know... get His permission, and all that...?
Oh, do stop whining, Melachus-- it's all standard procedure. And keep your bloody voice down.
"Besides, I'm quite sure Coleridge doesn't care..."

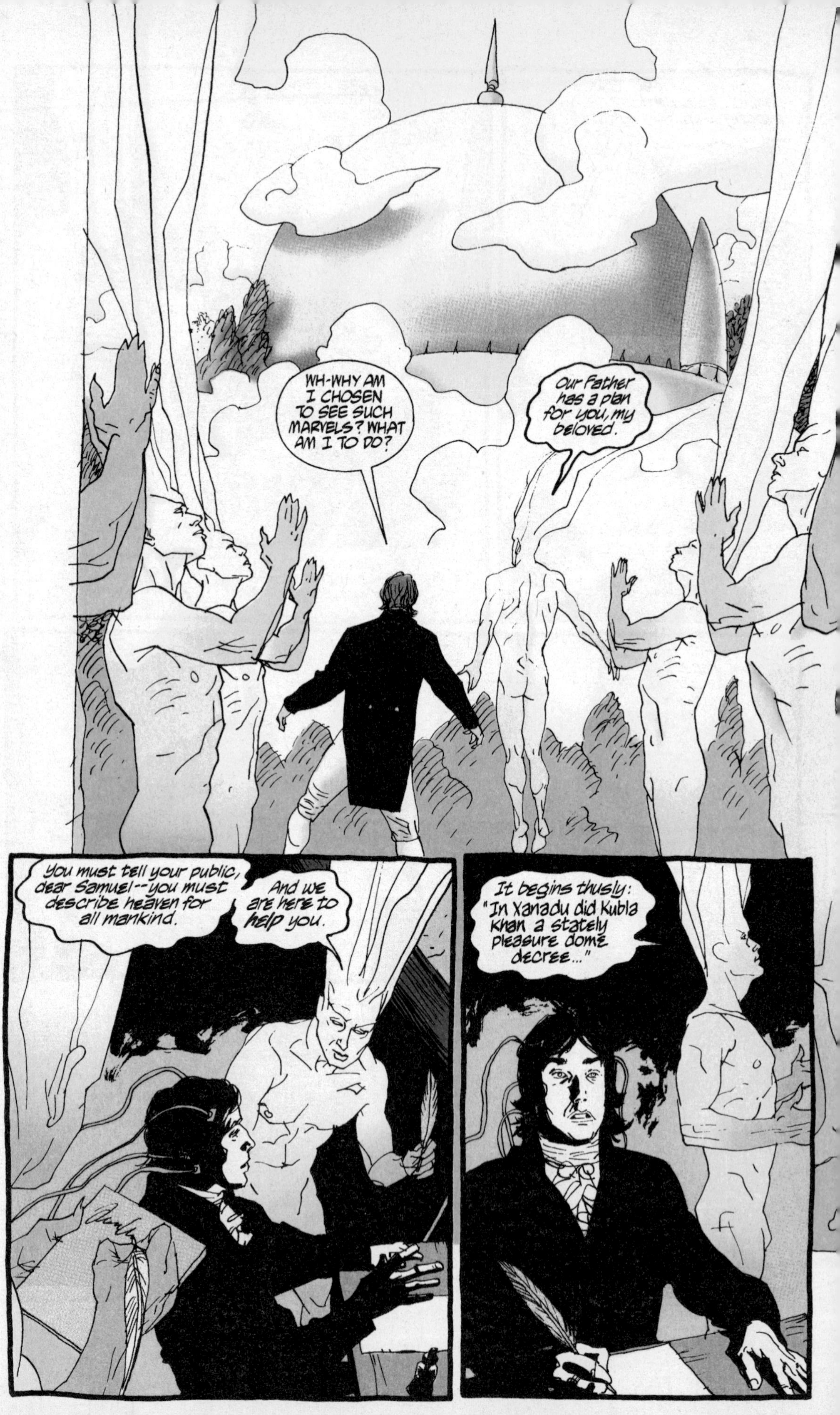
WH-WHY AM I CHOSEN TO SEE SUCH MARVELS? WHAT AM I TO DO?
Our Father has a plan for you, my beloved.
You must tell your public, dear Samuel--you must describe heaven for all mankind.
And we are here to help you.
It begins thusly: "In Xanadu did Kubla Khan a stately pleasure dome decree..."

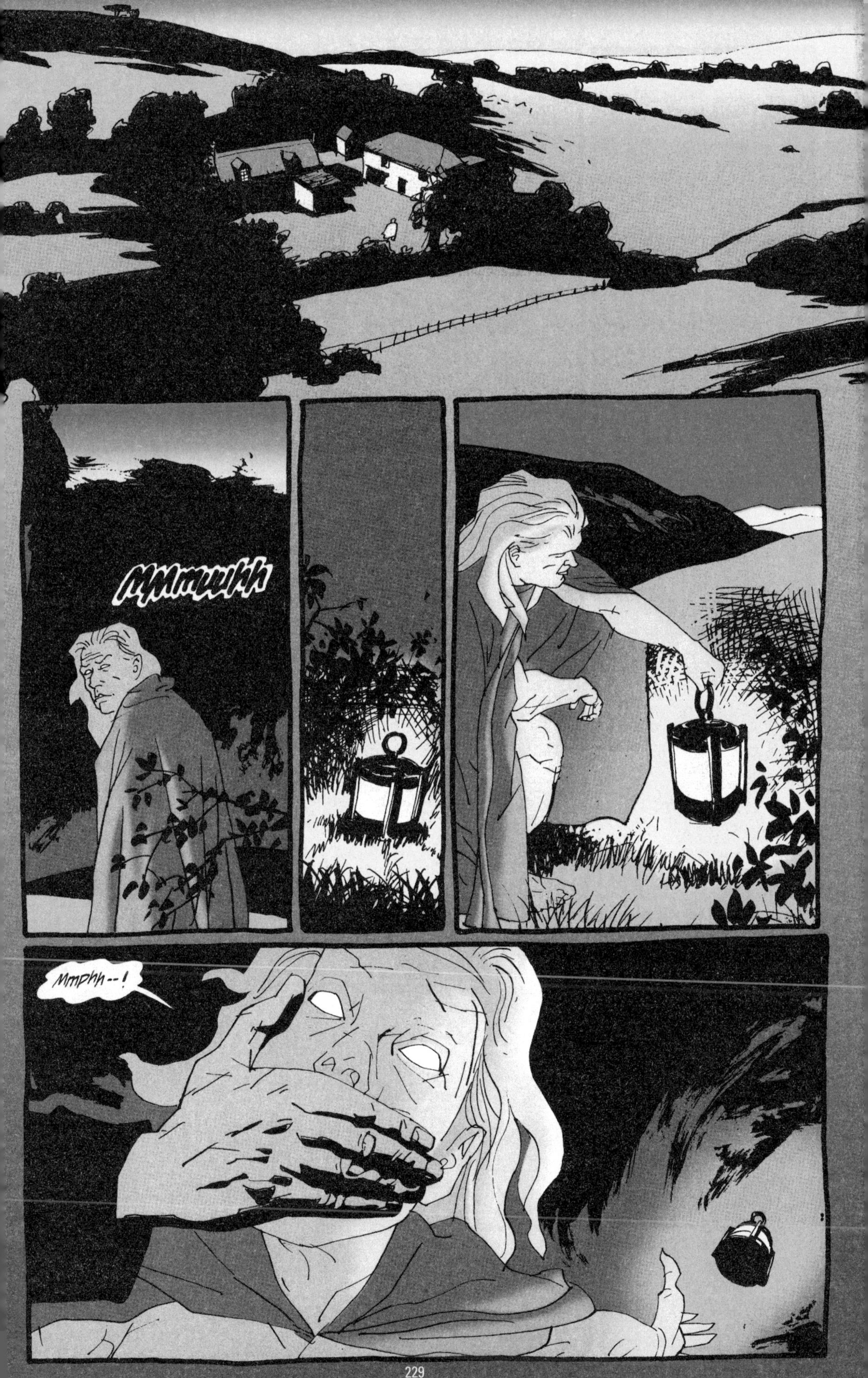
MMMmuuhh
Mmphh--!

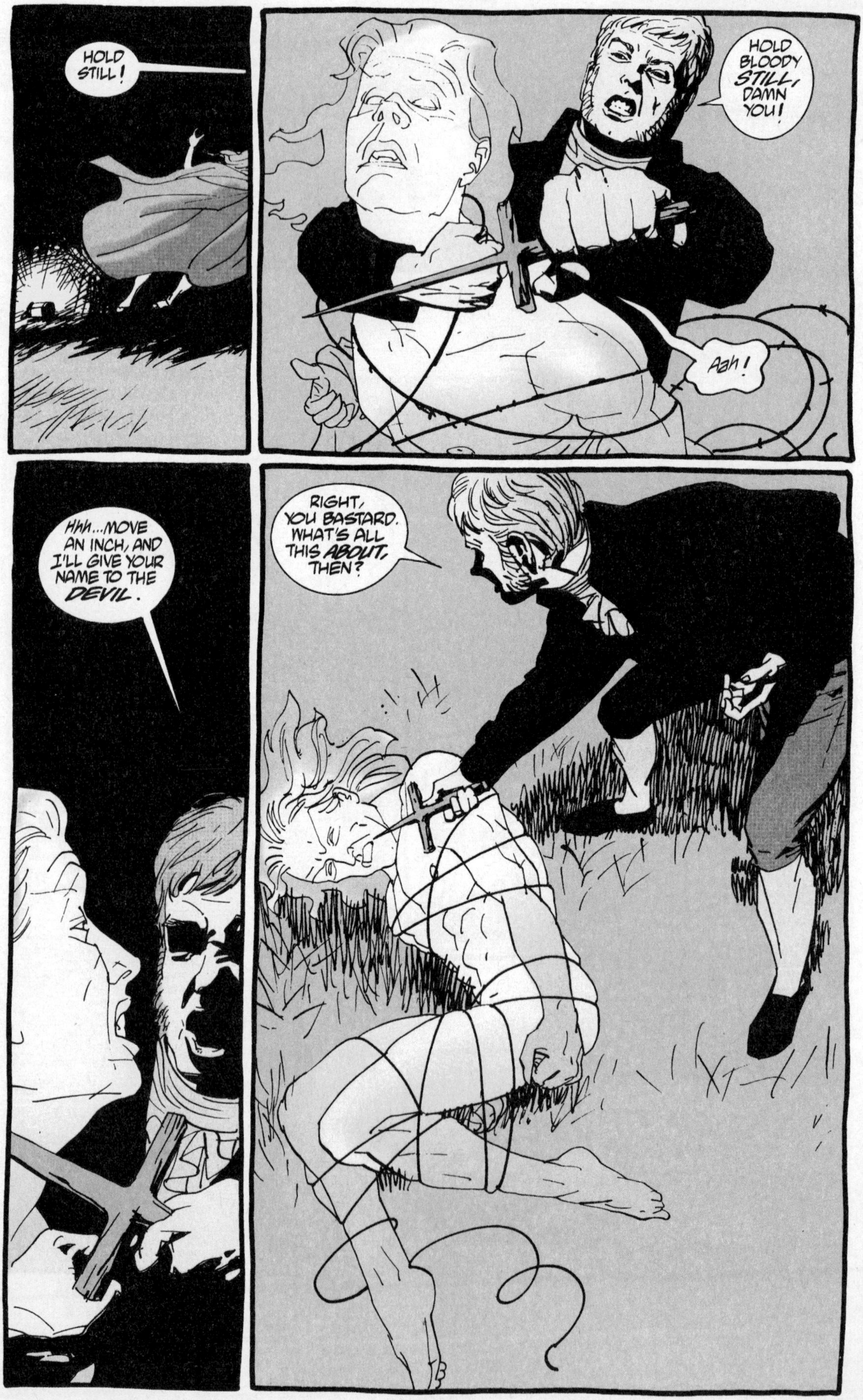
HOLD STILL!
HOLD BLOODY STILL, DAMN YOU!
Aah!
Hhh...MOVE AN INCH, AND I'LL GIVE YOUR NAME TO THE DEVIL.
RIGHT, YOU BASTARD. WHAT'S ALL THIS ABOUT, THEN?

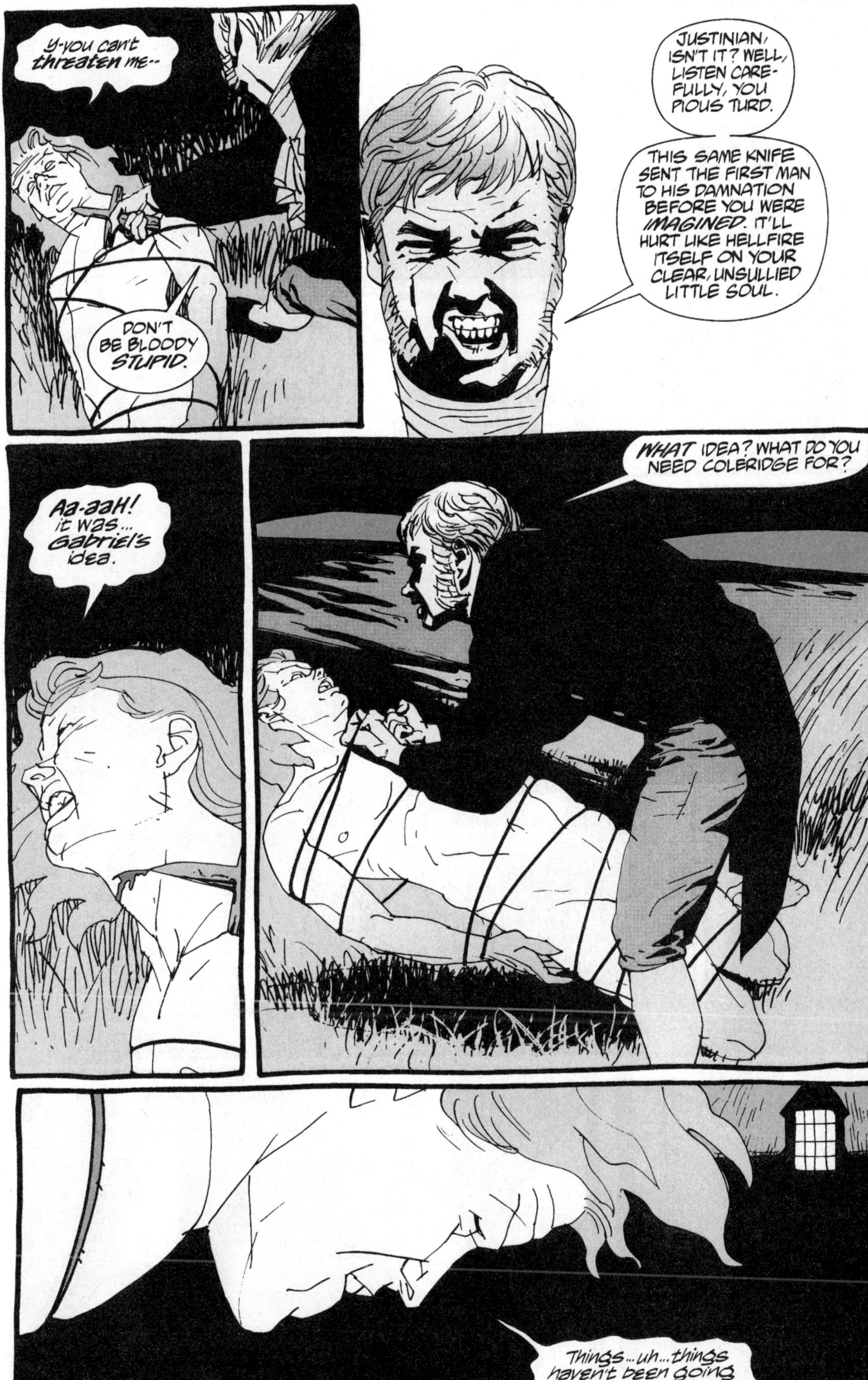
y-you can't threaten me--
JUSTINIAN, ISN'T IT? WELL, LISTEN CAREFULLY, YOU PIOUS TURD.
THIS SAME KNIFE SENT THE FIRST MAN TO HIS DAMNATION BEFORE YOU WERE IMAGINED. IT'LL HURT LIKE HELLFIRE ITSELF ON YOUR CLEAR, UNSULLIED LITTLE SOUL.
DON'T BE BLOODY STUPID.
Aa-aah! it was... Gabriel's idea.
WHAT IDEA? WHAT DO YOU NEED COLERIDGE FOR?
Things... uh... things haven't been going well for us lately...

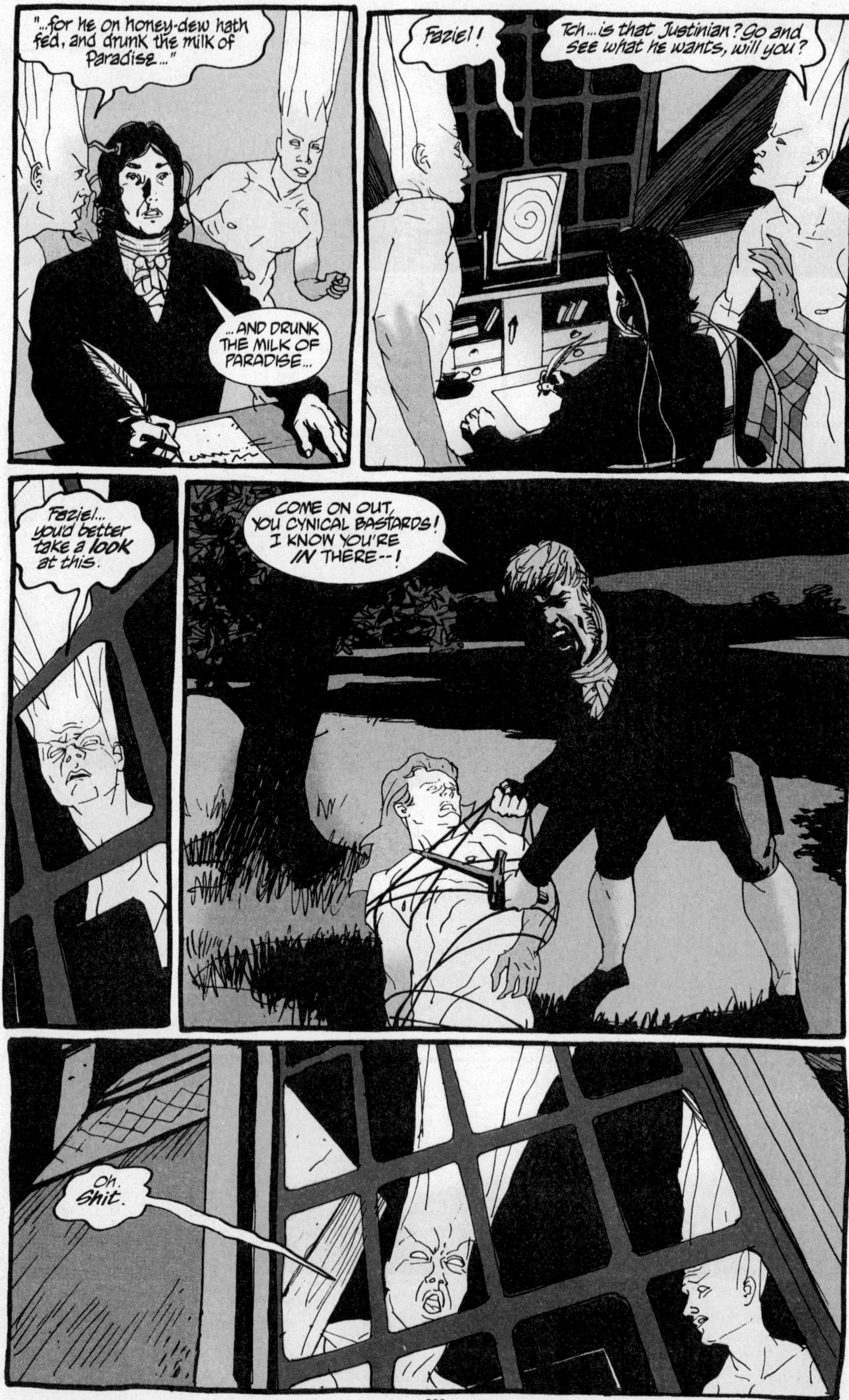
"...for he on honey-dew hath fed, and drunk the milk of Paradise..."
...AND DRUNK THE MILK OF PARADISE...
Faziel!
Tch... is that Justinian? Go and see what he wants, will you?
Faziel... you'd better take a look at this.
COME ON OUT, YOU CYNICAL BASTARDS! I KNOW YOU'RE IN THERE--!
Oh. Shit.

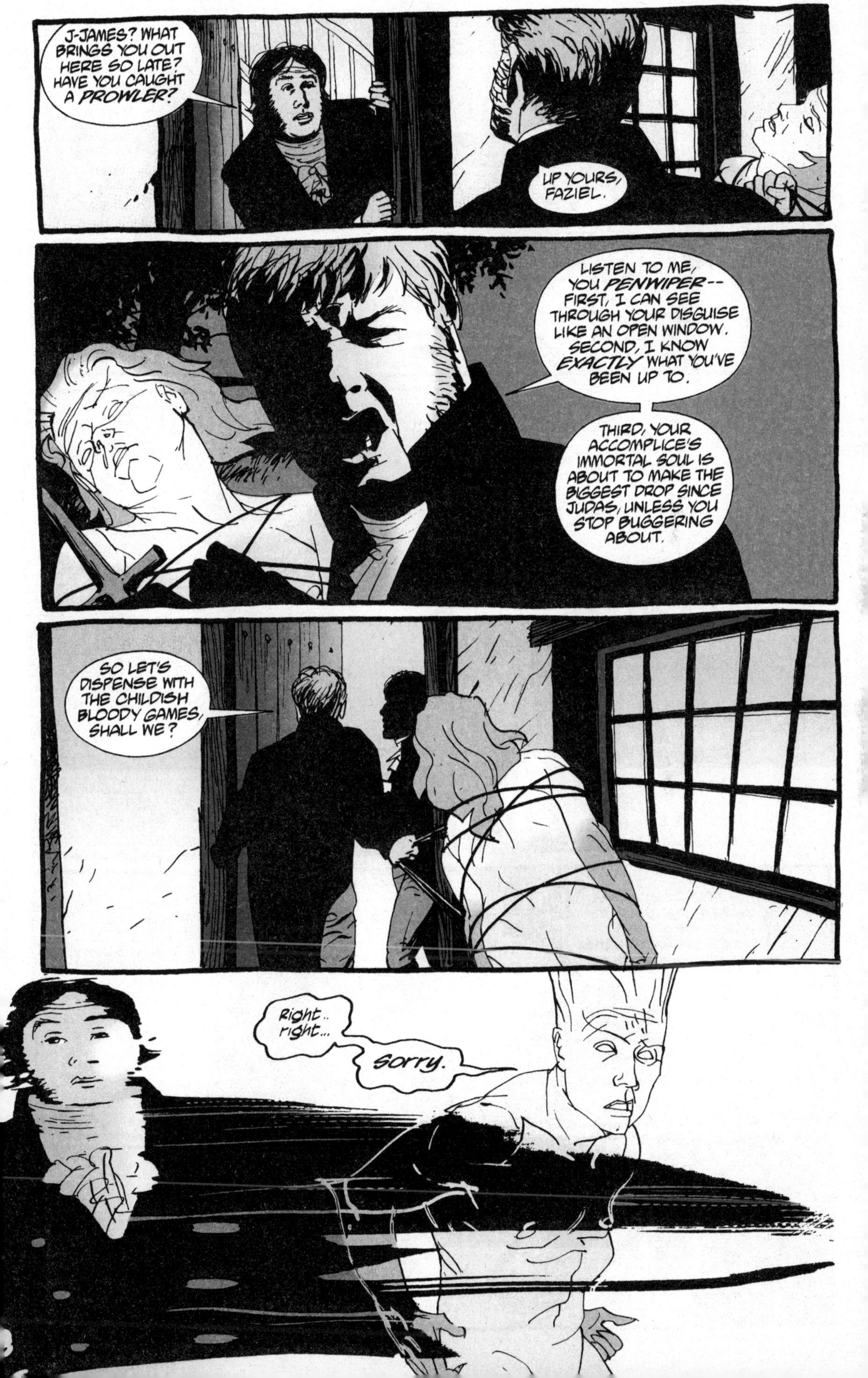
J-JAMES? WHAT BRINGS YOU OUT HERE SO LATE? HAVE YOU CAUGHT A PROWLER?
UP YOURS, FAZIEL.
LISTEN TO ME, YOU PENWIPER-- FIRST, I CAN SEE THROUGH YOUR DISGUISE LIKE AN OPEN WINDOW. SECOND, I KNOW EXACTLY WHAT YOU'VE BEEN UP TO.
THIRD, YOUR ACCOMPLICE'S IMMORTAL SOUL IS ABOUT TO MAKE THE BIGGEST DROP SINCE JUDAS, UNLESS YOU STOP BUGGERING ABOUT.
SO LET'S DISPENSE WITH THE CHILDISH BLOODY GAMES, SHALL WE?
Right.. right...
Sorry.

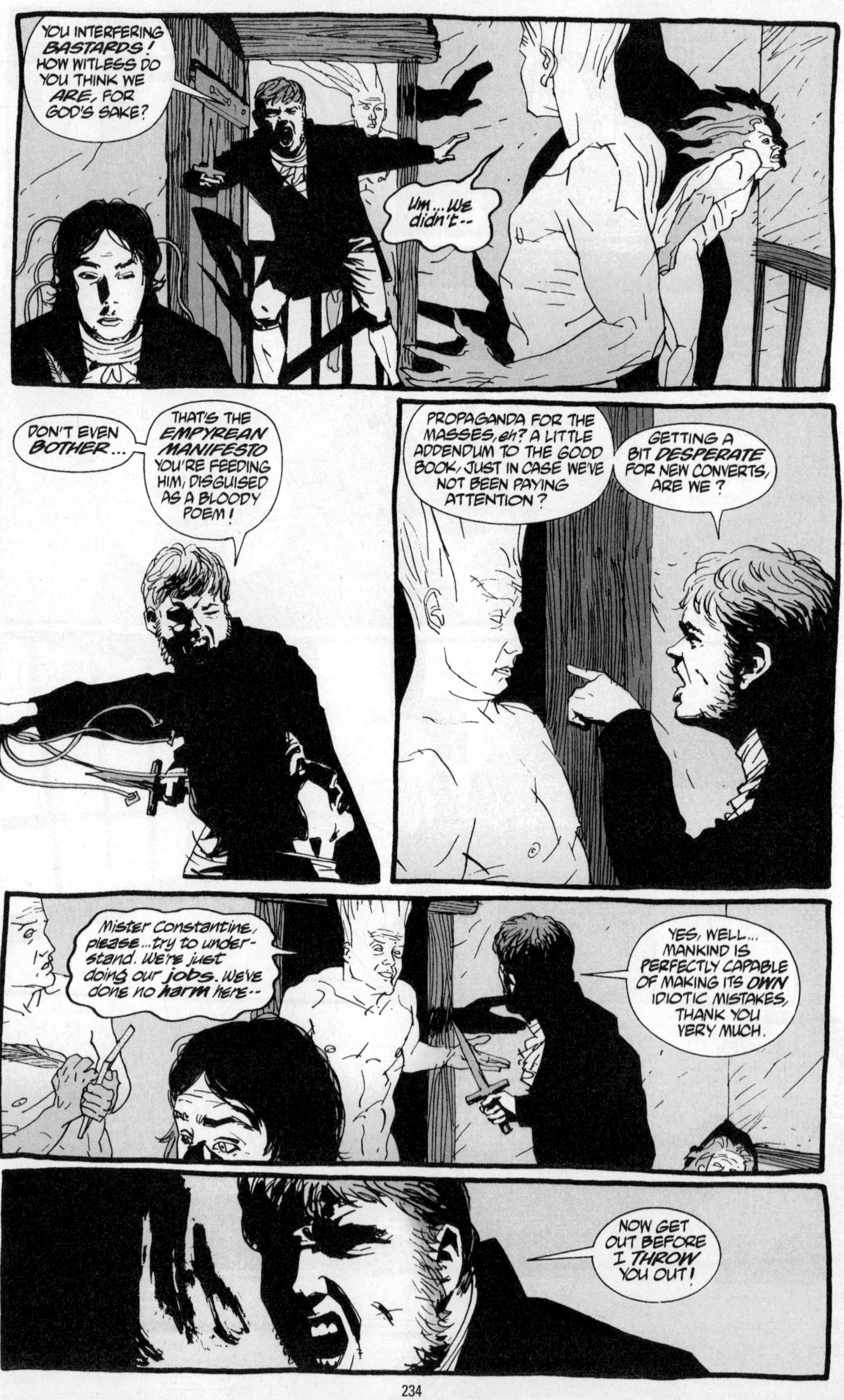
YOU INTERFERING BASTARDS! HOW WITLESS DO YOU THINK WE ARE, FOR GOD'S SAKE?
Um... We didn't--
DON'T EVEN BOTHER...
THAT'S THE EMPYREAN MANIFESTO YOU'RE FEEDING HIM, DISGUISED AS A BLOODY POEM!
PROPAGANDA FOR THE MASSES, eh? A LITTLE ADDENDUM TO THE GOOD BOOK, JUST IN CASE WE'VE NOT BEEN PAYING ATTENTION?
GETTING A BIT DESPERATE FOR NEW CONVERTS, ARE WE?
Mister Constantine, please...try to understand. We're just doing our jobs. We've done no harm here--
YES, WELL... MANKIND IS PERFECTLY CAPABLE OF MAKING ITS OWN IDIOTIC MISTAKES, THANK YOU VERY MUCH.
NOW GET OUT BEFORE I THROW YOU OUT!

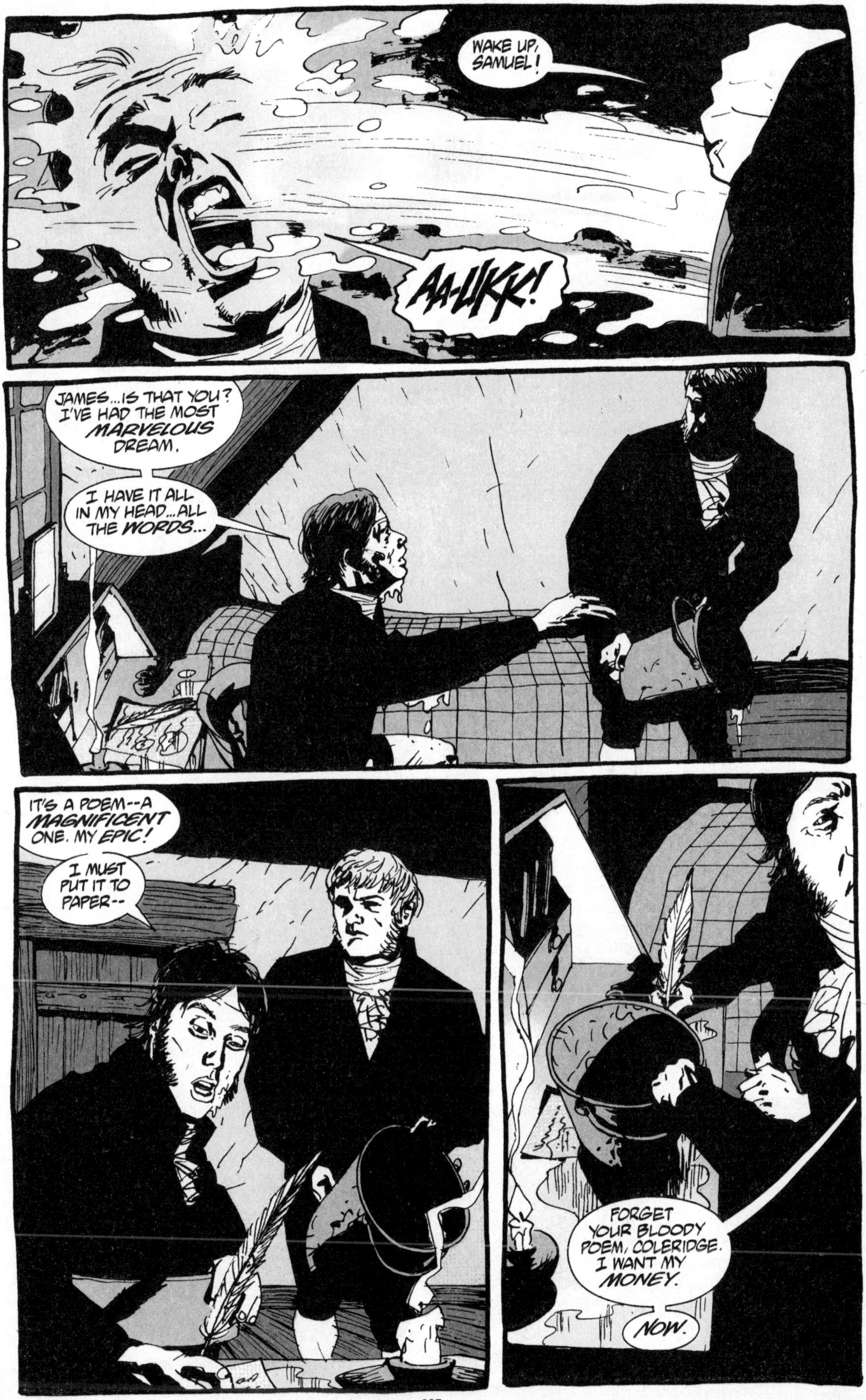
WAKE UP, SAMUEL!
AA-UKK!
JAMES...IS THAT YOU? I'VE HAD THE MOST MARVELOUS DREAM.
I HAVE IT ALL IN MY HEAD...ALL THE WORDS...
IT'S A POEM--A MAGNIFICENT ONE. MY EPIC!
I MUST PUT IT TO PAPER--
FORGET YOUR BLOODY POEM, COLERIDGE. I WANT MY MONEY.
NOW.

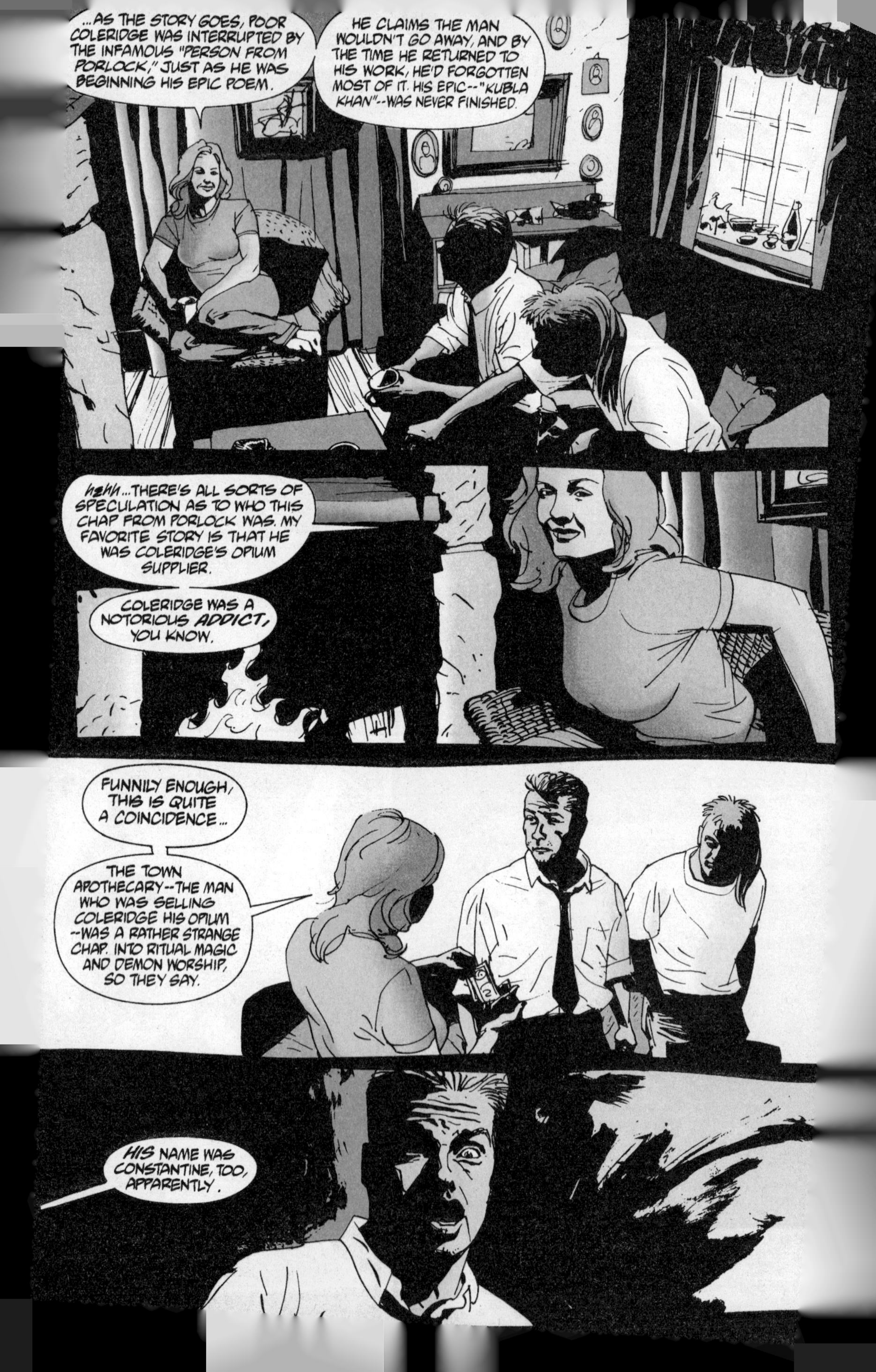
...AS THE STORY GOES, POOR COLERIDGE WAS INTERRUPTED BY THE INFAMOUS "PERSON FROM PORLOCK," JUST AS HE WAS BEGINNING HIS EPIC POEM.
HE CLAIMS THE MAN WOULDN'T GO AWAY, AND BY THE TIME HE RETURNED TO HIS WORK, HE'D FORGOTTEN MOST OF IT. HIS EPIC--"KUBLA KHAN"--WAS NEVER FINISHED.
hehh... THERE'S ALL SORTS OF SPECULATION AS TO WHO THIS CHAP FROM PORLOCK WAS. MY FAVORITE STORY IS THAT HE WAS COLERIDGE'S OPIUM SUPPLIER.
COLERIDGE WAS A NOTORIOUS ADDICT, YOU KNOW.
FUNNILY ENOUGH, THIS IS QUITE A COINCIDENCE...
THE TOWN APOTHECARY--THE MAN WHO WAS SELLING COLERIDGE HIS OPIUM --WAS A RATHER STRANGE CHAP. INTO RITUAL MAGIC AND DEMON WORSHIP, SO THEY SAY.
HIS NAME WAS CONSTANTINE, TOO, APPARENTLY.

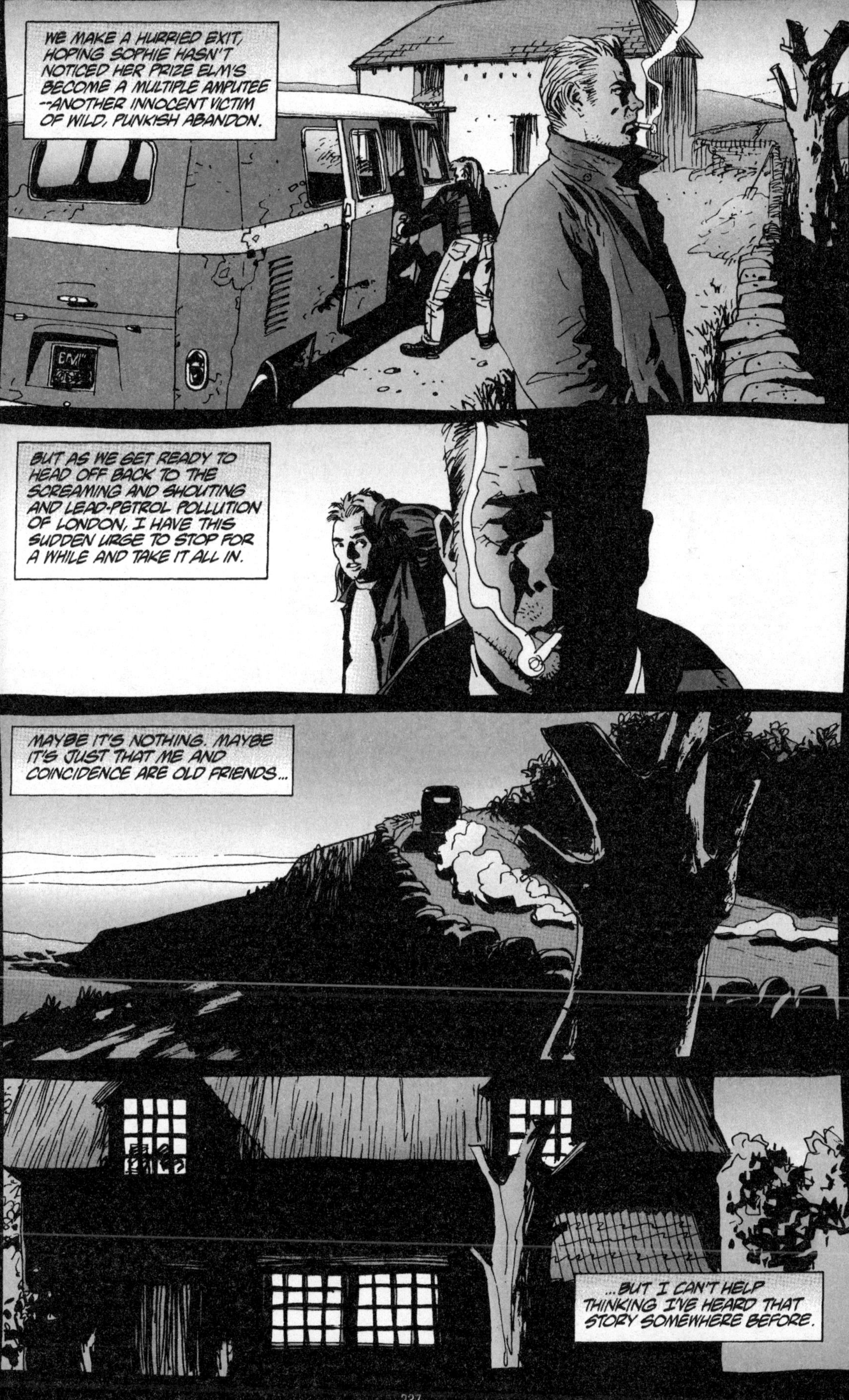
WE MAKE A HURRIED EXIT, HOPING SOPHIE HASN'T NOTICED HER PRIZE ELM'S BECOME A MULTIPLE AMPUTEE --ANOTHER INNOCENT VICTIM OF WILD, PUNKISH ABANDON.
BUT AS WE GET READY TO HEAD OFF BACK TO THE SCREAMING AND SHOUTING AND LEAD-PETROL POLLUTION OF LONDON, I HAVE THIS SUDDEN URGE TO STOP FOR A WHILE AND TAKE IT ALL IN.
MAYBE IT'S NOTHING. MAYBE IT'S JUST THAT ME AND COINCIDENCE ARE OLD FRIENDS...
...BUT I CAN'T HELP THINKING I'VE HEARD THAT STORY SOMEWHERE BEFORE.

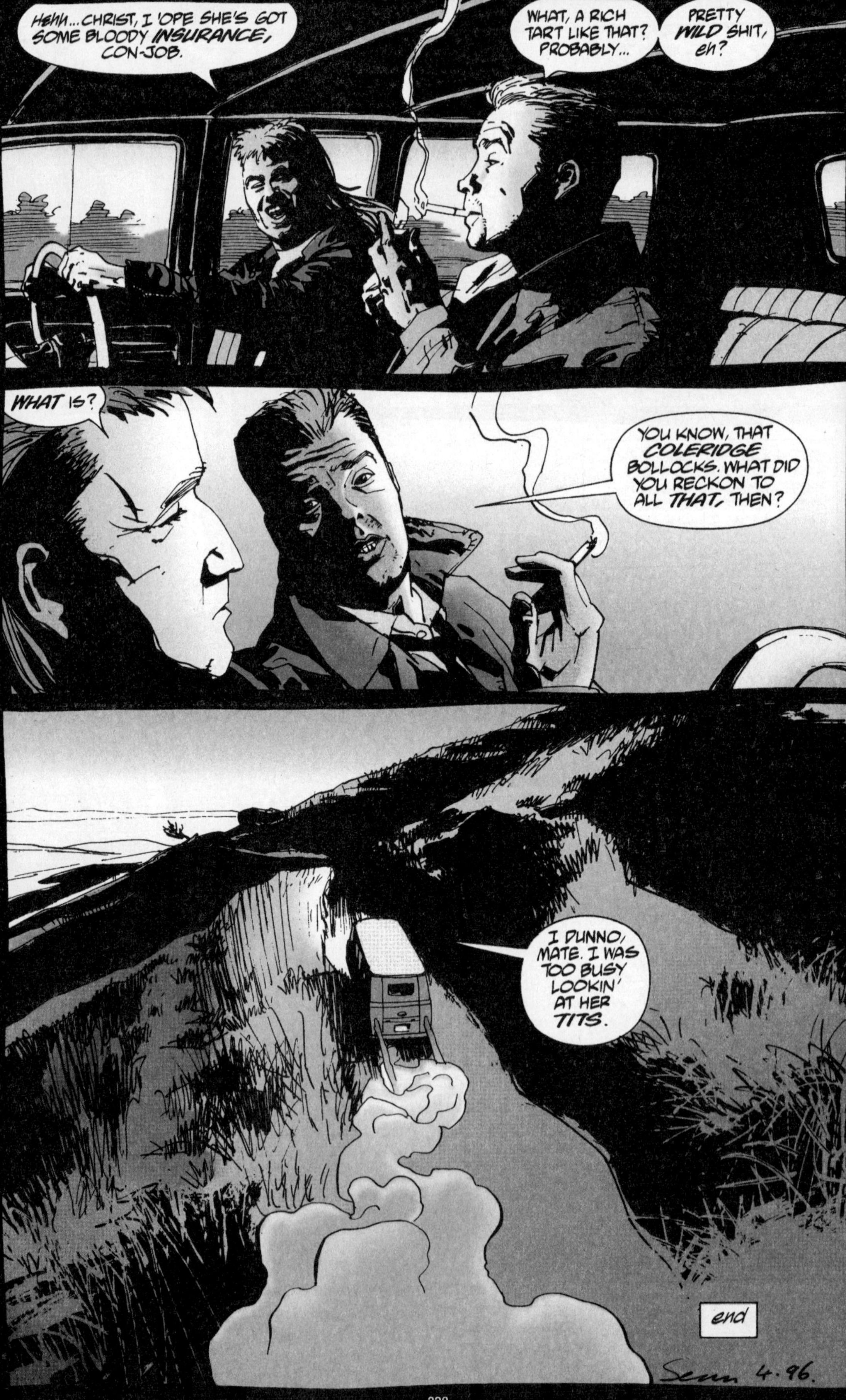
Hehh... CHRIST, I 'OPE SHE'S GOT SOME BLOODY INSURANCE, CON-JOB.
WHAT, A RICH TART LIKE THAT? PROBABLY...
PRETTY WILD SHIT, eh?
WHAT IS?
YOU KNOW, THAT COLERIDGE BOLLOCKS. WHAT DID YOU RECKON TO ALL THAT, THEN?
I DUNNO, MATE. I WAS TOO BUSY LOOKIN' AT HER TITS.
end
Sean 4.96.

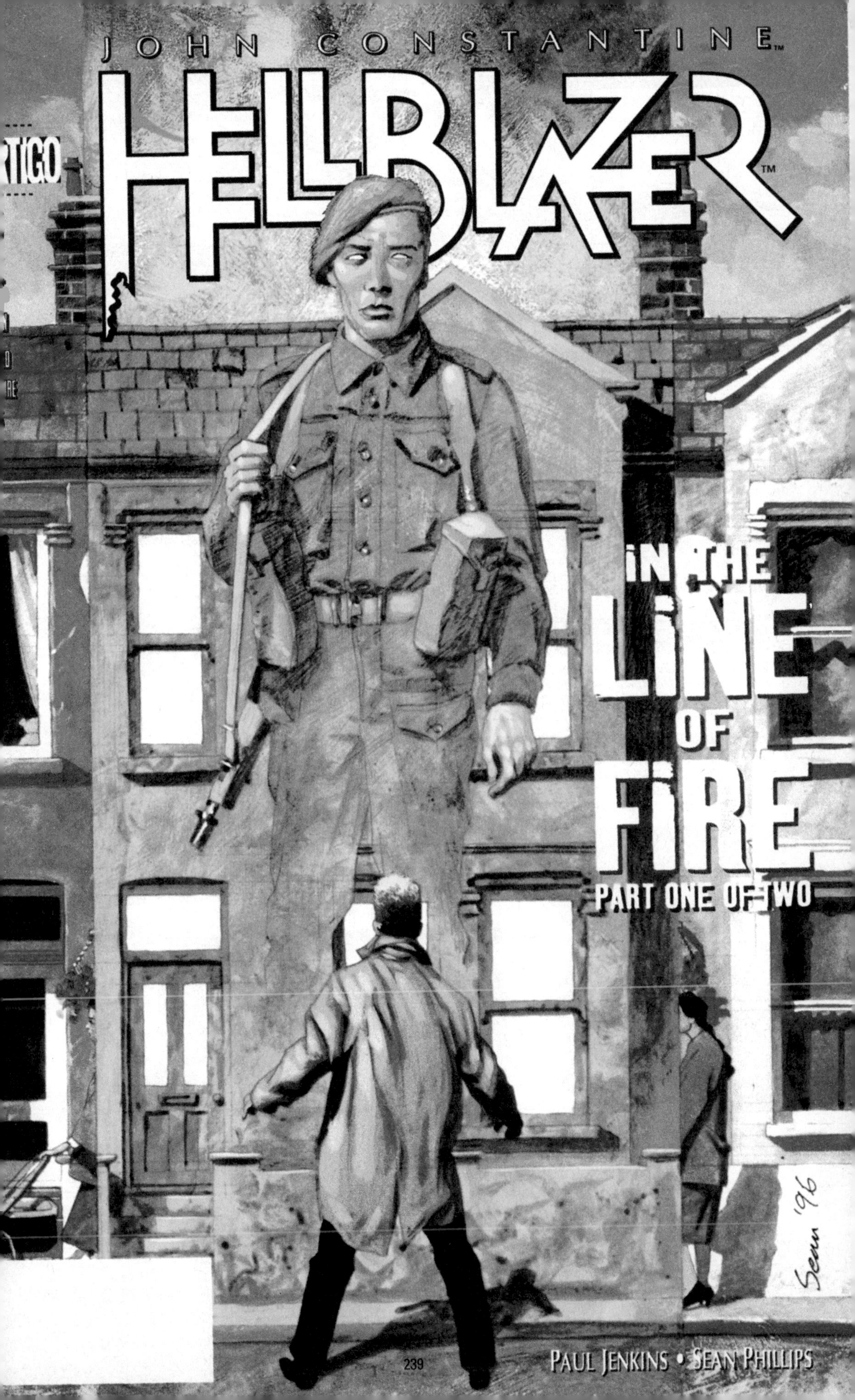
JOHN CONSTANTINE™
HELLBLAZER™
IN THE LINE OF FIRE
PART ONE OF TWO
Sean '96
PAUL JENKINS • SEAN PHILLIPS

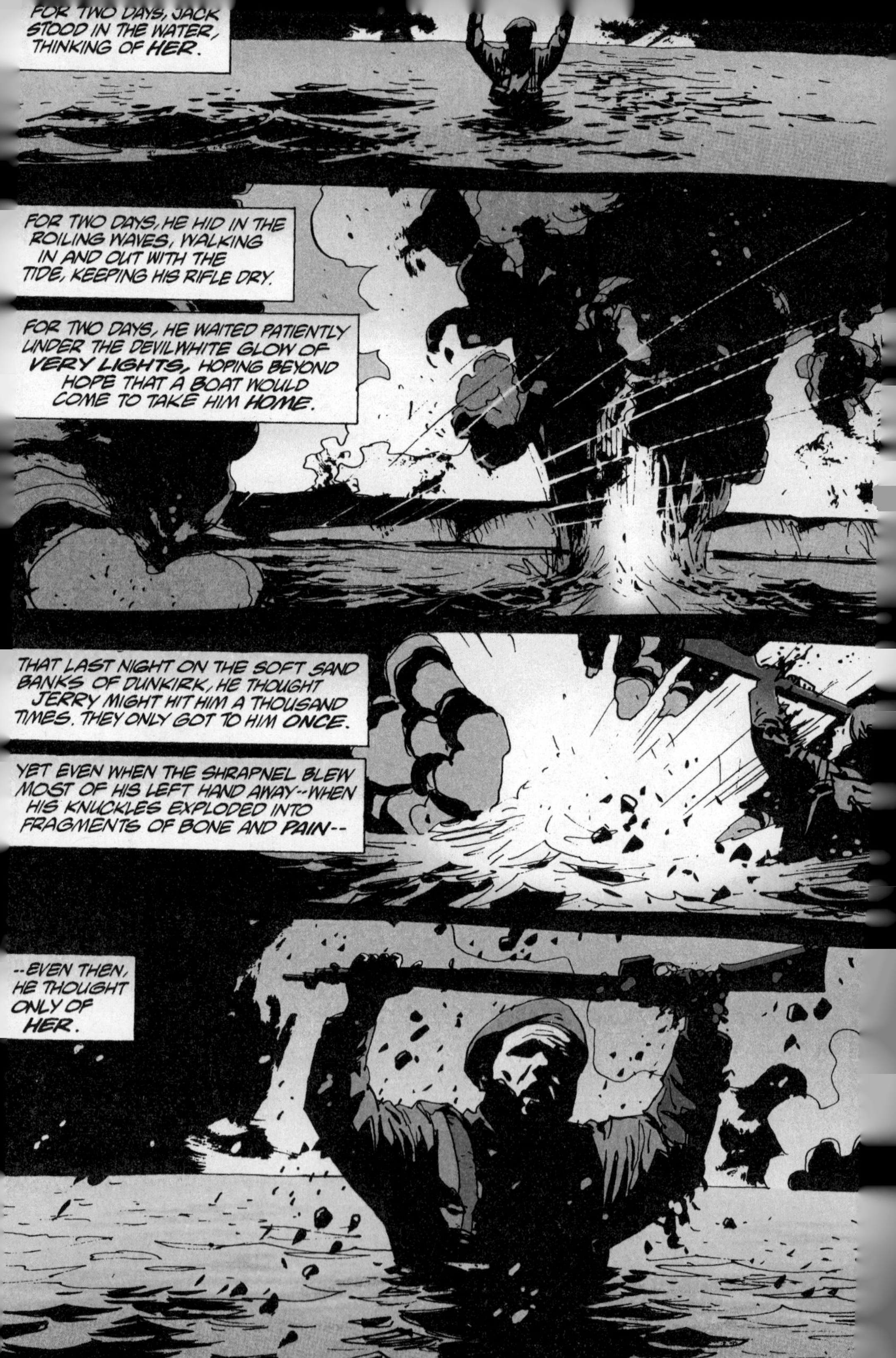
FOR TWO DAYS, JACK STOOD IN THE WATER, THINKING OF HER.
FOR TWO DAYS, HE HID IN THE ROILING WAVES, WALKING IN AND OUT WITH THE TIDE, KEEPING HIS RIFLE DRY.
FOR TWO DAYS, HE WAITED PATIENTLY UNDER THE DEVILWHITE GLOW OF VERY LIGHTS, HOPING BEYOND HOPE THAT A BOAT WOULD COME TO TAKE HIM HOME.
THAT LAST NIGHT ON THE SOFT SAND BANKS OF DUNKIRK, HE THOUGHT JERRY MIGHT HIT HIM A THOUSAND TIMES. THEY ONLY GOT TO HIM ONCE.
YET EVEN WHEN THE SHRAPNEL BLEW MOST OF HIS LEFT HAND AWAY--WHEN HIS KNUCKLES EXPLODED INTO FRAGMENTS OF BONE AND PAIN--
--EVEN THEN, HE THOUGHT ONLY OF HER.

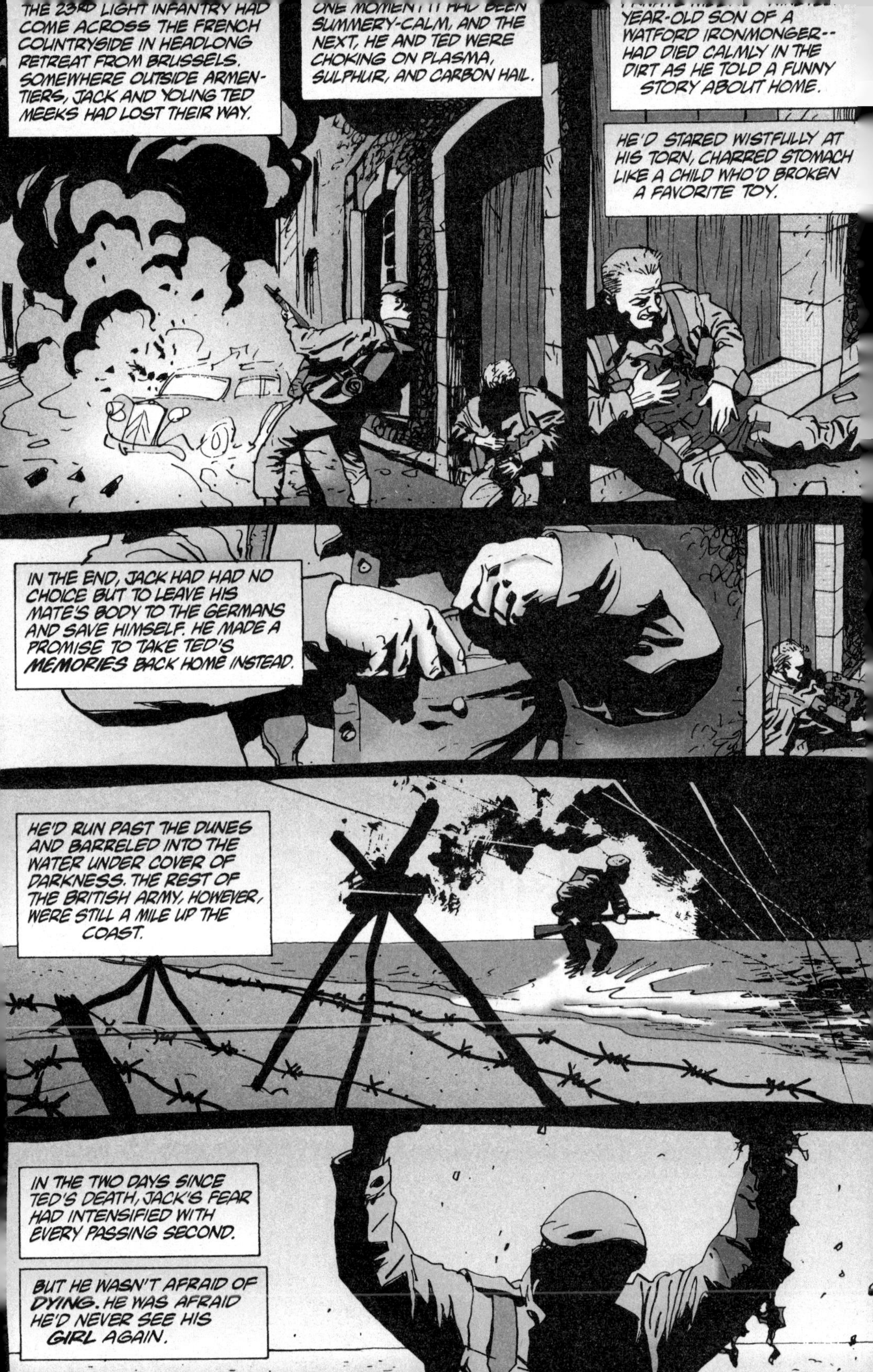
THE 23RD LIGHT INFANTRY HAD COME ACROSS THE FRENCH COUNTRYSIDE IN HEADLONG RETREAT FROM BRUSSELS. SOMEWHERE OUTSIDE ARMENTIERS, JACK AND YOUNG TED MEEKS HAD LOST THEIR WAY.
ONE MOMENT IT HAD BEEN SUMMERY-CALM, AND THE NEXT, HE AND TED WERE CHOKING ON PLASMA, SULPHUR, AND CARBON HAIL.
YEAR-OLD SON OF A WATFORD IRONMONGER-- HAD DIED CALMLY IN THE DIRT AS HE TOLD A FUNNY STORY ABOUT HOME.
HE'D STARED WISTFULLY AT HIS TORN, CHARRED STOMACH LIKE A CHILD WHO'D BROKEN A FAVORITE TOY.
IN THE END, JACK HAD HAD NO CHOICE BUT TO LEAVE HIS MATE'S BODY TO THE GERMANS AND SAVE HIMSELF. HE MADE A PROMISE TO TAKE TED'S MEMORIES BACK HOME INSTEAD.
HE'D RUN PAST THE DUNES AND BARRELED INTO THE WATER UNDER COVER OF DARKNESS. THE REST OF THE BRITISH ARMY, HOWEVER, WERE STILL A MILE UP THE COAST.
IN THE TWO DAYS SINCE TED'S DEATH, JACK'S FEAR HAD INTENSIFIED WITH EVERY PASSING SECOND.
BUT HE WASN'T AFRAID OF DYING. HE WAS AFRAID HE'D NEVER SEE HIS GIRL AGAIN.

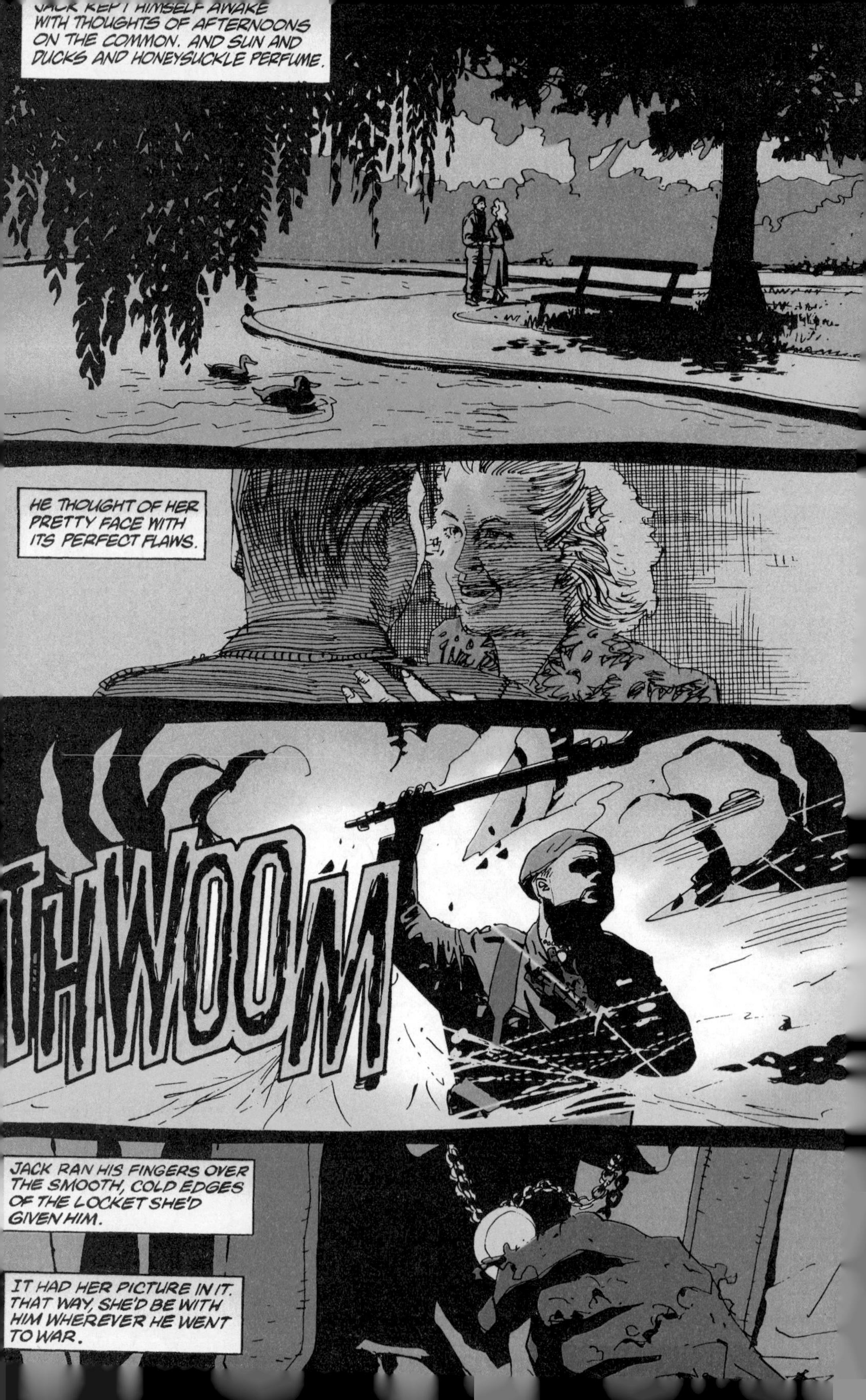
JACK KEPT HIMSELF AWAKE WITH THOUGHTS OF AFTERNOONS ON THE COMMON. AND SUN AND DUCKS AND HONEYSUCKLE PERFUME.
HE THOUGHT OF HER PRETTY FACE WITH ITS PERFECT FLAWS.
THWOOM
JACK RAN HIS FINGERS OVER THE SMOOTH, COLD EDGES OF THE LOCKET SHE'D GIVEN HIM.
IT HAD HER PICTURE IN IT. THAT WAY, SHE'D BE WITH HIM WHEREVER HE WENT TO WAR.

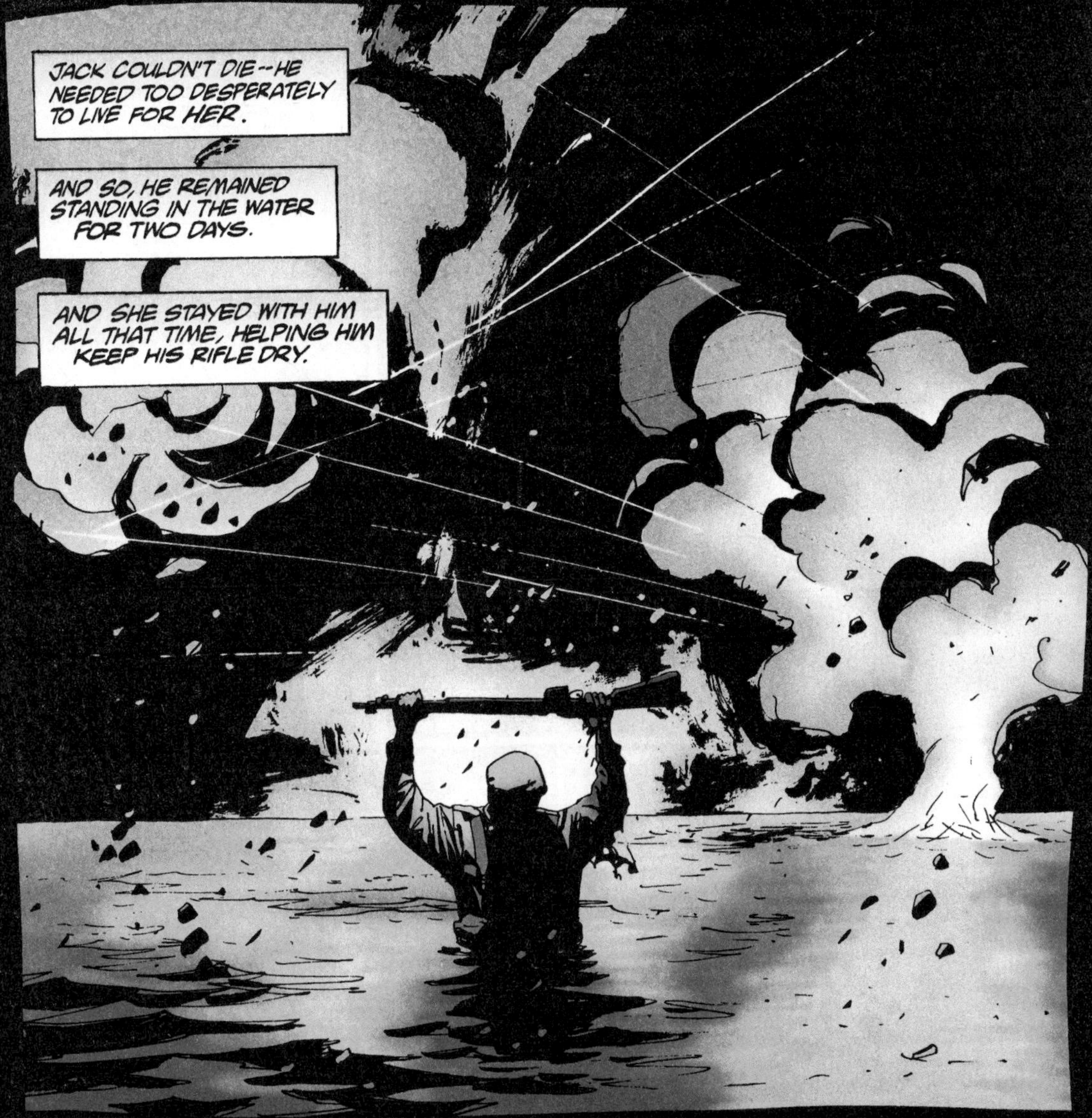
JACK COULDN'T DIE--HE NEEDED TOO DESPERATELY TO LIVE FOR HER.
AND SO, HE REMAINED STANDING IN THE WATER FOR TWO DAYS.
AND SHE STAYED WITH HIM ALL THAT TIME, HELPING HIM KEEP HIS RIFLE DRY.

In the LINE of FIRE

1

PAUL JENKINS Writer
SEAN PHILLIPS Artist
JAMES SINCLAIR Colors
CLEM ROBINS Letters
DIGITAL CHAMELEON Seps
AXEL ALONSO Asst Editor
LOU STATHIS Editor

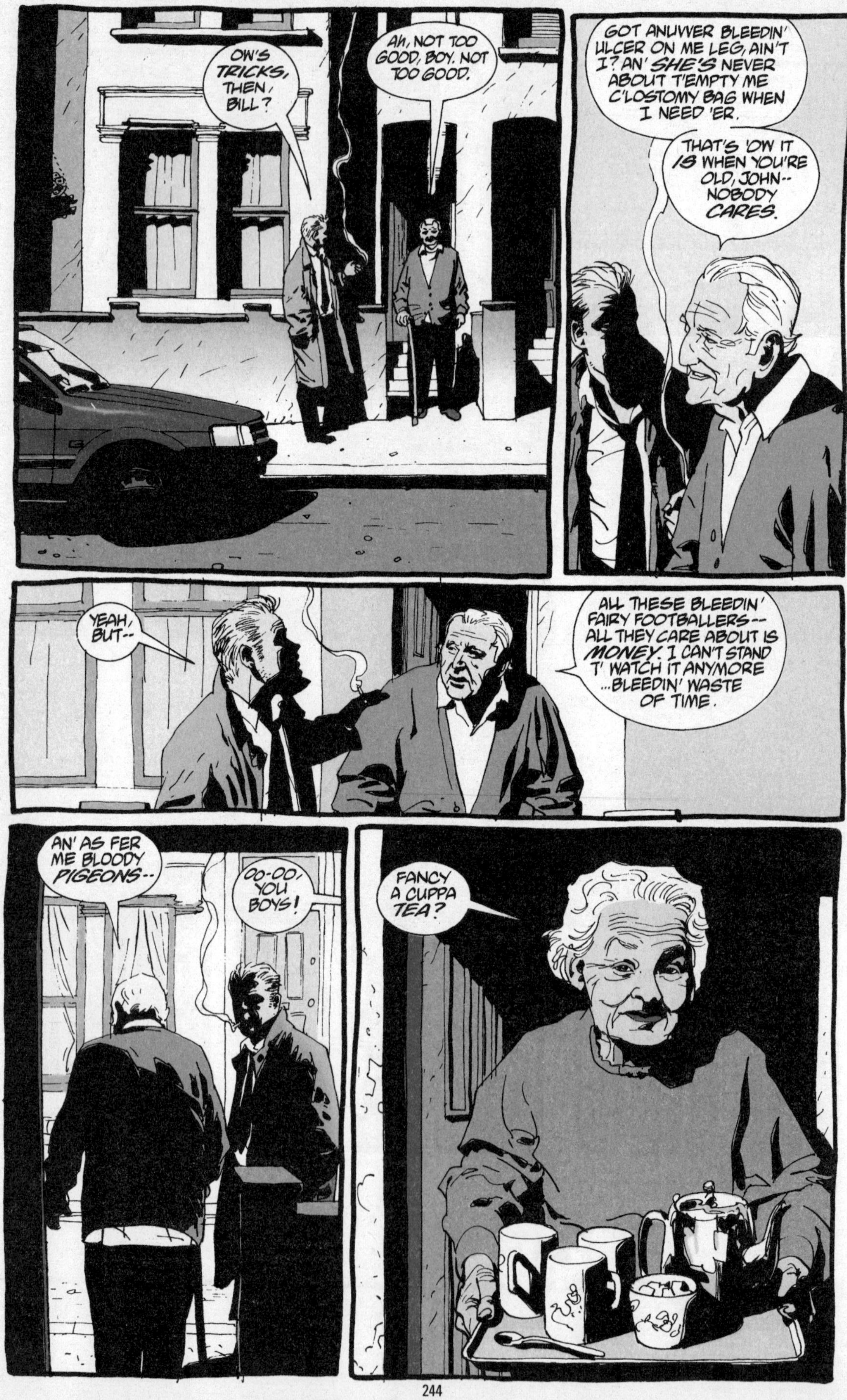
OW'S TRICKS, THEN, BILL?
AH, NOT TOO GOOD, BOY. NOT TOO GOOD.
GOT ANUVVER BLEEDIN' ULCER ON ME LEG, AIN'T I? AN' SHE'S NEVER ABOUT T'EMPTY ME C'LOSTOMY BAG WHEN I NEED 'ER.
THAT'S 'OW IT IS WHEN YOU'RE OLD, JOHN-- NOBODY CARES.
YEAH, BUT--
ALL THESE BLEEDIN' FAIRY FOOTBALLERS-- ALL THEY CARE ABOUT IS MONEY. I CAN'T STAND T' WATCH IT ANYMORE ...BLEEDIN' WASTE OF TIME.
AN' AS FER ME BLOODY PIGEONS--
OO-OO, YOU BOYS!
FANCY A CUPPA TEA?

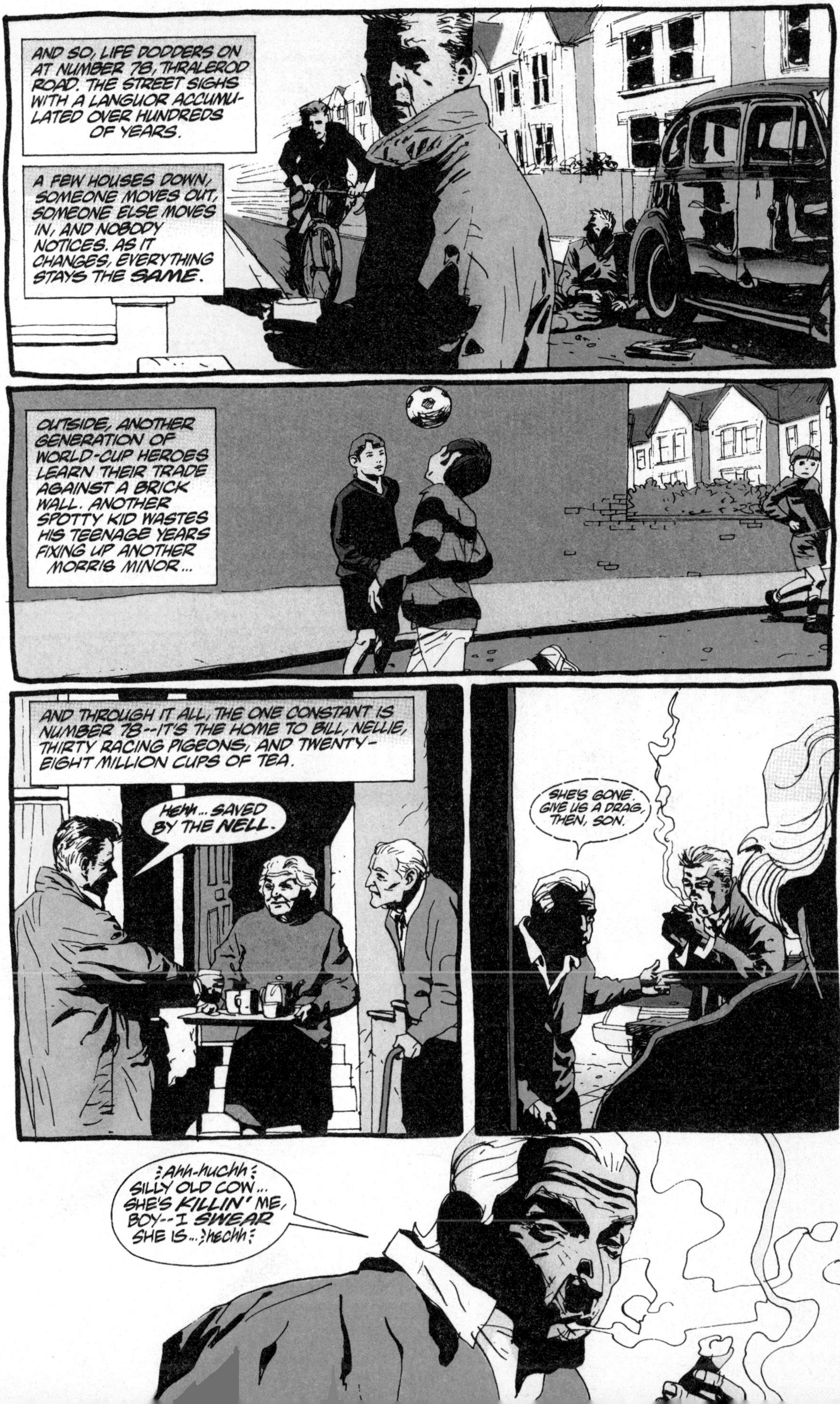
AND SO, LIFE DODDERS ON AT NUMBER 78, THRALEROD ROAD. THE STREET SIGHS WITH A LANGUOR ACCUMULATED OVER HUNDREDS OF YEARS.
A FEW HOUSES DOWN, SOMEONE MOVES OUT, SOMEONE ELSE MOVES IN, AND NOBODY NOTICES. AS IT CHANGES, EVERYTHING STAYS THE SAME.
OUTSIDE, ANOTHER GENERATION OF WORLD-CUP HEROES LEARN THEIR TRADE AGAINST A BRICK WALL. ANOTHER SPOTTY KID WASTES HIS TEENAGE YEARS FIXING UP ANOTHER MORRIS MINOR...
AND THROUGH IT ALL, THE ONE CONSTANT IS NUMBER 78--IT'S THE HOME TO BILL, NELLIE, THIRTY RACING PIGEONS, AND TWENTY-EIGHT MILLION CUPS OF TEA.
Hehh... SAVED BY THE NELL.
SHE'S GONE. GIVE US A DRAG, THEN, SON.
Ahh-huchh SILLY OLD COW... SHE'S KILLIN' ME, BOY--I SWEAR SHE IS... hechh

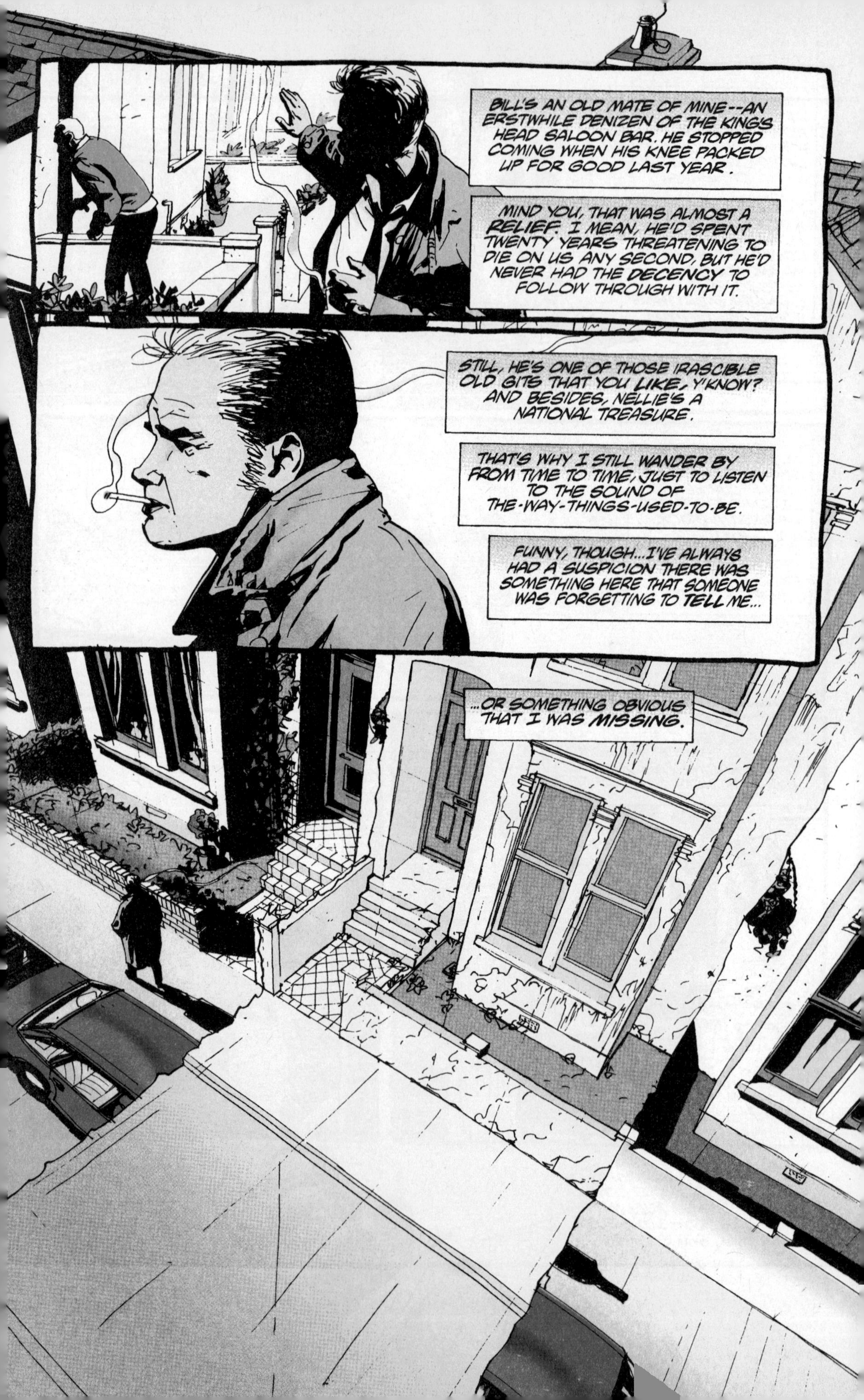
BILL'S AN OLD MATE OF MINE--AN ERSTWHILE DENIZEN OF THE KING'S HEAD SALOON BAR. HE STOPPED COMING WHEN HIS KNEE PACKED UP FOR GOOD LAST YEAR.
MIND YOU, THAT WAS ALMOST A RELIEF. I MEAN, HE'D SPENT TWENTY YEARS THREATENING TO DIE ON US ANY SECOND, BUT HE'D NEVER HAD THE DECENCY TO FOLLOW THROUGH WITH IT.
STILL, HE'S ONE OF THOSE IRASCIBLE OLD GITS THAT YOU LIKE, Y'KNOW? AND BESIDES, NELLIE'S A NATIONAL TREASURE.
THAT'S WHY I STILL WANDER BY FROM TIME TO TIME, JUST TO LISTEN TO THE SOUND OF THE-WAY-THINGS-USED-TO-BE.
FUNNY, THOUGH...I'VE ALWAYS HAD A SUSPICION THERE WAS SOMETHING HERE THAT SOMEONE WAS FORGETTING TO TELL ME...
...OR SOMETHING OBVIOUS THAT I WAS MISSING.

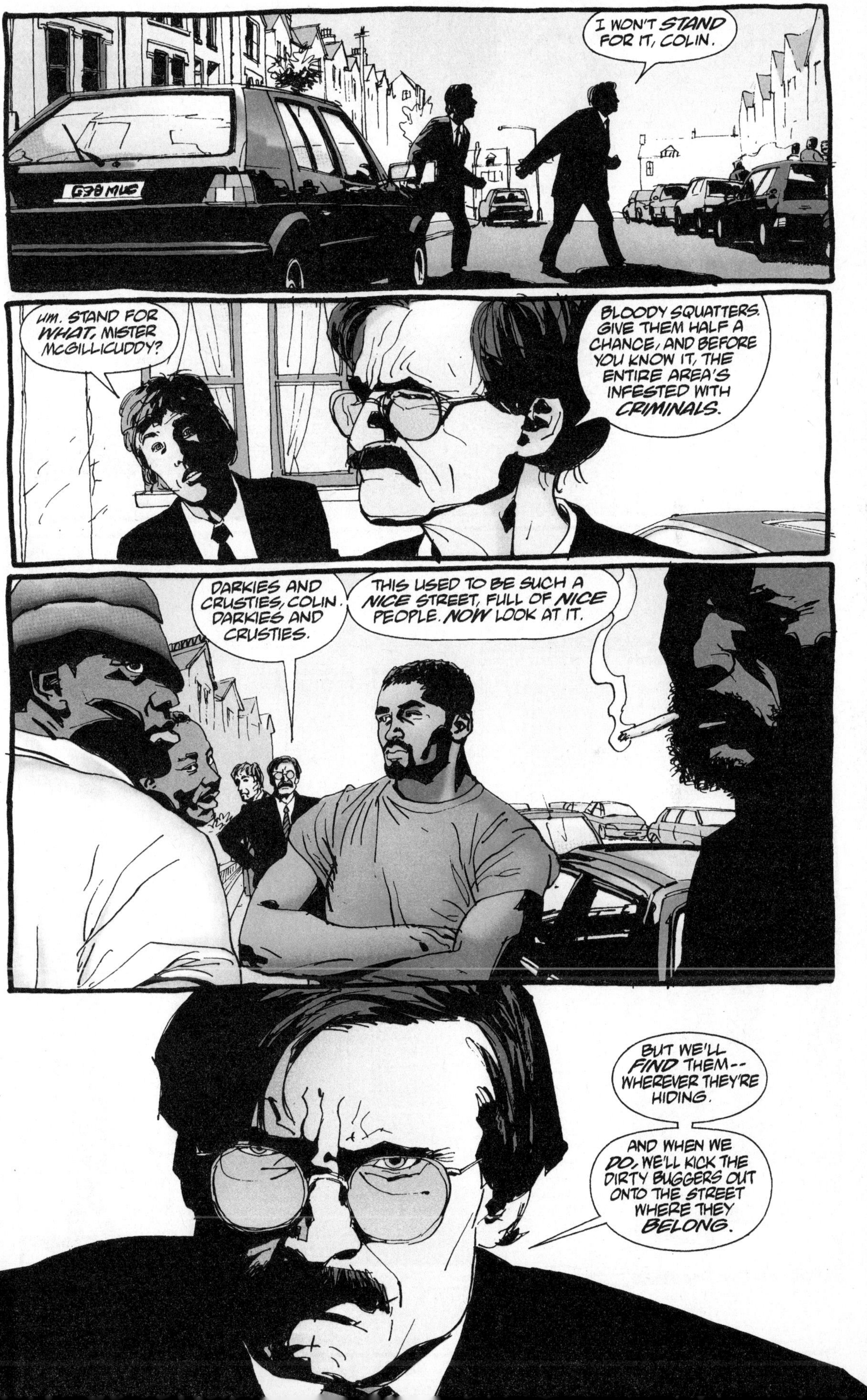
I WON'T STAND FOR IT, COLIN.
UM. STAND FOR WHAT, MISTER McGILLICUDDY?
BLOODY SQUATTERS. GIVE THEM HALF A CHANCE, AND BEFORE YOU KNOW IT, THE ENTIRE AREA'S INFESTED WITH CRIMINALS.
DARKIES AND CRUSTIES, COLIN. DARKIES AND CRUSTIES.
THIS USED TO BE SUCH A NICE STREET, FULL OF NICE PEOPLE. NOW LOOK AT IT.
BUT WE'LL FIND THEM-- WHEREVER THEY'RE HIDING.
AND WHEN WE DO, WE'LL KICK THE DIRTY BUGGERS OUT ONTO THE STREET WHERE THEY BELONG.

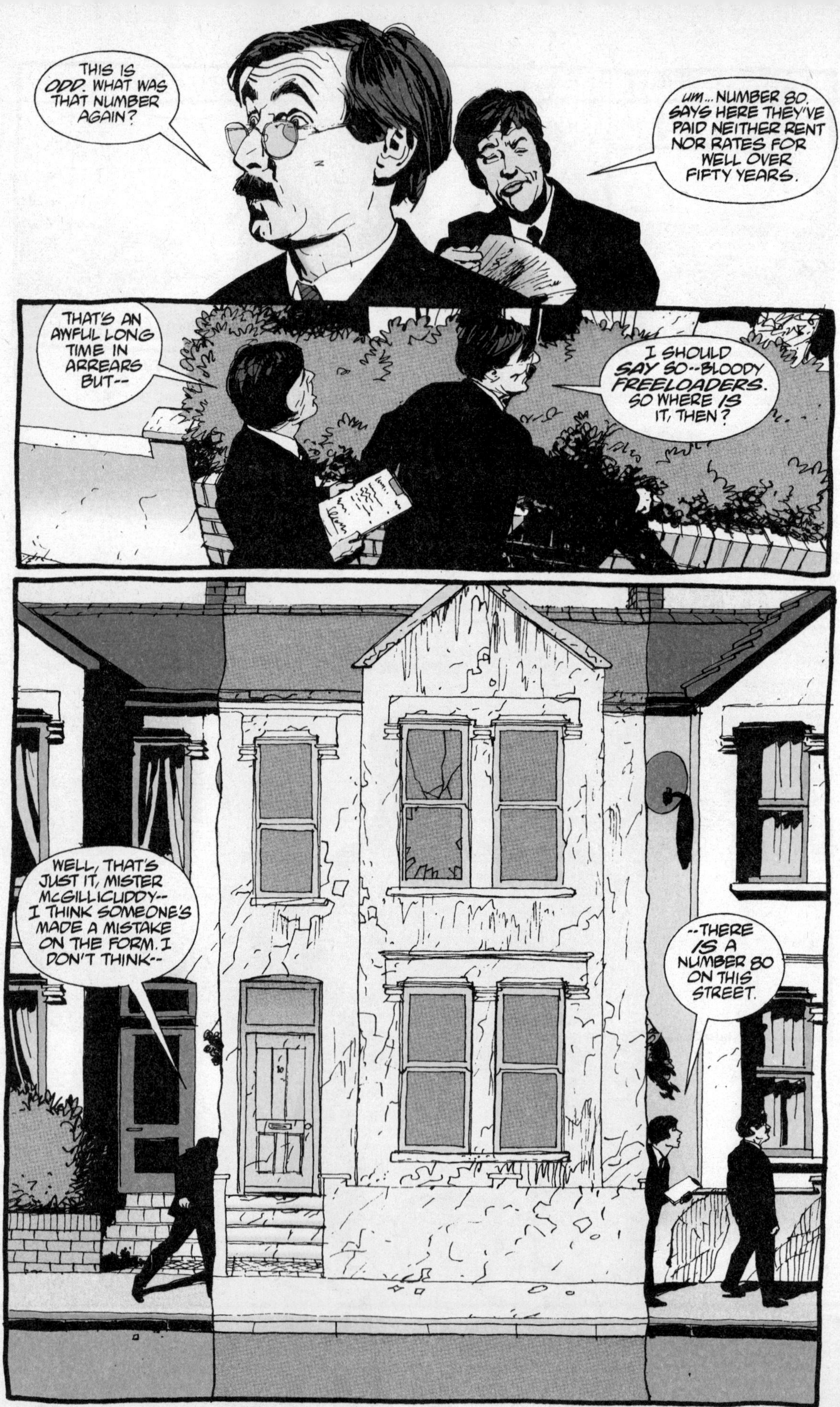
THIS IS ODD. WHAT WAS THAT NUMBER AGAIN?
UM... NUMBER 80. SAYS HERE THEY'VE PAID NEITHER RENT NOR RATES FOR WELL OVER FIFTY YEARS.
THAT'S AN AWFUL LONG TIME IN ARREARS BUT--
I SHOULD SAY SO--BLOODY FREELOADERS. SO WHERE IS IT, THEN?
WELL, THAT'S JUST IT, MISTER McGILLICUDDY-- I THINK SOMEONE'S MADE A MISTAKE ON THE FORM. I DON'T THINK--
--THERE IS A NUMBER 80 ON THIS STREET.

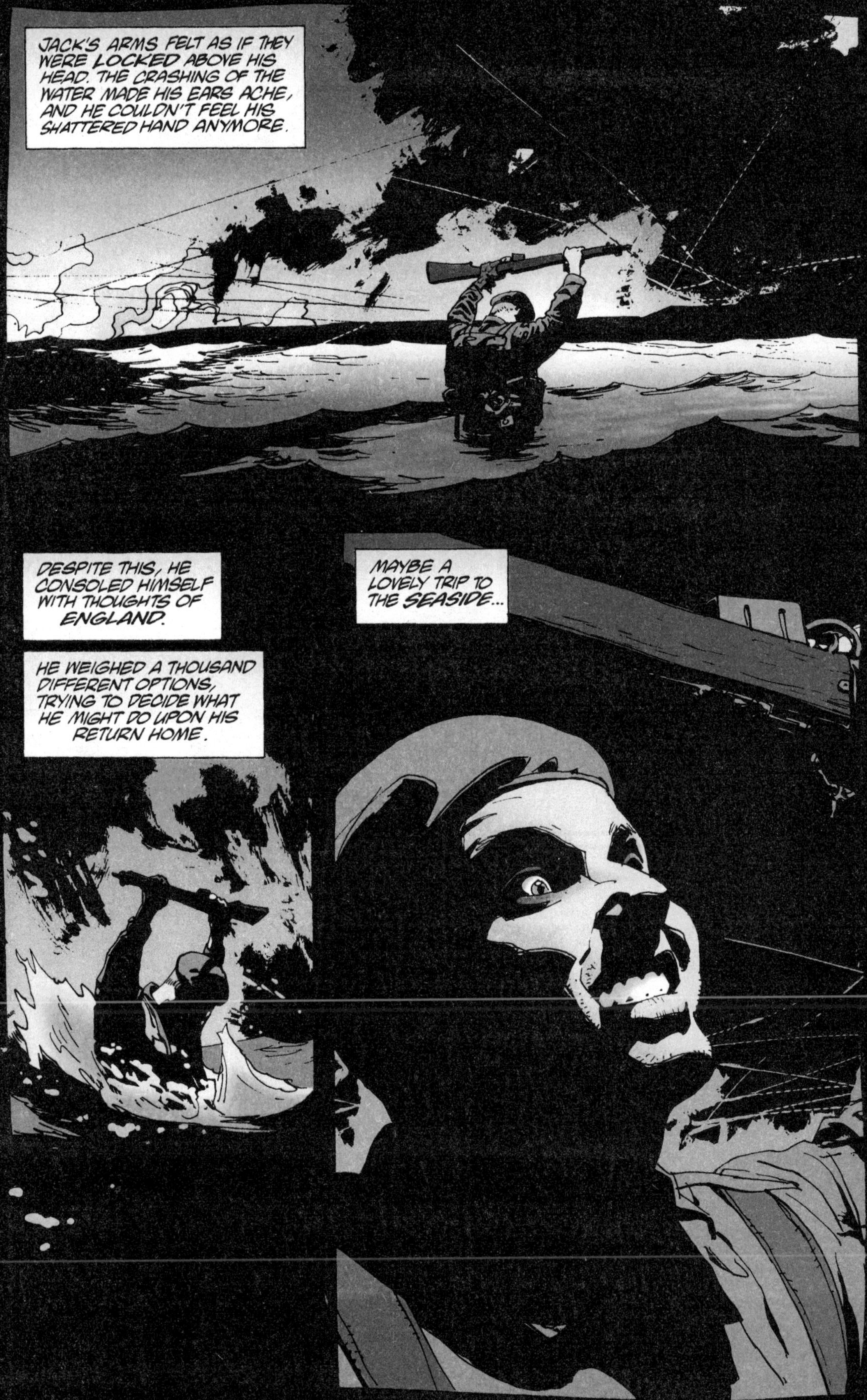
JACK'S ARMS FELT AS IF THEY WERE LOCKED ABOVE HIS HEAD. THE CRASHING OF THE WATER MADE HIS EARS ACHE, AND HE COULDN'T FEEL HIS SHATTERED HAND ANYMORE.
DESPITE THIS, HE CONSOLED HIMSELF WITH THOUGHTS OF ENGLAND.
HE WEIGHED A THOUSAND DIFFERENT OPTIONS, TRYING TO DECIDE WHAT HE MIGHT DO UPON HIS RETURN HOME.
MAYBE A LOVELY TRIP TO THE SEASIDE...

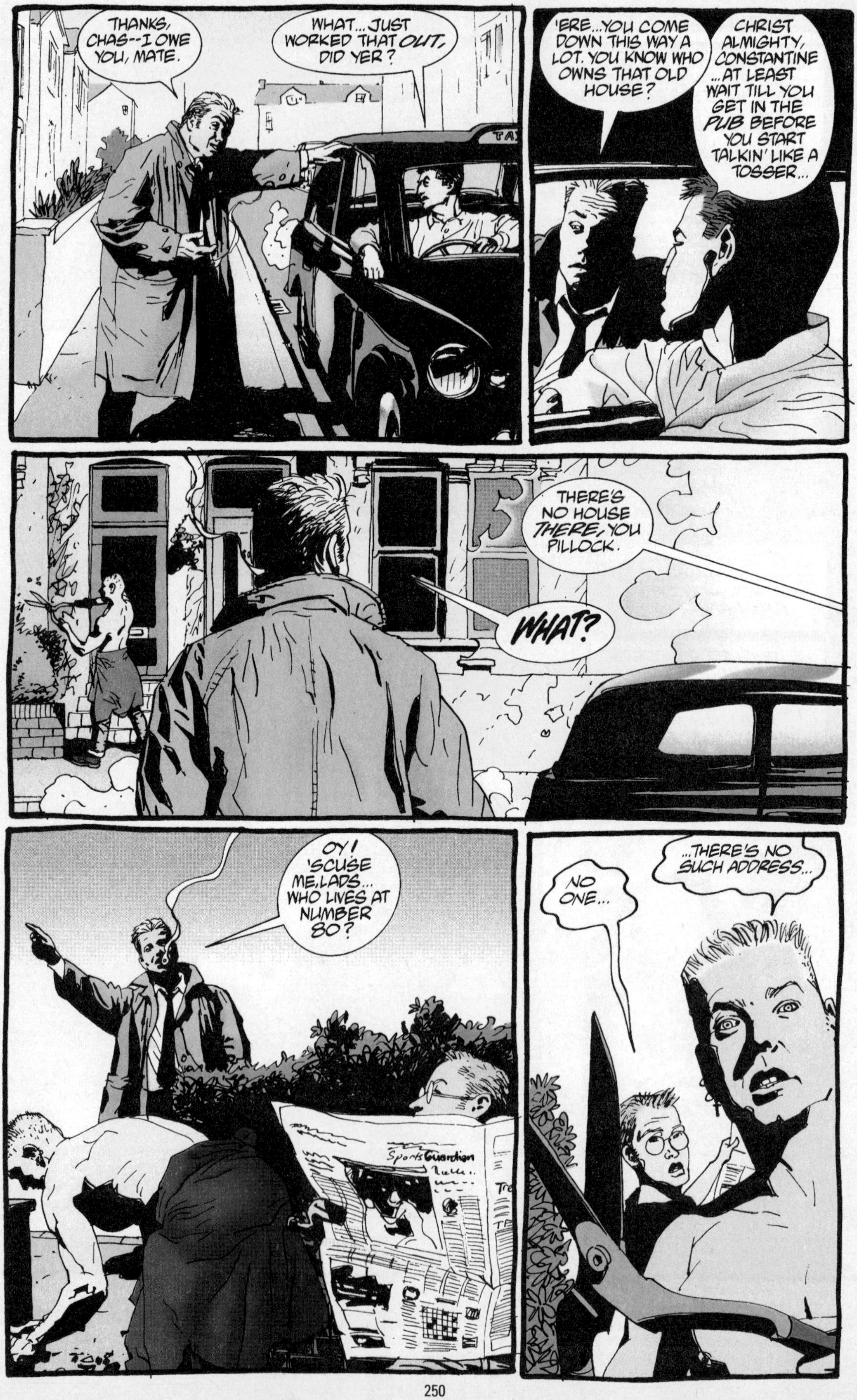
THANKS, CHAS--I OWE YOU, MATE.
WHAT... JUST WORKED THAT OUT, DID YER?
'ERE...YOU COME DOWN THIS WAY A LOT. YOU KNOW WHO OWNS THAT OLD HOUSE?
CHRIST ALMIGHTY, CONSTANTINE ...AT LEAST WAIT TILL YOU GET IN THE PUB BEFORE YOU START TALKIN' LIKE A TOSSER...
THERE'S NO HOUSE THERE, YOU PILLOCK.
WHAT?
OY! 'SCUSE ME, LADS... WHO LIVES AT NUMBER 80?
NO ONE...
...THERE'S NO SUCH ADDRESS...

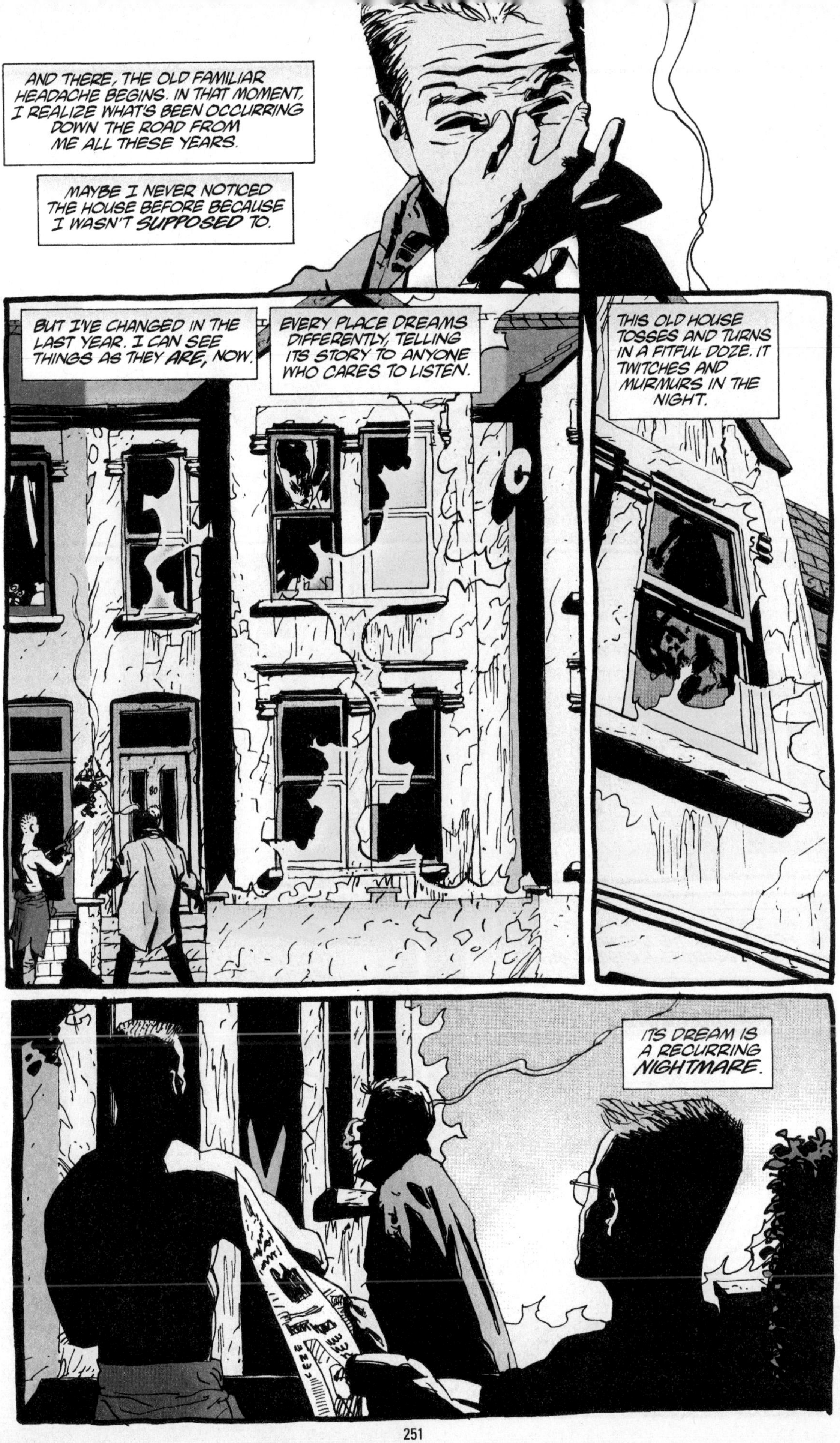
AND THERE, THE OLD FAMILIAR HEADACHE BEGINS. IN THAT MOMENT, I REALIZE WHAT'S BEEN OCCURRING DOWN THE ROAD FROM ME ALL THESE YEARS.
MAYBE I NEVER NOTICED THE HOUSE BEFORE BECAUSE I WASN'T SUPPOSED TO.
BUT I'VE CHANGED IN THE LAST YEAR. I CAN SEE THINGS AS THEY ARE, NOW.
EVERY PLACE DREAMS DIFFERENTLY, TELLING ITS STORY TO ANYONE WHO CARES TO LISTEN.
THIS OLD HOUSE TOSSES AND TURNS IN A FITFUL DOZE. IT TWITCHES AND MURMURS IN THE NIGHT.
ITS DREAM IS A RECURRING NIGHTMARE.

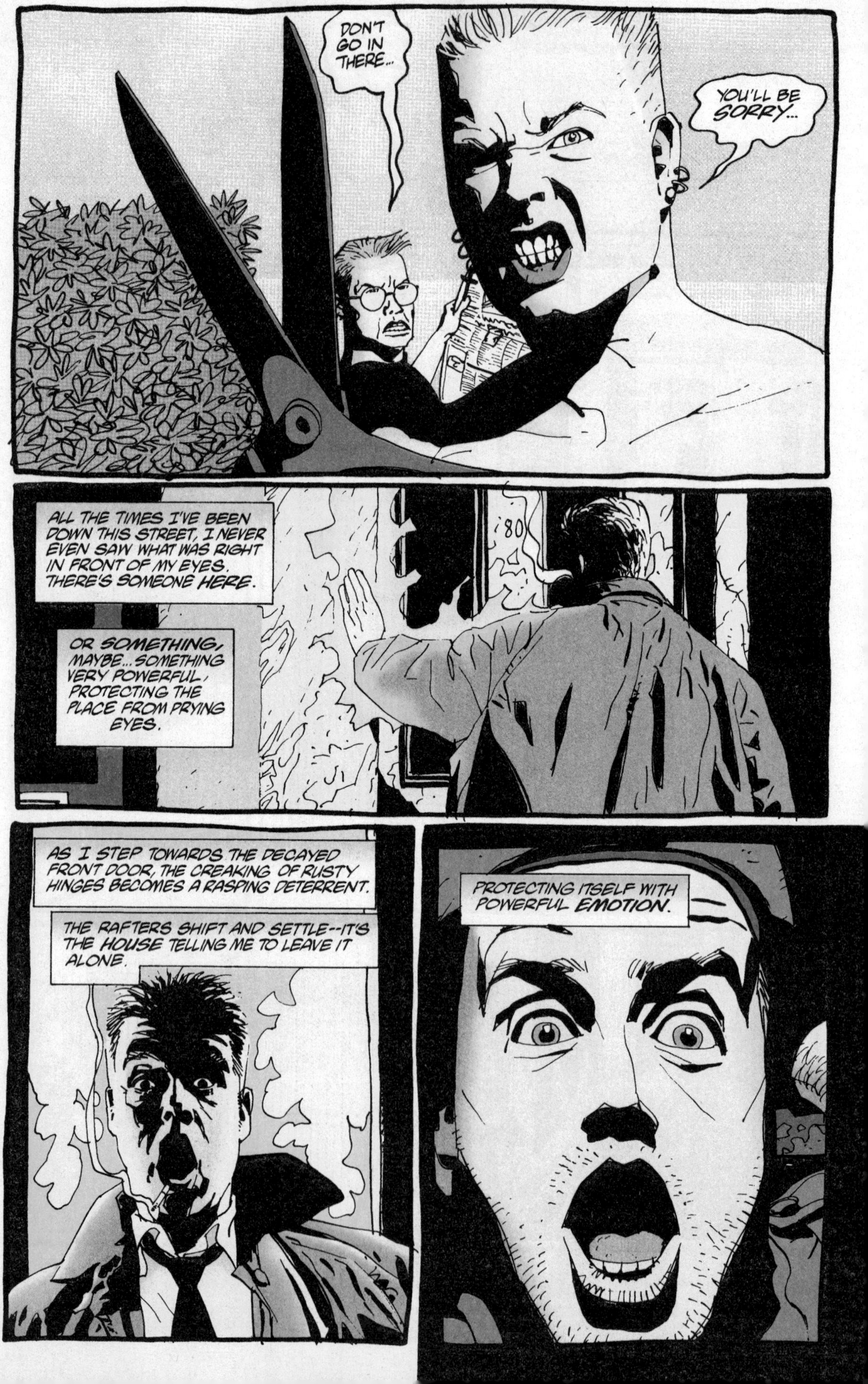
DON'T GO IN THERE...
YOU'LL BE SORRY...
ALL THE TIMES I'VE BEEN DOWN THIS STREET, I NEVER EVEN SAW WHAT WAS RIGHT IN FRONT OF MY EYES. THERE'S SOMEONE HERE.
OR SOMETHING, MAYBE... SOMETHING VERY POWERFUL, PROTECTING THE PLACE FROM PRYING EYES.
80
AS I STEP TOWARDS THE DECAYED FRONT DOOR, THE CREAKING OF RUSTY HINGES BECOMES A RASPING DETERRENT.
THE RAFTERS SHIFT AND SETTLE--IT'S THE HOUSE TELLING ME TO LEAVE IT ALONE.
PROTECTING ITSELF WITH POWERFUL EMOTION.

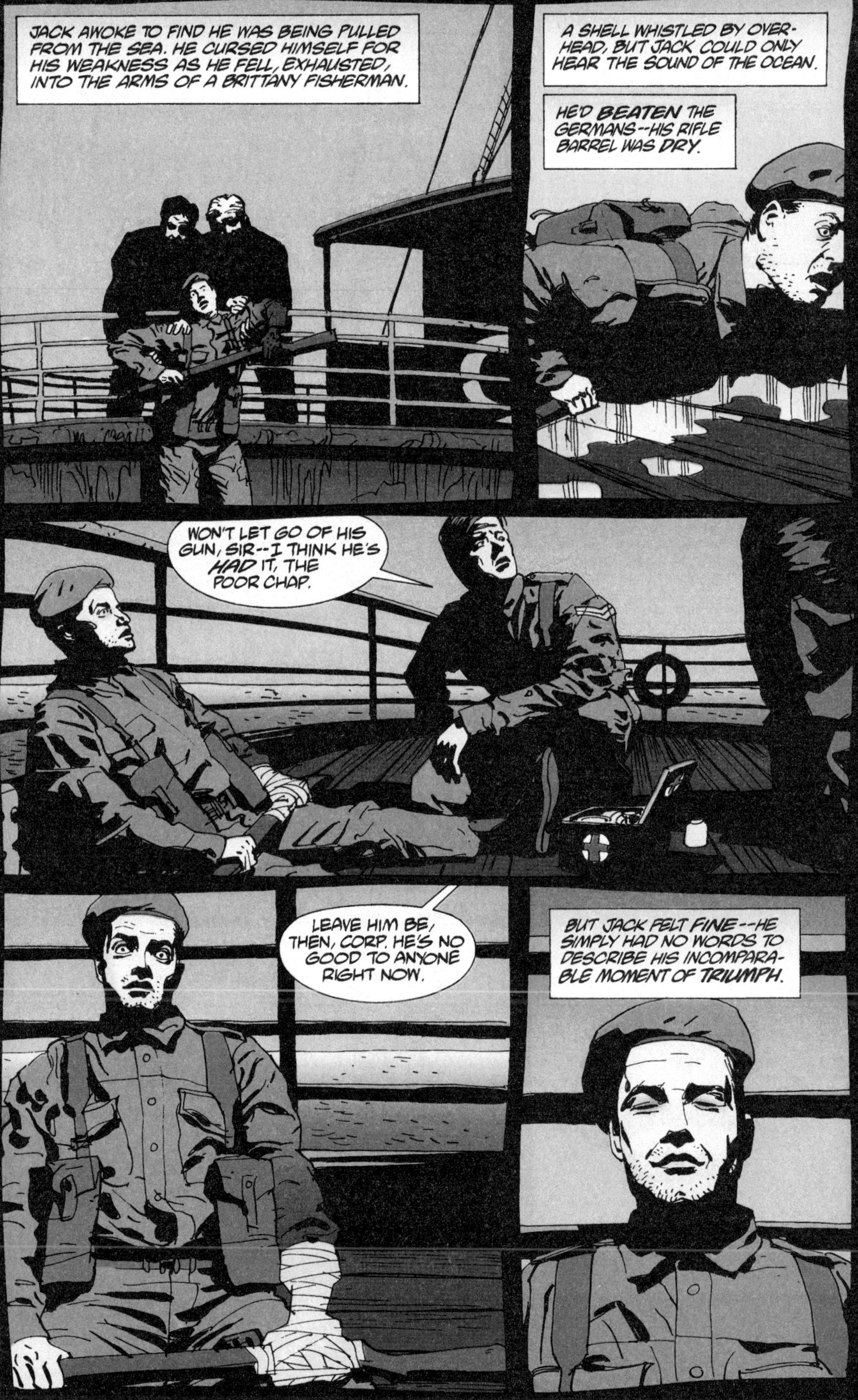
JACK AWOKE TO FIND HE WAS BEING PULLED FROM THE SEA. HE CURSED HIMSELF FOR HIS WEAKNESS AS HE FELL, EXHAUSTED, INTO THE ARMS OF A BRITTANY FISHERMAN.
A SHELL WHISTLED BY OVER-HEAD, BUT JACK COULD ONLY HEAR THE SOUND OF THE OCEAN.
HE'D BEATEN THE GERMANS--HIS RIFLE BARREL WAS DRY.
WON'T LET GO OF HIS GUN, SIR--I THINK HE'S HAD IT, THE POOR CHAP.
LEAVE HIM BE, THEN, CORP. HE'S NO GOOD TO ANYONE RIGHT NOW.
BUT JACK FELT FINE--HE SIMPLY HAD NO WORDS TO DESCRIBE HIS INCOMPARA-BLE MOMENT OF TRIUMPH.

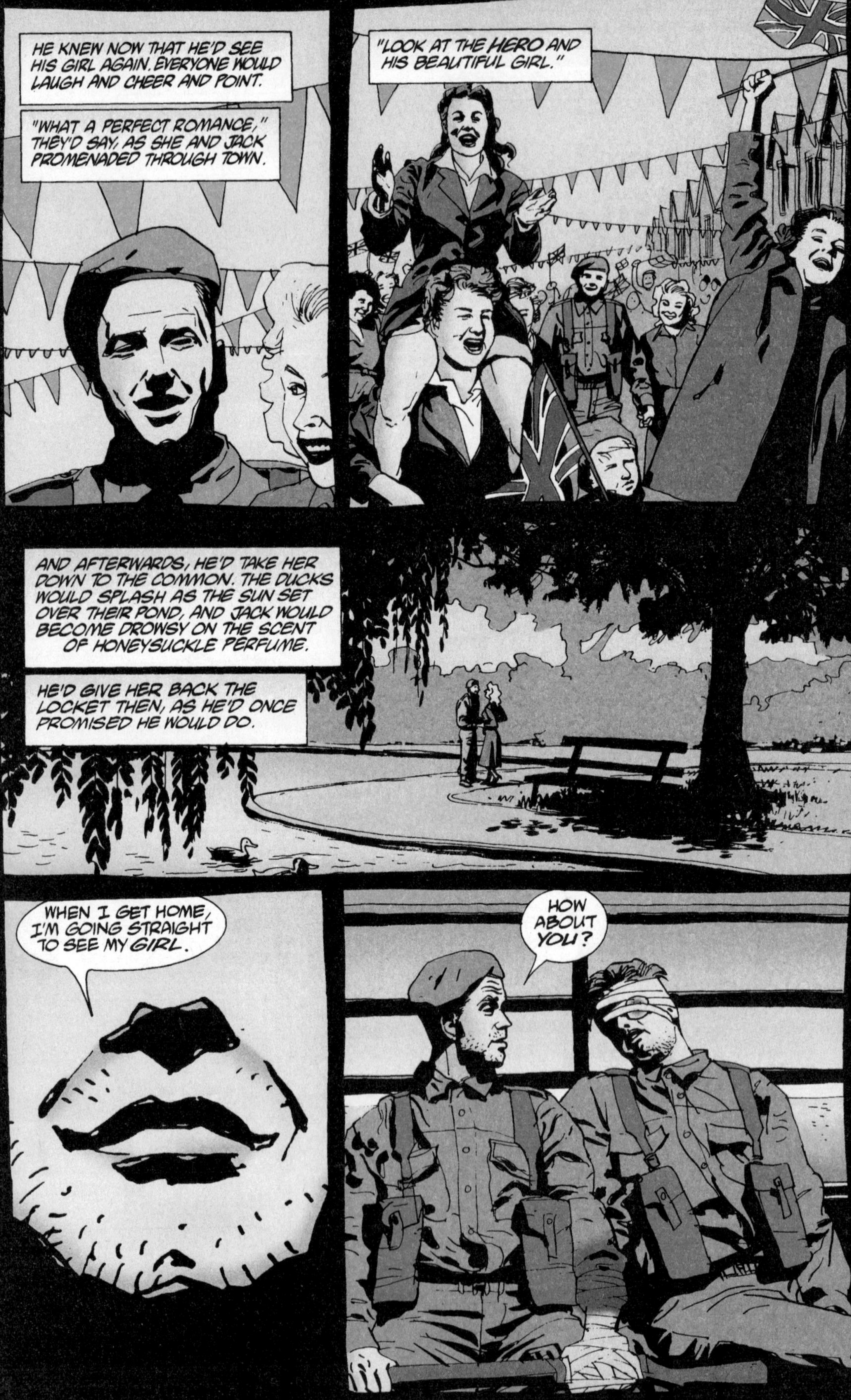
HE KNEW NOW THAT HE'D SEE HIS GIRL AGAIN. EVERYONE WOULD LAUGH AND CHEER AND POINT.
"WHAT A PERFECT ROMANCE," THEY'D SAY, AS SHE AND JACK PROMENADED THROUGH TOWN.
"LOOK AT THE HERO AND HIS BEAUTIFUL GIRL."
AND AFTERWARDS, HE'D TAKE HER DOWN TO THE COMMON. THE DUCKS WOULD SPLASH AS THE SUN SET OVER THEIR POND, AND JACK WOULD BECOME DROWSY ON THE SCENT OF HONEYSUCKLE PERFUME.
HE'D GIVE HER BACK THE LOCKET THEN, AS HE'D ONCE PROMISED HE WOULD DO.
WHEN I GET HOME, I'M GOING STRAIGHT TO SEE MY GIRL.
HOW ABOUT YOU?

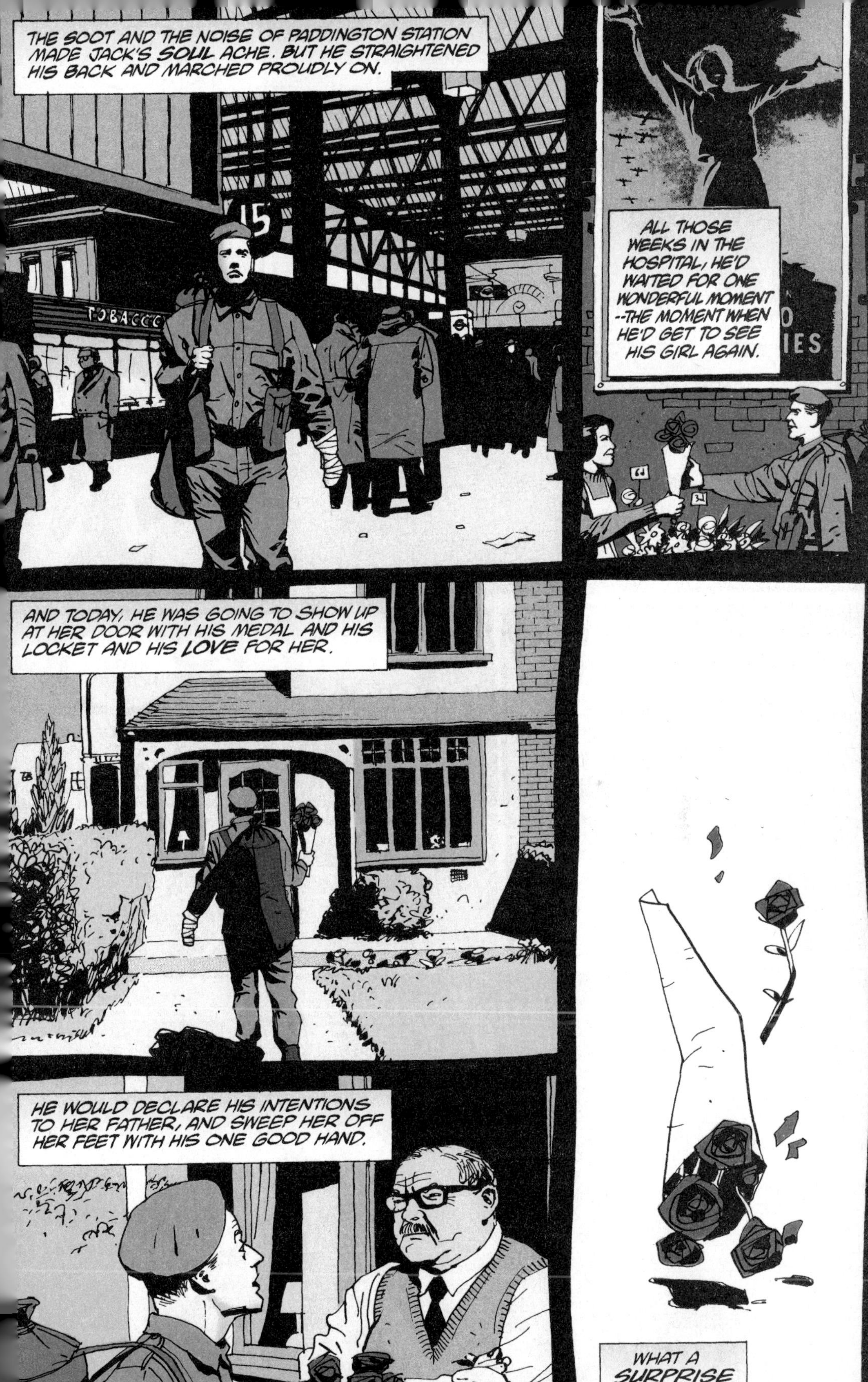
THE SOOT AND THE NOISE OF PADDINGTON STATION MADE JACK'S SOUL ACHE. BUT HE STRAIGHTENED HIS BACK AND MARCHED PROUDLY ON.
15
TOBACCO
ALL THOSE WEEKS IN THE HOSPITAL, HE'D WAITED FOR ONE WONDERFUL MOMENT --THE MOMENT WHEN HE'D GET TO SEE HIS GIRL AGAIN.
AND TODAY, HE WAS GOING TO SHOW UP AT HER DOOR WITH HIS MEDAL AND HIS LOCKET AND HIS LOVE FOR HER.
HE WOULD DECLARE HIS INTENTIONS TO HER FATHER, AND SWEEP HER OFF HER FEET WITH HIS ONE GOOD HAND.
WHAT A SURPRISE IT WOULD BE...

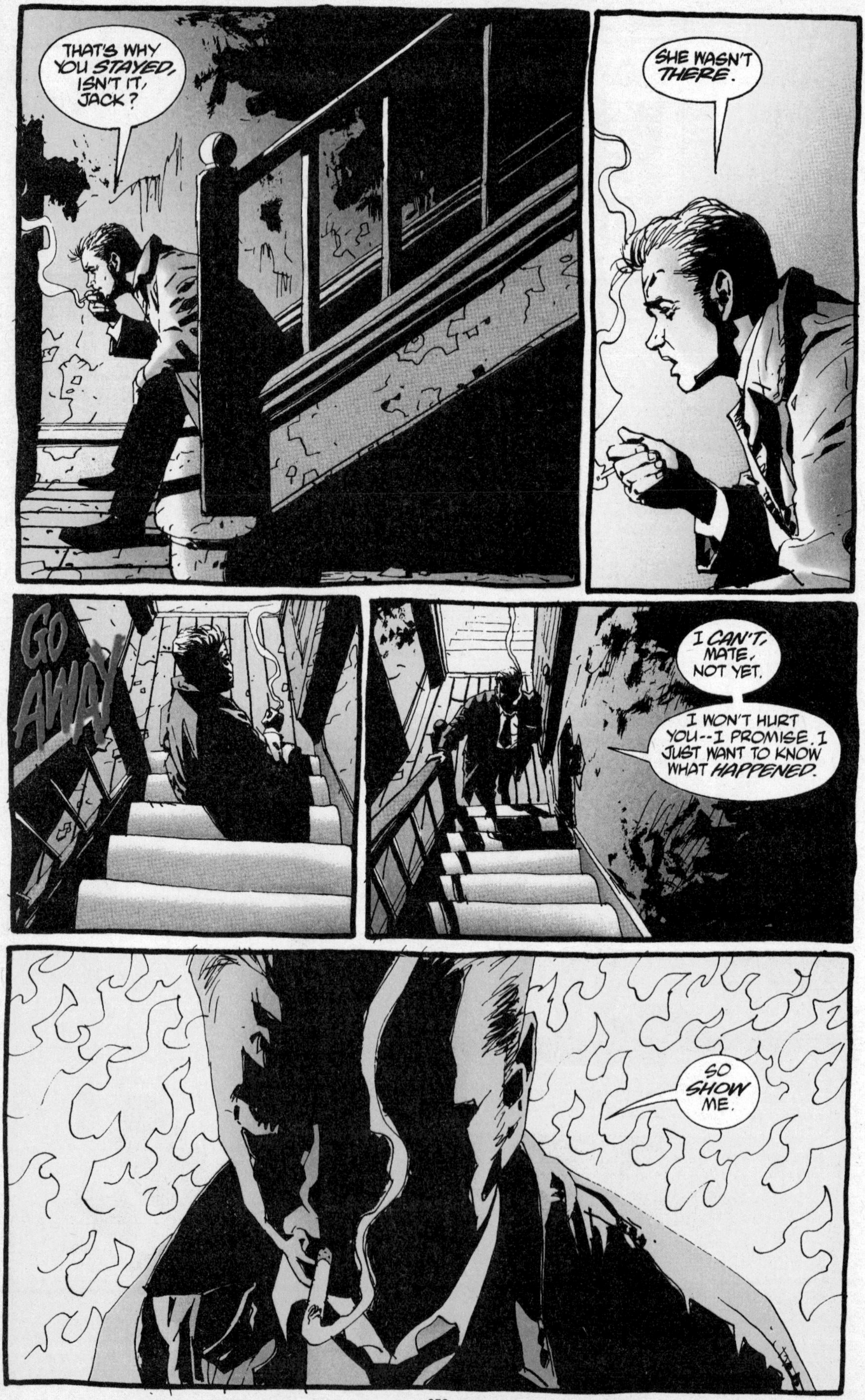
THAT'S WHY YOU STAYED, ISN'T IT, JACK?
SHE WASN'T THERE.
GO AWAY
I CAN'T, MATE, NOT YET.
I WON'T HURT YOU--I PROMISE. I JUST WANT TO KNOW WHAT HAPPENED.
SO SHOW ME.

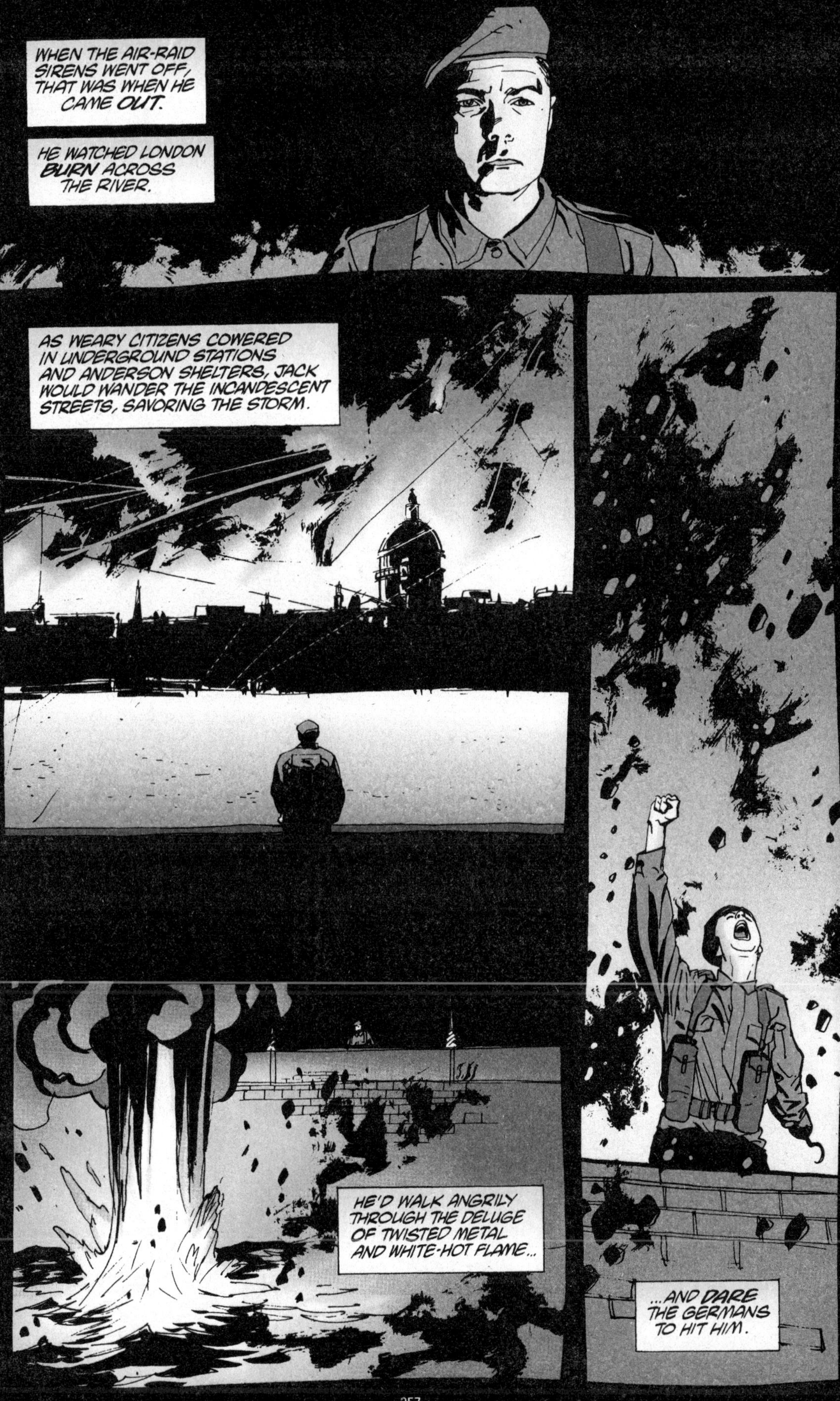

WHEN THE AIR-RAID SIRENS WENT OFF, THAT WAS WHEN HE CAME OUT.
HE WATCHED LONDON BURN ACROSS THE RIVER.
AS WEARY CITIZENS COWERED IN UNDERGROUND STATIONS AND ANDERSON SHELTERS, JACK WOULD WANDER THE INCANDESCENT STREETS, SAVORING THE STORM.
HE'D WALK ANGRILY THROUGH THE DELUGE OF TWISTED METAL AND WHITE-HOT FLAME...
...AND DARE THE GERMANS TO HIT HIM.

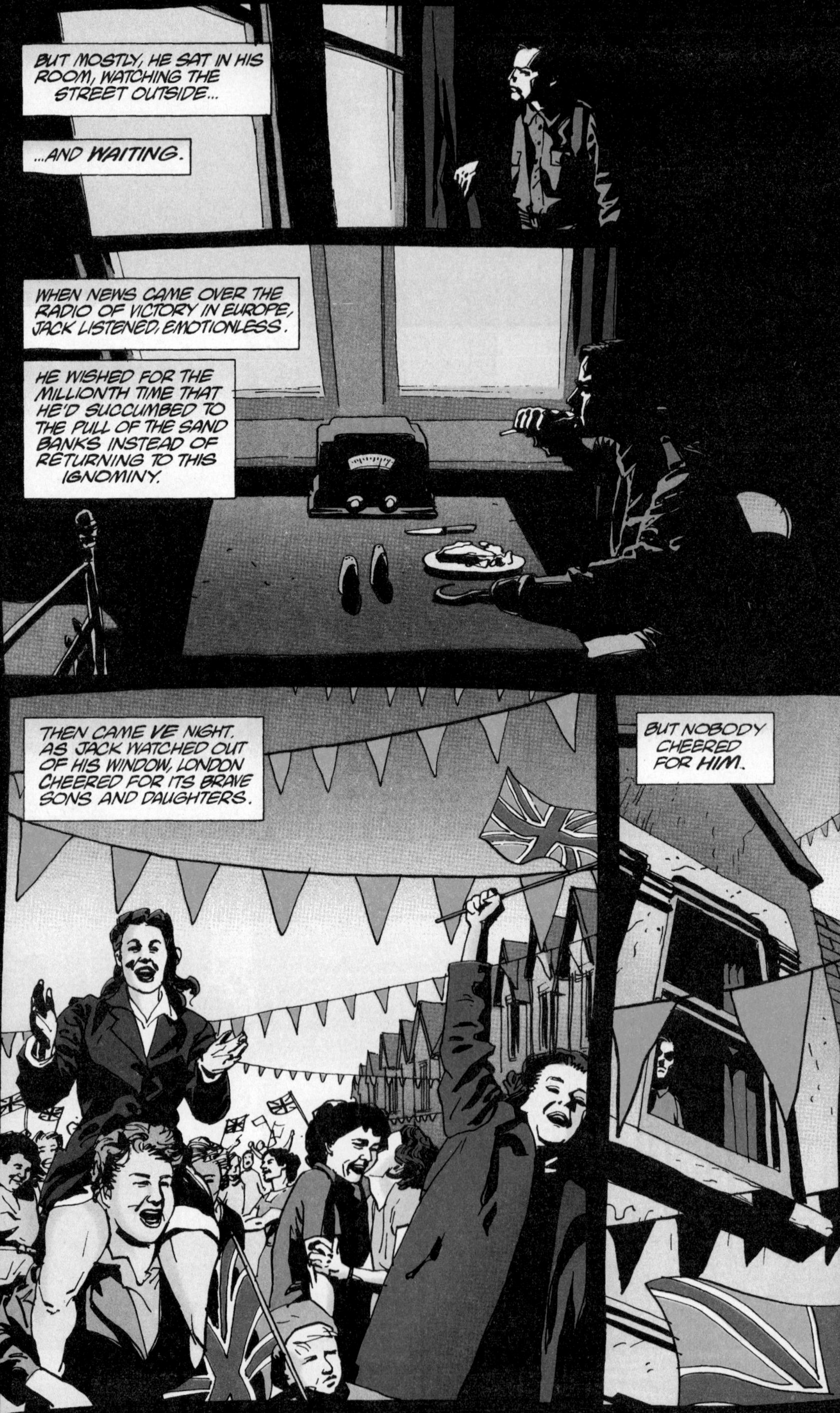
BUT MOSTLY, HE SAT IN HIS ROOM, WATCHING THE STREET OUTSIDE...
...AND WAITING.
WHEN NEWS CAME OVER THE RADIO OF VICTORY IN EUROPE, JACK LISTENED, EMOTIONLESS.
HE WISHED FOR THE MILLIONTH TIME THAT HE'D SUCCUMBED TO THE PULL OF THE SAND BANKS INSTEAD OF RETURNING TO THIS IGNOMINY.
THEN CAME VE NIGHT. AS JACK WATCHED OUT OF HIS WINDOW, LONDON CHEERED FOR ITS BRAVE SONS AND DAUGHTERS.
BUT NOBODY CHEERED FOR HIM.

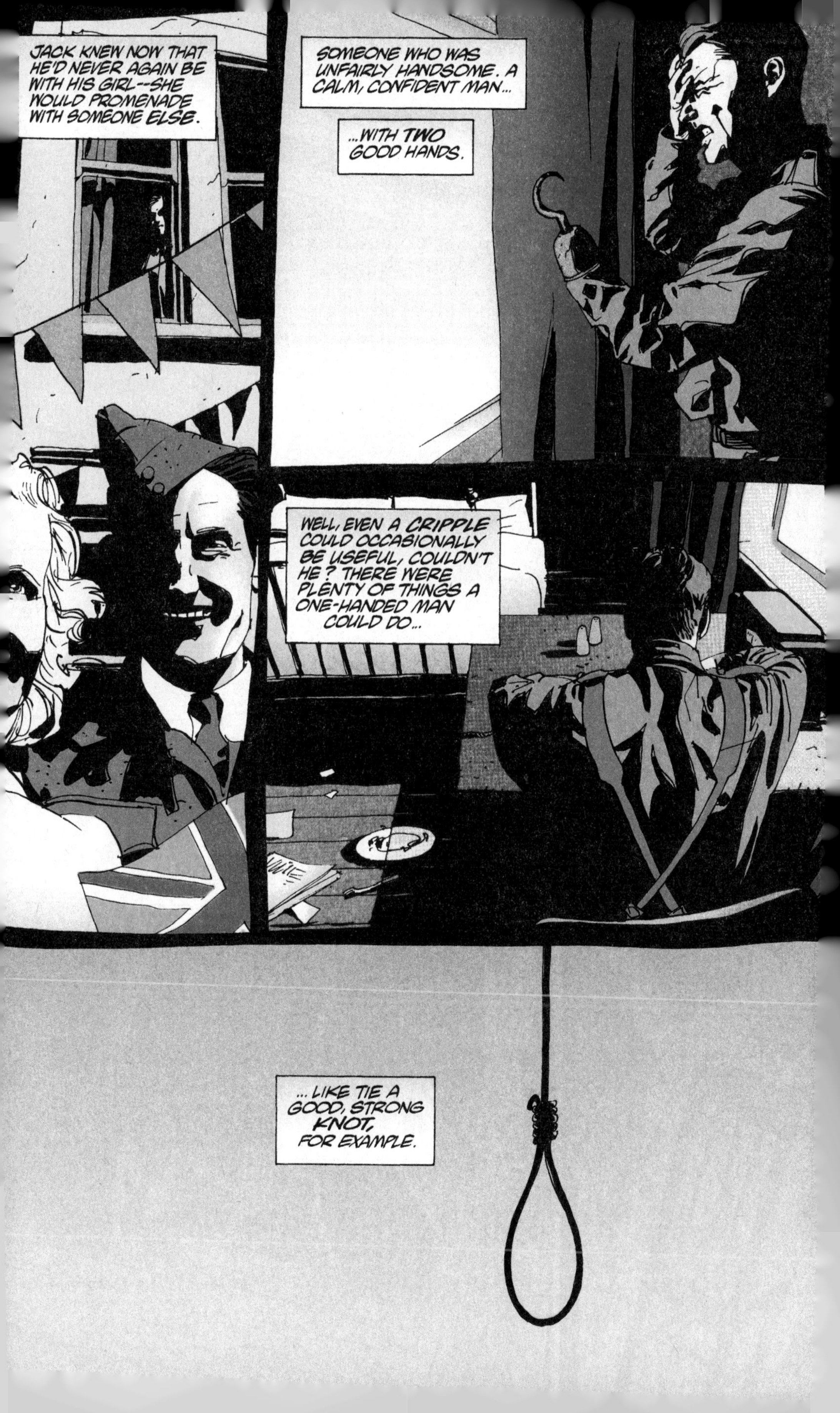
JACK KNEW NOW THAT HE'D NEVER AGAIN BE WITH HIS GIRL--SHE WOULD PROMENADE WITH SOMEONE ELSE.
SOMEONE WHO WAS UNFAIRLY HANDSOME. A CALM, CONFIDENT MAN...
...WITH TWO GOOD HANDS.
WELL, EVEN A CRIPPLE COULD OCCASIONALLY BE USEFUL, COULDN'T HE? THERE WERE PLENTY OF THINGS A ONE-HANDED MAN COULD DO...
...LIKE TIE A GOOD, STRONG KNOT, FOR EXAMPLE.

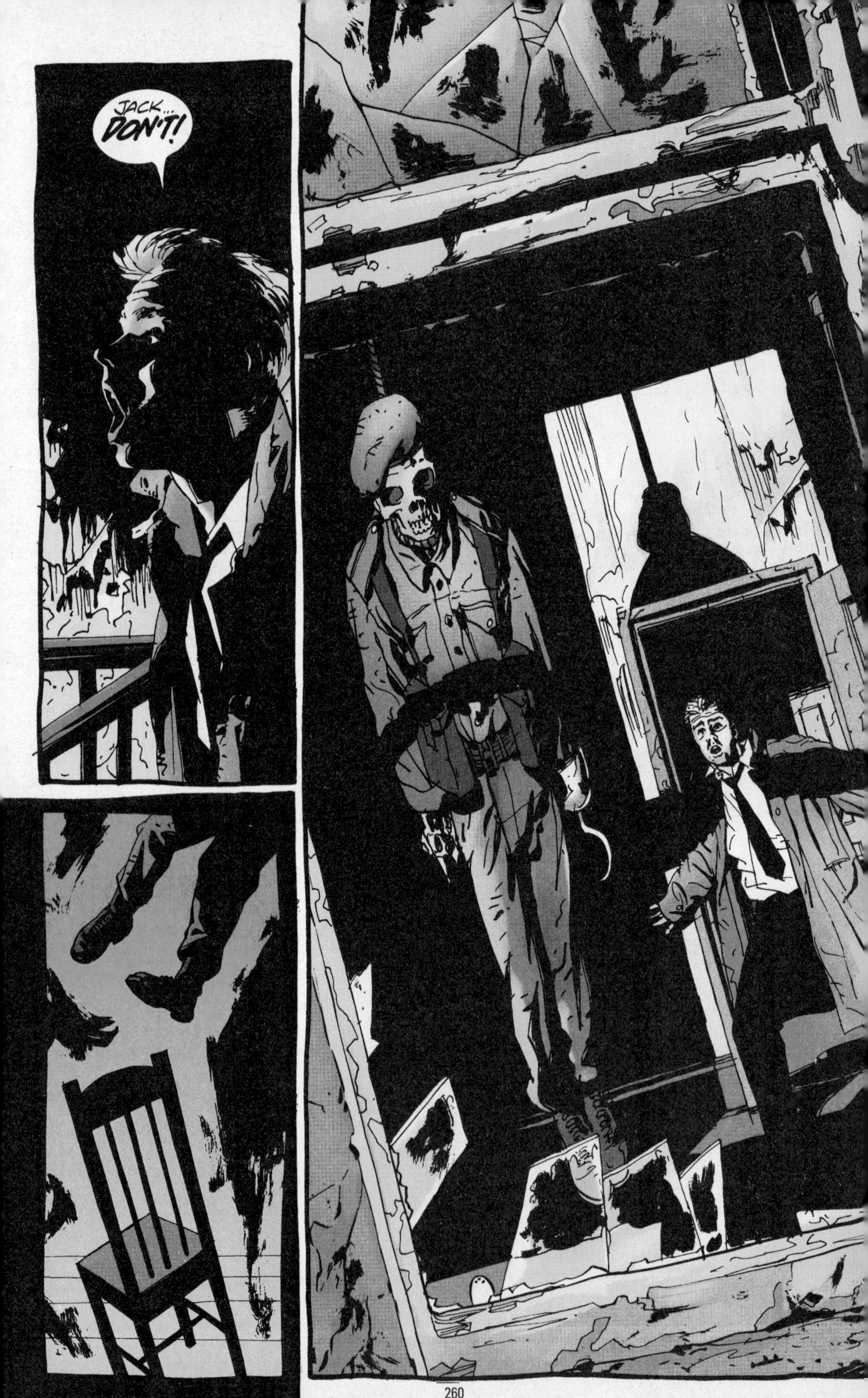
JACK... DON'T!

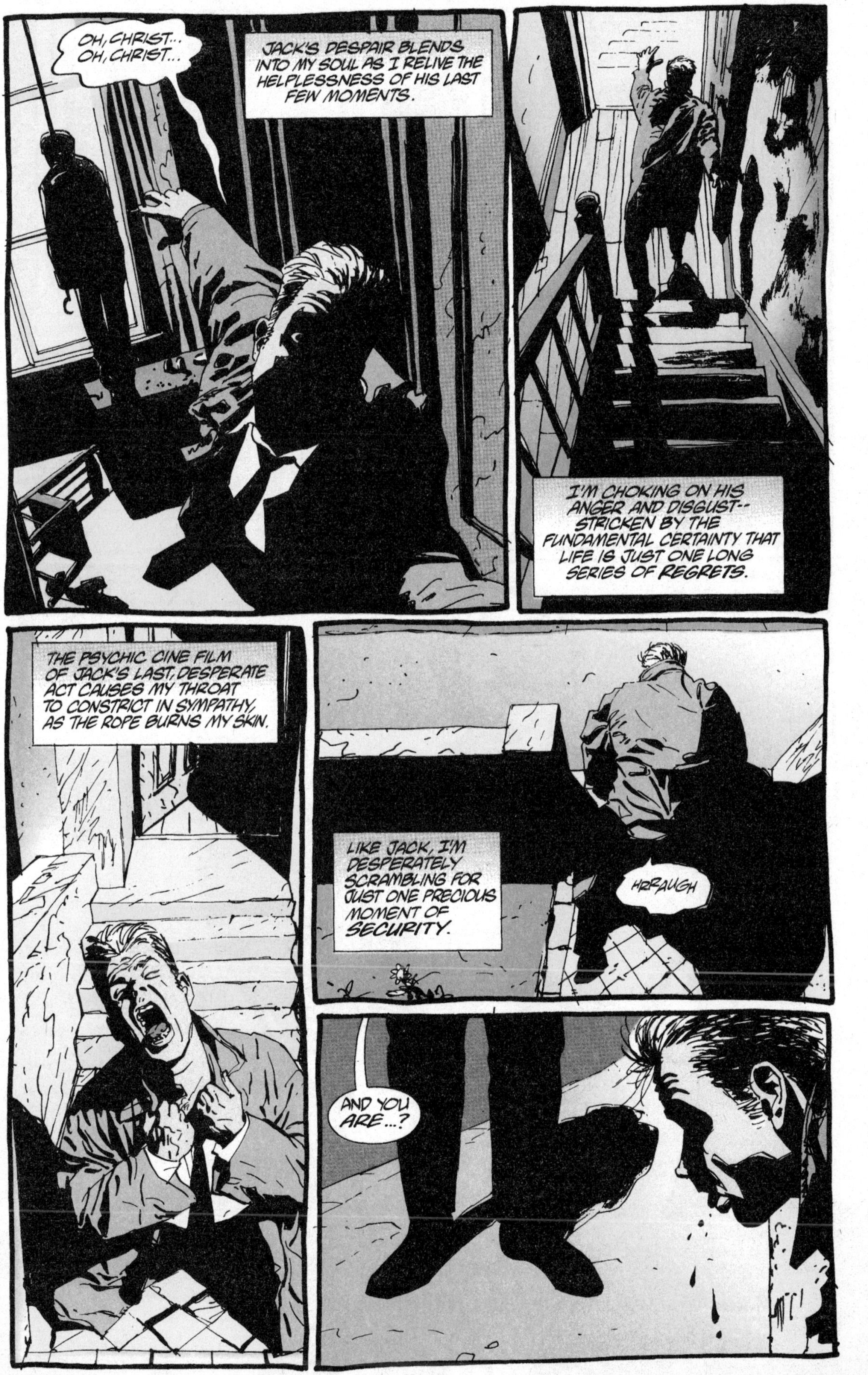
OH, CHRIST...
OH, CHRIST...
JACK'S DESPAIR BLENDS INTO MY SOUL AS I RELIVE THE HELPLESSNESS OF HIS LAST FEW MOMENTS.
I'M CHOKING ON HIS ANGER AND DISGUST--STRICKEN BY THE FUNDAMENTAL CERTAINTY THAT LIFE IS JUST ONE LONG SERIES OF REGRETS.
THE PSYCHIC CINE FILM OF JACK'S LAST, DESPERATE ACT CAUSES MY THROAT TO CONSTRICT IN SYMPATHY, AS THE ROPE BURNS MY SKIN.
LIKE JACK, I'M DESPERATELY SCRAMBLING FOR JUST ONE PRECIOUS MOMENT OF SECURITY.
HRRAUGH
AND YOU ARE...?

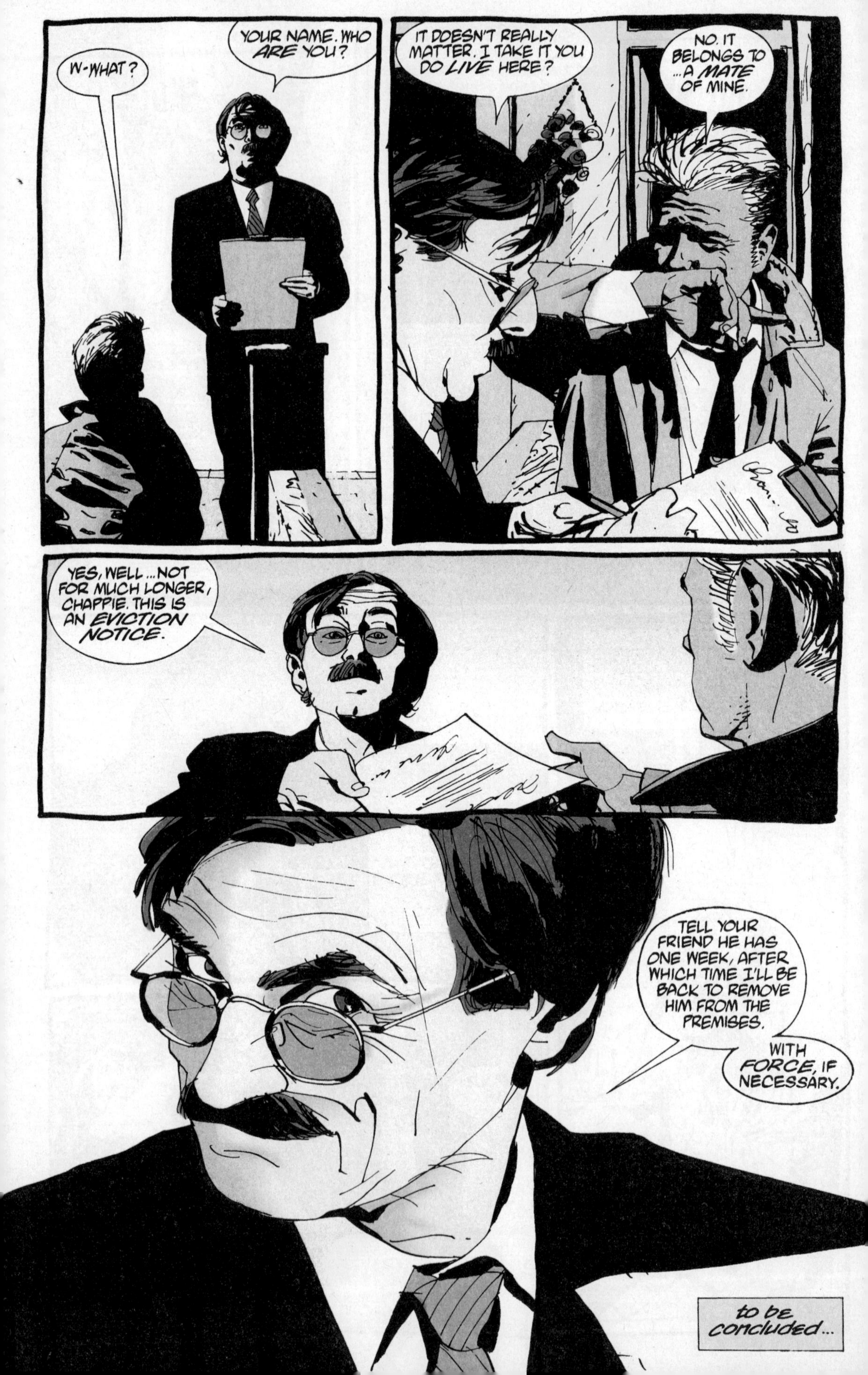
W-WHAT?
YOUR NAME. WHO ARE YOU?
IT DOESN'T REALLY MATTER. I TAKE IT YOU DO LIVE HERE?
NO. IT BELONGS TO ...A MATE OF MINE.
YES, WELL ...NOT FOR MUCH LONGER, CHAPPIE. THIS IS AN EVICTION NOTICE.
TELL YOUR FRIEND HE HAS ONE WEEK, AFTER WHICH TIME I'LL BE BACK TO REMOVE HIM FROM THE PREMISES.
WITH FORCE, IF NECESSARY.
to be concluded...

JOHN CONSTANTINE
HELLBLAZER
IN THE LINE OF FIRE
PART TWO OF TWO
PAUL JENKINS
SEAN PHILLIPS
Sean '96

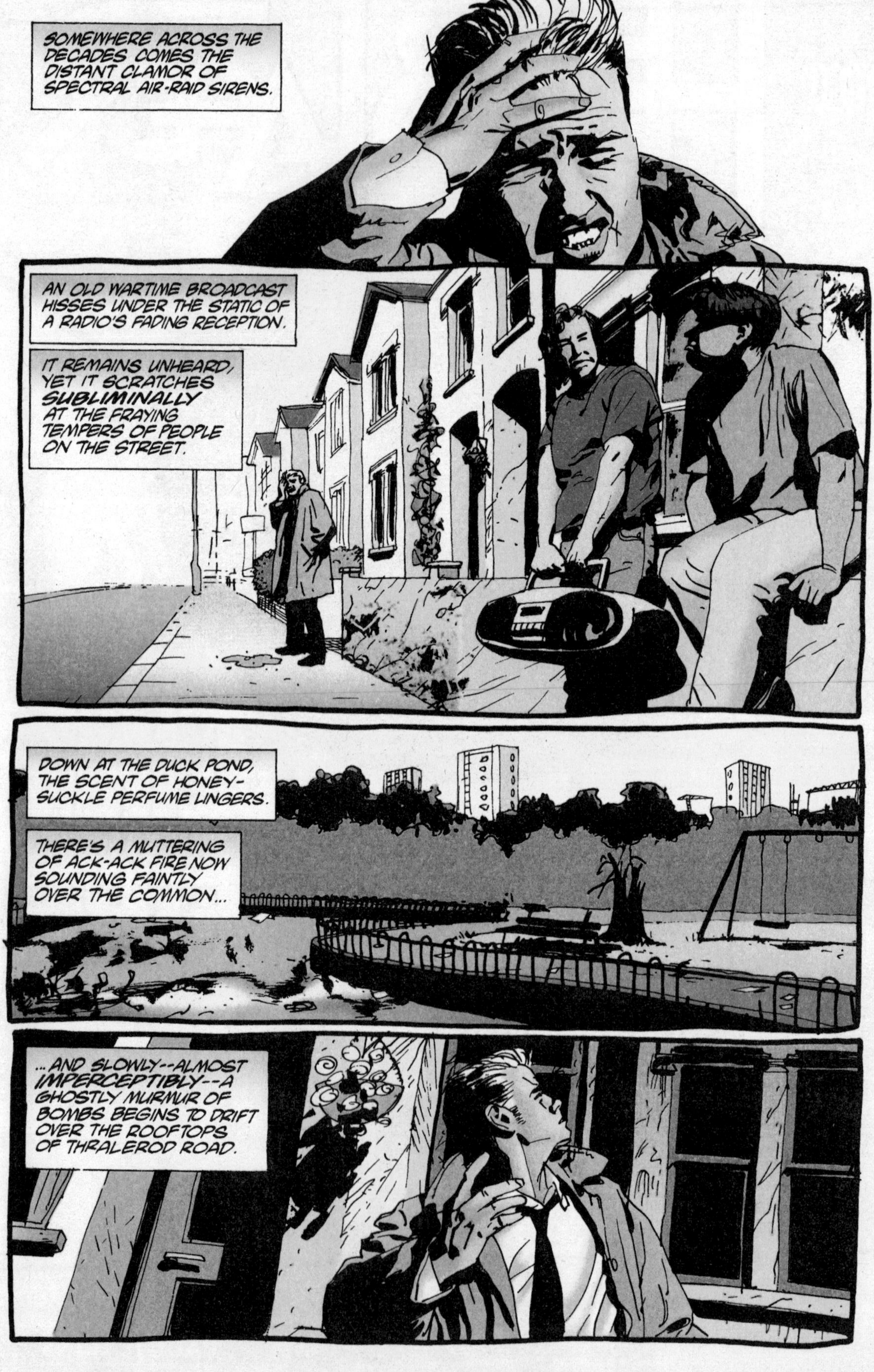
SOMEWHERE ACROSS THE DECADES COMES THE DISTANT CLAMOR OF SPECTRAL AIR-RAID SIRENS.
AN OLD WARTIME BROADCAST HISSES UNDER THE STATIC OF A RADIO'S FADING RECEPTION.
IT REMAINS UNHEARD, YET IT SCRATCHES SUBLIMINALLY AT THE FRAYING TEMPERS OF PEOPLE ON THE STREET.
DOWN AT THE DUCK POND, THE SCENT OF HONEY-SUCKLE PERFUME LINGERS.
THERE'S A MUTTERING OF ACK-ACK FIRE NOW SOUNDING FAINTLY OVER THE COMMON...
...AND SLOWLY--ALMOST IMPERCEPTIBLY--A GHOSTLY MURMUR OF BOMBS BEGINS TO DRIFT OVER THE ROOFTOPS OF THRALEROD ROAD.

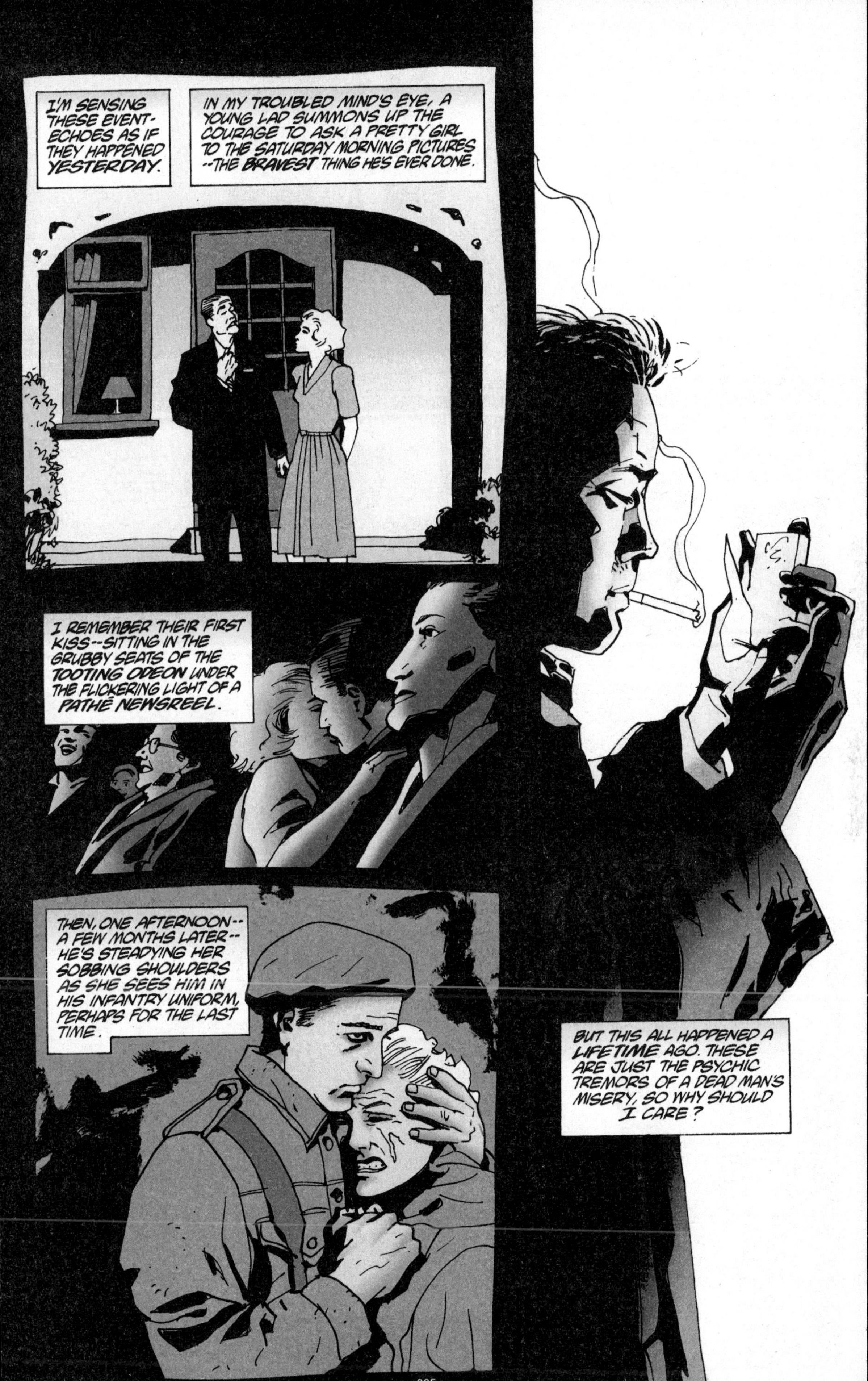
I'M SENSING THESE EVENT-ECHOES AS IF THEY HAPPENED YESTERDAY.
IN MY TROUBLED MIND'S EYE, A YOUNG LAD SUMMONS UP THE COURAGE TO ASK A PRETTY GIRL TO THE SATURDAY MORNING PICTURES --THE BRAVEST THING HE'S EVER DONE.
I REMEMBER THEIR FIRST KISS--SITTING IN THE GRUBBY SEATS OF THE TOOTING ODEON UNDER THE FLICKERING LIGHT OF A PATHÉ NEWSREEL.
THEN, ONE AFTERNOON-- A FEW MONTHS LATER-- HE'S STEADYING HER SOBBING SHOULDERS AS SHE SEES HIM IN HIS INFANTRY UNIFORM, PERHAPS FOR THE LAST TIME.
BUT THIS ALL HAPPENED A LIFETIME AGO. THESE ARE JUST THE PSYCHIC TREMORS OF A DEAD MAN'S MISERY, SO WHY SHOULD I CARE?

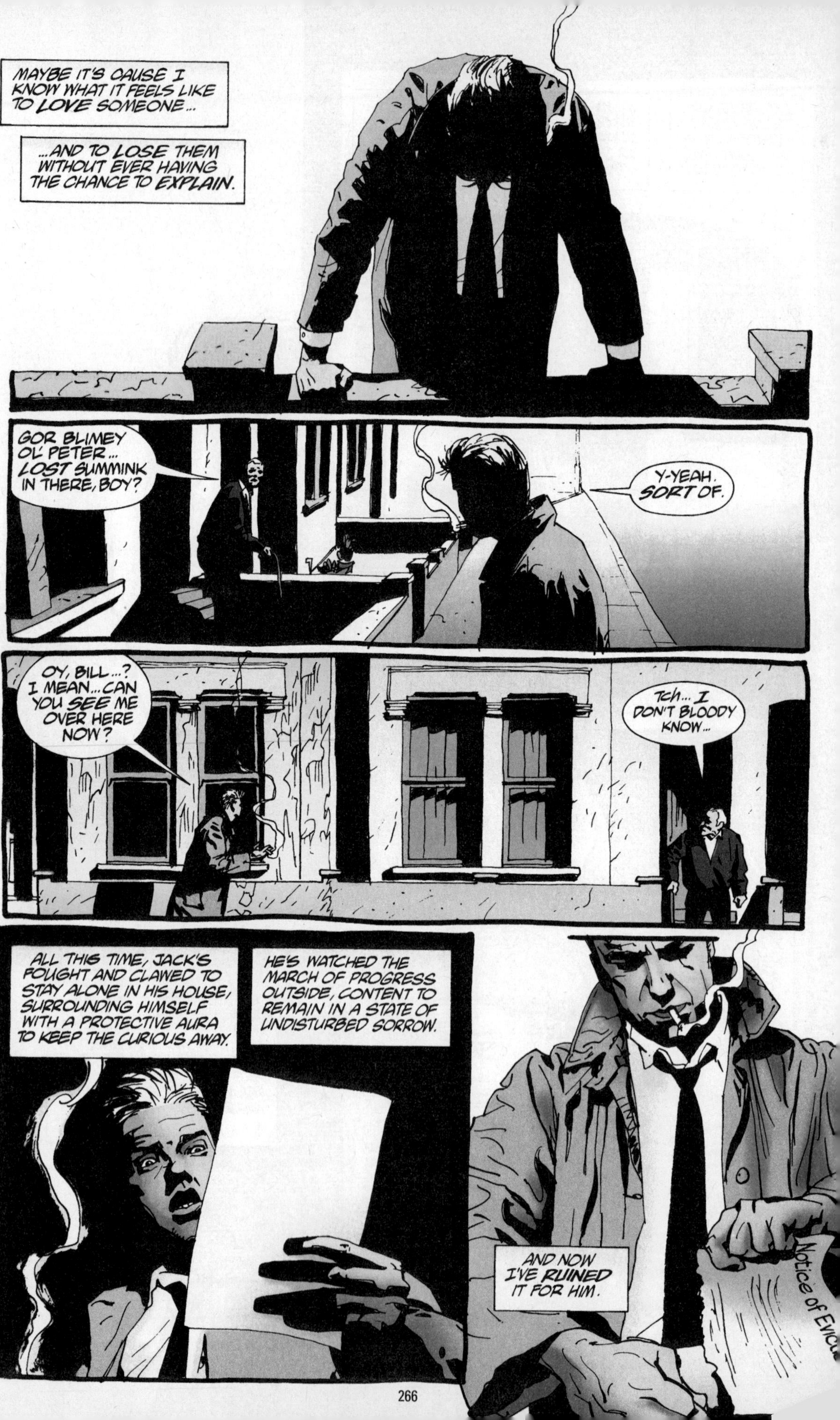
MAYBE IT'S CAUSE I KNOW WHAT IT FEELS LIKE TO LOVE SOMEONE...
...AND TO LOSE THEM WITHOUT EVER HAVING THE CHANCE TO EXPLAIN.
GOR BLIMEY OL' PETER... LOST SUMMINK IN THERE, BOY?
Y-YEAH. SORT OF.
OY, BILL...? I MEAN...CAN YOU SEE ME OVER HERE NOW?
Tch... I DON'T BLOODY KNOW...
ALL THIS TIME, JACK'S FOUGHT AND CLAWED TO STAY ALONE IN HIS HOUSE, SURROUNDING HIMSELF WITH A PROTECTIVE AURA TO KEEP THE CURIOUS AWAY.
HE'S WATCHED THE MARCH OF PROGRESS OUTSIDE, CONTENT TO REMAIN IN A STATE OF UNDISTURBED SORROW.
AND NOW I'VE RUINED IT FOR HIM.
Notice of Evic

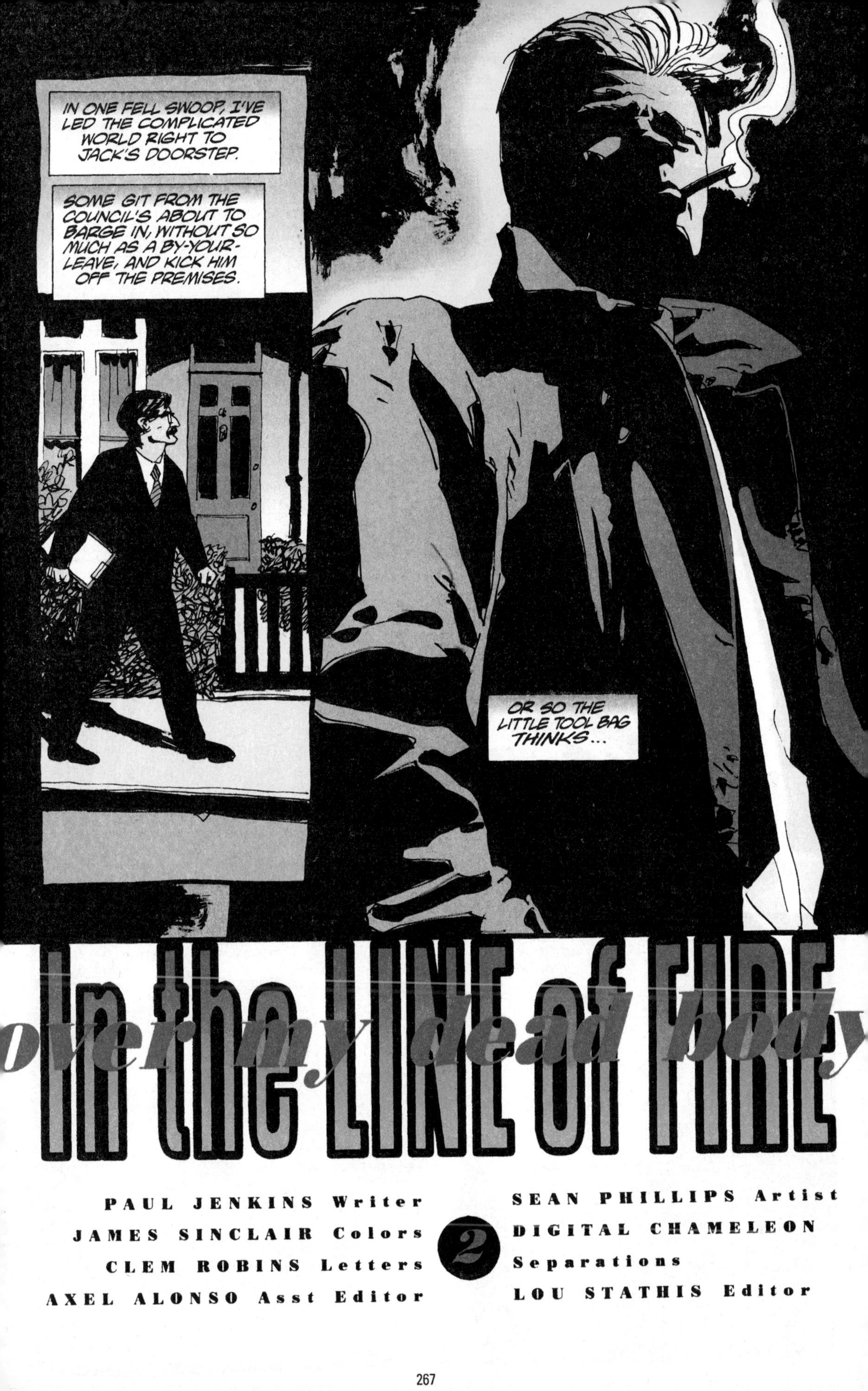
IN ONE FELL SWOOP, I'VE LED THE COMPLICATED WORLD RIGHT TO JACK'S DOORSTEP.
SOME GIT FROM THE COUNCIL'S ABOUT TO BARGE IN, WITHOUT SO MUCH AS A BY-YOUR-LEAVE, AND KICK HIM OFF THE PREMISES.
OR SO THE LITTLE TOOL BAG THINKS...

In the LINE of FIRE

over my dead body

2

PAUL JENKINS Writer
JAMES SINCLAIR Colors
CLEM ROBINS Letters
AXEL ALONSO Asst Editor
SEAN PHILLIPS Artist
DIGITAL CHAMELEON Separations
LOU STATHIS Editor

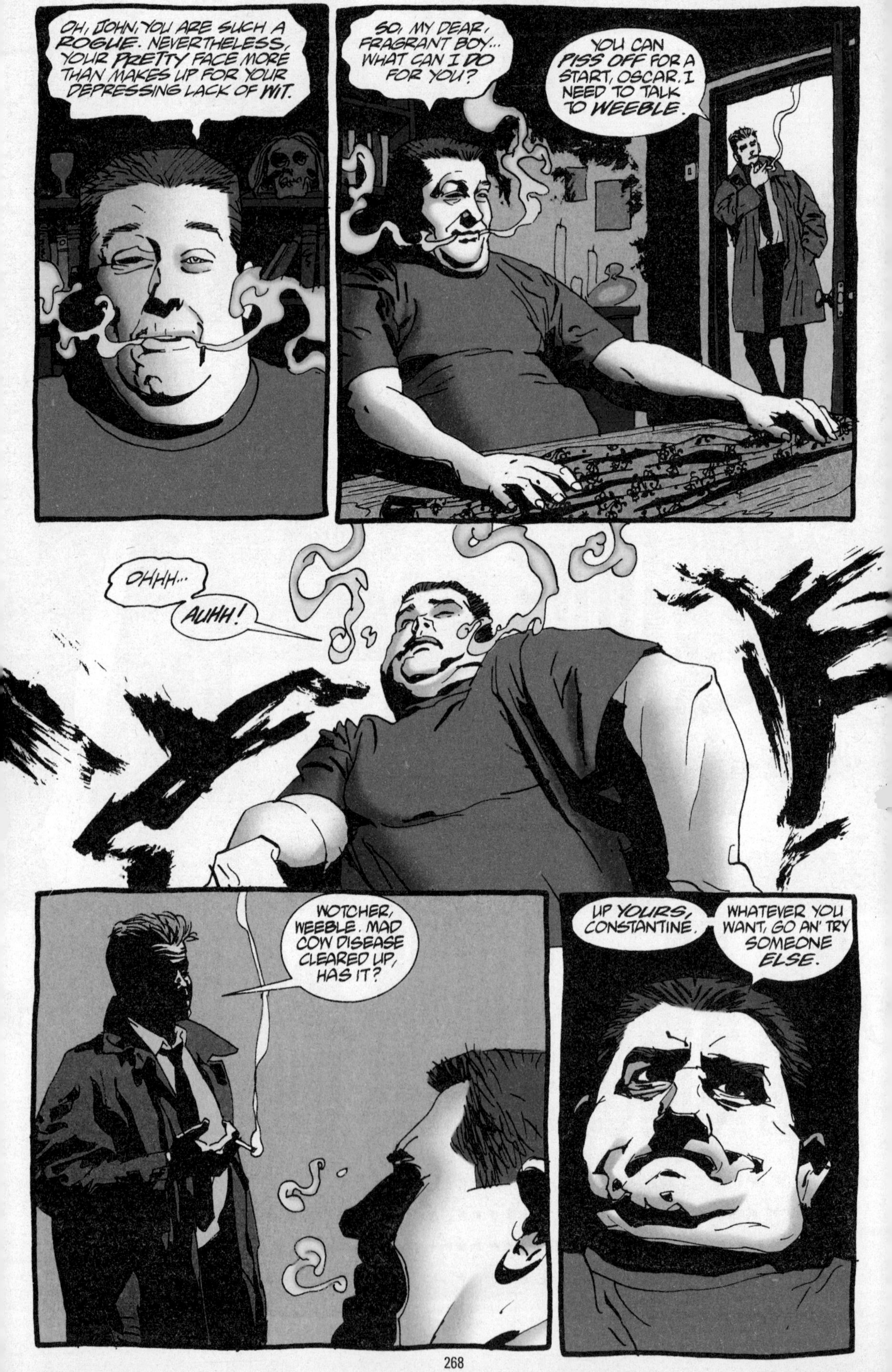

OH, JOHN, YOU ARE SUCH A ROGUE. NEVERTHELESS, YOUR PRETTY FACE MORE THAN MAKES UP FOR YOUR DEPRESSING LACK OF WIT.
SO, MY DEAR, FRAGRANT BOY... WHAT CAN I DO FOR YOU?
YOU CAN PISS OFF FOR A START, OSCAR. I NEED TO TALK TO WEEBLE.
OHHH...
AUHH!
WOTCHER, WEEBLE. MAD COW DISEASE CLEARED UP, HAS IT?
UP YOURS, CONSTANTINE.
WHATEVER YOU WANT, GO AN' TRY SOMEONE ELSE.

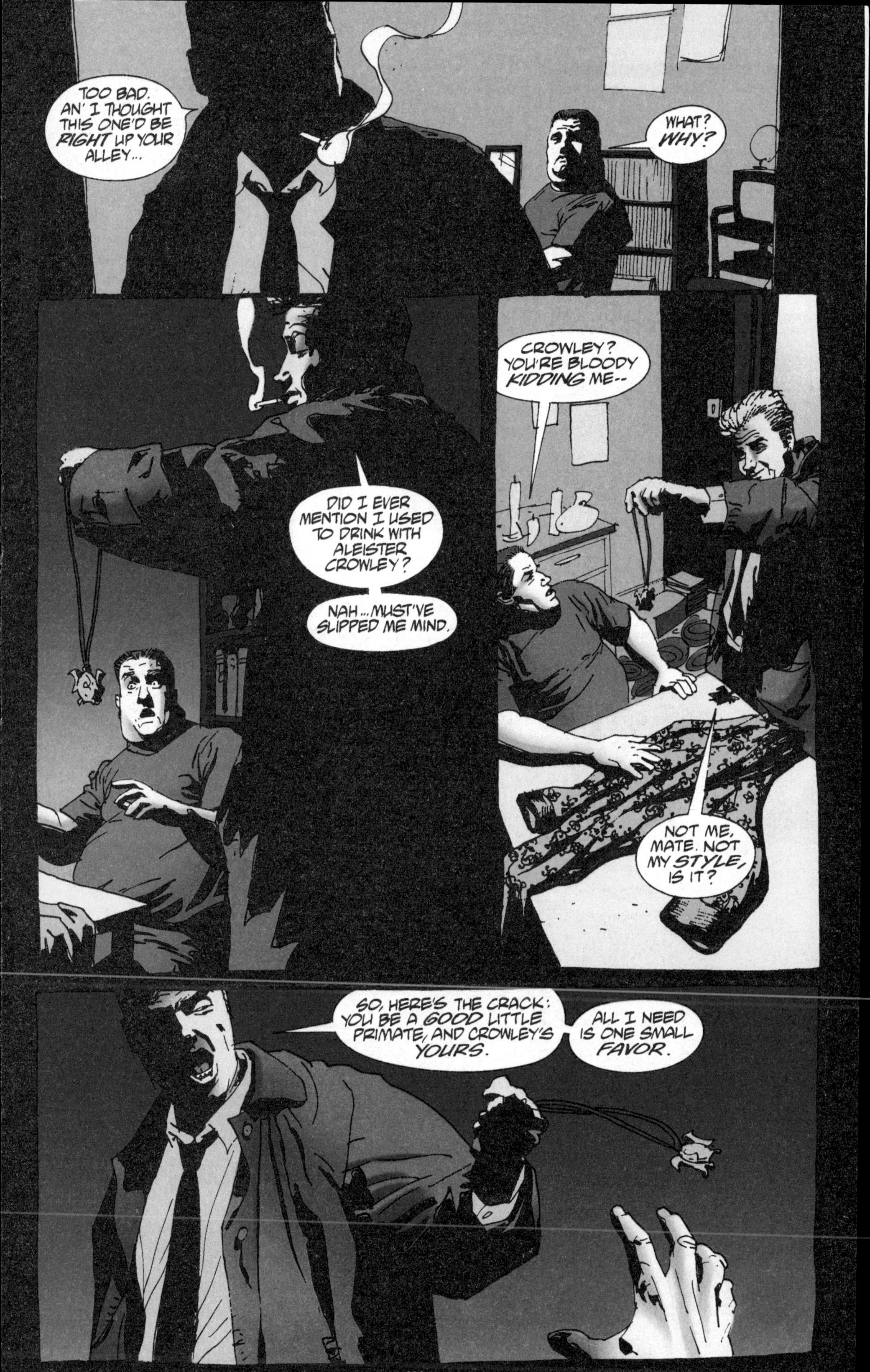
TOO BAD. AN' I THOUGHT THIS ONE'D BE RIGHT UP YOUR ALLEY...
WHAT? WHY?
DID I EVER MENTION I USED TO DRINK WITH ALEISTER CROWLEY?
NAH... MUST'VE SLIPPED ME MIND.
CROWLEY? YOU'RE BLOODY KIDDING ME--
NOT ME, MATE. NOT MY STYLE, IS IT?
SO, HERE'S THE CRACK: YOU BE A GOOD LITTLE PRIMATE, AND CROWLEY'S YOURS.
ALL I NEED IS ONE SMALL FAVOR.

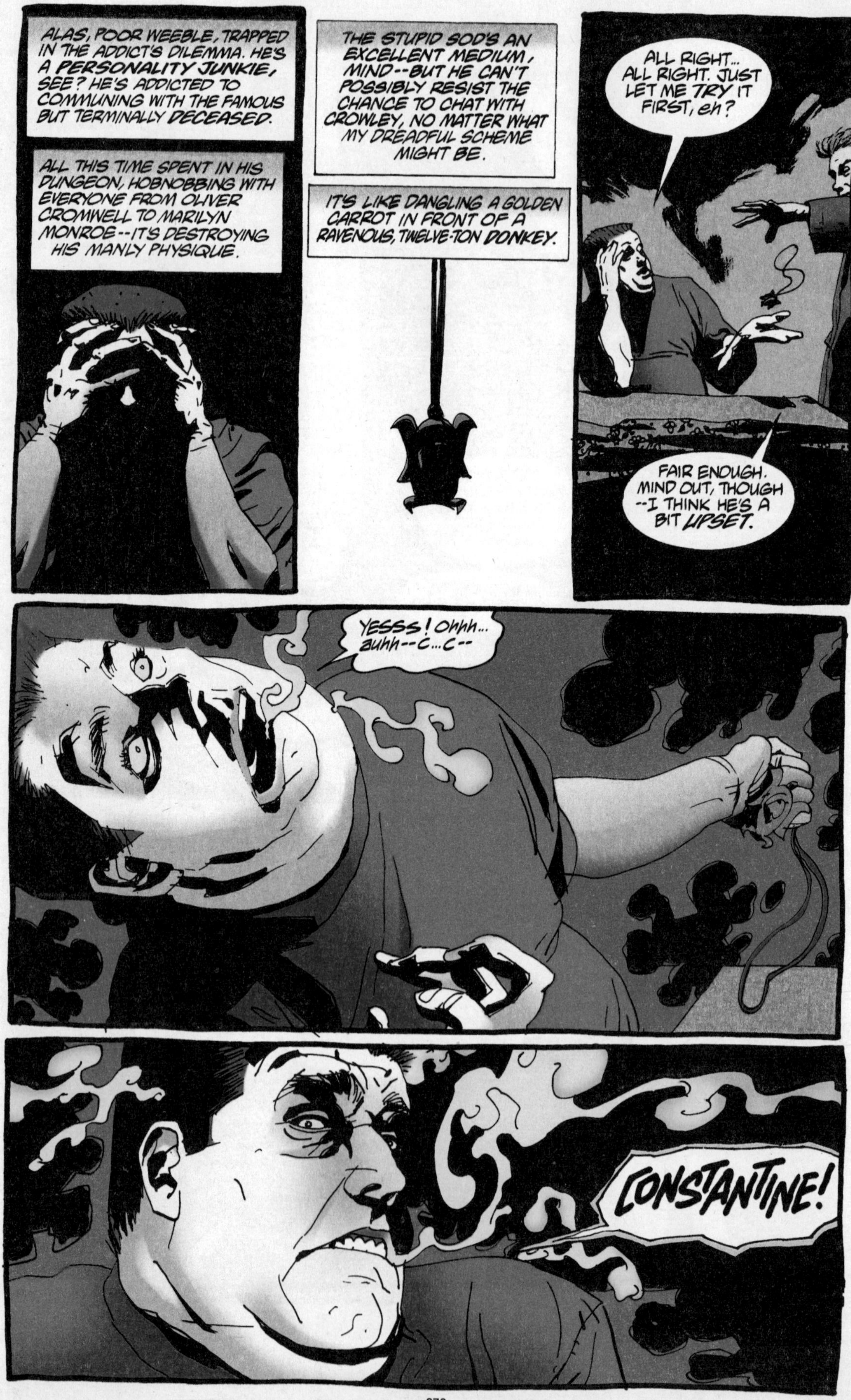
ALAS, POOR WEEBLE, TRAPPED IN THE ADDICT'S DILEMMA. HE'S A PERSONALITY JUNKIE, SEE? HE'S ADDICTED TO COMMUNING WITH THE FAMOUS BUT TERMINALLY DECEASED.
ALL THIS TIME SPENT IN HIS DUNGEON, HOBNOBBING WITH EVERYONE FROM OLIVER CROMWELL TO MARILYN MONROE--IT'S DESTROYING HIS MANLY PHYSIQUE.
THE STUPID SOD'S AN EXCELLENT MEDIUM, MIND--BUT HE CAN'T POSSIBLY RESIST THE CHANCE TO CHAT WITH CROWLEY, NO MATTER WHAT MY DREADFUL SCHEME MIGHT BE.
IT'S LIKE DANGLING A GOLDEN CARROT IN FRONT OF A RAVENOUS, TWELVE-TON DONKEY.
ALL RIGHT... ALL RIGHT. JUST LET ME TRY IT FIRST, eh?
FAIR ENOUGH. MIND OUT, THOUGH --I THINK HE'S A BIT UPSET.
YESSS! Ohhh... auhh--c...c--
CONSTANTINE!

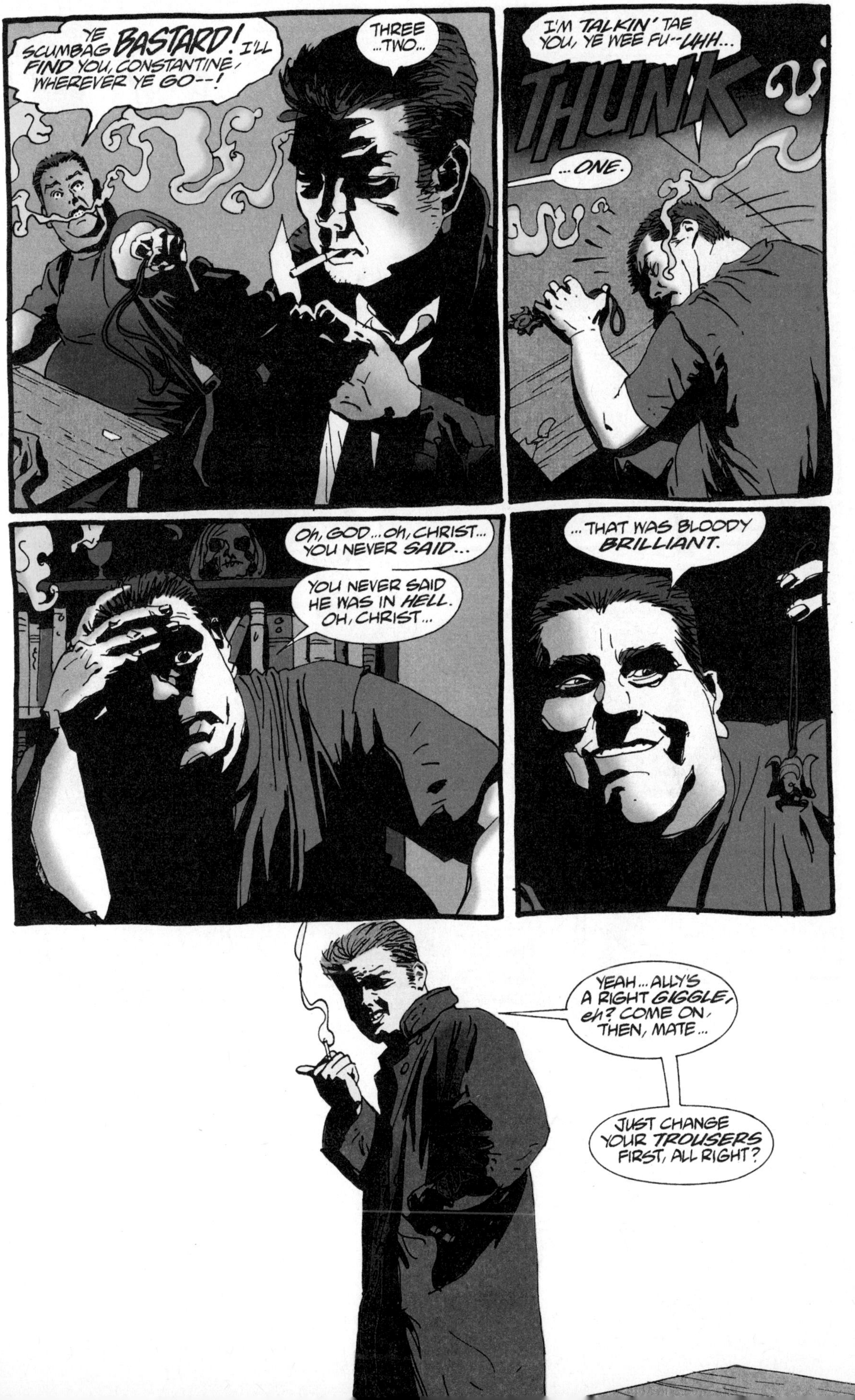
YE SCUMBAG BASTARD! I'LL FIND YOU, CONSTANTINE, WHEREVER YE GO--!
THREE ...TWO...
I'M TALKIN' TAE YOU, YE WEE FU--UHH...
THUNK
...ONE.
Oh, GOD...oh, CHRIST... YOU NEVER SAID...
YOU NEVER SAID HE WAS IN HELL. OH, CHRIST...
...THAT WAS BLOODY BRILLIANT.
YEAH...ALLY'S A RIGHT GIGGLE, eh? COME ON, THEN, MATE...
JUST CHANGE YOUR TROUSERS FIRST, ALL RIGHT?

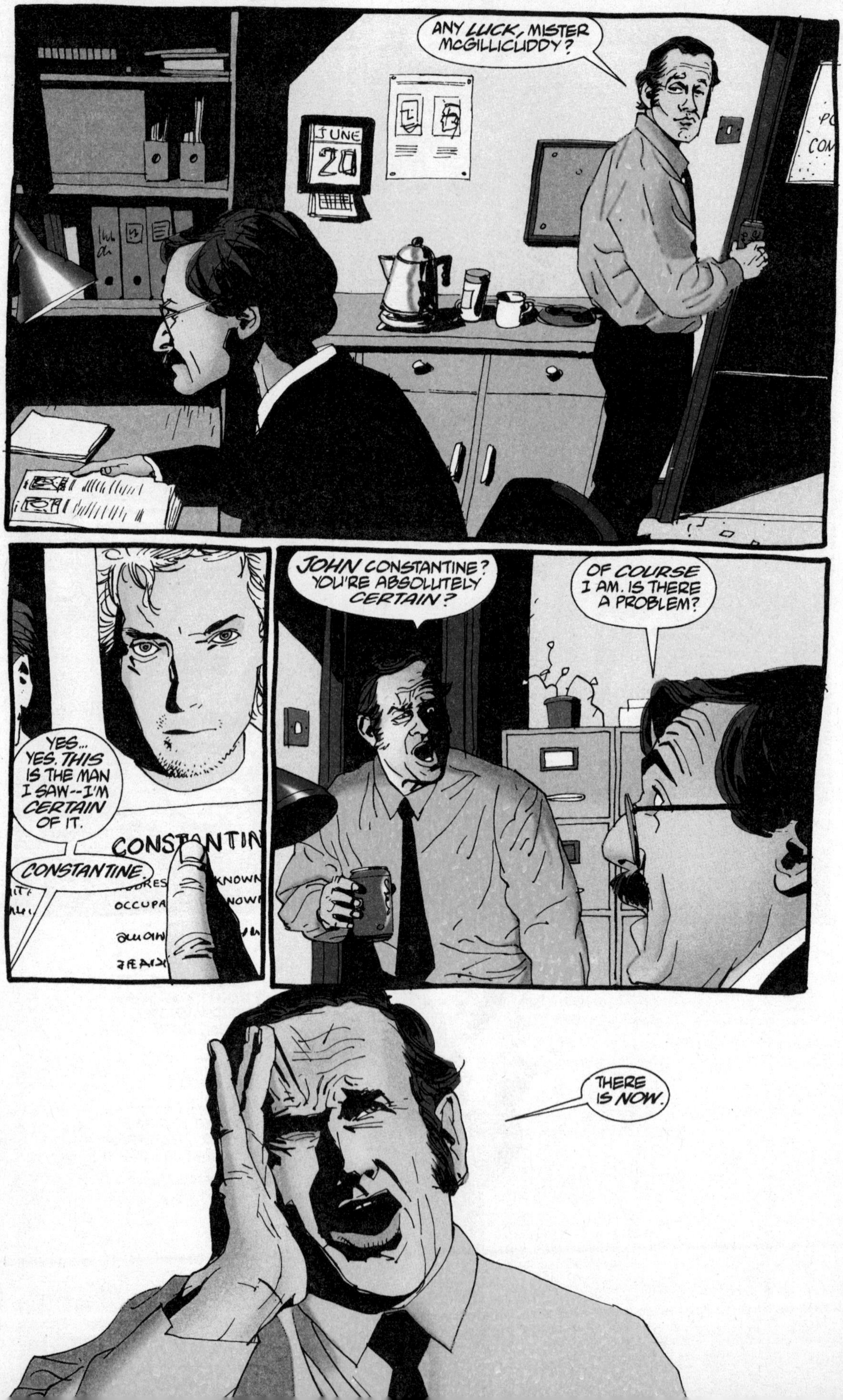

ANY LUCK, MISTER McGILLICUDDY?
JUNE 20
YES... YES. THIS IS THE MAN I SAW--I'M CERTAIN OF IT.
CONSTANTINE.
JOHN CONSTANTINE? YOU'RE ABSOLUTELY CERTAIN?
OF COURSE I AM. IS THERE A PROBLEM?
THERE IS NOW.

WHO *IS* HE?

HE'S BAD BLOODY *NEWS*, THAT'S WHO HE IS.

LOOK...THIS LITTLE *TREASURE'S* IN UP TO HIS *EYEBALLS.* DID TIME IN THE NUTHOUSE FOR KILLING SOME KID, SUSPECTED IN THE BRINKS MAT JOB...

OTHER STUFF, TOO--AND ALL OF IT'S BLOODY *IMPOSSIBLE* TO PIN ON HIM.

HONESTLY, SERGEANT --SURELY YOU CAN STIFLE THE ACTIVITIES OF ONE JUMPED-UP LITTLE STREET THUG. ISN'T THAT WHAT YOU *DO?*

WELL, YEAH. I *SUPPOSE* SO...

GOOD. THEN THEN WHAT ON EARTH SHOULD I BE WORRIED ABOUT?

OH, *COME* ON, MISTER McGILLICUDDY --USE YOUR *IMAGINATION.*

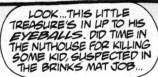

POLICE

I'M NOT *PAID* TO HAVE AN IMAGINATION, SERGEANT.

TCH... HURRY UP, YOU FAT BASTARD, WHAT *ARE* YOU--A MEDIUM OR A SODDIN' EXTRA LARGE?

BOLLOCKS, YOU SKINNY GIT.

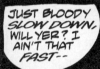

JUST BLOODY *SLOW DOWN,* WILL YER? I AIN'T THAT *FAST--*

YEAH... AND THE POPE'S CATHOLIC. IN *HERE--*

S-STAP ME--!

JUST *DO IT,* ALL RIGHT? HIS NAME'S JACK. LET ME TALK TO HIM.

IT'S NOT WORKING. HE'S FORGOTTEN *HOW...*

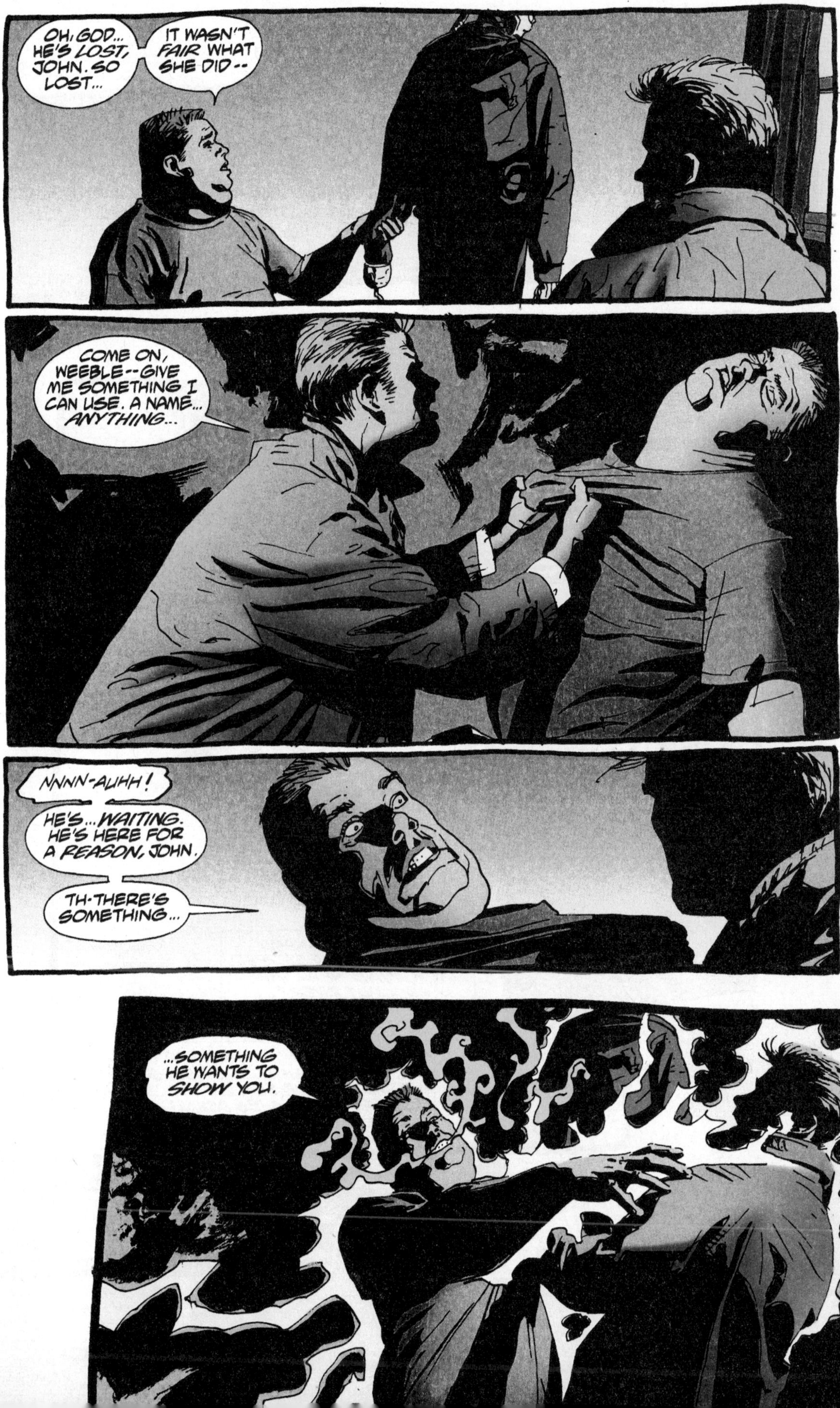
OH, GOD... HE'S LOST, JOHN. SO LOST...
IT WASN'T FAIR WHAT SHE DID--
COME ON, WEEBLE--GIVE ME SOMETHING I CAN USE. A NAME... ANYTHING...
NNNN-AUHH!
HE'S...WAITING. HE'S HERE FOR A REASON, JOHN.
TH-THERE'S SOMETHING...
...SOMETHING HE WANTS TO SHOW YOU.

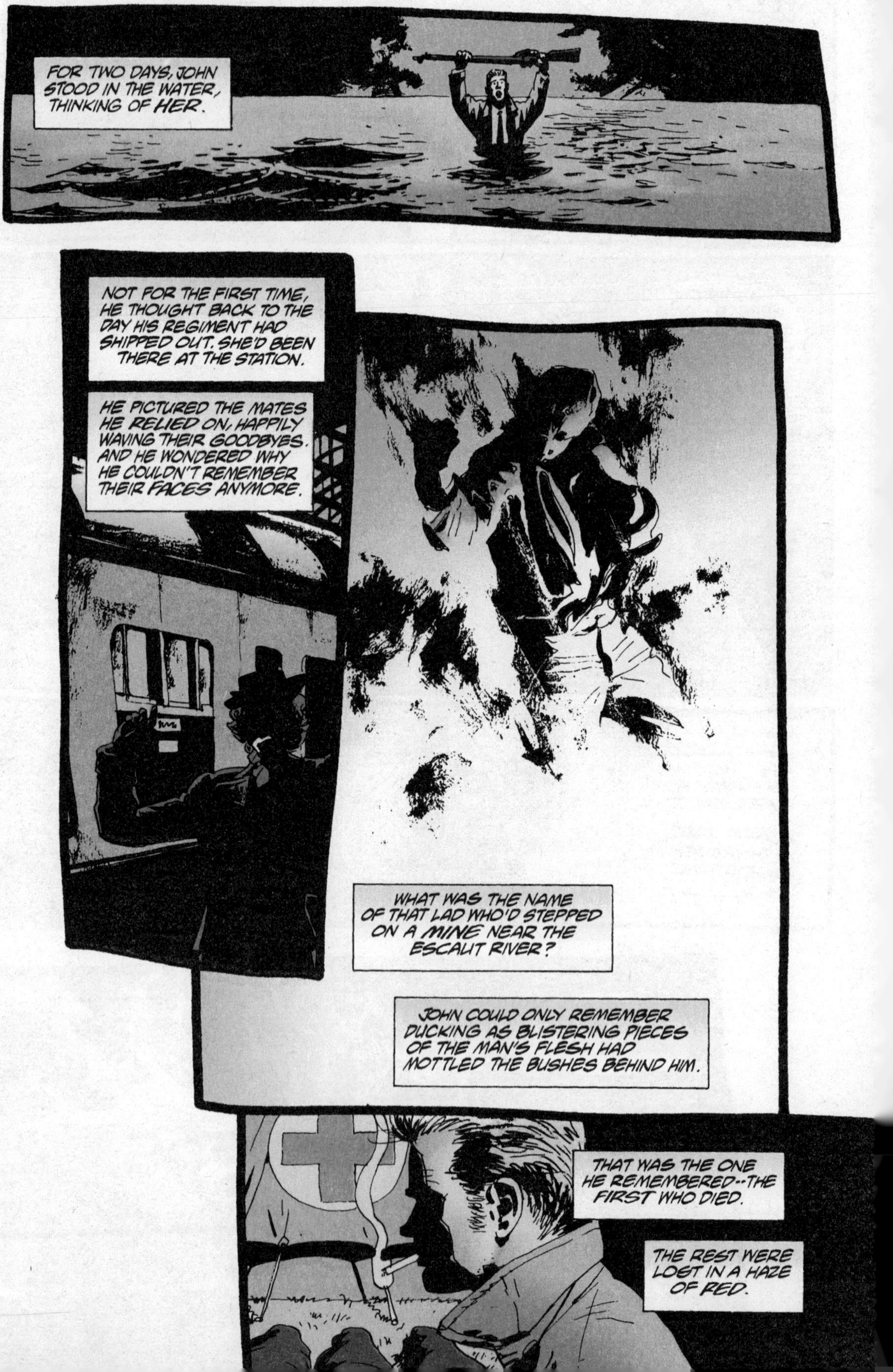
FOR TWO DAYS, JOHN STOOD IN THE WATER, THINKING OF HER.
NOT FOR THE FIRST TIME, HE THOUGHT BACK TO THE DAY HIS REGIMENT HAD SHIPPED OUT. SHE'D BEEN THERE AT THE STATION.
HE PICTURED THE MATES HE RELIED ON, HAPPILY WAVING THEIR GOODBYES. AND HE WONDERED WHY HE COULDN'T REMEMBER THEIR FACES ANYMORE.
WHAT WAS THE NAME OF THAT LAD WHO'D STEPPED ON A MINE NEAR THE ESCAUT RIVER?
JOHN COULD ONLY REMEMBER DUCKING AS BLISTERING PIECES OF THE MAN'S FLESH HAD MOTTLED THE BUSHES BEHIND HIM.
THAT WAS THE ONE HE REMEMBERED--THE FIRST WHO DIED.
THE REST WERE LOST IN A HAZE OF RED.

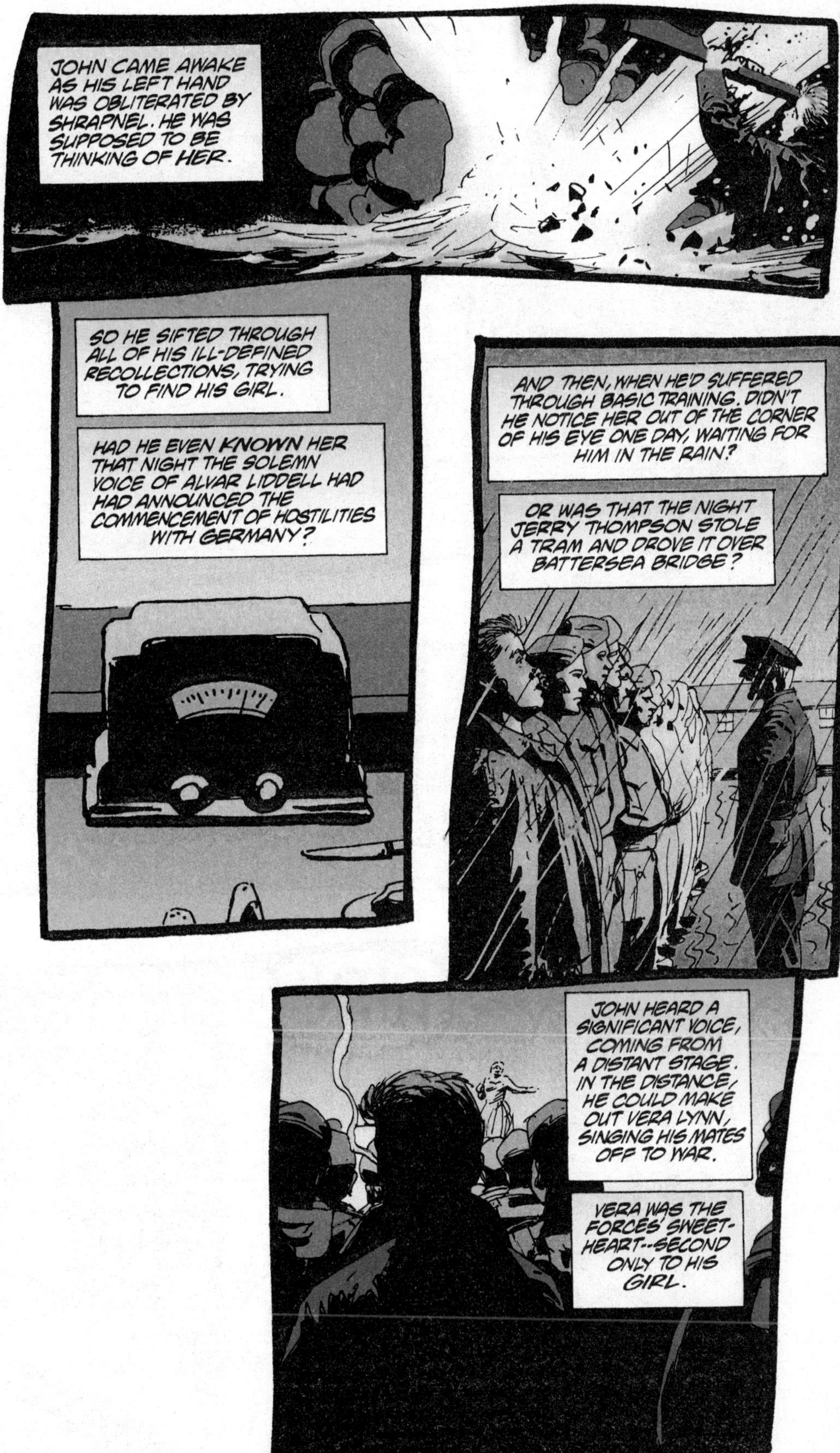
JOHN CAME AWAKE AS HIS LEFT HAND WAS OBLITERATED BY SHRAPNEL. HE WAS SUPPOSED TO BE THINKING OF HER.
SO HE SIFTED THROUGH ALL OF HIS ILL-DEFINED RECOLLECTIONS, TRYING TO FIND HIS GIRL.
HAD HE EVEN KNOWN HER THAT NIGHT THE SOLEMN VOICE OF ALVAR LIDDELL HAD HAD ANNOUNCED THE COMMENCEMENT OF HOSTILITIES WITH GERMANY?
AND THEN, WHEN HE'D SUFFERED THROUGH BASIC TRAINING. DIDN'T HE NOTICE HER OUT OF THE CORNER OF HIS EYE ONE DAY, WAITING FOR HIM IN THE RAIN?
OR WAS THAT THE NIGHT JERRY THOMPSON STOLE A TRAM AND DROVE IT OVER BATTERSEA BRIDGE?
JOHN HEARD A SIGNIFICANT VOICE, COMING FROM A DISTANT STAGE. IN THE DISTANCE, HE COULD MAKE OUT VERA LYNN, SINGING HIS MATES OFF TO WAR.
VERA WAS THE FORCES' SWEET-HEART--SECOND ONLY TO HIS GIRL.

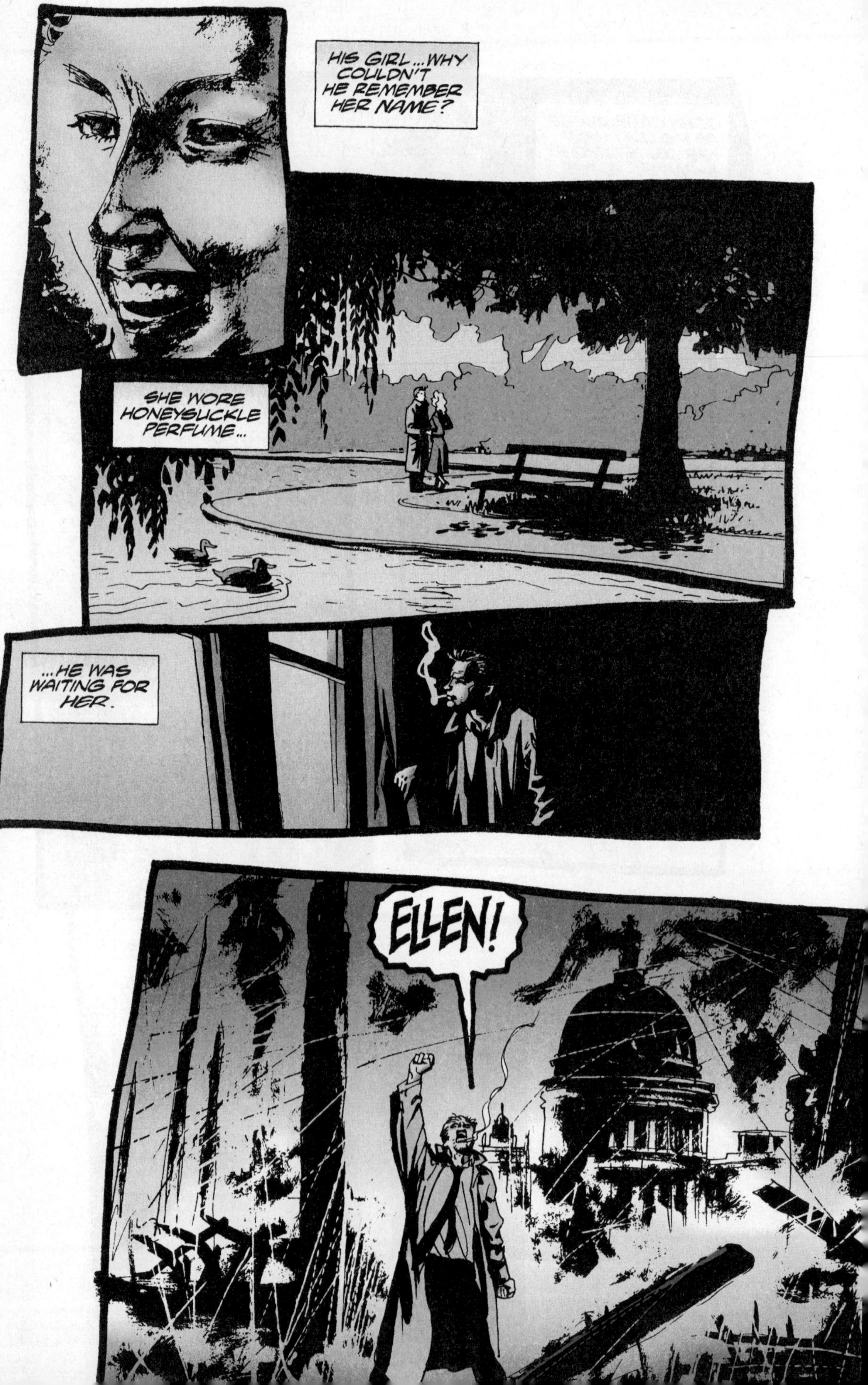
HIS GIRL...WHY COULDN'T HE REMEMBER HER NAME?
SHE WORE HONEYSUCKLE PERFUME...
...HE WAS WAITING FOR HER.
ELLEN!

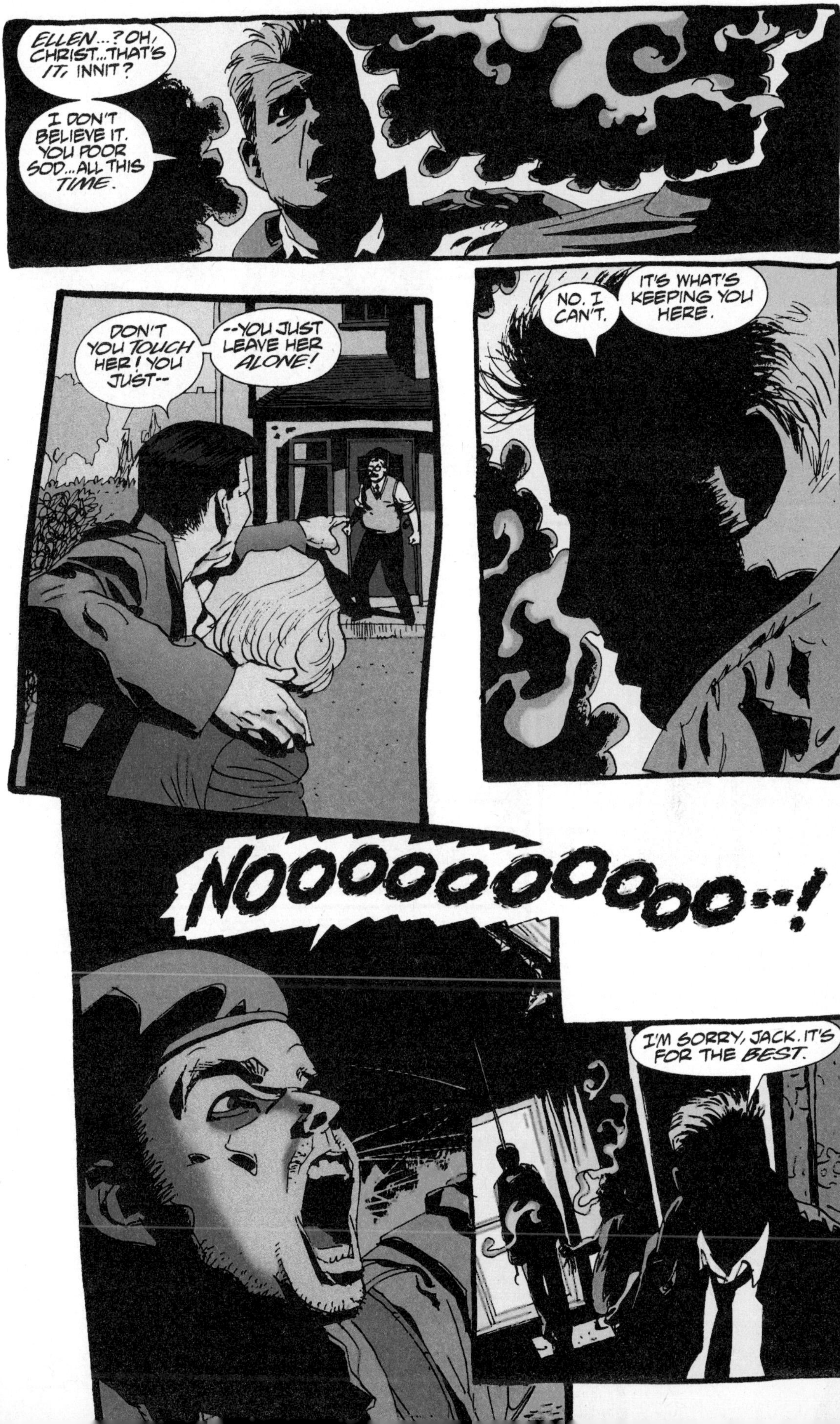
ELLEN...? OH, CHRIST...THAT'S IT, INNIT?
I DON'T BELIEVE IT. YOU POOR SOD...ALL THIS TIME.
DON'T YOU TOUCH HER! YOU JUST--
--YOU JUST LEAVE HER ALONE!
NO. I CAN'T.
IT'S WHAT'S KEEPING YOU HERE.
NOOOOOOOOOOO--!
I'M SORRY, JACK. IT'S FOR THE BEST.

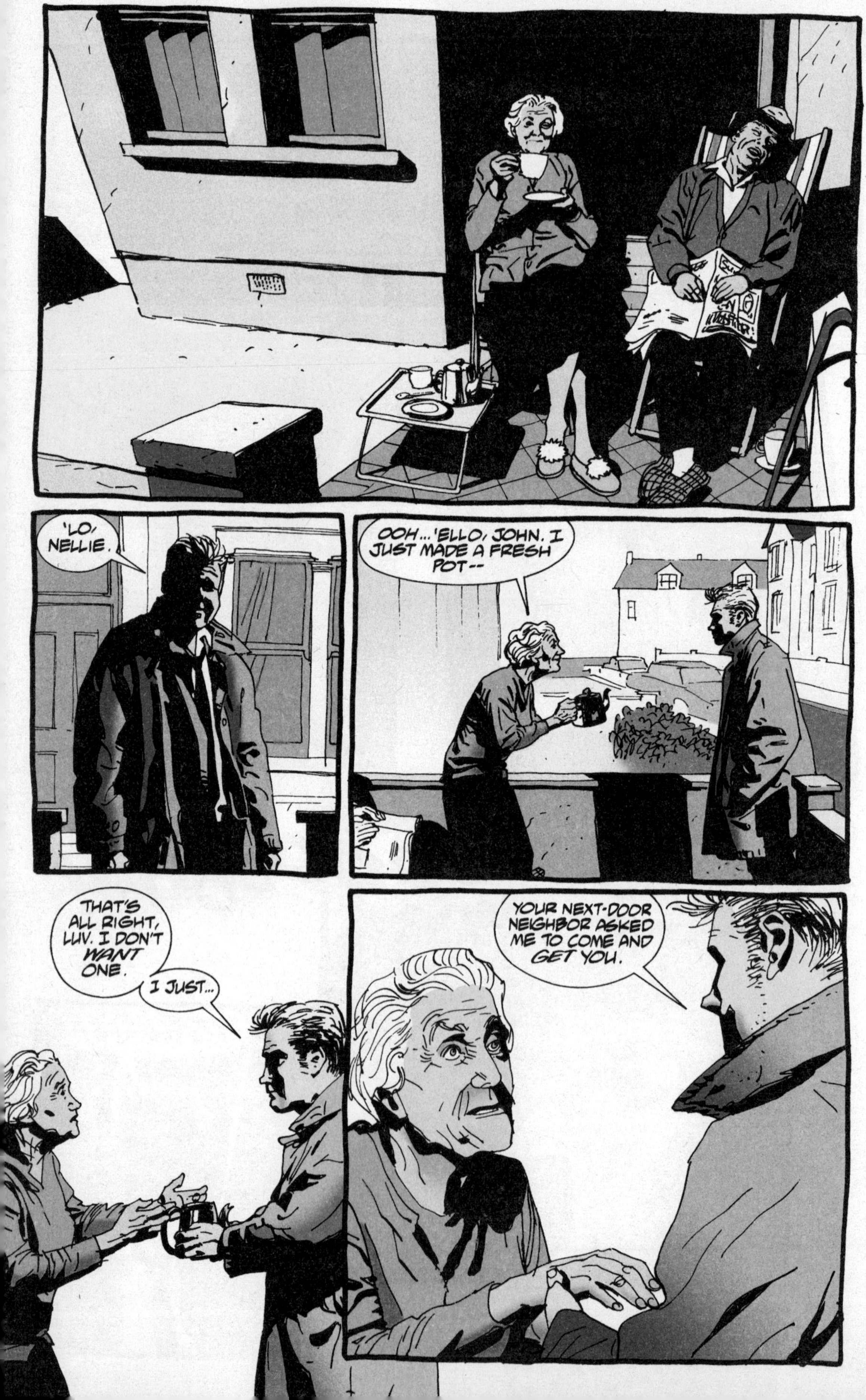
'LO, NELLIE.
OOH... 'ELLO, JOHN. I JUST MADE A FRESH POT--
THAT'S ALL RIGHT, LUV. I DON'T *WANT* ONE.
I JUST...
YOUR NEXT-DOOR NEIGHBOR ASKED ME TO COME AND *GET YOU*.

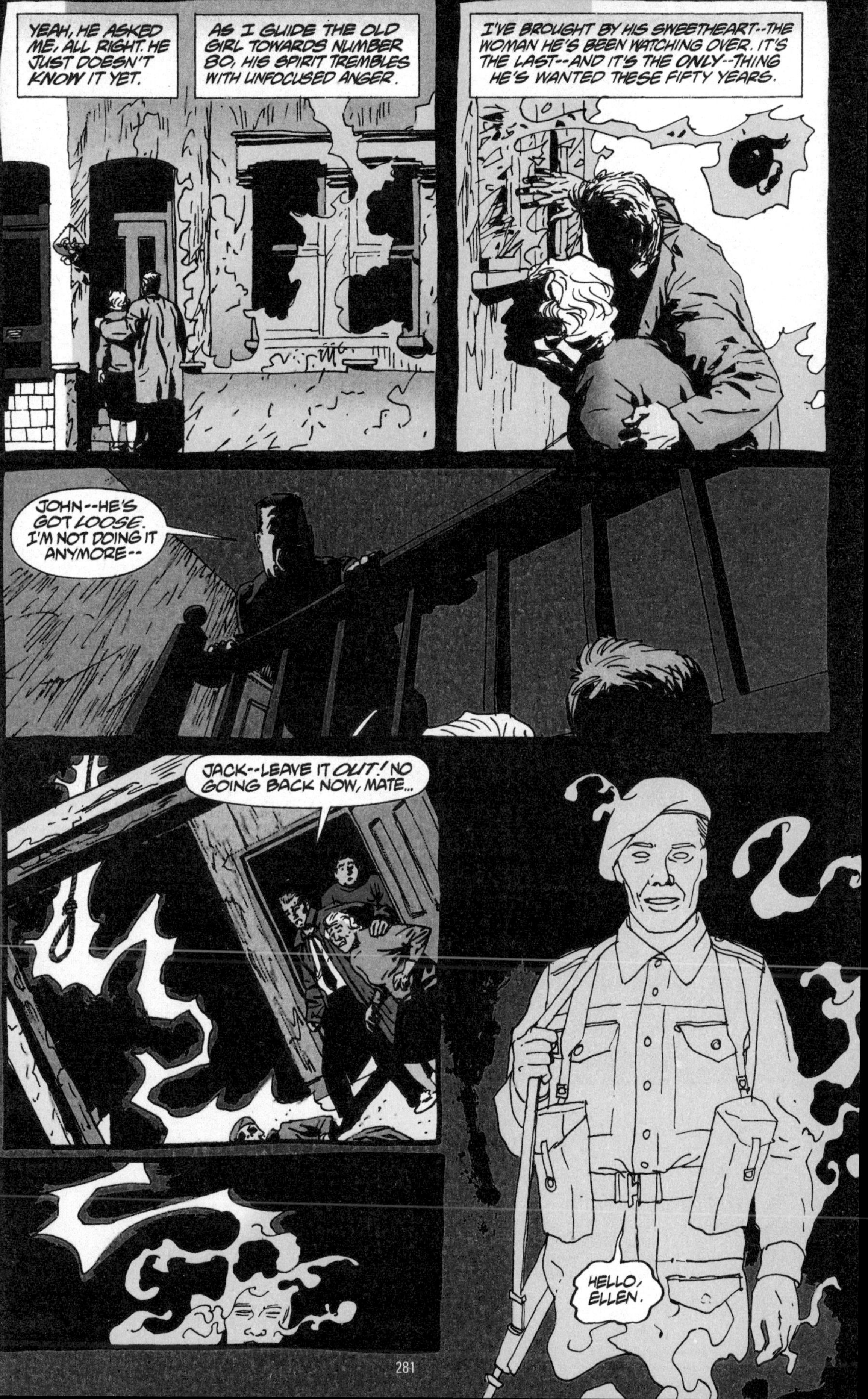

YEAH, HE ASKED ME, ALL RIGHT. HE JUST DOESN'T KNOW IT YET.
AS I GUIDE THE OLD GIRL TOWARDS NUMBER 80, HIS SPIRIT TREMBLES WITH UNFOCUSED ANGER.
I'VE BROUGHT BY HIS SWEETHEART--THE WOMAN HE'S BEEN WATCHING OVER. IT'S THE LAST--AND IT'S THE ONLY--THING HE'S WANTED THESE FIFTY YEARS.
JOHN--HE'S GOT LOOSE. I'M NOT DOING IT ANYMORE--
JACK--LEAVE IT OUT! NO GOING BACK NOW, MATE...
HELLO, ELLEN.

JACK? JACK LOUDFOOT? IS THAT *YOU*?

OH, JACK... WHEREVER DID YOU GO?

I KNOW YOU DIDN'T *MEAN* IT, ELLEN. YOU COULDN'T WAIT FOREVER.

"BILLY GREENWOOD--HE'S A GOOD MAN, LOVE. I SAW YOU BOTH, YOU KNOW."

SO, IT'S ALL RIGHT--EVERY-THING'S ALL RIGHT.

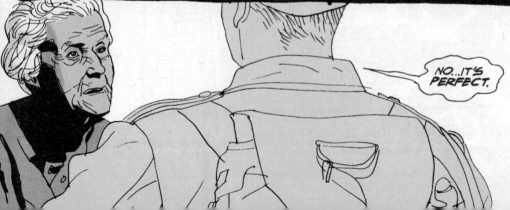

NO...IT'S PERFECT.

OH, JACK, YOU HAVEN'T CHANGED A BIT.

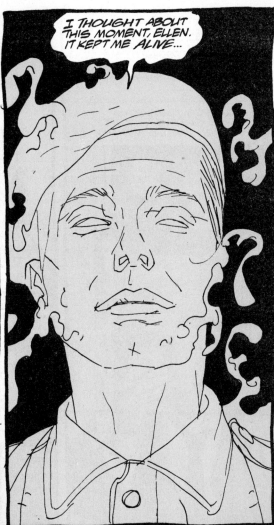

I THOUGHT ABOUT THIS MOMENT, ELLEN. IT KEPT ME ALIVE...

AND I'LL STAY HERE, LOVE--UNTIL YOU GO.

I'LL WAIT.

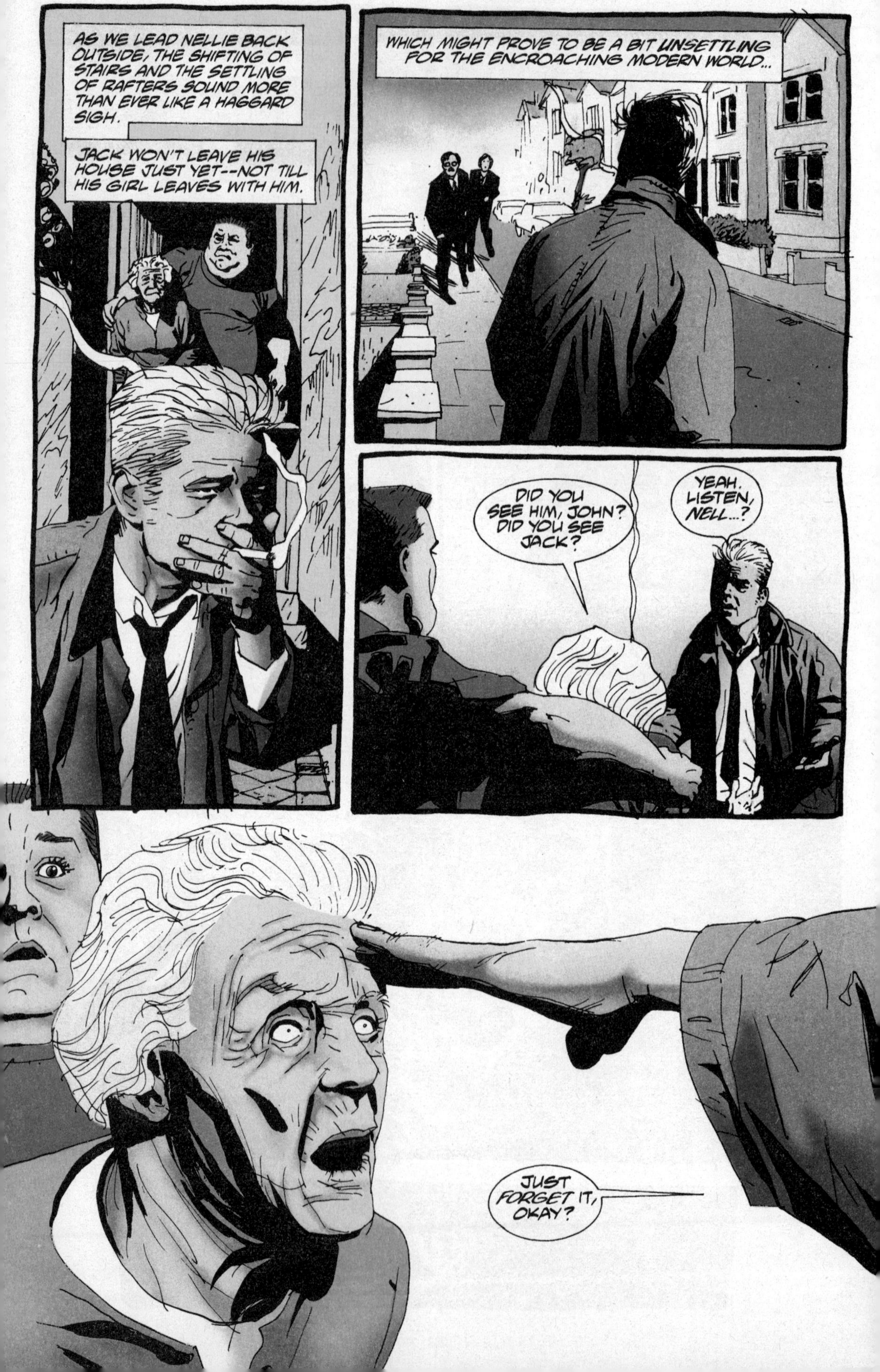
AS WE LEAD NELLIE BACK OUTSIDE, THE SHIFTING OF STAIRS AND THE SETTLING OF RAFTERS SOUND MORE THAN EVER LIKE A HAGGARD SIGH.
JACK WON'T LEAVE HIS HOUSE JUST YET--NOT TILL HIS GIRL LEAVES WITH HIM.
WHICH MIGHT PROVE TO BE A BIT UNSETTLING FOR THE ENCROACHING MODERN WORLD...
DID YOU SEE HIM, JOHN? DID YOU SEE JACK?
YEAH. LISTEN, NELL...?
JUST FORGET IT, OKAY?

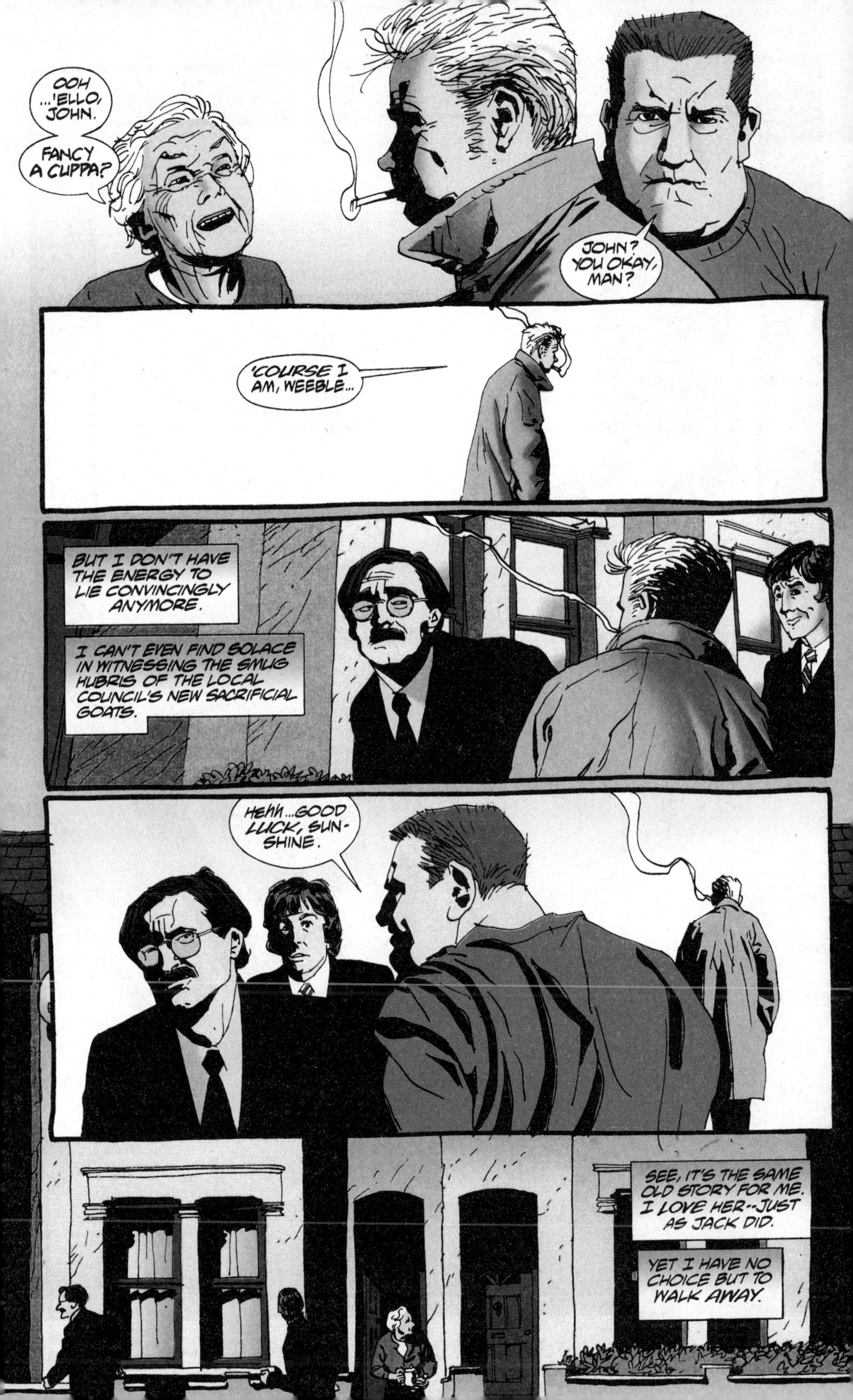
OOH ...'ELLO, JOHN.
FANCY A CUPPA?
JOHN? YOU OKAY, MAN?
'COURSE I AM, WEEBLE...
BUT I DON'T HAVE THE ENERGY TO LIE CONVINCINGLY ANYMORE.
I CAN'T EVEN FIND SOLACE IN WITNESSING THE SMUG HUBRIS OF THE LOCAL COUNCIL'S NEW SACRIFICIAL GOATS.
HEHH ...GOOD LUCK, SUNSHINE.
SEE, IT'S THE SAME OLD STORY FOR ME. I LOVE HER--JUST AS JACK DID.
YET I HAVE NO CHOICE BUT TO WALK AWAY.

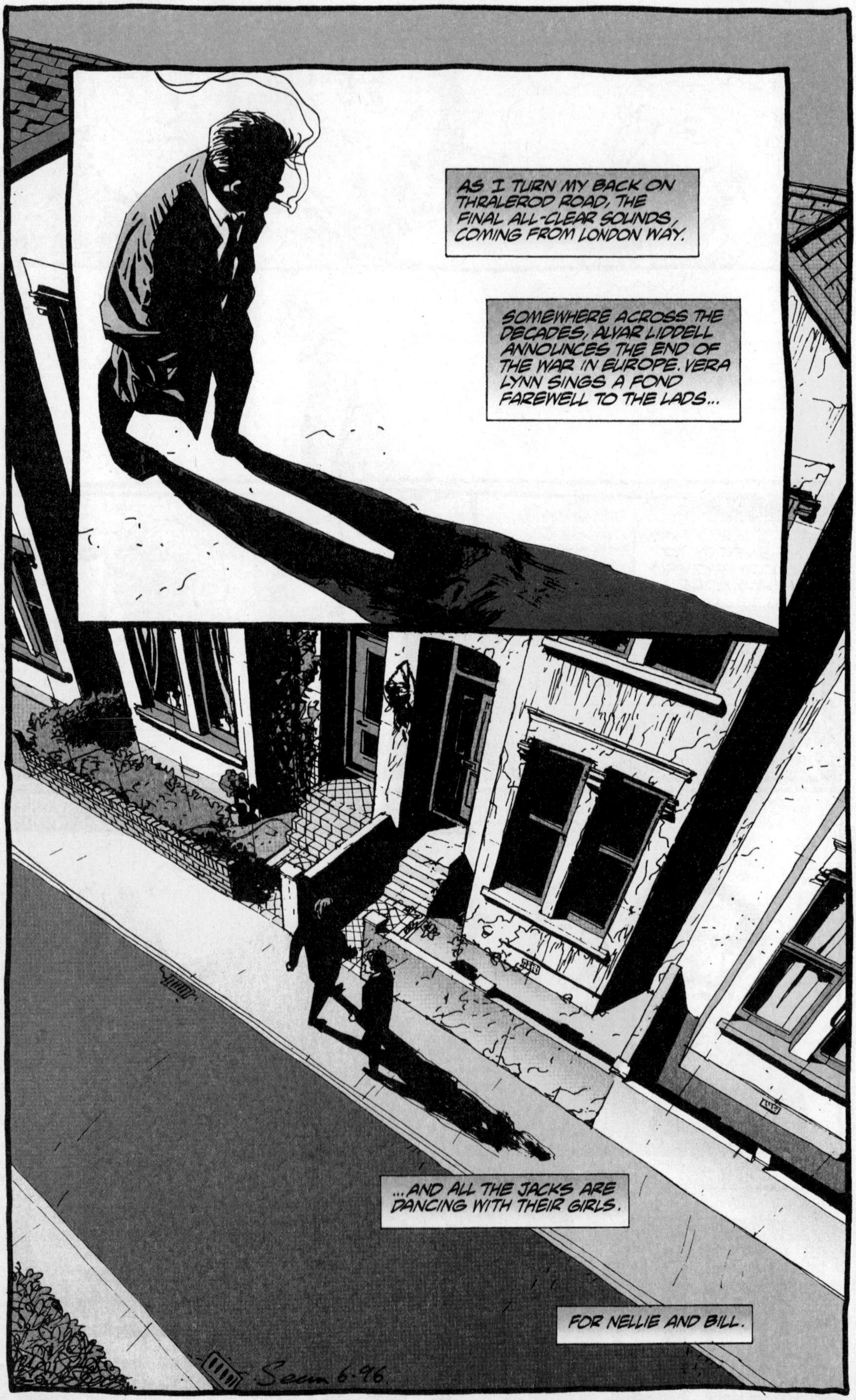
AS I TURN MY BACK ON THRALEROD ROAD, THE FINAL ALL-CLEAR SOUNDS, COMING FROM LONDON WAY.
SOMEWHERE ACROSS THE DECADES, ALVAR LIDDELL ANNOUNCES THE END OF THE WAR IN EUROPE. VERA LYNN SINGS A FOND FAREWELL TO THE LADS...
...AND ALL THE JACKS ARE DANCING WITH THEIR GIRLS.
FOR NELLIE AND BILL.
Sean 6·96.